Lecture Notes in Computer Science 5149

Commenced Publication in 1973
Founding and Former Series Editors:
Gerhard Goos, Juris Hartmanis, and Jan van Leeuwen

T0224425

Wolfgang Nejdl   Judy Kay   Pearl Pu
Eelco Herder (Eds.)

Adaptive Hypermedia and Adaptive Web-Based Systems

5th International Conference, AH 2008
Hannover, Germany, July 29 – August 1, 2008
Proceedings

 Springer

Volume Editors

Wolfgang Nejdl
Eelco Herder
L3S Research Center and University of Hannover
Appelstr. 9a, 30167 Hannover, Germany
E-mail: {nejdl, herder}@L3S.de

Judy Kay
University of Sydney, School of Information Technologies
Building J12, Sydney, NSW 2006, Australia
E-mail: judy@it.usyd.edu.au

Pearl Pu
Ecole Polytechnique Fédérale de Lausanne (EPFL)
Station 14, 1015 Lausanne, Switzerland
E-mail: pearl.pu@epfl.ch

Library of Congress Control Number: Applied for

CR Subject Classification (1998): H.5.4, H.4, H.5, H.3

LNCS Sublibrary: SL 3 – Information Systems and Application, incl. Internet/Web and HCI

ISSN	0302-9743
ISBN-10	3-540-70984-3 Springer Berlin Heidelberg New York
ISBN-13	978-3-540-70984-8 Springer Berlin Heidelberg New York

Springer is a part of Springer Science+Business Media

springer.com

© Springer-Verlag Berlin Heidelberg 2008
Printed in Germany

Typesetting: Camera-ready by author, data conversion by Scientific Publishing Services, Chennai, India
Printed on acid-free paper   SPIN: 12440269   06/3180   5 4 3 2 1 0

Preface

Adaptive Hypermedia has emerged as an important area of both academic and deployed research. It encompasses a broad range of research that will enable personalized, adaptive hypermedia systems to play an even more effective role in people's lives. The Web has enabled the widespread use of many personalized systems, such as recommenders, personalized filters and retrieval systems, e-learning systems and various forms of collaborative systems. Such systems have been widely deployed in diverse domains such as e-Commerce, e-Health, e-Government, digital libraries, personalized travel planning as well as tourist and cultural heritage services. They are particularly promising for users with special needs. The exciting possibilities of such deployed adaptive hypermedia systems rely on research progress in a broad range of areas such as: user profiling and modeling; acquisition, updating and management of user models; group modeling and community-based profiling; recommender systems and recommendation strategies; data mining for personalization; the Semantic Web; adaptive multimedia content authoring and delivery; ubiquitous computing environments and Smart Spaces; personalization for the plethora of mobile devices, such as PDAs, mobile phones and other hand-held devices; and pragmatics such as privacy, trust and security. Empirical studies of adaptive hypermedia and Web systems are also critical to informing future directions.

The Adaptive Hypermedia conferences have become the major forums for the scientific exchange and presentation of research results on adaptive hypermedia and adaptive Web-based systems. The field emerged from a series of successful workshops which matured into the conferences, starting with Adaptive Hypermedia 2000 in Trento, Italy, followed by Adaptive Hypermedia 2002 in Malaga, Spain, Adaptive Hypermedia 2004 in Eindhoven, The Netherlands and Adaptive Hypermedia 2006 in Dublin, Ireland. This fifth and final Adaptive Hypermedia was organized by the L3S Research Center in the city of Hannover, Germany. It is momentous, as it represents the marriage of the Adaptive Hypermedia and User Modeling communities, both of which are major sponsors. This also marks the increased maturity of the field, as it will become an annual conference.

Central to the success of a conference and a research community is the peer review process. It ensures that researchers can gain high-quality peer review of their work while it informs the selection of the papers. The process of review and selection for this conference had three main phases. First the Program Committee members completed their reviews. Then the Program Chairs studied each reviewer's comments as well as their scores and called upon reviewers to discuss discrepancies. We then held an international Program Meeting of the Program Co-chairs and Local Chair where we considered each paper, its reviews, reviewer discussions and handled discrepancies. We are very grateful to the Program Committee and the additional reviewers who completed high-quality reviews, on

time, and promptly responded to requests for discussion. We particularly want
to acknowledge the following reviewers who stood out in providing outstanding
reviews with detailed feedback to the authors and helpful explanations and comments for their scores: Tim Brailsford, Peter Brusilovsky, Owen Conlan, Mehmet
Goker , Anthony Jameson, Joseph A. Konstan, Jon Oberlander, Alan Smeaton,
Barry Smyth and Stephan Weibelzahl.

We had a large number of high-quality submissions to the conference for all
the categories. For the full papers, we selected relevant submissions that had high
levels of originality, were significant, built upon relevant previous work and were
validated in ways that matched the goals of the work. There were 78 full paper
submissions and 24 were selected for the conference. We also applied rigorous
standards in the selection of short papers during the Program Meeting. For these,
we were particularly concerned about the novelty and potential of the work and
the value of bringing this to the community. Of the 88 papers considered for this
category, 26 were accepted. We accepted four demonstration papers. We thank
the Publicity Chair, Stephan Weibelzahl, for an outstanding job in ensuring that
information reached the research community.

An important part of the conference is the Doctoral Consortium, which nur-
tures the next generation of researchers. We are grateful for the care with which
this was managed by Paul De Bra (Technische Universiteit Eindhoven, The
Netherlands) and Susan Gauch (University of Arkansas, USA). Of the 19 submissions, 11 were accepted.

The workshop program is a critical part of the conference. It provides opportunities for smaller group discussion, with a tight focus on an area of emerging importance. The Workshop Chairs, Cristina Conati (University of British
Columbia, Canada) Geert-Jan Houben (Vrije Universiteit Brussel, Belgium) selected a program of six workshops in the areas of "Adaptive Collaboration Support," "Adaptation for the Social Web," "Authoring of Adaptive and Adaptable
Hypermedia," "Personalized Access to Cultural Heritage," "User Model Integration and technologies for Mobile and Wireless Adaptive Elearning Environments." This year's conference featured a new element called bl.AH, a series
of thought-provoking discussion sessions on adaptive learning systems, blended
learning and quality of experience.

The Adaptive Hypermedia community is indebted to the local organizers who
performed the many and varied tasks that ensured an outstanding experience
for all participants, from the time of their first visit to the website, through
the online reviewing software experience, to the outstanding venue of the conference at the beautiful Hotel Wienecke XI and the program throughout the
conference.

June 2008

Wolfgang Nejdl
Judy Kay
Pearl Pu
Eelco Herder

Organization

Adaptive Hypermedia 2008 was organized by the L3S Research Center and the Leibniz University Hannover. The conference took place between 29 July and August 1, 2008 in Hannover, Germany.

Organizing Committee

General Chair

Wolfgang Nejdl (L3S Research Center and University of Hannover, Germany)

Program Chairs

Judy Kay (University of Sydney, Australia)
Pearl Pu (Ecole Polytechnique Fédérale de Lausanne, Switzerland)

Local Chair

Eelco Herder (L3S Research Center, Hannover, Germany)

Workshop and Tutorials Chairs

Cristina Conati (University of British Columbia, Canada)
Geert-Jan Houben (Delft University of Technology, The Netherlands)

Doctoral Consortium

Paul De Bra (Technische Universiteit Eindhoven, The Netherlands)
Susan Gauch (University of Arkansas, USA)

Publicity Chair

Stephan Weibelzahl (National College of Ireland, Dublin)

Keynote Speakers

Peter Brusilovsky (University of Pittsburgh, USA)
Jan Borchers (RWTH Aachen, Germany)
John Riedl (University of Minnesota, USA)

Workshops

The Adaptive Hypermedia 2008 Conference featured six workshops. In addition, a special discussion event took place throughout the conference.

Workshop 1: Adaptive Collaboration Support

Alexandros Paramythis, Johannes Keppler University, Linz, Austria
Stephan Weibelzahl, National College of Ireland, Ireland

Workshop 2: Adaptation for the Social Web

Rosta Farzan, University of Pittsburgh, USA
Jill Freyne, University College Dublin, Ireland
David Millen, IBM T.J. Watson Research Center, USA

Workshop 3: Authoring of Adaptive and Adaptable Hypermedia

Alexandra Cristea, University of Warwick, UK
Rosa Carro, Universidad Autònonoma de Madrid, Spain

Workshop 4: Personalized Access to Cultural Heritage

Lora Aroyo, Vrije Universiteit Amsterdam, The Netherlands
Tsvi Kuflik, University of Haifa, Israel
Oliviero Stock, ITC-IRST Trento, Italy
Massimo Zancanaro, ITC-IRST Trento, Italy

Workshop 5: User Model Integration

Shlomo Berkovsky, University of Melbourne, Australia
Francesca Carmagnola, University of Turin, Italy
Dominikus Heckmann, University of Saarland, Germany
Antonio Krüger, University of Münster, Germany
Tsvi Kuflik, University of Haifa, Israel

Workshop 6: Technologies for Mobile and Wireless Adaptive Elearning Environments

Cristina Hava Muntean, National College of Ireland, Ireland
Gabriel-Miro Muntean, Dublin City University, Ireland
Jennifer McManis, Dublin City University, Ireland

Discussion Event: bl.AH

Bertram (Chip) Bruce, University of Illinois, USA
Jennifer McManis, Dublin City University, Ireland
Sabine Moebs, Dublin City University, Ireland
Christine Neidhardt, ecomenta, Germany
Stephan Weibelzahl, National College of Ireland, Ireland

Program Committee

Ignacio Aedo, Universidad Carlos III de Madrid, Spain
Elisabeth Andre, University of Augsburg, Germany
Liliana Ardissono, University of Turin, Italy
Lora Aroyo, Vrije Universiteit Amsterdam, The Netherlands
Helen Ashman, University of South Australia, Australia
Mark Bernsteim, Eastgate, USA
James Blustein, Dalhousie University, Canada
Tim Brailsford, University of Nottingham, UK
Peter Brusilovsky, University of Pittsburgh, USA
Daniel Burgos, ATOS Origin Research & Innovation, Spain
Ricardo Conejo Muñoz, University of Málaga, Spain
Owen Conlan, Trinity College Dublin, Ireland
Alexandra Cristea, University of Warwick, UK
Paul Cristea, Politehnica University Bucharest, Romania
Hugh Davis, University of Southampton, UK
Paul De Bra, Technical University Eindhoven, The Netherlands
Vania Dimitrova, University of Leeds, UK
Peter Dolog, University of Aalborg, Denmark
Erich Gams, Salzburg Research, Austria
Franca Garzotto, Politecnico di Milano, Italy
Susan Gauch, University of Arkansas, USA
Mehmet Göker, PwC Center for Advanced Research, USA
Nicola Henze, University of Hannover, Germany
Eelco Herder, L3S Research Center, Hannover, Germany
Geert-Jan Houben, Delft University of Technology, The Netherlands
Anthony Jameson, International University, Germany
Judy Kay, University of Sydney, Australia
Declan Kelly, National College of Ireland, Ireland
Peter King, University of Manitoba, Canada
Alfred Kobsa, University of California, Irvine, USA
Joseph A. Konstan, University of Minnesota, USA
Rob Koper, Open Universiteit Nederland, The Netherlands
Miloš Kravčík, Open Universiteit Nederland, The Netherlands
Henry Lieberman, MIT, USA
Paul Maglio, IBM Almaden Research Center, USA
Lorraine McGinty, University College Dublin, Ireland
Alessandro Micarelli, University of Rome III, Italy
Maria Milosavljevic, Capital Markets Co-operative Research Centre, Australia
Antonija Mitrovic, University of Canterbury, New Zealand
Dunja Mladenic, Jozef Stefan Institute, Slovenia
Adam Moore, University of Nottingham, UK
Wolfgang Nejdl, L3S Research Center and University of Hannover, Germany
Jon Oberlander, University of Edinburgh, UK
Pearl Pu, EPFL, Lausanne, Switzerland

Gustavo Rossi, Universidad Nacional de La Plata, Argentina
Lloyd Rutledge, Open Universiteit Nederland, The Netherlands
Frank Shipman, Texas A&M University, USA
Marcus Specht, Open Universiteit Nederland, The Netherlands
Jose-Luis Perez de la Cruz, University of Málaga, Spain
Demetrios G Sampson, University of Piraeus & CERTH, Greece
Vittorio Scarano, University of Salerno, Italy
Alan Smeaton, Dublin City University, Ireland
Barry Smyth, University College Dublin, Ireland
Craig Stewart, Queen Mary University of London, UK
Carlo Strapparava, FBK-IRST Trento, Italy
Carlo Tasso, Universitá degli Studi di Udine, Italy
Jacco van Ossenbruggen, CWI, The Netherlands
Fabio Vitali, University of Bologna, Italy
Vincent Wade, Trinity College Dublin, Ireland
Gerhard Weber, PH Freiburg, Germany
Stephan Weibelzahl, National College of Ireland, Ireland
Ross Wilkinson, CSIRO, Australia
Massimo Zancanaro, FBK-IRST Trento, Italy

External Reviewers

Oisin Boydell, University College Dublin, Ireland
Janez Brank, Jozef Stefan Institute, Slovenia
Elizabeth Brown, University of Nottingham, UK
Christopher Campbell, IBM Almaden Research Center, USA
Francesca Carmagnola, University of Turin, Italy
Bonaventura Coppola, FBK-IRST Trento, Italy
Hendrik Drachsler, Open Universiteit Nederland, The Netherlands
Jure Ferlež, Jozef Stefan Institute, Slovenia
Andres Fortier, Universidad Nacional de La Plata, Argentina
Blaz Fortuna, Jozef Stefan Institute, Slovenia
Jill Freyne, University College Dublin, Ireland
Jaime Galvez, University of Málaga, Spain
Christian Glahn, Open Universiteit Nederland, The Netherlands
Miha Grcar, Jozef Stefan Institute, Slovenia
Marco Guerini, FBK-IRST Trento, Italy
Esther Guerra, Universidad Carlos III de Madrid, Spain
Eduardo Guzman, University of Málaga, Spain
Maurice Hendrix, University of Warwick, UK
Angelo Di Iorio, University of Bologna, Italy
Marco Kalz, Open Universiteit Nederland, The Netherlands
Styliani Kleanthous, University of Leeds, UK
Karin Leichtenstern, University of Augsburg, Germany
Carla Limongelli, University of Rome III, Italy

Danish Nadeem, Open Universiteit Nederland, The Netherlands
Michael O'Mahony, University College Dublin, Ireland
Bostjan Pajntar, Jozef Stefan Institute, Slovenia
Filippo Sciarrone, University of Rome III, Italy
Sergey Sosnovsky, University of Pittsburgh, USA
Natalia Stash Technical University Eindhoven, The Netherlands
Mónica Trella López, University of Málaga, Spain
Alessandro Valitutti, ITC-IRST Trento, Italy
Giulia Vaste, University of Rome III, Italy
Michael Yudelson, University of Pittsburgh, USA
Stefano Zacchiroli, University of Bologna, Italy
Jiyong Zhang, EPFL, Lausanne, Switzerland

Local Organization Support

Marion Wicht, L3S Research Center, Germany

Table of Contents

Short Papers

Demo Papers

Doctoral Consortium

Baroque Technology

Jan Borchers

RWTH Aachen University, Germany
borchers@cs.rwth-aachen.de

Abstract. As new interactive systems evolve, they frequently hit a
sweet spot: A few new tricks to learn, and users gets tremendous benefits,
simplifying their lives. But beyond that lies the dark phase of baroque
technology: increasing complexity with little payoff. We will look at examples for both sweet-spot and baroque interactive technologies, from
GPS devices to window systems, find out how to identify each kind, and
become better interaction designers in the process.

1   Introduction

Think back to two recent events in your daily life: First, when was the last
time you came across a new interactive electronic device or service that truly
simplified your life, making things easier than before by removing or cutting
down on an unnecessary task?

Second, when was the last time you used an interactive system and felt that,
actually, it was making your life more complicated, requiring complicated steps
without providing the simplification of your task that you had expected?

The first kind of system was a device in the sweet spot of its evolution. The
second one was likely already in its baroque phase. The rest of this article will
explain the difference.

2   Why "Device"?

I mostly talk about consumer devices here, because they have a broad user base
so you can probably relate to my examples. But the principle applies equally
to desktop productivity applications, ticketing machines, web shops, and many
other interactive technologies and services we encounter on a daily basis. So
when I say "device" in the remainder of this article, please interpret it in this
broader sense, and see if you can come up with additional examples from these
other domains from your own experience.

3   The Phases of Technology Adoption

In [2], David Liddle describes three phases of adoption for consumer technology: An initial enthusiast phase that only invites "hackers" to exploit the new

W. Nejdl et al. (Eds.): AH 2008, LNCS 5149, pp. 1–5, 2008.
© Springer-Verlag Berlin Heidelberg 2008

technology, a second professional phase in which it becomes mature enough to let professionals work with it to help their business, and a third consumer phase in which it becomes useable, cheap, and attractive enough for users to enjoy in their daily lives.

4   The Sweet Spot

Somewhere in the early consumer stage, products can hit their sweet spot: The device offers a new kind of support that so fundamentally simplifies everyday routines that it experiences an explosive growth in adoption by consumers. The system is lean, it does not offer unnecessary extras, its design just concentrates on delivering that new functionality as unobtrusively and conveniently as possible. After a little while, we even start using it without really noticing it, because it works so fluently and unobtrusively that it hardly becomes our "locus of attention" [3] anymore.

Not every product reaches this spot of course. Most will either not be of enough utility in their core functionality to warrant the additional hassle of integrating them into consumer's lives at a large scale, or they combine so many things in one that, despite a lot of added uses, their usability also suffers too much. In both cases they are not making it beyond Saffo's "threshold of indignation" [4]. This threshold claims that, for the general user population, the willingness to put effort into using an artifact will only be as high as its perceived usefulness for the respective kind of user.

Some indicators that the sweet spot has been reached include that a new market segment of consumer devices establishes itself; that non-technical users quickly understand and may even evangelize the usefulness of the new device category; and that social behavior around the device and its tasks changes.

5   The Baroque Stage

Unfortunately, development usually does not stop at the sweet spot (if it ever reaches it). Assuming that to compete in the marketplace, products need to continue to grow in their amount of features, companies keep adding extra "stuff" to their sweet-spot product. And consumers who had their lives simplifies by a sweet-spot device, will buy the upgrades, expecting similar additional life-simplifying effects.

Unfortunately, the opposite happens: The added features, often functions that already existed elswhere before, lead to a much more complicated user interface, but provide little added benefit compared to the original sweet-spot idea.

This means we need to add a fourth stage, the baroque phase, to Liddle's three-stage model of technology adoption (figure 1).

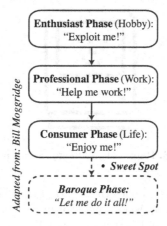

Fig. 1. Four phases of technology adoption

6   Examples

The best way to understand this model is by looking at some examples. In-car navigation systems have been attempted ever since GPS became commercially available, but were not for the faint-of-heart in their beginnings. After several years, logistics companies began equipping their fleet of trucks or cars with the technology, but only since the introduction of all-in-one, simple navigation systems such as TomTom's and Garmin's devices, the technology has spread like a virus into the consumer market.

Fig. 2. TomTom GO 910 Car Navigation System. Courtesy of TomTom.

And the effects are noticeable: You stop asking people for directions when planning to visit them; an address is enough (better, in fact). You may start to un-learn how to get from A to B because your GPS tells you about each required turn. Following manual driving directions, and the ensuing high stress levels during driving, become a hassle quickly forgotten.

But the latest slew of GPS devices keeps adding features, from photo slide shows to messaging with buddies, bringing the in-car GPS into the baroque phase.

Fig. 3. Happy Mac. Design: Susan Kare

Another example are cell phones that started as a high-tech device for technologists, soon became an indispensable tool in the form of car phones for entrepreneurs on the move, and in the 90s had their breakthrough as network coverage, prices, and device size and battery life met to create a sweet spot with an astonishingly quick adoption rate in many countries. Call anybody, or be called by anybody, wherever you are! The effects are also clearly visible in our society. But the latest all-in-one communicators and smart phones are squarely in the baroque phase of the traditional mobile phone.

Other examples include home DSL flatrates (a sweet spot), modern microwaves (extremely baroque), or even the graphical user interface metaphor of the desktop (with its sweet spot in the 80s).

7   Solutions

Sometimes, consumers simply backpedal to the sweet spot - take the microwave ovens that still only have two dials, go bing at the end, and sell extremely well.

Another solution is to innovate out of the baroque phase by rethinking the device, its form factor and interaction metaphors. Apple's iPhone is a good example.

But some will argue that the baroque phase is actually essential, because its pool of complex, hard-to-use devices is actually the enthusiast phase of the next generation of devices: the primordial soup out of which the next technology will arise and go through the same cycle again.

Fig. 4. Microwave. Photo: Thorsten Karrer.

Fig. 5. Apple iPhone. Courtesy of Apple.

Whether that is always true or not, it certainly pays off to look for more sweet spots in our research and development of interactive systems, products and services, instead of spending time on baroque extensions. And one of the keys to hitting this sweet spot lies in Human-Computer Interaction: Getting the interface right, supporting a task in an innovative and simplifying, enjoyable way.

Acknowledgements

A more extensive discussion of this topic can be found in [1] or at http:// hci.rwth-aachen.de/sweetspot. This work was funded by the German B-IT Foundation.

References

1. Borchers, J.: An ode to tomtom: Sweet spots and baroque phases of interactive technology lifecycles. Interactions of the ACM 15(2), 62–66 (2008)
2. Moggridge, B.: Designing Interactions. MIT Press, Cambridge (2007)
3. Raskin, J.: The Humane Interface. Addison-Wesley, Reading (2000)
4. Winograd, T.: Bringing Design to Software. Addison-Wesley, Reading (1996)

Adaptive Navigation Support for Open Corpus Hypermedia Systems

Peter Brusilovsky

University of Pittsburgh, School of Information Sciences
135 North Bellefield Avenue, Pittsburgh, PA 15232 USA
peterb@pitt.edu

Abstract. Open corpus adaptive hypermedia could be considered one of the major challenges of the adaptive hypermedia community since it can dramatically extend the range of applicability of adaptive hypermedia systems. An open corpus adaptive hypermedia system can be defined in as an "adaptive hypermedia system which operates on an open corpus of documents, e.g., a set of documents that is not known at design time and, moreover, can constantly change and expand" [6]. For the last five years open corpus adaptive hypermedia has been one of the priorities of our research group at the University of Pittsburgh. The goal of this presentation is to discuss the problems of open corpus adaptive hypermedia, review major approaches for developing adaptive navigation support for open corpus AHS system, and report our experience with some of these approaches.

Keywords: Adaptive navigation support, adaptive hypermedia, open corpus.

1 Introduction

Adaptive hypermedia systems (AHS) are known as an alternative to the traditional "one-size-fits-all" hypermedia and Web systems. AHS are able to provide a superior level of support by adapting to the goals, interests, and knowledge of individual users represented in the individual *user models*. The models are built by observing user navigation through a hyperspace and are used to deliver two main kinds of adaptation. The AHS manipulates link anchors to guide users towards interesting, relevant information. This functionality is known as *adaptive navigation support* [2]. In order to ensure that the content of a page contains the appropriate information for the given user at the given time, the AHS can conditionally show, hide, highlight or dim page fragments when presenting it. This functionality is known as *adaptive presentation* [2]. Both adaptive navigation support and adaptive presentation aim to modify the user interactive experience with the hypermedia system in order to help individual users locate, recognize, and comprehend relevant information. Existing empirical studies of AHS demonstrate that AHS are generally able to achieve that goal [3]. For example, educational AHS are known to reduce navigation effort, time to achieve the learning goal, and learner retention, and to increase quality of learning [5, 7, 11, 17, 18, 19, 20].

Unfortunately, nearly all popular and efficient adaptive hypermedia technologies were built to operate with a relatively small set of documents that were structured and

W. Nejdl et al. (Eds.): AH 2008, LNCS 5149, pp. 6–8, 2008.

enhanced by metadata annotations at design time. Classic AHS are predominantly closed corpus hypermedia since the *document space* of these adaptive systems is a closed set of information items. What makes closed corpus hypermedia special, from the adaptation point of view, is the fact that all documents and relations on the documents are known to the authors of an adaptive hypermedia system at design time. It allows the authors to augment the documents and relationships with additional information that can be used later by the adaptation algorithms to deliver the adaptation effectively to every user.

Closed corpus AHS demonstrate what is possible to achieve with adaptive hypermedia technologies, but they are impractical in an open corpus context such as the constantly growing digital libraries or the Web. In a range of important real world applications, neither system developers no content providers are able to invest time to structure and index thousands of documents in the way required by classic adaptive hypermedia systems. Without constant maintenance any structuring and indexing attempts are futile because new information becomes available daily.

The apparent contradiction between the potential power of adaptive hypermedia and its predominant close-corpus application content has caused a number of researchers to focus on what we call the *open corpus adaptive hypermedia* [1, 6, 13, 16]. An open corpus adaptive hypermedia system is defined in [6] as an "adaptive hypermedia system which operates on an open corpus of documents, e.g., a set of documents that is not known at design time and, moreover, can constantly change and expand". Open corpus adaptive hypermedia could be considered one of the major challenges of the adaptive hypermedia community since it can dramatically extend the range of AHS applicability.

For the last five years open corpus adaptive hypermedia has been one of the priorities of our research group at the University of Pittsburgh [4, 8, 9, 10, 21].

The goal of this presentation is to discuss the problems of open corpus adaptive hypermedia, review major approaches for developing adaptive navigation support for open corpus AHS system, and report our experience with some of these approaches such as service-based approach to provide navigation support for external interactive educational resources [9, 21] and social navigation support [4, 12, 14, 15].

References

1. Aroyo, L., De Bra, P., Houben, G.-J., Vdovjak, R.: Embedding information retrieval in adaptive hypermedia: IR meets AHA! New Review of Hypermedia and Multimedia 10(1), 53–76 (2004)
2. Brusilovsky, P.: Methods and techniques of adaptive hypermedia. User Modeling and User-Adapted Interaction 6(2-3), 87–129 (1996)
3. Brusilovsky, P.: Adaptive hypermedia. User Modeling and User Adapted Interaction 11(1/2), 87–110 (2001)
4. Brusilovsky, P., Chavan, G., Farzan, R.: Social adaptive navigation support for open corpus electronic textbooks. In: De Bra, P., Nejdl, W. (eds.) AH 2004. LNCS, vol. 3137, pp. 24–33. Springer, Heidelberg (2004)
5. Brusilovsky, P., Eklund, J.: A study of user-model based link annotation in educational hypermedia. Journal of Universal Computer Science 4(4), 429–448 (1998)

6. Brusilovsky, P., Henze, N.: Open corpus adaptive educational hypermedia. In: Brusilovsky, P., Kobsa, A., Nejdl, W. (eds.) Adaptive Web 2007. LNCS, vol. 4321, pp. 671–696. Springer, Heidelberg (2007)
7. Brusilovsky, P., Pesin, L.: Adaptive navigation support in educational hypermedia: An evaluation of the ISIS-Tutor. Journal of Computing and Information Technology 6(1), 27–38 (1998)
8. Brusilovsky, P., Rizzo, R.: Using maps and landmarks for navigation between closed and open corpus hyperspace in Web-based education. The New Review of Hypermedia and Multimedia 9, 59–82 (2002)
9. Brusilovsky, P., Sosnovsky, S., Yudelson, M.: Adaptive Hypermedia Services for E-Learning. In: Proc. of Workshop on Applying Adaptive Hypermedia Techniques to Service Oriented Environments at the Third International Conference on Adaptive Hypermedia and Adaptive Web-Based Systems (AH 2004), pp. 470–479. Technische University Eindhoven (2004)
10. Brusilovsky, P., Sosnovsky, S., Yudelson, M.: Addictive links: The motivational value of adaptive link annotation in educational hypermedia. In: Wade, V., Ashman, H., Smyth, B. (eds.) AH 2006. LNCS, vol. 4018, pp. 51–60. Springer, Heidelberg (2006)
11. Davidovic, A., Warren, J., Trichina, E.: Learning benefits of structural example-based adaptive tutoring systems. IEEE Transactions on Education 46(2), 241–251 (2003)
12. Dieberger, A., Dourish, P., Höök, K., Resnick, P., Wexelblat, A.: Social navigation: Techniques for building more usable systems. Interactions 7(6), 36–45 (2000)
13. Dolog, P., Gavriloaie, R., Nejdl, W., Brase, J.: Integrating Adaptive Hypermedia Techniques and Open RDF-Based Environments. In: Proc. of The Twelfth International World Wide Web Conference, WWW 2003. Vol. Alternative paper tracks, pp. 88-98 (2003)
14. Farzan, R., Brusilovsky, P.: Social navigation support through annotation-based group modeling. In: Ardissono, L., Brna, P., Mitrović, A. (eds.) UM 2005. LNCS (LNAI), vol. 3538, pp. 463–472. Springer, Heidelberg (2005)
15. Farzan, R., Coyle, M., Freyne, J., Brusilovsky, P., Smyth, B.: ASSIST: adaptive social support for information space traversal. In: Proc. of 18th conference on Hypertext and hypermedia, HT 2007, pp. 199–208. ACM Press, New York (2007)
16. Henze, N., Nejdl, W.: Adaptation in open corpus hypermedia. International Journal of Artificial Intelligence in Education 12(4), 325–350 (2001)
17. Kavcic, A.: Fuzzy User Modeling for Adaptation in Educational Hypermedia. IEEE Transactions on Systems, Man, and Cybernetics 34(4), 439–449 (2004)
18. Ng, M.H., Hall, W., Maier, P., Armstrong, R.: The Application and Evaluation of Adaptive Hypermedia Techniques in Web-based Medical Education. Association for Learning Technology Journal 10(3), 19–40 (2002)
19. Triantafillou, E., Pomportis, A., Demetriadis, S., Georgiadou, E.: The value of adaptivity based on cognitive style: an empirical study. British Journal of Educational Technology 35(1), 95–106 (2004)
20. Weber, G., Specht, M.: User modeling and adaptive navigation support in WWW-based tutoring systems. In: Jameson, A., Paris, C., Tasso, C. (eds.) Proc. of 6th International Conference on User Modeling, pp. 289–300. Springer, Wien, NewYork (1997)
21. Yudelson, M., Brusilovsky, P.: Adaptive Link Annotation in Distributed Hypermedia Systems: The Evaluation of a Service-Based Approach. In: Kay, J., Pu, P., Nejdl, W., Herder, E. (eds.) Proc. of 5th International Conference on Adaptive Hypermedia and Adaptive Web-Based Systems (AH 2008). LNCS, vol. 5149, pp. 245–254. Springer, Heidelberg (2008)

Altruism, Selfishness, and Destructiveness on the Social Web

John Riedl

GroupLens Research
Computer Science Department
University of Minnesota

Abstract. Many online communities are emerging that, like Wikipedia, bring people together to build community-maintained artifacts of lasting value (CALVs). What is the nature of people's participation in building these repositories? What are their motives? In what ways is their behavior destructive instead of constructive? Motivating people to contribute is a key problem because the quantity and quality of contributions ultimately determine a CALV's value. We pose three related research questions: 1) How does intelligent task routing—matching people with work—affect the quantity of contributions? 2) How does reviewing contributions before accepting them affect the quality of contributions? 3) How do recommender systems affect the evolution of a shared tagging vocabulary among the contributors? We will explore these questions in the context of existing CALVs, including Wikipedia, Facebook, and MovieLens.

1 Introduction

Groups of people, working loosely together, have demonstrated the ability to deliver an amazing amount of volunteer person-power. Sites like del.icio.us have shown that people can catalog the Web, Flickr and YouTube have shown that the desire to express themselves will drive people to create innovative content, and to provide search terms to help other people find it, and Wikipedia has demonstrated that they will even write the largest encyclopedia in history, with an astonishing lack of structured organization.

In fact, the history of Wikipedia has demonstrated that too much organization can lead these volunteer systems to fail: Nupedia only ever had a few pages work its way through the careful review process, before Wikipedia wiped it out. However, recent studies have shown that vandalism is growing dangerously fast on Wikipedia. Is it in danger of failing?

Overall, the take-away lessons are that: (1) volunteers can create a tremendous amount of value; (2) if volunteer communities are over-organized, they fail; (3) if volunteer communities are under-organized, they might fail; (4) semi-automated techniques that support lightweight organization may offer a middle path to success. In this paper we will look at two examples: Tagging and Wikipedia.

W. Nejdl et al. (Eds.): AH 2008, LNCS 5149, pp. 9–11, 2008.

2 Tagging

Tagging systems enable users to attach keywords or phrases ("tags") to items. Tags can help organize items, help people find them later, or enable users to share their opinions about the items with other users. Tags have exploded since their inception: one Web site for books, LibraryThing.com, has in just three years attached 20 million tags to books.

One important challenge for tagging systems is that the tags applied are often just for personal consumption. For instance, one common tag on LibraryThing is "to read", which is of little value to anyone except the person applying the tag. The fundamental question underlying this behavior is: "for whom am I tagging?" If tagging is primarily an individual activity, then tags like "to read" are valuable, because they help me organize my personal information space. On the other hand, if tags are primarily a community activity, both the vocabulary used, and the types of opinions expressed should change. One possible middle ground adopted by some sites is that tags can be classified as "shared" or "private". By labelling tags, users can avoid cluttering the community information space, while still helping others when they wish. However, it is difficult to build interfaces that are easy-to-use and easy-to-understand for managing privacy rules. One possible middle ground is to build tools that automatically detect tags that other users do not find valuable, and hide those tags.

A second important challenge for tagging systems is that the vocabulary used by their users can grow sloppy over time. For instance, the most popular tags for the movie "Pulp Fiction" on MovieLens include "Quentin Tarantino" (the director), and "Tarantino Rocks!". In general, synonyms or misspellings are not cleared out of tagging systems easily. Furthermore, once a term has been used, the interface of most tagging systems encourages its reuse; research has shown that this reuse has a strong influence on the vocabulary that emerges as a "standard" for the tagging system. For these (and other) reasons, information specialists are often skeptical of tagging systems. They argue that intentionally designed ontologies have many advantages. Ongoing research is exploring a middle ground: is it possible to encourage the evolution of a folksonomy to capture some of the benefits of designed vocabulary systems? Can this ontology evolution be managed semi-automatically with machine learning tools, without destroying the motivation of the tagging users?

3 Wikipedia

Wikipedia took many of us by surprise: how could such a tremendously valuable resource be created by such an diverse community, with so little structure or management? As of this writing, though, Wikipedia has firmly established its relevance: with millions of articles in English, and more articles than the Encyclopedia Britannica in languages such as Finnish, Catalan, and Esperanto, Wikipedia is consistently one of the top 10 most popular sites on the Internet.

One ongoing debate is how much of the value of Wikipedia is contributed by a few super-contributors, versus micro-contributions from millions of users.

People on both sides of the debate perceive Wikipedia as having more stability if it has a broader base of contributions. Recent studies tend to support the super-contributor perspective. Yes, there are millions of editors, but just a few users are having enormous impact. Some wikipedians believe that technology, such as intelligent task routing, should be used to encourage more effective micro-contributions by the masses.

From its beginnings, information experts have argued that Wikipedia's open-ness will be its Achilles heel. Vandals have always defaced articles, especially controversial articles. There are even small communities who compete to commit vandalism in a way that will last as long as possible before being reverted. Will vandalism eventually destroy Wikipedia? Since 2006 software robots have been effectively cleaning up many types of vandalism automatically. However, the vandals are now adapting to the techniques used in the robots. Is there a type of intelligent task routing that can help Wikipedia gain the upper hand on the vandals forever?

4   Looking Forward

The broad variety of Social Web techniques, and their remarkably rapid adoption across the Web creates a unique opportunity for technologies who are interested in developing tools that help communities of human work together more effectively across the boundaries of time and space. The key challenges are (1) to develop technologies that add value to these communities; (2) to deploy those technologies in ways that meld with the sense of purpose in the community; and (3) to measure the effects of the new technologies on the communities, the individuals who participate in them, and the community-maintained artifacts of lasting value (CALVs) they are creating. We should seek to move from stumbling in the dark to developing a science of online communities.

A Rule-Based Recommender System for Online Discussion Forums

Fabian Abel[2], Ig Ibert Bittencourt[1], Nicola Henze[2], Daniel Krause[2], and Julita Vassileva[3]

[1] Federal University of Alagoas, Computer Science Institute
Maceio, AL, Brazil
ibert@dsc.ufcg.edu.br
[2] IVS - Semantic Web Group, Leibniz University of Hannover
Appelstr. 4, D-30167 Hannover, Germany
{abel,henze,krause}@kbs.uni-hannover.de
[3] Department of Computer Science, University of Saskatechwan
110 Science Place, Saskatoon SK S7N 5C9, Canada
jiv@cs.usask.ca

Abstract. In this paper we present a rule-based personalization framework for encapsulating and combining personalization algorithms known from adaptive hypermedia and recommender systems. We show how this personalization framework can be integrated into existing systems by example of the educational online board *Comtella-D*, which exploits the framework for recommending relevant discussions to the users. In our evaluations we compare different recommender strategies, investigate usage behavior over time, and show that a small amount of user data is sufficient to generate precise recommendations.

1 Introduction

Online discussion forums allow people to discuss different topics using the World Wide Web. While a discussion forum has often one large overall topic, it is normally divided into subtopics, called subforums or topics. The subforums are further divided into single threads. In these threads, one specific question, defined by the thread opener, is discussed by several users. Every user who wants to contribute can create text snippets, called posts which are ordered by the time they have been created. Posts can be displayed as a list and enable other users to follow the discussion easily.

The tree-like structure of the discussion forums enables users to navigate quickly to the topics which they are interested in. A drawback of the structure is that it is hard to find interesting threads if the thread is either not classified correctly by the thread opener or the user does not know how a specific topic of his interest is classified into the static discussion forum's hierarchy. Another drawback is that every thread can be assigned to one category, making threads matching to multiple categories hard to find. A commonly used approach to handle the problems caused by the described classification is to display a flattened

W. Nejdl et al. (Eds.): AH 2008, LNCS 5149, pp. 12–21, 2008.

list of all topics which encountered recent changes as a starting point. However, when forums become popular and hence large or the community discusses various topics, these lists contain a high percentage of threads which are not relevant for the user. This results in the situation that interested users encounter serious problems to find relevant threads when the forum grows.

Collaborative recommender systems can be used to cope with the issue of bringing users and relevant tasks together. In an E-Learning Online Discussion Forum like Comtella-D there are different kinds of input data which can be used to create recommendations. In this paper we evaluate a) which kind of input data fits best and b) how much input data is required to generate appropriate recommendations. Based on the results of this evaluation, we propose a rule based framework which chooses the optimal input data source: Recommender systems based on different input data sources are implemented as Web Services of the Personal Reader Framework [1]. A rule layer enables on the one hand to pass parameters to single personalization Web Services, PServices for short, and on the other hand to combine the results of different PServices. Default rules allow Comtella-D users to use this personalization framework immediately without any interaction. Moreover, user adjustable parameters in the rule allow for fine tuning of the rules if a user is not satisfied with the recommendations.

The paper is structured as follows: In Section 2 we describe our rule-based personalization system. In Section 3 we describe the Comtella-D system and outline the need for personalization in this system. Afterwards, by evaluating different recommender strategies, we define a flexible personalization rule in Section 4 that performs best in creating recommendation in different scenarios. Section 5 contains related work and Section 6 gives a conclusion and some further ideas to be exploited.

2 Rule-Based Personalization System

Personalization techniques have been investigated extensively in different areas of computer science. Especially in the domains of recommender systems [2] and adaptive hypermedia [3], personalization algorithms have been developed and deployed in various systems.

These personalization techniques are generic as the algorithms can be deployed in different domains, changing the domain specific input data without the need of modifying the algorithm itself. Hence, personalization algorithms are perfect candidates for being encapsulated to become reusable. However, in current systems these algorithms are often strongly coupled with the system as the data is often domain specific pre- or postprocessed or combined with other algorithms. In our system we decouple personalization algorithms, data sources and pre- and postprocessing from each other and allow the creation of rules which describe the interaction of the single components.

Figure 1 shows the architecture of the rule-based recommender system. It emphasizes two aspects. First, it assures the integration of different recommendation algorithms based on the use of Web Services. Second, show how to integrate

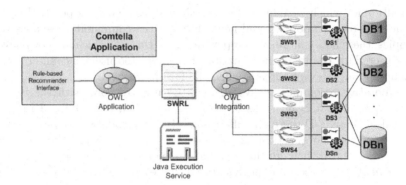

Fig. 1. Architecture of the System

external personalization functionality like recommendations. A description of the components of the architecture is listed below. However, it is not the focus of this paper to describe each component in detail. The technologies used in the development of the system were Java, *Protégé*[1], *SWRL*[2], *OWL-S Editor*[3], and *MindSwap*[4].

DB represents all databases that can be used for personalization, for e.g. user profiles or data provided in the Web

DS. Each data source represents an encapsulated personalization algorithm like a collaborative recommender system

SWS (Web Services). Each data source can be accessed as Web Service.

Comtella Application. It represents the Comtella application (more details are described in the next section)

Rule-based Recommendation Interface. This interface is used to specify personalization rules. Section 4.5 gives an example of such a rule.

SWRL (Semantic Web Rule Language). It is used to specify the conversion of information between the Comtella-D application and the data sources.

3   The Comtella-D System

Comtella Discussions (Comtella-D) [4] is an online community for discussing the social, ethical, legal and managerial issues associated with information technology and biotechnology. It was used to support the coursework related to a 4th year undergraduate class on Ethics and IT taught in the spring of 2006 at the University of Saskatchewan. Access to content is restricted to registered members, but anyone may create an account at http://fire.usask.ca after consenting to release their access data for research purposes. A nickname/alias,

---

[1] http://protege.stanford.edu/
[2] http://www.w3.org/Submission/SWRL/
[3] http://owlseditor.semwebcentral.org/
[4] http://www.mindswap.org/

e-mail address, and password are required to create an account. Members are relatively anonymous because they are identified just by their alias. The purpose of using Comtella-D in the class was sharing and discussing information (Internet publications, popular magazine, articles, etc.) related to the course topics. The students had to share at least one link to an online article related to the weekly topic and summarize the article in a way that it stimulates discussion. As a part of their coursework, the students also had to reply/discuss two of their colleagues' postings each week. In parallel with the students of the Ethics and IT class, (4th year Computer Science students), the Comtella-D system was used in a class on Ethics and Technology offered by the Philosophy department. These students used the system only as an additional resource, recommended by the instructor. The system was not related to their coursework and it was used entirely voluntary.

In the context of Comtella-D, a 'forum is an initial theme related to a course topic (usually weekly), defined and created by the instructor. A 'thread is started when a student contributes a link (URL) of a paper related to the topic of the forum. The first 'post in a new thread contains the URL and a summary of the paper (usually half a page). Further 'posts in the thread are added as other students respond to/discuss the first post of the thread. Each post can be commented. A 'comment is usually a very specific local comment to the post rather than to the entire thread. In Comtella-D comments were used mostly by the marker to give feedback on the quality of arguments raised in the students posts.

Comtella-D allows students to rate posts by adding or removing 'energy to or from it. A user can rate every post once, but only if there is free energy in the system available. The system provides a limited number of energy units, depending on the level of activity in the system. The number of energy units in the system increases every time when a new post is created (2 new units are added), and it decays with time. In this way, the scarcity of energy in the system prevents users from overrating their colleagues posts, and encourages them to carefully read a post before assigning energy to it. This mechanism is described in [4].

As every week several new threads are started and popular threads attract many posts, keeping an overview of the discussion is a time consuming task. A student who does not spend the time to read all new posts could easily miss important topics of his/her interest. Hence, a recommender system is needed which points the student to relevant posts. Using our rule-based personalization framework, we can utilize collaborative recommender services to solve this task. Based on the features of Comtella-D, there are different possibilities on which input data such a collaborative recommender can perform: a) recommendations based on explicit feedback gained from the user's energy rating and b) recommendations based on implicit feedback gained from co-posting in the same thread.

In the following section we will evaluate which kind of user feedback fits better to recommend threads a user might be interested in. Therefore, we also evaluate how much input data is required and over which time frame this input data has to be provided to generate high quality recommendations.

4   Evaluation

For the evaluation we took a snapshot of the Comtella-D system of the *Ethics and Computer Science* course 2006. Overall, there were 110 registered users. From these users only 36 contributed actively by posting a least one message in the discussion forum. Users rated other users 183 time and posted 756 messages in 173 threads over a time period of approximately 3 months. In these three months, the lectures deal every week with a new topic.

To define a personalization rule which recommends threads a user could be interested in, we use the existing user interaction with the system. Before creating this rule, we have to examine different questions: a) How much training data is required to generate precise recommendations (Section 4.1)? b) What kind of input data (explicit or implicit) gives the best quality to recommend threads (Section 4.2)? c) Does the behavior of users in the discussion forum change over time (Section 4.3)? d) Are active users, i.e. users who have posted frequently and hence are more experienced, more reliable as source for recommendations (Section 4.4)?.

For all of the following measurements, we used a recommender library[5] which implemented the collaborative recommender algorithm described in [5].

4.1   Required Amount of Training Data

According to the first question we divided our data set into weeks corresponding to the different topics of the lectures. Afterwards, we iterated over the weeks, selecting every week x as training set and tried to calculate the posts a specific user will create in week $x + 1$. Therefore, we classified the users into different classes, these classes contain sets of users who have posted at least y posts in different threads and at least 1 post in the test set. Furthermore, as a non-personalized baseline algorithm, we recommend the top-k threads having the most posts. Our hypothesis is that the more data from a user is available in the training set, the more precise the recommendation for the test set are.

The precision-recall distribution is build by iterating over all users in the class and calculating the top-k recommendations for these users. k is chosen from 1 to the number of all posts. For every k, the precision and recall is calculated as the average mean of all precision and recall values of all users in the class. Therefore, the recommendation system is invoked as follows: First, the posts generated in the training set are passed to the recommender system to determine the similarity between the users. Afterwards, the recommendations are calculated by passing all posts to the recommender system which were created in the test set.

Figure 2 displays the precision-recall distribution for the non-personalized base-line algorithm and the personalized recommendations based on users who have contributed at least 2, 3, 4, or 5 posts in the training set. While for $k <= 3$ the classes 3 to 5 perform better than class 2, class 2 performs better for $k > 4$. However, none of the different classes results in significantly better results than the other classes. Furthermore, all approaches are able to retrieve not more than 80%

---

[5] http://www.l3s.de/~diederich/SW/renkground-2006-09-07-1030.zip

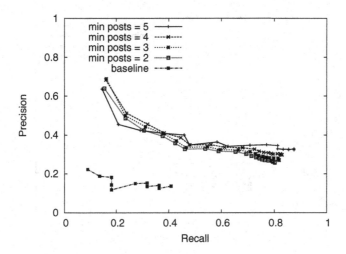

Fig. 2. The precision-recall diagram based on implicit user feedback for users who have posted at least 2, 3, 4, or 5 times in the training set week

of the threads the users have contributed to. This can be explained by the characteristics of the recommendation process: When a thread is recommended, a user who is similar to the current user must have contributed to this thread. Hence, threads which are discussed by only a few users are recommended rarely. This issue is known as *new item* problem in collaborative recommender systems [6].

Overall, the results imply that a) the non-personalized baseline algorithm is outperformed by the personalized algorithm and that b) two posts in a week are sufficient to generate precise personalized recommendations while more posts do not improve this the results significantly.

4.2   Implicit vs. Explicit User Feedback

Based on the classes defined in the previous section which used implicit user feedback by engaging the posts a user created, we define equivalent classes of explicit user feedback: These classes contain users who have at least added or removed x energy points to posts from other users in the training set week and have at least posted once in the test set week.

To recommend posts by using user ratings we modified the similarity function of the recommender system. Instead of comparing the similarity of user vectors containing threads a user has posted in, we use vectors containing the energy distribution. Two users are considered as similar when they gave energy to the same post, hence expressing interest in the same post. We did not take into account if users added or removed energy as we interpreted every form of energy assignment as interest in a post. The recommender algorithm itself was not modified.

Figure 3 gives an overview of the precision-recall ratio of recommendations based on explicit feedback for the classes of users having rated at least 2, or 3 other users in the training set period. The class with 5 energy assignments was

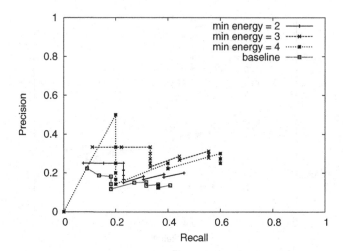

Fig. 3. The precision-recall diagram based on explicit user feedback for users who have rated at least 2, 3, or 4 posts of other users in the training set week

omitted as it contained not enough users to deliver reliable results. The graph outlines that – like in the previous section – a comparable small amount of input data, namely two energy assignments, are sufficient to create appropriate recommendations and that increasing the amount of input data does not increase the precision or recall of the recommendations significantly. Compared to the precision-recall distribution generated by implicit user feedback, the quality of the results generated by explicit feedback, in respect of both, precision and recall, are lower.

We also tried to combine explicit feedback and implicit feedback as we expected that input from different sources could improve the overall performance. We used the average mean to combine the weighted result sets of the recommendations based on explicit feedback and implicit feedback. We examined that the more we increased the weight of the explicit user feedback, the worse our recommender system performed. Our conclusion for the given setting is that explicit feedback performs always worse than implicit feedback and cannot be used to improve recommendation based on implicit feedback. However, if no implicit feedback is given for a specific user, explicit feedback performs better than the non-personalized baseline algorithm. Hence, explicit feedback based recommendations can be used as a fallback if no implicit feedback is available.

Based on these results we used implicit user feedback as source for the recommendations applied in the following evaluations.

4.3   User Behavior

The Comtella-D system was strongly coupled with the timeline of the lectures. This means that the users discussed every week a new topic. We assume that the behavior of users changes over time (and over different topics) which means that

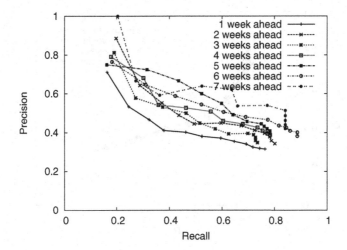

Fig. 4. User behavior over time

the more weeks ahead recommendations are created, the more imprecise they are. Furthermore, as topics discussed in a given week should be still somewhat fresher in the memory of the students, we assume that the forecast for the next week would be more precise than forecasts for two or more weeks ahead.

To verify our assumptions, we iterated over all weeks and used them as training data. We calculate the recommendations for n weeks ahead, where $n = 1, 2, .., 7$ and compared them with the test data. Afterwards, we created the precision-recall diagram displayed in Figure 4.

The figure displays a result which does not comply with our assumptions: The one week ahead precision-recall values for small top-k result sets are worse than all other forecasts. Furthermore, the forecasts for more weeks ahead do not comply to any rule or trend. This means that the behavior of the users indeed changes over time and topic, but that the change of behavior is not monotonic and cannot be forecasted. However, we have to remark that our dataset covers only three months of data. Thus, we can only infer about the short time behavior of users but cannot conclude that there is not a long time trend in user behavior.

4.4 Size of the Time Frame

In the previous section we have shown that the user behavior changes over the weeks making a constantly high forecast for several weeks ahead impossible. To lower this effect, we increase the input data timeframe by aggregating several weeks as training set and creating recommendations for one week ahead. We expect that aggregating several weeks of input data normalizes the behavior of a user on one hand and increases the amount of input data one the other. Both effects should result in an increased quality of the recommendations. Figure 5 displays the measurement aggregating one to five weeks of input data and calculating the precision and recall of the recommendations for the following week.

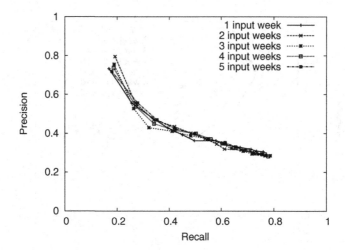

Fig. 5. Variation of the amount of weeks used as training data

All input periods result in similar results. Our expectation that more input weeks could improve the result could not be proven. This also underlines our previous observation that the changes of quality regarding precision and recall seem to follow no rule or trend.

4.5   Results

The results show that a small amount of input data (two posts or energy assignments) is enough to generate precise information. Furthermore, we have shown that the implicit user feedback, given by the posting behavior of users gives much better recommendations than explicit user feedback given by the energy assignment of the users. Also we have shown that more input data does not automatically result in better recommendations. According to these observations, an optimal personalization strategy to recommend threads in the Comtella-D system is the following:

```
if exist 2 or more posts of the user:
  -> recommendation based on implicit feedback
    else if exist 2 or more energy assignments of the user:
      -> recommendation based on explicit feedback
        else use the non-personalized baseline algorithm
```

5   Related Work

Our framework aims on decoupling personalization functionality from a specific application. For single domains, for e.g. the e-learning domain, there already exist approaches that realize such a decoupling [7]. However, to the best of our knowledge there exists no generic approach describing such an encapsulation of personalization functionality.

Also different personalization techniques are already combined to overcome the disadvantages of single personalization techniques. In the domain of recommender systems, these combination techniques are known as hybrid recommender systems systems [6], utilizing for example both, collaborative and content based recommender systems to overcome the *new item* or *new user* problem. The rule-based framework, however, does not only allow for a static combination of different personalization techniques. Instead, every rule can combine arbitrary personalization techniques.

6 Conclusion and Future Work

In this paper we presented a rule-based framework to combine arbitrary personalization techniques. Therefore, personalization techniques are encapsulated and separated from their input data to be reusable in different applications. We used the Comtella-D system to outline how the framework could be used to recommend forum threads. We specified a rule which selects the optimal recommendation technique according to the existing user information. To determine the best strategies, we evaluated which kinds of input data and which quantity is required to provide accurate recommendations.

In the future, we plan to make the rule user-adjustable. This can be done by introducing user adjustable weights in the rule which enable the combination of different techniques according to a user's preferences. Additionally, we plan to engage content-based recommender systems which take the text of the posts into account to improve the quality of recommendations further.

References

1. Abel, F., Baumgartner, R., Brooks, A., Enzi, C., Gottlob, G., Henze, N., Herzog, M., Kriesell, M., Nejdl, W., Tomaschewski, K.: The personal publication reader, semantic web challenge 2005. In: 4th International Semantic Web Conference (November 2005)
2. Adomavicius, G., Tuzhilin, A.: Toward the next generation of recommender systems: A survey of the state-of-the-art and possible extensions. IEEE Transactions on Knowledge and Data Engineering 17(6), 734–749 (2005)
3. Brusilovsky, P.: Adaptive Hypermedia. User Modeling and User-Adapted Interaction 11, 87–110 (2001)
4. Webster, A., Vassileva, J.: Visualizing personal relations in online communities. In: Wade, V.P., Ashman, H., Smyth, B. (eds.) AH 2006. LNCS, vol. 4018, pp. 223–233. Springer, Heidelberg (2006)
5. Shardanand, U., Maes, P.: Social information filtering: Algorithms for automating "word of mouth". In: Proceedings of ACM CHI 1995 Conference on Human Factors in Computing Systems, vol. 1, pp. 210–217 (1995)
6. Burke, R.: Hybrid recommender systems: Survey and experiments. User Modeling and User-Adapted Interaction 12(4), 331–370 (2002)
7. Brusilovsky, P., Henze, N.: Open corpus adaptive educational hypermedia. In: Brusilovsky, P., Kobsa, A., Nejdl, W. (eds.) Adaptive Web 2007. LNCS, vol. 4321, pp. 671–696. Springer, Heidelberg (2007)

Locally Adaptive Neighborhood Selection for Collaborative Filtering Recommendations

Linas Baltrunas and Francesco Ricci

Free University of Bozen-Bolzano,
Domeninkanerplatz 3,
Bozen, Italy
{lbaltrunas,fricci}@unibz.it

Abstract. User-to-user similarity is a fundamental component of Collaborative Filtering (CF) recommender systems. In user-to-user similarity the ratings assigned by two users to a set of items are pairwise compared and averaged (correlation). In this paper we make user-to-user similarity adaptive, i.e., we dynamically change the computation depending on the profiles of the compared users and the target item whose rating prediction is sought. We propose to base the similarity between two users only on the subset of co-rated items which best describes the taste of the users with respect to the target item. These are the items which have the highest correlation with the target item. We have evaluated the proposed method using a range of error measures and showed that the proposed locally adaptive neighbor selection, via item selection, can significantly improve the recommendation accuracy compared to standard CF.

1 Introduction

The World Wide Web, interconnecting a myriad of information and business services, has made available to on-line users an over abundance of information and very large product catalogues. Hence, users trying to decide what information to consult or what products to choose may be overwhelmed by the number of accessible options. Collaborative Filtering (CF) is a recommendation technique which emulates a simple and effective social strategy called "word-of-mouth" and is now largely applied in Web 2.0 platforms. CF, given a target user, uses the opinions (i.e., user ratings of items) of similar users to generate the personalized recommendation for the target[1]. A CF system represents users with their ratings on a set of items (ratings vectors). When requested to generate a recommendation for a target user, a memory based CF system first selects a set of users that are similar to the target according to a similarity measure computed on their ratings vectors (neighborhood selection). Then, it generates rating predictions for items not rated yet by the target user. Finally the system recommends the items with the highest predicted rating.

User-to-user similarity plays a very important role in CF; it is used in the neighborhood selection and in the final rating prediction, and it is normally

W. Nejdl et al. (Eds.): AH 2008, LNCS 5149, pp. 22–31, 2008.

computed using *all* the items co-rated by the two users whose similarity is required. The work presented in this paper is aimed at improving CF by adapting the user-to-user similarity function used in the neighbor selection step, taking into account: a) the user for whom a rating prediction is sought (target user), and b) the particular target item whose rating the system is predicting. We hypothesized that the neighbor, and consequently the goodness of the rating prediction, can be improved if the user-to-user similarity is based on a well selected subset of commonly co-rated items: those items highly correlated with the target item. The rationale is that certain ratings may not be relevant, and even detrimental, when predicting a particular item rating. For example, if we try to predict the rating for the movie "The Matrix", it could be better to take into account ratings on similar action or sci-fi movies and ignore ratings on documentary movies.

We shall show that the proposed adaptive user-to-user similarity method improves precision and increases the diversity of the profiles of the neighbor users, yielding a better recall. The rationale is that when similarity is computed on a different subset of items (depending on the target item), this is leading to a different neighborhood for each target item. Hence these two sets of neighbors are more likely to cover different parts of the item space. In fact, the proposed locally adaptive neighbor selection method brings improvements for all the error measures we used.

The paper is organized as follows. Section 2 discusses the related work on the item selection. Section 3 describes item selection methods for CF and in Subsection 3.1 we describe the item weighting methods that were used to determine importance of the item. The proposed locally adaptive item selection method is evaluated in Section 4. Finally, Section 5 draws the conclusions and presents future work.

2   Related Work

Item selection techniques are well know tools used in Machine Learning (ML). In ML they are called feature selection and are widely used to improve the prediction accuracy of supervised classification [2,3]. Recently they are receiving a new interest because of their exploitation in Information Retrieval methods based on learning [4,5]. In fact, a user-based CF system can be described as a collection of instance-based classifiers, one for each item, whose' rating is sought. Given a target item (class) and a target user, the user ratings on all other items provide the instance description (predictive items). In this perspective, the rating prediction step of a CF system can be described as a classification or regression learning problem, i.e., one classification/regression problem for each target item's rating prediction. The similarity measure is based on users' preferences, i.e., item ratings. Hence, these items can be regarded as user's features, and item ratings are the values of the feature. In general, the huge search space of thousands or millions of items makes the available feature selection methods hard to apply to CF. In fact, to our best knowledge item selection has not been explored in the context of the CF.

Classical feature selection methods assume that features are either relevant in the whole instance space or irrelevant throughout. However, it can often be the case that features are relevant only in the context of other features. To address this situation local feature selection was studied in [6,7]. Here, features are selected depending on the target instance whose class must be predicted, and the other features which are present in the selection set. Both works are related to our approach, as in these cases the selected features depend on the target instance (user in CF setting). However, they study and exploit the relationships between predictive features rather than the dependency between predictive items (features) and target item (feature), as we do.

Item weighting for CF is another related approach, which tries to adapt user-to-user similarity depending on the prediction task and the profiles of the users [8,9,10]. Here, the items with larger weights will have a major influence in the user-to-user similarity computation. Due to the huge amount of items and the sparseness of data, non localized item weighting methods give only minor improvements over classical CF (not shown here for lack of space).

3   Item Selection for Collaborative Filtering

Finding the optimal subset of items would require to conduct an extensive search in the space of all the subsets of the items [3]. Applying this to a recommender system scenario would require to conduct a search procedure for every target item (the item playing the role of the class to be predicted) and for a large number of subsets of the predictive items. This is clearly extremely expensive, and therefore, we propose to use a more parsimonious approach (filter method) that uses information provided by a item weighting method to select, for each target item and user pair, an appropriate set of predictive items.

Hence, first we compute item weights, using one of the methods described later in Section 3.1, and then we filter out irrelevant items, i.e., those with the smallest weights, for a given target item rating prediction. Following this procedure, every item weighting method generates one or more corresponding item selection method depending on how the weights are used to select items.

Extremely sparse rating matrix makes classical filter method ineffective. Imagine for instance, that there are two users that are perfectly correlated but have co-rated just a few items and these items have small weights. One of the two users could be used to predict the ratings of the second user. But, if we straight-forwardly select a small number of items, according to a precomputed weights (i.e., just the items with largest weights), there is a very small chance that the profiles of these users will overlap on the selected items. Therefore, using classical filter method many good neighbors could be discarded hence decreasing the prediction quality.

For these reasons, we propose a localized item selection method called **BIPO** (Best Items per Overlap). BIPO selects the subset of items with largest weights from the set of items co-rated by both users whose similarity we want to determine. We shall explain BIPO method using a simple example of user-item rating matrix showed bellow:

	i_1	i_2	i_3	i_4	i_5	i_t
w_{ti}	0.1	0.2	0.3	0.4	0.5	
u_1	5	3	2	1	?	6
u_2	4	2	4	?	5	?

The table consist of two user and six items. The question marks indicate the unknown ratings. Let us assume that we want to predict user's u_2 rating for the item i_t. Moreover, suppose that we have computed item weights beforehand, using an item weighting algorithm. The weights are showed in the second row of the table. For example, the weight of item i_1 for predicting the target item i_t is $w_{t1} = 0.1$.

In the example above, BIPO method would select items with the highest weights that are rated by both users. Suppose we want to compute user-to-user similarity on the 2 largely correlated items. In such a case BIPO would select items 3 and 2, and the other items would be not considered, despite the fact that they have a larger correlation with the target item. We note that in BIPO the items used in the prediction change for every target item and neighbor user pairs.

3.1 Weight Computation Methods

We use item weighting to estimate how much a particular item is important for predicting the ratings for another (target) item. Only the items with the highest weights are selected using BIPO to compute the user-to-user similarity. In CF, item weights can be learned while exploring training data consisting of user ratings, or using external information associated with the items. In this paper we introduce five item weighting methods used for item selection: Random, Variance, Mutual Information, Tag, and IPCC.

Random. The first method is used only as the baseline for comparisons and uses a random item weighting. Random weights in $[0, 1]$ are selected for each target and predictive items combination.

Variance. Variance method was originally proposed by [11] and gives to an item a weight equal to the variance of the ratings given by all users to that item:

$$w_{ji}^V = w_i^V = \frac{\sum_{u \in U(i)} (v_{ui} - \bar{v}_i)^2}{|U(i)|}$$

here $\bar{v}_i$ is the mean of the ratings of item i, $U(i)$ is the set of users who rated item i. Variance weighting method uses only information about the predictive item (i) and does not take into account the target item (j) for which a prediction is sought.

IPCC. This method computes the weight for item i using the Pearson Correlation Coefficient (PCC) between the item i ratings (i.e., the ratings of all users for item i) and the target item j ratings.

$$w_{ji}^P = \frac{\sum_u (v_{ui} - \bar{v}_i)(v_{uj} - \bar{v}_j)}{\sqrt{\sum_u (v_{ui} - \bar{v}_i)^2 \sum_u (v_{uj} - \bar{v}_j)^2}}$$

here u runs over all the users that have rated both i and j, and $\bar{v}_i$ is the mean of item i ratings.

Mutual Information. Mutual Information measures the information that a random variable provides to the knowledge of an other. Mutual Information between two items is defined as :

$$w_{ji}^M = \sum_{x \in j} \sum_{y \in i} p(x,y) \log \frac{p(x,y)}{p(x)p(y)}$$

and in practice it is implemented using the entropy as in [8].

Genre weighting. The previous methods exploit statistics of the users' rating data to compute item weights. The last method we present here computes weights using description of the items. In the movie recommendation data set, which we are going to use for our experiments, movies are tagged with movie genres. Hence, we make the assumption that the larger the number of common tags, here genres, the higher is the dependency. The weight of the predictive item i for a prediction of the ratings of the target item j is given by:

$$w_{ji}^T = \frac{\#\ comon\ tags\ of\ items\ i\ and\ j}{\#tags}$$

Genre weighting is related to the methods presented in [12] where item description information is used to selectively choose the items to be used in the user-to-user correlation.

For efficiency reasons, for all the item selection algorithms, we computed off-line all the weights and later we used these stored values in the user-to-user similarity computation. In practice, to store all the weights, we need an $M \times M$ matrix of weights, where M is the cardinality of the item set. In other words, one vector of weights of size M is used for each item prediction.

4   Experimental Evaluation

In this section we present the evaluation of BIPO item selection method for neighbor selection. As we mentioned above, our method is computing first the item weights and later is using them to select items considered in the user-to-user similarity. We note that PCC between users *with BIPO item selection* is used while computing the neighborhood of the active user, whereas *the standard PCC, without item selection,* is used to compute the predicted rating. This is because in this paper we want to measure the effect of item selection in neighbor formation, and consequently in CF performance. CF rating prediction is computed as follows:

$$v_{xj}^* = \bar{v}_x + \frac{\sum_{y \in N(k,x,j)} PCC(x,y) \times (v_{yj} - \bar{v}_y)}{\sum_{y \in N(k,x,j)} |PCC(x,y)|}$$

here the sum runs on the k-nearest neighbors of the user x, $N(k,x,j)$, that in our approach depend on the target item j. In our implementation of CF, as done in other studies [12], we do not take into account neighbors which have less than six co-rated items. Moreover, in our experiments k is equal to 60.

In our evaluation we used MovieLens [13] dataset with ratings in $\{1, 2, 3, 4, 5\}$. It contains 100K ratings, for 1682 movies by 943 users, who have rated 20 and more items. The data sparsity is 96%. To evaluate the proposed methods the data set was randomly divided into train (80%) and test (20%) subsets. We used the train data to learn the weights and also to generate a prediction for the test ratings. We evaluated the performance of the proposed methods with a wide range of error measures.

To measure the accuracy we used: MAE, High MAE, F measure, precision and recall [11,14]. To compute F, precision and recall, we considered items worth recommending (relevant items) only if their ratings were 4 or 5. Since, we are interested in recommending only the top items, we propose to modify the MAE error measure to see how an algorithm performs on the predictions of items with highest ratings. For this purpose we defined High MAE measure as MAE computed only on the items that were rated by the user 4 or 5. To compute the weights we used the five item weighting methods described in section 3.1. In figure 1 the performance of BIPO with all these methods is depicted. We note that **all** item weighting methods used for BIPO item selection showed a better performance over the baseline CF ,i.e., collaborative filtering without item selection, for all the error measures used. This result is important since it clearly

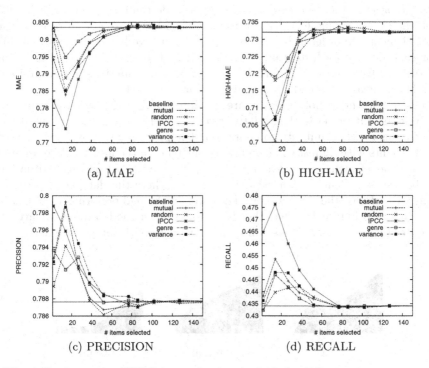

(a) MAE   (b) HIGH-MAE

(c) PRECISION   (d) RECALL

Fig. 1. Performance of BIPO item selection methods for different error measures

shows the robustness of item selection, and clearly shows that the improvements are due to item selection rather than weighting.

In fact, there is no single best item weighting approach and the winner depends on the particular error measure used. For example, weighting based on Mutual Information (in fig. "mutual") produces an item selection that performs best for High-MAE error measure, whereas IPCC weighting performs better for recall measure and gives improvement up to 6.6%. Random item selection and genre labelling methods are the worst, however, they also improve the performance of the baseline method. Note that the Variance based method performs as good as IPCC and Mutual Information with respect to precision, MAE, and High MAE. This is important, because in the Variance approach the weight of the item does not depend on the target item, hence this method can be easily applied for large data sets with many items. It can be also efficiently computed and cashed.

Similar performances can be seen using other datasets. Due to the lack of space, we could not include the full description of result in this paper. The method was tested on Yahoo! WebScope dataset[15], which contains extremely sparse data. We discovered, that the improvements are smaller, however, they increase when the average overlap between users increases (achieved by filtering out users with small number of ratings). Our conclusion is that in order to make a meaningful item selection we must have enough co-rated items to choose from. In order to explain why some weighting methods perform better than others we analyzed the distribution of correlation values between items. For each target item we ordered the item computed weights in descending order and then we took the average value for each position. In such a way we got an ordered list of M elements. In order to be able to depict this list we further compressed this representation into a histogram with 100 bins, where each bin averages 1% of the ordered list values. In Figure 2 three different distributions of item-to-item correlation measures for MovieLens dataset are depicted.

It is important to note that we are not interested in the absolute values of the weights, but rather in their relative size. Given the target item, we select the top f items for the similarity computation. The problem arises when we have a lot of weights with almost equal values. In such a case the items will be ordered in a pseudo random order, leading to a wrong item selection. Such situation can be seen for Genre weighting (Figure 2(c)), where the flat part represents items with almost the same weight. This explain the bad performance of Genre weighting (see Figure 1). The other two weighting methods produce relatively good ordering, i.e., there is a small number of items with similar weights.

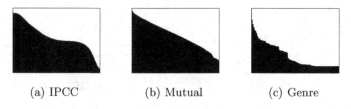

(a) IPCC   (b) Mutual   (c) Genre

Fig. 2. Various correlation distributions

Table 1. Performance of BIPO and standard CF on different set of ratings

	common ratings		CF-only ratings	BIPO-only ratings
Measure	CF	BIPO	CF	BIPO
# rat. predicted	17833	17833	117	**1146**
MAE	0.8024	**0.7663**	0.9656	0.8939
HIGH-MAE	0.7305	0.6954	1.1055	0.9776

In the previous experiments we showed that BIPO item selection method gives good results using a small number of items in user-to-user similarity. In the next analysis we investigated whether BIPO can generate predictions for the same user-item pairs that standard CF will predict[1]. Hence we evaluated the performance of BIPO on the subsets of the items whose rating is predicted by both BIPO and CF, and items that where predicted only by one of the two methods.

The performance of BIPO item selection method with a fixed number (14) of selected items was compared against the baseline CF. Both methods used 60 k-nearest neighbors. The test set was divided into three subsets: "common" subset contains ratings predicted by both methods; $CF - only$ contains the ratings predicted only by baseline CF and $BIPO - only$ contains those predicted only by BIPO. In table 1 summary of the results is shown.

These result shows that both methods can predict a large common subset user-item pairs in the test data set, namely 17833. On this set of user-item pairs that both can predict, BIPO decreases MAE by 4.5%. Moreover, BIPO can make more predictions compared to the baseline method (117 vs 1146 items not in the common subset). This result is surprising and shows that despite data sparsity, carefully selecting items for neighborhood formation increases recall and could also improve recommendation diversity.

The increase in recall (and also in the ability to make more predictions) shown by BIPO can be explained by better analyzing the way user-to-user similarity is computed by this method. First of all, BIPO computes the similarity using only the items that have the highest correlation with the target item. This can explain why it is more likely that the target item is also rated by the neighbors found by this method, and therefore the collaborative filtering prediction rule can actually compute a prediction for it.

Secondly, by computing the similarity on a smaller subset of items we tackle a problem related to users, who rated many items. At the first glance, such users should be easier to serve, and will be provided with better recommendations, because they have a large rating history. However, when looking for neighbors it is likely that there will be many users highly correlated to this target user but only on a small number of overlapping items. At the end, without item selection, we could select neighbors who are highly correlated but on a small number of items. Using item selection we compute overlap only on a small but **highly selected** items, making more likely that other users with larger profiles become

---

[1] Thanks to J. Konstan for suggesting this study in a personal communication.

neighbors of the target user. This may decrease the average correlation with the neighbor users but it computes correlations with higher reliability.

Moreover, since the selection of items is made by analyzing both the target user and the neighbor profile, the neighbors found are more diverse, as they can be correlated on different subsets of items. This is very important and is explaining the increase in recall as the increased diversity of the neighbors increases the chance that a neighbor rated the target item.

5   Discussion and Conclusions

In this paper we introduced locally adaptive item selection method for an improved neighbor selection in CF. We evaluated the proposed method along with a range of error measures. In summary, BIPO item selection approach, using a small number of items, can achieve significant improvements for all the considered error measures. This result is important because it shows that CF user profiles contain a lot of redundancy and even if the data set is sparse the information is not uniformly distributed among users.

We showed that CF performances can be improved with a careful selection of the item ratings, i.e., acquiring ratings for certain items can greatly improve the performance of the recommendation algorithm. In fact, since BIPO select items according to the target item, the outcome can be a different neighborhood for the same target user depending on the prediction that must be computed. Hence BIPO is in fact an item selection and user selection method. The idea is that when we must make a prediction for a particular type of item, not all the neighbors computed by the classical CF may be relevant. If a neighbor user is highly correlated to the target, but on items not highly correlated with the target item, then this user should not be considered.

We have also shown that in item selection the precise weighting method is not crucial. In other words, as we use only ranking of the item weights, but not the absolute values, even a suboptimal weighting can generate a good item selection. This observation is the base for a future extension of this work where we plan to consider fast sub-optimal weighting schemes for large data sets. We stress again that we used item selection only in the neighborhood formation step, therefore, we state that item selection leads to a better neighborhood formation. A natural extension of the method would be to validate item selection also in the prediction step.

In the future we shall better analyze the user selection problem, in addition and in combination with item selection. We want to compare pure item weighting and selection methods with instance (user) selection methods. Moreover, the computation of the item weights is an expensive step. We need to recompute the weights when new ratings are registered to the system. Therefore, for this reason we are currently working on the design of an item weighting method based on RELIEF [16] feature estimator in order to avoid item weights recomputation. Using this method with every new rating we could gradually adapt the overall weighting schema.

References

1. Schafer, J.B., Frankowski, D., Herlocker, J., Sen, S.: Collaborative filtering recommender systems. In: The Adaptive Web, pp. 291–324. Springer, Heidelberg (2007)
2. Wettschereck, D., Aha, D.W., Mohri, T.: A review and empirical evaluation of feature weighting methods for a class of lazy learning algorithms. Artif. Intell. Rev. 11(1-5), 273–314 (1997)
3. Kohavi, R., John, G.H.: Wrappers for feature subset selection. Artificial Intelligence 97(1-2), 273–324 (1997)
4. Radlinski, F., Joachims, T.: Query chains: learning to rank from implicit feedback. In: KDD 2005: Proceeding of the eleventh ACM SIGKDD international conference on Knowledge discovery in data mining, pp. 239–248. ACM Press, New York (2005)
5. Geng, X., Liu, T.-Y., Qin, T., Li, H.: Feature selection for ranking. In: SIGIR 2007: Proceedings of the 30th annual international ACM SIGIR conference on Research and development in information retrieval, pp. 407–414. ACM, New York (2007)
6. Atkeson, C., Andrew Moore, S.S.: Locally weighted learning. AI Review 11, 11–73 (1997)
7. Puuronen, S., Tsymbal, A.: Local feature selection with dynamic integration of classifiers (2001)
8. Yu, K., Xu, X., Ester, M., Kriegel, H.-P.: Feature weighting and instance selection for collaborative filtering: An information-theoretic approach*. Knowl. Inf. Syst. 5(2), 201–224 (2003)
9. Jin, R., Chai, J.Y., Si, L.: An automatic weighting scheme for collaborative filtering. In: SIGIR 2004: Proceedings of the 27th annual international ACM SIGIR conference on Research and development in information retrieval, pp. 337–344. ACM Press, New York (2004)
10. Breese, J.S., Heckerman, D., Kadie, C.M.: Empirical analysis of predictive algorithms for collaborative filtering. In: Cooper, G.F., Moral, S. (eds.) UAI, pp. 43–52. Morgan Kaufmann, San Francisco (1998)
11. Herlocker, J.L., Konstan, J.A., Borchers, A., Riedl, J.: An algorithmic framework for performing collaborative filtering. In: SIGIR, pp. 230–237. ACM, New York (1999)
12. Berkovsky, S., Kuflik, T., Ricci, F.: Cross-domain mediation in collaborative filtering. In: Conati, C., McCoy, K.F., Paliouras, G. (eds.) UM 2007. LNCS (LNAI), vol. 4511, pp. 355–359. Springer, Heidelberg (2007)
13. MovieLens: Movielens dataset, http://www.grouplens.org/
14. Herlocker, J.L., Konstan, J.A., Terveen, L.G., Riedl, J.T.: Evaluating collaborative filtering recommender systems. ACM Trans. Inf. Syst. 22(1), 5–53 (2004)
15. Yahoo!: Webscope movie data set (Version 1.0), http://research.yahoo.com/
16. Robnik-Šikonja, M., Kononenko, I.: Theoretical and empirical analysis of relieff and rrelieff. Mach. Learn. 53(1-2), 23–69 (2003)

Adaptive Retrieval of Semi-structured Data

Yosi Ben-Asher[1], Shlomo Berkovsky[1], Paolo Busetta[2],
Yaniv Eytani[3], Sadek Jbara[1], and Tsvi Kuflik[1]

[1] University of Haifa, Haifa, Israel
{yosi,slavax}@cs.haifa.ac.il, tsvikak@is.haifa.ac.il
[2] ITC-irst, Trento, Italy
busetta@itc.it
[3] University of Illinois at Urbana-Champaign, Illinois, USA
yeytani2@uiuc.edu

Abstract. The rapidly growing amount of heterogeneous semi-structured data available on the Web is creating a need for simple and universal access methods. For this purpose, we propose exploiting the notion of UNSpecified Ontology (UNSO), where the data objects are described using a list of attributes and their values. To facilitate efficient management of UNSO data objects, we use LoudVoice, a multi-agent channeled multicast communication platform, where each attribute is assigned a designated communication channel. This allows efficient searches to be performed by querying only the relevant channels, and aggregating the partial results. We implemented a prototype system and experimented with a corpus of real-life E-Commerce advertisements. The results demonstrate that the proposed approach yields a high level of accuracy and scalability.

1 Introduction

Nowadays, the amount of available semi-structured, heterogeneously represented, and highly dynamic data is growing, making it difficult for users to find and access the data relevant to their needs. Hence, mechanisms are required that will facilitate access to and matching of such data and thus free users from the need to know a priori how the data objects are structured (e.g., schemata or ontologies [9]).

This issue is being approached from different angles. Information retrieval techniques [10] cannot handle semantic and syntactic heterogeneity in the data. Semantic Web research [6] focuses on treating the Web as a knowledge base that defines semantic concepts and their relationships, whereas knowledge representation languages allow the meaning of concepts to be represented using ontologies. The key challenge of the semantic approach is the large number of such ontologies. Data integration [3] and schema matching [8] research studies aim at addressing this challenge by, respectively, reconciling the ontologies and matching between the concepts pertaining to different ontologies. A global ontology allows a uniform data access mechanism and defines rules encapsulating the differences between the ontologies. Despite their relative success, neither data integration nor ontology matching have fully succeeded in resolving the issues related to the dynamic and variable nature of the ontologies.

W. Nejdl et al. (Eds.): AH 2008, LNCS 5149, pp. 32–41, 2008.

This work uses an alternative approach to accessing the data: UNSpecified Ontologies (UNSO) [2]. UNSO assumes that the ontologies are not fully defined and can be dynamically specified by the data providers. Hence, instead of basing the data description on a set of a-priori defined ontologies, the data objects are described in the form of an unspecified list of attributes and their values, where both the attributes and the values in the data object descriptions are determined by the data providers. In this work we investigate the accuracy and efficiency of the UNSO approach implemented over the LoudVoice multi-agent platform [4]. In this setting, an agent can either provide a new data object (i.e., contribute data and define new concepts) or search for the existing data objects. To handle these functions, LoudVoice provides a set of channels that allow the agents to be tuned to existing channel or to create new ones.

The practical part of this work implements UNSO over LoudVoice, and experiments with a set of real-life E-Commerce ads from various domains. The experimental results demonstrate that the proposed approach yields both accurate and efficient data management and search capabilities. Hence, our contribution is two-fold. First, we propose and evaluate a scalable approach for storing data objects over a multi-agent platform, which allows search queries to be posed to a dynamic mechanism that captures the descriptions of the data objects. Second, the LoudVoice communication mode facilitates the extraction of domain meta-data reflecting the dynamic quality of the data objects, which is exploited for optimizing the search and improving the efficiency of the proposed approach.

2   Unspecified Data Management over Multi-agent Platform

Ontologies are referred to as standardized, well-defined, and formal models of a domain, agreed upon all the users [9]. Conversely, the main assumption behind UNSO is that the domain ontologies are not fully specified and their parts can be dynamically specified by the data providers [2]. As such, UNSO allows the data providers to describe the data objects in a relatively unconstrained form of a list of *<attribute:value>* pairs, where neither the attributes nor their values are defined a priori. Although such a description of the data objects may be inapplicable for complex entities, it is sufficient for simple data and real-life objects, e.g., files, products or computing resources.

UNSO may suffer from inconsistent symbolism, since the data providers may insert different descriptions of the same objects. For example, consider the two descriptions of an object shown in Figure 1. There, the same object is described in different ways and using different attributes. Moreover, the same value of the attribute *engine* is described using different values. In [2], this problem is addressed by standardizing the *<attribute:value>* pairs mentioned in UNSO descriptions using WordNet [7]. In WordNet, nouns, verbs, adjectives, and adverbs are organized into synonym sets,

```
<product:car, type:Mazda>            <product:car, type:Mazda>
<volume:engine1600, year:2000>       <volume:1.6l, year:2000>
<color:red, distance:Km100000>       <condition:good, owners:2>
```

Fig. 1. Different descriptions of the same data object using UNSO

representing the underlying lexical concepts. To overcome the inconsistent symbolism, UNSO data object descriptions are standardized by substituting the original terms used in the descriptions with their most frequent synonyms.

To facilitate efficient data management of UNSO data objects, we extend the notion of implicit organizations [5]. An implicit organization is "a group of agents playing the same role and coordinating their actions." The term implicit stresses that there is no explicit group formation stage, and joining an organization is a matter of sharing functionality with other members of the organization. In the context of UNSO descriptions, implicit organizations reflect the attributes mentioned in the descriptions, such that each attribute is assigned to a single organization. The resulting set of organizations facilitates dynamic management and access to the underlying data objects.

The selected LoudVoice communication platform [4] has been designed to support implicit organizations inherently, as every LoudVoice channel represents an individual organization. To adjust UNSO to an agent-based environment, the data object descriptions are partitioned among agents, mimicking a real-life matching scenario, where real agents represent users offering or searching for a product. Each unique attribute mentioned in the descriptions is assigned a designated channel, such that the agents join the channels through 'tuning' to them. Hence, each agent joins multiple channels, according to the attributes mentioned in the descriptions it stores.

The above mapping of data objects to LoudVoice channels is shown in Figure 2. Data object descriptions in the form of an *<attribute:value>* list (left) are inserted by an agent (middle), which is tuned to a channel representing one of the mentioned attributes (right). Note that other agents, storing data object descriptions with the same attribute, are also tuned to that channel. For example, consider the following description of a file: [*name:myfile.txt, author:JohnDoe, size:1.23*K]. The agent storing this description is tuned to channels representing *name*, type *author*, and *size* attributes. For the sake of simplicity, we refer to the channels using the attribute names only.

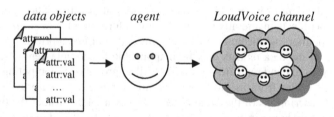

Fig. 2. Mapping of data object descriptions to implicit organizations

LoudVoice implements a channeled multicast communication mode, where messages sent over a channel are received by all the agents tuned to it. Channeled multicast reduces the amount of communication and allows overhearing, i.e., 'eavesdropping' on messages addressed to others. Overhearing, in turn, allows advanced data management functionalities, e.g., domain meta-data extraction (will be presented later), which are achieved through so-called *mediating* agents. These agents are tuned to both the channels pertaining to attributes and the inter-organization communication channels used for transferring information between the channels and coordinating between agents. For example, consider two channels A and B and their mediating agents tuned also to an inter-organization communication channel, as shown in Figure 3.

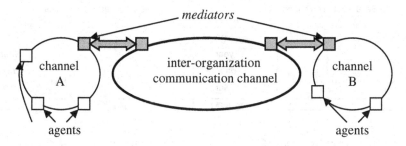

Fig. 3. Organization of LoudVoice channels

3   Semantic Search and Matching over LoudVoice

One of the main characteristics of UNSO is the efficient storage, search, and matching of data objects. This work focuses on the E-Commerce applications, and, in particular, on buy/sell interactions, where sellers offer products, buyers search for products offered by the sellers, and the products are represented by the data objects. We use this setting to demonstrate a protocol for search and matching of the data objects. Various enhancements, such as the highest bid selection and product ranking, can be added to this protocol. The protocol is schematically shown in Figure 4.

Consider three objects offered by two sellers: (O1) Mazda produced in *2000* and having *2* past owners, (O2) Nissan produced in *2002* that costs *$12,000*, and (O3) red Van that costs *$9,000*. Objects O1 and O2 are stored by *seller1* agent, while O3 is stored by *seller2*. In addition, there are two buyers: *buyer1* and *buyer2*, such that *buyer1* is searching for a red car below *$10,000* and *buyer2* is searching for a *Mazda* car having *2* or less past owners. The proposed protocol consists of two steps executed by the buyers and two steps executed by the sellers.

- Step1 (sellers listen): The sellers are tuned to the channels corresponding to the attributes of their objects and wait for queries indicating that the buyers are looking for products represented by *<attribute:value>* pairs. For example, *seller1* is tuned to the channels *product, type, year, price* and *owners*.
- Step 2 (buyers broadcast): The buyers send the desired values of the attributes they are searching. For example, *buyer2* broadcasts *car* on the channel *product*, *Mazda* on the channel *type*, and *less than 2* on the channel *owners*.
- Step 3 (sellers respond): The sellers inform the buyers that they have a product with the mentioned *<attribute:value>* pair. For each buyer, the seller sends one message $seller_{id} \rightarrow buyer_{id}$ specifying all the objects matching the desired value. For example *seller2* sends two messages on the *product* channel indicating that the Van matches the *car* value of *buyer1* and *buyer2*.
- Step 4 (buyers aggregate responses): The buyers collect all the messages sent at the previous step and identify matchings. Thus, *buyer1* obtains a complete matching for the O3 and *buyer2* obtains a complete matching for O1.

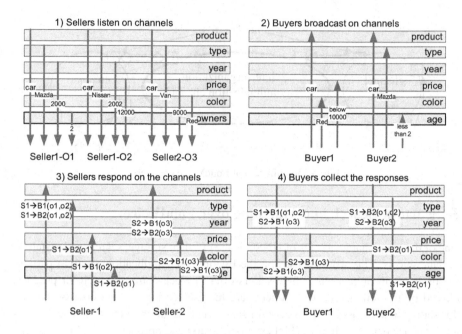

Fig. 4. Stages of the matching protocol

An interesting observation appears when analyzing the overhearing in LoudVoice channeled multicast communication. Due to the overhearing, the mediating agents can learn the attributes used to describe domain objects. Hence, in addition to the matching capability, the proposed structure facilitates autonomous generation of domain meta-data. This is achieved as follows. The mediating agents receives all the messages sent over the channel. Hence, it can collect the data referring to the statistical properties (e.g., distribution, values, frequencies and so on) of the attributes. Using the inter-organization channel, the mediating agents can communicate and collect domain meta-data. For example, the mediating agent of a channel can collect meta-data regarding the possible values of the attribute, or several agents can manage a list of the most frequently mentioned domain attributes.

3.1 Search Optimizations

Now we consider two optimizations of the above protocol, aimed at reducing the number of messages in the system and the overhead related to their processing. The first optimization, referred to as a *dedicated channel*, allows each buyer to use a dedicated channel, where the sellers respond in step 3 of the protocol. In this way, the number of processed messages is reduced, as the sellers send the messages destined for a buyer on a separate channel, to which only the seller and the buyer (and, possibly, a small number of other agents concurrently sending their responses) are tuned. As a result, the number of messages that are received and processed is reduced in comparison to the original protocol, where all the responses are received by all the sellers and buyers that are tuned to the channels.

The second optimization, referred to as *meta-data*, uses the collected domain meta-data to reduce the number of response messages. This is done by substituting the con-current execution of steps 2 and 3 over multiple channels with sequential execution, such that the order of sequential operations is determined by the frequencies of the attributes. We will illustrate this optimization with an example. Assume that a buyer is searching for an object $<a_1{:}v_1,..., a_k{:}v_k>$, whose attributes are ordered according to the attribute frequency (a_1 is the most frequent attribute). The cardinality of the set of objects having a complete match with the query is bounded by the frequency of the least frequent attribute a_k. Hence, sequential querying of channels is ordered such that they are launched first on the channels of the least frequent attributes (starting from the channel of a_k) and then on the channels of more frequent attributes.

To implement this optimization, we use an additional set of candidate object identi-ties, a *CO*. Initially, a *CO* contains the identities of all the available objects. The following operations are repeated for the $<a_i{:}v_i>$ pairs, according to the attribute frequencies, from the least frequent to the most frequent attribute:

- Broadcast the query for the desired v_i and the current *CO* on the channel a_i
- Sellers, storing the objects containing the desired v_i, respond to the query only if the identity of the data object having the desired v_i appears in the *CO*
- Buyers receive the responses and remove from the *CO* the identities of the objects that were not included in the sellers' responses.

Hence, in each iteration the buyers filter out from the *CO* the identities of the objects not satisfying the desired $<a_i{:}v_i>$ pair, but only previous $<a_{i+1}{:}v_{i+1}, ..., a_k{:}v_k>$ pairs. This reduces the number of messages sent, received and processed, as the sellers do not respond to all the identified matchings.

4 Experimental Evaluation

To evaluate the proposed approaches, we collected 5 corpora of real-life E-Commerce *supply* ads from the following application domains: refrigerators, cameras, televi-sions, printers, and mobile phones. The ads were downloaded from *www.recycler.com* and converted by annotators to UNSO format. For example, "Nokia 5190 phone, charger and leather case, good condition, $125" ad was converted to *<manufac-turer:Nokia, model:5190, charger:yes, case:leather, condition:good, price:$125>*. Conversions were kept as close as possible to the original contents of the ads. A set of *demand* ads was built by modifying the attributes and values of the supply ads. Due to space limitations, we present in this section only the results obtained for a corpus of mobile phones ads. The other corpora demonstrate a similar behavior.

In the first experiment, we evaluated the matching accuracy of the system through the traditional Information Retrieval metric of recall[1] [10]. For this, we used a corpus of *130* supply ads imitating the available data objects and a corpus of *64* demand ads imitating the search queries. For each one of the *64* queries, the recall was computed as the number of retrieved relevant ads divided by the total number of relevant ads in the system. The average recall for all *64* queries was computed in two conditions: (1)

---

[1] Precision was not measured, as all the ads pertaining to one domain are considered relevant.

for the original terms mentioned in the ads, and (2) after standardizing the <*attribute:value*> pairs using WordNet.

The original average recall was *0.29*. The low result is explained by the observation that when the data objects were defined using UNSO format, the users mentioned different terms in their UNSO descriptions, and only the exact string matching ads were retrieved. Using WordNet standardization, the average recall was *0.8*. This is explained by the nature of the standardization, which substitutes semantically close terms with their most frequent synonym. Note that even after the standardization the recall did not reach the optimal value of *1* due to the fact that WordNet standardization with the most frequent synonym failed to identify syntactic errors, hyponyms and hypernyms, polysemy, and other discrepancies.

We used the same corpora of *130* supply and 64 demand ads also in the second experiment, which was aimed at measuring the communication overhead of the proposed mechanism. We gradually increased the number of inserted ads N_c from *1* to *125* and for each value of N_c launched the same set of *64* queries. In the experiments we measured four metrics: (1) the number of established channels, i.e., channels to which at least one agent was tuned, (2) the overall number of messages sent for every query, (3) the overall number of ads received and processed for every query, and (4) the average size of the messages. For each value of N_c, the 64 searches were repeated *1,000* times, for randomly selected sets of supply ads. Figures 5, 6, and 7 show the results of all four metrics for the original protocol (Figure 5), *dedicated channel* optimization (Figure 6), and *meta-data* optimization (Figure 7). Note that the average message size values were scaled down to be shown with the other metrics.

Figure 5 shows that the number of channels established converges fast. This is explained by the observation that even a small number of ads provides most of the domain attributes, whereas further ads contribute few new attributes. Also the number of messages sent in a single search converges. This is explained by the fact that the sellers respond to the queries regardless of the number of matching ads they store. Hence, even for a small number of ads they respond if a matching is identified, whereas further insertions contribute few new responses. It can be seen that both the number of channels and the number of messages sent reach over *80%* of their maximal values when inserting approximately *20%* of the ads.

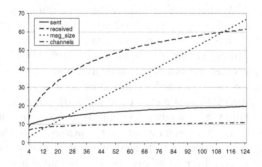

Fig. 5. Original protocol

The number of received messages converges more slowly than the number of sent messages, as every message sent on a channel is received by multiple agents tuned to it. Thus, a minor increase in the number of sent messages is reflected by a stronger increase in the number of received messages. Since the response messages include the identity of the data object having the desired attribute value, the average message size increases linearly with the number of ads. The results obtained for the original protocol serve as a baseline for following two protocol optimization experiments.

Figure 6 shows that *dedicated channel* optimization leads to a major improvement in terms of the number of received messages. Since in this case the messages are sent over a dedicated channel, they are received by a smaller number of agents. As a result, the number of received messages is significantly lower than in the original protocol. However, this is reflected by the number of channels established, which is higher by *1*, i.e., the channel where the responses are sent, than in the original protocol.

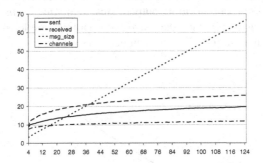

Fig. 6. *Dedicated channel* optimization

Figure 7 shows that *meta-data* optimization leads to an improvement in three metrics: the number of messages sent and received, and the average message size. The first two are explained by the fact that the set of seller responses in this optimization is smaller than in the original protocol, as the set of candidate objects *CO* inherently limits the data objects for which the sellers can potentially respond. Hence, the number of sent messages decreases and, as a result, the number of received messages. Surprisingly, also the average message size decreases. Unlike in the original protocol, where the sellers respond to all the matchings, in this optimization they respond to

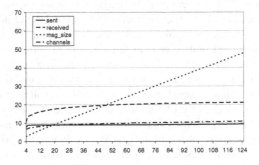

Fig. 7. *Meta-data* optimization

only the identity of the data object appearing in the *CO*. Thus, the average size of the response messages decreases. As for the number of channels established, the performance of this optimization is identical to the performance of the original protocol.

Finally, to compare the advantages and disadvantages of the above optimizations, we computed the overall communication overhead by multiplying the average message size by the sum of the number of sent messages and the number of received messages, i.e.,

$$overall\ overhead = (sent\ messages + received\ messages) * message\ size\ \cdot$$

Intuitively, this computation reflects the observation that every message sent over a channel requires communication and every message received requires processing overhead, where the overheads are proportional to the size of the message. The overall communication overheads of the original protocol and two optimizations are shown in Figure 8. As can be seen, both optimizations are superior to the original protocol, while *meta-data* optimization outperforms *dedicated channel* optimization. These results allow us to conclude that *meta-data* optimization leads to the most significant improvement in terms of the communication overhead.

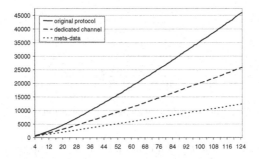

Fig. 8. Overall communication overhead

5 Conclusions and Future Research

This work was motivated by the abundance and dynamic nature of semi-structured and heterogeneous data on the Web. While many previous studies were focused primarily on overcoming the heterogeneity challenge, this study focused on overcoming the dynamicity of the data. For this, we used the flexible UNSO descriptions of the data objects and implemented a multi-agent system for the management and matching of the data objects over the LoudVoice channeled multicast communication platform.

Experimental evaluation comprised two parts. In the first part, we evaluated the contribution of semantic standardization to the retrieval capabilities. The results showed their dramatic improvement with respect to the recall metric. In the second part, we evaluated the scalability of the proposed approach. For this, we measured four factors: the number of channels established, the number of messages sent and received, and the average size of the messages. We evaluated the original search protocol and two optimizations based on (1) slightly modified communication policy, and (2) domain meta-data learned from the existing data objects. Experimental results showed that both optimizations lead to a decrease in the communication overheads. Although the reported results pertain to one corpus of ads from one application domain, in other corpora and domains the results were similar, allowing us to hypothesize that the results will be valid also for large-scale Web-based data.

In the future, we plan to evaluate the performance of another optimization, combining the advantages of the optimizations presented and evaluated in this work. That is, according to the envisaged optimization, the sellers will use a dedicated channel for responding to queries, whereas querying the channel will be sequential and ordered according to the frequencies of the attributes. We hypothesize that this optimization will decrease further the communication overheads of the proposed approach.

The manual generation of UNSO data object descriptions by human annotators constitutes a serious drawback (and, in fact, scalability limit) of the current work. However, to provide their descriptions in UNSO format may emerge as a controversial and unreliable task for the users. Hence, we plan to investigate text processing and language technologies for the purpose of automatically extracting UNSO descriptions from the free-text natural language descriptions inserted by the users.

We also plan to exploit the collected domain meta-data for advanced functionalities aimed at improving users' interaction with the system. For example, we plan to consider the deployment of user modeling agents, which will collect information about users and their needs by analyzing the queries launched by them. In turn, availability of this information will facilitate the use of personalization agents, which will suggest query modifications (e.g., a widely-used domain attribute, or another value) and notify the users about recently inserted data objects that would match their needs.

References

[1] Adali, S., Candan, K., Papakonstantinou, Y., Subrahmanian, V.: Query Caching and Optimization in Distributed Mediator Systems. In: Proceedings of the SIGMOD Conference, Montreal (1996)

[2] Ben-Asher, Y., Berkovsky, S.: Management of Unspecified Semi-Structured Data in a Multi-Agent Environment. In: Proceedings of the SAC Conference, Dijon (2006)

[3] Bernstein, P.A., Melnik, S.: Meta Data Management. In: Proceedings of the ICDE Conference, Boston (2004)

[4] Busetta, P., Dona, A., Nori, M.: Channeled Multicast for Group Communications. In: Proceedings of the AAMAS Conference, Bologna (2002)

[5] Busetta, P., Merzi, M., Rossi, S., Legras, F.: Intra-Role Coordination Using Group Communication: A Preliminary Report. In: Proceedings of the Workshop on Agent Communication Languages and Conversation Policies, Melbourne (2003)

[6] Dean, M., Connolly, D., van Harmelen, F., Hendler, J., Horrocks, I., McGuinness, D., Patel-Schneider, P., Stein, L.: OWL Web Ontology Language. W3 Consortium (2002)

[7] Fellbaum, C.: WordNet - An Electronic Lexical Database. MIT Press, Cambridge (1998)

[8] Gal, A., Modica, G., Jamil, H.M., Eyal, A.: Automatic Ontology Matching Using Application Semantics. AI Magazine 26(1), 21–31 (2005)

[9] Gruber, T.R.: A Translation Approach to Portable Ontology Specifications. Knowledge Acquisition Journal 6(2), 199–220 (1993)

[10] Witten, I.H., Moffat, A., Bell, T.C.: Managing Gigabytes: Compressing and Indexing Documents and Images. Morgan Kaufmann Publishers, San Francisco (1999)

Using Collaborative Models to Adaptively Predict Visitor Locations in Museums

Fabian Bohnert[1], Ingrid Zukerman[1],
Shlomo Berkovsky[2], Timothy Baldwin[2], and Liz Sonenberg[2]

[1] Monash University
Clayton, Victoria 3800, Australia
{Fabian.Bohnert,Ingrid.Zukerman}@infotech.monash.edu.au

[2] The University of Melbourne
Carlton, Victoria 3010, Australia
{shlomo,tim}@csse.unimelb.edu.au,
l.sonenberg@unimelb.edu.au

Abstract. The vast amounts of information presented in museums can be over-whelming to a visitor, whose receptivity and time are typically limited. Hence, s/he might have difficulties selecting interesting exhibits to view within the available time. Mobile, context-aware guides offer the opportunity to improve a visitor's experience by recommending exhibits of interest, and personalising the delivered content. The first step in this recommendation process is the accurate prediction of a visitor's activities and preferences. In this paper, we present two adaptive collaborative models for predicting a visitor's next locations in a museum, and an ensemble model that combines their predictions. Our experimental results from a study using a small dataset of museum visits are encouraging, with the ensemble model yielding the best performance overall.

1 Introduction

Museums offer vast amounts of information, but since a visitor's receptivity and time are typically limited, s/he is confronted with the challenge of selecting interesting exhibits to view during a visit. A personal human guide who is knowledgeable about the museum's exhibits and aware of the visitor's interests and time limitations could support the visitor in this selection process, but the provision of personal guides is generally impractical. Advances in mobile, context-aware computing and user modelling point towards an alternative solution: electronic handheld guides. These guides have the potential to (1) make recommendations about items of interest, and (2) personalise the content delivered for these items; based on predictions of a visitor's activities and interests estimated from non-intrusive observations of his/her behaviour.

In this paper, we describe the first step in this process. We consider two collaborative predictive models of visitor behaviour, *Interest* and *Transition*, and an ensemble model that combines their predictions. These models are employed to predict the next $K (= 3)$ exhibits to be viewed by a visitor, using two prediction approaches: *set*, which predicts a set of exhibits, and *sequence*, which predicts a sequence. Accurately predicting a visitor's next locations will enable us to deliver useful recommendations about

W. Nejdl et al. (Eds.): AH 2008, LNCS 5149, pp. 42–51, 2008.

exhibits to visit, e. g., by excluding from the set of potential recommendations the exhibits that a visitor is likely to see anyway in the near future. We trained and tested our models on a small dataset collected at the Marine Life Exhibition in Melbourne Museum. Our results show that the *Transition Model* outperforms the *Interest Model*, indicating that the layout of a physical space with homogeneous exhibits (e. g., marine theme) is a dominating factor influencing visitor behaviour. However, the ensemble model yielded the best performance overall with an average accuracy of 59%, demonstrating the importance of considering also a visitor's interests. Additionally, we found that our sequence-based prediction model has a significantly higher accuracy than our set-based prediction model (59% vs. 49%).

The rest of this paper is organised as follows. In Section 2 we outline related work, and in Section 3 we introduce the domain. Our predictive approaches are described in Sections 4 and 5. In Section 6 we present the results of our evaluation, followed by our conclusions in Section 7.

2 Related Research

Our work lies at the intersection of statistical user modelling [1] and personalised guide systems for physical museum spaces.

Personalised guide systems in physical domains have often employed adaptable user models, which require visitors to explicitly state their interests in some form, e. g., [2,3]. Less attention has been paid to predicting preferences from non-intrusive observations, and to utilising adaptive user models that do not require explicit user input. In the museum domain, adaptive user models have usually been updated from the user's interactions with the system, with a focus on adapting content presentation [4,5,6] rather than predicting or recommending exhibits to be viewed. These systems, like most systems in the museum domain, rely on *knowledge-based user models*, which require an explicit and a-priori built representation of the domain knowledge.

In contrast, this work investigates non-intrusive statistical user modelling techniques that do not require an explicit representation of the domain knowledge, and takes into account spatial constraints — a factor that has not been considered to date.

3 Domain and Dataset

The data used in the experiments reported in this paper was obtained by manually tracking visitors to the Marine Life Exhibition of Melbourne Museum in 2006. This exhibition consists of 56 exhibits in four sections, displaying marine-related topics. With the help of curators, we transformed the original set of 56 exhibits into a set of 22 grouped exhibits by unifying logically related exhibits, such as a visual display and its accompanying explanatory panel. Figure 1 depicts the layout of the exhibition space and the exhibition highlight "Whale meets Squid". In the initial stage of their visit, visitors pass through a highly constrained entrance area where they behave similarly. This area leads to a space with several open sections, where visitor behaviour is less prescribed. However, at around the 55%–60% point of their visit, most visitors enter the area from which the "Whale meets Squid" exhibit is visible, and gravitate towards it.

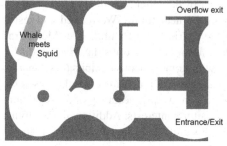
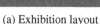

(a) Exhibition layout   (b) "Whale meets Squid" exhibit

Fig. 1. The Marine Life Exhibition

Owing to the difficulties associated with collecting data in a physical space, our dataset consists of only 44 visitor pathways, which comprise a total of 317 stops at grouped exhibits. On average, visitors viewed 7.20 exhibits, with the shortest and longest pathways being 3 and 16 exhibits respectively.

4   Using Collaborative Models Based on Spatio-temporal Information to Predict Location Probabilities

In this work, we consider two collaborative approaches for estimating the probability of a visitor viewing a particular exhibit given his/her previous visit trajectory: interest-based (Section 4.1) and transitional (Section 4.2). The interest-based approach predicts a visitor's next location on the basis of his/her interest in unseen exhibits, which in turn is estimated from the time the visitor spent at the exhibits s/he saw. The transitional approach predicts a visitor's next location on the basis of the pathways followed by other visitors in the museum. In Section 4.3 we propose an ensemble approach that combines the predictions generated by these models [7,8]. The utilisation of the estimated location probabilities to predict a set or sequence of next items is described in Section 5.

Recent developments in the area of positioning technology have made possible the non-intrusive indoor tracking of visitors equipped with a positioning device. The availability of such technology as a basis for inferring a visitor's high-level activities from sensing data is crucial to this work, i. e., to perform non-intrusive, adaptive user modelling. In this research, we assume access to a visitor's pathway in the form of a time-annotated sequence of visited items. That is, for each visitor u, we have an ordered sequence of viewing durations $t_{ui_1}, t_{ui_2}, \ldots$ for items $i_1, i_2, \ldots$ respectively. As stated above, this information was obtained by tracking people manually, but is of the same type as information inferable from sensing data in a real-world setting.[1]

4.1   Interest Model

In an information-seeking context, users are expected to spend more time on relevant information than on irrelevant information, as viewing time correlates positively with

---

[1] The consideration of the impact of instrument accuracy on user models is outside the scope of this work.

preference and interest [9]. Hence, viewing time can be used as a measure of interest. However, viewing time is also positively correlated with item complexity. Additionally, viewing times vary over different visitors depending on the time available for their visit.[2] In order to infer the interests of visitors in different items while taking into account these factors, we have devised the *relative interest* measure below. It reflects the interest of a visitor in an exhibit in the context of the time s/he has spent on previously seen exhibits, and the time spent by other visitors on this exhibit. This measure implicitly takes into account item complexity, as complex items are likely to be viewed for a longer time than simpler items.

Definition 1 (Relative Interest: RI)
The *relative interest* of visitor u in a seen exhibit i is defined as follows.

$$RI_{ui} = \frac{t_{ui}}{\bar{t}_{u\cdot}} - \frac{1}{n_{\cdot i}} \sum_{v \in U} n_{vi} \frac{t_{vi}}{\bar{t}_{v\cdot}} \tag{1}$$

where t_{ui} is the time visitor u spent at exhibit i, $\bar{t}_{u\cdot}$ is the average viewing time of visitor u, $n_{\cdot i}$ is the number of visitors that viewed exhibit i, U is the set of visitors, and $n_{vi} = 1$ if visitor v viewed exhibit i, and 0 otherwise.

The first term in Equation 1 reflects visitor u's viewing time for item i relative to his/her average viewing time, and the second term represents the average relative viewing time spent at item i (over all the visitors that viewed this item). Hence, RI_{ui} measures whether visitor u is (relative to his/her average viewing time) more or less interested in item i than the average interest in item i.[3]

The collaborative *Interest Model (IM)* is built by calculating RI_{ui}, the relative interest of visitor u in exhibit i, for all visitors $u = 1, \ldots, |U|$ and all items $i = 1, \ldots, |I|$, where $|U|$ is the number of visitors and $|I|$ is the number of exhibits. This yields a relative interest matrix $\mathcal{RI}$ of size $|U| \times |I|$, which contains defined values for all combinations of visitors u and items i that occurred, i. e., combinations referring to an item i viewed by a visitor u. These values, which may be regarded as implicit ratings given by visitors to exhibits, do not take into account the order in which the exhibits were visited.

Following the collaborative approach described in [10], we use Algorithm 1 to predict the missing relative interest values of the active user a from the values in $\mathcal{RI}$. These values are mapped into the $[0, 1]$ range to estimate the probability of visiting an unseen exhibit [11]. Formally, given a visit where a user a has viewed k items so far, the probability of the $(k + 1)$-th item being item i is represented by the expression $\Pr(X_{k+1} = i \mid v_a^k)$, where v_a^k is the user's visit history so far. Approximating this expression by a probability estimated using our *Interest Model* yields the following formula.

$$\Pr\left(X_{k+1} = i \mid v_a^k\right) \approx \Pr_{IM}\left(X_{k+1} = i \mid t_a^k\right)$$

where t_a^k is the time component of the visit history v_a^k (the *Interest Model* depends on viewing times, rather than transitions between locations).

---

[2] Viewing time was also found to be negatively correlated with familiarity, positively correlated with novelty, and decreases from beginning to end within a sequence of stops [9]. However, these factors are not yet considered in our model.

[3] Clearly, other measures of interest are possible. The measure proposed here outperformed other variants of relative interest we have explored.

Algorithm 1. Estimating the relative interests of the active visitor in unseen exhibits

---

1: Estimate from the observed viewing times the relative interests of all visitors —
   including the active visitor a — in the items viewed during their visit (Equation 1).
2: **for all** i such that i is an unvisited exhibit **do**
3:   Find a set of *item mentors*, who have viewed item i, and whose relative interests
     are most similar to those of the active visitor. To calculate a visitor-to-mentor
     similarity, use Pearson's correlation coefficient.
4:   Estimate the active visitor's relative interest in item i as the weighted mean of the
     relative interests of his/her item mentors in i, where the weights are the visitor-
     to-mentor similarities.
5: **end for**

4.2 Transition Model

In contrast to the *Interest Model*, the *Transition Model (TM)* considers the order in
which exhibits were visited. The *Transition Model* is represented by a stationary 1-stage
Markov model, where the transition matrix $\mathcal{TM}$ approximates the probabilities of moving between exhibits. Specifically, the element $\mathcal{TM}(i, j)$ approximates the probability
of a visitor going from exhibit i to exhibit j, where $i, j = 1, \ldots, |I|$ and $|I|$ is the num-
ber of exhibits. This probability is estimated on the basis of the frequency count of
transitions between i and j. In order to overcome the data sparseness problem (which
is exacerbated by our small dataset) and to smooth out outliers, we added a flattening
constant ε $(= 1/|I|)$ to each frequency count before normalising each row of $\mathcal{TM}$ to 1.

When we employ the *Transition Model* to approximate the probability that the
$(k + 1)$-th exhibit viewed by the active user a is item i, we obtain the following formula.

$$\Pr\left(X_{k+1} = i \mid v_a^k\right) \approx \Pr_{TM}\left(X_{k+1} = i \mid I_a^k\right)$$

where I_a^k are the exhibits visited by the active user.

Since our *Transition Model* is a 1-stage Markov model, the probability of the next
exhibit being item i is further approximated by

$$\Pr_{TM}(X_{k+1} = i \mid I_a^k) \approx \Pr_{TM}(X_{k+1} = i \mid X_k = i_k) = \mathcal{TM}(i_k, i)$$

where i_k is the current item. Although visitors sometimes return to previously viewed
exhibits, our observations indicate that this rarely happens. Hence, we focus on unseen
exhibits. That is, prior to calculating the transition probabilities, we set to 0 the entries
of $\mathcal{TM}$ that correspond to the visited items, i. e., the items in I_a^k, and appropriately
renormalise the rows.

The *Transition Model* implicitly captures the physical layout of the museum space,
i. e., the physical proximity of items, on the basis of the assumption that transitions
to spatially close items occur more frequently than movements to items that are further
away. However, in the future, we intend to experiment with spatial models that represent
more directly the spatial proximity between exhibits.

4.3 Combining Interest Model and Transition Model

As outlined above, the probabilities computed by the *Interest Model* are based on temporal information, while the predictions made by the *Transition Model* implicitly capture spatial information. Additionally, while the *Interest Model* adapts to the behaviour of a visitor, the *Transition Model* is not personalised. In this section, we propose an ensemble *Hybrid Model (HM)* that combines the predictions made by these models [7,8], thereby jointly taking into account transitional and temporal information.

Formally, we use the probability $\Pr_{HM}(X_{k+1} = i \mid v_a^k)$ generated by our ensemble model to approximate $\Pr(X_{k+1} = i \mid v_a^k)$.

$$\Pr\left(X_{k+1} = i \mid v_a^k\right) \approx \Pr_{HM}\left(X_{k+1} = i \mid v_a^k\right)$$

This probability in turn is calculated by means of a weighted average of the predictions generated by our *Interest Model* and *Transition Model*, i. e.,

$$\Pr_{HM}\left(X_{k+1} = i \mid v_a^k\right) = \omega \Pr_{IM}\left(X_{k+1} = i \mid t_a^k\right) + (1 - \omega)\Pr_{TM}\left(X_{k+1} = i \mid I_a^k\right)$$

where the weight ω is chosen from the range $[0, 1]$. We experimented with different values for ω, with the assignment $\omega = \beta/(\alpha + \beta)$ yielding the best performance,[4] where

$$\alpha = \min_{i \in I \setminus I_a^k} \Pr_{IM}\left(X_{k+1} = i \mid t_a^k\right) \quad \text{and} \quad \beta = \min_{i \in I \setminus I_a^k} \Pr_{TM}\left(X_{k+1} = i \mid I_a^k\right)$$

and $I \setminus I_a^k$ is the set of exhibits not yet visited. This choice of ω assigns more weight to the model with the lower minimum prediction, which may be viewed as the more discriminating model.

5 Building Models to Predict the Next K Exhibits

In this section, we describe two approaches for using the probabilities estimated in Section 4 to predict the next K exhibits to be viewed by a visitor: *TopK*, which predicts the next K items as a set and ranks them in descending order of estimated probability; and *SeqK/N*, which predicts the next K items as the initial portion of a sequence of N items.

5.1 *TopK* Prediction

The *TopK* approach assumes that the current history of the active visitor a is sufficient to predict his/her future behaviour, and that it is unnecessary to consider the impact of future transitions on the visitor's subsequent behaviour. Hence, in order to predict the next K items to be visited (having visited k items), we find the set of K unvisited items $i_{k+1}, \ldots, i_{k+K}$ which maximises the product of their visit probabilities by solving

$$\underset{i_{k+1},\ldots,i_{k+K} \in I \setminus I_a^k}{\arg\max} \prod_{m=1}^{K} \Pr\left(X_{k+1} = i_{k+m} \mid v_a^k\right)$$

This approach is equivalent to computing the probabilities $\Pr(X_{k+1} = i \mid v_a^k)$ for all (unvisited) exhibits $i \in I \setminus I_a^k$ (pretending that each of these exhibits is the next

---

[4] In the future, we intend to apply machine learning techniques to learn the optimal ω.

one — hence the subscript $k + 1$), then sorting these items in descending order of their estimated visit probability, and selecting the top K items.

5.2 *SeqK/N* **Prediction**

In contrast to the *TopK* approach, the *SeqK/N* approach assumes that future transitions influence a visitor's subsequent behaviour. Hence, in order to predict the next K items to be visited (having visited k items), we first find the maximum-probability sequence of N unvisited items $i_{k+1}, \ldots, i_{k+N}$ by solving

$$\underset{i_{k+1},\ldots,i_{k+N}\in I \setminus I_a^k}{\arg \max} \Pr\left(X_{k+1} = i_{k+1}, \ldots, X_{k+N} = i_{k+N} \mid v_a^k\right)$$

and then select the first K items $i_{k+1}, \ldots, i_{k+K}$ within this sequence. Assuming that X_{k+m} depends only on the past, this probability is decomposed as follows.

$$\Pr\left(X_{k+1} = i_{k+1}, \ldots, X_{k+N} = i_{k+N} \mid v_a^k\right) = \prod_{m=1}^{N} \Pr\left(X_{k+m} = i_{k+m} \mid v_a^{k+m-1}\right) \qquad (2)$$

Due to this decomposition, the joint probability in Equation 2 can be maximised by recursively spanning a search tree of depth $N - 1$, and performing an exhaustive search for a maximising path from its root to one of its leaves.

The probability $\Pr(X_{k+m} = i_{k+m} \mid v_a^{k+m-1})$ in Equation 2 depends on the active user's visit history up to exhibit i_{k+m-1}, but in practice this history is available only up to item i_k. Future exhibits are incorporated into a "potential history" for the *Transition Model* by iteratively adding predicted unseen exhibits to construct different potential sequences. In order to incorporate such a potential history into the *Interest Model* (and hence the *Hybrid Model*), we also need to predict viewing times. The calculation of the estimated viewing times is similar to that performed for the estimation of relative interests, and is described in detail in [11].

6 Evaluation

In our experiments, we evaluated the performance of our two approaches for predicting the next K exhibits to be viewed by a visitor, *TopK* and *SeqK/N*, for $K = 3$ and $N = 3$, yielding the two variants *Top3* and *Seq3/3*. For both prediction modes, we considered the three prediction models defined in Section 4 — *Interest Model (IM)*, *Transition Model (TM)* and *Hybrid Model (HM)* — yielding a total of six variants. Due to the small size of our dataset (Section 3), we used leave-one-out validation, i. e., we trained our prediction models on 43 of the 44 visitors in our dataset, and tested them on the remaining visitor (the active visitor). Additionally, we considered only the portion of a museum visit for which a collaborative *Interest Model* could be constructed (i. e., for which the active visitor's similarity with the other visitors could be computed). Hence, we report on the results obtained only after at least three observations have been made for the active visitor. Also, to be able to evaluate the predictions of the final three items viewed in a visit, we stopped simulating the visit history of the active visitor at that point. To obtain statistically valid results, we considered only visit percentages where at least 10 visitors were observed. Owing to these considerations, the results presented in this paper pertain to the middle part of a museum visit, spanning between 25% and 70% of a visit.

For each visit percentage, we averaged the values obtained for the following evaluation measures for all the active visitors in the test set (we considered visit percentage, rather than number of viewed exhibits, because this number varies across visitors).[5]

- **Precision (Pre)** – $Pre = |\mathcal{K} \cap \mathcal{M}|/|\mathcal{K}|$, the proportion of the $|\mathcal{K}|$ (= 3) predicted exhibits in $\mathcal{K}$ that appear in the set $\mathcal{M}$ of exhibits viewed during the remainder of the visit; and
- **Modified Spearman (mSP)** – a modified version of Spearman's rank correlation [13], measuring the fit between the predicted exhibit sequence and the sequence of actually visited exhibits (a modified version is required because the sequences being compared may be of different lengths [11]).

The results of our experiments are summarised in Figure 2. For both measures and both prediction modes, the overall performance of *HM* is at least as good as the performance of *TM*, and both of these methods perform considerably better than *IM*. Specifically, for the *Pre* measure (Figures 2a and 2b), the difference between the performance of *HM* and that of *IM* is statistically significant ($p < 0.05$) for most of the visit for both *Top*3 and *Seq*3/3.[6] The difference between *HM* and *TM* is statistically significant ($p < 0.1$) for *Seq*3/3 for up to 50% of a visit, but it is not significant for *Top*3. For the *mSP* measure (Figures 2c and 2d), *HM* and *TM* perform similarly in the *Top*3 mode (the difference is not statistically significant), while *HM* significantly outperforms *IM* for the initial stages of a visit and for visit percentages larger than 45% ($p < 0.05$). For the *Seq*3/3 mode, *HM* outperforms *IM* ($p < 0.05$) throughout a visit, and *TM* ($p < 0.05$) for the first 50% of a visit. Comparing the prediction modes *Top*3 and *Seq*3/3, *Top*3 *IM* and *Seq*3/3 *IM* perform similarly, as do *Top*3 *TM* and *Seq*3/3 *TM*. However, *Seq*3/3 *HM* yields a higher precision than *Top*3 *HM* for most of a visit ($p < 0.1$), and a higher value for *mSP* for 30%–50% of a visit ($p < 0.1$). On average, *Seq*3/3 *HM* yields 59% for *Pre* and 46% for *mSP*, whereas *Top*3 *HM* performs at 49% with respect to *Pre* and at 40% with respect to *mSP*.

The results in Figure 2 highlight the relationship between the exhibition layout and the relative performance of our predictive models. Figures 2b–2d show a divergence in the performance of *TM* and *IM* during the initial stages of a visit (the accuracy of *TM* is relatively high, while the accuracy of *IM* is relatively low), and Figures 2a–2c show such a divergence around the 55%–60% point of a visit. These regions of divergence coincide with those visit percentages where a visitor's behaviour is constrained by the physical layout (the entrance area and the point where the highlight exhibit becomes visible, Section 3). Additionally, our results show a performance decrease for the *IM* variants as the visit percentage increases (Figures 2a–2c). This may be due to our *Interest Model* disregarding the fact that viewing time decreases within a sequence of stops (Section 4.1).

---

[5] In agreement with Herlocker *et al.*'s observations regarding the impracticality of using recall for recommender systems [12], we eschew the calculation of recall. That is, due to the large number of exhibits left to be viewed at most stages of a visit (i. e., $|\mathcal{M}| \gg 3$), our setup would yield low recall values, which are not comparable to the values obtained for precision.

[6] Throughout this paper, the statistical tests performed are paired two-tailed t-tests. Also, we consider $p > 0.1$ to indicate a lack of statistical significance.

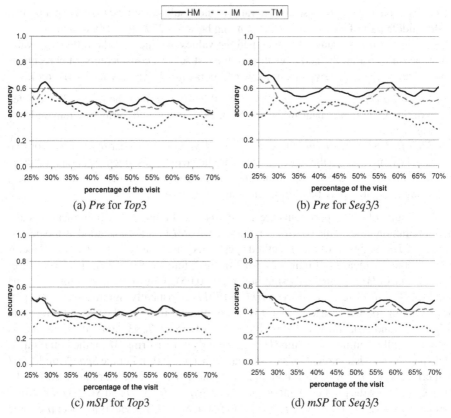

Fig. 2. Performance of predictive models

In summary, when predicting a sequence of $K = 3$ exhibits, (1) *Seq3/3* is superior to *Top3*, meaning that sequence information aids prediction, and (2) *TM* and *IM* should be hybridised, as their combined predictive accuracy surpasses that of the individual methods.

7   Conclusions and Future Work

We have offered two models for predicting visitor locations in a museum — a *Transition Model* implicitly capturing spatial information, and an *Interest Model* based on viewing times — and we have combined these models into a hybrid ensemble model. The performance of these models was tested on a small dataset collected from visitors to the Marine Life Exhibition in Melbourne Museum. Our results show that the *Transition Model* outperforms the *Interest Model*, indicating that the layout of a physical space with homogeneous exhibits is a dominating factor influencing visitor behaviour. Nevertheless, the *Hybrid Model* yielded the best performance overall, which demonstrates the importance of also considering a visitor's interests. Additionally, our results show that when predicting the next three exhibits to be viewed, a model that predicts a sequence of items has a higher accuracy than a model that predicts a ranked set.

In this work, our experiments were conducted using a small dataset obtained from a single exhibition comprising a homogeneous set of exhibits. The small size of the dataset affects the applicability of probabilistic models. Additionally, its homogeneity reduces the impact of a visitor's interests on his/her behaviour, and consequently the usefulness of a predictive model of interest. In the near future, we intend to address these problems by collecting additional traces of visit trajectories over areas of the museum with more heterogeneous content.

Acknowledgements. This research was supported in part by grant DP0770931 from the Australian Research Council. The authors thank Enes Makalic for his assistance with ensemble models. Thanks also go to Carolyn Meehan and her team from Museum Victoria for fruitful discussions, their support of this research, and the dataset.

References

1. Zukerman, I., Albrecht, D.W.: Predictive statistical models for user modeling. User Modeling and User-Adapted Interaction 11(1-2), 5–18 (2001)
2. Cheverst, K., Mitchell, K., Davies, N.: The role of adaptive hypermedia in a context-aware tourist guide. Communications of the ACM 45(5), 47–51 (2002)
3. Aroyo, L., Stash, N., Wang, Y., Gorgels, P., Rutledge, L.: CHIP demonstrator: Semantics-driven recommendations and museum tour generation. In: Aberer, K., Choi, K.-S., Noy, N., Allemang, D., Lee, K.-I., Nixon, L., Golbeck, J., Mika, P., Maynard, D., Mizoguchi, R., Schreiber, G., Cudré-Mauroux, P. (eds.) ISWC 2007. LNCS, vol. 4825, pp. 879–886. Springer, Heidelberg (2007)
4. Petrelli, D., Not, E.: User-centred design of flexible hypermedia for a mobile guide: Reflections on the HyperAudio experience. User Modeling and User-Adapted Interaction 15(3-4), 303–338 (2005)
5. Hatala, M., Wakkary, R.: Ontology-based user modeling in an augmented audio reality system for museums. User Modeling and User-Adapted Interaction 15(3-4), 339–380 (2005)
6. Stock, O., Zancanaro, M., Busetta, P., Callaway, C., Krüger, A., Kruppa, M., Kuflik, T., Not, E., Rocchi, C.: Adaptive, intelligent presentation of information for the museum visitor in PEACH. User Modeling and User-Adapted Interaction 18(3), 257–304 (2007)
7. Lekakos, G., Giaglis, G.M.: A hybrid approach for improving predictive accuracy of collaborative filtering algorithms. User Modeling and User-Adapted Interaction 17(1-2), 5–40 (2007)
8. Polikar, R.: Ensemble based systems in decision making. IEEE Circuits and Systems Magazine 6(3), 21–45 (2006)
9. Parsons, J., Ralph, P., Gallager, K.: Using viewing time to infer user preference in recommender systems. In: Proceedings of the AAAI Workshop on Semantic Web Personalization (SWP 2004), pp. 52–64. AAAI Press, Menlo Park (2004)
10. Herlocker, J.L., Konstan, J.A., Borchers, A., Riedl, J.: An algorithmic framework for performing collaborative filtering. In: Proceedings of the 22nd Annual International ACM Conference on Research and Development in Information Retrieval (SIGIR 1999), pp. 230–237 (1999)
11. Bohnert, F., Zukerman, I., Berkovsky, S., Baldwin, T., Sonenberg, L.: Using interest and transition models to predict visitor locations in museums. Technical Report 2008/219, Faculty of Information Technology, Monash University, Clayton, Victoria 3800, Australia (2008)
12. Herlocker, J.L., Konstan, J.A., Terveen, L.G., Riedl, J.T.: Evaluating collaborative filtering recommender systems. ACM Transactions on Information Systems 22(1), 5–53 (2004)
13. Siegel, S., Castellan, N.J.: Non-Parametric Statistics for the Behavioral Sciences, 2nd edn. McGraw–Hill, Inc, New York (1988)

Supporting Users in Creating Pedagogically Sound Personalised Learning Objects

Aoife Brady, Owen Conlan, Vincent Wade, and Declan Dagger

School of Computer Science and Statistics,
Trinity College, Dublin, Ireland
{Aoife.Brady,Owen.Conlan,Vincent.Wade,Declan.Dagger}@cs.tcd.ie
http://kdeg.cs.tcd.ie

Abstract. Successful eLearning is predicated on the application of pedagogies appropriate to online education that respond to the capabilities and needs of the learners. Typically, designing and assembling personalized learning objects that respond to the pedagogical needs of a variety of different learners is an expensive and time-consuming process requiring both domain and educational expertise. Educators have the domain expertise and formal or informal pedagogical knowledge to create quality learning objects. However, they lack the tools and often the specific knowledge of online pedagogical approaches that make it time efficient for them to do so. This paper describes the motivation behind, the workflow supported by and the evaluation of the LO Generator, a tool that offers personalized support and scaffolding for users, who are not necessarily content creation or pedagogical experts, in assembling pedagogically sound personalized learning objects.

Keywords: Personalization, Pedagogy, eLearning, Learning Object Creation.

1 Introduction

One of the key difficulties in achieving a large-scale take up of Adaptive Hypermedia for eLearning is the cost, complexity and technical barriers to allow non technical teachers and learners to design their own adaptive eLearning experiences. The principle of 'one size not fitting all' is evident not only in static learning content, but also in adaptive content, such as Adaptive Hypermedia, that is created within a particular context that may not suit other uses. Over the last few years a number of adaptive eLearning tools for authoring have begun to appear as witnessed by the success of the A3H Workshop [1]. A number of these tools have been little more than technical editors to allow for the generation of adaptive content [2]. Others have focused on designing complete adaptive courses, e.g. ACCT [3], WHURLE [4]. However, in blended learning a frequent requirement from teachers, academics and end users [5] is for a specific learning resource on a particular topic that is capable of adapting to the pedagogical needs of individual students. This requirement for finer grained learning objects should be satisfied with minimal user design effort. That said, this effort needs to be balanced against a requirement for pedagogically appropriate and adaptive learning objects (LO) that meet the needs of the end user. This paper describes the LO

W. Nejdl et al. (Eds.): AH 2008, LNCS 5149, pp. 52–61, 2008.

Generator, a tool that provides personalized support to users in the creation of pedagogically sound personalized learning objects.

This research is focused on developing a unique pedagogical tool to allow end users to generate personalized learning objects on the fly. These learning objects will be semi-automatically generated for a user (either a learner or a teacher) with direct pedagogical and design guidance offered. This process is both empowering and effective as the user can create a learning object that is not only specific to their needs as an educator or learner, but also personalized to learning preferences. This personalization will take two different forms; the personalization of the process of the generation of the learning object, thus tailoring the options that the LO composer is offered, and also the ability to add personalization to the learning object that is generated. The need for a system of this type is driven by the general situation that when you, as a user, search for and retrieve a piece of content the likelihood is that you will not get back exactly what you require. There is a need to bridge this gap between what is requested, what is returned and what the user actually wanted. The aim of this research is to provide pedagogically sound, personalized and context sensitive learning object composition on the fly, enabling both teachers and learners to manipulate LOs suggested by the system to produce exactly what they require.

The research in this paper extends existing adaptive composition tool research by addressing the problems of personalizing the design process, enabling end user personalization design and more rigorously integrating pedagogical strategies and techniques into adaptive eLearning composition.

This paper describes the pedagogically sound and user-friendly workflow supported by the LO Generator. The need for this type of workflow is placed within the context of the state of the art in this area. The paper then describes how personalization is applied and presents the evaluation and its results. The paper concludes by describing the future work that will be carried out on this system.

2 State of the Art

This section briefly reviews and compares four recent authoring systems aimed at producing eLearning courses. Each occupies a subtly different niche in the area of Adaptive Hypermedia Authoring Systems. My Online Teacher (MOT) [6] is a tool developed at Eindhoven University of Technology for authoring Adaptive Hypermedia courses. MOT utilizes a three-layer model for authoring adaptation [7] that provide a conceptual hierarchical layer of atomic and composite concepts, a lesson layer, which provides the manner and sequencing of the concepts, and a third layer which consists of an adaptation engine. Its output is at the course level and matches the AHA! Model (AHAM) closely. A consequence of this is that the tool does not explicitly support specific pedagogies and requires the author to have some knowledge of the AHA! system upon which the courses are deployed.

The Dialog Plus learning design toolkit [8] approaches authoring from a very different perspective. It is a toolkit that guides users through the process of designing pedagogically sound learning activities, known as learning nuggets. These nuggets are made up of various tasks that are to be undertaken in a specified context in order to attain certain learning outcomes [9]. The toolkit is highly pedagogic as it offers various pedagogical approaches. After the user has selected an approach, the toolkit provides guidance to the user in building the individual nuggets. Unlike MOT, Dialog Plus does not have a specific target platform on which it is deployed and as a consequence aids the user in assembling the model of a course rather than in deploying a specific course instance.

The ASK Learning Designer Toolkit (ASK-LDT) [10] provides a graphical authoring system to create learning scenarios based on IMS LD Level B [11]. This tool is much more programmatic in nature than the previous tools and requires the author to have a strong knowledge of the IMS LD specification and its capabilities. As such there is no explicit pedagogic guidance offered to the author, but it could be argued that IMS LD has in built pedagogical biases. The authoring process supported in ASK-LDT consists of several steps [2]. The first allows the definition of the pedagogical elements and is followed by the definition of the environment. The next step is the design of the learning scenario, after which comes the statistical analysis and is finished by the content packaging step. ASK-LDT is highly focused on producing IMS LD compliant outputs and as such has a number of platforms (e.g. Reload [12]) that are capable of playing the resulting LDs.

The final authoring system discussed in this section is the Adaptive Course Construction Toolkit (ACCT) [3] which is a system that allows a course developer to create both adaptive and non-adaptive activity-oriented courses based on sound pedagogical strategies. The ACCT offers many different tools available to the course developer: a concept space/domain ontology builder, a custom narrative builder, a content package assembler, learning resource repository interactivity and also a real time course test and evaluation environment. ACCT has two key features; it offers an abstracted pedagogy-based framework in which to construct courses and it enables the courses to be deployed to APeLS [13], as well as in IMS LD format. Its support of IMS LD is not as rich as that offered in ASK-LDT, nor is the pedagogic support offered by its framework as detailed as that in Dialog Plus, however ACCT strikes a balance that enables pedagogically sound courses to be created and deployed.

Table 1. Comparing MOT, Dialog Plus, ASK-LDT and ACCT

Feature / System	MOT	ACCT	Dialog Plus	ASK-LDT
Learner as Designer	No	No	No	No
Teacher as Designer	Yes (Knowledge of AHAM required)	Yes	Yes	No (Knowledge of LD Required)
Produce Individual LOs	No	No	No	No
Produce Courses	Yes (in AHA!)	Yes (in APeLS or LD)	Yes (as Activities)	Yes (as LD Act)
Explicit Pedagogic Guidance	No	Yes	Yes	No
Explicit Support for multiple Pedagogic Strategies	No	Potentially	Potentially	No

The above table summarizes the capabilities of each of the four authoring systems mentioned. As may be seen from this table each system occupies a different niche and offer authors different features. It is worth noting that none of the systems offer support for creating learning objects.

As a final piece of related work Generative Learning Objects (GLOs) [14] are based on the idea that for LOs to be adaptable, the structure of the learning design needs to be separated from the content. The construction of a GLO is broken up into two parts. The first part is the creation of a Learning Object Template. This template encompasses the learning design and is created by a team of experts, students, an artist and a facilitator. The job of the facilitator is to ensure that the design produced is suitable for a GLO. Once the Template is created web based forms allow either a tutor or a student to instantiate the GLO by adding subject specific content to the Template. This work is referenced here as the LO Generator presented in this paper is also template-based, but takes a fundamentally different approach.

3   Workflow of the LO Generation Process

As may be seen from the State of the Art section there is an unexplored niche in the area of personalized LO creation. However, the most successful systems not only present a tool that enables the creation of a personalized offering, but do so in a pedagogically supportive manner that scaffolds the non-expert. Supporting non-expert users in creating learning objects for their own or others consumption requires a logical and easy to follow workflow to be implemented. This section describes the workflow for creating pedagogically sound personalized learning objects that is enabled in the LO Generator. A wizard was implemented to allow the user to create a learning object by following a set of logical steps. The first two steps involve the user interacting with two separate ontologies, a learning domain concept ontology and a learning outcomes ontology, in order to refine the scope of the learning object to be created.

Step 1 allows the user to select the learning domain concepts that they would like covered by their LO. In this step the user is presented with a list of high level domain concepts, for example, *The Structure of the Human Eye* and *How We See*, in the domain of *Human Vision*. After selecting a high level concept, this concept is then decomposed by the system with the help of a domain specific concepts ontology. This decomposition allows the high level concept to be broken down into lower level concepts allowing the user to specify exactly the low level concepts that they require. For example, when *The Structure of the Human Eye* is selected as a high level concept, it may be decomposed into several low level concepts, such as *cornea*, *aqueous humour*, *iris*, etc. The user can then select or deselect the various concepts that they would like included.

After the user has specified the domain concepts that they wish to be included in the LO, they are invited to move on to the next step. During this step, the user is asked to choose the overall learning outcome of the LO. These overall learning outcomes are based on Bloom's Taxonomy [15] which comprises *Knowledge*, *Comprehension*, *Application*, *Analysis*, *Synthesis* and *Evaluation*. When a user selects one of these high level outcomes, in a similar manner to the high level domain concept in the previous step, the outcome may then be decomposed into various learning events or activities which support a pedagogically sound approach to fulfilling these outcomes. This decomposition is performed using the learning outcomes ontology. The user can again select or deselect any of these learning events or activities that they desire. Each learning activity and event is accompanied with supporting text that helps guide the user towards pedagogically appropriate events and activities for their outcomes. This process is shown in Figure 1, where the learning outcome is chosen on the left and the specific activities are chosen on the right. These activities can be turned on and off for each selected sub-concept from Step 1. In this example the higher level, *Knowledge*, outcome is selected and this is broken down into the activities *introduce*, *explain* and *self test*.

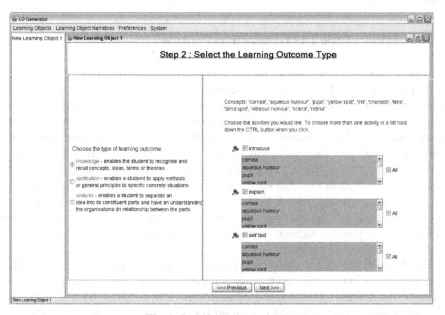

Fig. 1. Specifying the Activities

When these two steps are completed and the user is satisfied with their choices, the LO Generator then calls APeLS [13] to search for all Learning Object Narratives that fulfils the chosen learning outcome(s) across the desired concepts and utilises the learning events and activities specified by the user. An LO Narrative is a structure which comprises a pedagogical strategy and is composed of a set of rules which governs the selection and sequencing of learning activities and content. When these LO Narratives are chosen, they are presented to the user for inspection and selection. The LO Narrative that the system deems to be most relevant is highlighted, although the user can change the selected one if they feel that another matches their requirements more closely. The user can access information about each of these LO Narratives, such as the pedagogical description, the author, etc., as well as compare the narratives so as to make an informed decision. The LO Narrative chosen in our example is the one that encompasses the three required learning activities chosen above.

When the LO Narrative is chosen by the user, the system moves onto the next step. At this stage a skeleton LO is created with actual pre-selected content assets that would be used in the generated LO. These content assets are chosen based on the pairings of each low level concept, a complementary learning event or activity. The user can make changes to this LO skeleton by reordering or deleting these pairings. This stage is shown in Figure 2, with the tree on the left representing the skeletal structure of the LO. Using drag and drop the activities can be re-sequenced in any order desired. At any stage during the generation process the user can choose to go backwards and change any of their selections.

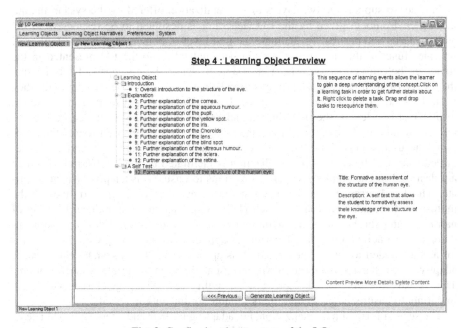

Fig. 2. Confirming the structure of the LO

The support for the two forms of adaptivity offered by the LO Generator are described in the next section, but it is at this stage that the first personalization of the LO will be applied.

Once the user is satisfied with the skeleton that is presented, they can then choose to generate the learning object. When the LO is generated it is output as an IMS Learning Design (IMS LD) [11] compliant manifest using an XSLT transform. An IMS Content Package [16] is created that combines this manifest with the appropriate learning assets and it is this package that the user is offered as a download at the end of the generation process. This package can then be played in an IMS LD compliant player such as Reload [12].

4 Supporting Personalization in LO Authoring

Personalization in this workflow is represented in two different ways. The first form of personalization is within the LOs produced by the system. When the composer is creating an LO they have access to several adaptive LO (sub-) Narratives that they may compose together to provide adaptivity, e.g. to prior knowledge, across the learning activities added to the LO Generator. Secondly, there is the personalization of the experience of the LO composer. Through repeated use of the LO Generator the desires of the composer will be observed and automatically accounted for. These desires are manifest as frequent deviations from the recommendations offered by the LO Generator. For example, if the composer frequently adds specific learning activities to all suggested structures this pattern will be recorded and in future these additions would be automatically performed.

In order to support the two layers of personalization offered by the system the authoring environment given by the LO Generator is designed to be responsive to the authors needs and desires. To facilitate the first layer of personalization, the tool itself provides functionality to the user to add personalization to the LO presented in the final step before generation. The user is able to select the concept and activity that they would like to enable adaptivity on and then select the type of adaptivity they want, be it adaptivity due to prior knowledge or progression. This personalization is available at two levels, the first allowing adaptivity to be added to the entire LO and the second adding the adaptivity to elements within the LO. In order to add the adaptivity the user simply drags the appropriate adaptivity icon onto the part of the required learning object. This personalization is facilitated by the LO Narratives which are designed to encompass rules and conditions to ensure this adaptivity is appropriate. The LO Narratives, as the name suggests, are derived from narratives in the multi-model metadata driven approach [17], which enable a hierarchical layering of narratives and sub-narratives to facilitate personalization. Concept domain and adaptation are reconciled through LO Narratives applied at design time by the LO Generator and are added to the LO generated. This approach facilitates scalable and generic adaptivity, but has the potential downside of enabling inappropriate personalizations. This is why the "on the fly" preview capability and pedagogical scaffolding are important to ensure the generated LO is suitable for the author's needs.

The second form of personalization, i.e. adapting to their authoring style and needs, is performed by assessing their pattern of LO creation. This pattern may only be observed through repeated use of the tool and is manifest as recording the modifications the author makes to the templates that are suggested to them. When the conditions are met for a similar template to be given these differences are analysed for commonalities. The most popular commonalities are added to the template automatically and are tagged as user preferred modifications.

5 Trial and Evaluation

This section provides an overview of the trial and evaluation process carried out in order to assess the suitability of the LO Generator. The initial results are overwhelmingly positive, particularly in the area of flexibility of the tool and the suitability of the produced LOs, where the trial participants expressed satisfaction with both the process and product. Many of the advanced features of personalisation were not implemented at this stage, but the fundamental pedagogical process and learning object construction paradigms were in place.

An initial experiment for the LO Generator took place in early August 2007 with the aim to trial the prototype LO Generator with five users to get their feedback on the usability of the software in relation to the user interface and importantly on the perceived educational effectiveness of the tool. The users that participated in the evaluation all had teaching experience. This tool has been designed to be used by both teachers and learners, but it was decided to initially trial it with teachers. During the trial the users were asked to complete two surveys. The first dealt primarily with usability and user interface issues and will only be briefly discussed. The more pertinent survey with regard to the focus of this paper addressed the perceived educational benefit of LO Generator.

Assessing the fundamental usability of the LO Generator as a tool is important in order to ensure its basic technical suitability for the purpose of constructing personalized learning objects. The usability evaluation questionnaire was originally developed in Trinity College, Dublin as part of an approach to evaluate educational courseware [18]. During this survey the users were asked to agree or disagree with statements about the user interface in the areas of naturalness, navigation, user support, consistency, non redundancy and flexibility. The general responses given were very positive with all users agreeing that the LO Generator was usable for its envisaged purpose. The primary comments centered around the quantity and quality of instructions and scaffolding available in the use of the tool. Most users agreed that they were sufficient, but a minority desired more.

The second survey in the evaluation concentrated on the perceived educational effectiveness of the system and the composed learning object. The goals of this evaluation were to determine if the learning object composed by the system reflected what the user wanted (Goal 1), to discover whether the composed learning object is usable (Goal 2) and to discover whether the teacher felt that they had control over the composition and whether this was the composition that they wanted, i.e. could they produce a learning object for their needs (Goal 3).

Each of these three goals was broken down into a series of discrete objectives upon which the users would be questioned. The results of this survey were mixed but overall positive about the use of the LO Generator.

With reference to the first goal, the users responded that their initial educational requirements were fulfilled while using the LO Generator. They believed that all the topics they selected were covered in the resulting LO and for the most part were taught in the manner expected. Unfortunately, at this stage the manner they were taught in was linear which was pointed out as being a drawback. The sequence of activities matched their expectations and they felt that they could specify the required topics though they were limited by the selection of topics available. On a negative note it was commented that the choice of activities did not necessarily fulfil the requirements of the learning outcome, but maybe would suffice when the system was complete and more content available for later trials. It is planned that further implementations of the tool will provide more available activities.

Regarding the second goal, which was to determine the usability of the composed learning object, for the most part the users thought that they had sufficient information to make use of the LO. However, a minority believed that there was not enough information to make use of the LO. They were then asked whether the design process resembled one that they would normally use to design an LO. Those who had actually given some thought to designing an LO before answered yes. They reported that the steps involved in the process were appropriate and the flow between them was logical. They reported that the mapping between concepts and content was readily understood, but that the mapping between the learning outcomes and the activities was not as transparent. This mapping may require some scrutable reasoning to explain to the user why these activities were chosen. When asked whether they would have the confidence to actually use the LO as part of their course they all answered yes, but with some stipulations. One mentioned that it would be useful to have proper training with using the tool, another mentioned that she would need to see the end result before committing and to have relevant course material available.

With respect to the third goal, the users were first asked whether they could compose the learning object that they wanted using this tool and they all answered yes. Using the LO Generator to generate an LO was not thought to be a difficult process. They felt that they had adequate control over the various stages, except for the sequencing of activities which got a mixed response, mainly due to the usability of the sequencing tool. They agreed that the granularity of both topics and activities were suitable. They liked the fact that they could define the activities they wanted, but would like a way of adding their own as they believed that there were not enough available. To qualify this it was expressed that this could be remedied with more development. With regard to the learning objectives, there was a mixed response as to whether you could specify the ones that you wanted. It was reported that it would be great to be able to specify clearer objectives and also it would be good to be able to specify or add your own. It was also reported that the users would like to be able to create their own LO Narratives.

In summary the reaction to the LO Generator as a tool was a positive one. As regards its usefulness the users believed that they could see the potential in a system like this but would like some additional features to be added to make it more useful.

6 Conclusions

This paper has detailed the workflow of the current version of the LO Generator which has focused on the importance of appropriate pedagogical scaffolding and usability. The LO Generator empowers an author who is not a pedagogical expert in assembling a learning object on the fly to suit their needs. The next version is under development with the refinement of the personalization components being the main focus. With this personalization in place, the vision of the generation of fully adaptive learning objects created in an adaptive environment will become a reality. Plans for a second phase of evaluation are planned to discover the usability and educational effectiveness of this completed approach.

References

1. A3H International Workshop on Authoring of Adaptive and Adaptable Hypermedia, http://www.win.tue.nl/~acristea/A3H/
2. Karampiperis, P., Sampson, D.G.: A Flexible Authoring Tool Supporting Learning Activities. In: Proceedings of the IADIS International Conference on Cognition and Exploratory Learning in Digital Age, CELDA 2004, Lisbon, Portugal, pp. 51–58 (2004)
3. Dagger, D., Wade, V., Conlan, O.: Personalisation for All: Making Adaptive Course Composition Easy. Educational Technology & Society 8(3), 9–25 (2005)
4. Web-based Hierarchical Universal Reactive Learning Environment (WHURLE), http://whurle.sourceforge.net/
5. Intelligent Distributed Cognitive-based Open Learning System for Schools (iClass), European Commission FP6 IST Project, http://www.iclass.info
6. Cristea, A.I., De Mooij, A.: Adaptive Course Authoring: My Online Teacher. In: 10th International Conference on Telecommunications, ICT 2003, Papeete, French Polynesia, pp. 1762–1769. IEEE, Los Alamitos (2003)
7. Cristea, A., Aroyo, L.: Adaptive Authoring of Adaptive Educational Hypermedia. In: De Bra, P., Brusilovsky, P., Conejo, R. (eds.) AH 2002. LNCS, vol. 2347, pp. 122–132. Springer, Heidelberg (2002)
8. Conole, G., Fill, K.: A learning design toolkit to create pedagogically effective learning activities. Journal of Interactive Media in Education (2005)
9. Bailey, C., Zalfan, M.T., Davis, H.C., Fill, K., Conole, G.: Panning for Gold: Designing Pedagogically-inspired Learning Nuggets. Educational Technology & Society 9(1), 113–122 (2005)
10. Sampson, D.G., Karampiperis, P., Zervas, P.: ASK-LDT: A Web-Based Learning Scenarios Authoring Environment Based on IMS Learning Design. International Journal on Advanced Technology for Learning (ATL), 207–215 (October 2005)
11. IMS Global Learning Consortium Learning Design Specification (IMS LD), http://www.imsglobal.org/learningdesign/
12. Reusable eLearning Object Authoring and Delivery (RELOAD), http://www.reload.ac.uk/
13. Conlan, O., Wade, V.: Evaluating the Multi-model, Metadata-driven Approach to producing Adaptive eLearning Services. In: De Bra, P.M.E., Nejdl, W. (eds.) AH 2004. LNCS, vol. 3137. Springer, Heidelberg (2004)
14. Morales, R., Leeder, D., Boyle, T.: A Case in the Design of Generative Learning Objects (GLOs): Applied Statistical Methods. In: Kommers, P., Richards, G. (eds.) Proceedings of World Conference on Educational Multimedia, Hypermedia and Telecommunications 2005, pp. 2091–2097. AACE, Chesapeake, VA (2005)
15. Major Categories in the Taxonomy of Educational Objectives (Bloom (1956), http://faculty.washington.edu/krumme/guides/bloom1.html
16. IMS Global Learning Consortium Content Packaging Specification (IMS CP), http://www.imsglobal.org/content/packaging/
17. Conlan, O., Wade, V., Bruen, C., Gargan, M.: Multi-Model, Metadata Driven Approach to Adaptive Hypermedia Services for Personalized eLearning. Second International Conference on Adaptive Hypermedia and Adaptive Web-Based Systems, Malaga (May 2002)
18. Lyng, M.: Experience Improving WWW based Courseware through evaluating User Satisfaction, M.Sc. in Computer Science, Trinity College, Dublin

Supporting Interaction Preferences and Recognition of Misconceptions with Independent Open Learner Models

Susan Bull, Andrew Mabbott, Peter Gardner, Tim Jackson, Michael J. Lancaster, Steven Quigley, and P.A. Childs

Electronic, Electrical and Computer Engineering, University of Birmingham, U.K.
{s.bull,axm891,p.gardner,t.j.jackson,m.j.lancaster,
s.f.quigley,p.a.childs}@bham.ac.uk

Abstract. Misconceptions have been identified in many subjects. However, there has been less investigation into students' interest in their misconceptions. This paper presents two independent open learner models used alongside seven university courses to highlight the state of their knowledge to the learner as a starting point for their independent study. Many students used the environments; many had misconceptions identified at some point during their learning; and most of those with misconceptions viewed the statements of their misconceptions. Students were able to use the independent open learner models in a variety of ways to suit their interaction preferences, at different levels of study.

1 Introduction

There is much interest in misconceptions, with research in various subjects: materials engineering [1]; chemistry [2]; astronomy [3]; statistical reasoning [4]; special relativity [5]; electrical circuits [6]; java [7]; cardiovascular phenomena [8]. Given the prevalence of misconceptions, a method of helping students recognise such problems would be useful. We introduce two independent open learner models (OLM) to support preferred ways of interacting, to help students identify difficulties in order that they may undertake appropriate independent work according to this information.

Jameson defines a user-adaptive system as "an interactive system which adapts its behaviour to individual users on the basis of processes of user model acquisition and application which involve some form of learning, inference, or decision-making" [9]. A *learner model* is typically inferred based on the user's responses to questions or attempts at problem solving. This relates to the model acquisition part of Jameson's definition. The learner model is compared by the system to its expert model to predict appropriate tutoring or guidance actions for the user according to their learning needs, for example: individualised feedback or explanations; revision material or suitable new material; relevant link adaptations; tasks and exercises on an appropriate topic at an appropriate level. This relates to model application in Jameson's definition.

Usually the learner model is not accessible to the user. An *open learner model* is a learner model that the user can access. An advantage of OLMs is that they can help raise awareness of knowledge, prompting metacognitive activities such as reflection, self-evaluation and planning (see [10]). Presentation of the model can be in a variety

W. Nejdl et al. (Eds.): AH 2008, LNCS 5149, pp. 62–72, 2008.

of forms, from high level overviews such as skill meters [11], [12]; to OLMs incorporating information about conceptual relationships [13], [14].

In *independent open learner models* the model is constructed in the usual way (inferred from user input). However, rather than providing user guidance in line with their inferred needs, responsibility for decisions in learning remains with the learner. Independent OLMs help students identify their learning requirements in order to undertake appropriate work, often outside the system. The independent OLM is therefore a means of encouraging learner independence and responsibility for learning. Adaptation based on "user model acquisition and application" [9] is thus different for independent OLMs. Model application usually relates to inferences based on the model (e.g. for adaptive tutoring as described above). In an independent OLM, model application primarily refers to externalising the model contents. The user then decides appropriate application of the model information to further their learning. The traditional roles of adapting presentation or navigation support in adaptive hypermedia [15] also differs in focus when independent OLMs are employed: adaptive presentation relates to the display of model information (e.g. presentations of descriptions of misconceptions held); adaptive navigation support can be an automatic outcome of displaying the learner model. (Of course, further adaptations may also be made, e.g. misconception descriptions that take account of knowledge of prerequisite concepts required to understand certain statements.)

While some adaptive learning environments adapt or recommend based on learning or cognitive style, it has been suggested that matching an interaction to style is not necessarily effective [16], [17]. Therefore our OLMs allow the user to interact as suits them (accessing the OLM in their preferred format; extensive/limited use; consulting materials during/after an interaction; returning/not returning to check new knowledge). Survey results suggest that students would be interested in obtaining information about their misconceptions from an OLM [18]. In this paper we consider the extent to which students will consult descriptions of their misconceptions in practice in an independent OLM, as a starting point for independent study; interacting in a manner that suits their preferred approaches to learning.

2   Independent Open Learner Models: OLMlets and Flexi-OLM

Our first system, OLMlets, is subject-independent: it can be used in any course for which appropriate multiple choice questions can be created. Instructors input questions and define misconceptions. The OLMlets learner model is inferred based on the most recent five attempts at a topic, with current knowledge level and misconceptions represented in the underlying model by a number between 0 and 1. Use of simple modelling techniques allows easy deployment in a range of courses, as OLMlets does not require instructors to define detailed relationships between concepts. Simple modelling necessarily results in simple model presentations.

The most common simple OLM is the skill meter. OLMlets also uses this format, as in Figure 1 (left). Medium shading (green) in the first, second and last topics of the skill meters shows level of knowledge. The dark shaded (red) portion of the skill meter in the first and last topics indicates the extent to which the learner holds misconceptions. Misconception descriptions are viewed by clicking on the 'misconceptions' link.

Lighter shading (grey) shows more general difficulties (not linked to specific misconceptions). White means that insufficient questions have been attempted to model user understanding. There are four additional views of the model, to accommodate learner preferences. Figure 1 also shows the graph view. Similar to the skill meters, the graph represents knowledge level by the proportion of the area of a meter that is green; with red and grey also used in the same way as in the skill meter view. The main difference between these views is that in the graph, the positive information is on one side of an axis, and the negative information is on the other. A text view is also available, giving a text statement of knowledge level. A table view shows knowledge level in ranked order. Boxes portray knowledge level by the colour of a box surrounding the topic name, using one box for each topic. Learners can use this information in a variety of ways, for example: to plan their study; to navigate to relevant materials (M icon); to select areas on which to answer further questions (Q icon).

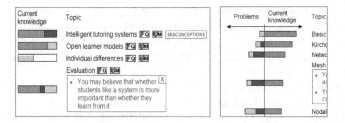

Fig. 1. Excerpts from the OLMlets skill meter and graph views

The misconception statements are based on common difficulties identified from diagnostic tests, tutorials, lab exercises, coursework and examinations. Misconception examples from our courses include the following, with the misconception statement (italics) seen by the student (prefixed by "you may believe that...").

- *Voltages are summed at a node (1st year Circuit Analysis)*
  In nodal analysis of circuits, currents at nodes are summed in accordance with Kirchoff's current law, and the resulting simultaneous equation solved to find the currents in the various branches of the circuit. In mesh analysis, drops in voltage around each branch are summed according to Kirchoff's voltage law. The misconception arises from confusion between the two methods of circuit analysis.
- *The fundamental frequency of a square wave is 1/T (1st year Info. Engineering)*
  Students may remember an equation from previous studies, giving frequency as the reciprocal of period. Thus they may associate 1/T with the fundamental frequency. However, in this context T is only half the period of the waveform, because one period is made up of a positive going pulse of duration T and a negative going pulse of duration T. So the actual period is 2T and the fundamental frequency is 1/(2T). The misconception is likely to be held by students who try to remember formulae rather than working from sketches or mental images.
- *A control group that does nothing is an ideal comparison for evaluating learning gains (3rd year Interactive Learning Environments)*

Students sometimes believe that measuring learning gains resulting from some feature of an interactive learning environment should be achieved by comparing to a control group that had no instructional intervention. This often seems to be based on an assumption that a control group 'controls' by doing nothing (any learning gains are therefore due to the learning environment). However, this does not allow for effects such as time on task or multiple variables in the experimental condition.

Our second system, Flexi-OLM, uses multiple choice and short answer questions for C programming. As with OLMlets, Flexi-OLM models users over the last five attempts and represents knowledge by a number between 0 and 1, but because it was designed for a specific subject, the modelling is at a more fine-grained level in terms of the breakdown of topics and concepts - therefore allowing more detailed OLM views. Figure 2 shows excerpts from the lecture hierarchy/tree and concept map. The colour of nodes indicates knowledge level, with further breakdown of concepts and statements of misconceptions available from the links. In total there are 7 views, the other 5 being: related concepts (tree), prerequisites (map), alphabetical index (list), ranked (list), statement of knowledge level (text). Misconceptions include the following (prefixed by "you may believe that", when seen by students):

- *The '=' operator is used for comparison (1st year C programming)*
  Equality testing is performed with the '==' operator (e.g. if(x == y)...). Because the '=' operator is used for assignment (i.e. when setting the value of a variable), some students assume the same operator is used to test for equality. Further confusion arises because some programming languages *do* use '=' for this purpose.

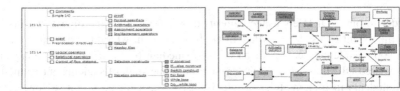

Fig. 2. Excerpts from the Flexi-OLM lecture structure and concept map views

3 Student Use of Independent Open Learner Models

In this section we focus on six OLMlets courses selected to illustrate use of OLMlets in introductory (1st year) and advanced (3rd year) modules; and use of Flexi-OLM in an introductory (1st year) C Programming course, to allow comparison of simple and more complex OLMs at the same educational level.

The OLMs aim to help learners recognise their needs in order to make more informed decisions about their learning. We therefore do not attempt to measure learning gains, since a low level of knowledge in the learner model might relate to a user who successfully identified their difficulties when viewing their OLM, and worked to overcome them away from the system. Not all users will feel a need to return to check their new knowledge. It is assumed students will use an independent OLM to the extent that they benefit, which may differ for different students. This study therefore complements work demonstrating learning with OLMs (e.g. [11],[19]). We investigate whether students will consult descriptions of their misconceptions at introductory and advanced levels, using simple and complex OLMs. We also investigate the range of study approaches that can be supported by an independent OLM.

3.1 Participants, Materials and Methods

Participants were 276 students taking courses in the Electronic, Electrical and Computer Engineering department at the University of Birmingham. 211 students were using OLMlets in 6 modules (1st year – Circuit Analysis; Semiconductors; Information Engineering; Mathematics; 3rd year – Computer Hardware and Digital Design; Interactive Learning Environments). 3rd years were experienced OLMlets users, having used it previously in other courses. We focus on courses at these levels in which lecturers had defined a range of misconceptions. 65 students were using Flexi-OLM (1st year C Programming). The above figures exclude the few students who logged in and then attempted only a small number of questions.

The OLMs were offered alongside the courses throughout a term in the case of OLMlets, and 2 terms in the case of Flexi-OLM. The learner models were assessed in the Semiconductors and Interactive Learning Environments modules; use was optional in the other modules. The logs and learner models were examined to reveal usage patterns and misconceptions, and questionnaires were used to obtain user comments (we here use the open-ended comments). Student data was anonymised.

3.2 Results

In order to place OLMlets usage patterns of our 6 modules in context, we first consider the extent of use of OLMlets in all 14 courses in which it was deployed in the 2006-2007 academic year. A mean of 66% (median 64%) of students taking the 14 courses used OLMlets. This ranged from around one sixth of students in two modules, to all students in four modules. Table 1 shows usage for each course considered in this paper, measured by percentage of students using the systems. Table 1 also shows the percentage of users who held misconceptions at some point, and the percentage of those holding misconceptions, who viewed their misconception descriptions. Most of those with misconceptions had between 1 and 4, but some held as many as 8-10.

Table 1. Usage of OLMlets and Flexi-OLM

Year	Course	OLMlets/Flexi-OLM users		Users with miscon.	Viewed miscon.
1	C Programming	48%	(F-O)	95%	83%
1	Circuit Analysis	94%	(O)	97%	93%
1	Semiconductors	94%	(O)	87%	73%
1	Information Engineering	65%	(O)	88%	83%
1	Mathematics	120%	(O)	94%	71%
3	Comp. Hardware & Digital Design	59%	(O)	95%	87%
3	Interactive Learning Environments	100%	(O)	100%	97%

The percentage of students using the OLMs differed for each course, ranging from almost one half, to over 100% (i.e. there were also students answering questions who were not actually registered to take the module). Students were attempting different numbers of questions, from around 20 to well over 1000. Across the courses 71% of users attempted over 50 questions, with 56% attempting more than 100 questions. In all courses, a large majority of users held misconceptions at some point during their learning. Most of these students viewed the descriptions of their misconceptions. Student comments further illustrate the utility of the misconception statements, and how students used the information about their misconceptions. For example:

- The misconceptions link was useful as it gave me a chance to see exactly what problems I faced.
- The way my misconceptions are highlighted encouraged me to resolve the misconceptions.
- The misconceptions feedback was useful - I went back to the notes and the books, revised the material and then got the questions right.
- I talked to my friends about our misconceptions and we helped each other.
- It helped talking to other students who had got further than me to overcome my misconceptions and problematic areas within the weaker topics.

Using one topic from a course in each case, Figures 3 and 4 illustrate the way in which students typically used OLMlets. There were no differences across courses or levels. Figure 3 gives an example of a student making extensive use, and Figure 4 an example for a student with lower use. The x axis shows the number of questions answered for that topic (in chronological sequence), with the peaks/highest levels showing correct responses; the middle levels, general problems (incorrect answers or selection of the unsure option); and the lowest level, misconceptions. There was no difference in the extent of use depending on the number of misconceptions held; though those with very strong knowledge identified at the start tended to use OLMlets less.

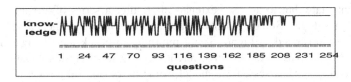

Fig. 3. Pattern of responses of an extensive user

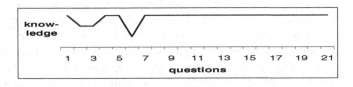

Fig. 4. Pattern of responses of a lower level user

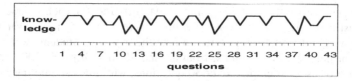

Fig. 5. Pattern of responses of a non-returning user

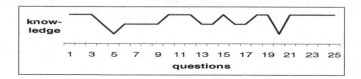

Fig. 6. Pattern of responses of a user being assessed (ceased using OLMlets)

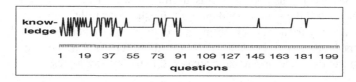

Fig. 7. Pattern of responses of a user examining questions as a learning strategy

Students often worked with OLMlets until they achieved a level of knowledge of which *they* were confident – i.e. they did not cease answering questions immediately upon achieving an 'excellent' model (indicated in Figures 3 and 4 by the fact that there are many points at which they could have stopped towards the end of the interaction, with excellent knowledge: a series of 5 questions indicating correct responses). The user in Figure 3 required many questions to eradicate their difficulties and specific misconceptions, and to become sufficiently confident in their knowledge; the user in Figure 4 achieved this with fewer questions. Others continued use beyond achieving an 'excellent' state, but to a lesser extent - often after a series of around 10 correct responses on a topic. Some students stopped using OLMlets when it still showed difficulties as illustrated in Figure 5, not returning to check their knowledge. Thus students appeared to use OLMlets in different ways, to suit their individual needs.

In the modules that assessed the model, some users stopped answering questions on a topic once they had achieved an 'excellent' representation, as in Figure 6 where, following a misconception (question 20) and previously fluctuating knowledge, the user answered 5 more questions correctly and then ceased interacting on the topic.

Sometimes students adopted a different strategy as shown in Figure 7 for an extensive user. We show here a learner who appears to start answering questions according to their understanding, but on determining their knowledge, switches to studying the questions and answering 'unsure' on most attempts. The learner eventually returns to answering questions according to their beliefs, demonstrating the disappearance of the earlier misconceptions.

The above examples show the most common usage patterns (with Figures 3, 4 and 5 showing very common patterns), which were found across all courses at both levels. A student tended to use a similar approach for each topic where they had similar levels of difficulty, with a lower level of use on topics for which they had good knowledge. (It should be remembered that the Figures show just one topic from a course – e.g. the student who answered 254 questions in Figure 3 attempted similar numbers of questions in the other topics.)

For consistency we have here used OLMlets usage patterns to illustrate students' interactions with an independent OLM. Use of Flexi-OLM was similar. For example, there were differences in the extent of use of Flexi-OLM, and whether students continued to use it until they achieved a good level of knowledge in the various areas. There were also many users who continued interacting on a topic beyond the point at which excellent knowledge had been demonstrated. Thus the complexity of the model display did not appear to affect usage patterns.

3.3 Discussion

Although there is no reason why students should necessarily use OLMlets or Flexi-OLM if they are already confident of their strengths and weaknesses, sufficient numbers were using the OLMs to suggest provision of this approach is worthwhile. Indeed, in some courses students were using OLMlets optionally at the same level as in courses where the learner models were assessed. As there were a greater number of OLMlets users in the mathematics module than were registered on the course, we hypothesise that the additional users had recognised a need to improve their mathematics skills in order to progress well in another course. The smaller percentage of Flexi-OLM users may be because it was used in one course, whereas OLMlets has more prominence in the department as it is deployed in several courses; or it may be due to the greater complexity of the OLM - some may have found Flexi-OLM harder to use. This issue warrants further investigation. Nevertheless, it appears that both simple and detailed independent OLMs can be found useful by many, and this may be applicable at different levels of learning or OLM familiarity as illustrated by the simpler system (OLMlets) used at both introductory and advanced levels.

Although there has been much interest in identifying misconceptions and their underlying causes, and how knowledge of common misconceptions may be used in teaching, there has been less research into students' interest in their misconceptions. We do not claim that showing a student their misconceptions will be sufficient for them to understand their problems: our aim is to assist users in identifying that they have certain difficulties to help them focus on these problems in their independent learning (we aim to facilitate formative assessment and encourage learner independence). Table 1 shows that many students had misconceptions during their learning. Although the number seems quite high, it should be noted that these figures refer to students who had misconceptions *at some stage*. Nearly all those holding misconceptions inspected the descriptions of their misconceptions, thereby gaining information about their understanding that would not normally be available. Student comments suggest that they perceived the misconceptions statements to be helpful, and they used them to facilitate their learning in a variety of ways - both in individual study and in collaboration with peers. Given the extent of misconceptions across subjects indicated in the literature, our results may have relevance to a variety of course types.

Both users who make extensive use of an independent OLM (Figure 3), and users who make lesser use (Figure 4), may continue beyond the point at which their models display excellent knowledge. This suggests that, even where the OLM had identified strong understanding, some were keen to continue until they themselves felt confident of their knowledge. Given that this pattern occurred with students who used the OLM different amounts, this may reflect different strategies. The extensive user may adopt an approach of learning through observing the occurrence of errors (a trial and error strategy), while the less frequent user may be consulting lecture notes once having pinpointed their problems, then returning to test their newly acquired knowledge. This is, of course, speculation. However, the key point is that an independent OLM was used optionally by students with different interaction strategies, suggesting the potential of independent OLMs to support students with different approaches to learning.

Figure 5 demonstrates a user who ceased answering questions without returning to OLMlets, although their OLM still showed difficulties. In this case, after identifying difficulties, the learner may have independently overcome them - not needing to return to OLMlets for confirmation. As stated above, unless an OLM is used to summatively assess students, there is no expectation that they should return to a topic if confident in their knowledge, and so interaction patterns such as Figure 5 are considered equally acceptable as those that demonstrate improvement (Figures 3 and 4).

In the modules that assessed the learner models, some students stopped using OLMlets at the point where it showed excellent knowledge (Figure 6). There may be a tradeoff, therefore, between summative assessment aiming to ensure use of a system intended primarily to support formative assessment, and the formal assessment leading some to restrict their use in order to achieve the maximum mark. However, those not taking full advantage of the benefits of formative assessment may also do the minimum in other forms of assessment and assessment preparation. This is therefore an issue to investigate further. Would these students use an OLM more appropriately if there were no associated summative assessment? Or would they perhaps use it less, as the external assessment pressure would not apply? This also raises the question of validity of the summative assessment - knowledge levels in the OLMs tend to fluctuate when unstable knowledge is represented. In OLMlets in particular, where topics are often broader, if students cease using it at a point when they think it shows the maximum knowledge levels they believe themselves able to achieve, it may be overestimating knowledge. However, this may not differ from other strategic approaches to assessment that students adopt, and so it may be a more general problem.

An interesting strategy was observed amongst some, where they initially answered questions according to their knowledge, then examined questions/response options by repeatedly selecting 'unsure'. Figure 7 demonstrates the success of this approach, with a learner initially having difficulties but after extensive interaction where no attempt was made to select the correct response, the learner then answered accurately, demonstrating the disappearance of their earlier problems.

The interaction examples used reflect the most common interaction strategies. However, as stated above, the important point is not that these particular strategies were more common (or, indeed, the relative frequencies of the interaction types), but that independent OLMs can support *different* approaches to independent study. This may account for the fact that many students were using the OLMs optionally (in only two OLMlets courses did the learner models form part of the assessment).

4 Summary

This paper has described use of two independent OLMs. There were sufficient levels of use to suggest that many students found the information about their knowledge to be helpful. Most users had misconceptions during their learning, and most viewed descriptions of their misconceptions. Independent OLMs were shown to be able to support students with different usage strategies. We therefore suggest that an independent OLM approach may be of benefit to students in promoting understanding of their conceptual knowledge, including their misconceptions, in order to help them focus their study. This appears to apply for many learners with both simple and more detailed learner model presentations, and at different levels of study.

References

1. Krause, S., Decker, J.C., Nisca, J., Alford, T., Griffin, R.: Identifying Student Misconceptions in Introductory Materials Engineering Classes. In: ASEE Annual Conf., Nashville TN (2003),
   http://www.foundationcoalition.org/publications/journalpapers/asee2003
2. Taber, K.S.: Chemistry Lessons for Universities? A Review of Constructivist Ideas. University Chemistry Education 4(2), 63–72 (2000)
3. Zeilik, M., Schau, C., Mattern, N.: Conceptual Astronomy: Replicating Conceptual Gains, Probing Attitude Changes Across 3 Semesters. American J. of Physics 67(10), 923–927 (1999)
4. Hirsch, L.S., O'Donnell, A.M.: Representativeness in Statistical Reasoning: Identifying and Assessing Misconceptions. J. of Statistics Education 9(2) (2001),
   http://www.amstat.org/publications/jse/v9n2/hirsch.html
5. Scherr, R.E.: Modeling Student Thinking: An Example from Special Relativity. American J. of Physics 75(3), 272–280 (2007)
6. Engelhardt, P.V., Beichner, R.J.: Students' Understanding of Direct Current Resistive Electrical Circuits. American J. of Physics 72(1), 98–115 (2004)
7. Fleury, A.E.: Programming in Java: Student-Constructed Rules. In: Proceedings of 31st SIGCSE Tech. Symposium on Computer Science Education, pp. 197–201. ACM Press, New York (2000)
8. Michael, J.A., Wenderoth, M.P., Modell, H.I., Cliff, W., Horwitz, B., McHale, P., Richardson, D., Silverthorn, D., Williams, S., Whitescarver, S.: Undergraduates' Understanding of Cardiovascular Phenomena. Advances in Physiology Education 26(2), 72–84 (2002)

9. Jameson, A.: Adaptive Interfaces and Agents. In: Jacko, J.A., Sears, A. (eds.) Human-Computer Interaction Handbook, 2nd edn. Lawrence Erlbaum Publishers, Mahwah (2007)

10. Bull, S., Kay, J.: Student Models that Invite the Learner. The SMILI Open Learner Modelling Framework. Int. J. of Artificial Intelligence in Education 17(2), 89–120 (2007)

11. Mitrovic, A., Martin, B.: Evaluating the Effect of Open Student Models on Self-Assessment. Int. J. of Artificial Intelligence in Education 17(2), 121–144 (2007)

12. Weber, G., Brusilovsky, P.: ELM-ART: An Adaptive Versatile System for Web-Based Instruction. Int. J. of Artificial Intelligence in Education 12, 351–384 (2001)

13. Dimitrova, V.: StyLE-OLM: Interactive Open Learner Modelling. Int. J. of Artificial Intelligence in Education 13(1), 35–78 (2003)

14. Perez-Marin, D., Pascual-Nieto, I., Alfonseca, E., Rodriguez, P.: Automatically Generated Inspectable Learning Models for Students. In: Luckin, R., Koedinger, K., Greer, J. (eds.) Artificial Intelligence in Education, pp. 632–634. IOS Press, Amsterdam (2007)

15. De Bra, P., Brusilovsky, P., Houben, G.-J.: Adaptive Hypermedia: From Systems to Framework. ACM Press, New York (1999)

16. Papanikolaou, K.A., Mabbott, A., Bull, S., Grigoriadou, M.: Designing Learner-Controlled Educational Interactions Based on Learning / Cognitive Style and Learner Behaviour. Interacting with Computers 18(3), 356–384 (2006)

17. Uruchrutu, E., MacKinnon, L., Rist, R.: User Cognitive Style and Interface Design for Personal, Adaptive Learning. What to Model? In: Ardissono, L., Brna, P., Mitrovic, A. (eds.) User Modeling 2005, pp. 154–163. Springer, Heidelberg (2005)

18. Bull, S.: Supporting Learning with Open Learner Models. In: Proc. 4th Hellenic Conference: Information and Communication Technologies in Education, Athens, Greece (2004)

19. Shahrour, G., Bull, S.: Does 'Notice' Prompt Noticing? In: Nejdl, W., Kay, J., Pu, P., Herder, E. (eds.) AH 2008, LNCS, vol. 5149, pp. 173–182. Springer, Heidelberg (2008)

An Evidence-Based Approach to Handle Semantic Heterogeneity in Interoperable Distributed User Models

Francesca Carmagnola[1] and Vania Dimitrova[2]

[1] Department of Computer Science, University of Turin, Italy
`carmagnola@di.unito.it`
[2] School of Computing, University of Leeds, UK
`vania@comp.leeds.ac.uk`

Abstract. Nowadays, the idea of personalization is regarded as crucial in many areas. This requires quick and robust approaches for developing reliable user models. The next generation user models will be distributed (segments of the user model will be stored by different applications) and interoperable (systems will be able to exchange and use user model fractions to enrich user experiences). We propose a new approach to deal with one of the key challenges of interoperable distributed user models - semantic heterogeneity. The paper presents algorithms to automate the user model exchange across applications based on evidential reasoning and advances in the Semantic Web.

1 Introduction

User-adaptive systems are moving from research labs to practical environments where users are provided with rich personalized experiences. This enables information about the user to be collected and processed in diverse settings (home, work, travel, leisure) and from different platforms (web, mobile devices, sensors). Commonly, the computational effort to extract user models is repeated across applications and domains, due to the lack of interoperability and synchronization among user-adaptive systems. There is a strong appeal that the next generation user models (UMs) will be *distributed* (segments of the user model will be extracted and stored by different applications) and *interoperable* (two or more systems will be able to exchange user model fractions and to use the information that has been exchanged to enrich user experiences), [1], [4].

One of the major challenges to interoperable distributed user models (IDUMs) is handling the semantic heterogeneity[1]. Systems represent user data in different ways by using various syntactic and conceptual structures, rarely share vocabularies (even when dealing with the same domains), and often make different interpretations of the same terminology. This may hinder the exchange and reuse of user models, and can have a negative impact on the practical applications of IDUMs.

The paper proposes a new approach for user model interoperability which deals with semantic heterogeneity of UMs and automates the user model exchange across applications. We consider the user data coming from different systems to be pieces of evidence

---

[1] See [2] for a recent review of the challenges to IDUMs.

W. Nejdl et al. (Eds.): AH 2008, LNCS 5149, pp. 73–82, 2008.

about the user. This enables us to apply an evidential approach [16] to handle the exchange of user data by measuring the *relevance* and *credibility* of UM statements which come from different systems.

The paper will first position our work in the relevant literature (Section 2), and will then outline our evidence-based mechanism for user model data exchange (Section 3). Sections 4 and 5 will describe the main algorithms for measuring the relevance and credibility of user data, which have been evaluated with a study outlined in Section 6. Section 7 concludes and points at future research directions.

2 Related Work

A possible way to address heterogeneity in IDUMs is to impose the use of a common syntax and semantics. This advocates a *lingua franca* approach of cooperation among user-adaptive systems committing to a unified user profile that is easily exchangeable and interpretable [11]. However, in open and dynamic environments, such as the Web or decentralized ubiquitous settings, it is impractical, and in many cases impossible, to create a unified user profile infrastructure and to enforce applications to adhere to a shared vocabulary [13].

The opposite approach excludes the use of any semantic representation and proposes instead algorithms to bootstrap the user models in one system by using information from other systems [2]. This approach, however, loses the richness of semantics and domain specific knowledge the systems have accumulated about the user [13].

An intermediate solution would be to combine the benefits of both approaches to allow flexibility in representing user models and to provide *semantic mapping* of the user data from one system to another [13]. Recent proposals along this line of research exploit Semantic Web (SW) techniques. For example, [17] suggests that the exchange of IDUMs is facilitated by an additional phase wherein the user model schemata of different systems are mapped. However, the mapping requires additional human effort and may not always be feasible. Instead, [7] proposes the use of a semantics-based dialog for exchanging and clarifying user model data between applications. However, the dialog planning mechanism assumes that the applications share a common domain ontology, which may not always be the case.

The approach proposed in this paper is inspired by evidential reasoning and advances in the Semantic Web (SW), and contributes to research along the agenda of finding an intermediate solution. The distinctive characteristics of our approach are: (a) systems are not required to use a common user model, the only requirement is to adhere to a standard for exchange of semantic-enriched user data; (b) different ontologies can be used to represent the domain (even if the domain is the same); (c) exchange of user data is done automatically without the need for manual mapping of user schema.

3 Evidence-Based Approach for User Data Exchange

The work presented in this paper is part of a larger research which developed a framework for IDUMs, including (a) a mechanism for user identification; (b) privacy constraints; and (c) a mechanism for user data exchange. A detailed description of the

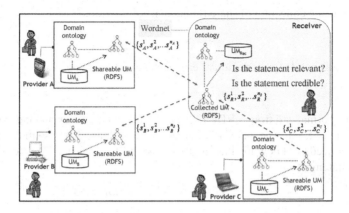

Fig. 1. Architecture of the evidence-based approach for user data exchange

framework and its implementation is given in [5]. This paper focuses on the mechanism for exchange of user data. We will present first its main principles and architecture.

User data can be stored in more than one application. An application, which we will call *receiver R*, may request data about a user U from other systems, called *providers P*. This may happen for different purposes, e.g. when R's data about U is insufficient, conflicting, or out-of-date [4]. Figure 1 illustrates the mechanism for user data exchange using three providers (A, B, and C) that offer data about the same user U.

To ensure syntactic interoperability, a standard representation language of the user model has to be considered. We exploit RDFS[2], one of the most widely used SW languages which ensures interoperability of semantic data. We consider that to take part in the interoperability process every provider system maintains a *shareable user model* which includes RDFS statements representing those fragments of the user model that can be shared with other systems. Furthermore, we assume that each shareable user model is linked to a semantic representation of the domain exported by the provider as an RDFS ontology. The following extract illustrates part of a shareable user model from the experimental study reported in Section 6. The provider P in this case is a mobile tourist guide called UbiquiTO [8] which maintains a profile of the user's interests and offers personalized recommendations with places to visit in the cities. The user is called *Carlo*[3] and the example represents his interests in Rock music as an overlay upon the domain ontology (where the class Rock is defined).

```
<rdf:Description rdf:about="http://www.di.unito.it/~cena/ubiquito/carlo.rdf">
<rdf:type rdf:resource="http://www.di.unito.it/~cena/ubiquito/um.rdf#User"/>
<um:has_interest rdf:resource="http://www.di.unito.it/~cena/ubiquito/dm.rdf#Rock"/>
</rdf:Description>

<rdf:Description rdf:about="http://www.di.unito.it/~cena/ubiquito/dm.rdf#Rock">
<rdf:type rdf:resource="http://www.w3.org/2000/01/rdf-schema#Class"/>
<um:has_value>0.8</um:has_value>
</rdf:Description>
```

---

[2] http://www.w3.org/TR/rdf-schema/
[3] This is an alias used for privacy reasons.

We will denote the collection of shared statements of provider P as

$$S_P = \left\{ s_P^1, s_P^2, s_P^3, \ldots s_P^n \right\}$$

We consider a general representation of each statement as a tuple

$$s = < subject, property, object, value >$$

which can be formalized trough RDF reification (a mechanism for making statements about statements[4]). Imagine that Carlo interacts also with another system (Receiver in Fig.1) which needs to know his interest for Rock and Roll music. This can be represented as a statement s_R:

$$s_R = < Carlo, interested\_in, Rock\_and\_Roll, ? >$$

The interoperability process is performed as a SeRQL query[5] from R in the form of s_R over the sharable user models of the provider systems, as shown below:

$$select * from\{< http://www.di.unito.it/cena/ubiquito/carlo.rdf >\}X\{Carlo\}$$

As a result, R receives the complete collection of statements about the user U from each provider, on the basis of which R will extract the relevant statements for its purposes and will update its model of U. To formalize this process, we will adopt an evidence-based approach. Each statement about U coming from a provider system can be considered by the received R as a *piece of evidence*, i.e. "something known or assumed as fact and made the basis of reasoning or calculation"[6] from which inferences about the user will be drawn. To analyze the evidence, we will adopt Schum's evidential reasoning approach [16] which explains how evidence coming from different sources can be evaluated. The first step in the analysis of evidence concerns its *relevance*, i.e. "How is the evidence linked to matters at issue in the case?". In our context, the relevance of an evidence measures how close the provider's statement is to what the receiver is searching for. The second step concerns the *credibility* of an evidence, i.e. "Can we believe that the event(s) reported in the evidence actually occurred?". Applied to user model data, the credibility of a statement coming from a provider measures the trustworthiness and reliability of both the user model data and the provider of data itself. This will also allow dealing with incorrect or contradictory UM data coming from different providers. The following sections describe algorithms for calculating the relevance and credibility of user model statements.

4   Relevance of User Model Statements: Semantic Similarity

To measure the relevance of a provider's statement s_P with regard to a receiver's statement s_R, we will calculate the similarity between the objects and the properties of s_P

---

[4] An example of reification is shown in the above RDF statement when assigning a value of the user's interest in Rock.

[5] We exploited SeRQL [3] as RDFS language and Sesame ($http://www.openrdf.org/$) as a RDFS repositories server.

[6] http://www.oed.com/

and s_R. To illustrate, let us consider the example s_R above where the receiver wants to know Carlo's interest in Rock and Roll. P can provide the following statements:

$$s_P^1 =< Carlo, interested\_in, Rock, 0.6 >$$

$$s_P^2 =< Carlo, interest, Music, 0.5 >$$

$$s_P^3 =< Carlo, knowledge, Art, 0.8 >$$

where Rock, Music, and Art are linked to P's domain ontology. To measure how relevant s_P^1, s_P^2, s_P^3 are to s_R, we calculate the similarity between their objects (Rock, Music, Art) and the object of s_R (Rock_and_Roll), as well as the similarity between their properties ("interested_in", "interest", "knowledge") and the property of s_R ("has_interest").

4.1 Object Similarity (Osm Algorithm)

In the absence of a unique user model ontology, the computation of semantic similarity among the objects of statements linked to different domain model ontologies cannot rely on direct comparison of terms. For instance, it may happen that the same terms represent completely different concepts, e.g. Rock (music genre) and Rock (geological object), or different terms present similar concepts, e.g. Rock and Music. To compare the semantics of $object(s_P)$ and $object(s_R)$ we follow the word sense disambiguation theory which postulates that two terms are semantically equivalent if their *micro-contexts* are equivalent [12]. We define the micro-context of a term as a set of its semantically related concepts. The *Osm algorithm* first derives the micro-contexts for $object(s_P)$ and $object(s_R)$, and then measures the similarity between both micro-contexts.

Step 1: Find the micro-contexts of $object(s_P)$ **and** $object(s_R)$**.** To define the micro-contexts of $object(s_P)$ and $object(s_R)$ we use the domain ontologies of P and R. Given an ontology Ω and a concept $C \in \Omega$, the micro-context of C is defined as:

$$microContext(C, \Omega) = DirectSuperClasses(C, \Omega) \cup DirectSubClasses(C, \Omega) \cup Siblings(C, \Omega)$$

We find $microContext(object(s_P), \Omega_P)$ and $microContext(object(s_R), \Omega_R)$ by using corresponding SeRQL queries over the provider's ontology Ω_P and receiver's ontology Ω_R. Figure 2 shows the micro-context for object Rock from s_P^1 given above.

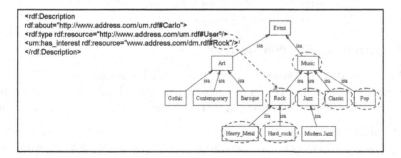

Fig. 2. Micro-context for Rock from the domain ontology of P (used in the study in Section 6)

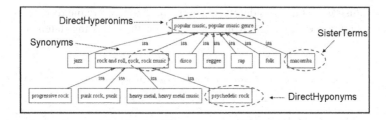

Fig. 3. Micro-context for object Rock and Roll in Wordnet (used in the study in Section 6)

To widen the application of our approach, we consider that it may be possible the receiver not to have a pre-defined domain ontology. In this case, the micro-context of $object(s_R)$ is extracted by using Wordnet [7]. We consider that $object(s_R)$ is associated with a corresponding *word meaning* of an Wordnet entity[8]. To define the micro-context of $C = object(s_R)$ we extract its neighbors [9] (see Figure 3), as follows:

$DirectSuperClasses(C, \Omega_R) \Leftrightarrow DirectHyperonims(C, Wordnet)$
$DirectSubClasses(C, \Omega_R) \Leftrightarrow DirectHyponyms(C, Wordnet)$
$Siblings(C, \Omega_R) \Leftrightarrow SisterTerms(C, Wordnet)$

Step 2: Calculate similarity among the micro-contexts of $object(s_P)$ **and** $object(s_R)$.
We consider each micro-context as a vector of keywords in the form of strings. To compare the elements in the vectors, we use the *Dice coefficient* - a term based similarity measure - used in Information Retrieval [9]. It ranges from 0.0 to 1.0, where a coefficient of 1.0 indicates identical vectors, whilst a coefficient of 0.0 indicates orthogonal vectors. The Dice coefficient measures the similarity of two vectors X and Y:

$$DC(X, Y) = 2 * \frac{|X \cap Y|}{|X| + |Y|}$$

The *Osm algorithm* returns the Dice coefficient of both micro-contexts:

$Osm(object(s_P), object(s_R)) = DC(microContext(object(s_P), \Omega_P), microContext(object(s_R), \Omega_R))$

The *Osm algorithm* was tested with several combinations. For instance, the similarity of the objects in the example statement given above is:

$Osm(object(s_P^1), object(s_R)) = Osm(Rock\_and\_Roll, Rock) = 0.37;$
$Osm(object(s_P^2), object(s_R)) = Osm(Rock\_and\_Roll, Music) = 0.25;$
$Osm(object(s_P^3), object(s_R)) = Osm(Rock\_and\_Roll, Art) = 0.02.$

4.2 Property Similarity (Psm Algorithm)

The *Psm Algorithm* measures the semantic similarity among $property(s_P)$ and $property(s_R)$. We cannot rely on the domain ontology of the provider, which may not include a taxonomy of the properties. There is also a high heterogeneity, both at

---

[7] http://wordnet.princeton.edu/
[8] Since there can be many senses for the same word, the receiver should specify which sense should be used, e.g. Rock as music genre or Rock as geological object.
[9] If there are any synonyms they are included as well in the micro-context.

a semantic level (different verbs may have different meanings) and at a syntactic level (a verb may assume many different forms according to the tense used). Furthermore, properties are normally verbs[10] (e.g., *has_interest*, *interested_in*), so Wordnet similarity algorithms, which deal mostly with noun comparison, cannot be employed for understanding the semantics of the properties included in the s_P.

We assume that semantic similarity of properties dovetails to syntactic similarity, i.e. properties having a similar syntax (e.g. *has_interest* and *interested_in*)are likely to have a similar semantics. The *Psm algorithm* measures the similarity among $property(s_P)$ and $property(s_R)$ using the *Levenshtein distance* [14] that assigns a unit cost to all edit operations required to convert one string ($property(s_P)$ in this case) into another ($property(s_R)$)[11]. The Levenshtein distance is 1 when there is no similarity between the compared terms, i.e. the *Psm algorithm* returns values close to 1 when $property(s_P)$ and $property(s_R)$ are not similar at all. However, the *Osm algorithm* returns values close to 1 when $object(s_P)$ and $object(s_R)$ are similar. Hense, in order to combine the *Osm* and *Psm* values, the *Psm* measure is normalized, as shown below:

$$Psm = (1 - \frac{LD}{max\{|property(s_P)|, |property(s_R)|\}})$$

The *Psm algorithm* was tested with several combinations. For instance, Psm scores for the statements used as example at the beginning of Section 4 are:

$Psm(property(s_P^1), property(s_R)) = Psm(has_interest, interested\_in) = 0.42$
$Psm(property(s_P^1), property(s_R)) = Psm(has\_interest, interest) = 0.73$
$Psm(property(s_P^1), property(s_R)) = Psm(has\_interest, knowledge) = 0.1$

Finally, the similarity measure (Sm) between s_P and s_R is derived as the average of *Osm* and *Psm*. The highest similarity measure between a provider's statement s_P and the receiver's statement s_R gives the highest relevance of s_P for the receiver R. The algorithms for similarity measure have been implemented in Java using Sesame and SeRQL and are described in more detail in [5].

5   Credibility of User Model Statements

Following Schum's evidential approach we consider that the receiver R should check the credibility of each relevant UM statement s_P coming from a provider P. To measure the credibility of use data we exploit corresponding *description of context*, including a description of the provider P and adescription of the statement s_P:

– *description(P)* - used by the receiver R to judge the reliability of P in general. This includes general information from the shareable user model of P (e.g. *name* of provider, *domain* of the application, *method* used by P to derive the user model), as well as a measure of P's credibility based on R's past experiences with P.
– *description(s_P)* - used by R to judge the reliability of the statement s_P. This includes any additional information P can provide about s_P, e.g. *last update* of

---

[10] http://www.w3.org/RDF/

[11] The Dice coefficient is not applicable in this case, as it is used to compare large vectors, while we need to compare two terms expressing a property.

the statement, *duration* for which the statement is valid, *length of interaction* on the basis of which the statement has been derived, *method of derivation* indicating whether s_P was stated by the user or derived by P.

Both *description*(P) and *description*(s_P) are expressed as RDF statements and stored in the shared user model of each provider. We assume that *description*(P) is provided as general information and is applicable to all statements given by P, while *description*(s_P) is assigned using RDF reification and applies only to statement s_P. Since credibility can be related to *trust*, we adapt the mechanism from [15][12] by using a set of heuristics to define for each element in the description of context an *impact value* $\lambda \in [-1, 1]$ of this element on the overall value of trust ψ. Let us denote the impact of an element i on the initial trust value φ with λ_i. Let us denote with ψ_i the trust value applying element λ_i. To calculate ψ_i we apply the formula:

$$\psi_i = \varphi + (1 - \varphi) * \lambda_i$$

For example, if the trust value of a provider is $\varphi = 0.7$, the length of interaction is short and impacts the trust negatively, i.e. $\lambda_1 = -0.6$, and the method of derivation indicates that the statement is made by the user, i.e. will have a positive impact on trust $\lambda_2 = 0.9$, the corresponding trust values ψ_i are calculated as follows:

$$\varphi = 0.7; \ \psi_1 = \varphi + (1 - \varphi) * \lambda_1 = 0.52; \quad \varphi = 0.52; \ \psi_2 = \varphi + (1 - \varphi) * \lambda_2 = 0.952;$$

The overall trust measure ψ is derived as an average measure of the values for ψ_i (in the above example, $\psi = 0.724$). Based on the value of ψ, the receiver can decide which of the relevant statements should be accepted. By calculating the relevance and credibility of each statement, we avoid dealing with conflicting information coming from different providers. The receiver always takes as valid the statements which are most relevant. If there are two highly relevant statements about the same object, e.g. Rock, coming from two providers A and B, the receivers takes the statement with higher credibility value. It is theoretically possible to arrive with the same relevance and credibility value for the same object with conflicting values. In the algorithms defined above, such combination is unlikely to happen often. In case it does, some additional heuristic rules can be used, e.g. prefer the most recent statement or the most trusted provider [13].

6 Initial Evaluation

We conducted an experimental study to test the algorithms and validate the overall framework. We also looked at the potential benefit of IDUMs by analyzing whether a receiver system would get a better UM based on the data provided by a provider. Due to space constraints, we discuss briefly only the improved UM accuracy [10], see [5] for more detail about the evaluation.

We used two systems in a tourist domain which exchanged data about the same users but exploited different domain ontologies:

---

[12] Note that trust in our case concerns systems which is much simpler than measuring trust between users in [15].

[13] A more detailed description of the algorithms for credibility of user models is given in [5].

- **Provider** - iCITY, a mobile user-adaptive guide which provides users with suggestions about events [6]; the UMs collected by iCITY were shared with a receiver.
- **Receiver** - UbiquiTO, a mobile tourist guide which supports users in visiting cities[8]; it asked the provider for more information about users to improve its UMs.

Method. A group of 20 users, 23-40 years old, volunteered to take part in the study. They were asked to register to UbiquiTO and use it every day for one month. This enabled UbiquiTO to generate a fairly detailed and accurate model of each user. The users were also asked to register to iCITY and use it only for one week. This enabled iCITY to generate a partial model of each user. The users were then asked to evaluate their scrutable user models in iCITY by examining whether the scores the system assigned to each domain category matched their real interest in that category. In case of a discrepancy, the users had to assign the correct values for the categories. After this, iCITY acted as a receiver and for each user requests UbiquiTO to provide information about the interests of the user in every domain category from iCITY's domain ontology. The statements provided from PPP were evaluated according to their relevance and credibility (following description of context assigned by UbiquiTO and considering iCITY's trust in UbiquiTO 0.7). The users were then asked to examine again their scrutable user models and indicate possible corrections.

Results. To evaluate the accuracy of the system's predictions we calculated the Mean Absolute Error (MAE). The initial MAE, before using data from UbiquiTO, was 0.35 (in a range from 0 to 1). After the interoperability process, the obtained MAE was 0.11 (in a range from 0 to 1). A decrease of about 68% was observed. This was result of adding more information about the users and updating some of the incorrect information, based on information iCITY received from UbiquiTO. Because there have not been other factors influencing the changes in the user models apart from the interoperability process, we can conclude that the distance between the system's predictions and the user's opinion has been reduced due to the user model interoperability process.

7 Conclusion

The paper has proposed a new approach for user model interoperability which deals with semantic heterogeneity of user models and automates the user model exchange across applications. With respect to the works proposed in the community, our approach is not performed through the use of a lingua franca approach, nor exploiting any semantic representation to employ machine learning or hybrid recommendation algorithms to bootstrap user models in one system by using information from other systems. On the contrary, we propose an intermediate solution inspired by evidential reasoning and recent advances in SW to allow flexibility in representing user models and to provide semantic mapping of the user data from one system to another.

In the immediate future work we plan an evaluation of the overall framework with a greater number of real users in order to extend the results with an appropriate significance degree. This will also include the evaluation of the IDUMs process in a multi-provider scenario, with particular relevance to the resolution of conflicts (different assumptions about the user) which may occur in this case. Furthermore, we are interested in considering the benefits of the IDUMs process in improving the quality of the information provided to users for different kinds of adaptive web systems, e.g. we are currently working on the integration of the IDUM algorithm within an existing personalised mashup system. In the long run, we want to incorporate also the sharing of user modeling *reasoning strategies* across systems, to provide interoperability not just of user data but also of the procedures used to derive this data.

References

1. Berkovsky, S., Cheverst, K., Dolog, P., Heckmann, D., Kuflik, T., Picault, J., Mylonas, P., Vassileva, J.: Ubiquitous and decentralized user modeling. In: Workshop UBIDEUM 2007, 10th International Conference on User Modelling (UM 2007), Corfu (June 2007)
2. Berkovsky, S., Kuflik, T., Ricci, F.: Mediation of user models for enhancing personalized services delivery. User Model. User-Adapt. Interact (published online) (2007)
3. Broekstra, J., Kampman, A.: Serql: An rdf query and transformation language. In: Proc. of International Semantic Web Conference, Hiroshima, Japan (2004)
4. Carmagnola, F.: The five ws in user model interoperability. In: Workshop on Ubiquitous User Modeling, in International Intelligent User Interface Conference (IUI 2008) (2008)
5. Carmagnola, F.: From User Models to Interoperable User Models. PhD thesis, Department of Computer Science, Torino, Italy (December 2007)
6. Carmagnola, F., Cena, F., Console, L., Cortassa, O., Ferri, M., Gena, C., Goy, A., Parena, M., Torre, I., Toso, A., Vernero, F., Vellar, A.: iCITY - an adaptive social mobile guide for cultural events. In: Proc. of Mobile Guide 2006 (2006)
7. Cena, F., Aroyo, L.: A semantics-based dialogue for interoperability of user-adaptive systemsin a ubiquitous environment. In: Proc. of User Modelling Conference 2007 (2007)
8. Cena, F., Console, L., Gena, C., Goy, A., Levi, G., Modeo, S., Torre, I.: Integrating heterogeneous adaptation techniques to build a flexible andusable mobile tourist guide. AI Commun. 19(4), 369–384 (2006)
9. Dice, L.: Measures of the amount of ecologic association between species. In: Ecology (1945)
10. Chin, D.N.: Introduction to the special issue on empirical evaluation of user models and user modeling systems. User Modeling and User-Adapted Interaction 12(5), 105–109 (2002)
11. Heckmann, D., Schwartz, T., Brandherm, B., Schmitz, M., Wilamowitz-Moellendorff, M.: Gumo - the general user model ontology. In: Proc. of International Conference on User Modeling, Edinburgh, Scotland, pp. 428–432 (2005)
12. Ide, N., Veronis, J.: Introduction to the special issue on word sense disambiguation: The state of the art. Computational Linguistics 24(1), 1–40 (1998)
13. Kuflik, T.: Semantically-enhanced user models mediation: Research agenda. In: Workshop on Ubiquitous User Modeling, in International Intelligent User Interface Conference (IUI 2008) (2008)
14. Levenshtein, V.: Binary codes capable of correcting deletions, insertions, and reversals. Technical Report 8 (1966)
15. Masthoff, J.: Computationally modelling trust: An exploration. In: Proceedings of the SociUM workshop associated with the User Modeling conference (June 2007)
16. Schum, D.: The Evidential Foundations of Probabilistic Reasoning. J. Wiley and Sons, Chichester (1994)
17. van der Sluijs, K., Houben, G.J.: Towards a generic user model component. In: Proc. of Workshop on Decentralized, Agent Based and Special Approaches toUser Modelling, In International Conference on User Modelling (July 2005)

Concept-Based Document Recommendations for CiteSeer Authors[*]

Kannan Chandrasekaran[1], Susan Gauch[2], Praveen Lakkaraju[1],
and Hiep Phuc Luong[2]

[1] EECS Department, University of Kansas
[2] CSCE Department, University of Arkansas
kannanc@ku.edu, sgauch@uark.edu, lakkaraju.praveen@gmail.com,
hluong@uark.edu

Abstract. The information explosion in today's electronic world has created the need for information filtering techniques that help users filter out extraneous content to identify the right information they need to make important decisions. Recommender systems are one approach to this problem, based on presenting potential items of interest to a user rather than requiring the user to go looking for them. In this paper, we propose a recommender system that recommends research papers of potential interest to authors known to the CiteSeer database. For each author participating in the study, we create a user profile based on their previously published papers. Based on similarities between the user profile and profiles for documents in the collection, additional papers are recommended to the author. We introduce a novel way of representing the user profiles as trees of concepts and an algorithm for computing the similarity between the user profiles and document profiles using a tree-edit distance measure. Experiments with a group of volunteers show that our concept-based algorithm provides better recommendations than a traditional vector-space model based technique.

Keywords: Recommender System, CiteSeer, Digital Library, Conceptual Recommender.

1 Introduction

The web has grown tremendously since its inception. Traditional search engines gave the same results to all the users without considering their specific user needs. However, the nature of information available on the web, its applications, and its user base has diversified significantly. In addition, a user's ability to locate relevant content would be based on their ability to construct good queries. This has lead to the development of systems that identify the needs of individual users and provide them with very specific information to satisfy their requirements. "Recommender systems"

---

[*] This research was supported in part by the National Science Foundation grant number 0454121: CRI: Collaborative: Next Generation CiteSeer.

W. Nejdl et al. (Eds.): AH 2008, LNCS 5149, pp. 83–92, 2008.

which recommend items to the users by capturing their interests and needs, are one approach to implementing personalized information filtering systems [19].

Recommender systems have been used to recommend many different types of items. For example, websites such as Amazon.com use recommendation engines to make personalized recommendations of the products to its users, and digital libraries like CiteSeer [22] make recommendations of technical papers to its users. Most existing recommender systems use a form of recommendation called collaborative filtering [21]. In this approach, every user in the system has a neighborhood of similar users who share many of the current user's interests. The recommendations provided for the current user are provided as a function of ratings provided by the users in their neighborhood. However, even when there are a large numbers of users to provide recommendations and large numbers of items to be recommended; only a small portion of items receive a sufficient number of ratings to form the neighborhood. Consequently, the recommendations are isolated to only a subset of the available items. Also, when a new item is introduced, there are no ratings available for its recommendation. These problems can be avoided if the recommendation is based on the content of the item.

Previous research has shown that recommendation is a very valuable service to the users of digital libraries [20]. The large amount of textual information in the library collections, such as CiteSeer, can be exploited to provide content-based recommendations. Traditional content-based recommender systems [23] have used the tf*idf [3] similarity measure to compute the similarity between documents. In this model, the documents are modeled as keyword vector and similarity is computed using a distance metric such as cosine similarity measure. However, this model relies heavily on the exact keyword match and does not consider ambiguities present in natural language such as synonymy and polysemy. In this work, we propose a content-based recommender system that represents documents and the user profiles as trees of concepts and computes the similarity between the documents and user profile using a version of the tree-edit distance algorithm. We demonstrate that this approach outperforms a traditional keyword vector-based recommender system.

2   Related Work

In the section, we present sample recommender systems with more emphasis given to recommendations of textual data such as book recommendations and digital library recommendations since these are directly related to our work. [8], [10] and [17] use content-based recommendations whereas [11] and [15] use collaborative recommendations to recommend different items. [2] and [5] take a hybrid approach by combining both content and collaborative recommendations.

Basu et al [8] model the task of assigning technical papers to conference reviewers as a problem of recommending technical papers to the authors based on their interests and background. Using WHIRL [9], they analyze the effect of combining different information sources about papers and reviewers in providing recommendations. Pazzani et al [10], describe a content-based recommender system for recommending news items for users of handheld devices such as PDA's and cell phones. Implicit information about the user is collected based on the activities such as selecting or skipping a news item and is modeled as a profile describing the user's interest. The content-based machine learning algorithm then learns the user's short-term and long-term interests and provides recommendations for future news items. Zhang et al [17], developed a content-based recommender system that extends information filtering systems by recommending papers that are not just relevant, but also novel. They use set theory, cosine similarity measure and Kullback-Leibler measure to propose different models that assign a redundancy score to the new items based on previously seen items.

Si and Jin [11], propose a probabilistic model for collaborative filtering in which they extend the existing partitioning algorithms used for collaborative filtering by clustering both the users and the items simultaneously. They use a modified version of the EM algorithm to predict the ratings for the unseen items for individual users based on their past ratings. Rather than using clustering to address the problem of limited data, Sarwar et al [15] apply dimensionality reduction techniques to the sparsely-populated user-product matrix. Then they perform latent semantic indexing [16] before using the cosine similarity measure to select items to recommend.

In work related specifically to digital libraries, Torres et al [2] use a combination of content-based and collaborative algorithms to build a recommender system for digital libraries. The content-based algorithms find similar papers based on the text of the current paper using cosine similarity measure while collaborative algorithms use the standard K-nearest neighbor algorithm on the input list of citations to output an ordered list of citations as recommendations. These content and collaborative algorithms are then combined together to generate the hybrid recommendation algorithms. They find that the hybrid algorithms perform better than the individual algorithms. Huang et al [5] also take a hybrid approach to recommendations from a digital library. They employ a two stage approach to build a graph based recommender system for a Chinese book store. Books, customers and the purchase information are modeled as a two layered graph. Once the model is set up the task of recommendation reduces to a graph search problem.

3 Approach

The system consists of three main modules, i.e., the classifier module, the profiler module, and the recommender module. The architectural diagram for our system is shown in Fig. 1.

3.1 Classifier Module

This module classifies the documents in the CiteSeer database into a predefined set of concepts, in particular, ACM's Computing Classification System (or CCS). A vector-space classifier was trained the categories of this taxonomy using published papers labeled with the CCS category codes and evaluated as part of prior work [26]. The output from the module is a concept vector for each document in the CiteSeer collection. Since these vectors are sparse, they are stored in the database as lists of (*conceptId, wt*) pairs in which the *wt* represents the degree of association between the document and the concept.

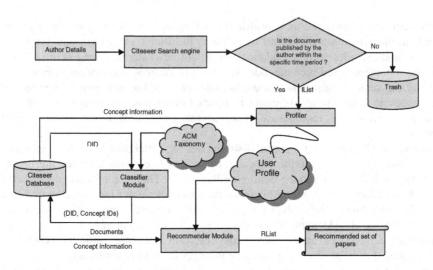

Fig. 1. Author Recommender System for CiteSeer

3.2 Profiler Module

The main objective of the profiler module is to create a conceptual user profile for the author for whom we are trying to recommend papers. The input to the profiler module is a list of documents from the CiteSeer database that were published by the author, called the *IList*. For authors in our study, we create this list by manually querying the CiteSeer search engine with the author's first, last or other common names provided by as part of the registration process. For each document in the *IList*, we retrieve the set of associated concepts and sort them in decreasing order by their weights. They are then added together to create a weighted concept vector representing user's interests.

3.3 Recommender Module

The recommender module uses the user profile to create the list of recommended papers, or *RList*. For each non-zero concept x in the user profile, the recommender module searches the CiteSeer database for documents which have non-zero values for x in their concept vectors. These documents are then added to the *RList*. The number of concepts (β) in the user profile used by the recommender module is provided as a parameter and only the highest weighted β concepts are used.

After processing the concepts in the user profile, the *RList* holds the list of documents that are associated with concepts in the author's profile. The final step is to rank order these documents in decreasing order of their likely interest to the author. To begin this ranking, the recommender module retrieves the concept vectors for each document in the *RList*. Traditionally, recommender systems would calculate the cosine similarity measure between the document and user keyword vectors in order to rank them by similarity. We extend this approach by calculating the similarity between the user and the documents using concept, rather than keyword vectors.

The cosine similarity measure assumes that the elements of the vectors being compared are independent, which is not true. In order to exploit the relationships between concepts in a hierarchical concept space such as the CCS, we next convert the concept vectors for the user profile and the documents in the *RList* into weighted concept trees. This conversion is performed by creating a full taxonomy of all CCS concepts with zero weights for each concept. Then, for each non-zero concept in the original vector, we add the concept's weight to the tree. Finally, we recursively propagate weights up the tree until the root is reached. A tuning parameter, α, is introduced to control the proportion of weight that is propagated to a parent by its child.

Once the user profile and the documents are represented as trees, the problem of computing the distance between them is reduced to finding the distance between the two trees. Based on previous research [26], we use the tree-edit distance measure to calculate the cost of transforming one tree into another with the minimum number of operations. By matching each pair of nodes in two trees, we have three kinds of operations as following:

1. Insertion: The cost of inserting a new node into the tree
2. Deletion : The cost of deleting a existing node from the tree
3. Substitution: The cost of transforming the one node into another

The cost of deletion or insertion of a node is equal to the weight associated with the node and the cost of substitution is equal to the difference between weights of the substituted nodes.

This algorithm calculates the cost of modifying the document profile to match the user profile. The closer the two profiles, the lower the cost of the required modifications. It then sorts the documents in the *RList* in increasing order so that the closest documents appear first and the most distant documents appear last. The closest 10 documents are then displayed to the author as the set of recommended papers.

4   Evaluation and Results

We used the ACM's Computing Classification taxonomy to classify the documents in the CiteSeer database into a predefined set of concepts. This taxonomy consists of 368 categories and is three levels deep. After the classification, each document had three concepts associated with it. We used the documents in CiteSeer database published between 1994-2005 as dataset for building the profile and generating the recommendations. In order to establish truth for the recommendations, we conducted a user study involving 8 published professors from the computer science and computer engineering departments from various universities.

During registration, the professors entered basic information such as their First Name, Last Name, Email Address and any common names that they used in their published papers. This information is used to manually create the queries provided to the CiteSeer search engine to generate the *IList* for each subject.

4.1   Baseline Method

CiteSeer has a built-in recommender system that can compute the similarity between documents using different semantic features [1]. In order to compare our conceptual approach to a keyword approach, we used the tf*idf scheme implemented by CiteSeer as our baseline algorithm. In order to identify the most similar documents for a registered author, for each document in the author's *IList*, we used CiteSeer to retrieve a rank-ordered list of the most similar documents based on tf*idf similarity. These lists, one list per document in the *IList*, are then combined to create the final list for the author. If a document occurred in more than one list, then the weights were accumulated to produce the total weight for that document. The top 10 documents from the final list are then treated as the final set of recommendations produced by the baseline method and is then presented to the author for evaluation.

4.2 Conceptual Recommendation Method

As discussed in the previous section, there are 2 input parameters to our algorithm, i.e., α (the propagation factor) and β (the number of concepts in the user's concept vector to be used to find documents for the *RList*). We tested with four different values for α: 0, 0.33, 0.67 and 1.0. When $\alpha = 0$, no weight is propagated from the child concept to the parent concept during the concept vector to concept tree conversion. Since we are not exploiting the hierarchical relationships of the concepts, this is essentially a concept vector approach. When $\alpha > 0$, weight is propagated from child concepts to their parents and we consider these variations of a concept tree approach. In order to evaluate whether authors are more interested in receiving recommendations for papers on all their interests, or just their major ones, we also evaluated the three values of β: 5, 10 and 15.

We compared the concept tree, concept vector and the baseline algorithm with each other to test the hypothesis that the algorithm computing the similarity using the concept tree ($\alpha > 0$) is better than the algorithm computing the similarity using concept vector ($\alpha = 0$) which is in turn better than the algorithm computing the similarity using keyword vector.

For each value of α, we varied β to obtained three different outputs of the concept-based algorithm. Thus, for each author we obtained 12 different lists, each containing 10 recommended papers. To reduce the work of authors we merged these lists and removed duplicates. To receive unbiased judgments, this list was randomized before being presented to the subjects for evaluation. Once the recommended papers were identified, the author was emailed to notify them that they have papers to review. For easier and more efficient interactions, a web interface was provided for rating the documents. For each recommended document, the title, abstract and the link to the original document were provided and the author was asked to rate the documents using a scale of 1-4 with 1 representing the most relevant and 4 representing the least relevant documents.

4.3 Results

Our hypothesis is that a recommender system based on the concept tree algorithm would be more accurate than the one using concept vectors which in turn should be more accurate than a recommender system based on keyword vectors.

We compared the approaches using the number of correct recommendations within the top 10. Unlike simple "relevant-not relevant" judgments, we had judgments on a scale of 1-4. We report the results when only documents with a user judgment of 1 are considered good recommendations, a very strict definition of correct. The middle ground occurs when we consider documents with ratings of 1 or 2 as correct. Finally, we report results we considering documents with any rating except 4 as being correct.

The first experiment was designed to identify the best performing concept tree algorithm, i.e., algorithms that propagate of α to create a connected tree. Thus, we compared results for the three non-zero values of the propagation factor α, i.e., 0.33, 0.67, and 1.0. For each value of α, we evaluated three values of β, the number of concepts in the user profile used to create the *RList*. Thus, for each value of α we identified the value of β that gave the highest accuracy overall. Fig. 2 displays the results with the best-performing β for each non-zero value of α.

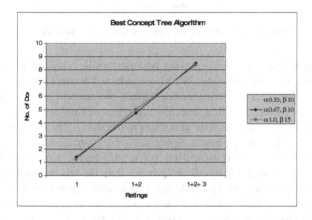

Fig. 2. Best Concept Tree Algorithm for each Value of α

With a high propagation factor, the best results were obtained when 15 concepts from the user profile were used. However, for the other two propagation factors, slightly better results were obtained when only 10 concepts were used. The best overall results occurred with $\alpha = 0.33$ and $\beta = 10$. From this figure, we observe that this version provided the best performance for all definitions of "correct." However, we also observe that the algorithms provide very similar performance, so that the results do not seem to be particularly sensitive to the choice of α or β. Only one of the recommended documents, on average, would satisfy the strictest definition of correct, i.e., be judged 1. However, when we consider a reasonable definition of "correct", i.e., documents judged 1 or 2, roughly half of the 10 documents presented to the authors were of interest to them. With the loosest definition of correct, documents judged 3 or above, 9 of the 10 documents are of interest.

We next compared the best concept tree algorithm to the best concept vector algorithm and the keyword vector baseline. To find the best concept vector algorithm, we evaluated the algorithm with no propagation, i.e., $\alpha = 0$, for the same three values of β. The best concept vector algorithm occurred when 10 concepts in the user profile were used. To find the keyword vector algorithm, we merely evaluated the results on the 10 documents recommended by combining the results from CiteSeer's built-in tf*idf recommender system as described in Section 4.1.

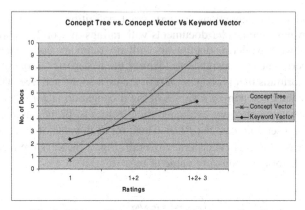

Fig. 3. Concept Tree vs. Concept Vector vs. Baseline

Fig. 3 shows the results comparing the best performing concept tree and concept vector algorithms with the baseline. We also conducted a two-tailed t-test of significance. We found that, for all definitions of correct, the concept tree algorithm outperforms the concept vector algorithm, but this difference was not statistically significant, perhaps because of the small number of authors in the study. The keyword-based algorithm outperforms the concept-based algorithms for the strictest definition of correct only. Although it was only statistically significantly better than the concept vector approach (p=0.005), it was not significantly better than the concept tree approach. The keyword vector approach would provide the author with approximately 1 more highly relevant document, 2.5 vs 1.5 judged 1, in the list of 10. In contrast, the concept tree approach would provide an additional document judged 1 or 2 (5 vs 4). The biggest different occurs when we consider documents judged 3 or above. On average, only 5 documents provided by the keyword approach meet this criteria, meaning that roughly half of the recommended documents are totally irrelevant. However, with the conceptual approaches, only 1 of the 10 documents is not at least somewhat relevant. For documents judged 2 or above and 3 or above, both methods based on a conceptual representation of the documents outperform the keyword-based algorithm and these results are statistically significant (p= 0.001).

5   Conclusions

In this work, we presented a novel way recommending technical papers to the users of the CiteSeer. We represent the user profiles and the documents as content tree and used a tree matching algorithm to compute the similarity between them. To evaluate our system we conducted a user study involving 8 authors with published papers in the CiteSeer collection. We compared recommendations provided by CiteSeer's built-in tf*idf keyword vector representation, a concept vector-based matching algorithm, and a concept-tree based algorithm based on the tree-edit distance measure. We obtained the best results when the propagation factor used to convert the concept vector into concept tree was 0.33 and we used the highest weighted 10 concepts in the user profile to create the unranked set of candidate documents to recommend.

We conclude the following from our results:

1. The concept tree matching algorithm performed much better than the traditional algorithm based on keywords for providing recommendations. The result was found to be statistically significant. We found an improvement of 8% and 31% on average for the documents judged 2 and above and 3 and above, respectively.
2. The concept tree method performed better than the concept vector method. We found an improvement of 6% to 9% on the average. However, this result was not statistically significant.

The list of documents used to build the user profile for an author was created by manually querying the CiteSeer system. Future work will focus on automating this process so that this improved recommender system can be deployed on the CiteSeer site. In addition, we want to explore the effect of a hybrid approach combining keyword and conceptual matches to see if we can get improvements for highly relevant documents.

References

1. Bollacker, K., Lawrence, S., Giles, C.L.: Citeseer: an autonomous web agent for automatic retrieval and identification of interesting publications. In: Bollacker, K., Lawrence, S., Giles, C.L. (eds.) Agents 1998, 2nd International ACM Conference On Autonomous Agents, pp. 116–123. ACM Press, New York (1998)
2. Torres, R., McNee, S.M., Abel, M., Konstan, J.A., Riedl, J.: Enhancing digital libraries with techlens. In: Digital Libraries. Proceedings of the Joint ACM/IEEE Conference, June 2004, pp. 228–236 (2004)
3. Salton, G., Buckley, C.: Term weighting approaches in Automatic Text Retrieval. Information Processing and Management 24(5), 513–523 (1988)
4. Burke, R.: Hybrid recommender systems: survey and experiments. User Modeling and User-adapted Interaction 12(4), 331–370 (2002)
5. Huang, Z., Chung, W., Ong, T.-H., Chen, H.: A graph-based recommender system for digital library. In: Proc. Joint Conf. on Digital Libraries, Portland, pp. 65–73 (2002)
6. Chen, H., Ng, T.: An algorithmic approach to concept exploration in a large knowledge network (automatic thesaurus consultation): symbolic branch-and-bound search vs. connectionist hopfield net activation. Journal of the American Society for Information Science 46(5), 348–369 (1995)
7. Balabanović, M., Shoham, Y.: Fab: content-based, collaborative recommendation. Communications of the ACM 40(3), 66–72 (1997)
8. Basu, C., Hirsh, H., Cohen, W., Nevill-Manning, C.: Technical paper recommendation: a study in combining multiple information sources. Journal of Artificial Intelligence Research (14), 231–252 (2001)
9. Cohen, W.: The WHIRL approach to information integration. In: Hearst, M. (ed.) Trends and Controversies, IEEE Intelligent Systems, pp. 20–23 (October 1998)
10. Billsus, D., Pazzani, M.J., Chen, J.: A learning agent for wireless news access. In: Proc. of the International Conference on Intelligent User Interfaces, pp. 33–36 (2000)
11. Si, L., Jin, R.: Flexible mixture model for collaborative filtering. In: Proc. 20th Int'l Conf. Machine Learning, August 2003, pp. 704–711 (2003)

12. Hofmann, T., Puzicha, J.: Latent class models for collaborative filtering. In: The Proceedings of IJCAI, pp. 688–693 (1999)
13. Dempster, A., Laird, N., Rubin, D.: Maximum likelihood from incomplete data via the EM algorithm. Journal of the Royal Statistical Society 39(1), 1–38 (1977)
14. Hofmann, T., Puzicha, J.: Statistical models for co-occurrence data (Technical Report). Artificial Intelligence Laboratory Memo 1625, M.I.T (1998)
15. Sarwar, B., Karypis, G., Konstan, J., Riedl, J.: Application of dimensionality reduction in recommender systems-a case study. In: ACM WebKDD Wk. shop (2000)
16. Deerwester, S., Dumais, S.T., Furnas, G.W., Landauer, T.K., Harshman, R.: Indexing by latent semantic analysis. Journal of the American Society for Information Science 41(6), 391–407 (1990)
17. Zhang, Y., Callan, J., Minka, T.: Novelty and redundancy detection in adaptive filtering. In: Proc. ACM SIGIR 2002, pp. 81–88 (2002)
18. http://en.wikipedia.org/wiki/Kullback-Leibler_divergence
19. Gauch, S., Speretta, M., Chandramouli, A., Micarelli, A.: User Profiles for Personalized Information Access. In: Brusilovsky, P., Kobsa, A., Nejdl, W. (eds.) Adaptive Web 2007. LNCS, vol. 4321, pp. 54–89. Springer, Heidelberg (2007)
20. Geisler, G., McArthur, D., Giersch, S.: Developing recommendation services for a digital library with uncertain and changing data. In: Proceedings of the 1st ACM/IEEE-CS. JCDL 2001, pp. 199–200. ACM Press, New York (2001)
21. Schafer, J.B., Frankowski, D., Herlocker, J., Sen, S.: Collaborative Filtering Recommender Systems. In: Brusilovsky, P., Kobsa, A., Nejdl, W. (eds.) Adaptive Web 2007. LNCS, vol. 4321, pp. 291–324. Springer, Heidelberg (2007)
22. CiteSeer.IST Scientific Literature Digital Library, http://citeseer.ist.psu.edu/
23. Pazzani, M.J., Billsus, D.: Content-Based Recommendation Systems. In: Brusilovsky, P., Kobsa, A., Nejdl, W. (eds.) Adaptive Web 2007. LNCS, vol. 4321, pp. 325–341. Springer, Heidelberg (2007)
24. Adomavicius, G., Tuzhilin, A.: Toward the next generation of recommender systems: A survey of the state-of-the-art and possible extensions. IEEE Trans. On Knowledge and Data Engineering 17(6), 734–749 (2005)
25. Breese, J.S., Heckerman, D., Kadie, C.: Empirical analysis of predictive algorithms for collaborative filtering. In: Proc. 14th Conf. Uncertainty in AI, July 1998, pp. 43–52 (1998)
26. Lakkaraju, P., Gauch, S., Speretta, M.: Document Similarity Based on Concept Tree Distance. In: 19th International Conference on Hypertext and Hypermedia (Hypertext 2008), Pittsburgh, PA, June 19-21 (to appear, 2008)
27. The ACM Computing Classification System, http://acm.org/class/1998/

Social Information Access for the Rest of Us: An Exploration of Social YouTube

Maurice Coyle[1], Jill Freyne[1], Peter Brusilovsky[2], and Barry Smyth[1]

[1] School of Computer Science and Informatics,
University College Dublin, Belfield, Dublin 4, Ireland
{maurice.coyle,jill.freyne,barry.smyth}@ucd.ie
[2] University of Pittsburgh, Pittsburgh, USA
peterb@sis.pitt.edu

Abstract. The motivation behind many Information Retrieval systems is to identify and present relevant information to people given their current goals and needs. Learning about user preferences and access patterns recent technologies make it possible to model user information needs and adapt services to meet these needs. In previous work we have presented ASSIST, a general-purpose platform which incorporates various types of social support into existing information access systems and reported on our deployment experience in a highly goal driven environment (ACM Digital Library). In this work we present our experiences in applying ASSIST to a domain where goals are less focused and where casual exploration is more dominant; YouTube. We present a general study of YouTube access patterns and detail how the ASSIST architecture affected the access patterns of users in this domain.

1 Introduction

For many people, access to online information is a pervasive feature of everyday life. A recent report by ComScore [1] found that more than 61 billion searches were carried out in August 2007 (with Google search properties accounting for over 37 billion of these searches). At the same time, however, users are frequently finding it increasingly difficult to access the right information at the right time; for example, recent research points to search failure rates of 50% [10]. Personalization and recommendation techniques are often proposed as potential solutions to these information access difficulties. By learning about users' preferences and interests, these technologies make it possible to model their information needs with a view to adapting modern information services in response to these needs. To date there has been considerable research when it comes to the development of the "algorithmics of recommendation" (the development of the core algorithms that underpin recommendation engines) but relatively little attention has been paid to the interfaces that are needed to deliver recommendations to end-users.

Recently we have developed ASSIST, a general-purpose platform that can be used to incorporate various types of *social cues* into existing information access systems. ASSIST is a proxy-based architecture that facilitates the tracking of

W. Nejdl et al. (Eds.): AH 2008, LNCS 5149, pp. 93–102, 2008.

user information access requests in order to build a repository of community preferences that can then be used to enhance the interactions of future users as they search and navigate for information. ASSIST capitalizes on two earlier streams of research in the field of social information access: social search and social navigation. Social search systems such as AntWorld [7], I-SPY [11], or SERF [6] archived past search successes of their users to recommend relevant resources to the future users, who are looking for similar information. Social navigation support systems such as Footprints [12], CoWeb [4], and Knowledge Sea II [2] archived past browsing traces of their users and visualized them to help new users to make navigation decisions. ASSIST is, however, unique among these systems in that it archives and integrates both navigation and search cues to provide users with information access *hints* that reflect the past experiences of other users. Combining the search and browsing experiences of past users allows ASSIST to generate more reliable social recommendations and provide coherent support in the context of integrated search and browsing [9].

To date a number of studies have been conducted to evaluate the benefits of ASSIST in the context of traditional information access services. For example, in [5] we focus on the application of ASSIST to the ACM Digital Library, where users search and navigate for particular items of information that fulfill specific information needs; in this context ASSIST is used in the support of *goal-driven* information access. This type of access is typical for information systems aimed at professional users; however, it is not a dominant form of information access for the average Web user. Nowadays, the majority of Web information systems such as Web stores, news agencies, and entertainment services, strive to support both goal-driven and *exploratory* information access. It reflects the fact that many of their users do not have a specific information goal in mind and thus are not in a position to express a detailed information need. To support both kinds of information access, modern systems pay attention to both search and browsing support, which, as we expected provide a good application context for our framework. YouTube serves as an excellent example of a modern Web information system. It supports search, but also provides many opportunities for exploration through several types of featured videos connected to the system home page and rich opportunities to navigate from one video to related videos.

In this paper, we describe our attempt to explore the applicability of the ASSIST framework in this context. We chose YouTube as our target and implemented the ASSIST-YouTube proxy, which provides social recommendation for YouTube users. In the following sections, we describe how the ASSIST platform can be used to capture user interactions and the ways in which this interaction data can be used to adapt the YouTube interface. We also present the results of a recent live-user trial of ASSIST-YouTube. In particular we will examine the influence that ASSIST's social recommendations have on the manner in which YouTube users search for information and how they explore the YouTube information space. We will also consider how these results differ from those found for the application of ASSIST to the ACM Digital Library, highlighting a number of features that emphasise important differences between the interaction patterns that are commonplace in these different information access scenarios.

2   ASSIST Engine

ASSIST is a proxy-based architecture for social information access. It resides between a user and an information system (such as YouTube), intercepts user requests to an information repository, and enhances the source of the returned pages with social guidance features such as re-ranking lists of *related videos* or recommending a specific item to the user (Figure 2). A store of past user interactions with the system maintained by ASSIST constitutes a store of "community wisdom", which is used to bring forward content to users in order to allow more informed relevance judgements to be made and to recommend content from beyond the current page. For reasons of space we have omitted many of the technical details of the ASSIST architecture; for more details please refer to [3].

2.1   Monitoring User Interactions

ASSIST records three different types of click behaviour: search result selections, simple browsing clicks, and contextual browsing clicks by capturing implicit relevancy feedback through user click behaviour within the system. A search result selection occurs each time a user selects a result, I_T, from a result-list generated by ASSIST in response to a query. A record of this selection is noted in the search hit-matrix maintained by ASSIST (Figure 1). A simple browsing click occurs when a user views a video whose link is contained within a "Featured" or

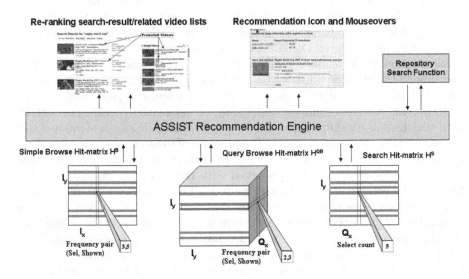

Fig. 1. ASSIST Architecture

"Most rated" list. Contextual browsing clicks are clicks which are made in the context of a previous selection or query submission. An item I_T is considered to have an associated item context I_C if I_C contains a hyperlink to I_T and a contextual click is recorded if a user follows the link. An item I_T is seen to have a *query browsing context*, Q_C and a *browsing item context* I_C if the path being navigated by the user started at the result-list for q_C and the user has navigated away from the result-list to an item I_C which contains a hyperlink to I_T.

2.2 Exploiting User Interactions for Recommendations

ASSIST helps the users of an information system by providing both active and passive social guidance (recommendations). Both types of guidance provided by the ASSIST engine are based on the past search and browsing interactions of community members. In the context of the YouTube system, social guidance provided by ASSIST-YouTube offers a number of enhancements to the standard YouTube interface, providing both improved search and browsing capabilities.

To provide active recommendations, ASSIST re-ranks lists of videos offered by YouTube to reflect accumulated community preferences. In the search context, ASSIST re-ranks the search results returned by YouTube in response to a user query Q according to their *relevance* to Q. ASSIST leverages the search hit-matrix data to assign relevance scores to videos based on their search interactions. The relevance of video item I to query Q can be calculated by calculating the number of times I has been selected in response to Q as a percentage of the total number of selections across all items for Q. ASSIST also identifies videos which have been selected for *similar* queries (using a simple term-overlap similarity metric) and weights their relevance to their associated query Q_i by the similarity of Q_i to Q. These *promotion candidates* are ranked according to their weighted relevance score and placed at the top of the result-list for the query Q.

In a browsing context, ASSIST re-ranks the list of YouTube generated related videos which are displayed alongside a video which is being watched. This list is a valuable source of complementary content for engaging in browsing activities and thus the position of videos within the list is important. ASSIST reranks the related video list according to the items *contextual browsing popularity*.

To provide passive recommendation, ASSIST augments hyperlinks to content with visual *social cues* throughout the interface, highlighting areas of interest and suggesting paths through the space. The presence of these cues indicates previous encounters by community members with the content behind the link. If the user mouses over the icon, they are presented with the item's search and browsing history with community members (Figure 2). The search history information in a mouseover aims to convey to users that the associated content has been chosen by a community member in relation to a query and also the strength of the item-query relationship (i.e. the relevance score). This mouseover includes a list of all queries which have led to the selection of the video (see Figure 2). Users may click on these queries to commence a new search, which essentially allows them to query YouTube for 'more videos like this' with very little effort. The query list is ordered by the strength of the item-query relationship.

Fig. 2. By mousing over the 'recommended' icon presented alongside recommended videos, users may access recommendations for queries or additional video content

The mouseovers are also used to provide the user with *contextual recommendations* to provide the user with an Amazon-style *"users who watched this video subsequently watched these"* feature. As mentioned in Section 2.1, if previous users engaged in browsing behaviour after viewing a particular video (i.e. they selected a related video), this fact is recorded in the browse hit matrices. By recommending videos that were subsequently watched in the mouseover provided alongside a hyperlink, the user may choose to skip watching the top-level video and go straight to one of the recommended videos.

3   ASSIST-YouTube User Studies

In the context of the ASSIST-YouTube project we ran two user studies. The first study was a short 7 week monitoring of students using the official YouTube video sharing site (http://www.youtube.com). This study was used for data collection and observation and was performed before ASSIST-YouTube was implemented, to analyse activity patterns in YouTube. The results of the study were reported in [3]. The data, amongst other findings, uncovered the presence of long navigational trails through the repository, motivating the need for social support in the domain. The second study, reported below, attempted to assess the effect of social guidance provided by ASSIST-YouTube. This study took place over 14 weeks in the winter semester of 2007. The trial monitored 21 participants from the School of Computer Science and Informatics in University College Dublin in their regular activities with YouTube. All participants communicated with

YouTube through the ASSIST-YouTube proxy server, which enhanced their interaction with active and passive social support as described above. This study pursued two goals. First, we were interested in analyzing patterns of user interaction in YouTube and investigating the need for social support beyond the results of our earlier smaller-scale study. Second, we wanted to investigate how the social support provided by ASSIST-YouTube influenced user interaction with YouTube. The following two sections address each of these issues.

4   YouTube Usage Analysis

The most important thing, which we discovered when analyzing YouTube user logs is the differing nature of YouTube usage in comparison with more traditional information systems, such as the ACM Digital Library, which we explored in the process of evaluation of ASSIST [5]. A typical ASSIST-ACM user came to the ACM Digital Library with a reasonably well-defined goal in mind: to find papers on a specific topic. The vast majority of user sessions started with search, while browsing from a paper to related papers was most popular as a search follow-up. This was the context for which the original ASSIST system was engineered.

As we discovered, a similar type of access (searching for a video on a specific topic or with specific features) happens in YouTube as well, but it accounts only for one (and by far not the dominant) type of YouTube usage. Out of 1230 sessions recorded in the ASSIST-YouTube logs, only 366 (i.e, less than 30%) started with search. These goal-directed sessions displayed similar characteristics to those observed in ASSIST-ACM: searching for videos, which matched their goal, the users were eager to examine related videos creating session trails. 47% of sessions initiated by search activity resulted in a trail and the average length of the trail was quite considerable (3.07 clicks). To clarify, the submission of a search query was not counted as part of the trail.

The majority of sessions (864) started directly with video browsing. Most of these sessions are unlikely to have been driven by a specific goal (i.e. an attempt to find a video on a specific topic). Only 125 of these browsing sessions resulted in a trail and the average trail length was shorter than for search-initiated sessions (2.69 clicks). The remaining 739 browsing sessions (> half of all sessions) produced no trail. To shed light on the nature of user browsing-initiated activity in YouTube, we classified all sessions which started with browsing by the origin of the session. The data uncovered another eye-opening fact: 47% of browsing-initiated sessions (or about 30% of all sessions) were external accesses to YouTube through a specific video URL. These URLs can be considered as direct social recommendations, which the user most likely received in an email from another user (44%) or found on such social sites such as FaceBook, MySpace and Bebo, inside blogs and other sites (3%), which allow users to embed videos on their pages. This shows the collaborative nature of YouTube and highlights the social recommendation potential in this context.

The remaining browsing-initiated activity could be classified as casual browsing. Here the users were not trying to find something specific, but were simply trying to watch interesting videos with no apparent goal in mind. Surprisingly, user casual browsing was not dominated by exploring links, which were specifically engineered by YouTube to support this kind of browsing (what's being watched right now, featured videos and the menus on the videos page). These links only contribute to 11% of clicks showing their relatively low value to our users. These menu lists are generated by YouTube as recommendations to all of their users (in the case of the featured and directors videos) and as a response to general popularity figures (in the case of "what's being watched right now" and the popular links on the videos page). The content of these lists inspired our users less frequently than might be expected, which is another fact motivating the need for support at the level of communities and groups in YouTube. At the same time, the users were quite eager to follow various kinds of related links from the videos they liked. For example, 7% of all browsing sessions were started by follow-up links shown by YouTube at the end of watching a movie. It hints that navigating through related videos is a valuable approach not only for goal-directed, but also for casual browsing.

Overall, our analysis uncovered three major types of user behavior in YouTube: traditional goal-directed search, direct browsing (following an externally recommended link) and casual browsing (watching interesting, but not specific videos). While the ASSIST-YouTube social recommendation engine was designed to assist only the first type of activity, the nature of its browsing support component makes it also quite useful for social support of casual browsing. However, social support of casual browsing may be more challenging than social support of goal-directed browsing. While the search goals of the users of a specific community have some reasonable overlap [10], their casual browsing is driven by their general interests, not goals. Since these general interests could be much more diverse even in a small community, it may be hard to expect that users in a small community will see movies recommended by other community members during their search and browsing (the context supported by ASSIST-YouTube). Indeed, the users in our trial watched 1257 unique videos 2027 times in total. It gives a relatively low watch repetition rate of 1.6. To leverage social support in this context, alternative social recommendation tools for casual browsing should be considered, such as a list of recent popular movies in the community. The next section will analyse to what extent we can demonstrate the success of social navigation support in a relatively small group in this new context.

5   Socially Supported Exploration in YouTube

In previous trials using ASSIST [5] we examined the speed, accuracy and effort exerted of the users using the traditional versus the socially enhanced versions of the repository in question. We also set the users specific tasks which were representative of how the systems are generally used and monitored their performance in terms of the task at hand. The emphasis of this trial differed in two ways. Firstly we moved from a focus driven environment into a more leisure-oriented environment which was undoubtedly going to produce differing results and secondly we allowed users to use the system without setting an agenda or task to be completed. In order to observe the user in their natural interaction mode with the YouTube system we opted for non disruptive feedback methodologies and opted to consider two implicit indicators *success rates* and *view percentages* when comparing the performance of YouTube and ASSIST-YouTube. When measuring the quality of ranked lists of videos, we calculate the *success rate* of a set of lists to be the percentage of lists that had at least one item selected (that is a list is *successful* if the user finds at least one apparently interesting item). The second metric of performance is the *view percentage* of a video, since it seems likely that the proportion of a video that is watched by a user could be used as a proxy for the user's opinion of the video content. We will also examine the effort exerted by users as they navigate, with comment on how this compares to ASSIST deployments in a more goal-focussed domain.

Effects of Social Recommendation on Search. Figure 3(a) graphs the success rates for different types of search sessions; we can see that search sessions that had some results with social explanations attached (*Expln*) had at least 1 result selected 11% more often than sessions without explanations (*!Expln*). When we examine sessions in which the searcher accessed more detailed explanatory information by mousing over an icon (*MO*), we see that the difference is more pronounced still, with a 31% increase observed. These findings suggest that

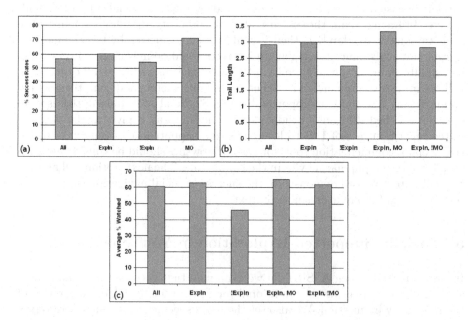

Fig. 3. (a)Success rates of search sessions with explanations (*Expln*), without explanations (*!Expln*) and with explanation icon mouseovers (*MO*). (b) Average trail length when explanations are encountered (c) Average percentage of videos along a trail that were watched when explanations were encountered.

augmenting search result lists in the YouTube repository with social recommendations results in a greater likelihood of the user finding a video of interest and speaks to the utility of reusing such community preference information.

Effects of Social Recommendation on Exploratory Behaviour. In an environment such as the ACM DL where users are likely to be searching for a specific paper or a number of papers on a given topic, we can assume that users want to get to these articles as quickly possible. Indeed, the ASSIST-ACM system received positive qualitative feedback regarding the ease and speed of finding information while empirical data showed an overall reduction in user effort both in search and browsing contexts (see Farzan et al. [5]). However, as we can see from Figure 3(b), ASSIST-YouTube caused users to exert *more* effort when navigating through the site. For navigation trails which had explanations presented along the way, users travelled 33% further on average than they did in trails where no explanations were present. Indeed, when the user moused over an explanation icon at some point in a trail, they browsed $\sim$ 47% further on average than on trails with no explanations. To investigate the reason for this increase in effort exerted, we turn our attention to the average view percentages for different trail types, as graphed in Figure 3(c). As we can see, the presence of explanations along a trail corresponds to an increase in view percentages over trails with no explanations of $\sim$ 37%, on average, with a slightly higher increase ($\sim$ 42%) observed when a mouseover occurs along the trail. Assuming that users watch more of videos that they are interested in, we can claim that the presence of ASSIST's social enhancements improves the user experience by aiding them in selecting videos which they are likely to watch more of.

6 Conclusions

Evaluating ASSIST within a multimedia site with a casual and leisure-oriented focus has enriched our insight into the value of social support in information spaces. The results of the current study suggest that the effects and type of social enhancements have to be engineered to match the user task and target repository. The original social support in ASSIST was engineered for a goal-driven search task which needs to be done with minimal effort versus an entertaining exploratory task with fewer time constraints. Social support of casual browsing may require some modifications to the ASSIST approach. For example, a high number of items examined in a goal-driven search task could reflect user dissatisfaction. In the context of casual browsing, a high number of examined items can reflect continued user interest in the retrieved items. In addition, the need to support casual browsing calls for additional social recommendation tools such as the most popular or currently watched videos within a community.

Our work also demonstrated that the users are eager to share links to interesting videos with others as well as to follow such direct social recommendations. While the majority of modern research focuses on indirect recommendations, our data shows that in a multimedia domain it could be wise to return to the roots of collaborative recommender system research [8] and to embed a direct recommendation mechanism into the system. In addition to the convenience provided to the recommending users, it allows the exploring user to take advantage of the recommendation in the context of using the system and while spending time with the system. As our result suggests, receiving a video through an email or external site can interfere with the user's current task and will result in less exploration of the system while social recommendation provided in the system encourages even higher exploration. We hope to address some of these ideas in our future research with ASSIST-YouTube.

References

1. 61 Billion Searches Conducted Worldwide in August (2008),
   http://www.comscore.com/press/release.asp?press=1802
2. Brusilovsky, P., Chavan, G., Farzan, R.: Social Adaptive Navigation Support for Open Corpus Electronic Textbooks. In: De Bra, P.M.E., Nejdl, W. (eds.) AH 2004. LNCS, vol. 3137. Springer, Heidelberg (2004)
3. Coyle, M., Freyne, J., Farzan, R., Smyth, B., Brusilovsky, P.: Reducing Click Distance through Social Adaptive Interfacing. In: Proceedings ReColl 2008 - International Workshop on Recommendation and Collaboration. In conjunction with International Conference on Intelligent User Interfaces (2008)
4. Dieberger, A., Guzdial, M.: CoWeb–Experiences with Collaborative Web Spaces. Computer Supported Cooperative Work. In: From Usenet to CoWebs: Interacting with Social Information Spaces, pp. 155–166. Springer, Heidelberg (2003)
5. Farzan, R., Coyle, M., Freyne, J., Brusilovsky, P., Smyth, B.: Adaptive Social Support for Information Space Traversal. In: Proceedings of the 18th ACM Conference on Hypertext and Hypermedia, Manchester, UK, pp. 199–208 (2007)
6. Jung, S., Harris, K., Webster, J., Herlocker, J.L.: SERF: integrating human recommendations with search. In: Proceedings of the Thirteenth ACM conference on Information and knowledge management, pp. 571–580 (2004)
7. Kantor, P.B., Boros, E., Melamed, B., Meñkov, V., Shapira, B., Neu, D.J.: Capturing human intelligence in the net. Communications of the ACM 43(8), 112–115 (2000)
8. Maltz, D., Ehrlich, K.: Pointing the Way: Active Collaborative Filtering. In: Proceedings of the SIGCHI conference on Human factors in computing systems, pp. 202–209 (1995)
9. Olston, C., Chi, E.D.H.: ScentTrails: Integrating Browsing and Searching on the Web. ACM Transactions on Computer-Human Interaction 10(3), 177–197 (2003)
10. Smyth, B., Balfe, E., Boydell, O., Bradley, K., Briggs, P., Coyle, M., Freyne, J.: A Live-User Evaluation of Collaborative Web Search. In: Proceedings of the 19th International Joint Conference on Artificial Intelligence (IJCAI 2005), Edinburgh, Scotland, pp. 1419–1424 (2005)
11. Smyth, B., Balfe, E., Freyne, J., Briggs, P., Coyle, M., Boydell, O.: Exploiting Query Repetition and Regularity in an Adaptive Community-Based Web Search Engine. User Modeling and User-Adapted Interaction: The Journal of Personalization Research 14(5), 383–423 (2004)
12. Wexelblat, A., Maes, P.: Footprints: history-rich tools for information foraging. In: Proceedings of the SIGCHI conference on Human factors in computing systems: The CHI is the limit, pp. 270–277 (1999)

(Web Search)^{shared}: Social Aspects of a Collaborative, Community-Based Search Network

Maurice Coyle and Barry Smyth

Adaptive Information Cluster, School of Computer Science & Informatics,
University College Dublin, Belfield, Dublin 4, Ireland
{maurice.coyle,barry.smyth}@ucd.ie

Abstract. Collaborative Web search (CWS) is a community-based approach to Web search that supports the sharing of past result selections among a group of related searchers so as to personalize result-lists to reflect the preferences of the community as a whole. In this paper, we present the results of a recent live-user trial which demonstrates how CWS elicits high levels of participation and how the search activities of a community of related users form a type of social search network.

1 Introduction

The Web is evolving into a much more social place, with user-driven sites such as Wikipedia and Flickr and social networking sites such as FaceBook and Bebo[1] connecting users and facilitating communication in a community-oriented environment. At the same time, the field of Web search is also changing, with the traditional *one-size-fits-all* paradigm for result selection and ranking being abandoned in favour of a more personalized approach where, for example, *user profiles* store the preferences of each searcher and this profile information is reused in the future to formulate more specific queries [4] or re-rank the results returned by a search engine to reflect the profile contents [11]. Past user behaviour is also increasingly being used to inform Web search processes, with a *mass consensus*-style approach being used to determine which items within a repository are most relevant to a user's query [12]. Clickthrough data and other implicitly-collected user data have been shown to be useful for inferring global user preferences [1,7] and for identifying useful query expansion terms [3].

Collaborative Web search (CWS) is a technique that combines both personalization and implicit feedback reuse with today's *social Web* ethos, operating at the level of a *search community* of users with overlapping search interests to generate focussed, relevant result rankings. CWS harnesses implicitly-collected *search knowledge* in the form of past queries and their associated result selections to enhance future search sessions by promoting and inserting previously-selected results. This ensures not only that users' natural searching behaviour is

---

[1] http://www.facebook.com, http://www.bebo.com

W. Nejdl et al. (Eds.): AH 2008, LNCS 5149, pp. 103–112, 2008.

not interrupted but also that contributions towards the collective store of search knowledge are made by a large proportion of the community, which reduces the *participation inequality* often observed in user-driven online sites [8,13].

In the past we have presented detailed accounts of the collaborative Web search approach [10], including a number of evaluations that have demonstrated the potential benefits of CWS at the level of the individual searcher. More recently we have begun to explore what might be termed the *social benefits* of CWS. For example, in [5] we focused on the hypothesis that much of the benefits of CWS were derived from the sharing of search histories among community members, in the sense that many users seemed to benefit from result promotions that come from the histories of *other* users. In fact we found that searchers more frequently selected promotions that came from the search histories of other community members, rather than their own. In this paper we present some evaluation results related to the search performance of CWS in addition to examining more of the social aspects of CWS. To this end we describe the *social search network* that evolves in a CWS setting as users forge and strengthen connections with other community members as a direct result of their search activities with emphasis on the participation levels across the community. We identify 2 different searching roles that emerge within this network: *search leaders* produce high quality search knowledge in the form of their result selections that are promoted and selected in future sessions, while *search followers* tend to select the promotions that have been derived from the search histories of other users.

The remainder of this paper is organised as follows. In Section 2 we will briefly describe the core CWS technique and mechanisms for result promotion. In Section 3, we present the results of a live-user trial, using the employees of a company as a search community. We will briefly highlight some performance benefits of CWS, along with an examination of participation levels within the community before presenting a visualisation of the CWS social search network that emerges, which illustrates graphically the social dimension of the technology.

2   Collaborative Web Search

Collaborative Web search (CWS) is a technique for personalizing the results returned by an existing Web search engine. Instead of maintaining individual preference profiles as some of the techniques mentioned in the introduction to this paper do, CWS maintains a community profile in which the contributions of individual users are unknown. In essence, CWS uses the implicitly-collected searching histories of a community of like-minded users to tailor the result selection and ranking processes. The computational details of CWS have been presented previously (see [10,5]) and so in this section only a brief description of the core technique is provided.

For our purposes, a community may be defined as any ad hoc or structured group of searchers who share some set of interests; in this work we are not concerned with the precise origins of a community of searchers and only assume that such a community can be identified. Very briefly, given a target query

q_T^C submitted by some member of community C, CWS will identify a set of similar queries $\{q_1, ..., q_n\}$ previously submitted by the community; typically using a standard term-overlap query-similarity metric $Sim(q_T, q_i)$ [10]. Each similar query q_i is associated with a set of previously-selected results and the relevance score $Rel(p_j, q_T, q_1, ..., q_n)$ for each such result p_j can be calculated (see Equation 1) based on how often p_j has been selected for similar queries. Then the top ranking results can be promoted within a result-list that is returned by some underlying search engine; once again the details are purposefully light here and the interested reader is directed to [10] for a more detailed account of these relevance ranking and result promotion techniques.

$$Rel(p_j, q_T, q_1, ..., q_n) = \frac{\sum_{i=1...n}(\frac{H_{ij}}{\sum_{\forall j} H_{ij}}) \bullet Sim(q_T, q_i)}{\sum_{i=1...n} Exists(p_j, q_i) \bullet Sim(q_T, q_i)} \qquad (1)$$

Figure 1 illustrates how the result-list returned by Google for the query *michael jordan* is re-ranked so that results that relate to the shared interests of a search community are promoted. Within a community of computer science researchers, results relating to the well-known Berkeley professor of artificial intelligence and machine learning have attracted selections in the past for similar queries and thus they are promoted ahead of results about the basketball star. Note that the promoted results are identified as such using graphical icons that summarise the result's interaction history (see [6] for more details and an evaluation of this explanation-oriented interface).

Fig. 1. For the query 'michael jordan', CWS promotes previously-selected results related to the Berkeley professor within a community of computer science researchers

3   Evaluation

The objective of this trial was to evaluate the impact of CWS in a more realistic or natural search setting than previous evaluations (see [10]), involving live users over a significant period of time. To this end, the trial was conducted in conjunction with the 66 employees (ranging in age from their early 20s to early 50s) of a Dublin software company, who used the CWS system as their primary search front-end over a 17-week period. In addition to evaluating the baseline effectiveness of CWS we were particularly interested in exploring some of the social dynamics of the search community that evolves as a result of shared search behaviours.

3.1   Methodology

One of the key challenges in evaluating search technologies in a natural setting concerns the determination of relevance. Since we were unable to directly elicit feedback from the participants regarding the relevance of a particular result list, we used 2 indirect measures of search success which allow us to compare alternative search strategies in a systematic way. For our purposes, a *search session* is defined as a single query submission, including any result selections from the list returned by the underlying engine. We define a *successful session* as one in which at least one result was selected (i.e. the searcher found a search result which was at least *apparently* relevant to their search). In addition, we will consider the selection of the top result in a ranked list to be an indicator of success in so far as it tells us that a result which looked relevant enough for the user to select it was chosen by the ranking method as being the most relevant result; see [2] for an analysis of the importance of the top result. Thus, the percentage of sets of sessions which have the first result selected can be used as a means for comparing the success of different ranking functions.

It might be argued that the presence of explanation icons alongside promoted results (see Figure 1) might affect the selection probability of a result and thus skew the success rates of search sessions containing promotions. To control for this we disguise the promoted results in certain sessions by eliminating the explanation icons altogether. Thus we have 3 basic session types; a *standard session* (STD) is a search session for which CWS failed to identify any promotion candidates and so the default Google results were returned to the searcher, without modification; an *identified session* (ID) is one for which CWS made promotions and these promotions were annotated with appropriate explanation icons (see Figure 1); finally a *disguised session* (DISG) is identical to an identified session, except that promoted results were not annotated with explanation icons. Promotions were disguised for 20% of sessions containing promotions and this feature was not communicated to the trial participants.

It should also be noted here that although the core CWS technique requires no user identification to operate, for certain parts (see Sections 3.6 and 3.7) of this evaluation the identities of participants were extracted and logged.

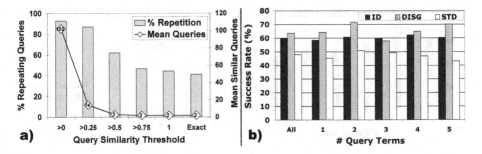

Fig. 2. a) Percentage of query repetition at various similarity thresholds and mean number of similar queries, b) The percentage of sessions with at least 1 result selected for identified (ID), disguised (DISG) and standard (STD) sessions

3.2 Preliminary Observations

Over the 17 weeks a total of 20,448 search sessions were generated, covering a total of 15,977 result selections. The average query contained 2.73 terms, which is in line with the findings of Silverstein et al. [9]. One of the basic assumptions of this trial was that the participants would behave as a search community with broadly similar search interests, on the basis that the vast majority of their searches would be work-related and thus somewhat aligned to a shared set of business interests. In Figure 2, we graph the percentage of (stopword-stripped) queries whose terms overlap to various degrees with at least one other query and we see, for example, that more than 65% of queries share at least half of their terms with other queries (for this trial, a query similarity threshold of 0.5 was applied). We can also see, in Figure 2, how each query sharing half of its terms with at least one other query, actually shares half of its terms with 3 other queries, on average. These results indicate the trial participants search for similar information in similar ways on a regular basis.

3.3 Session Success Rates

To begin with, we compare the success rates of the three different types of session (standard, identified, and disguised) across all queries and also for queries of different lengths. The results are presented in Figure 2b) and clearly indicate a performance advantage for both types of promoted sessions (identified and disguised) compared to the standard (Google) sessions. For example, on average (across all query lengths — "All" in Figure 2b)) we found a 48% success rate for the standard sessions containing the default Google result-lists; this means that searchers failed to find any apparently relevant results in more than half of the standard Google sessions. In comparison, the success rates for promoted sessions are significantly higher (at the 99% confidence level), with success rates of 60% and 64% reported for the disguised and identified sessions, respectively. Improvements of between 25% and 33% are found across different query lengths and once again all differences are statistically significant at the 99% confidence level.

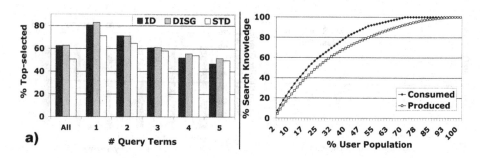

Fig. 3. a) Percentage of successful search sessions with top result selected for each session type, b) The percentage of the total number of selected promotions produced and consumed by different percentages of the user population

It is worth noting that the success rates for disguised sessions are found to be higher than those for identified sessions for all but one of the query lengths considered. The increased success rates due to the disguised sessions may suggest a *Google bias* inherent in participant selection behaviour: the participants appear to be somewhat sceptical of the annotated CWS promotions in identified sessions and, all other things being equal, are more likely to select results from the more Google-esque disguised sessions; see also Section 3.4.

3.4   Ranking Success

Figure 3a) shows, for each session type, the percentage of successful sessions that had the top result selected. We can see that across all query lengths (i.e. the bars labelled *All* in Figure 3a)), successful identified and disguised sessions will have the top result selected 23% more frequently than successful standard sessions.

When we examine the results across different query lengths, we see that the difference between promoted (i.e. identified and disguised) and standard sessions steadily decreases for longer queries; indeed for queries with 4 or more terms, standard sessions will have the top result selected more often than identified sessions[2]. This is an indication that within a CWS setting, performance is optimal for shorter queries and it is increasingly difficult to ensure that the *most* relevant result appears at the top as more terms are added to a query. We argue that this is an acceptable tradeoff in the context of Web search, since it has been shown that most user queries are of the order of 2-3 terms [9] and indeed for the trial described here, we found that over 75% of queries have 1, 2 or 3 terms.

3.5   Discussion

One very important point to note before conclusions may be drawn regarding the performance metrics (i.e. success rates and top result selection) used here concerns the *nature* and ease of different search tasks. The presence of promotions in a search session correlates with a higher likelihood of at least one result

---

[2] This could also be affected by the Google bias mentioned in Section 3.3.

selection. In addition, the top result in a promoted session (which, it should be noted, will always be a promotion by definition) is more likely to be selected that that in a standard session for shorter, more ambiguous queries. However, before firm conclusions can be drawn, further analysis into the characteristics of promoted and standard sessions is required to investigate whether search tasks that lend themselves to promotion (i.e. in which user queries overlap, enabling promotions to be made) are inherently *easier* for a search engine to satisfy for some reason.

In the context of the analysis of the social rather than the purely performance-based aspects of CWS as presented in this paper, the interested reader is directed to [5] for an investigation into the extent to which users select promotions that come from the search histories of other users above their own and the likelihood of promotions (when present) being selected over standard results.

3.6   Participation Levels in a CWS Search Community

One of the limitations of more traditional forms of user-generated content is that a relatively small number of users (i.e. in the order of 1-2% [8]) actively engage in content production. Such *participation inequality* [13] may be undesirable, since the few who contribute are unlikely to be representative of the views and opinions of the entire user base [8].

Before continuing with the discussions in this and the subsequent section, some basic definitions are required. A *search leader* is a user who is the first user to select a result which is not only promoted in a future search session, but also *selected*; that is, search leaders *produce* valuable search knowledge by selecting results that future searchers find useful. A *search follower* is a user who is presented with a result promotion which they then select; that is, they *consume* the search knowledge produced by previous users. Note that a search leader is the user who executes the *first click* on a result which is later promoted; all future selections of that result where it is promoted are examples of search knowledge consumption. Finally, since we are interested in the social nature of CWS, when examining a user's search history, we consider only search knowledge that is produced or consumed by community members other than the searcher themselves (the searcher's *peers*).

Figure 3b) shows the cumulative percentage of *first clicks* on promotions ascribed to different proportions of the test community along with the percentage of promotions consumed by increasing percentages of the community. We can see that 80% of valuable search knowledge is produced by 50% of the community. Also, the maximum contribution of any individual community member is just under 5%, and thus there are no users that dominate the production of search knowledge. Similarly, we see a gradual increase in the percentage of promotions consumed by increasing percentages of users, with 80% of the search knowledge consumed by just under 38% of the community population. An examination of the most active producers and consumers finds that they share only 48% of their members, which is important because it highlights that the store of valuable search knowledge is not useful to only a small proportion of the community.

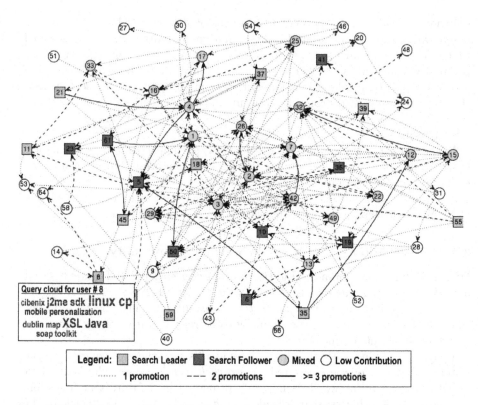

Fig. 4. The social search network that evolved from a CWS deployment within an organisational setting. The colour-coded nodes and weighted edges allow at-a-glance determination of search leaders and search followers within the community. This information can be used to improve knowledge management, expert identification and internal communications.

3.7 Search Relationships

In this final section, we will attempt to graphically depict the relationships between search knowledge producers and consumers in more detail. Figure 4 contains a visualisation of the CWS social search network (generated by the JUNG suite of network analysis tools[3]) which shows the extent to which community members interact and provides at-a-glance recognition of the most active search knowledge producers and consumers.

The vertices correspond to community members and search relationships are shown as directed arcs between the producer and consumer of search knowledge. The strength of each such relationship is encoded by the weight of the arcs, as indicated. Community members are coded by shape and colour according to whether they are *search leaders* or *search followers*, or a mixture of the 2. For example, the link from user 11 (a search leader) to user 33 (a search leader *and a*

---

[3] http://jung.sourceforge.net

search follower) in Figure 4 indicates that user 11 has provided promotions that user 33 has subsequently selected twice (i.e. the arc is a heavy dashed line). This visualisation supports the quantitative analyses of previous sections, by showing that CWS fosters a social searching environment, in which people are actively creating and using search knowledge in a manner that is not prone to *cliques* or solely local sharing.

Figure 4 also demonstrates the ability of CWS to produce *query clouds* for community members which could be used in an application setting to identify search *experts* on various topics, thereby enhancing communication and knowledge sharing opportunities within the community.

4 Conclusions

Collaborative Web search (CWS) harnesses the search behaviour of a community of users in order to adapt the result lists of a conventional Web search engine so that they reflect collective community interests. In this paper we have presented the results of a comprehensive evaluation of CWS within a corporate search setting. We have highlighted how CWS has the potential to deliver significant performance increases, in terms of session success rates and top result selection, when compared with standard Google rankings.

A key contribution of this paper has been to highlight how the production and consumption of valuable search knowledge (i.e. promotions that are reused rather than simply presented) is shared right across the community so that no small subset of users dominates either activity. We believe this highlights the utility of CWS as a means for effective implicit relevance feedback collection without the drawbacks that some other more explicit user-driven online services suffer from.

We have also defined distinct search roles within communities in the form of search leaders (users who create valuable search knowledge) and search followers (users who reuse the search knowledge produced by others). A visualization of the social search network for the particular community used in our evaluation enables the identification of the most active search leaders and followers, while highlighting the social interactions that occur throughout the community.

Combined with the results presented in [5] in which the value of leveraging the search histories of *other* users was highlighted, we feel the work presented in this paper supports the view of CWS as a social medium for sharing valuable search knowledge within a search community.

References

1. Agichtein, E., Brill, E., Dumais, S., Ragno, R.: Learning user interaction models for predicting web search result preferences. In: Proceedings of the 29th Annual International ACM SIGIR Conference on Research and Development in Information Retrieval (SIGIR 2006), pp. 3–10 (2006)
2. Agichtein, E., Zheng, Z.: Identifying "best bet" web search results by mining past user behavior. In: Proceedings of the 12th ACM SIGKDD International Conference on Knowledge Discovery and Data Mining (KDD 2006), pp. 902–908 (2006)

3. Billerbeck, B., Scholer, F., Williams, H.E., Zobel, J.: Query expansion using associated queries. In: Proceedings of the 12th International Conference on Information and Knowledge Management (CIKM 2003), pp. 2–9 (2003)
4. Chirita, P.-A., Firan, C.S., Nejdl, W.: Summarizing local context to personalize global web search. In: Proceedings of the 15th ACM international conference on Information and knowledge management (CIKM 2006), Arlington, Virginia, USA, pp. 287–296 (2006)
5. Coyle, M., Smyth, B.: Information Recovery & Discovery in Collaborative Web Search. In: Amati, G., Carpineto, C., Romano, G. (eds.) ECiR 2007. LNCS, vol. 4425, pp. 356–367. Springer, Heidelberg (2007)
6. Coyle, M., Smyth, B.: On the Community-Based Explanation of Search Results. In: Proceedings of the 10th International Conference on Intelligent User Interfaces (IUI 2007), pp. 282–285 (2007)
7. Joachims, T., Granka, L., Pan, B., Hembrooke, H., Gay, G.: Accurately Interpreting Clickthrough Data as Implicit Feedback. In: Proceedings of the 28th International Conference on Research and Development in Information Retrieval (SIGIR 2005), pp. 154–161 (2005)
8. Nielsen, J.: Participation inequality: Lurkers vs. contributors in internet communities (2006), http://www.useit.com/alertbox/participation_inequality.html
9. Silverstein, C., Henzinger, M., Marais, H., Moricz, M.: Analysis of a Very Large AltaVista Query Log. Technical Report 1998-014, Digital SRC (1998), http://gatekeeper.dec.com/pub/DEC/SRC/technical-notes/abstracts/src-tn-1998-014.html
10. Smyth, B., Balfe, E., Freyne, J., Briggs, P., Coyle, M., Boydell, O.: Exploiting query repetition and regularity in an adaptive community-based web search engine. User Modeling and User-Adapted Interaction: The Journal of Personalization Research 14(5), 383–423 (2004)
11. Teevan, J., Dumais, S.T., Horvitz, E.: Personalizing search via automated analysis of interests and activities. In: Proceedings of the 28th Annual International ACM SIGIR Conference on Research and Development in Information retrieval (SIGIR 2005), pp. 449–456 (2005)
12. Truran, M., Goulding, J., Ashman, H.: Co-active intelligence for image retrieval. In: Proceedings of the 13th ACM International Conference on Multimedia, pp. 547–550 (2005)
13. Whittaker, S., Terveen, L., Hill, W., Cherny, L.: The dynamics of mass interaction. In: Proceedings of the 1998 ACM conference on Computer-supported Cooperative Work (CSCW 1998), pp. 257–264 (1998)

Evaluation of ACTSim: A Composition Tool for Authoring Adaptive Soft Skill Simulations

Conor Gaffney, Declan Dagger, and Vincent Wade

Knowledge and Data Engineering Group
Trinity College Dublin
Dublin, Ireland
{cgaffne,Declan.Dagger,Vincent.Wade}@cs.tcd.ie

Abstract. Adaptivity in technology enhanced learning has proven to be an effective and efficient approach in education. While simulations are include in the top end of eLearning there has been few if any real attempts to develop adaptive educational simulations. The key problem with their incorporation is their expense, cost and the effort involved in developing them. This ground breaking paper is the first publication to show a unique way for non-technical domain experts to compose and generate adaptive eLearning simulations. In particular it presents ACTSim, an innovative and unique composition tool used to author adaptive soft skill simulations.

Keywords: composition, simulation, education, soft skills.

1 Introduction

Simulations are at the high end of sophistication in eLearning and in recent years have become more common place within education [1]. While educational simulations provide a safe and immersive environment for a learner to practice the application of their knowledge [2], the simulations can be rather flat and repetitive. One of the most obvious solutions to this problem is the use of adaptivity within the simulations. Not only does adaptivity insure that the simulations are engaging but more importantly, adaptivity improves the educational effectiveness of the simulations by enhancing their functionality [3]. However, the problem with incorporating adaptive simulations is the huge cost involved in their composition. While traditional adaptive composition tools have focused exclusively on courseware or adaptive content presentation, there has been little to no research in the domain of simulation composition.

This ground breaking paper is the first publication to research and develop a tool which specifically supports composition of adaptive simulation based eLearning. It presents a new and unique approach to adaptivity in educational simulations and also gives a detailed account of ACTSim, an innovative authoring tool used to compose adaptive soft skill simulations. Typically adaptive simulations tend to combine content and adaptivity. This results in adaptivity which is hard coded into the content of the simulation. This makes it very difficult to alter the adaptivity or reuse the content. The approach presented in this paper and which is incorporated in the ACTSim

W. Nejdl et al. (Eds.): AH 2008, LNCS 5149, pp. 113–122, 2008.

composition tool is to separate the content and adaptivity. This allows adaptivity to become extendable and content more available for reuse. This approach also supports a more effective and intuitive methodology of composition. By separating the two concerns composition becomes clearer and more manageable for the author. ACTSim is the first authoring tool to use this approach to composition and this is the only paper in the eight years of Adaptive Hypermedia to address adaptivity within educational simulations.

2   Soft Skill Simulations

There are of many types of educational simulations, from Microsoft's famed Flight Simulator [4] to the lesser known Future Lab [5] which simulates laboratories for second level education. Although a wide variety of educational simulations exist, there are two principle categories [6]. The first and most common category are *'hard skill'* simulations, used to teach procedural or physical skills such as machine or software operation. Vortex Training Simulators [7] is a typical example of this type of educational simulation, used to help train heavy equipment operators. The second of the two categories are *'soft skill'* simulations which are generally used for teaching skills based on interpersonal relationships. In this category of simulation based learning, the focus is on the human communication skills and learning to communicate in different scenarios by applying different communication skills. Examples of soft skill simulations include SkillSim Simulations [8] and ForceTen 4.0 [9]. Educational simulations in this category typically teach skills which include interviewing, marketing, negotiation or sales. This paper focuses on teaching such soft skills. Of particular interest is the manner in which soft skill simulations incorporate adaptivity and the key impediment of their use which is their composition [10].

The models that soft skill simulations operate on are dialogue based. The visualization of this dialogue (and branching of the dialogue) in authoring is very important as it needs to capture and display the features and attributes of communication between two people. These models are known as the dialogue models.

The dialogue model details all the dialogue possibilities that can occur in the simulation. This paper focuses on semi-structured dialogue, for example interview dialogue between interviewer and interviewee. However even semi-structured dialogue models are very complex and considerably large [11]. While there have been many different approaches to modeling human-to-human dialogue, for example Chat Circles [12], there has been very little research of the addition of adaptivity which further complicates development.

The use of adaptive soft skill simulations has its advantages but the major difficulty with their application is the complex and expensive task involved in composing them [13]. This is true of any type of simulation but with the addition of modeling conversation and introducing adaptivity the task becomes especially difficult. With conventional soft skill simulations, multiple (but very similar) models need to be composed. Any soft skill simulations that do include adaptivity tend to be rather naive, for example simply classing learners into broad categories (novice, intermediate, expert) or incorporating a system of different skill levels such as those used in The Human Intelligence Collector [14]. These simulations do not separate adaptivity from content and hard code the adaptivity into the simulation. As can be seen with the research in adaptive courseware [15] there needs to be move away from this approach and towards a more fine grained form of adaptivity. There is also a need for adaptivity that supports topics other than learner experience such as roles, learning outcomes and subject relevancy.

3   Design of the ACTSim Composition Tool

In order to identify the major design concerns of creating a composition tool for authoring adaptive soft skill simulations, existing composition tools were examined through a state of the art survey. There were four requirements identified as being pivotal to the authoring process, dialogue representation, complexity, scalability and adaptivity [16].

Due to the complexities involved in developing a composition tool for authoring adaptive soft skill simulations its design was separated into two phases. The first phase addresses the design requirements of the dialogue representation, complexity and scale. These issues were grouped together as they are closely related to the composition of the dialogue model and describe all the requirements needed to author a conventional soft skill simulation. The second phase of design concerned the application of adaptivity across the dialogue model being created.

The separation of the design of the composition tool not only reduced complexity but by separating the two concerns it was ensured that adaptivity would not be hard coded into the dialogue model. The need to separate the dialogue model composition and to add adaptivity across this model is also reflected in the approach to the evaluation. The two phases of design are described in the following sections.

3.1   Dialogue Model Composition Design

The first challenge of composing a soft skill simulation is the representation of the dialogue which is required to be intuitive for the author and expressive enough to capture the complex knowledge models needed to generate the simulations. To achieve this, a dialogue is decomposed into basic components known as dialogue elements. Each of these dialogue elements represents a statement and response that occurs within the dialogue and are graphically depicted as nodes. The flow of the dialogue is represented by connecting these nodes with directed arrows. The connected nodes form a graph which is constructed in an area in the composition tool known as the dialogue space. Figure 1 presents a screen shot of the ACTSim composition tool which contains a typical dialogue model. Within the simulation each connection represents a choice that a learner can select within the simulation which then guides them to another node and another set of routes.

The requirements of dialogue representation address the low level issues of constructing the dialogue model. However a higher level methodology is needed to handle the complexities of composition. In order to achieve this, a process was developed which directs the author to initially create the most optimal path through the simulation known as the main stem. This stem consists of a single string of connected

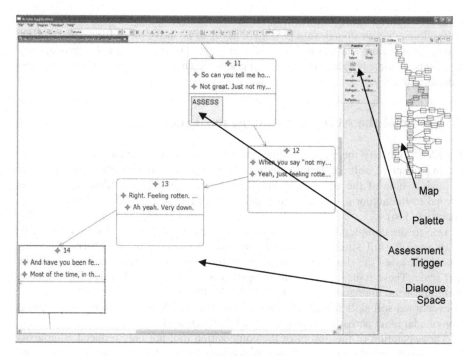

Fig. 1. ACTSim Composition Tool

dialogue elements. Once the main stem is completed the author adds dialogue elements in groups which are connected to the optimal path. Each of these groups of dialogue elements would typically cover a relevant subject or learning outcome the author would want included in the simulation. These groups of added dialogue elements are referred to as branches.

With complex simulations many branches are required. The result is that the dialogue model can become very large, with some models reaching in excess of 150 dialogue elements. In order to address this issue of scalability, navigational aids are incorporated into the design of the composition tool. To offer the author different perspectives of the dialogue space, functionality such as zoom and a map of the dialogue space, as observed in the top right corner of Figure 1, were included. Another feature incorporated into the composition tool to aid in navigation is an *"arrange"* feature, which, when selected reorders the dialogue model into a clearer formation. Finally, a note feature is also included in the design which allows the authors to add comments to the dialogue model.

Once the dialogue model composition design is completed the incorporation of adaptivity can be considered this is outlined in the next section.

3.2   Adaptivity Design

While separate to the design of the dialogue model, the incorporation of adaptivity in the composition tool is considered from the beginning of the design process. With the necessary functionality in place to compose the dialogue models, the types of adaptivity and methods of applying them across the dialogue model can be more informatively considered.

There were two principal goals in incorporating adaptivity with soft skill simulations. The first is to reduce the burden of composition by decreasing the number of similar dialogue models produced. This is accomplished by allowing the author to compose a single model per subject domain and applying adaptivity across it to produce several simulations. In the past the author would need to compose several dialogue models that were very alike. The second goal is to allow the author to produce soft skill simulations that would adapt to the individual needs of each learner. The areas identified as being most effective at addressing individual needs are learner role, learning outcomes, subject or topic relevancy, prerequisites (requirements) and adaptive triggers. The remainder of this section indicates how providing adaptivity based on each of these aspects can enhance the learner experience.

Adaptivity Based on Role: Within a soft skill simulation it is necessary for the learner to play a role as they interact with the simulation and often there are multiple similar roles. With conventional soft skill simulations the author is required to compose a model for each of the separate roles that exist within a domain. To alleviate this effort the concept of incorporating multiple roles into a single dialogue model has been included in the design of the composition tool. Thus dialogues can be authored and the multiple roles assigned to dialogue elements. The adaptive simulation generated by the composition tool can reason about the role assignments and render appropriate dialogues depending on the particular role chosen by the learner.

Adaptivity Based on Learning Outcomes: Adaptivity can be incorporated into the simulation by allowing the author to create learning outcomes and associate them with dialogue elements. The adaptive simulations generated by the composition tool when using adaptivity and learning outcomes can render the most appropriate dialogues depending on the learning outcomes of that particular learner. A dialogue simulation composed with adaptivity in this way would be able to cope with much greater student diversity.

Adaptivity Based on Subject or Topic Relevancy: In a similar way the relevant subjects or topics that a dialogue models cover can also be incorporated to produce adapted models, with simulations tailored to a learner with respect to the subjects they are being taught. The dialogue elements created are assigned to relevant subjects that the author also creates. The adaptive simulations that are generated by the composition tool can reason about the assignments and only dialogues that are relevant to learner are included in the simulation.

Adaptivity Based on Prerequisites: To further complement individually tailored simulations, sections of the dialogue model can be assigned as a prerequisite to other sections of the dialogue model. This means that within the simulation, certain sections would not be accessible by the learner until they had completed a previous section. The author would designate the association in the composition tool and the learner's user model could then track the sections of the simulation that the learner has completed. This insures that the learner does not enter into dialogues for which they have not attained prerequisite skills from previous dialogues. This and other adaptivity can be included in the simulation at the discretion of the author.

Adaptivity Based on Triggers (Assessment, Feedback & Reflection): The use of adaptive triggers completes the learning experience with three kinds of trigger incorporated into the composition tool. These are triggered events that they learner can interact with during the simulation and are included at the discretion of the author. The triggers are based on the learning principles assessment, feedback and reflection. Assessments test the learner's knowledge, feedback delivers to the learner information regarding their progress and reflection allows the learner to annotate and add to the knowledge they have been presented. The triggers are graphically represented as separate nodes and can be placed on the dialogue elements to indicate their location. This approach allows the trigger to be easily moved from one dialogue element to another. The triggers are adaptive as they are event driven meaning they will only activate based on previous events. For example, the assessment triggers are associated by the author with learning outcomes, if a learner arrives at this trigger in the simulation and has not completed the associated learning outcomes the trigger will not be activated during the simulation. The incorporation of adaptive triggers into the simulation results in the entire learning experience being adaptive.

3.3 Representing Adaptivity within a Dialogue

In order for the author to apply adaptivity and display its location in the dialogue model, graphical representation is required in the composition tool. This was applied using two approaches. The first of these is a tagging methodology which allows the author to label a dialogue element with a certain type of adaptivity while also indicating the adaptivity value. This approach is incorporated in the areas of role, learning outcomes, relevant subjects and prerequisites. In order for the author to apply adaptivity of these kinds, they initially select the dialogue elements that are to be tagged. The author then chooses the appropriate function in the composition tool which allows them to tag the dialogue elements with a relevant value. To allow the author to examine which dialogue elements have been tagged the composition tool also includes a highlight operation for each type of adaptivity. Currently tagged dialogue elements are indicated with a change of color to the dialogue elements however to insure accessibility multiple techniques will be employed.

The second approach to representing adaptivity in the dialogue model is with the introduction of nodes to represent the adaptive triggers. Nodes were identified as being the most optimal approach of graphically displaying adaptive triggers as it is necessary to allow the author to move the triggers between dialogue elements. Triggers also appear less frequently than other types of adaptivity within the simulation and have their own properties associated with them so the use of nodes is most suitable. To accommodate the triggers being placed on dialogue elements compartments were added to the dialogue element node. An example of an assessment trigger can be viewed in the top most dialogue element in Figure 1. The trigger is represented using a square in the lower section of the dialogue element with ASSESS printed across the top. The trigger can be easily dragged and dropped into other dialogue element compartments which can also be seen in the diagram.

With the adaptivity design being so ambitious it is clear there was a need to separate it from the design of the dialogue model composition. The remainder of this paper details the evaluation of the first phase of design and outlines the approach to be employed with the evaluation of the adaptivity design.

4 Evaluation

The purpose of this initial evaluation is to examine the first phase of the composition tools design. As the second phase of design is so reliant on the success of the first it was necessary to initially evaluate the requirements for composing the dialogue models. If the composition tool cannot be successfully used to compose soft skill simulations without adaptivity, the addition of adaptivity would certainly result in failure. This approach also allowed the design decisions regarding adaptivity to be made in a more informed manner. This section describes the first phase of evaluation including the objectives of the evaluation, the methodology incorporated, results and a description of next iteration of evaluation.

4.1 Objectives of the Evaluation

The objective of this evaluation was to determine the ability of the ACTSim composition tool to address the key issues for authoring adaptive (dialogic) simulations, namely dialogue representation, complexity and scalability. It should be noted that these key issues are not independent from one another. There is an overlap between each of them and so the performance of one affects the other two. In this section, each of the issues are described and examined with regard to their effectiveness, efficiency and usability [17].

In order to evaluate dialogue representation a task based evaluation approach was employed. Evaluation experiments were conducted to assess the ease of creating and adding a dialogue element, deleting dialogue elements, moving dialogue elements within the dialogue space as well as evaluating the dialogue element representation and visualization.

The second key issue with authoring adaptive (dialogic) simulations is complexity. In order to address complexity the composition tool has associated with it a methodology for authoring, i.e. the main stem and branching technique previously described. While dialogue representation is concerned with the ease of use of the tool, complexity focuses on author's ability to use this authoring methodology.

The final issue to be addressed by this evaluation is scalability. In order to address this issue the composition tool includes navigational aids which assist the author in managing the large graphs that they create. To evaluate scalability it was necessary to examine these features, which included the zoom, list, map and note functionality. The arrange operation was another feature that was evaluated which also addressed the issue of scalability.

4.2 Evaluation

Once the objectives of the evaluation were outlined a suitable method of evaluation was determined. As this is a user based application, with the author central to its development, a trial based user study was determined to be the most appropriate approach. The evaluation process included the selection of authors from a particular domain and a specific series of stepwise tasks that the authors would complete in order to examine the composition tools different functionality. The authors were then to complete a questionnaire in order to evaluate each of the objectives previously outlined.

While the ACTSim composition tool was designed to be flexible enough to allow authors to compose a wide variety of soft skill simulations, a single domain was chosen to carry out the evaluation. The first pilot of the tool was developed to support medical students in the department of psychiatry as part of the ADAPT [18] project. Five authors were selected for the evaluation; each author was a practicing psychiatric doctor, involved in the training of medical students with respect to their communication skills. This example is an authentic evaluation which incorporates the target audience of the composition tool. Each author was given the task of developing an initial interview that would take place between a doctor and a patient. The objective of this dialogue was to create a simulation which would be used to simulate an initial introductory interview with a patient.

The task required the author to create a dialogue model which included eight topics and consisted of at least forty dialogue elements. The task also required the author to use the main stem branching methodology for authoring and that the authors should utilize the different features if the composition tool. Once the authors had created the dialogue models they completed a questionnaire designed to gather data regarding the three key objectives of the evaluation as previously outlined.

4.3 Results

With the task completed and questionnaires collected the data was examined. The data was grouped so as to address the respective issues, the results of which are detailed in this section.

Dialogue Representation: The feedback regarding the dialogue representation was very positive with all authors successfully composing a dialogue model and utilizing the composition tools associated functionality. The functions associated with dialogue representation included adding and connecting dialogue elements along with accessing and editing their properties. In terms of efficiency and usability the dialogue representation was very well received with one author commenting *"It represents flow of dialogue from one exchange to the next"*. All operations and functionality regarding efficiency and usability of dialogue representation returned an average between three and four in a Likert scale of zero to four where four is the most favorable result. There was in fact only a single negative response with respect to the issue of dialogue representation with one author finding it difficult to move dialogue elements within the dialogue space.

Complexity: The feedback concerning the complexity of composing the dialogue models was also very favorable. Unlike the dialogue representation some of the authors did not utilize all of the functionality associated with the authoring methodology. For example, three of the five authors did not successfully delete multiple dialogue elements (a single branch) with one commenting *"I'm sure deleting multiple* *elements would have been no problem – just didn't do it"*. Although not utilized by all the participants in the evaluation, the authors that were successful in using this functionality found it efficient and user friendly. The reason for this (and similar) functionality not being utilized by authors may have been that the authors were only creating relatively small dialogue models and so were not often required to delete an entire branch of their dialogue. The results that were returned for this functionality, similarly unused functionality and all other functionality associated with complexity were very positive. All functionality scored an average between three and four on the on a Likert scale identical to the scale previously described.

Navigational Aids for Scalability: Of the three issues being address in this evaluation the assessment of the navigational aids used to address the scale of the dialogue model returned the most inconclusive results. This was due to the small number of authors that used the navigational aids incorporated in the composition tool. Of the five navigational aids being evaluated, only the map functionality was utilized by all of the authors. The remainder of the navigational aids were only utilized by two or three of the authors. This may also have been due to the small nature of the dialogue model being composed by the authors. It could be that the navigational aids are probably needed for large dialogue models (>100 dialogue elements). The results accumulated for the navigational aids that were utilized were very positive. Each of the navigational aids scored an average between three and four in the Likert scale in terms of their efficiency but further evaluations need to be completed.

4.4 Approach to Adaptivity Evaluation

User based applications require many iterations of evaluation. The purpose of the initial evaluation was to examine the issues of dialogue representation, complexity and scalability. The primary purpose of the next evaluation is to address the key issue of adaptivity applied to the dialogue model. To accomplish this, the authors will be supplied with identical dialogue models and be required to apply the different types of adaptivity across these models. The contrast between the tasks of the initial evaluation and the task that users will be required to complete in the following evaluation again highlights the necessity of separating the two evaluations. By supplying a suitably large model this evaluation will also allow scalability to be more satisfactorily addressed as the navigational aids will become more effective then with the previously user authored dialogue models.

Another issue to be addressed in the next iteration of evaluation is the flexibility of the composition tool. While the composition tool has been successfully tested in the domain of healthcare it was designed to be flexible enough to be used to author soft skills from other domains. Future evaluations will take place in the areas of business, human resources and telephone customer service.

5 Conclusion

The composition of adaptive soft skill simulations is a very complex undertaking and so, to develop an authoring tool that allows non-technical domain experts to compose these simulations is very difficult. The development of ACTSim, an authoring tool which addresses this problem, needed to be divided into two phases such was the complexities involved. The purpose of this paper was to describe the two phases of development and detail the evaluation of the first.

The results of this evaluation were very positive with users describing the ACTSim composition tool as being *"intuitive"* and *"easy to use"*. With the composition tool now considered competent at allowing the authoring of dialogue models, the second phase of the design development can be evaluated. The paper also describes a methodology to be employed to achieve this next iteration of the evaluation process.

References

1. Katz, J.A.: Institutionalizing Elegance: When Simulation Becomes a Requirement. Simulation & Gaming 30(3), 332–336 (1999)
2. Issenberg, S.B., Gordon, M.S., Gordon, D.L., Safford, R.E., Hart, I.R.: Simulation and new learning technologies. Medical Teacher 23(1), 16–23 (2001)
3. Brusilovsky, P.: Methods and techniques of adaptive hypermedia. In: Brusilovsky, P., Vassileva, J. (eds.) Spec. Iss. on Adaptive Hypertext and Hypermedia, User Modeling and User-Adapted Interaction, vol. 6(2-3), pp. 87–129 (1995)
4. Microsoft Flight Simulator,
   http://www.microsoft.com/games/flightsimulatorx/
5. Future Lab: Circuits for Physical Science, http://www.futurelab.org.uk/
6. Brandon Hall: Online Simulations 2006, Section III (2006)
7. Vortex Training Simulators, http://www.vortexsim.com/
8. SkillSoft, http://www.skillsoft.com/
9. Eedo Knowledgeware, http://www.eedo.com/
10. Page, E.H., Opper, J.M., McLean, V.A.: Observations on the complexity of composable simulation. In: Simulation Conference Proceedings, Winter, vol. 1, pp. 553–560 (1999)
11. Allen, J., Miller, B.W., Ringger, E.K.: A Robust System for Natural Spoken Dialog. In: Thirty-Fourth Annual Meeting of the Association for Computational Linguistics (1996)
12. Viégas, F.B., Donath, J.S.: Chat Circles. In: SIGCHI conference on Human factors in computing systems, pp. 9-16 (1999)
13. Waziruddin, S., Brogan, D.C., Reynolds Jr., P.F.: The Process for Coercing Simulations. In: Proceedings of the Fall Simulation Interoperability Workshop (2003)
14. Hainley, V.: Challenges of Developing Web-Based Soft Skills Training. In: The Interservice/Industry Training, Simulation & Education Conference (2005)
15. Conlan, O.: The Multi-Model, Metadata driven approach to Personalised eLearning Services. Doctoral Thesis, Submitted to the University of Dublin, Trinity College (2005)
16. Gaffney, C., Dagger, D., Wade, V.: A Survey of Soft Skill Simulation Authoring Tools. In: Proceedings of Hypertext Conference (2008)
17. Frøkjær, E., Hertzum, M., Hornbæk, K.: Measuring usability: are effectiveness, efficiency, and satisfaction really correlated? In: Proceedings of CHI 2000, pp. 345–352. ACM Press, New York (2000)
18. ADAPT: Adaptive Plug-in for Run-time Composition of Personalised eLearning and Adaptive Simulations, http://www.empowertheuser.com

Modelling Semantic Relationships and Centrality to Facilitate Community Knowledge Sharing

Styliani Kleanthous and Vania Dimitrova

School of Computing, University of Leeds
{stellak,vania}@comp.leeds.ac.uk

Abstract. Some of today's most widely spread applications are social systems where people can form communities and share knowledge. However, knowledge sharing is not always effective and communities often do not sustain. Can user modelling approaches help to identify what support could be offered and how this would benefit the community? The paper presents algorithms for extracting a model of a closely-knit virtual community following processes identified as important for effective communities. The algorithms are applied to get an insight of a real virtual community and to identify what support may be needed to help the community function better as an entity.

Keywords: Knowledge Sharing, Community Model, Community Adaptation.

1 Introduction

Social systems, which enable people to form communities and share knowledge, are becoming increasingly popular nowadays. Studies have shown that having technology and people present does not guarantee the sustainability of a virtual community (VC) [4]. Appropriate support is needed to facilitate the functioning of a community where the members actively engage and share knowledge effectively [6]. Along this line, personalisation and adaptation can play a crucial role, as illustrated by recent user-modelling approaches [2, 13]. However, existing adaptation techniques focus mainly on supporting individual members, rather than supporting the community to function *as an entity*. We propose a new method for community-tailored support which is aimed at facilitating processes related to the effectiveness and sustainability of VCs [9] and is based on a community model derived from analysis of log data.

In a broad sense, virtual communities vary from fairly large, loosely structured communities to relatively small, closely-knit ones. In this paper we consider closely-knit VCs for knowledge sharing, which are characterised by common interests, participants' commitment to the sharing of information and generation of new knowledge, and equal membership inside the community. Closely-knit VCs usually exist in relatively well-defined organisational or educational settings, and can share common characteristics with teams. Following research in organisational psychology [7], we have identified several processes important for effective team functioning which can be applied to VCs and can be examined or facilitated by analysing community log data. These processes include: good *transactive memory system* (members are aware

W. Nejdl et al. (Eds.): AH 2008, LNCS 5149, pp. 123–132, 2008.
© Springer-Verlag Berlin Heidelberg 2008

how their knowledge relates to the knowledge of the others), *shared mental models* (members develop a shared understanding of the key processes and the relationships that occur between them), and *cognitive centrality* (members who hold strong relevant expertise can be influential; it has been shown that members of effective communities gradually move from being peripheral to becoming more central and engaged in the community [11]).

Based on the above processes, we have defined algorithms to extract a *community model* that includes: (a) individual user models of all members, (b) a model of the semantic relationships in the community, (c) a list of the cognitively central members, (d) a list of the popular and peripheral topics in the community, and (e) the community context defined by the key topics of interest within the community [10]. This paper will present the application of the community modelling algorithms to get an understanding of what is happening in a real community, and to identify what support can be provided to improve the functioning of this community. We will focus on semantic relationships and cognitive centrality, which are the kernel of the community model in our approach, see [10] for a description of all components. Section 2 describes the algorithms developed to extract the community model. Section 3 presents the study performed using a VC and Section 4 discusses application of the community model and points out possibilities for community tailored support. Finally, we compare with related work and outline future work plans.

2 Semantic Relationships and Cognitive Centrality

This section will outline the main algorithms to capture the semantic relationships and centrality within a community. As input we consider the *metadata of the resources* shared in the community, such as: (a) keywords associated with each resource (*rKeywords*), which can be provided by the publisher or by the members in terms of tags, (b) the person who shared or accessed a specific resource, and (c) the time when a resource is uploaded or read. We also consider the *community context* C_T which is the list of key topics for this community. We consider four types of semantic relationships between users: *ReadRes* relationship indicates links based on reading resources uploaded by others, *ReadSim* and *UploadSim* relationships are based on similarity of read or uploaded resources, respectively, and *InterestSim* indicates similarity in members' interests. We combine these relationships to calculate the cognitive centrality of each member.

The algorithms below utilise a mechanism for measuring similarity between two lists of terms. If L_1 and L_2 are two lists of terms, we define a similarity procedure $Sim(L_1, L_2)$ which returns a number that indicates how close semantically the terms in both lists are. For this, we adapt the algorithm presented in [12] which calculates the semantic similarity between two words based on the WordNet's taxonomic structure. The algorithm accepts nouns as input and returns a decimal number (0, no similarity – 1, the same meaning) as an output, which represents the semantic similarity between two words. We have made a slight modification to the original algorithm in [12] to allow measuring the similarity between two phrases (e.g. "knowledge management" and "knowledge capture").

2.1 ReadRes Relationship

ReadRes(a,b) relationship indicates that resources uploaded by member *b* are read by member *a*, and its strength corresponds to the relevance of the resources to the community context. *ReadRes* can be used to identify complementary knowledge among people, and this helps to improve the community's *transactive memory*[15].

Consider a resource r_i uploaded by *b* and read by *a*. We will denote its keywords with *rKeywords$_i$*. Considering the community context C_T, we define the value of r_i for the community as $V_{r_i} = Sim(rKeywords_i, C_T)$, where the similarity is calculated based on the WordNet algorithm described above.

Let us denote $N_r^{a \leftarrow b}$ to be the number of resources uploaded by *b* and read by *a*. The value of *ReadRes(a,b)* is the sum of all values of the resources uploaded by *b* and read by *a*, based on their relevance to the community context, i.e.:

$$ReadRes(a,b) = \sum_{i=1}^{N_r^{a \leftarrow b}} V_{r_i}$$

2.2 ReadSim and UploadSim Relationships

ReadSim(a,b) indicates that members *a* and *b* have read semantically similar resources, while *UploadSim(a,b)* indicates that *a* and *b* have uploaded similar resources. These relationships can be important for discovering similarities that members may not know of. Making people aware of who else is holding knowledge similar to theirs can improve the community's *transactive memory system* [15]. This can also improve the understanding of what is happening in the community which can be related to the development of *shared mental models[7]*. *UploadSim* can also be used to identify people who are not uploading and to encourage them to contribute by pointing at their *ReadRes* or *ReadSim* relationships with others.

To calculate *ReadSim(a,b)* we derive an extended list of keywords for each member by combining the keywords of every resource read by this member. Let us denote these extended keyword lists as *aKeywords* and *bKeywords*. These lists are compared to find the similarity between them by using again the WordNet similarity algorithm. Hence, the *ReadSim(a,b)* is calculated as follows:

$$ReadSim(a,b) = Sim(aKeywords, bKeywords)$$

UploadSim(a,b) is calculated similarly using the resources uploaded by *a* and *b*.

2.3 InterestSim Relationship

InterestSim(a,b) relationship represents the similarity of interests between members *a* and *b*. This relationship can identify interest complementarities. Furthermore, making members aware how their interests relate to the others can motivate participation. Finding people with similar interests and making them aware of this similarity can indicate possibilities for *collaboration*. Awareness of other people's interests can improve the shared understanding the members have about the community and help the development of *shared mental models* [7].

To derive interests of a member, we considered the resources he/she has uploaded and downloaded. Using the keywords *rKeywords* for each resource uploaded or downloaded by a user, his/her interests are represented as a list of terms with weights. For example, all terms that member a has shown any interest in are aggregated in the list T_a, where every term $t \in T_a$ has weight $w(t, T_a)$ that indicates the frequency of t in T_a. If $w(t, T_a) \geq \sigma$ (σ is a threshold), t is added to the interests of a denoted with I_a.

I_a is presented as the member a's personal list of interests. The same algorithm is used to derive the personal list of interests for member b. The lists I_a and I_b are compared to calculate the interest similarity between a and b:

$$InterestSim(a,b) = Sim(I_a, I_b)$$

2.4 Cognitive Centrality (CCen)

Cognitive centrality measure is used to locate knowledge inside the community that is important to the community members. This can be helpful to identify the central members and how they contribute to the community. It can also be useful in identifying unique knowledge held by peripheral members. This is important for the community's sustainability and flexibility - interests might shift in time [11], knowing where unique knowledge is located can facilitate the transition from one subject area to another [15]. Being aware of the central and peripheral members of the community can also help the improvement of *shared mental models* and *transactive memory*.

To calculate each member's centrality within the community, we adapt the degree centrality algorithm used in social networks [5]. *CCen(a)* of member a is calculated as the number of all members b to whom a is connected considering the four relationship types defined above:

$$CCen(a) = \sum_{b=1}^{n} ReadRes(a,b) + ReadSim(a,b) + UploadSim(a,b) + InterestSim(a,b)$$

The above algorithms were applied to extract a community model based on tracking data from an existing closely-knit virtual community. The next section describes a study that shows how the community model derived can be used to determine what support may be offered to improve the functioning of the community.

3 Study with a Virtual Community

To validate the community modelling algorithms we have employed them to extract a model of a real community which both authors belonged to. The VC in our study included 34 members (researchers and doctoral students) from two research groups working on similar research areas, sharing documents and research papers with the BSCW system that provides general support for collaboration over the web [14]. The groups were based in two European countries, some members knew each other but many had never met. The community was established in 2003. We collected log data from October 2005 until December 2006 using BSCW features allowing every member to see what is happening in the community.

The activity monitored included uploading and downloading resources, 244 resources in total. Four members were only uploading while thirteen were only downloading. Eight members were isolates and never uploaded or downloaded resources. There was a gradual decline in the uploading and downloading of resources in the observed period. During the beginning of the monitored period (October – December 2005) members were uploading and downloading papers. After that the activities minimised for all members, and during the last few months of the monitored period (September – December 2006) there was no uploading and very little downloading. The community was gradually declining and has almost stopped its activity at the moment. The study was conducted to examine whether the application of the community modelling algorithms to analyse the log data could identify problems that could have been spotted earlier and addressed properly to help this community sustain.

4 Application of the Community Model

The community log data was stored in a text file, fully anonymised, and then converted to database tables. The tables were used as input for the community modelling algorithms described in Section 2, and in [10], and implemented in Java. All keywords converted into nouns in order to be used as an input to the WordNet similarity algorithm [12]. We will show here representative examples of phenomena discovered about the community, and will discuss how this can be used for adaptive support. In the illustrations below, excerpts from the community model are rendered with NetDraw[1].

4.1 Application of the Relationships Model

The relationship model indicated strong semantic links between members which were often not explored in the community.

According to the community model, the members who never uploaded resources in the community had in fact *ReadRes* similarity (see figure 1). There are links with two groups – the group including members 31, 29, 15, 3, 13, 22, 23, 29, and 17 and with the group of members 33, 20, and 12.

The situation in figure 1 indicates that the community's transactive memory system is not well-developed, which points at the need for appropriate support. For example, automatic messages can be generated to point out to member 29 (who is actively engaged in the community) that he/she has a relation with member 19 (who is not uploading). Providing such awareness can improve the transactive memory, develop members' understanding of what the others are doing and facilitate collaboration.

Another interesting case concerns members 7, 24 and 26 who have ReadSim relation with almost the same people but have no connection among themselves (figure 2).

---

[1] Network visualization software: http://www.analytictech.com/Netdraw/netdraw.htm

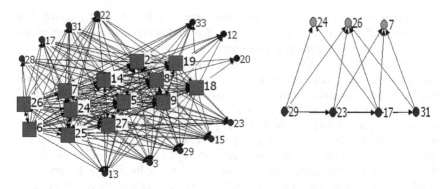

Fig. 1. The members not uploading to the community, in rectangles, had *ReadRes* similarity with the same people. These links were unexplored in the community.

Fig. 2. *ReadSim* between members 24, 26 and 7, who are reading resources uploaded by the same people but are not aware of this similarity

Interestingly, these people are coming from the same research group and, as indicated in the community model, they have not explored (and are perhaps unaware of) their connections via the community. Making these members aware of their similarities with others may motivate them to better participate in the community, see [6]. It can also facilitate knowledge sharing between these people, who appear to be interested in the same topics [4], and may promote collaboration.

Most nodes of the graphs representing *ReadSim*, *UploadSim*, and *InterestSim* relationships appeared strongly connected. This confirmed our expectations for the community model (when people are working in similar areas their interests and the resources shared tend to be semantically similar). However, it also pointed out that further tuning of the similarity algorithms could be beneficial. For this, we are currently integrating an enhanced model of the community context represented with an external ontology and a taxonomy of resource folders.

4.2 Application of Cognitive Centrality

The centrality of each member (figure 3) was calculated based on the formula presented in Section 2.4. Members 31, 29 and 17 are indicated as the three most central members of this community. This closely corresponds to the real world - members 17 and 31 are the facilitators of the two research groups involved in this community, while member 29 is a researcher who actively contributed to the VC.

Centrality can be influenced by different circumstances. For example, members 6 (newcomer) and 25 (oldtimer) gained some centrality due to actively downloading from the community. Such members might be aware of the cognitive processes in the community and can provide valuable information to the others. Member 13 on the other hand, is an old-timer actively engaged by both reading and uploading resources to the community. This member is indeed involved in most projects and can be quite influential to the community.

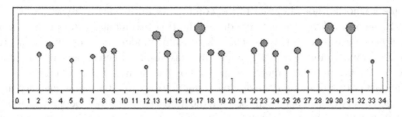

Fig. 3. Community members' cognitive centrality. Numbers represent community members and bubble size and height represent members' cognitive centrality.

It is interesting to compare the centrality of two members 5 (newcomer) and 26 (old-timer) – who have not uploaded resources. Member 26 appears to be more central to the community than member 5 although 26 has read fewer resources (twenty-one in total) than 5 (who read fifty resources in total). This indicates that 26 has read resources that are closer to the community's interests and illustrates the effect of the community's context on deriving relationship values (Section 2).

The centrality measure can be a way to motivate people to contribute and remain active, e.g. in [2] centrality is visualised to encourage participation. We consider *push mechanisms* where tailored messages can be sent to members based on their centrality. For example, members 5, 6 and 25 can be encouraged to contribute to the community since they already have similarities with the rest of the community. Indicating the most central members can be beneficial for the community. They can be asked to point others at valuable resources, e.g. when member 28 (peripheral) is searching for a topic which member 31 (central) seems to have information about, we can display a message to direct 28 to 31 for further help. Also, a newcomer like 6 can be integrated faster if they are mentored by a cognitively central member with similar interests.

4.3 Interesting Individual Cases

Information about individual users' engagement can be combined with the relationships model to identify cases where individuals can be given support in order to improve the functioning of the community as a whole.

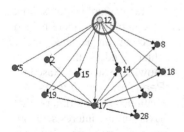

Fig. 4. *ReadRes* relationships of member 12. The graph shows the members who have read the resource uploaded by 12.

For instance, member 12, who was actively involved in projects with community members, has not downloaded anything, and has uploaded only one resource read by many members (figure 4). 12, was identified as a fairly central member, as what he/she shared was important to the community. This member can be informed that people are interested in his/her resources and that there are other members uploading similar resources. This can motivate member 12 to engage and can improve the knowledge sharing.

A typical problem for the effective functioning of communities is the *integration of newcomers* (newly joining members). There were several newcomers who did not integrate in the community during the analysed period. For example, member 14 was very active during the first two months after his/her joining but then became fully disengaged. The relationships model indicates that 14 has read resources similar to those read by others and has similar interests to other members (figure 5). The community model helped recognise similar behaviour followed by other members (e.g. 25 and 19) - downloading actively for some time and becoming disengaged afterwards. This might be an indication that these members are struggling to find their way in the community's knowledge space and are uncertain about their role in the community. Such members can be helped to become aware of their cognitive relationships with others, so they may be motivated to remain actively involved.

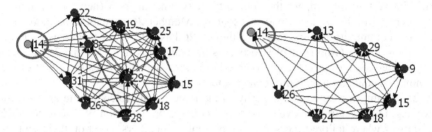

Fig. 5. *ReadSim* (left) and *InterestSim* (right) ego networks for member 14. The above networks show that the resources member 14 was reading were similar to the resources several members on the community were reading too. Also the derived interests of member 14 are similar to the interests of other community members. These links were unexplored, and member 14 became disengaged from the community.

Another interesting newcomer case is member 33 who was inactive at the beginning but then started contributing to the community. He/she uploaded a total of eleven resources but only one resource was read by one other member (figure 6). Member 33 was a collaborator for a year at one of the research groups whose leader was member 31. The relationship model indicated that many members uploaded similar resources to 33. Unfortunately, these links were never exploited and the VC as a whole did not benefit from the knowledge "shared" by 33.

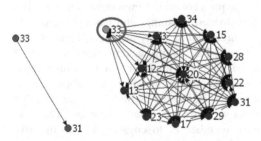

The example shows how the community model helped detecting an isolated niche which hinders the effective knowledge sharing. Based on *ReadSim* or *InterestSim* relationships, oldtimers that have similar interests or are reading similar resources and are actively engaged in the community can be approached.

Fig. 6. *ReadRes* for member 33 (left) and ego networks for *UploadSim*(33) (right). Despite the similarity with other member, 33 did not integrate in the community.

For instance, a message can be sent to member 31 to help the newcomer 33 to integrate in the VC. Member 33 could also be reminded that others have similar interest and are uploading relevant resources. At the same time, oldtimers can be encouraged to look into interesting resources uploaded by newcomers. In general, such support aims at improving the community's transactive memory and can motivate members to remain engaged.

The study enabled us to identify patterns of community behaviour detected with the community model, and provide the basis for dynamic community-tailored support.

5 Related Work

There is a growing interest in providing adaptive support for teams, groups and communities. A well-researched area is that of expertise finding. Different tools and algorithms have been developed to support people in locating expertise on a specific subject inside small or large VCs [13]. Our approach does not aim at identifying expertise alone, but also derives a person's influence in the VC based on the relationships he/she has developed with others, which benefits the VC as a whole.

Visualisation techniques are another approach for providing awareness of what is happening in a community, and thus, supporting participation and collaboration in a VC. For example, graphical representations are used to make people aware of the relevance to the activity or to the position of a particular member in the group [8] or to show the status (or popularity) of a resource [14]. The key limitation of visualisation techniques is their passive influence on the functioning of the community, e.g. while examining graphical representations members may not be able to see how their contribution could be beneficial for the community. In contrast, our approach proposes the use of an extended community model to *automatically detect* problematic cases which can be used to decide when and how to intervene.

Recently research on modelling communities employed graph theory to model relationships between members [8] or members' interactions in general [3]. The key contribution of our approach to community modelling is the considering of semantic relationships, i.e. an edge connecting two members represents their semantic similarity to each other, and the relevance of this link to the community's context.

The relationship model in [1] is the closest to ours but there is a crucial difference. Users' interests are modelled in [1] based on how frequently and how recently users have searched for a specific area from the ACM taxonomy, and user relationships are derived based on any successful download or service that took place between two users. In contrast, our approach employs the metadata of the resources shared in the community and derives a semantically relevant list of interests for every user.

6 Conclusion and Future Work

We have proposed a new approach for modelling relationships and centrality in a virtual community, aimed at supporting processes that facilitate the effective knowledge sharing and sustainability of VCs. The community modelling algorithms have been employed to derive a model of a real VC, which has indicated when and how community-tailored support can be offered.

The goal of this research is to develop computational means to provide community-tailored support for knowledge sharing. We are currently tuning the community modelling algorithms by integrating an existing ontology to represent the community context. A possible step is also a study to gather the community members' feedback on the results discussed above. Possibilities for future work include also the use of data from a different virtual community, e.g. Comtella [2], to further evaluate the extracted community model in real settings. Our future work will also include developing algorithms that automatically detect changes in the behaviour of a closely-knit VC, which will help us examine the possible effect of adaptive support offered.

References

1. Bretzke, H., Vassileva, J.: Motivating Cooperation on Peer to Peer Networks. In: 9th Int. Conf. on User Modelling, USA (2003)
2. Cheng, R., Vassileva, J.: Design and evaluation of an adaptive incentive mechanism for sustained educational online communities. UMUAI V16(3), 348 (2006)
3. Falkowski, T., Spiliopoulou, M.: Users in Volatile Communities: Studying Active Participation and Community Evolution. In: User Modeling, pp. 47–56 (2007)
4. Fischer, G., Ostwald, J.: Knowledge Management: Problems, Promises, Realities, and Challenges. IEEE Intelligent Systems 16(1), 60–72 (2001)
5. Freeman, L.: Centrality in social networks conceptual clarification. Social Networks 1(3), 239 (1979)
6. Harper, M., et al.: Talk amongst yourselves: inviting users to participate in online conversations. In: IUI 2007. ACM Press, New York (2007)
7. Ilgen, D.R., et al.: Teams in Organizations: From Input - Process - Output Models to IMOI Models. Annual Review of Psychology, 517–543 (2005)
8. Kay, J., et al.: The Big Five and Visualisations of Team Work Activity. In: Intelligent Tutoring Systems, pp. 197–206 (2006)
9. Kleanthous, S.: Semantic-Enhanced Personalised Support for Knowledge Sharing in Virtual Communities. In: Conati, C., McCoy, K., Paliouras, G. (eds.) UM 2007. LNCS (LNAI), vol. 4511, pp. 465–469. Springer, Heidelberg (2007)
10. Kleanthous, S., Dimitrova, V.: Semantic-Enhanced Approach for Modelling Cognitive Relationships in Virtual Communities. In: SociUM workshop at UM 2007 (2007)
11. Lave, J., Wenger, E.: Situated Learning: Legitimate Peripheral Participation. Cambridge University Press, New York (1991)
12. Seco, N., Veale, T., Hayes, J.: An Intrinsic Information Content Metric for Semantic Similarity in WordNet. In: ECAI 2004, pp. 1089–1090 (2004)
13. Song, X., et al.: ExpertiseNet: Relational and Evolutionary Expert Modeling. LNCS, p. 108. Springer, Heidelberg (2005)
14. Wang, Y., Graether, W., Prinz, W.: Suitable notification intensity: the dynamic awareness system. In: Proc. of the int. ACM conf. on Supporting Group Work (2007)
15. Wegner, D.M.: Transactive Memory: A Contemporary Analysis of the Group Mind. In: Mullen, B., Goethals, G.R. (eds.) Theories of Group Behavior, pp. 185–208. Springer, Heidelberg (1986)

LS-PLAN: An Effective Combination of Dynamic Courseware Generation and Learning Styles in Web-Based Education

Carla Limongelli, Filippo Sciarrone, and Giulia Vaste

"Roma Tre" University
Department of Computer Science and Automation
AI-Lab
Via della Vasca Navale, 79 00146 Rome, Italy
{limongel,sciarro,vaste}@dia.uniroma3.it

Abstract. This paper presents LS-PLAN, a system capable of providing Educational Hypermedia with adaptation and personalization. The architecture of LS-PLAN is based on three main components: the Adaptation Engine, the Planner and the Teacher Assistant. Dynamic course generation is driven by an adaptation algorithm, based on Learning Styles, as defined by Felder-Silverman's model. The Planner, based on Linear Temporal Logic, produces a first Learning Objects Sequence, starting from the student's Cognitive State and Learning Styles, as assessed through pre-navigation tests. During the student's navigation, and on the basis of learning assessments, the adaptation algorithm can propose a new Learning Objects Sequence. In particular, the algorithm can suggest different learning materials either trying to fill possible cognitive gaps or by re-planning a newly adapted Learning Objects Sequence. A first experimental evaluation, performed on a prototype version of the system, has shown encouraging results.

1 Introduction

Personalization and adaptation in learning environments are two very important requirements for providing an effective educational service on the Internet. In this context, Dynamic Courseware Generation [6] and Instructional Planning [15] are two of the most important research areas.

In this work we address the problem of helping the student during his learning activity by means of a synergy based on his cognitive state, his learning styles and the teacher's didactic strategy. The main contribution of our work is given by an adaptation algorithm, capable to modify the student's model and to guide the student step by step, especially in recovery activity. At the same time the system lets the student free to navigate in the learning hyperspace in accordance with the constructivist pedagogical theory [16]. Here we propose LS-PLAN, a Web-based system, capable of providing Educational Hypermedia with adaptation and personalization. The system is based on the synergy between classical planning techniques and Learning Styles refinement procedures.

W. Nejdl et al. (Eds.): AH 2008, LNCS 5149, pp. 133–142, 2008.

The architecture of LS-Plan includes three main modules: the Adaptation Engine, the Planner and the Teacher Assistant. The Adaptation Engine manages the adaptivity mechanism and the user model, from its initialization to its update. The Planner produces a Learning Objects Sequence (LOS), on the basis of the current Student Model and of the learning strategies previously set by the teacher. The Teacher Assistant allows the teacher to modify the teaching strategies related to the learning material. The pedagogical background of the Student Model is based on the student's Cognitive State (CS) and Learning Styles (LS). The student's CS is defined as a set of Knowledge Items, i.e., atomic elements of knowledge concerning the learning domain, according to the Knowledge Space Theory [9]. Learning Styles are the student's learning preferences as defined by Felder-Silverman's (FS) Learning Styles Model [10]. Moreover, the system models the student's knowledge by an Overlay Model [5], based on three of the five levels of Bloom's Taxonomy [2]. Our system is based on the idea that LS are tendencies and may change through educational experiences [11]. In fact, the system takes into account the information gathered from the student's self-assessments and navigation, in order to evaluate the effectiveness of the current teaching strategy, modifying it, if necessary.

In the literature, different systems have been proposed on the basis of the FS Model and for generating LOS. In the system proposed in [1], an adaptive interface has been presented, while the CS383 system [8] and the Intelligent Web Teacher system [7] propose an adaptive presentation based on learning material typologies. Our system generates LOS by means of planning techniques, similarly to the Dynamic Course Generation (DCG) system [6] following the style of the systems AHA! [3] and ELM-ART [17]: while AHA! does not exploit assessment for adaptivity, ELM-ART and DCG do not make use of LS. Our adaptation mechanism provides both features and it is very fine grained: a specific learning material has associated its own LS, thus providing the teacher with the possibility to implement suitable didactic strategies for different learners.

The rest of the paper is organized as follows. Section 2 illustrates the architecture of LS-Plan together with its main components. Section 3 shows a first experimentation of the system to a real instructional environment. In Section 4 our conclusions are drawn.

2   The Adaptive System

The overall system, that is LS-Plan together with the Adaptive Educational Hypermedia (AEH), is shown in Figure 1, where the main components are highlighted with grey blocks. The teacher, through a suitable framework, the *Teacher Assistant*, arranges a pool of learning objects, i.e., learning nodes, building the Domain Knowledge, stored in a special repository inside the AEH system. The teacher also prepares the initial *Cognitive State Questionnaire* for evaluating the starting knowledge of the student, that is the knowledge already possessed by the student with respect to the topic to be learned. Moreover, the teacher provides each student with his own instructional goal, and specifies the

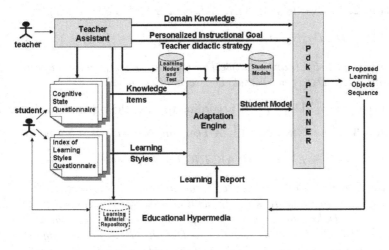

Fig. 1. The Functional Schema of the Adaptive System. Grey blocks form LS-PLAN.

didactic strategies. The *Index of Learning Styles (ILS) Questionnaire*, developed by Felder and Soloman [1], is also submitted to the student with the aim of mapping his learning preferences to the four dimensions of the FS Model: active-reflective, sensing-intuitive, visual-verbal, sequential-global [10]. The information gathered through the two questionnaires, is processed by the *Adaptation Engine* module, that builds the initial Student Model and updates the *Student Models Database* that collects all of them. The *Pdk Planner*, described in Section 2.3, takes in input the Domain Knowledge, the current Student Model, the Personalized Instructional Goal, and the teacher didactic strategies, giving in output to the AEH a new *LOS* tailored to that particular student. According to the constructivist theory, the student is not forced to follow the *LOS* generated by the planner. The *Adaptation Engine* builds a Learning Report on the basis of the student's navigation in the AEH. Consequently, it builds a new Student Model starting from the current one. If significant variations are detected, the adaptation algorithm provides an alternative *LOS*, as it will be discussed in Section 2.1.

Before entering in details of the Student Model, its updating procedures and the planner, we introduce some definitions about the elements we are going to work with.

Definition 1. (KNOWLEDGE ITEM). *A Knowledge Item KI is an atomic element of knowledge about a given topic. KI is a set:*

$$KI = \{KI_K, KI_A, KI_E\}$$

where KI_ℓ, with $\ell \in \{K, A, E\}$, represents a cognitive level taken from Bloom's Taxonomy: Knowledge, Application and Evaluation.

---

[1] Available at http://www.engr.ncsu.edu/learningstyles/ilsweb.html

Definition 2. (LEARNING STYLE). *A Learning Style LS is a 4-tuple:*

$$LS = \langle D_1, D_2, D_3, D_4 \rangle, \quad with \ D_i \in [-11, \ldots, +11], \quad i = 1, \ldots, 4$$

where each D_i is a FS Learning Style Dimension, i.e., D_1: active-reflective, D_2: sensing-intuitive, D_3: visual-verbal, D_4: sequential-global.

We used the range $[-11, \ldots, +11]$ according to the Felder-Soloman *ILS* scale.

Definition 3. (LEARNING NODE). *A Learning Node LN is a 5-tuple:*

$$LN = \langle LM, AK, RK, LS, T \rangle \quad where$$

LM is the Learning Material, i.e., any instructional digital resource.

AK Acquired Knowledge. It is a KI_ℓ, with an associated success threshold σ_{KI_ℓ} defined in Definition 4, that represents the knowledge that the student acquires at a given level as specified in Definition 1, after having passed the assessment test related to the KI_ℓ of the node. If such a test is not present in the node the AK is considered acquired anyway.

RK Required Knowledge. It is the set of KI_ℓ necessary for studying the material of the node, i.e., the cognitive prerequisites required by the AK associated to the node.

LS is given in Definition 2.

T   is a pair of reals $T = (t_{min}, t_{max})$ which represents the estimated time interval for studying the material of the node, as prefixed by the teacher. A fruition time, t_f, less than t_{min} is not a realistic time to learn that material; for a fruition time, t_f, greater than t_{max} we have the so-called "coffee break" effect, i.e., the student is supposed to have done something else.

Definition 4. (THRESHOLD σ_{KI_ℓ}). *A threshold value σ_{KI_ℓ} is a real number associated to KI_ℓ, defined as:*

$$\sigma_{KI_\ell} = \frac{S_T}{S_{max}}, \qquad 0 < \sigma_{KI_\ell} \le 1$$

being S_T the lowest score of an assessment test, as fixed by the teacher, in order to consider the KI_ℓ acquired; S_{max} is the highest possible score for that test [2].

Definition 5. (POOL). *A pool is the particular set of LN, selected or created by the teacher in order to arrange a course about a particular topic.*

Definition 6. (DOMAIN KNOWLEDGE). *The Domain Knowledge DK is the set of all the KI present in a pool.*

Definition 7. (COGNITIVE STATE). *The Cognitive State CS is the set of all the KI_ℓ possessed by the student with respect to the given topic: $CS \subseteq DK$.*

---

[2] Here and in the following we suppose that the teacher gives to S_T and S_{max} positive values.

Definition 8. (STUDENT MODEL). *The Student Model SM is a pair:*

$$SM = (CS, LS)$$

where, CS is given in Definition 7 and LS is given in Definition 2.

Definition 9. (TEST). *A Test is a set of k items, i.e., questions, with $k \in \mathcal{N}$. To each item is associated a weight $Q_j \in \mathcal{R}$. Each item has m answers, with $m \in \mathcal{N} - \{0,1\}$ and to each answer is associated a weight $w_i \in \mathcal{R}$.*

Let S_{KI_ℓ} be the score associated to a test; it assesses the student knowledge of the single KI_ℓ:

$$S_{KI_\ell} = \sum_{j=1}^{k} (Q_j \cdot \sum_{i=1}^{m} w_i)$$

where $w_i = 0$ for the answers the student does not select.

Definition 10. (ACQUISITION OF A KI_ℓ). *A KI_ℓ is supposed to be acquired by the student if:*

$$S_{KI_\ell} = \sum_{j=1}^{k} (Q_j \cdot \sum_{i=1}^{m} w_i) \geq \sigma_{KI_\ell}$$

where σ_{KI_ℓ} is given in Definition 4 and k, m, Q_j, w_i and S_{KI_ℓ} are given in Definition 9.

2.1   The Adaptation Engine

In this section we show the mechanisms of the SM management, i.e., the initialization and the updating processes, and adaptation strategies.

Student Model Initialization. At the first access to the system the student fills in the *Cognitive State Questionnaire* composed by some tests (see Definition 9), related to the KI of the Domain. The acquisition of a KI_ℓ is described in Definition 10. All the acquired KI_ℓ initialize the CS, which can also be an empty set if the student does not know anything about the domain. The student also fills in the *ILS Questionnaire* whose result is used to initialize his own LS.

Student Model Updating and Adaptation Methodology. In order to update the SM and guide the student during the learning process, we propose the algorithm presented in Figure 2, where the function UPDATEANDLEARN returns the SM after studying the node LN, and proposes the next node to be learned. When the student studies a LN, the function is activated taking in input the LN and the current SM. The function TIMESPENTONTHENODE computes and returns the time t_f, that is the time spent by the student on the node. The function COMPUTESCOREPOSTTEST computes and returns the score taken by the student in the post-test related to the KI_ℓ of the node, that is the AK related to LN. If the post-test does not exist we assume a score equal to 0. The student's LS is updated by means of the function UPDATELS, according to the

---

UPDATEANDLEARN (LearningNode LN, StudentModel SM)

$t_f \leftarrow$ TIMESPENTONTHENODE(LN)
$S_{KI_\ell} \leftarrow$ COMPUTESCOREPOSTTEST(KI_ℓ)
$SM \quad \leftarrow (CS,$ UPDATELS(LS, LN, t_f, S_{KI_ℓ}))
if ((not post-test) or (KI acquired)) then
$\quad\quad SM \leftarrow (CS \cup AK, LS)$
$\quad\quad$ if ($\exists D_i$ that changed sign) then REPLAN(SM); return (LN^{first}, SM)
$\quad\quad$ else return (LN^{next}, SM)
else if (time-out(t_f)) then $\quad$ return (LN, SM)
$\quad\quad$ else $LN' \leftarrow$ CHECKCLOSESTNODE(LN, SM)
$\quad\quad\quad$ if ($LN' \neq NIL$) then $\quad$ return (LN', SM)
$\quad\quad\quad$ else $L \leftarrow$ ORDEREDPREDECESSORSLIST(LN)
$\quad\quad\quad\quad$ if ($L \neq NIL$) then
$\quad\quad\quad\quad\quad \forall LN_i \in L$, if ($AK \in CS$) then $CS \leftarrow CS - AK$
$\quad\quad\quad\quad\quad$ ADD_L_TOPLAN(L); return (LN^{first}, SM)
$\quad\quad\quad\quad$ else REPLAN(SM); return (LN^{first}, SM)

Fig. 2. UPDATEANDLEARN: *LearningNode × StudentModel → (LearningNode × StudentModel)*

LS associated to the chosen node, to the time t_f, to the score obtained with the post-test assessment and to the knowledge level of the node. If the node does not provide any post-test assessment, i.e., the boolean variable "post-test" is "false", or if the student passes the test, the SM acquires the KI_ℓ related to that node. If a D_i (as given in Definition 2) changes sign, we consider that a significant variation in the student LS is present, and it is necessary to replan the LOS: the algorithm suggests the first LN of the new LOS computed by the planner. If the student does not pass the test, the time t_f is examined: the boolean function "time-out" checks whether t_f is out of range and if it is the first time that the LN has been studied. In positive case, the system proposes once again the same node to the student. After the second unsuccessful trial, the system applies the function CHECKCLOSESTNODE, that looks for the "closest" node similar to the current student's LS, with the same RK and AK of that LN. If such a node does not exist, the algorithm by means of the function ORDEREDPREDECESSORSLIST, computes the list L of the LN predecessors, i.e., the nodes connected to LN by an incoming link, in order to verify the acquisition of prerequisites, RK, related to LN. The AK of the prerequisite nodes, if present, are removed from the CS, because we are in presence of a sort of "loss" of knowledge. Then the algorithm puts L on the top of the LOS and suggests the first LN, of such a new LOS. If both the attempts to explain the concepts with different learning material and the prerequisite checks fail, the algorithm replans a new LOS and proposes the first node of such a sequence. The functions UPDATELS, CHECKCLOSESTNODE and ORDEREDPREDECESSORSLIST are explained in the following.

UPDATELS. Each D_i related to a student LS is updated on the basis of the value of the previous D_i, and on the basis of the difference between the D_i of the node and the D_i of the student (ΔD_i). The updating shown in equation (1) is a function that takes into account some of the possible feedbacks that the student gives to the system when he deals with the contents of a given node: the fruition time, the score obtained with the test and the difficulty level.

$$D_{i_{new}} = D_{i_{old}} + (\alpha(t_f) + \beta(S_{KI_\ell}, \ell)) \mid \Delta D_i \mid \tag{1}$$

The second addendum of the sum in the equation (1) ranges between -1 and 1, and $\alpha(t_f)$ is a function of the fruition time. If KI is acquired, the student LS is reinforced towards the node LS; the less is the t_f, the more is the reinforcement. Function β is a function of the score S_{KI_ℓ}, obtained by the student in the post-test, and of the knowledge level ℓ associated to the KI. Let us note that the updating of the LS is computed apart from the acquisition of a KI.

CHECKCLOSESTNODE. The closest node is computed by selecting an alternative node, LN_{alt} with the same RK and the same AK of the current LN, that is the node with the smallest distance to the student's LS, computed on the basis of the following Euclidean distance metric:

$$d(LS_{LN_{alt}}, LS_{student}) = \sqrt{\sum_{i=1}^{4}(D_i^{LN_{alt}} - D_i^{student})^2} \tag{2}$$

ORDEREDPREDECESSORSLIST. The list is composed by all the nodes that are predecessors of LN, ordered according to the following priorities: (i) the predecessor nodes that have not been visited by the student. In fact it is possible that the student got the AK related to that node, by giving a correct answer to the initial test, but he lacks that concept indeed; (ii) the nodes that do not provide tests are proposed on the basis of the difficulty levels: K, A, E; (iii) the nodes that provide test whose LS are closest to the student's LS, by following the equation (2).

2.2   The Teacher Assistant

The *Teacher Assistant* is responsible for the management of the functionalities provided for the teacher, i.e., for the management of the pool. The teacher also selects the items and the threshold for the *Cognitive State Questionnaire* and manages the students' registration to the course. In particular he decides the student's instructional goal and specifies his didactic strategies, such as the desired level of the course, or the particular way he prefers to explain a given concept.

2.3   The Pdk Planner

In automated planning, *planning languages* are used to specify problems in a uniform and simple way. In the context of course configuration, planning problems are described by "actions" (LN), specifying action preconditions (RK) and action effects (AK), as well as the initial state (initial SM) and the goal. Besides all these basic elements a teacher would be allowed to express his didactic strategies, e.g., preferences related to a concept explanation. Unfortunately standard planning language, such as PDDL [13], and classical planners are not suitable to describe such kind of learning problems. To this aim we use the planning language PDDL-K and the Pdk planner (Planning with Domain Knowledge) [14][3]. It conforms to the "planning as satisfiability" paradigm: the logic used to encode planning problems is propositional Linear Time Logic (LTL). The related planning language PDDL-K [14], conforming to standard PDDL, guides the teacher, through the Teacher Assistant, in the specification of heuristic knowledge, providing a set of control schemata, that is a simple way of expressing control knowledge. The language is given an executable semantics by means of its translation into LTL. In the following section, in the framework of empirical evaluation, we show how the planner can configure different courses.

3   A First Evaluation

In this Section we show a first evaluation of our pilot system. According to [4] and [12] we propose a layered evaluation of our system. We assume that our student modeling approach is a suitable one, and we check if the LOSs computed by the planner are considered by experts didactically suitable for the SMs taken into account. This experiment has been performed starting from a pool of 20 LN related to the *recursion* topic and arranged in a such a way that the teacher could decide to explain *recursion* either with the induction principle or activation records (run time stack management).

Experimental Setup. We consider the two following case studies.

First Student Model: $SM_1 = (CS_1, LS_1) = (\emptyset, \langle 3, 3, 7, 7 \rangle)$, that is, the student is supposed to know nothing about the DK, while his LS_1 are: reflective, intuitive, verbal, global.

First Pedagogical Strategy: The teacher desires to configure the course at the Evaluation Level and decides to explain recursion through activation records.

Second Student Model: $SM_2 = (CS_2, LS_2) = (\{recursive\_programs, rec\_fun\_K\}, \langle -3, -5, -7, -9 \rangle)$, that is, the student is supposed to know something about recursive programs and the functional approach to recursion at the Knowledge level, while his LS_2 are: active, sensing, visual, sequential.

Second Pedagogical Strategy: The teacher desires to configure the course at the Application level and decides to explain recursion in a functional manner.

The instructional goal is in both cases learning *Recursion*.

Experimental Results. The planner produced the following two LOS, for the first and second SM with their related pedagogical strategies, respectively.

---

[3] Available at http://pdk.dia.uniroma3.it/

LOS 1	LOS 2
1) Unit_Description	1) Rec_Fun_StringReverse
2) Recursive_Programs	2) Rec_Exercises
3) Rec_RunTimeStack_Intro	3) Rec_List_VI
4) Rec_RunTimeStack_Factorial	4) Rec_List_Examples
5) Rec_RunTimeStack_Use_Examples	5) Rec_List_Exercises
6) Rec_List_VE	6) Complements_GroupWorking
7) Rec_List_Examples	
8) Rec_Exercises	
9) Rec_List_Exercises	
10) Complements_Reflection_Proposals	

Discussion. The first planned learning path included nodes related to activation records at all the difficulty levels, i.e., K, A and E, to obtain the Evaluation level is necessary to know the previous ones: K and A. The learning path is also suitable for the student because it reflects his LS and starting knowledge: all the contents are proposed because the student has an empty starting knowledge; list recursion is explained in a *verbal* way; suggested complements are proposals for thinking about the learning material. Moreover the proposed LOS presents all the theoretical components before proposing exercises. The LOS includes a node that provides an overall picture of the topics of the unit. These are suitable features for *global* learners. The second LOS is also suitable for the student: it does not include the *Recursive_Programs* and the *Rec_Fun_Intro* nodes because the student knows these concepts; it proposes *visual* didactic material. It suggests complements for group working, this is motivating for an *active* learner. Moreover, theoretical material is immediately followed by exercises, because the learner prefers studying in a *sequential* manner. Finally the LOS reflects the teacher didactic strategies, i.e.: *functional* nodes. These two learning sequences were assessed by a sample of 14 teachers who were required to assess the instructional validity of the two proposed didactic plans according to their related SMs. To this aim, we submitted to our experimental group the following sentence both for LOS_1 and LOS_2: *This Learning Objects Sequence is a valid Learning Objects Sequence on the basis of the starting student model SM*, with a 5-points Likert scale (strongly disagree, disagree, neither agree nor disagree, agree, strongly agree). The experimental results have shown that: 7.1% disagree, 7.1% neither agree nor disagree, 71.4% agree and 14.4% strongly agree with the LOS_1; 78.6% agree and 21.4% strongly agree with LOS_2.

4   Conclusion and Future Work

In this work we proposed a Web-based system for personalizing and adapting sequences of learning objects. The main contribution of this work consists of combining course generation with an adaptation algorithm, based on Learning Styles. During the learning activity, the student navigates through learning nodes and its model is constantly updated. If the student fails a post-test assessment, the adaptation algorithm proposes alternative learning strategies. Let us note that the use of control knowledge in planning domain description languages, such as the PDDL-K, enriches the expressivity of relations among concepts to be taught and helps the teacher both in configuring optimized courses and managing the pool of learning nodes. We plan to extend the PDDL-K with new syntactic elements that help the teacher in building the pool of learning nodes.

References

1. Bajraktarevic, N., Hall, W., Fullick, P.: Incorporating learning styles in hypermedia environment: Empirical evaluation. In: Proceedings of the Fourteenth Conference on Hypertext and Hypermedia, pp. 41–52 (2003)
2. Bloom, B.S.: Taxonomy of Educational Objectives. David McKay Comp. Inc. (1964)
3. De Bra, P., Smits, D., Stash, N.: Creating and delivering adaptive courses with AHA. In: EC-TEL, pp. 21–33 (2006)
4. Brusilovsky, P., Karagiannidis, C., Sampson, D.: Layered evaluation of adaptive learning systems. International Journal of Continuing Engineering Education and Lifelong Learning 14(4/5), 402–421 (2004)
5. Brusilovsky, P., Millan, E.: User models for adaptive hypermedia and adaptive educational systems. In: Brusilovsky, P., Kobsa, A., Nejdl, W. (eds.) Adaptive Web 2007. LNCS, vol. 4321. Springer, Heidelberg (2007)
6. Brusilowsky, P., Vassileva, J.: Course sequencing techniques for large-scale web-based education. International Journal of Continuing Engineering Education and Life-long Learning 13, 75–94 (2003)
7. Capuano, N., Gaeta, M., Micarelli, A., Sangineto, E.: Automatic student personalization in preferred learning categories. In: 3rd International Conference on Universal Access in Human-Computer Interaction (2005)
8. Carver, C.A., Howard, R.A., Lane, W.D.: Enhancing student learning through hypermedia courseware and incorporation of student learning styles. IEEE Transactions on Education 42(1), 33–38 (1999)
9. Falmagne, J.C., Koppen, M., Villano, M., Doignon, J.P., Johannesen, L.: Introduction to knowledge spaces: How to build, test, and search them. Psychological Review 97(2), 201–224 (1990)
10. Felder, R.M., Silverman, L.K.: Learning and teaching styles in engineering education. Engineering Education 78(7), 674 (1988)
11. Felder, R.M., Spurlin, J.: Application, reliability and validity of the index of learning styles. Int. Journal of Engineering Education 21(1), 103–112 (2005)
12. Gena, C.: Methods and techniques for the evaluation of user-adaptive systems. Knowl. Eng. Rev. 20(1), 1–37 (2005)
13. Ghallab, M., Howe, A., Knoblock, C., McDermott, D., Ram, A., Veloso, M., Weld, D., Wilkins, D.: Pddl—the planning domain definition language (1998)
14. Cialdea Mayer, M., Limongelli, C., Orlandini, A., Poggioni, V.: Linear temporal logic as an executable semantics for planning languages. J. of Logic, Lang. and Inf. 1(16), 63–89 (2007)
15. Mohan, P., Greer, J., McCalla, G.: Instructional planning with learning objects. In: Baumgartner, K.M., Cairns (eds.) n IJCAI 2003 Workshop Knowledge Representation and Automated Reasoning for E-Learning Systems (2003)
16. Piaget, J.: Language and thought of the child. Harcourt, New York (1926)
17. Weber, G., Brusilovsky, P.: Elm-art: An adaptive versatile system for web-based instruction. International Journal of AI in Education 12(4), 351–384 (2001)

Pervasive Personalisation of Location Information: Personalised Context Ontology

William T. Niu and Judy Kay

School of Information Technologies
The University of Sydney, Australia
{niu,judy}@it.usyd.edu.au

Abstract. There is considerable value in personalising information about people's location. Personalised Context Ontology (PECO) is an ontology for a building, and with PECO, we can provide personalised descriptions of the relevant people. For pragmatic reasons, it is important that PECO is created semi-automatically, making flexible use of a range of sources. For reasons of user control, it is important that PECO can be used to explain the personalisation. This paper describes PECO and how it is created for reasoning about a building. We also describe its use in an application called Locator, which presents information about the people in a building. PECO enables Locator to provide personalised information in two ways: it shows people of relevance and it makes use of personalised location labels. At the same time, PECO enables the user to scrutinise the reasoning about the personalisation. We report a study with eight users in which we compare a personalised and a non-adaptive versions of Locator. This indicates that people preferred the personalised version even though they could complete the designed tasks with both systems.

Keywords: personal ontology, ontological reasoning, personalised location label, scrutability.

1 Introduction

Location modelling is a core concern of pervasive computing because it has a key role in personalised service delivery. In addition, one of the valuable uses of this technology is to enable people to determine the location of other people. This operates at diverse levels. At one extreme, Alice may want to know where Bob is because she needs to discuss an urgent matter. Another extreme is the notion of presence and awareness: for example, Carol may find comfort in glancing at an ambient display that shows when her son David is at home.

There is considerable value in personalising information about people's location. Firstly, people describe locations differently depending on their audience because different people use different names for places. For example, Alice may not even know the address of the local fruit shop, so she would not understand it if a system reported that Bob was at that address. But she would understand

W. Nejdl et al. (Eds.): AH 2008, LNCS 5149, pp. 143–152, 2008.

it if the system stated that he was at Bondi Fresh Fruit. Secondly, to avoid information overload, it is important to have ways to select which people's location should be reported. This paper tackles both of these problems exploiting ontological reasoning.

For modelling people and entities in a pervasive environment, a key problem in most ontologies is their *static* nature: a predicate holds in all contexts (e.g. Sydney is a city). This often constrains the flexibility in personalised reasoning. Therefore, we propose to take advantage of populating an ontology from different domain-specific document sources by accumulating evidence for each concept-relation pair found. We call this a personalised context ontology (PECO) because it adapts semantics to different people and contexts. PECO is also carefully designed to support the user's scrutiny of personalisation: its operations can be explained in terms of the accreted evidence for each relationship of the ontology.

Figure 1 illustrates our approach in terms of the ways that PECO models a concept. The underlined text under or above each concept indicates the evidence sources from which the concept-relation pair was derived. So, for example, the predicate of "Room 125 is a common room" was derived from both the technical building data and a building manual. So this applies generally, to most people. By contrast, the predicate of "Room 125 is a social hub" was extracted from a postgraduate student handbook and, therefore, might only apply to postgraduate students. The predicate of "Room 125 is a recharging corner" was given by Bob and, thus, it is only valid for Bob.

In this paper, we explore PECO's power in two critical areas in user modelling: facilitate personalised reasoning, and help generate explanations understandable to end-users. So, for example, when Bob's location is queried, a system may reason with PECO to produce "Bob is at the social hub". Should the user find the reasoning incorrect or incomprehensible—or they are just curious—the system can then provide an explanation, such as "From the 2008 postgraduate student handbook, Room 125 is a social hub".

In the next section, we present related work on context ontologies and personal ontologies. Section 3 describes PECO's structure and operation in depth,

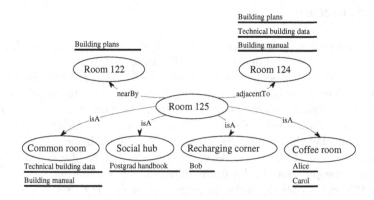

Fig. 1. A snippet of a personalised context ontology

followed by an evaluation that consists of an implemented prototype using PECO for the reasoning and a user study.

2   Related Work

Context ontologies have been shown to have the potential to provide person-alised information in a pervasive computing environment: for example, Strang, Linnhoff-Popien and Frank [1] showed how a specific ontology language could improve interoperability for service interaction architecture; the ontologies in GAIA [2] aimed to tackle the problem of interoperability between different sets of context ontologies in order to deliver personalised services; the Semantic Space [3] demonstrated that context querying and reasoning with an ontology would be useful—even with noticeable delay caused by computational complexity; Chen, Finin and Joshi [4] proposed to use a set of context ontologies to address knowledge sharing and context reasoning in a pervasive computing environment; Wishart, Henricksen and Indulska [5] proposes an *obfuscation* approach with an ontology to address the issue of partial location privacy. They focus on interoperability [1,2,4], ontological reasoning in performance [3], representation languages [1,4] and privacy [5]. By contrast, we focus on ontological reasoning in personalised location information delivery and explanation generation, using a personalised ontology.

The notion of a *personal ontology* is appealing and has been explored previously, for example [6,7,8,9,10,11,12]. However, in that work, the personal ontologies were generally managed in a user-centred, distributed manner: each person would have an ontological profile of contextual information, similar to a hierarchical user model. By contrast, PECO has a more modular architecture: we have ontologies for users, location and devices, and each concept-relation pair in the ontologies has at least one source that may give evidence to relevant individuals and/or groups. For example, the predicate of "Room 125 is a recharging corner" only applies to Bob according to Figure 1. In terms of application, previous work mainly focused on personal ontology comparison [6], general personal information modelling [7,11], Web navigation [8,9] and personal ontology elicitation [10,12]. In this paper, we show that PECO is capable of delivering personalised location information as well as generating adaptive explanation in the scope of a building.

3   Personalised Context Ontology

PECO is built on an ONCOR location ontology [13] and a collection of models of devices and people. The core of the location ontology is the Middle Building Ontology (MIBO), which can be extended to a large range of building ontologies. Even though handcrafted, MIBO is carefully separated from its extension, which can be created semi-automatically. MIBO is also designed to potentially be plugged into a more general ontology, such as the Cyc [14] and SOUPA [15].

3.1   Ontology Population

The building ontology is further populated with relations and concepts extracted from multiple sources. Each source can constitute different degrees of reliability and relevance in different contexts. In the following, we describe our approach to the sources used to populate the ontology and how each affects personalised reasoning.

Location sensors. There is a range of location sensors in the building and these constantly collect evidence of device and user movements, as described in [16]. Those evidence sources populate the ontology as evidence of X *isLocatedAt* Y predicate, where X is a person or a device and Y is a location.

Building plans. Building plans are a natural source for extracting spatial relations about the building.

We use computational geometry to extract relations like: *Room 126 is adjacent to Room 125*. We can establish informal definitions of these concepts and these indicate how a map might be used to such relationships in a building. *Adjacent to* is defined as: when two locations are physically connected to each other, by having touching walls, touching corners, or a corner of one location touching a wall of the other. *Nearby* can be defined as—from the point of view of a two-dimension building map—when two objects are within some distance away from each other, between corners, walls, or a corner and a wall.

There are very valuable applications for such spatial relationship models. For example, they can be used to model the detecting range of a sensor in terms of the locations within some set distance. A very different example is to infer about likely acquaintanceships between people who have offices very close to each other.

Technical building data. Table 1 shows a sample of extracted information from the technical building data. The first row shows that Room 125 is a *common room*, and the usual activities conducted there is *casual breakout*; it is accessible for *all staff* and should be next to the *boardroom*. Possible uses for the extracted information include: obtaining a more human-understandable name for a room; better location estimation and way-finding by knowing nearby locations; the "Primary Users" information may help systems deliver personalised information to different groups of users. For example, Room 125 may be relevant in an

Table 1. A sample view of extracted technical building data

Rm No.	Room Name	Principal Activities	Primary Users	Essential Link
125	common room	casual breakout	all staff	boardroom
203	pervasive computing lab	experimental space	academic staff	

orientation tour to undergraduate advisors, but not Room 203, as it is only relevant to academic staff.

Staff directories. Staff and postgraduate student directories also contain valuable information to populate the ontology. For example, they help provide more human-understandable names for personal offices and work spaces. The roles for staff (e.g. lecturers) and students (e.g. full-time PhD students) can also facilitate personalised information delivery. For example, a reminder for a board meeting may be valuable to academic staff, but would be irrelevant to students.

Internal email aliases. The assumption is that people who are on the same email list—normally representing a research group—know each other. This might not always be true; for example, a new student normally gets to know the academic staff quicker than the other way around.

Direct user input. A key aspect of our approach is that the system must deal with the possibility that some sources may be inaccurate. For example, the staff directory details of people's work roles might be out of date, and people may change office. In such cases, users should be able to control their own models and correct the information.

Other sources. There are many other useful document sources, such as the building manual, postgraduate and undergraduate student handbooks, the university calendar and university publications, that could yet be mined to further populate PECO. For example, opening hours of school reception can be extracted from the building manual; the relevant contact and location about submitting a thesis dissertation can be found in a postgraduate student handbook.

3.2 Reasoning with PECO

PECO makes use of evidence from a range of sources to populate an ontology and it generates a personalised ontology depending on the user and context. It does this using the *accretion-resolution* [17] approach, where it *accretes* evidence, adds it to the ontology, and *resolves* a value at the time, and in the context, that a value is needed. We call a function that resolves a value with the accreted evidence a *resolver*. With the dynamic nature of a pervasive environment, being able to postpone the resolution of a value is invaluable. This not only saves potentially unnecessary machine calculation and complex non-monotonic reasoning, but it also, critically, provides flexibility to deliver personalised and scrutable information. We have successfully extended this approach to ontological reasoning for location conflict resolution in a multi-sensor environment [16]. In this paper, we focus on provision of personalised information and sensible system explanations using such reasoning.

4   Evaluation of PECO

We used an application-based approach to evaluate PECO: that is, we implemented an application that used PECO and evaluated the results. This is one of the four main evaluation techniques reviewed in [18]. The system is called Locator and it displays the location of people in our building (Figure 2) making use of PECO to provide personalised and scrutable information. In our study, we compared the full version of Locator against a non-adaptive. Key goals of the evaluation were: to assess the accuracy and value of personalised location labels; to assess the accuracy and value of the selection of people relevant to the user; to assess the understandability of the explanations for the personalisation. We designed two sets of task that Locator would normally be used for: locating individuals and groups in the building [19].

Before the main task-sets, participants did four familiarisation tasks. This gave familiarity with the map interface. They then completed a task-set for each of the two systems using a double-blind, cross-over methodology to reduce inter-subject variability: half the participants used the adaptive system first, and the other half used the non-adaptive one first. After the task-sets, participants completed an online questionnaire with eight questions. Each asked for level of agreement on a seven-point Likert scale, with space for comments and justifications of the answer. Participants were observed by the first author throughout.

4.1 Participants

Eight participants were recruited: two women and six men; two staff members, two graduate students and four undergraduates. Their ages range was 19 to 57. Six worked regularly in the building for over six months, and the others for four and one month respectively. All but one had used an earlier non-personalised version of Locator [20], and the other person knew about it before the study. As we made use of inferences about social networks, we deliberately recruited the participant group as users of the building and familiar with the maps.

4.2 The Adaptive System

Figure 2 shows level 3 in the Locator interface. The top left allows navigation to other levels: as there were no people detected on level 2, it is hidden at this time. Each dot on the map represents a person; its darkness indicates the strength of the relationship to the current user. The user can click "What do the colours mean?" to see this explained. Below the map is personalised information of the people on that floor. Holding the cursor over a person's description highlights the dot presenting that person. Clicking place (e.g. his desk) or person (e.g. User L) gives an explanation. In the figure, the user has clicked where the hand appears on User L's location: his desk. The pop-up explains this part of the personalisation. PECO omits people whom it infers to be unknown to the user, but the user can choose to display them by clicking "show" after "3 Person(s) hidden" at the bottom left.

The system reasons about the user's relationship with people to determine who to display and who to hide. For this evaluation, the system models relationships via mining available resources. A person is assessed as more closely related if they work at a nearby office or desk and if they are on the same internal mailing aliases.

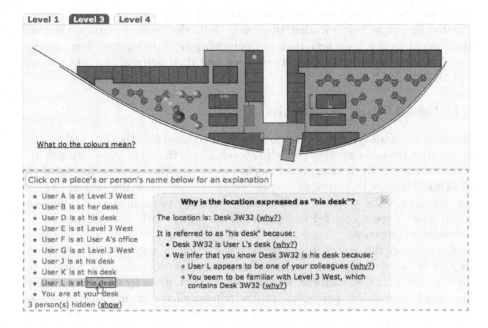

Fig. 2. A user view of the adaptive system

To personalise location labels (e.g. `his desk`), a range of evidence is used. As shown in Figure 2, the system uses the following evidence for User L's location:

- User L's work space is Desk 3W32, for mapping the place to their desk
- The user knows User L, for "User L's Desk" to be meaningful
- The user knows where Desk 3W32 is, inferred because the user has been to the wing containing that place

4.3 Data Collection

The response to the familiarisation tasks was collected, as one of them was designed to also determine how each participant would refer to a place which they were familiar with. For the system tasks, we collected the time each participant took to complete each task and the answers for the tasks. In addition, before they scrutinised the adaptive system's explanation about personalised location labels, they were asked to think about what the system would need for such reasoning. We also kept a record of the participants' clicks on the map interface, explanations, and the link to show and hide less relevant people.

As for the non-adaptive system, the participants were asked to indicate— from the 20 people shown by the system—whom they would and would not be interested in knowing location of, and why. For the questionnaire, we aimed to collect the participants' quantified opinions on three aspects of the adaptive system: determining relevant people, displaying personalised location labels, and generating explanations about the personalisation. In particular we would like to determine how satisfied they were with the personalisation, whether they would prefer a system that presents adaptive information, how understandable and useful the explanations were, and their perception about system scrutability.

4.4   Data Analysis and Results

We used log data to assess the time required to complete the tasks. We used observation to assess whether participants completed the set of tasks successfully. Time data needs to be interpreted cautiously as participants were not asked to work quickly and they tended to talk aloud as they used the system. There was no statistically significant difference in the time to complete the tasks. All participants were successful in completing all tasks, with both adaptive and non-adaptive systems.

We assessed the accuracy of the personalisation of selecting the people to display in tasks that asked people to indicate whose location they wanted to know about compared with the personalised selection made by the system. They also rated their overall perception on the number of system mistakes in seven-point Likert scale. Figure 3 shows the percentage of the actual (lighter line) and user perceived (darker line) mistakes, which are 24% and 25% in average respectively. Most chose the rating closest to the percentage of actual mistakes. Participants D and F under-rated by one point on the seven-point scale. While A over-rated by one point, they commented, "my need to find them (i.e. the people hidden by the system) is less (often) than those that did show up", hence the better rating than the actual system performance. Participants indicated that they preferred—with an average of 6.4 out of 7.0 rating—the personalisation, although three stated they wanted more information on hidden people. Two participants indicated that they wanted more control over the data.

Participants strongly agreed (average rating 6.8) that personalised labels (e.g. Bob's office) are more useful than the actual room number (e.g. Room 300).

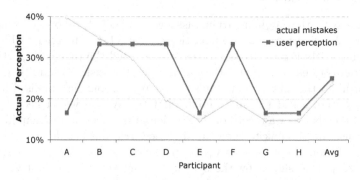

Fig. 3. The actual and user perceived system mistakes

They all preferred (average 6.6) personalised location labels in the system, but five participants indicated that they also wanted to see the room number displayed along with the personalised labels. In one of the familiarisation tasks, participants were asked how they would refer to the office of one of the authors. They unanimously put down "Judy's office".

In terms of scrutability, participants indicated that the explanations were understandable (average rating 6.5) and that it explained what they wanted to know (average 6.4), except for the cases of hidden people, as expressed by three participants. For that, the system's explanation would be, for example, "You do not appear to know Bob". This explanation was judged adequate unless the system had made a mistake. In that case, participants indicated they wanted more details of the reasoning process. They gave a strong rating of 6.6 in agreeing that explanations are important for personalisation. The participant who gave the lowest rating of 5 stated that in some cases they would not care how the system made the personalisation.

5   Discussions and Conclusions

We have described the design and operation of PECO, an ontological reasoner that can provide personalised ontologies for a pervasive computing that personalises information about the people present in a building. We have reported its evaluation, within the Locator application. While the evaluation had to be restricted to people who use our instrumented building, the results are a strong indication of the power of our approach. All participants were able to complete the set of tasks with both systems. The system achieved a mean 24% of error in displaying relevant people, which mostly correlated with the users' perceptions of its accuracy. Participants preferred the personalised location labels although the majority favoured the addition of the absolute room number as well. Participants considered the system explanations extracted from PECO were both understandable and told them what they wanted to know. All considered the explanation of personalisation was important, and three participants explicitly stated that they wanted the ability to control the information delivered to them. This result matches the strong concern for user control in pervasive computing. Overall, all participants preferred the adaptive system.

Key contributions of this work are a new form of personal ontology, use of that ontology to deliver personalised location information to display relevant people nearby and to personalise location labels, demonstrated usefulness of the explanations from PECO to explain personalised ontological reasoning.

Acknowledgements. The Smart Internet Technology CRC partially funded this project. We would like to thank all the experiment participants for their time and participation. We also want to thank David Carmichael, Vincent Daviet and Carolin Plate for their valuable feedback on the design of the experiment.

References

1. Strang, T., Linnhoff-Popien, C., Frank, K.: Applications of a context ontology language. In: Begusic, D., Rozic, N. (eds.) Int. Conf. on Software, Telecommunications and Computer Networks, pp. 14–18 (2003)
2. Ranganathan, A., McGrath, R.E., Campbell, R.H., Mickunas, M.D.: Use of ontologies in a pervasive computing environment. Knowl. Eng. Rev. 18, 209–220 (2003)
3. Wang, X., Dong, J.S., Chin, C., Hettiarachchi, S., Zhang, D.: Semantic Space: An infrastructure for smart spaces. IEEE Pervasive Computing 3, 32–39 (2004)
4. Chen, H., Finin, T., Joshi, A.: An ontology for context-aware pervasive computing environments. Knowl. Eng. Rev. 18, 197–207 (2004)
5. Wishart, R., Henricksen, K., Indulska, J.: Context obfuscation for privacy via ontological descriptions. In: Location- and Context-Awareness, pp. 276–288 (2005)
6. Dieng, R., Hug, S.: Comparison of personal ontologies represented through conceptual graphs. In: Prade, H. (ed.) 13th European Conf. on Artificial Intelligence, pp. 341–345 (1998)
7. Huhns, M.N., Stephens, L.M.: Personal ontologies. IEEE Internet Computing 3, 85–87 (1999)
8. Gauch, S., Chaffee, J., Pretschner, A.: Ontology-based personalized search and browsing. Web Intelligence and Agent System 1, 219–234 (2003)
9. Noh, S., Seo, H., Choi, J., Choi, K., Jung, G.: Classifying web pages using adaptive ontology. In: IEEE Conf. on Systems, Man and Cybernetics, pp. 2144–2149 (2003)
10. Cimolino, L., Kay, J., Miller, A.: Concept mapping for eliciting verified personal ontologies. Int. Journal of Continuing Engineering Education and Life-Long Learning 14, 212–228 (2004)
11. Golemati, M., Katifori, A., Vassilakis, C., Lepouras, G., Halatsis, C.: Creating an ontology for the user profile: Method and applications. In: Rolland, C., Pastor, O., Cavarero, J.L. (eds.) RCIS: 1st Int. Conf. on Research Challenges in Information Science, pp. 407–412 (2007)
12. Katifori, A., Vassilakis, C., Daradimos, I., Lepouras, G., Ioannidis, Y., Dix, A., Poggi, A., Catarci, T.: Personal ontology creation and visualization for a personal interaction management system. In: Personal Information Management (2008)
13. Kay, J., Niu, W., Carmichael, D.J.: ONCOR: Ontology- and evidence-based context reasoner. In: 12th Int. Conf. on Intelligent User Interfaces, pp. 290–293 (2007)
14. Lenat, D.B.: CYC: A large-scale investment in knowledge infrastructure. Communications of the ACM 38, 33–38 (1995)
15. Chen, H., Perich, F., Finin, T., Joshi, A.: SOUPA: Standard ontology for ubiquitous and pervasive applications. In: Int. Conf. on Mobile and Ubiquitous Systems: Networking and Services, pp. 258–267 (2004)
16. Niu, W., Kay, J.: Location conflict resolution with an ontology. In: Int. Conf. on Pervasive Computing (to appear, 2008)
17. Carmichael, D.J., Kay, J., Kummerfeld, B.: Consistent modelling of users, devices and sensors in a ubiquitous computing environment. User Modeling and User-Adapted Interaction 15, 197–234 (2005)
18. Brank, J., Grobelnik, M., Mladenić, D.: A survey of ontology evaluation techniques. In: Conf. on Data Mining and Data Warehouses (2005)
19. Assad, M., Carmichael, D.J., Niu, W., Kay, J., Kummerfeld, B.: Location in the workplace: How is it used? In: Workshop on Ubicomp in the Office (2007)
20. Assad, M., Carmichael, D., Kay, J., Kummerfeld, B.: PersonisAD: Distributed, active, scrutable model framework for context-aware services. In: Int. Conf. on Pervasive Computing, pp. 55–72 (2007)

Using Decision Models for the Adaptive Generation of Learning Spaces

Eric Ras and Dimitri Ilin

Fraunhofer IESE
Fraunhofer-Platz 1
67663 Kaiserslautern
eric.ras@iese.fraunhofer.de,
dimitri.ilin@iese.fraunhofer.de

Abstract. This paper presents an approach that uses a decision model for resolving variations in a so-called learning space, which aim is to enhance the reuse of explicitly documented experiences by providing context-aware learning content. Decision models promise a better possibility to separate the variabilities in e-learning content, and address the problem of closed corpus of adaptive hypermedia systems. Adaptation is not coupled to a fixed set of learning resources, but to types of learning space concepts. The system adapts and personalizes the learning space to the learner's situation. A controlled experiment provides first statistically significant results, which show an experience package reuse improvement regarding knowledge acquisition and application efficiency. Further, it provides a baseline for future evaluations of different adaptation methods and techniques.

Keywords: adaptation, decision model, experience management, learning space.

1 Introduction

Most of our daily learning is, in fact, experience-based. Software engineering is a very knowledge-intensive activity and strongly relies on individual competencies. The field of *experience management* (EM) has increasingly gained importance. EM supports the collection, pre-processing, analysis, and dissemination of experiences. However, different problems occur when experiences documented by experts are reused by novices. Experience is often documented by domain experts. Expert knowledge is somehow 'routine'. This makes it challenging for experts to document experiences appropriately and to make them reusable for others. Novices lack software engineering background knowledge and are not able to connect the experience to their knowledge base (see [1] for more details about the problems).

To address the problems, an adaptive educational hypermedia system has been developed to produce so-called context-aware *learning spaces* for enhancing understanding, know acquisition, and application during the reuse of experience packages. The success of adaptation techniques depends for example on how good an AHS

W. Nejdl et al. (Eds.): AH 2008, LNCS 5149, pp. 153–162, 2008.

separates the content from its structure and its presentation. The so-called *closed corpus* problem in adaptive hypermedia states that the systems are working with a closed set of artifacts (e.g., fined grained learning objects or documents) [2] [3], and that the alterations or modifications are defined in-between the documents (e.g., by using the relation "required prerequisites"). This makes it difficult to reuse the adaptive functionality of the system, and does not allow extending the document space or even work in an open environment like the Web (example for open corpus).

The aim of this paper is to describe the approach of decision models for adaptation in order to cope with the problem of "closed corpus". The goal of the presented results of a controlled experiment is first to demonstrate that learning spaces significantly enhances experience reuse and second to provide a first baseline of effect sizes that can be used for future evaluations of the adaptive characteristics of the learning space approach. The next section briefly describes the kind of adaptation mechanisms that exists in the domain of adaptive hypermedia systems. Section 3 explains the variable concepts of a learning space. Section 4 shows how a decision model can solve the issue of adaptation in learning spaces. Section 5 provides statistically significant results of a recently conducted controlled experiment regarding the effect of context-aware learning spaces on experience reuse. Section 6 concludes the paper.

2 Adaptive Hypermedia Systems

Adaptive hypermedia systems (AHS) have enhanced classical hypermedia by using an intelligent agent that supports a user during work with hypermedia. The intelligent agent is able to adapt the content of a hypermedia page to the user's knowledge and goals or suggests the most relevant links to follow [2]. In the domain of education, so-called intelligent tutoring systems (ITS) use knowledge about the domain, the learner, and about teaching strategies to support flexible individualized learning and tutoring. Adaptive hypermedia systems are, in fact, a ,more recent research domain than ITS. AHS allow the adaptation of learning to specific user needs and requirements. Some well known systems are AHA!2.0, ActiveMath, ELM-ART, INTERBOOK, and KBS Hyperbook. Over the years, many different adaptation techniques have been developed. Several classifications exist that are mostly derived based on the classification of Brusilovsky [2]. He distinguishes between adaptive navigation and adaptive presentation:

Adaptive navigation alters the structure presented to the learner according to the individual learner characteristics. The most popular methods of adaptive navigation [4] are: global, local guidance, local orientation support, global orientation support, personalized views. *Adaptive presentation* refers to content adaptation and alters the way content is visually displayed to the user based on a user model. The most popular methods of adaptive presentation [4] are additional explanations, explanation variants, sorting, prerequisite explanations, comparative explanations.

The architecture of an adaptive hypermedia system (such as AHA!) usually consists of three components [5]: a domain model that contains the concepts with its relations and the learning goals, a user model that represents a system user's characteristics, and an adaptation model that consists of adaptation rules. These rules define how the concepts and content resources, which are suitable for the learning process, are selected. A common problem of AHS is that the dependencies between learning resources and system user characteristics are often too complex to characterize them all. This complexity leads to a number of problems with adaptation rules [6] [7]:

- Inconsistency, if several rules are conflicting,
- Confluence, if several rules are equivalent,
- Insufficiency, if one or several necessary rules are not defined, and
- Because of the faulty cooperation of the adaptive rules it can happen, that the adaptation engine does not terminate.

There are different approaches which try to avoid the above mentioned problems. Wu and De Bra [6] suggest so-called sufficient conditions. These constraints help authors to write such adaptation rules, which guarantee termination and confluence. Karampiperis [7] suggests, to abandon the adaptive rules and to use so-called decision models. The proposed alternative method at first generates all possible learning paths that correspond to the learning goal, and then selects the best one. The selection relies on a decision model, which estimates the suitability of learning resources for the user. A so-called decision-making function is used for the estimation of the suitability.

During the last years, technologies from AHS and semantic web are combined to profit on the one hand from the knowledge in the domain of user modeling and adaptation of hypermedia content and on the other hand from ontology description languages (e.g., RDF, and OWL) and reasoning and inference techniques. Now, ontologies based on semantic web technologies are increasingly used for modeling knowledge in adaptive web systems.

3 Adaptive Learning Spaces

From a technical point of view, a learning space consists of a hypermedia space with linked pages. A learning space follows a specific global learning goal and is created based on context information about the current situation and the context description of an experience package. The learning space is technically presented by means of linked Wiki pages within the Software Organization Platform (SOP). SOP intends to support specific software engineering activities such as experience management, requirements engineering, or project management. Hence, by integrating the learning space generation and presentation functionality into SOP, knowledge management and e-learning were merged into one system [8].

Fig. 1 depicts the concepts of a learning space and their relationships. The generation process starts with the adaptation of a so-called generic *LearningSpaceStructure-Template* (this step is elaborated in more detail in a subsequent section). This template reflects the high-level structure of a learning space. Each *LearningSpaceStructure-Template* is refined by a set of *LearningGoalTemplates*. These templates reflect a concrete learning activity structure and refer to a learning goal level (details about the learning goals and the didactical structures can be found in [1, 8]).

Each of these templates is implemented by a *LearningPage* (which physically corresponds to a Wiki page, see Fig. 4). Such a page contains a *LearningComponent* consisting of *LearningElements*. Learning elements are the most basic learning

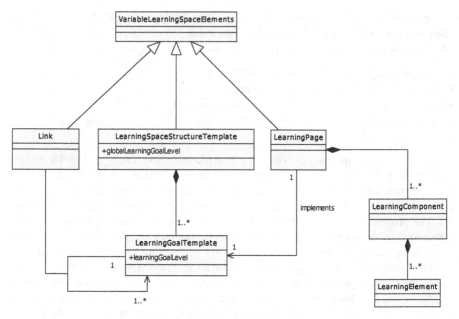

Fig. 1. Variable Learning Space Concepts

resources. They are electronic representations of media, such as images, text, sound, or any other piece of data that can serve as a learning resource when aggregated with other learning elements to form a learning component. Learning components are units of instruction that contain at least one learning element. A learning component represents the lowest granularity of a learning resource that can be reused by the system for learning purposes.

Some of the learning space concepts can be adapted according to the context: a *LearningSpaceStructureTemplate* contains variable elements in terms of the *LearningGoalTemplates* used and/or the *Links* between them; *LearningPages*, which implement the learning goal templates, could possess alternatives in terms of selected *LearningComponents* and their sequence in a learning page; adaptation related to the presentation is done on the *LearningComponent* and *LearningElement* level. The variabilities cover navigation as well as presentation adaptation.

4 Decision Models for Adaptive Learning Space Generation

Decision models are used in different domains. The work in this paper uses a decision model based on results from the domain of software product line engineering. Product line engineering aims at the "systematic development of a set of similar software systems by understanding and controlling their common and distinguishing characteristics" [9]. The so-called variabilities are characteristics that may vary from learning space to learning space. In order to control these so-called variabilities, they need to be identified, their interrelationships have to be defined, and alternatives have to be modeled. Returning to the learning spaces, variabilities can depend on different context characteristics (i.e., individual, group, process, product, project, organization; see [10] for details). Individual context characteristics such as learning style or selected global learning goal can have an impact on the adaptation of a learning space.

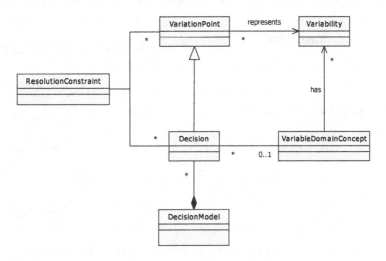

Fig. 2. Information Model of Decision Model (adapted from [9])

The variabilities are defined by means of so-called optional and alternative variation points. Usually, a variation point can capture any kind of variability. *Optional variation points* refer to two choices, with one choice having to be selected. More than one choice can be selected in case of an *alternative variation point*. A *decision model* contains a set of decisions that describe and document these variation points, i.e., their inter-relationships and dependencies. Each decision contains a question that resolves the decision, i.e., the variation point. A decision possesses a set of choices, i.e., answers to the questions. After answering the decisions, the answers are used to resolve the variation points. If a decision refers to one variation point, the decision is called a *simple* decision. *Complex* decisions refer to more than one variation point. Relations between variation points and decisions are described by so-called resolution constraints [9]. There are three types of resolution constraints: complete, partial, and exclude. Complete resolution means that a decision completely resolves a variation point. Partial resolution resolves a part of a variation point, i.e., other decisions are necessary to resolve the variation point completely. Exclude resolution constraints exclude other decisions, i.e., those decisions become obsolete. Variation points can be resolved in different ways. Each alternative corresponds to one different resolution.

4.1 Resolving Process

Only one learning space structure template and one related decision model exist for creating a learning space. Adaptation within a learning space is done by resolving variabilities in the template by using the context information, the selected global

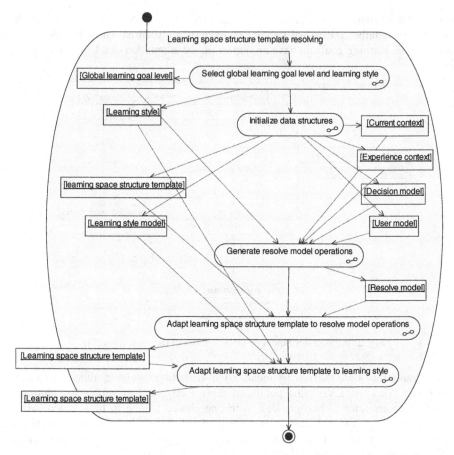

Fig. 3. Template Resolving Activity Diagram

learning goal level, and the learning style chosen by the software engineer. All steps of this process are shown in Figure 3.

First, the *GlobalLearningGoalLevel* (remember, understand, and apply) and the *LearningStyle* (e.g., theory followed by examples, examples followed by theory) are selected by the user. The next step initializes the data structures for the following activities: the *LearningSpaceStructureTemplate*, the *DecisionModel*, the *UserModel*, and the *LearningStyleModel* are retrieved from the system repository; the *ExperienceContext* (see introduction of this section) has been determined by the developer when he or she decides to reuse the experience package before using the learning space. The *UserModel* is initialized and adapted according to the *CurrentContext*. The *UserModel* contains the known processes, products, and knowledge concepts. The *CurrentContext* is an ontology that reflects the current relationships between the user and applied processes, developed products, involvement in development groups and project, etc. The *UserModel* is adapted by performing queries to this ontology. The next step resolves the decisions of the *DecisionModel* and generates the

ResolveModel operations by using the information about the *CurrentContext*, the *ExperienceContext*, the *UserModel*, and the *GlobalLearningGoalLevel*. For each question in the *DecisionModel* a SPARQL query is forwarded to the *CurrentContext* ontology or to the *UserModel* of the current user in order to resolve the different decisions. Queries are built based on the context information stored in the description of the experience package.

The answers, respectively the selected choices (i.e., alternative answers to the query), are stored in the *ResolveModel*, since they will be used for resolving variation points in the *LearningSpaceStructureTemplate*. Each choice of a decision is related to a set of generic operations that resolve the variation points in the *LearningSpaceStructureTemplate*. They are not explicitly related to specific variations points, but to types of variable elements: e.g., hide the *LearningGoalTemplate(s)* (see Section 3 for this concept) of the learning level type "apply", etc. Than, the *ResolveModel* operations are executed to adapt the *LearningSpaceStructureTemplate*.

After the adaptation process the attributes that define the visibility of *LearningGoalTemplate* (they correspond to one learning page, respectively one Wiki page) are set. Therefore, only the appropriate *LearningGoalTemplates* will be displayed to the user in the learning space presentation step. The last process step adapts the *LearningSpaceStructureTemplate* to the *LearningStyle*, which was selected by the current user. The order of the learning components in the *LearningGoalTemplate* is changed based on the selected *LearningStyle*.

4.2 Technical Implementation

The techniques of the adaptive navigation and presentation, which implement the above mentioned methods of the adaptive navigation and presentation, are addressed in the following. The adaptive navigation techniques direct guidance, link sorting, link hiding, link generation, and map adaptation were implemented by means of the adapted values of the attributes in the learning space structure template and the order of the learning elements in the learning goal templates that are shown to the learner. The adaptive presentation techniques conditional text, page variants, fragment variants, and frame-based technique were implemented by means of the implemented possibilities to interact with the created learning space.

The context vector refers to the concepts of the ontology that is available in the OWL-DL format. The learning space structure template, the decision model, the user model, the resolve model, and the learning style model are stored in XML and conform to corresponding XML schemas. The experience packages are stored in the experience database. All classes were implemented with the object-oriented programming language PHP 5. MySQL was used as relational database management system. The open source ontology editor Protégé was used for developing Ontologies and exporting OWL files. The application programming interface RAP-RDF API was used for the building, storage, and retrieval of the RDF models, and the RDF query language SPARQL was used as the query language for the OWL files. The Reload editor was used to build IMS Learning Design conform *LearningSpaceStructureTemplate*.

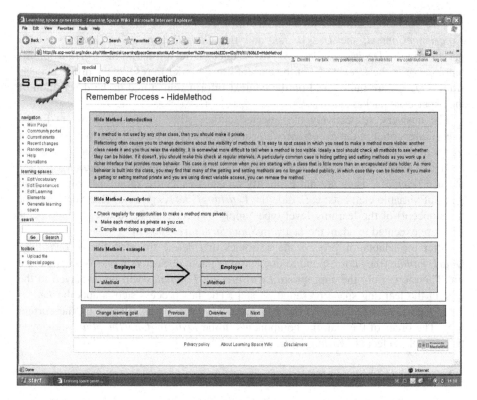

Fig. 4. Learning Space in SOP

5 Empirical Results and Conclusion

In order to evaluate the effect of adaptive learning spaces on experience reuse, a balanced within-subject experiment was conducted with 19 students of the University of Kaiserslautern. With this design, higher power can be achieved because such a "crossover" design removes the inter-subject variability from the comparison between treatments, and can provide unbiased estimates for the difference between treatments. The independent variable (factor) was the set of information provided, i.e., experience package (EP) or experience package enriched with learning space (LSEP). The experimental group (ten subjects) was assigned to use LSEP, while the control group (nine subjects) used EP at the same time. For the experiment, the software engineering maintenance task of refactoring in Java was chosen. All experience packages, questionnaires, and assignments were related to the topic of refactoring. The subjects were asked to read two experience package descriptions (either in EP or LSEP mode) and to use these descriptions for solving specific assignments. For the LSEP option, an adaptive learning space was created according to the process described before. Amongst several other dependent variables the results of *knowledge acquisition* and *application,* will be presented here:

- Knowledge acquisition difference (know_diff) is measured via the difference of a pre-test score and the post-test score by using a questionnaire with 65 items.
- Application efficiency *(a_eff)* is measured via the number of correctly found defects per time unit (i.e., minutes)
- Application completeness *(a_comp)* is measured via the correctly found defects divided by the total amount of defects that can be found
- Application accuracy *(a_accu)* is measured via the correctly found defects divided by the total amount of defects indicated as a defect by the subject

A one-sided dependent samples t-test was applied with the alternative hypothesis H_{1x}: $\mu(dep_{LSEP}) > \mu(dep_{EP})$ and the null hypothesis H_{0x}: $\mu(dep_{LSEP}) \leq \mu(dep_{EP})$. A significance level of $\alpha = 0.05$ (error type I) and an error type II of $\beta = 0.20$ was chosen. The effect size is a measure of the strength of the relationship between two variables. A post-hoc power analysis was done based on effect size d, sample size N, and α.

Table 1. Results of the Hypotheses Tests

One-Tailed Dependent Samples T-Test *(Control Group vs. Experimental Group)*						
	t	*df*	*Crit. T$_{0..95}$*	*p-value*	*effect size (d)*	*power*
know_diff H$_{01}$	7.17	18	1.734	0.000	1.64	1.00
a_eff H$_{02}$	3.171	17	1.740	0.006	0.75	0.92
a_comp H$_{03}$*	3.132	16	1.746	0.006	1.47	0.91
a_accu H$_{04}$	2.111	18	1.734	0.049	0.48	0.65

First, outliers and anomalies in the data were removed. These deletions were in favor of the control group. Hence, the differences did not increase (i.e., the means of the experiment group decreased and the means of the control group rose). The differences were normally distributed, so that a parametric test could be used (for H$_{03,}$ an independent sample t-test on cross-over differences was performed in order to correct for a period effect that confounded the treatment effect). For all dependent variables, p-values lower than $\alpha = 0.05$ were obtained. In addition, the effect sizes almost pass the level of 0.5, which means that learning spaces have at least a "medium" effect on the dependent variables. For know_diff a very high difference was obtained. The reason for this is that current approaches in experience reuse do not explicitly support learning processes respectively knowledge acquisition at all. Experience packages are transferred according to the "copy model", i.e., as they have been documented by experts – no didactical structuring of the information is done. Therefore, a high improvement was expected beforehand. A high correlation between know_diff and a_comp was found, i.e., a high knowledge acquisition results in a high performance regarding application completeness. For application know_diff, acomp, and a_eff, the power was higher than 0.80, which corresponds to a β lower than 0.20, i.e., a chance of less than 20% of failing to detect an effect that is there. Hence, all null hypotheses can be rejected. However, H$_{14}$ cannot be accepted due to the fact that the power is lower than 0.80. Nevertheless, H$_{14}$ could probably have been accepted with a larger sample size (we would have needed 29 subjects in total).

6 Conclusion

Decision models promise a better possibility to separate the variabilities in e-learning content, and address the problem of closed corpus because adaptation is not coupled to a fixed set of learning resources, but to types of variable learning space concepts. This leads to one main advantage: adaptation can be defined on an evolutionary basis, i.e., variation points, resolution constraints as well the resolving of the variation points can be developed step by step by addressing new requirements for adaptation that appear during the lifecycle of the adaptive system. The results of the experiment have demonstrated that learning spaces improve experience reuse regarding knowledge acquisition and application of experience packages. Because software engineering is a very knowledge-intensive activity and strongly relies on experiences, adaptive hypermedia approaches have a high potential for enhancing an engineer's daily work. The experiment has to be replicated to other domains than refactoring and the impact of adaptation has to be investigated in more detail. This experiment and the effect sizes in particular can be used as a baseline for future evaluations that concentrate especially on the different methods and techniques of adaptation.

References

1. Rech, J., Ras, E., Decker, B.: Riki: A System for Knowledge Transfer and Reuse in Software Engineering Projects: Strategies beyond Tools. In: Lytras, M., Naeve, A. (eds.) Open Source for Knowledge and Learning Management. Idea Group, Inc (2007)
2. Brusilovsky, P.: Adaptive Hypermedia. User Modeling and User-Adapted Interaction 11, 87–110 (2001)
3. Henze, N., Nejdl, W.: Extendible adaptive hypermedia courseware: Integrating different courses and web material. In: Brusilovsky, P., Stock, O., Strapparava, C. (eds.) AH 2000. LNCS, vol. 1892. Springer, Heidelberg (2000)
4. Brusilovsky, P.: Adaptive Hypermedia. User Modeling and User Adapted Interaction Nr. 11, 87–110 (2001)
5. De Bra, P., Stash, N., De Lange, B.: AHA! Adding Adaptive Behavior to Websites. In: NLUUG Conference, Ede, The Netherlands (2003)
6. Wu, H., De Bra, P.: Sufficient Conditions for Well-behaved Adaptive Hypermedia Systems. In: First Asia-Pacific Conference on Web Intelligence, Maebashi City, Japan, pp. 148–152 (2001)
7. Karampiperis, P., Sampson, D.: Adaptive Learning Resources Sequencing in Educational Hypermedia Systems. Journal of Educational Technology & Society 8, 128–147 (2005)
8. Ras, E., Rech, J., Decker, B.: Lernräume für erfahrungsbasiertes Lernen mit Wiki-Systemen im Software Engineering. Zeitschrift für E-Learning - Lernkultur und Bildungstechnologie 2, 22–35 (2007)
9. Muthig, D.: A Lightweight Approach Facilitating an Evolutionary Transition Towards Software Product Lines. PhD Thesis, Series of in Experimental Software Engineering. University of Kaiserslautern, Kaiserslautern (2002)
10. Ras, E., Rech, J., Decker, B.: Workplace Learning in Software Engineering Reuse. In: Tochtermann, K., Maurer, F. (eds.) I-KNOW 2006, Special track on "Integrating Working and Learning", Graz, Austria, pp. 437–445 (2006)

Accuracy in Rating and Recommending Item Features

Lloyd Rutledge[1,*], Natalia Stash[2], Yiwen Wang[2], and Lora Aroyo[3]

[1] Telematica Instituut, Enschede, The Netherlands
[2] Technische Universiteit Eindhoven, Eindhoven, The Netherlands
[3] Vrije Universiteit, Amsterdam, The Netherlands

Abstract. This paper discusses accuracy in processing ratings of and recommendations for item features. Such processing facilitates feature-based user navigation in recommender system interfaces. Item features, often in the form of tags, categories or meta-data, are becoming important hypertext components of recommender interfaces. Recommending features would help unfamiliar users navigate in such environments. This work explores techniques for improving feature recommendation accuracy. Conversely, it also examines possibilities for processing user ratings of features to improve recommendation of both features and items.

This work's illustrative implementation is a web portal for a museum collection that lets users browse, rate and receive recommendations for both artworks and interrelated topics about them. Accuracy measurements compare proposed techniques for processing feature ratings and recommending features. Resulting techniques recommend features with relative accuracy. Analysis indicates that processing ratings of either features or items does not improve accuracy of recommending the other.

1 Introduction

Recommender systems have acquired an important role in guiding users to items that interest them. Traditionally, recommendation systems work exclusively with tangible objects (such as films [1], books or purchasable products [2]) as what they let users rate and what they consequently recommend. More recently, however, abstract concepts related to such items play an increasingly important role in extended hypertext environments around recommender systems. For example, Amazon.com's recommender system[1] lets users select categories to fine-tune recommendation lists. In addition, Amazon.com lets users assign tags to items, which extends not only search for and navigation between items but also recommendation of them. As tags, categories and other concepts become more important to users in interaction with recommender systems, users will benefit from help with finding appropriate ones. The context of recommender systems offers an obvious tool for this: the rating and recommendation of such concepts.

---

[*] Lloyd Rutledge is also affiliated with CWI and the Open Universiteit Nederland.
[1] http://www.amazon.com/gp/yourstore/

W. Nejdl et al. (Eds.): AH 2008, LNCS 5149, pp. 163–172, 2008.

Fig. 1. CHIP Artwork Recommender display

Such rating and recommending of abstract concepts occurs in the CHIP project Artwork Recommender[2] [3]. Figure 1 shows an example display. The system's users can rate and recommend items in the form of artworks from the collection of the Rijksmuseum Amsterdam. Users can also rate and recommend features in the form of abstract topics (such as artist, material and technique) related to these artworks, which fall in a hyperlinked network joining artworks with related topics and topics with each other. Recommending artworks and topics brings users to interface displays from which they can rate related artworks and topics, improving their profiles. In this process, users not only find artworks they like, they learn about personally interesting art history topics that affect their taste. Studies show that users benefit from feature recommendation in such an integrated environment [4].

This paper explores how to maximize both the accuracy of feature recommendation and the exploitation of feature ratings. It starts by discussing related work and describing the evaluation methods it applies. The first core section discusses the differences between how users rate features and how they rate items. The paper then shows the impact on collaborative filtering accuracy that feature rating and recommending bring. The final core section proposes an adaptation of established content-based techniques to recommend features. This paper wraps up with conclusions from the study.

2   Related Work

This section discusses work related to navigating and rating features in recommender systems. This work tends to fall in the separate subfields of feature-based navigation in recommender systems, rating of tags and browsers for extensively annotated items. These fields combine in the implementation this work applies in exploring recommender accuracy for these topics.

Amazon.com uses both categories and tags in its recommender service by letting users specify that each can refine recommendation lists. Amazon, however,

---

[2] http://www.chip-project.org/demo

lets users rate neither categories nor tags, only items. In addition, they do not use categories and tags in recommendation generation processing. MovieLens recently added tags to its recommender service, giving users both the ability to assign tags to movies and to rate tags assigned by others [5]. This rating of tags relates closely to this work's rating of features. In MovieLens, however, a user's rating of a tag indicates the user's confidence in its informative accuracy rather than how appealing the user finds that topic.

While Amazon.com and MovieLens only let users rate items, Revyu.com lets users rate "anything" by assigning ratings (and descriptive reviews) to community-defined tags [6]. These ratings represent level of user interest. Revyu.com does not distinguish between items and their features because tags can represent either in the same manner. However, Revyu.com does not process these ratings for recommendations.

Amazon.com and MovieLens offer tags as part of recommendation, providing community-defined features. Amazon.com also provides centrally maintained item features in the form of categories. Facetted browsers offer the current state-of-the-art for accessing items by exploiting their centrally maintained features, where the features are more complex in nature. Typically, with facetted browsers, items can have many features and each feature is a property assignment using one of multiple property types. The E-Culture browser[3] offers such facetted access for museum artworks, processing data for over 7000 artworks from multiple institutions that cooperatively apply common vocabularies in making typed properties of these artworks [7]. The annotations from the CHIP Artwork Recommender use the same vocabularies and property types, which has enabled incorporation of the Rijksmuseum artworks and annotations into the E-Culture browser.

Studies with the CHIP Artwork Recommender show that coordinated rating and recommending of features with items improves how novices learn art topics of interest [4]. Other studies with this system show that explaining item recommendation in terms of common features is important for user assessment of recommender system competence and other aspects of trust [8]. This work now performs similar accuracy analyses for feature recommendation and for processing feature ratings for recommendation in general.

3   Method

This section presents the methods that evaluate the techniques this work proposes. It first discusses the user tasks to which the evaluating measurements apply. It then describes the application of the leave-n out approach that provides accuracy measurements here. This section wraps up by presenting the specific metrics for measuring the satisfaction of these user tasks.

The CHIP recommender interface display in Figure 1 illustrates several user tasks. This work's evaluation focuses on two of these tasks. Both involve providing recommendations as a list of all things the user is likely to like. One task is showing all recommendations of items, to which the interface provides access

---

[3] http://e-culture.multimedian.nl/demo/search

from the link "See all recommended artworks" at the bottom right of Figure 1. The area above this links shows the top five of these recommendations. The second task is show all recommended features, which the link "See all recommended topics" links to at the bottom left of Figure 1.

This work's evaluations of the techniques it proposes apply the leave-n out approach. This starts by withholding 10% of the sample ratings as a truth set. The algorithms to evaluate then process the remaining ratings to calculate predictions for the ratings in this truth set. Comparing the predictions with their corresponding true values forms the basis for the various metrics these evaluations use.

The metrics that this work calculates in its evaluations are NMAE, precision and recall. They are common in recommender system and information retrieval research. As both main user tasks involve retrieval of all appropriate matches, these classic metrics of precision and recall apply well.

The *NMAE* (normalized mean absolute error) measures predictive accuracy by showing by what percentage the system's predictions for the truth set ratings differ from their real values. The remaining metrics provide classification accuracy, which measures how well the system generates list of recommendations. *Precision* shows how many of the recommendations the user truly likes. *Recall* indicates how many desired items and features appear among the recommendations. Precision and recall depend on a recommendation threshold, which is a value above which predicted ratings form recommendations for their corresponding concepts. That is, the system recommends an item or feature if the predicted interested for it exceeds this threshold.

4   User Ratings for Items and Features

This section discusses patterns that emerge in comparing how users rate items with how they rate features. This analysis uses two sets of ratings for artworks and related art topics entered by users of the CHIP Artwork Recommender. One set of ratings comes from the online demo, with no restriction on use. The other is from a directed user study. By having ratings for both artworks and topics, this set represents ratings for items and features respectively.

Figure 2 shows the distribution of these ratings across the users. The sample sets for this current work includes only users who gave at least 10 ratings, of which at least one is for a feature, in order to ensure there is substantial data from each user from which to calculate recommendations. The bar charts on the right half of Figure 2 show overall a large amount of five-star (value is 1) and four-star (value is 0.5) ratings.

One rating set comes from the main online demo for the CHIP Artwork Recommender. These users have *"free use"* of the online demo in the sense that they are unsupervised and can have as many sessions as they want whenever they want with no particular tasks to fulfill and no restrictions in how to use the demo. This usage represents the general target use of a recommender system.

One pattern that Figure 2 shows is that users given free use of such a system tend to enter many more, in this case almost three times as many, ratings for

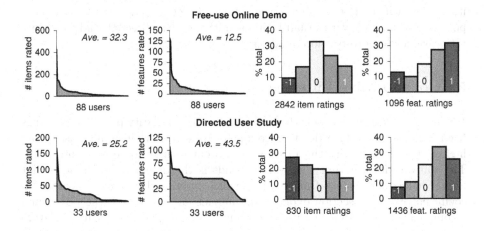

Fig. 2. User-rating distributions

items as they do for features. Another pattern is that feature ratings tend to be more positive and extreme than item ratings. Users were almost twice as likely to rate a feature with five stars (value is 1) than an item. They were also almost twice as likely to rate an item as neutral (value is 0) than a feature. One possible explanation is that users have more extreme opinions about features than items because features are abstract generalizations whereas an item can have many potentially contrasting characteristics that affect user interest in it.

Another possible explanation for the more frequently positive feature ratings is that previous familiarity has a different impact on rating items than on rating features. Perhaps users are more familiar with topics that influence their interest, particularly if this influence is positive. Because users see images of items, they can quickly make a rating for any item, even if they have not seen it before. Features, on the other hand, appear as text labels instead of images, meaning that users must be previously familiar with a topic to enter a rating for it.

While the previous rating set comes from free use of the online demo, another sample set comes from a *directed user study* of this system. This study starts by showing its users 45 topics, which this work considers features, and asking the user to rate them. It then has the user interact with the main demo for a minimum amount of time.

The directed user study brought different patterns in the charts in Figure 2 than for the free-use online demo. The two left-most charts, with distributions of each type of rating across the users, are flatter than for the free-use demo. One factor is that, in the directed study, ratings for each user came from a single session with a time duration minimum. The plateau in the curve for the distribution of feature ratings across users reflects the 45 features the study asks users to rate. The values for the ratings also spread more evenly for the directed study than for the free-use demo. This may be because the directed study compels users to rate a particular variety of features and, to a lesser degree, items. As with the free-use demo, users of the directed study tend to give more positive ratings to features than to items, although the directed study's feature rating values tend to be more moderate.

5   Collaborative Filtering

Collaborative filtering (CF) is the determination of similarity patterns in ratings from multiple users in order to recommend to a user what similar users rate highly. This is typically the processing of item ratings to recommend items. The software for CF that this work extends is the open source Duine toolkit for recommender system frameworks[4], which applies the Pearson correlation coefficient [9]. This section explores the impact on CF of both the rating and recommendation of item features, showing that CF provides accurate feature recommendation but does not improve accuracy when processing ratings from both features and items together.

Figure 3 indicates the accuracy of the proposed techniques. It plots the corresponding precision and recall values from 21 thresholds evenly spread in the full range of rating values. The threshold for recommendation that the precision and recall measurements here use is the top 20% of the range. The bar charts along

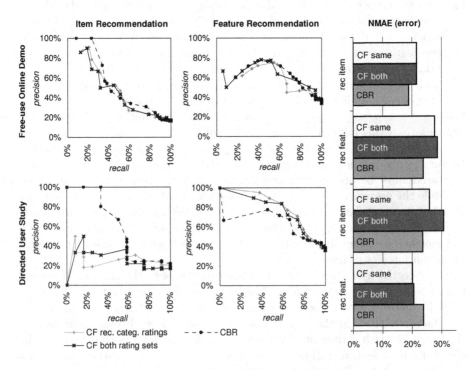

Fig. 3. Accuracy charts for proposed techniques

---

[4] http://sourceforge.net/projects/duine

the right show predictive accuracy for these techniques. The top half comes from the free-use set, while the bottom half comes from the directed user study. In each case, the NMAE charts show measurements for recommending items and features separately. Here, the bar "CBR" indicates the accuracy of content-based recommendation, which the next section discusses. "CF both" measures the error resulting from processing ratings of items and features together with collaborative filtering. Finally, "CF same" processes only item ratings for recommending items and feature ratings for recommending features.

The charts in Figure 3 show that, given this work's rating sets, CF works as well for features as for items. This indicates that systems can recommend features with comparable accuracy as they do for items. One indication of this comparable performance is in predictive accuracy, which the NMAE bar charts on the right of Figure 3 show. Here, CF predictive accuracy from the larger feature rating set has the same average error, if not slightly less, than CF recommendation from the larger item rating set. This comparison uses the largest available set for each recommendation category because CF relies on large amounts of ratings. As Figure 2 shows, the larger set of feature ratings comes from the directed study, which Figure 3's bottom-most bar triple conveys. The larger set of item ratings comes from the free-use demo, which the top-most bar trio conveys.

Another indication of CF's accuracy in feature recommendation comes from the precision-recall plot graphs in Figure 3. They convey that CF provides better classification accuracy for recommending features than items. As with the predictive accuracy comparison, this comparison is between CF for the larger ratings sets: the predictive accuracy for the directed study's feature ratings, which the lower right plot graph in Figure 3 shows, with the predictive accuracy for the feature ratings from the online demo in the upper left plot graph. The curve for features is clearly higher, with the points for each threshold having higher precision and recall than the corresponding points in the plot graph for items. While it is tempting to conclude from this that features in general result in such strongly more accurate CF classification than items, a primary factor in the better classification in this comparison may be the strong overlap in ratings between users for the directed study's set of 45 topics. However, even if this overlap screws the comparison, the conclusion would still be that CF provides accurate classification at least when it compels users to rate overlapping sets.

While this work shows that accurate feature CF is possible, it fails to show how feature ratings can benefit item CF, and vice versa. Figure 3's NMAE bar charts shows that combining ratings sets in CF provides less predictive accuracy than CF processing of only ratings for the type of recommended concept. Here, the "CF same" bars show accuracy for CF processing of ratings for the type of recommendation, either for items or for features. The "CF both" bars show accuracy for processing both item and feature ratings together and equivalently for each type of recommendation. Although processing both ratings sets provides more information than either alone, in all four cases there is either no discernable change or substantial decrease in accuracy in CF for the combined rating sets.

Figure 3's classification plot graphs show the equivalent degradation in accuracy for CF with combined rating sets. In three of the four graphs, the curve for combined processing is clearly lower than the other CF curve. The exception is feature CF with the free-use ratings, which show slight increase in precision but larger decrease in recall. That CF accuracy for both prediction and classification mostly decreases indicates that CF system should use only item ratings for item recommendation and only feature ratings for feature recommendation.

One possibility for having CF improved accuracy by combine rating sets is to treat items and features as domains in cross-domain mediation [10]. This approach shows that CF in one domain can improve with ratings from another by first computing user similarity in each domain separately, combining them and then applying the result for recommendation in the current domain. It remains an open challenge for cross-domain mediation or other techniques to exploit user ratings for either items or features to improve recommendation of the other.

6   Role-Reversed Content-Based Recommendation

Content-based recommendation (CBR) is the typical companion recommender algorithm to CF. While CF uses similarities between users in terms of ratings in order to recommend items similar users like, CBR uses similarities between items in terms of their features in order to recommend items similar to other items the current user likes. CF is typically more accurate than CBR when there are enough ratings for enough items from enough users. However, in the cold-start period leading up to this point, CBR typically performs better. Hybrid recommender systems provide best overall recommendation by selecting which of the two to apply in each recommendation situation [11]. With the previous section having established that CF can accurately recommend features, this section adapts CBR to do so as well, providing in combination the components needed for accurate hybrid recommendation of features. This adaptation is a "role-reversed CBR" to recommend features instead of items.

Core issues in CBR include assigning appropriate features for the items to recommend and determining appropriate processing for these features. This work uses a CBR technique for processing features that are item properties encoded with Semantic Web formats. The item and feature set are the museum artworks and annotations from the CHIP Artwork Recommender. This paper adapts established CBR algorithms in the following ways:

- Treating semantically assigned properties as features (instead of keywords)
- Assigning weights to features by adjusting tf-idf for frequency of properties
- Processing cosine similarity on the resulting feature vectors

This technique represents the typical perspective of recommender systems, in which items to recommend are tangible objects, with features that are abstract concepts related to them. This section proposes *role-reversed CBR* for effective feature recommendation as CBR that switches the roles items and features play in its processing. That it, role-reversed processes features as "items" to recommend and applies cosine similarity with tf-idf weights on vectors consisting of the original items that each original feature annotates.

Figure 3 shows that this role-reversed CBR for features has similar precision and recall as CF for features. The curves in both feature recommendation plot graphs follow roughly the same pattern. For the free-use rating set, the curves are very close. For the directed study set, however, CBR precision tends to be less, albeit with roughly the same recall. A factor here may be that the second set has more ratings overall and many more ratings per user, conditions which typically improve CF in comparison to CBR. These measurements indicate that role-reversed CBR provides effective cold-start feature recommendation and can combine well with feature CF in hybrid systems for overall accurate feature recommendation. As with CF, while CBR can accurately recommend features, it remains an open challenge to have CBR exploit feature ratings to improve item recommendation, and vice versa.

7   Summary

This paper shows how to improve feature recommendation and what role processing ratings of either features or items has in recommending the other. Systems can recommend features with accuracy that is comparable to item recommendation. Techniques for doing so include CF and this work's role-reversed CBR. Users choose freely to rate features, although they rate items more frequently. Users tend to rate features more positively than items. It remains a challenge in both CF and CBR to have processing ratings for either items or features improve the recommendation of the either.

Acknowledgements

This work was a collaboration with the Rijksmuseum Amsterdam within the CHIP project[5] of the CATCH program[6], funded by the Dutch Organization for Scientific Research (NWO). The MultimediaN/E-Culture project[7] provides the encoding of the Getty vocabularies that define some of this work's items features, along with mappings to them from original curator annotations. The CATCH/STITCH project[8] provides an encoding for Iconclass, which defines other item features this work uses. The implementation here uses the open source Duine Toolkit[9] for recommendation processing. The Rijksmuseum Amsterdam gave permission for the use of its images.

---

[5] http://www.chip-project.org/
[6] http://www.nwo.nl/catch
[7] http://e-culture.multimedian.nl/
[8] http://stitch.cs.vu.nl/
[9] http://sourceforge.net/projects/duine

References

1. Good, N., Schafer, J.B., Konstan, J.A., Borchers, A., Sarwar, B.M., Herlocker, J.L., Riedl, J.: Combining collaborative filtering with personal agents for better recommendations. In: Proceedings of the Sixteenth National Conference on Artificial Intelligence (AAAI 1999), Orlando, Florida, USA, July 18-22, 1999, pp. 439–446 (1999)
2. Linden, G., Smith, B., York, J.: Amazon.com recommendations: item-to-item collaborative filtering. Internet Computing 7(1), 76–80 (2003)
3. Aroyo, L., Brussee, R., Rutledge, L., Gorgels, P., Stash, N., Wang, Y.: Personalized museum experience: the Rijksmuseum use case. In: Museums and the Web 2007, San Francisco, USA, April 11-14 (2007)
4. Wang, Y., Aroyo, L., Stash, N., Rutledge, L.: Interactive User Modeling for Personalized Access to Museum Collections: The Rijksmuseum Case Study. In: Proceedings of User Modeling 2007, Corfu, Greece, June 2007, pp. 385–389 (2007)
5. Sen, S., Lam, S.K., Rashid, A.M., Cosley, D., Frankowski, D., Osterhouse, J., Harper, F.M., Riedl, J.: Tagging, communities, vocabulary, evolution. In: CSCW 2006: Proceedings of the 2006 20th anniversary conference on Computer supported cooperative work, pp. 181–190. ACM, New York (2006)
6. Heath, T., Motta, E.: Revyu.com: A reviewing and rating site for the web of data. In: Aberer, K., Choi, K.-S., Noy, N., Allemang, D., Lee, K.-I., Nixon, L., Golbeck, J., Mika, P., Maynard, D., Mizoguchi, R., Schreiber, G., Cudré-Mauroux, P. (eds.) ISWC 2007. LNCS, vol. 4825, pp. 895–902. Springer, Heidelberg (2007)
7. Schreiber, G., Amin, A., van Assem, M., de Boer, V., Hardman, L., Hildebrand, M., Hollink, L., Huang, Z., van Kersen, J., de Niet, M., Omelayenko, B., van Ossenbruggen, J., Siebes, R., Taekema, J., Wielemaker, J., Wielinga, B.J.: Multimedian e-culture demonstrator. In: Cruz, I., Decker, S., Allemang, D., Preist, C., Schwabe, D., Mika, P., Uschold, M., Aroyo, L.M. (eds.) ISWC 2006. LNCS, vol. 4273, pp. 951–958. Springer, Heidelberg (2006)
8. Cramer, H., Wielinga, B., Ramlal, S., Evers, V., Rutledge, L., Stash, N.: The effects of transparency on perceived and actual competence of a content-based recommender. In: CHI 2008 Semantic Web User Interaction Workshop (SWUI 2008), Florence, Italy, April 5 (2008)
9. Herlocker, J.L., Konstan, J.A., Borchers, A., Riedl, J.: An algorithmic framework for performing collaborative filtering. In: SIGIR 1999: Proceedings of the 22nd annual international ACM SIGIR conference on Research and development in information retrieval, pp. 230–237. ACM Press, New York (1999)
10. Berkovsky, S., Kuflik, T., Ricci, F.: Cross-domain mediation in collaborative filtering. In: Conati, C., McCoy, K., Paliouras, G. (eds.) UM 2007. LNCS (LNAI), vol. 4511, pp. 355–359. Springer, Heidelberg (2007)
11. Balabanovic, M., Shoham, Y.: Fab: content-based, collaborative recommendation. Commun. ACM 40(3), 66–72 (1997)

Does 'Notice' Prompt Noticing? Raising Awareness in Language Learning with an Open Learner Model

Gheida Shahrour and Susan Bull

Electronic, Electrical and Computer Engineering, University of Birmingham, U.K.
{GJS607,s.bull}@bham.ac.uk

Abstract. Open learner models (OLM) are learner models that are accessible to the learner they represent. Many examples now exist, often with the aim of prompting learner reflection on their knowledge. In language learning, this relates to research on noticing and awareness-raising. We here introduce an open learner model to investigate the potential of OLMs to facilitate noticing. Results suggest that an OLM could be a useful way of helping students to notice language features, with all students noticing some of the features tested, a result that was maintained in a delayed post-test one week after the experimental session.

1 Introduction

Traditional approaches to learner modelling keep the learner model internal to the adaptive environment, invisible to the learner, as its purpose is to allow the system to adapt to the learner's needs. The desire to facilitate reflection on learning and raise learner awareness of their knowledge has prompted some researchers to make the learner model visible to learners: hence the development of open learner models (OLM), e.g. [1], [2], [3], [4], [5].

In language learning, reflection and awareness-raising could be likened to 'noticing' [6]. An important function of awareness-raising is to help learners 'notice the language feature' [6] and 'notice the gap' between their own production and the correct grammatical feature as produced by native speakers [7]. For example, in the input (i.e. the language available to learners) *"she bought two loaves of bread"*, the target word is 'loaves'. Learners may note the correct form of 'loaves' and compare it to their own form 'loafs'. They see that 'f' is replaced by 'ves', and may realise the grammar rule (which is: *to get a plural form from a singular countable noun ending in 'f', one has to change 'f' into 'v' and add 'es'*). Such noticing can enable learners to integrate a rule into their language system. Raising awareness of language features, or noticing items available in the input, may help direct learner attention to these features [6], [8] (see also [9] for a recent overview on language awareness); and increasing the saliency of target items has been recommended for computer-assisted language learning [10].

This paper investigates the potential for prompting noticing in language learning using an OLM. We consider both noticing language features and noticing the distance between one's own language and the native speaker language. The specific example

W. Nejdl et al. (Eds.): AH 2008, LNCS 5149, pp. 173–182, 2008.

for this study is English as a Second or Other Language (ESOL), focusing on irregular verbs and irregular plural nouns as these are amongst the grammatical morphemes commonly overgeneralised by learners [11].

2 The Notice Open Learner Model

Mackey and Abbuhl [12] prompt us to use a salience technique in the OLM to: help learners notice a grammar feature; compare their production with awareness-raising examples, which in this context are native speaker productions; and motivate them to self-repair instead of the system providing direct error correction (by showing learners representations of their knowledge and difficulties). 'Notice', an OLM for language learning, was developed to investigate whether students might immediately notice highlighted features presented in an OLM, and whether there may be retained noticing, measured in a delayed post-test. Notice aims to facilitate acquisition of irregular language forms, and reduce the occurrence of irregular verb and irregular plural noun overgeneralisation-related errors. It provides examples using a salience technique of highlighting the clues which may draw the learner's attention to the target items.

The Notice OLM consists of three parts: the learner model which is built and updated dynamically from the learner's answers to questions; the native model which shows the domain knowledge (i.e. the correct target language); and the comparison model which is a combination of both learner model and native model. The learner model of Notice is therefore open to the learner to view information about their knowledge of the target domain to promote reflection and to help them notice the language features (see [6]). The compare model consists of both the learner model and the domain model to help learners notice the distance or 'gap' between their knowledge and the domain knowledge (see [7]).

For the purpose of this study, the learner modelling in Notice has been kept simple. Learner knowledge is modelled through multiple choice questions, with distracters designed to elicit common difficulties. For example, the belief that: *all verbs in the simple past end in 'd' or 'ed'* (note: know-knew, drive-drove, light-lit, send-sent, teach-taught, set-set (which could be classified into groups such as verbs having a medial long vowel, verbs that require no change in the past)); and *all plural nouns add 's' or 'es'* (note: leaf-leaves, sheep-sheep, information-information, hypothesis-hypotheses, tooth-teeth (which could be classified into groups such as nouns ending in 'f' or 'fe', nouns ending in 'is')). The learner's language features are modelled over the last five attempts at questions relating to that feature. If learners answer five questions correctly, their knowledge is identified as excellent. If they have four questions with one misconception or incorrect response, their knowledge will be identified as very good. If they get three or more questions right, their knowledge level will be good. If they answer three or more questions indicating a misconception, their knowledge will be identified as a misconception (and associated with the specific misconception). If they have three or more questions incorrect, their knowledge will be identified as limited. If they have only one or two correct answers with two incorrect or two misconceptions, their knowledge will be identified as very limited. Beyond the above, other possibilities are classified as insufficient data.

In the externalisation of the learner model, as also in some other OLMs (e.g. [2], [13], [14]), colour is used to depict the level of the learner's understanding. This is combined with text (e.g. 'very good' and information about a misconception); graphically as in small boxes or nodes in front of the title of topics; a large (red) text box which contains information about a misconception, and the background colour of small text boxes which contain the target words. These are shown in Figure 1 (LM Basic: Learner Model Basic) and Figure 2 (LM CR Sentences: Learner Model Consciousness-Raising Sentences).

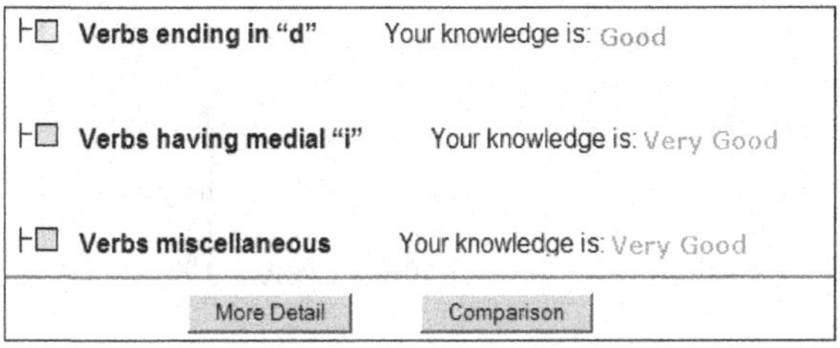

⊢☐ **Verbs ending in "d"**	Your knowledge is: Good
⊢☐ **Verbs having medial "i"**	Your knowledge is: Very Good
⊢☐ **Verbs miscellaneous**	Your knowledge is: Very Good
	More Detail Comparison

Fig. 1. The Notice OLM (LM Basic)

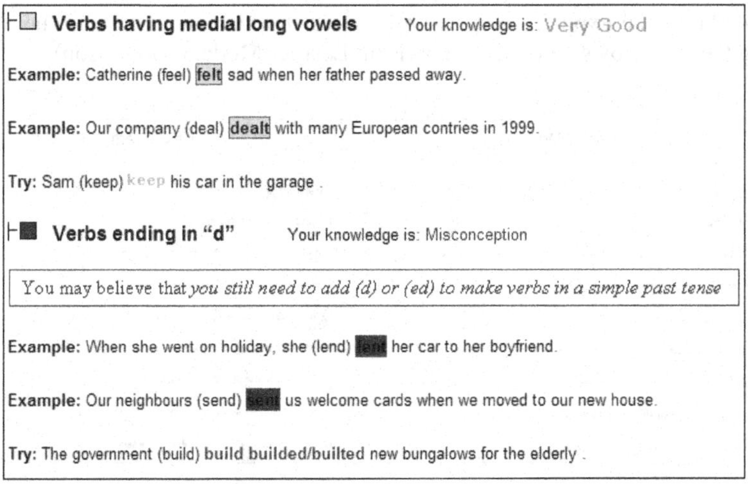

⊢☐ **Verbs having medial long vowels**   Your knowledge is: Very Good

Example: Catherine (feel) felt sad when her father passed away.

Example: Our company (deal) dealt with many European contries in 1999.

Try: Sam (keep) keep his car in the garage .

⊢■ **Verbs ending in "d"**   Your knowledge is: Misconception

You may believe that *you still need to add (d) or (ed) to make verbs in a simple past tense*

Example: When she went on holiday, she (lend) ▨▨▨ her car to her boyfriend.

Example: Our neighbours (send) ▨▨▨ us welcome cards when we moved to our new house.

Try: The government (build) build builded/builted new bungalows for the elderly .

Fig. 2. The Notice OLM (LM CR Sentences)

The learner's knowledge of the simple past tense for *verbs having medial long vowels* in Figure 2 is modelled as 'very good'. This is stated both textually, and with the target words *felt* and *dealt* and the box in front of the title of the topic, in light green – the colour that represents very good knowledge. A misconception is shown for *verbs ending in 'd'* (that the regular form ('d' or 'ed') is added. Highlighting words is designed to draw the learner's attention to the correct form, as this technique makes the target forms more explicit to learners. The aim of having a sentence which a learner can try, as in the fourth and last line of Figure 2, is to stimulate the learner into thinking about how the word should look in each form, and what rule should be followed to attain the relevant target form.

Of course, we are not claiming that if the learner reads the awareness raising sentences, they will necessarily notice the correct form. Instead, a new group of questions is provided after viewing the model, as in Figure 3, to identify whether there may have been any immediate noticing of forms. If a learner's knowledge of a certain feature improves after attempting these post model-viewing questions, we take this as an indication that some immediate noticing has occurred.

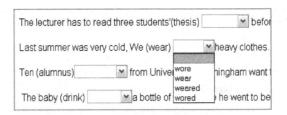

Fig. 3. Excerpt from questions to test for immediate noticing after viewing the learner model

The learner may choose to compare their model with the domain knowledge. Figure 4 shows the explicit comparison between the learner model and the domain, showing these side by side (LM Comparison: Learner Model Comparison).

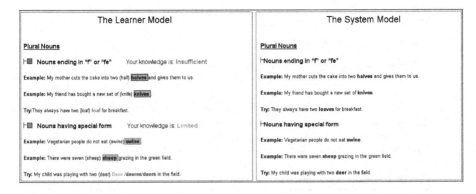

Fig. 4. Comparison of learner model and native (domain) model (LM Comparison)

Figure 4 shows the learner's (inaccurate) knowledge by providing examples of their (incorrect) beliefs written in the same colour that represents their knowledge of the topic (left and Figure 2). The domain model (the system/native model) contains information to draw the learner's attention not only to the target words, but also to the correct form of these words by emboldening them (right). The learner can compare very closely (on the same line) between their productions, whether correct or incorrect, and the domain model – in this case the correct words produced by a native speaker of the target language. If, after viewing LM Comparison, learners subsequently answer questions correctly (see Figure 3), we can assume that they have learned from the comparison, and that they may immediately 'notice the gap' [7].

There is currently no agreement over how instruction may best facilitate language learning, the extent to which focus on form may be useful, or the importance of noticing (see [15]), and we do not wish to argue that Notice should necessarily be deployed in a generally form-focused instructional context. Nevertheless, some attention to language form is likely to be helpful [16], [17]. We investigate this in the following section.

As stated above, Notice was developed to observe whether learners may be prompted to notice language features in an OLM. It is here used together with a delayed post-test to investigate whether any immediate noticing may be retained.

3 Does Notice Facilitate Noticing?

In this section we investigate the following research questions using Notice:

1. Will participants understand the OLM views?
2. Will participants consider the OLM views to be accurate?
3. Will participants find the OLM views useful for their learning?
4. Will the salience technique help participants to 'notice' the correct form and 'notice the gap' between their knowledge and the domain knowledge?
5. Will any 'noticing' be maintained over time?

3.1 Participants, Materials and Methods

Participants were 30 students taking an ESOL course at a U.K. College of Further and Higher Education, at intermediate or higher intermediate level, who were aiming for a higher level certificate in English. Two sessions were arranged for each participant in small groups of seven to eight, scheduled during their usual laboratory time. In the first session participants interacted with the Notice system (unconstrained), and in the second session held one week later, they took a delayed post-test.

In the first session participants were given information about the system and instructions for the session. The experimenter was present to help participants with the log on process, to answer any questions about Notice, and to explain any unknown words in English. During the session, participants answered questions and viewed their learner model showing the basic information (LM Basic), the learner model containing the awareness or consciousness raising sentences (LM CR Sentences), and the learner model comparing the learner's knowledge and the native model (LM Comparison). All interactions were logged by the system to enable identification of the frequency of model inspection; the knowledge level each learner had during model inspection; whether a participant immediately noticed the correct form of the word after inspecting the LM (CR Sentences); and whether s/he noticed the gap between his/her own rules and the correct rules when inspecting the LM (Comparison). The initial state of the learner model (as soon as the learner had answered sufficient questions for the learner model to be constructed), and the final learner model states were used to identify learner knowledge at the beginning and the end of the session (in place of a pre-test and post-test). The mid-point state of the learner model was used to identify learner knowledge in the middle of the session. At the end of the session a questionnaire was administered, with responses to statements required by circling one of the following: 'strongly disagree', 'disagree', 'neutral', 'agree' and 'strongly agree'. Here we combine the responses of 'strongly disagree' and 'disagree' as negative responses and 'strongly agree' and 'agree' as positive responses. The session was scheduled for one hour, but some students chose to continue interacting beyond this time.

The college lecturers refrained from teaching irregular verbs and irregular plural nouns until after a paper-based delayed post test one week later. 24 of the 30 participants took the post test containing fifty questions similar to the questions attempted during interaction with Notice. The session lasted for one hour (sufficient time for questions to be answered at participants' own pace), with the aim of determining whether the participants had retained the correct forms. In other words, to what extent they had or had not internalised the correct form into their language system one week after using Notice.

3.2   Results

In the questionnaire, participants rated whether they understood each view of the learner model, namely, LM Basic, LM CR Sentences and LM Comparison. As seen in Figure 5, most participants claimed to understand the learner model views, with a few responding neutrally to one or two views (different participants responded neutrally to different views, with only 2 participants responding neutrally to two views), and one responding negatively to one of the views (LM CR Sentences). Similarly, most participants agreed that the three views were accurate. Only 3 or 4 participants responded neutrally to one or two views, with different participants responding neutrally to different views. Only 2 participants responded neutrally to two views and 1 answered negatively about the accuracy of the LM Comparison view.

Figure 6 shows that most users claimed to find each of the views useful for identifying their knowledge (1), any general difficulties (2), and any misconceptions/ overgeneralisations (3). They also rated the views as useful in general (4).

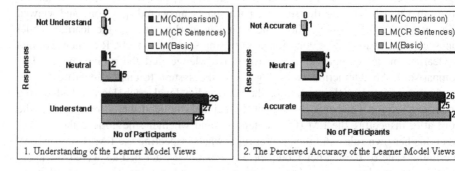

Fig. 5. Understanding and the perceived accuracy of the learner model views

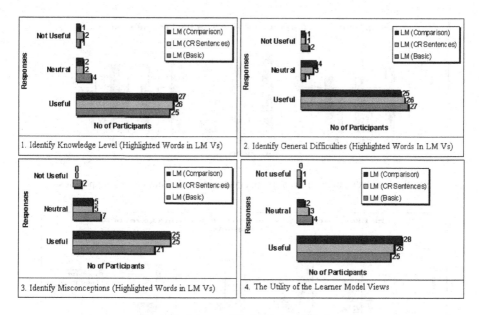

Fig. 6. Usefulness of the learner model views

The overall picture of the knowledge level averaged for all participants is given in Figure 7. 50% of the participants' initial LM was at a low level (either misconceptions or limited knowledge), and none was seen at the excellent level. In contrast, 90% of the final LM is identified at high levels (excellent, very good, or good), with progression throughout the session from initial to mid to final learner model. Although there was a decrease in excellent and very good levels identified in the post-test (one week after the final LM), this is still much higher than in the initial LM, and the differences between the final LM state and delayed post-test are small. All learners improved their knowledge between the initial LM and the delayed post-test.

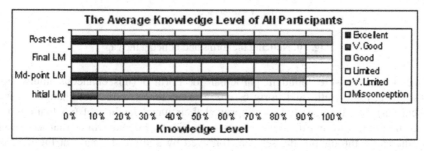

Fig. 7. Learner knowledge at initial, mid-point, final learner model state, and post-test

Figure 8 shows the average knowledge of each of the irregular plural noun and irregular verb features modelled, at the initial LM stage and the delayed post-test. For each, knowledge was greater in the delayed post-test than when students started using

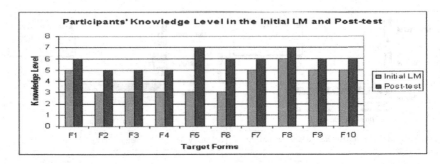

Fig. 8. Knowledge of each feature modelled at initial learner model and post-test

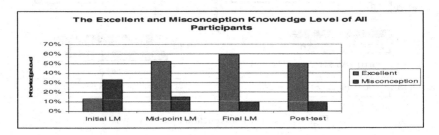

Fig. 9. Excellent (highest) level of knowledge and misconceptions at each stage

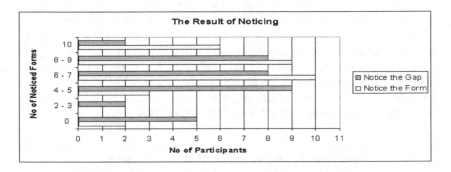

Fig. 10. Noticing the forms and noticing the gap

Notice. Increases were found in particular for Form 5 (miscellaneous nouns, e.g. mouse-mice, tooth-teeth) and Form 6 (unique verb forms, verbs not changing form, e.g. cut-cut). On average students improved their understanding of 6.5 features between the initial LM and the delayed post-test. Figure 9 demonstrates that as knowledge increased throughout the session, followed by a slight decrease at the delayed post-test stage, the misconceptions decreased.

Figure 10 shows the results for immediate noticing of language features and noticing the gap, revealed from students' answers to the test questions after accessing the LM CR Sentences and LM Comparison views (see Figure 3). This is averaged over the whole session, and indicates that students were immediately noticing some of the forms as well as the gaps between their knowledge and the target features.

3.3 Discussion

This section discusses the results with reference to our research questions: Will participants understand the OLM views? Will they consider them accurate? Will they find them useful? Will they notice correct forms? Will they notice the 'gap'? Will any noticing still be evident one week later?

It is important to first identify whether students understand what the OLM views represent, as this is crucial for fostering noticing in this context. It is also important to ascertain whether students consider the views to be accurate, since this is likely to influence their motivation to pay attention to the representations. In both cases a large majority responded positively in the questionnaire for each of LM Basic, LM CR Sentences and LM Comparison: 25-29 of the 30 participants (Figure 5). Students also found the model views useful – both generally and specifically for identifying knowledge level, general difficulties and misconceptions (Figure 6). This is also important with reference to motivation to use Notice.

Overall there was a strong increase in knowledge level between the initial learner model state and the delayed post-test (Figures 7 and 9), and all learners improved their level of knowledge. The post-test results remained quite similar to the final learner model state, dipping only slightly. Furthermore, there was an increase in average knowledge level of all forms between initial state and delayed post-test (Figure 8). Thus we argue that forms can indeed be noticed through use of an OLM such as Notice. This is also shown in Figure 10 with reference to immediate noticing, where learners were observed to notice after using both the individual learner model and the comparison view. The extent to which noticed forms might be retained beyond one week is a question for further investigation. Of course, if instructors are also teaching the forms at the same time, heightening their salience, this retention may be more likely.

In summary: the results suggest that an awareness-raising technique used in an OLM may help language learners to notice target forms. This holds true not only immediately after inspecting the learner model, but in many cases also after one week with no further instruction on the forms. It seems, therefore, that learners may be able to internalise correct forms into their language system, using an OLM such as Notice. This type of OLM has already been found able to support independent learning in a range of university courses [2], and it now seems that the approach may be particularly relevant for reflecting on, or noticing language. Further work would therefore be useful. In particular, we would like to investigate students' noticing experiences *after* using an awareness-raising OLM. Were they more aware of noticing elements in the everyday language around them?

4 Summary

This paper has presented Notice, an OLM to prompt noticing in second language learning. It was found that using a saliency technique in the context of an OLM can help to prompt noticing of language elements (here irregular noun plurals and verbs), and this can be maintained over a one week period. Further investigation of the potential for OLMs to prompt noticing in language learning is recommended.

References

1. Bull, S., Pain, H.: Did I Say What I Think I Said, And Do You Agree With Me?: Inspecting and Questioning the Student Model. In: Greer, J. (ed.) Proceedings of World Conference on Artificial Intelligence and Education, AACE, Charlottesville VA, pp. 501–508 (1995)
2. Bull, S., Quigley, S., Mabbott, A.: Computer-Based Formative Assessment to Promote Reflection and Learner Autonomy. Engineering Education: Journal of the Higher Education Academy Engineering Subject Centre 1(1), 8–18 (2006)
3. Dimitrova, V.: STyLE-OLM: Interactive Open Learner Modelling. International Journal of Artificial Intelligence in Education 13, 35–78 (2003)
4. Kay, J.: Learner Know Thyself: Student Models to Give Learner Control and Responsibility. In: Halim, Z., Ottomann, T., Razak, Z. (eds.) Proceedings of International Conference on Computers in Education, AACE, Charlottesville VA, pp. 17–24 (1997)
5. Mitrovic, A., Martin, B.: Evaluating the Effect of Open Student Models on Self-Assessment. International Journal of Artificial Intelligence in Education 17(2), 121–144 (2007)
6. Schmidt, R.: The Role of Consciousness in Second Language Learning. Applied Linguistics 11(2), 129–158 (1990)
7. Schmidt, R., Frota, S.: Developing Basic Conversational Ability in a Second Language, a Case Study of an Adult Learner of Portuguese. In: Day, R. (ed.) Talking to Learn: Conversation in Second Language Acquisition, Rowley MA, Newbury House, pp. 237–326 (1986)
8. Rutherford, W.E., Sharwood Smith, M.: Consciousness-Raising and Universal Grammar. Applied Linguistics 6(3), 274–282 (1985)
9. Svalberg, A.M.-L.: Language Awareness and Language Learning. Language Teaching 40, 287–308 (2007)
10. Chapelle, C.A.: Multimedia CALL: Lessons to be Learned from Research on Instructed SLA. Language Learning and Technology 2(1), 22–34 (1998)
11. Pica, T.: Methods of Morpheme Quantification: Their Effect on the Interpretation of Second Language Data. Studies in Second Language Acquisition 6(1), 69–78 (1983)
12. Mackey, A., Abbuhl, R.: Input and interaction. In: Sanz, C. (ed.) Mind and Context in Adult Second Language Acquisition: Methods, Theory and Practice, pp. 207–233. Georgetown University Press, Washington (2005)
13. Mabbott, A., Bull, S.: Alternative Views on Knowledge: Presentation of Open Learner Models. In: Lester, J.C., Vicari, R.M., Paraguacu, F. (eds.) Intelligent Tutoring Systems: 7th International Conference, pp. 689–698. Springer, Heidelberg (2004)
14. Zapata-Rivera, J.-D., Greer, J.: Interacting with Inspectable Bayesian Student Models. International Journal of Artificial Intelligence in Education 14(2), 127–163 (2004)
15. Truscott, J.: Noticing in Second Language Acquisition: A Critical Review. Second Language Research 14(2), 103–135 (1998)
16. Ellis, R.: Principles of Instructed Language Learning. Asian EFL Journal 7(3), 9–24 (2005)
17. Swan, M.: Legislation by Hypothesis: The Case of Task-Based Instruction. Applied Linguistics 26(3), 376–401 (2005)

Proactive Versus Multimodal Online Help: An Empirical Study

Jérôme Simonin and Noëlle Carbonell

LORIA, CNRS, INRIA, Nancy Université,
BP 239, F54506 Vandœuvre-lès-Nancy Cedex, France
{Jerome.Simonin,Noelle.Carbonell}@loria.fr

Abstract. Two groups of 8 participants experimented two enhancements of standard online help for the general public during one hour: adaptive proactive (AP) assistance and multimodal user support. Proactive help, that is, anticipation of the user's information needs raised very positive judgments, while dynamic adaptation to the user's current knowledge and skills went almost unnoticed. Speech and graphics (SG) messages were also well accepted, based on the observation that one can go on interacting with the software application while listening to instructions. However, several participants observed that the transience and linearity of speech limited the usability of this modality. Analysis of interaction logs and post-tests shows that procedural and semantic knowledge acquisition was higher with SG help than with AP assistance. Contrastingly, AP help was consulted more often than SG user support. Results also suggest that proactive online help may reduce the effectiveness of autonomous "learning by doing" acquisition of unfamiliar software concepts and procedures.

Keywords: Online help. Adaptive user interfaces. Proactive user support. Multimodal interaction. Speech and graphics help messages.

1 Context and Motivations

1.1 Context

The effectiveness of online help for the general public is still unsatisfactory despite continuous efforts from researchers and designers over the last twenty years. Help facilities are still ignored by most "lay users" who prefer consulting experienced users to browsing online manuals. This behavior is best accounted for by the "motivational paradox" [3], namely: users in the general public are reluctant to explore unfamiliar software and to learn how to use it efficiently as their main objective is to carry out the tasks they have in mind. The study presented here addresses the crucial issue of how to design online help that will *actually* be used by the general public, hence that will be truly effective.

To solve this issue, help systems should be capable of providing users with *appropriate* information *when* they need it [3]. To meet both requirements, these systems have to be aware of the user's current knowledge, skills, intent and activity; that is,

W. Nejdl et al. (Eds.): AH 2008, LNCS 5149, pp. 183–192, 2008.

they have to be capable of creating and updating an *adaptive* model of the current user's profile from interaction logs. Such a model is necessary for tailoring help information to the user's current knowledge, and for anticipating their information needs accurately in order to satisfy them through timely initiatives. This "push" strategy has the advantage to relieve users of requesting help information, thus alleviating their cognitive workload noticeably. We call it adaptive and *proactive* help (APH).

Using speech for conveying user support information may also contribute to increasing online help usage by significantly reducing the interference of help consultation in the user's current activity. Users have to stop interacting with the application in order to access standard help systems, and the visual information they obtain is usually superimposed on the current display. In contrast, oral messages do not use screen space. In addition, most users cannot read a message while simultaneously interacting with a graphical user interface; on the contrary, it is easy to go on interacting with a software application while listening to an oral information message, and to carry out a sequence of oral instructions while it is being delivered.

An attractive approach to achieve effective help in the sense mentioned above might be to combine multimodal (i.e., speech and graphics) presentations with dynamic adaptation of the system responses to the current user's profile as described above. However, this approach is not feasible. Text and graphics messages delivered to the user on the system initiative are likely to be well accepted because they can be looked at or ignored, while it is difficult, even impossible, to completely ignore oral messages. On the other hand, efficient speech and graphics help (SGH) messages are easy to design whereas the implementation of APH systems still raises many unsolved issues, such as, for instance: how to identify users' current intents and needs accurately from their interactions with unfamiliar software only?

The empirical study presented here contributes to assessing the respective advantages and limitations of APH versus SGH online help for the general public. It focuses on comparing the influence of these two enhancements on:

–   Help usage,
–   Learning of unfamiliar software operation, and
–   Users' subjective judgments.

1.2   Related Work

Adaptive online help has motivated large-scale research efforts, such as the Lumiere project [5] or the Berkeley Unix Consultant [14]. According to [4], [6] and [13], the bulk of research on adaptive human-computer interaction has been mainly focused on designing efficient user models. Contrastingly, empirical assessment of these models and evaluation of the effectiveness and usability of adaptive user interfaces, are research areas which need to be developed.

Evaluation of the ergonomic quality of speech as an output modality has motivated few studies compared to speech input. Recent research has been centered on ergonomic issues pertaining to the use of speech synthesis in specific contexts where displays are difficult to use; see, for instance, interaction with in-vehicle systems [15] and mobile devices [11], or speech synthesis for blind and sight impaired users [10, 9]. Speech synthesis intelligibility [1] and expressiveness (especially the use of prosody for conveying emotions [12]) have also motivated a number of evaluation studies.

In contrast, recent research on speech as an output modality for expressing help information has only been investigated by one research group, at least to our knowledge. Authors of [7] propose guidelines for the design and testing of help information presented via voice synthesis to users of current commercial computer applications; in [8], they describe how existing user assistance systems can be extended to incorporate an auditory interface and present an implementation of an oral assistance system.

2 Method

2.1 Overview

To assess the advantages and weaknesses of APH versus speech and graphics help (SGH), we observed the behaviors of two groups of participants who had to learn how to use the basic functionalities of an unfamiliar software application in a realistic context of use. One group benefited from AP help, and the other from SG user support.

We chose Flash, a software toolkit for creating graphical 2D animations, because computer-aided design of animations involves concepts which differ from those implemented in standard interactive software for the general public. Thus, participants in our study, who were unfamiliar with animation creation tools, had to acquire both semantic knowledge and procedural know-how in order to be able to complete simple animation creation tasks using Flash.

Each group of participants was gender-balanced and included 8 undergraduate students with ages ranging from 20 to 26 (23 on average) for the APH group, and from 18 to 21 (20 on average) for the SGH group. Participants had never used Flash or any other animation creation tool previously. Their computer experience was limited to Internet, games and application software for the general public (e.g., word processors and spreadsheets).

Once participants had filled in a background information questionnaire (10 min.), they got acquainted with Flash basic concepts (e.g., scenario, interpolation, etc.) using a short multimedia tutorial they could browse through as long as they wanted to (15-20 min.). Then, they created two animations (1 hour or so). When they were finished, they filled in two questionnaires, a verbal one and a non verbal one (Sam[1]). Both questionnaires were meant to elicit their subjective judgments on the help system (APH or SGH) they had had the opportunity to use. Next, their understanding and memorization of Flash basic concepts and operation were assessed using a written post-test. Finally, they participated in a debriefing interview. All-in, individual sessions lasted about 2 hours and a half.

2.2 Implementation of AP and SG Help

Adaptive Proactive Help
The display included two permanent windows (see figure 1): a sizeable Flash window and a small help window (on the right of the screen) meant to reduce interference

---

[1] Bradley, M.M., Lang, P.J.: Measuring emotion: the self-assessment manikin and the semantic differential. Journal of Behavioral Therapy and Experimental Psychiatry, 25: 49-59 (1994).

between help consulting and animation design activities. Based on earlier empirical work [2], participants could request four different types of help information using four dedicated buttons (see figure 1): procedural know-how (How?), semantic knowledge (What?), explanations of the application current state (Why?) and confirmation or invalidation of their recent actions on Flash (Confirm?).

Our objective being to assess the effectiveness of adaptive and proactive help rather than to evaluate a specific prototype, we used the Wizard of Oz technique to implement the APH system. To achieve adaptive user assistance, the Wizard was given the means to adapt the information content of help messages to the current participant's actual knowledge and skills as s/he perceived them through observing their interactions with Flash and with the help system. Three different versions were available to the Wizard for each message:

- An *initial version* including all the information needed by users unfamiliar with the topic of the message; the Wizard used it the first time s/he had to send the message to the current participant.
- Later, s/he had to choose between two other versions:
  - A *short reminder* of the information in the initial version, with or without additional technical details; s/he sent it to participants who had shown a good understanding of the information in the initial version through their subsequent interactions with Flash;
  - A *detailed presentation* of the information in the initial version, including explanations, examples and illustrations; s/he sent it to participants who had had difficulty in understanding and putting to use the information in the initial version.

Thus, when a message had to be sent to a participant, the Wizard just selected the version of the message that best matched this participant's current knowledge and skills, based on the observation of her/his interactions with Flash, and sent it to her/him. As participants' interactions with Flash and the simulated APH system lasted less than one hour, three versions of the same message were sufficient for achieving a realistic simulation of the behavior of a truly adaptive help system.

To implement proactive user support, the Wizard was instructed and trained to observe participants' interactions with Flash so as to be able to assist them in carrying out scenarios by anticipating their information needs and satisfying them on his own initiative using appropriate message versions.

Multimodal Help

The same help window was used for the SGH system. We just replaced textual information by buttons which activated speech messages (see figure 1); graphics and request buttons were unchanged. Initial versions of messages in the APH system (over 300 messages) were recorded by a female speaker who was instructed to sound friendly and vary her prosody according to the type of information that messages were meant to convey: instructions, warnings, examples or advice.

We used the same implementation of the Wizard of Oz technique for simulating the APH and SGH systems.

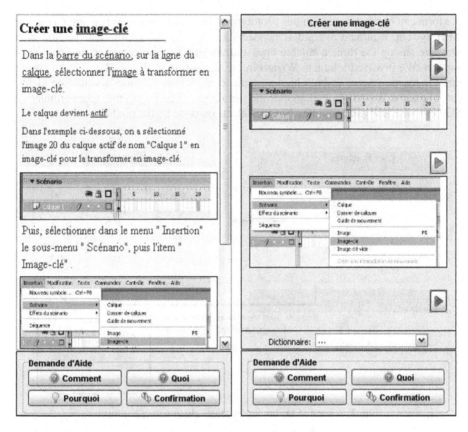

Fig. 1. The two help systems, APH on the left and SGH on the right. Answers to the same request, "How to create a key frame?", are displayed (initial message version for APH).

Software Assistance to the Wizard's Activity
To assist the Wizard in his/her task, we developed a client-server platform in Java (see figure 2) which can:

- Forward displays on the participant's screen to the Wizard,
- Display messages selected by her/him on the participant's screen, and
- Assist the Wizard in the simulation of the APH system by displaying, on selection of a message, a log (or history) of the various versions of this message received earlier by the current participant.

Messages, in the form of Web pages (one page per version for the APH system), are stored in a hierarchical database.

This software platform also records logs of participants' interactions with Flash (or any Windows software application) and either help system. Logs include user and system events, mouse positions and clicks, screen copies; they may also include speech, gaze and gestures from the user.

In addition, interpretation of the simple, unambiguous request language we designed is carried out by the platform. Each request is linked to a unique message, so that the platform can run as an autonomous prototype of the SGH system. When simulating the APH system, a human Wizard is needed for choosing the appropriate version of a message among the three available ones and, mostly, for implementing proactive user support. We involved a human Wizard in the simulation of the SGH system to ensure that the reaction times of both help systems to participants' requests would be identical. The same Wizard took charge of the simulation of both systems; when simulating SG help, s/he just validated message pre-selections done by the platform.

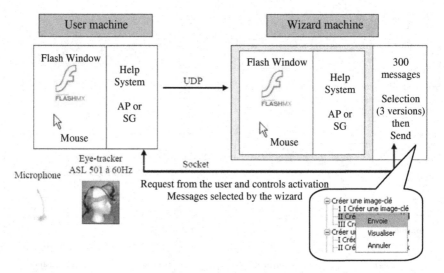

Fig. 2. Wizard of Oz implementation: client-server platform

2.3 Measures

Information in final questionnaires and debriefing interviews was analyzed to gain an insight into participants' subjective judgments on the help system (APH or SGH) they had experimented.

To assess the influence of APH and SGH help on performances and behaviors, we used post-test marks and manually annotated interaction logs. These data provided us with information on participants' assimilation of Flash concepts and operation, and enabled us to study participants' behaviors and activities, namely: help usage, task achievement, and exploration of Flash functionalities which denotes the use of an approach by trial and error.

Analysis of annotated logs was limited to the first scenario which lasted about 40 minutes on average, because participants seldom requested help or needed pro-active assistance during the second scenario which they completed in less than 20 minutes.

3   Results

We first present and discuss participants' subjective judgments. Then, we describe and interpret their activities and performances.

3.1 Participants' Preferences

6 participants out of 8 preferred the APH experimental system to standard online help, that is, help to the use of existing application software intended for the general public (help they were familiar with). Proactive user support raised enthusiastic comments while dynamic adaptation of message content went almost unnoticed. 6 participants rated the support provided by the APH system as very useful, and 7 judged its initiatives very effective. The 2 participants who preferred standard help to APH and SGH systems put forward the force of habit to explain their preference.

Similarly, 7 participants out of 8 globally preferred the SGH experimental system to standard online help. According to their non verbal judgments, these participants valued the substitution of speech for text in help messages. However, verbal comments were less positive. 5 participants only preferred audio to visual presentations of help information, based mainly on the argument that they could carry out instructions while listening to them. The 3 other participants preferred visual to audio presentations because taking in a spoken message is a more demanding cognitive task than assimilating the content of a textual message, due to the transience and linearity of speech. One can read displayed text at one's pace, and freely select or ignore parts of a textual message. Participants who used the SGH system could only replay oral messages from the start; they could not access or skip parts of a message, nor replay parts of it several times, nor modify the speech rate.

So, proactive online assistance is likely to arouse higher subjective satisfaction than speech and graphics help among novice users in the general public. Dynamic adaptation of message content may have gone unnoticed because it is a basic feature of human communication, especially tutor-novice dialogues; repetitions of identical messages might have been noticed and judged negatively. Further empirical research is needed to validate this interpretation.

Participants' rather balanced judgments on the usability of speech compared to text for expressing help information should not deter designers from considering speech as a promising alternative modality to text in help messages. Speech usability can easily be improved by implementing advanced audio browsing facilities. Taking up this research direction might prove to be more rewarding in the short term than implementing effective proactive help which at present represents a difficult scientific challenge. How to guess novice users' intents accurately from their sole actions on an unfamiliar software application, as these users tend to perform actions unrelated to, or even contrary to, the achievement of their goals? What is the highest prediction error rate they are likely to tolerate from the help system without getting confused or irritated to the point of switching it off?

3.2 Participants' Behaviors

Numbers of clicks in pre-defined areas on the display were used to study participants' activities. Distributions of actions were similar for the APH and SGH groups: 80% of participants' interactions involved Flash, 11% the help system (APH or SGH) and 9%

Windows. Exploration of Flash functionalities was marginal for both groups (less than 2.5% of actions), which suggests that approaches by trial and error were seldom resorted to. Participants in the APH group activated as many "How?"[2] requests as participants in the SGH group (58 versus 60) although the APH help system displayed 183 messages on its own initiative, most of them encapsulating instructional information. Numbers of "How?" requests varied from 4 to 15 in the APH group and from and 0 to 11 in the SGH group. These large inter-individual differences together with the small number of participants in each group explain why we did not carry out any statistical analysis on the data collected on participants' behaviors and their performances (see table 1 in the next paragraph).

These results suggest that pushing help information to novice users does not reduce rates of spontaneous requests for help. Proactive assistance appears as an efficient strategy for increasing the actual consultation and use of help information, as all participants in the APH group, according to their own comments, read most of the help messages displayed by the system on its own initiative.

3.3 Participants' Performances

Time spent on the first scenario greatly varied from one participant to another, ranging from 33 min. to 50 min. for the APH group, and from 33 min. to 47 min. for the SG group; the difference between averages per group is small (1 min. 45 sec.), hence not meaningful. Inaction rate measured by the percentage of time while the mouse was still is sensibly higher for the APH group than for the SGH group (62% versus 53%). This difference illustrates the efficiency of speech instructions compared to textual messages: one has to stop interacting with the application while reading a textual message as mentioned by participants in the SGH group.

Table 1. Task completion (1st scenario) and post-test evaluations: average marks per group

Participants	Task completion /20	Post-test /31
SGH group	12.6/20 (SD 3.4)	17.6/31 (SD2.8)
APH group	11.1/20 (SD 3.2)	15.6/31 (SD 5.2)

Evaluations of post-tests and task achievement (i.e., completion of the first scenario) are presented in table 1.

Data in the second column of table 1 suggest that SGH participants gained a better understanding of Flash specific concepts than APH participants and recollected how to operate its functions more accurately. This difference in knowledge and skill acquisition between the two groups may be explained as follows: efficient proactive help may have induced APH participants to put little effort into learning Flash concepts, and operation and to rely on help information to carry out scenarios successfully. However, further empirical data are needed to validate this hypothesis, as the number

---

[2] Other types of messages were scarcely used.

of participants is limited and the range of their individual performances is large (see SD ranges in table 1). In addition, the APH help system might prove more effective and efficient if used over a longer span of time; timely help information tailored to the user's current needs and knowledge and "pushed" to them may, in the long run, support learning of the operation of new software more effectively than standard online help. Empirical and/or experimental assessment of this assumption is a challenging open research issue.

As for task completion (1st column in table 1), the difference observed between the two groups is likely to have the same origins as the difference in inaction rates: APH participants had to interrupt interaction with Flash to read help messages while SGH participants could go on interacting with Flash while listening to them. These interruptions may have interfered with task achievement. This interpretation is a working hypothesis which deserves further empirical investigation.

4 Conclusion

We have reported an empirical Wizard of Oz study on the experimentation and evaluation, by two groups of 8 participants, of two enhancements of standard online help to the use of software intended for the general public: adaptive proactive assistance and multimodal user support. Proactive help to the use of an animation creation tool, Flash, raised very positive judgments while adaptation to the user's current knowledge and skills went almost unnoticed. Speech and graphics messages were also well accepted, based on the observation that one can go on interacting with a software application while listening to instructions. However, several participants observed that the transience and linearity of speech limited the usability of this modality. Procedural and semantic knowledge acquisition proved to be higher with the multimodal system than with the adaptive and proactive one. These results suggest that proactive (and, perhaps, adaptive) user support may reduce the effectiveness of "learning by doing" unfamiliar software concepts and operation. But, if used over a longer time span than the duration of participants' experimentation, adaptive and proactive help might improve conceptual and procedural knowledge acquisition since this strategy seems to be capable of increasing actual help usage.

Results of this comparative study open up several main research directions. First, further empirical research is needed to determine the exact influence of proactive help on conceptual and procedural knowledge acquisition. Secondly, online help interaction being inherently different from e-learning situations (see the motivational paradox in [3]), novice users' behaviors cannot be, a priori, assimilated to those of students whose main motivation is to acquire knowledge or skills. Therefore, research focused on the learning processes at work in this specific situation is essential. Finally, improving the usability of oral messages by remedying the intrinsic limitations of speech compared to text is another useful research direction. We are currently engaged in the first research direction.

References

1. Axmear, E., Reichle, J., Alamsaputra, M., Kohnert, K., Drager, K., Sellnow, K.: Synthesized Speech Intelligibility in Sentences: a Comparison of Monolingual English-Speaking and Bilingual Children. Language, Speech, and Hearing Services in Schools 36, 244–250 (2005)
2. Capobianco, A., Carbonell, N.: Contextual online help: elicitation of human experts' strategies. In: Proc. HCI International, vol. 2, pp. 824–828 (2001)
3. Carroll, J.M., Smith-Kerber, P.L., Ford, J.R., Mazur-Rimetz, S.A.: The minimal manual. Human-Computer Interaction 3(2), 123–153 (1987)
4. Chin, D.N.: Empirical Evaluation of User Models and User-Adapted Systems. User Modeling and User-Adapted Interaction 11, 181–194 (2001)
5. Horvitz, E., Breese, J., Heckerman, D., Hovel, D., Rommelse, K.: The Lumière Project: Bayesian User Modeling for Inferring the Goals and Needs of Software Users. In: Proc. UAI, pp. 256–265 (1998)
6. Jameson, A.: Adaptive Interfaces and Agents. In: Jacko, J., Sears, A. (eds.) Human-Computer Interaction Handbook, ch. 15, pp. 305–330. Erlbaum, Mahwah (2003)
7. Kehoe, A., Pitt, I.: Designing help topics for use with text-to-speech. In: Proc. DC 2006, pp. 157–163. ACM Press, New York (2006)
8. Kehoe, A., Neff, F., Pitt, I.: Extending traditional user assistance systems to support an auditory interface. In: 25th IASTED Int. Multi Conference: Artificial intelligence and applications, pp. 637–642. ACTA Press, Anaheim (2007)
9. Neo, S.-Y., Goh, H.-K., Yen-Ni Ng, W., Ong, J.-D., Pang, W.: Real-time Online Multimedia Content Processing: Mobile Video Optical Character Recognition and Speech Synthesizer for the Visually Impaired. In: Proc. Int. Conv. on Rehab. Eng. & Assist. Tech., pp. 201–206. ACM Press, New York (2007)
10. Ran, L., Helal, A., Moore, S.E., Ramachandran, B.: Drishti: An Integrated Indoor/Outdoor Blind Navigation System and Service. In: Proc. 2nd IEEEConference on Pervasive Computing and Communications (PERCOM 2004), pp. 23–30 (2004)
11. Roden, T.E., Parberry, I., Ducrest, D.: Toward mobile entertainment: A pardigm for narrative-based audio only games. Science of Computer Programming, Special Issue on Aspects of Game Programming 67(1), 76–90 (2007)
12. Ververidis, D., Kotropoulos, C.: Emotional speech recognition: Resources, features, and methods. Speech Communication 48(9), 1162–1181 (2006)
13. Weibelzahl, S., Weber, G.: Evaluating the Inference Mechanism of Adaptive Learning Systems. In: Brusilovsky, P., Corbett, A.T., de Rosis, F. (eds.) UM 2003. LNCS, vol. 2702, pp. 154–162. Springer, Heidelberg (2003)
14. Wilensky, R., Chin, D.N., Luria, M., Martin, J., Mayfield, J., Wu, D.: The Berkeley UNIX Consultant Project. Artificial Intelligence Review 14(1-2), 43–88 (2000)
15. Zajicek, M., Jonsson, I.-M.: Evaluation and context for in-car speech systems for older adults. In: Proc. ACM Latin American Conference on Human-Computer Interaction, pp. 31–39. ACM Press, New York (2005)

Re-assessing the Value of Adaptive Navigation Support in E-Learning Context

Sergey Sosnovsky, Peter Brusilovsky,
Danielle H. Lee, Vladimir Zadorozhny, and Xin Zhou

University of Pittsburgh, School of Information Sciences,
135 North Bellefield ave., Pittsburgh, PA, 15260, USA
{sas15,peterb,hyl12}@pitt.edu,
vladimir@sis.pitt.edu, reniorc@gmail.com
http://www.sis.pitt.edu/~paws/

Abstract. In a recent study, we discovered a new effect of adaptive navigation support in the context of E-learning: the ability to motivate students to work more with non-mandatory educational content. The results presented in this paper extend the limits of our earlier findings. We describe the implementation of adaptive navigation support for the SQL domain, and report the results of the classroom evaluation of our approach. Among other issues, we investigate whether the use in parallel of two different types of navigation support could change the nature or the magnitude of the previously observed effect. Our study confirms the motivational value of navigation support in the new domain. We observe the increase of this effect after adding the concept-based navigation layer to the existing topic-based adaptive navigation service. The results of the navigational pattern analysis allow us to determine the major source of this increase.

1 Introduction

Adaptive navigation support has emerged into a popular technology in modern e-learning. It is known to improve the learning outcome [1, 2], increase the speed of learning [3, 4], and encourage non-sequential navigation [5]. In our recent work, we discovered another effect of adaptive navigation support: an increase in the amount of students' work with non-mandatory educational content [6]. The magnitude of the observed effect was notably large – main usage parameters increased two to three times in the presence of navigation support. The effect also appeared to be stable: we were able to replicate it in three separate studies with two different systems – QuizGuide, which provided adaptive navigation support to a set of C programming quizzes, and NavEx, which offered adaptive navigation support for a repository of annotated C programming examples.

Our previous studies reported in [6] left several questions unaddressed. First, QuizGuide and NavEx implemented two different adaptation mechanisms. QuizGuide offered topic-based navigation support relying on a coarse-grained topic-level student model. NavEx implemented concept-based navigation support that employed a more

W. Nejdl et al. (Eds.): AH 2008, LNCS 5149, pp. 193–203, 2008.

traditional and finer-grained concept-level model. While both types of navigation support led to statistically significant increase of user activity, we never applied them at the same time. As a result, it was not clear whether we were observing the same effect caused by two slightly different technologies or two complementary effects, which could potentially magnify the value of each other. Second, while we explored the motivational value of adaptive navigation support in two different systems, both systems were developed for the same domain (C programming) and both operated on relatively simple content – quiz questions and examples, both requiring relatively low processing efforts from a student.

The work presented in this paper attempts to address both limitations of our earlier studies. We explored the value of adaptive navigation support in a different domain (SQL) and with more advanced educational content: SQL problems that require a student to write fragments of SQL code as a solution. We also investigated whether the simultaneous use of both types of navigation support in parallel could change the nature or the magnitude of the previously observed effect.

The following two sections briefly describe the details of SQL problems offered to students, and the new implementation of the QuizGuide adaptive hypermedia service. The evaluation part of the paper is divided into two sections: Section 4 analyses the differences between adaptive and non-adaptive access to the SQL problems and reports the results agreeing with the previous findings [6]; Section 5 compares two approaches of adaptive navigation support implemented in QuizGuide and investigates the added value of concept-based adaptation. Section 6 concludes the paper with final remarks and discussion.

2 SQL Knowledge Tester

SQL-KnoT (SQL Knowledge Tester) is a system performing generation, delivery, and assessment of online problems for testing and training on a basic subset of SQL concepts. Every problem in SQL-KnoT asks a student to write a query for a set of sample databases and a desired output. The system evaluates student answers on-the-fly and generates feedback indicating whether the answer is correct or not. For a number of recognized errors, SQL-KnoT also provides students with corrective messages. An important feature of SQL-KnoT is the dynamic generation of typical problems based on the collection of pre-defined templates. As a result, when a student repeats a problem accessed before, the problem definition, the original databases and, consequently, the answer to the problem will be different. This allows students to master a certain skill through the sequence of typical exercises. Students can access SQL-KnoT problems with and without adaptive navigation support. Fig. 1 demonstrates the non-adaptive access to SQL-KnoT problems served by the KnowledgeTree learning portal. The left frame of the portal allows students to browse SQL-KnoT problems (and other types of learning activities) by lecture. The right (content) frame presents the selected problem to a student. Every SQL-KnoT template is associated with a topic and a set of concepts, thus providing the basis for evaluating the student's knowledge and adapting to it. The adaptive navigation for the problems is provided by QuizGuide service. The next section describes the implementation of adaptive access to SQL-KnoT problems and compares two versions of the QuizGuide interface employed for this study.

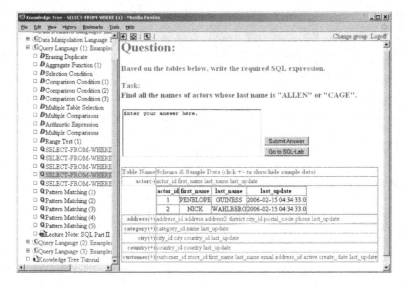

Fig. 1. Non-adaptive access to SQL-KnoT problems on the learning portal

3 Topic-Based and Concept-Based Adaptation in QuizGuide

QuizGuide is an adaptive hypermedia service providing students with individualized access to online educational content. It implements the principles of open learner modeling by showing a student the content of her/his user model in the form of navigational cues. QuizGuide groups learning resources into coarse-grained topics and annotates the topic links with adaptive icons. The new system prototype described in this paper implements two kinds of adaptive navigation support for the same set of SQL-KnoT problems. Fig. 2a shows a sample problem accessed with the pure topic-based version of QuizGuide. The list of topics in the left frame is annotated with "target-arrow" icons, where the number of arrows reflects the current level of knowledge of the topic, and the color of the target indicates the relevance of a topic to the current learning goal of the class. Fig. 3 provides the detailed explanation of QuizGuide topic-based annotations.

To explore the value of combined navigation support, we have implemented another version of the system with the added layer of concept-based annotations (see Fig. 2b). In this version, every problem icon represents the cumulative level of knowledge a student has demonstrated for the set of concepts underlying the problem. Concepts are much smaller knowledge elements than topics; a problem is usually indexed by multiple concepts. A concept itself can relate to several problems where it plays one of two roles: outcome or prerequisite. Concepts first introduced by the problem are called the outcomes of the problem. Concepts used in the problem, but introduced earlier in the course are the problem's prerequisites. The order of problems and the set of prerequisite-outcome relations are defined by the order of course lectures and problem-lecture associations. As in the topic-based version of the interface, problems answered correctly receive a checkmark.

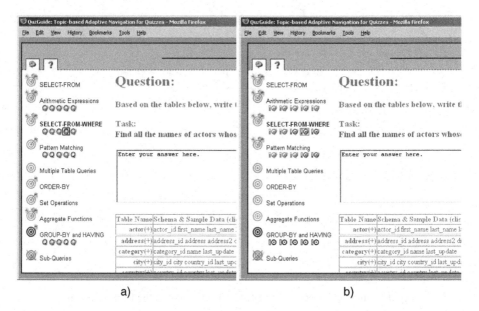

a)   b)

Fig. 2. Adaptive navigation for SQL-KnoT problems provided by QuizGuide: a) Topic-based;
b) Topic-based combined with concept-based

Fig. 3 summarizes all annotations used in both versions of QuizGuide interface. Large "target-arrow" icons (Fig. 3a) annotating topics are used in both versions; however, on the problem level the interfaces differ. The only navigation support provided by the pure topic-based QuizGuide is a checkmark denoting a problem solved correctly at least once (Fig. 3b). The interface combining topic-based and concept-based adaptation annotates problems using small targets with vertical progress bars (Fig. 3c). The progress of a student for the concepts underlying the problem is double-coded: as the knowledge level grows, the icon fades and the bar level rises. By means of this abstraction, QuizGuide tries to deliver to a student two kinds of information: where the progress has been made (higher bar level) and where the attention should be focused (brighter target color). To help a student understand the meaning of annotations, QuizGuide dynamically generates mouse-over hints for all icons. The detailed help explaining all interface elements is available as well.

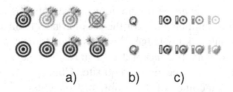

a)   b)   c)

Fig. 3. QuizGuide annotations: a) Topic-based: upper row – levels of topic relevance to the current learning goal (current goal, prerequisite for the current goal, passed goal, future goal); lower row – knowledge levels for the topic (from 0 to 3); b) Problem progress (done / not done); c) Concept-based (four knowledge levels combined with problem progress)

One of the challenges in developing the new interface of QuizGuide was the implementation of immediate feedback. To update the navigation state reflecting recent activity, the previous version of the system needed a user to click the reload icon. Practical evaluation showed that this feature was often neglected by students. It was not critical for the topic-based navigation as the topic knowledge levels grow relatively slowly. However, introduction of the concept-based annotation has demanded higher level of interactivity, as a single correct answer can change the annotations for several problems sharing the same outcome concepts. Therefore, for both versions of the QuizGuide interface we have implemented an AJAX-based component updating all relevant icons after each answer. This update increases the transparency and predictability of the system interface; a student can immediately observe the results of the correct answer to a problem and make an appropriate decision for the next step.

4 Confirming the Value of Adaptive Navigation Support

We evaluated QuizGuide in two classroom studies in the Fall, 2007. The system was used as a learning tool in one graduate and one undergraduate database class (38 and 36 students correspondingly) taught by the same instructor. Each version of the system provided access to 46 SQL-KnoT problem templates. Each template was accessible in both ways – through QuizGuide (adaptive mode) and though the learning portal (non-adaptive mode). Within QuizGuide, templates were grouped into 10 topics (Fig. 2). Within the course portal, they were placed in the corresponding lecture folder (Fig. 1). All user interactions with the systems were logged. For every problem-solving attempt, the associated log record contained template ID, time of the attempt, access point (QuizGuide or portal), and the attempt result (success or failure).

To investigate the value of adaptive navigation support, we looked at such usage parameters as the number of attempts, the number of distinct problems attempted, the number of topics for which at least one problem has been attempted, the number of sessions and the average session length. Totally, 19 graduate students and 26 undergraduate students have attempted at least one problem over the semester. Overall, students attempted 4081 problems in QuizGuide and 1218 problems in non-adaptive mode. Because the system was introduced to the graduate students later in the course, the total number of attempts made by the undergraduate students was larger. Nevertheless, the observed difference was stable for both courses – adaptive access to the problems dominated non-adaptive.

The results of the evaluation confirmed our hypothesis. The students were much more willing to access problems in the adaptive mode (through QuizGuide), and the use of the adaptive mode caused them to work more. The magnitude of the effect was comparable to the earlier study [6]. On average, students from both courses made about three times more attempts in the adaptive mode than they did in the non-adaptive. They also accessed twice as many distinct problems and explored almost twice as many topics while receiving adaptive navigation support from QuizGuide. The difference in the amount of work might be caused by more frequent access (greater number of sessions) and/or by longer sessions. For both these parameters we observed significantly higher values in adaptive mode than in non-adaptive. This as well agrees to our previous findings (see [6]), that in the presence of adaptive navigation support not only students access the system more often, but they also stay with the system longer and do more work per session: i.e., the use of the system becomes "addictive." Table 1 summarizes the results of statistical tests comparing major usage characteristics between adaptive and non-adaptive modes. Wilcoxon Matched-Pairs Signed-Rank Test was used in the analysis, since the assumptions of the parametric statistics were violated.

Table 1. Comparison of Cumulative Usage Parameters for Adaptive and Non-adaptive

	Adaptive	Non-Adaptive	p-value
Number of Attempts	90.69	27.07	0.005
Number of Attempted Problems	23.11	10.80	0.019
Number of Attempted Topics	5.56	3.31	0.016
Number of Sessions	3.27	2.09	0.047
Average Session Length	21.99	10.62	0.021

5   The Added Value of Concept-Based Adaptation

To investigate the difference between the two versions of QuizGuide interface and determine the added value of the concept-based navigation, we divided students from both courses into two groups. Over the semester, the experimental group used the combined version of the system (Fig. 2b), while the control group had access to the pure topic-based interface (Fig. 2a). The non-adaptive access to the same set of SQL-KnoT problems, as well as all other course tools, was equally available for both groups. The groups were balanced with respect to the gender and pre-test scores. After filtering out outliers, the experimental group contained 13 students (7 undergraduate and 6 graduate), and the control group consisted of 15 students (8 undergraduate and 7 graduate).

5.1   Evaluation of Student Motivation and Persistence

The analysis of main usage parameters, which could indicate further increase in user motivation with the introduction of an additional layer of navigation support (such as the number of attempts, the number of sessions, and the session length), did not show stable significant results [1]. However, the comparison of the average number of attempts per problem for both courses demonstrated statistically significant difference. The assumptions of parametric statistics were; therefore, we used the non-parametric Mann-Whitney test. The results of the test indicated that students using the concept-based interface on average made significantly more attempts per problem ($M=3.36$, $SD=2.66$) than those using the topic-based interface ($M=1.68$, $SD=0.42$), *Mann-Whitney U statistics=51.0, p=0.033.*

---

[1] While in the undergraduate course the usage parameters where significantly higher for the experimental group than for the control group, the effects did not hold for the graduate course.

Such an increase in problem persistence led to another statistically significant effect. The comparison of student knowledge levels taken from their user models at the end of the semester showed that the students from the concept-based group achieved higher knowledge levels (*M=0.45, SD=0.09*) than the students from the topic-based group (*M=0.39, SD=0.03*), *t(26) = 2.71, p=0.023.*

The comparison of students' activity has also shown that, on average, students from the experimental group used the system more consistently over the semester. Similar to what we observed in [6], students have been employing QuizGuide in two main learning scenarios: for routine self-assessment throughout the semester and as a preparation tool for the final exam. Consequently, we could identify two corresponding clusters of transactions, stable across all groups. The comparison of the ratios of transactions that belong to a particular cluster showed, that students from the concept-based groups worked more over the semester than those from the topic-based group (79.35% of all transactions compared to 66.04%). The examination of these clusters demonstrated considerable differences in students' work with the system in terms of exploring system content, reacting to the its feedback, and following its navigational cues.

The next section analyzes the low-level navigational patterns followed by the students in QuizGuide and reports on important differences in the distribution of these patterns between the experimental and the control group.

5.2 Navigational Pattern Analysis

To obtain a deeper understanding of how students of two groups work with QuizGuide and respond to adaptive guidance, we performed detailed evaluation of student sessions. As a result, we could identify eight basic patterns of navigation: four problem-based patterns characterizing the transition of a student from one problem to another, three topic-based patterns reflecting the moves between topics and one combined pattern.

The problem-based patterns define student's navigational behavior within a topic. Transitions between problems in such situation are largely determined by the adaptive guidance provided on the level of problem icons and the feedback generated by SQL-Knot. The problem-based patterns can be subcategorized into the following:

- *Sequential*: a student moves from one problem to another in the order they are placed inside the topic;
- *Repetition*: a student attempts the same problem again immediately after the previous attempt;
- *Go-Back*: a student decides to return to one of the previous problems in the same topic;
- *Skipping*: a student skips one or several problems by moving to the next problem within the same topic.

The topic-based patterns can be explained by the reaction of a student on the adaptive topic icons. Whenever a student decides to switch a topic, s/he can observe the current state of topic-based annotations and use it as a hint for choosing the most appropriate set of problems to work on. To differentiate the topic-based navigational decisions from the problem-based ones we identified following three patterns:

- *Next-Topic*: a student moves to the first problem of the topic next in the list;
- *Jump-Forward*: a student moves to the first problem of a topic, which is more than 1 step later in the list;
- *Jump-Backward*: a student moves to the first problem of a topic earlier in the list.

Sometimes, when moving to a different topic, a student might decide to skip the rest of the problems of the previous topic and/or start the new topic not from the first problem. In these situations the student's behavior is influenced by both: the topic icons on the top level and the problem icons within a topic. We considered such cases as combined patterns consisting of the corresponding topic-based pattern and one or two problem-based *Skipping* patterns (two *Skipping* patterns are registered if a student skips both the end of the previous topic and the beginning of the new one).

Fig. 4 represents all patterns in a graphical form.

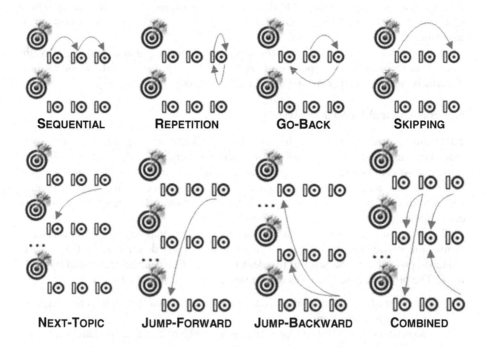

Fig. 4. Observed navigational patterns: upper row shows problem-based patterns; lower row shows three topic-based patters and the combined pattern

One of the goals of adaptive navigation support is to promote the non-sequential navigation and guide students in the most effective way to the relevant content. The analysis of the topic-based pattern distribution showed that on the level of topics both versions of QuizGuide encouraged students to choose topics in non-linear order: the combined ratio of the non-sequential patterns (*Jump-Forward* and *Jump-Backward*) varies from 65-70% for undergraduate students to 30-35% for graduate students. However, the evaluation of QuizGuide problem-based patterns showed that most of them are dominated by the sequential problem access. The ratios of such patterns as *Go-Back*, *Skipping* did not exceed 20% for any of the group. The presence of the concept-based adaptation did not have any significant effect on the occurrence of these patterns.

However, for the second most popular pattern – *Repetition* – the presence of the concept-based annotations had a dramatic effect. Generally, *Repetition* has two major sources depending on the result of the user's previous attempt:

- *Repetition$_0$*: when the previous answer is incorrect, a student is likely to retake the same problem to remedy the error, try a different answer and, finally, get a checkmark for the problem;
- *Repetition$_1$*: when the previous answer is correct, but the student still decides to solve the problem again.

While the *Repetition$_0$* portion is stable across all the groups, introduction of concept-based annotations increased the overall ratio of *Repetition$_1$* from 1.78% to 17.51% for the undergraduate students and from 2.51% to 17.92% in the graduate course. Hence, the adaptive concept-based problem icons caused students to repeat the same problem again and again even after the problem had been solved correctly. The presence of a checkmark in both version of the system ensured that the students were aware of the problem status, which singled out as the most probable reason for such behavior that the students were trying to earn a greater level icon for the problem. This observation explains two significant effects reported in the previous section:

- The average number of attempts per problem was greater for the experimental group, because students repeated the same problem more often in the presence of concept-based adaptive navigation support on the problem level;
- The resulting knowledge levels were greater for the experimental group, because students gave more correct answers to the same problems in order to receive an icon of the higher level corresponding to the higher level of knowledge;

This result also confirms the motivational value of adaptive annotation on the concept-based level. The students once again became "addicted" to the adaptive icons – they continued drilling in the same problem in order to achieve the maximum possible level of annotation.

The observed effect has both positive and negative outcomes. From one point of view, students follow the adaptive navigational cues, become involved and motivated by the system, which causes them work more and in a meaningful way. However, on the other hand, repeating the same problem multiple times after the problem is solved correctly is a suboptimal usage pattern. The goal of the concept-based navigation in QuizGuide is to help students shift focus from the problems that have been solved to those that have not been answered correctly yet. Drilling in the same material to obtain the maximum possible level of annotation and neglecting the rest of the problems is not the desired learning strategy.

6   Discussion

This paper reports two major experimental results:

- We could confirm our previous finding on the motivational effect of adaptive navigation support in a new domain with a new type of interactive content;
- We observed a further increase of this effect as the concept-based navigation support was added to the existing topic-based interface of QuizGuide system.

The detailed analysis of student sessions determines that the main pattern underlying the added-value of the concept-based adaptive navigation is a suboptimal drilling pattern. There are several possible remedies for this problem:

- Reducing the adaptive navigation support to the topic-based level (in this case the students will not become too "addicted" to the problem links and will be choosing the appropriate problem within a topic independently);
- A more accurate concept-based adaptation granting students the maximum levels of annotations without unnecessary repetitions (this will require much finer adjustment of the modeling formula as well additional analysis of conceptual models of the problem);
- Combination of the pure glass box approach [7] (implemented currently in QuizGuide) with the direct guidance (this would allow to break undesirable patterns when a better navigational option is available).

We plan to further investigate this issue and compare several possible strategies. The final goal of this study is the interface design for an E-Learning hypermedia service inheriting the addictive nature of adaptive navigation support and maximally promoting the non-sequential navigation within the limits of in-class usage.

Acknowledgements

This material is based upon work supported by the National Science Foundation under Grant No. DUE-0633494.

References

1. Kavcic, A.: Fuzzy user modeling for adaptation in educational hypermedia. IEEE Transactions on Systems, Man, and Cybernetics 34(4), 439–449 (2004)
2. Triantafillou, E., Pomportis, A., Demetriadis, S., Georgiadou, E.: The value of adaptivity based on cognitive style: an empirical study. British Journal of Educational Technology 35(1), 95–106 (2004)
3. Brusilovsky, P., Pesin, L.: An intelligent learning environment for CDS/ISIS users. In: Levonen, J.J., Tukianinen, M.T. (eds.) The interdisciplinary workshop on complex learning in computer environments (CLCE 1994), pp. 29–33. EIC, Joensuu, Finland (1994)
4. Davidovic, A., Warren, J., Trichina, E.: Learning benefits of structural example-based adaptive tutoring systems. IEEE Transactions on Education 46(2), 241–251 (2003)

5. Brusilovsky, P., Eklund, J.: A study of user-model based link annotation in educational hypermedia. Journal of Universal Computer Science 4(4), 429–448 (1998)
6. Brusilovsky, P., Sosnovsky, S., Yudelson, M.: Addictive links: the motivational value of adaptive link annotation in educational hypermedia. In: Wade, V.P., Ashman, H., Smyth, B. (eds.) AH 2006. LNCS, vol. 4018, pp. 51–60. Springer, Heidelberg (2006)
7. Höök, K., Karlgren, J., Wærn, A., Dahlbäck, N., Jansson, C.G., Karlgren, K., Lemaire, B.: A glass box approach to adaptive hypermedia. User Modeling and User-Adapted Interaction 6(2-3), 157–184 (1996)

The Effectiveness of Personalized Movie Explanations:
An Experiment Using Commercial Meta-data

Nava Tintarev and Judith Masthoff

University of Aberdeen,
Aberdeen, U.K.

Abstract. This paper studies the properties of a helpful and trustworthy explanation in a movie recommender system. It discusses the results of an experiment based on a natural language explanation prototype. The explanations were varied according to three factors: degree of personalization, polarity and expression of unknown movie features. Personalized explanations were not found to be significantly more Effective than non-personalized, or baseline explanations. Rather, explanations in all three conditions performed surprisingly well. We also found that participants evaluated the explanations themselves most highly in the personalized, feature-based condition.

1 Introduction

Recommender systems represent user preferences for the purpose of suggesting items to purchase or examine, i.e. recommendations. Our work focuses on explanations of recommended items [1,2,3], explaining how a user might relate to an item unknown to them. More concretely, we investigate explanations in the movie domain with the aim of helping users make qualified decisions, i.e. Effective explanations. An explanation may be formulated along the lines of *"You might (not) like Item A because..."*. The justification following may depend on the underlying recommendation algorithm (e.g. content-based, collaborative-based), but could also be independent. Our approach is algorithm independent, as it aims to explain a randomly selected item rather than the recommendation. In this way we implicitly differentiate between explaining the way the recommendation engine works (Transparency), and explaining why the user may or may not want to try an item (Effectiveness). In addition, since items are selected randomly the explanation can vary in polarity: being positive, neutral or negative.

The experiment described in this paper measures how different explanations affect the likelihood of trying an item (Persuasion) versus making informed decisions (Effectiveness) and inspiring user trust (Trust). We investigate the effects different types of explanations have on these three explanation aims.

As in a study by Bilgic and Mooney [1], we define an Effective explanation as one which helps the user make a correct estimate of their valuation of an item. Persuasion only reflects a user's initial rating of item, but not their final rating

W. Nejdl et al. (Eds.): AH 2008, LNCS 5149, pp. 204–213, 2008.
© Springer-Verlag Berlin Heidelberg 2008

after trying it. While the user might initially be satisfied or dissatisfied, their opinion may change after exposure. As in [1], Effectiveness can be measured by (1) the user rating the item on the basis of the explanation, (2) the user trying the item, (3) the user re-rating the item. While it would be preferable if users could actually try the item, in an experimental setting step 2 may be approximated by e.g. allowing users to read item reviews written by other users. The metric suggested by [1] is optimized when the mean difference between the two ratings (step 1 - step 3) is close to zero, has a low standard deviation, and there is a strong positive correlation between the two ratings. If an explanation helps users make good decisions, getting more (accurate and balanced) information or trying the item should not change their valuation of the item greatly.

Although [1] did not explicitly consider the direction of skew, the difference between the two ratings may be either positive (over-estimation of the item) or negative (under-estimation). Over-estimation may result in false positives; users trying items they do not end up liking. Particularly in a high investment recommendation domain such as real-estate, a false positive is likely to result in a large blow to trust in the system. Under-estimation may on the other hand lead to false negatives; users missing items they might have appreciated. If a user recognizes an under-estimation due to previous knowledge or subsequent exposure, this may lead to a loss of trust as well. Likewise, an under-estimation may needlessly decrease an e-commerce site's revenue.

2   Factors That May Impact Explanation Effectiveness

2.1   Features and Personalization

Users like to know what it is about a particular item that makes it worthy (or not) of recommendation. Bilgic and Mooney [1] did not find a significant result for Effectiveness for an 'Influence based explanation' which listed other books previously rated highly by the user as influential for the recommendation. Other work surveying a similar type of interface suggests that users would like to know the explicit relationship between a recommended item and similar items used to form the recommendation [4]. An explanation based on item features may be one way to do this, e.g. "You have rated books with the *same author* highly in the past."

Using item features also makes it possible to personalize explanations, as different users may place different importance on different feature, and have individual tastes with regard to these features (i.e. not everyone has the same favorite actor). The seminal study by Herlocker et al. [2] on explanation interfaces shows a strong *persuasive* effect for an explanation interface referring to a particular movie feature, namely "favorite actor or actress". This feature (favorite actor/actress) may be more important to some users than others since a high variance in acceptance for this type of explanation was found. Qualitative feedback from focus groups also shows that users vary with regard to which movie features they find important[5,6].

If it is the case that some features are more important for particular users, it would seem plausible that explanations that tailor which features to describe would be more Persuasive and Effective than explanations with randomly selected features, and non-feature based explanations. In the real-estate domain Carenini and Moore have shown that user-tailored evaluative arguments (such as *"the house has a good location"* for a user who cares about location) increase users' likelihood to adopt a particular house compared to non-tailored arguments [7].

While similar, our work differs from the studies in [7] and [2], which primarily considered the *Persuasive* power of arguments and explanations, but did not study Effectiveness. Arguably [7] varied the polarity of the evaluative arguments, but given the domain (real-estate) it was difficult for them to consider the final valuation of the items. Our aim is therefore to consider how user-tailoring of item features can affect explanation Effectiveness, Persuasion as well as Trust.

2.2   Polarity

An explanation may contain both positive and negative information, and in that sense may have a polarity in a similar way as a numerical rating of an item. [8] showed that manipulating a rating prediction can alter the user valuation of a movie, causing either an over- or underestimation. Modifying the polarity of an explanation is likely to lead to a similar skew in Effectiveness. In the study by Herlocker et al [2] participants were most likely to see a movie if they saw an explanation interface consisting of a barchart of how similar users had rated the item. This bar chart had one bar for "good", a second for "ok" and a third for "bad" ratings. A weakness of this result is a bias toward positive ratings in the used dataset[1]. Bilgic and Mooney [1] later showed that using this type of histogram causes users to overestimate their valuation of the items (books).

We have analyzed online movie reviews mined from the Amazon website, to see if we could distinguish the properties of reviews that are considered helpful [6]. We found that users were more prone to write positive reviews and that negative reviews were considered significantly less helpful by other users than positive ones. Similar correlations between item rating and review helpfulness were found in other domains such as digital cameras and mobile phones [9]. All of this makes us consider whether negative explanations are likely to be found less helpful by users, or may instead help mitigate users' overly optimistic beliefs about items.

2.3   Certainty

The Herlocker et al study [2] considered an interface which looked at recommendation confidence, which portrays to which degree the system has sufficient information to make a strong recommendation. Their study did not find that confidence displays had a significant effect on how likely a participant was to see a movie. McNee et al [10] also studied the effect of confidence displays on user acceptance. They found that users that were already familiar with their

---

[1] MovieLens - http://www.grouplens.org/node/12#attachments

recommender system (MovieLens) were less satisfied with the system overall after being exposed to confidence displays. On the other hand, more experienced users also found the confidence display more valuable than new users.

As part of a larger study comparing different types of explanation interfaces we held three focus groups (comprising of 23 participants) discussing the confidence display used in [2]. We found that many participants found information about confidence displays confusing. They did not understand what to do with the confidence rating or felt that the system should not make predictions if it was not confident. This raised the question of how lack of confidence would affect explanation Effectiveness, Persuasion as well as Trust. In particular, we were curious how users would react to missing information. In real data-sets as our data retrieved from Amazon's e-Commerce Service (ECS), detailed feature meta-data is sometimes missing. Is it better to refrain from presenting these items to users altogether, to talk about another feature which might not be as important to the user, or candidly state that the system is missing certain information?

2.4   Other Factors

Effectiveness of explanations can also be affected by a number of other factors. If the quality of the information used to form the recommendation or recommendation accuracy are compromised this is likely to lead to poor Effectiveness. Likewise, the nature of the recommended object and presentation of the recommended items are likely to be contributing factors. While these are highly relevant topics, they will not be discussed further in this paper. We conduct a study where no recommendation engine is used, in a single domain (movies), with all items presented in the same manner (one stand-alone item).

3   Experiment

This experiment is based on a prototype system which dynamically generates natural language explanations[2] for movie items based on meta-data retrieved from Amazon (ECS)[3]. The aim of this experiment was to see if using movie features (e.g. lead actors/actresses), and personalization could affect the Effectiveness of explanations. We studied if explanation polarity, and clearly stating that some information is missing could affect Effectiveness. We also wanted to know whether the effect was the same for Persuasion. When we help users make decisions that are good for them (Effectiveness), will they end up buying/trying fewer items (Persuasion)? Likewise, we are interested in the effects these factors have on user Trust.

---

[2] Realized with simpleNLG, a simple and flexible natural language generation system created by Ehud Reiter. See also http://www.csd.abdn.ac.uk/~ ereiter/simplenlg

[3] The used meta-data considers the finding of focus groups and analysis of online movie reviews [5,11,6] as well as which features are readily available via Amazon's ECS e.g. actors, directors, genre, average rating, and certification (e.g. rated PG).

3.1   Design

First, participants entered their movie preferences: which genres they were in the mood for, which they would not like to see, how important they found movie features (elicited in previous studies [6]), and their favourite actors/directors. The user model in our prototype can weigh the movies' features, according to feature utility as well as the participant's genre preferences.

Fifty-nine movies were pre-selected as potential recommendations to participants. Thirty are present in the top 100 list in the Internet Movie Database (IMDB[4]) and the other twenty-nine were selected at random, but all were present in both the MovieLens 100.000 ratings dataset[5] and Amazon.com.

Each participant evaluated *ten* recommendations and explanations for movies selected at random from the pre-selected set. Note that the explanations tell the user what they might think about the item, rather than how the item was selected. Moreover, these explanations differ from explanations of recommendations as they may be negative, positive, or neutral, as the movies shown to the user are selected at random. Since we did not want the users to have any pre-existing knowledge of the movies they rated, we prompted them to request a new recommendation and explanation if they felt they might have seen the movie. Next, we followed the experimental design of [1] for each movie:

1. Participants were shown the title and cover image of the movie and explanation, and answered the following questions:
   - *How much do you think you would like this movie?*
   - *How good do you think the explanation is?*
2. Participants read movie reviews on Amazon.com, care was taken to differentiate between our explanation facility and Amazon.
3. They re-rated the movie, the explanation and their trust of our system: *"Given everything you've seen **so far** how much do you now trust the explanation facility in this system?"*

On all questions, participants selected a value on a Likert scale from 1 (bad) to 7 (good), or opted out by saying they had "no opinion". They could give qualitative comments to justify their response. In a between subjects design, participants were assigned to one of three degrees of personalization:

1. **Baseline:** The explanation is neither personalized, nor describes item features. This is a generic explanation that could apply to anyone, e.g. *"This movie is one of the top 100 movies in the Internet Movie Database (IMDB)."* or *"This movie is not one of the top 100 movies in the Internet Movie Database (IMDB)."* No additional information is supplied about the movie.
2. **Random choice, feature based:** The explanation describes item features, but the movie feature is selected at random, e.g. *"This movie belongs to your preferred genre(s): Action & Adventure. On average other users rated this movie 4/5.0"*. The feature 'average rating' may not be particularly important to the user.

---

[4] http://www.imdb.com
[5] http://www.grouplens.org/node/12#attachments

3. **Personalize choice, feature based:** The explanation describes the item feature that is most important to the participant, e.g. *"Although this movie does not belong to any of your preferred genre(s), it belongs to the genre(s): Documentary. This movie stars Liam Neeson your favorite actor(s)"*. For this user, the most important feature is leading actors.

Our previous findings [11,6] suggest that genre information is important to most if not all users, so both the second and third condition contain a sentence regarding the movie genre in a personalized way. This sentence notes that the movie belongs to some of the user's disliked genres (negative polarity), preferred genres (positive polarity), or lists the genres it belongs to though they are neither disliked nor preferred (neutral polarity). In negative explanations, the movie belongs to a genre the user dislikes. We do not explicitly state what the user may think of the item, e.g. "You might like/dislike this movie" as this is likely to bias their rating. Also, there are times when Amazon is missing information. An example explanation for a negative explanation with unknown information is: *"Unfortunately this movie belongs to at least one genre you do not want to see: Horror. Director information is unknown."*. Seventeen movies lack director information and their explanations explicitly state that this is missing.

Also, a movie may star one of the user's favorite actors or director in which case this will also be mentioned as a *"favorite"*, e.g. "This movie starts Ben Kingsley, Ralph Fiennes and Liam Neeson your *favorite* actor(s)."

Fifty-one students and university staff participated in the experiment. Of these, five were removed based on users' comments suggesting that they had either rated movies for which they had a pre-existing opinion, or Amazon's reviews instead of our explanations. Of the remaining, 25 were male, 21 female and the average age was 26.5. Participants were roughly equally distributed among the three conditions (14, 17 and 15 respectively).

We hypothesize that personalized feature based explanations will be more Effective than random choice feature based explanations and the baseline explanations.

3.2   Results and Discussion

Table 1 summarizes the means of all the recorded values.

Table 1. Means (and StDev) of user ratings and percentage "no opinions". First ratings are given after viewing the explanation, second ratings after viewing the Amazon reviews.

Condition	Movie rating1	Movie rating2	Explanation rating1	Explanation rating2	Trust
Baseline	3.45 (1.26) 8.8%	4.11 (1.85) 0%	2.38 (1.54) 2.2%	2.85 (1.85) 0%	2.69 (1.94) 0.7%
Random choice	3.85 (1.87) 7.2%	4.43 (2.02) 3.6%	2.50 (1.62) 3.0%	2.66 (1.89) 3.0%	2.56 (1.74) 3.6%
Personalized	3.61 (1.65) 3.1%	4.37 (1.93) 0.6%	3.09 (1.70) 0.6%	3.14 (1.99) 0%	2.91 (1.60) 1.3%

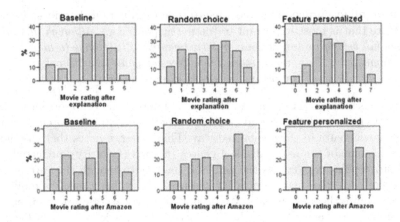

Fig. 1. First and second movie ratings - the distribution is considered with regard to *percentage* of ratings in each condition

Enough to Form an Opinion? Since our explanations are very short we first considered whether they were sufficient for the user to form an opinion of the movie. In Table 1 we note the percentage of no-opinions in each condition. We see that this is small though perhaps not negligible. The percentage for the first movie as well as for the first explanation is smallest in the personalized condition. In Figure 1 we consider the actual ratings of the movie. We see that the first and second rating of the movie are distributed beyond the mean rating of 4, suggesting that participants are able to form polarized opinions.

Are Personalized Explanations More Effective? Next we considered Effectiveness. Similar to the metric described by [1] we consider the mean of the difference between the two movie ratings. Unlike [1] (who considered the signed values) we consider the *absolute*, or unsigned, difference between the two ratings in Table 2. *Independent samples t-tests show no significant difference between the means of the three conditions.* This suggests that the degree of personalization or using item features does not increase explanation Effectiveness.

Figure 2 graphically depicts the *signed* distribution of Effectiveness. We see here that under-estimation is more frequent than overestimation in all three conditions. We also note the peak at zero in the random choice, feature based

Table 2. Effectiveness over absolute values with "no-opinions" omitted, and Pearson's correlations between the two movie ratings

Condition	$\overline{m}$ (StDev)	Correlation	p
Baseline	1.38 (1.20)	0.427	0.000
Random choice	1.14 (1.30)	0.650	0.000
Personalized	1.40 (1.21)	0.575	0.000

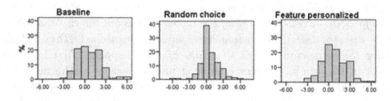

Fig. 2. Distribution of (signed) Effectiveness - "no opinions" omitted

condition. Around 40% of explanations in this condition are perfectly Effective, i.e. the difference between the two ratings is zero.

We investigated this further and found that the random choice condition has significantly higher initial ratings than the other two conditions. We compared this condition with the personalized condition to see if there was any factor that could cause this. The percentage of shown movies that were in the top 100 in IMDB was comparable, and the distribution of movie titles did not show an evident skew. In the personalized condition most participants chose "actors" as their most preferred movie feature (75%) while the participants in the random choice condition received explanations describing the four movie features in fairly equal proportions. The explanations in the random choice condition have *fewer* mentions of favorite actors and directors, *more* explanations with unknown information, and *fewer* movies in the participants' preferred genres than in the personalized condition. All of this, except the difference in features mentioned, would be expected to lead to a *lower* initial rating rather than the found higher rating. With regards to features, we speculated that the difference may be due to the feature "average rating by other users" being mentioned more often, as we observed a positive bias of average ratings on the Amazon website. However, we found that mentioning this feature correlated more with *low* ratings of movies. So, we have not yet found a satisfactory explanation.

Since [1] did not consider the sign of the difference between the two ratings, their metric of Effectiveness also requires that the two ratings are correlated. This correlation is still interesting for our purposes. Table 2 shows a significant and positive correlation between these two ratings for all three conditions. *That is, explanations in all three conditions perform surprisingly well.*

Explanations and User Satisfaction. In Table 1 we see that the second set of explanation ratings are higher than the first. This may be partly due to some participants confounding our explanations with the Amazon reviews, thus rating our explanation facility higher. The mean rating for trust and explanations is low overall, but users rate the first explanation rating significantly highest in the personalized condition (independent sample t-tests, p<0.001). This suggests that while the personalized explanations may not help users make better decisions, users may still be more satisfied. This is confirmed by the qualitative comments. Participants in the personalized condition appreciated when their preferred feature was mentioned: *"...explanation lists main stars, which attracts me a little to watch the movie..."*. Participants felt that vital information was missing in particular in the random choice condition: *"...I indicated that Stanley Kubrick is one of my favorite directors in one of the initial menus but the explanation didn't tell me he directed this. That would have piqued my interest. The explanation didn't have this important detail so a loss of trust happened here..."* Another participant in the random choice condition had set actors as the most important feature and left the following comment for an explanation with information about the director: *"...not much useful information in the explanation - I do not know many directors, so do not really care who directs a movie."*. In contrast, participants in the baseline condition expressed that they were dissatisfied with the explanation: *"Not very helpful explanation even if it is top 100..."*

Trust, Classification and Completeness. In Table 1 we see that the mean trust is low in all three conditions, but seems best in the personalized feature based condition. Many participants felt that the genres were misclassified, and that this reduced their trust in the explanation facility. Although the genre classification is automatically retrieved from the Amazon ECS there are two things we could change in our explanations to mitigate these effects. In our prototype when a movie belongs to any of the users' favorite genres, only preferred genres are mentioned in the explanation even if the movie belongs to other genres as well. Similarly for disliked genres, only these are mentioned. A first improvement would be to mention all the genres a movie belongs to. Secondly, the genre explanations can be improved by considering even more detailed genre specification such as "Period Drama" rather than just "Drama" for costume dramas.

We received similar feedback for actors, where we only mention the user's favorite actor in the explanation: *"Benicio del Toro is in it, but so are others who aren't listed and who I really like..."*. That is, users might like to hear the names of all the leading actors even if only one is known to be their favorite.

Certainty and Polarity. None of the seven users for which director information was missing noted this, nor were there any explicit complaints about negative explanations where the movie belonged to a genre the user did not like.

4   Conclusions

In all three conditions participants largely have an opinion of the movie, and in all conditions there was more underestimation than overestimation. The mean Effectiveness deviated ca 1.5 from the optimum discrepancy of zero on a 7 point scale (StD < 1.5), regardless of the degree of personalization or whether or not the explanation used features such as actors. In light of this under-estimation we reconsider the fact that movie ratings in general, and their Amazon reviews in particular, tend to lean toward positive ratings. If Amazon reviews are overly positive, this may have affected our results.

Since there is no significant difference between conditions w.r.t. Effectiveness we consider the factors that the three conditions share, which is that they all expose the participant to the movie title and movie cover. A number of participants justify their ratings in terms of the image in their qualitative comments, in particular for the baseline explanation. So it is fair to assume that at least some participants use the image to form their judgment.

We are now planning a repeated experiment accounting for the factors discussed in this paper. Firstly, the experiment will consider explanations without images. Secondly, explanations regarding genre and actor will be more detailed and complete. Thirdly, a clearer distinction will be made between the personalized and random choice condition. Explanations in the random choice condition will describe all the genres of the movie, but not relate them to the user's preferences. Likewise it will list all the lead actors, and the director, but will not relate whether they are the user's favorites. We will consider alternative sources for approximating the user's true evaluation of the item, or repeat the experiment in a domain which does not have as strong a positive bias as Amazon. A final evaluation in which participants will *view* the movie they rate is also planned.

Acknowledgments. This research was partially supported by the EPSRC platform grant (EP/E011764/1).

References

1. Bilgic, M., Mooney, R.J.: Explaining recommendations: Satisfaction vs. promotion. In: Beyond Personalization Workshop, IUI (2005)
2. Herlocker, J.L., Konstan, J.A., Riedl, J.: Explaining collaborative filtering recommendations. In: Computer supported cooperative work (2000)
3. Mcsherry, D.: Explanation in recommender systems. Artificial Intelligence Review 24(2), 179–197 (2005)
4. Hingston, M.: User friendly recommender systems. Master's thesis, Sydney University (2006)
5. Tintarev, N., Masthoff, J.: Effective explanations of recommendations: User-centered design. In: Recommender Systems (2007)
6. Tintarev, N.: Explanations of recommendations. In: Recommender Systems (2007)
7. Carenini, G., Moore, D.J.: An empirical study of the influence of user tailoring on evaluative argument effectiveness. In: IJCAI (2001)
8. Cosley, D., Lam, S.K., Albert, I., Konstan, J.A., Riedl, J.: Is seeing believing?: how recommender system interfaces affect users' opinions. In: CHI (2003)
9. Kim, S.M., Pantel, P., Chklovski, T., Pennacchiotti, M.: Automatically assessing review helpfulness. In: EMNLP (2006)
10. McNee, S., Lam, S.K., Guetzlaff, C., Konstan, J.A., Riedl, J.: Confidence displays and training in recommender systems. In: INTERACT IFIP TC13 (2003)
11. Tintarev, N.: Explaining recommendations. In: Conati, C., McCoy, K., Paliouras, G. (eds.) UM 2007. LNCS (LNAI), vol. 4511. Springer, Heidelberg (2007)

User-Centric Profiling on the Basis of Cognitive and Emotional Characteristics: An Empirical Study[*]

Nikos Tsianos[1], Zacharias Lekkas[1], Panagiotis Germanakos[1,2],
Costas Mourlas[1], and George Samaras[2]

[1] Faculty of Communication and Media Studies, National & Kapodistrian University of Athens,
5 Stadiou Str, GR 105-62, Athens, Hellas
[2] Computer Science Department, University of Cyprus, CY-1678 Nicosia, Cyprus
{ntsianos,pgerman,mourlas}@media.uoa.gr, zlekkas@gmail.com,
cssamara@cs.ucy.ac.cy

Abstract. In order to clarify whether extending learners' profiles in an adaptive educational system to cognitive and emotional characteristics may have a positive effect on performance, we conducted an empirical study that consists of two subsequent experiments. The human factors that were taken into consideration in the personalization process were cognitive style, visual working memory span, control/speed of processing and anxiety. With the exception of control/speed of processing, matching the instructional style to users' characteristics was revealed to be statistically significant in optimizing their performance (n=219). On the basis of this empirical assessment, this paper argues that individual differences at this intrinsic level are important, and their main effect can be manipulated by taking advantage of adaptive technologies.

Keywords: Cognitive style, working memory, anxiety, e-learning, personalization, user profiling.

1 Introduction

The notion of personalization and the development of adaptive hypermedia [1, 2] has indeed generated research in the area of e-learning, and corresponding educational applications have been developed [3, 4, 5, 6]. Learning style theories have been quite popular as a personalization parameter, even though researchers from the educational field express reservations regarding the use of such constructs [7, 8].

However, the popularity of learning and cognitive style theories in user/learner profiling could perhaps be attributed to the fact that the typologies that are derived from these approaches are viable for implementation in hypermedia environments. On the contrary, educational and psychological theories that introduce terms such as attention, perception, memory, reading processes, language comprehension, thinking and reasoning [9], are far more complex and profound in order to be mapped in a hypermedia setting.

---

[*] The project is co-funded by the Cyprus Research Foundation under the project EKPAIDEION (#ΠΛΗΡΟ/0506/17).

W. Nejdl et al. (Eds.): AH 2008, LNCS 5149, pp. 214–223, 2008.

Even though the entire spectrum of individual differences undoubtedly concludes the aforementioned constructs, learning and cognitive style theories seem to have a predominant role in the area adaptive hypermedia research. The function of these typologies as "...an important interface at the border of personality and cognition" [10] is certainly of importance, but an approach that disregards the rest of the human factors involved in information processing would be inadequate, at least in search of a significant difference.

In search of a model that combines the construct of cognitive style with other human information processing parameters, the authors have introduced a three dimensional model [11]: Cognitive Style, Cognitive Processing Efficiency and Emotional Processing. The first dimension is unitary, whereas Cognitive Processing Efficiency is comprised of (a) Visual Working Memory Span (VWMS) [12] and (b) speed and control of information processing and visual attention [13]. The emotional aspect of the model focuses on different aspects of anxiety [14, 15, 16] and self-regulation.

A corresponding adaptive hypermedia system has been built around this model [17] and there is a continuing process of evaluating our approach and reforming both the theoretical model and the system. This paper presents new results that are gathered from experiments conducted throughout the assessment procedure, in order to clarify at some extent whether such a combination of human factors is of importance in the area of educational adaptive hypermedia.

2 Theoretical Background

The rationale behind opting for the parameters that comprise our proposed user profiling model has been thoroughly presented in previous publications [18]. In short, the theories that are involved satisfy the criteria of scientific value and of the possibility to be integrated into a hypermedia system.

Firstly, the use of cognitive rather than learning style is due to the fact that the latter is "a construct that by definition is not stable- it was grounded in process and therefore susceptible to rapid change" [19] Moreover, we are research-wise interested in individual information processing parameters, whereas the social implications of other learning typologies are not examined.

More specifically, Riding and Cheema's Cognitive Style Analysis (CSA) has been opted for. The CSA is derived from a factor analytic approach on previous cognitive style theories, summarizing a number of different yet highly correlated constructs into two distinct independent dimensions [20]. This covers a wide array of the former cognition based style typologies, without going into unnecessary depth- for the needs of hypermedia education that is. The dimensions are the holist/analyst and the imager/verbalizer; the former alters the structure and amount of learner control, while the latter affects the type of resources that are presented to provide the necessary educational information.

As mentioned above, in search of a more coherent approach, the term of working memory [21] has also been introduced as a personalization factor. A brief description of the working memory system is that is consisted of the central executive that controls the two slave systems (visuo-spatial sketchpad and phonological loop), plus the episodic buffer that provides a temporary interface between the slave systems and the

Long Term Memory [22]. Due to the visual form of presentation in the web, we have focused especially on the visual working memory [23]. In any case, each individual has a specific and restricted memory span. As to decrease the possibility of cognitive load in hypermedia environments [24], our system takes into account each users' visual working memory span (VWMS), by altering the amount of simultaneously presented information.

In parallel to VWMS, a number of other individuals' "cognitive processing efficiency" parameters are also measured. This term refers to "hardware" functions of the brain, based on Demetriou's architecture of the mind [25]. It is not a unitary concept, but an aggregation of learners' abilities: (a) control of processing (refers to the processes that identify and register goal-relevant information and block out dominant or appealing but actually irrelevant information), (b) speed of processing (refers to the maximum speed at which a given mental act may be efficiently executed) and (c) visual attention (based on the empirically validated assumption that when a person is performing a cognitive task, while watching a display, the location of his / her gaze corresponds to the symbol currently being processed in working memory and, moreover, that the eye naturally focuses on areas that are most likely to be informative).

Lastly, an endeavor to take into account learners' emotional state has been carried out. Our approach is entirely differentiated from affective computing [26], since we have focused exclusively on learners' levels of anxiety and their ability to control their emotions. At this levet, we make use of the term "Emotional Processing", which includes (a) Emotional Arousal, which is the capacity of a human being to sense and experience specific emotional situations- with anxiety [14, 15, 16] as the main indication of emotional arousal, and (b) Emotion Regulation, which is the way that an individual perceives and controls his emotions [27, 28, 29, 30].

The greatest challenge is of course to extract from the abovementioned theories the corresponding implications for an educational hypermedia environment. As it concerns cognitive style and VWMS, such an elaboration is rather explicit. On the other hand, in order to experimentally assess the effect of individuals' cognitive processing efficiency, we necessarily imposed time limitations within the learning process. By manipulating time limits, we examine how learners perform (level of comprehension). Finally, in the ambiguous field of emotions, the aesthetic enhancement of the system was expected to have a positive effect on highly anxious learners. Therefore, our research questions may be set forth as follows:

i)   Does matching online instructional style to users' cognitive style have a significant effect on their performance?

ii)   Does providing the right amount of information according to users' VWMS alleviate cognitive overload?

iii)   Is users' cognitive processing efficiency related to the available amount of time, with an effect on comprehension and performance?

iv)   Is there a correlation between learners' performance and their levels of anxiety and emotional regulation? In that case, is the aesthetic enhancement of the environment any useful?

In order to elucidate the abovementioned issues, we conducted two subsequent experiments in parallel with the development of the system, whilst the assessment methods where derived from the field of experimental psychology. Our efforts were also focused on "translating" our theoretical framework into personalization rules; it should be mentioned that the mapping of such a user profile into a hypermedia system is a complex procedure, due to the non-linearity and the unforeseen interactions of human traits. However, this is the main challenge of our research work- the successful integration of theory into practice in a coherent way.

3 Method

The experimental design in both experiments was a between participants memory posttest. Users created their profiles through a series of psychometric tests, logged into the system, took the online course, and afterwards participated in an on-line exam in order to assess their level of comprehension. Therefore, in all cases the dependent variable was users' score at the memory posttest.

The total number of participants was 219; all of them were students in the Universities of Athens and Cyprus, and their age varied from 17 to 22 with a mean age of 19. About 70% of the participants were female and 30% were male. The academic subject was a computer science course on algorithms, which was chosen because at the departments where the experiments took place students have absolutely no experience or previous knowledge on programming, due to the theoretical orientation of their curriculum. Participation in the experiments was voluntary, but most students were willing to take the course, as an additional help on a very difficult academic subject.

Almost half of the participants received an online course that was personalized to their preferences, whilst the other half received courses that didn't coincide with their profiles. This allocation was quasi-random; each user that logged in was placed in the opposite, from the previous user, group (matched or mismatched).

The first experiment took place at the University of Cyprus, while the second was conducted at the University of Athens. The number of participants in each experiment was 138 and 81 respectively.

3.1 Materials

Cognitive style: Riding's Cognitive Style Analysis, standardized in Greek and implemented in the .NET platform.

Visual Working Memory Span: Visuospatial working memory test [31], firstly developed on the E-prime platform (a software tool for developing psychometrical applications), afterwards implemented in the .NET platform.

Cognitive Processing Efficiency: Speed and accuracy task-based tests that assess control of processing, speed of processing and visual attention. Originally developed in the E-prime platform, we integrated them into the .NET platform.

Core (general) Anxiety: Spielberger's State-Trait Anxiety Inventory (STAI) – 10 items (Only the trait scale was used) [16].

Application Specific Anxiety: Cassady's Cognitive Test Anxiety scale – 27 items [15].

Current Anxiety: Self-reported measures of state anxiety taken during the assessment phase of the experiment, in time slots of every 10 minutes – 6 Time slots.

Emotion Regulation: This questionnaire was developed by us; cronbach's α that indicates scale reliability reaches 0.718.

3.2 Personalization Rules

A short description of the way that our system adapts to users' preferences is needed in order to provide the reader an insight to our research framework.

(a) Cognitive style: There are two dimensions of users' cognitive style that are mapped in the educational environment: the holist/analyst scale affects the structure, the navigational patterns and the amount of learner control, whereas the imager/verbalizer is related to the textual or graphical representation of information (where possible of course).
(b) VWMS: Each users' visual working memory span is measured and classified. Users that have low levels of VWMS receive segmented content that is unfolded gradually. The main idea is to alleviate the possibility of cognitive overload, and is based on the notion that information processing is not sequential but parallel- therefore, the segmentation in clear-cut chunks may assist users' with low VWMS.
(c) Cognitive Processing Efficiency: Since the term efficiency refers mainly to speed, in order to distinguish whether there is a relationship between users' ability and the time required to complete an online course, we set different time limits for each category.
(d) Anxiety: In these first experiments, we were based on the results of the "core" and "application specific" anxiety questionnaires. The measurement of "current" anxiety and "Emotion Regulation" was used for exploratory reasons and for investigating the validity of such constructs- which is beyond the scope of this paper. In any case, if there were high levels of anxiety (on behalf of the user), we provided aesthetical enhancement of the environment and further annotations; in a sense, the aesthetical aspect predominates over functionality (in terms of font size, colours, annotations).

As mentioned above, the matched/mismatched methodology was followed, with the addition of control groups in the case of cognitive style and levels of anxiety (see results). We are still conducting experiments at the same departments with quite the same methodology, in order to improve the effectiveness of the system; these are the first of a series of experiments that provide statistically significant results. The actual system, the psychometric tests and the course can be reached at http://www3.cs.ucy.ac.cy/adaptiveweb/

4 Results

Experiment I
The first experiment focused only on the construct of cognitive style as a personalization factor. Besides users' cognitive style, their VWMS was also included in their profile as a control variable. Participants had either a cognitive style preference or were classified as intermediates (no cognitive style preference). The latter were treated as a control group that has no need for a personalized environment, and received a "baseline" balanced course. The remaining users were randomly allocated to

a "matched" or "mismatched" group of learners. If cognitive style is of any importance, these two groups should have statistically significant different scores.

A 3X3 analysis of variance was performed (three groups of cognitive style and three groups of VWMS), since the variance of the dependent variable was homogeneous, in order not only to assess the effect of matching the environment to users' style, but also to control for the effect of VWMS. Indeed, learners that received matched environment (n=53) outperformed mismatched learners (n=61): $F_{(2,137)}=4.395$, p=0.014. There was no main effect of VWMS, or interaction with cognitive style.

Post hoc analysis (see table 1) has demonstrated that the differences actually exist between matched and mismatched learners; intermediates (n=24) do not seem to vary from the former groups, and they are more dispersed. Perhaps in the absence of a cognitive style preference, some other factors mediate their performance in a hypermedia environment. In any case, our next experiment was to shed light on what happens with the rest of our theoretical model.

Table 1. Post hoc analysis of learners' scores in all three conditions of experiment I

Dependent Variable: Score %
Tukey HSD

(I) Matched Environment	(J) Matched Environment	Mean Difference (I-J)	Std. Error	Sig.	95% Confidence Interval	
					Lower Bound	Upper Bound
Matched	Mismatched	8.74(*)	3.455	.034	.55	16.93
	Intermediate	7.94	4.527	.189	-2.79	18.68
Mismatched	Matched	-8.74(*)	3.455	.034	-16.93	-.55
	Intermediate	-.80	4.433	.982	-11.31	9.72
Intermediate	Matched	-7.94	4.527	.189	-18.68	2.79
	Mismatched	.80	4.433	.982	-9.72	11.31

Based on observed means.
* The mean difference is significant at the .05 level.

In sum, the argument that personalization on the basis of cognitive style may improve learners' information processing in a hypermedia environment can be supported; those who demonstrate cognitive style preference are indeed benefited. The mean difference of app. 9 points should also be evaluated in relation to the small variation of participants score.

Experiment II

By controlling the cognitive style parameter (environment matched to this preference), users received either matched or mismatched environment in regards to each separate factor of our model (VWMS, cognitive processing efficiency and level of anxiety). In order to distinguish the effects of matching/mismatching each factor, since the distribution of the sample was homogenous, a 2X2X3 analysis of variance was performed; there were three groups of learners in the emotional categorization, since users with low levels of anxiety were treated as a control group. The composition of groups was the following: a) 19 mismatched low VWMS learners, b) 62 matched VWMS learners, c) 42 mismatched CPSE learners, d) 39 matched CPSE learners, e) 29 mismatched anxious learners, f) 22 matched anxious learners and g) 30 participants in the emotional control group.

There was a significant main effect of matching the instructional style to users' VWMS ($F_{(1,80)}=4.501$, $p=0.037$), and to their levels of anxiety ($F_{(2,80)}=3.128$, $p=0.05$). Cognitive processing efficiency was not found to have a main effect on score or interaction with the other parameters. The differences in mean scores are demonstrated in Tables 2 and 3.

Table 2. Differences of mean scores in the matched and mismatched condition with regards to users' levels of anxiety

Dependent Variable: Score %

Match_Emotion	Mean	Std. Error	95% Confidence Interval	
			Lower Bound	Upper Bound
matched	56.250	3.905	48.461	64.039
mismatched	43.107	3.667	35.792	50.421
control	51.826	4.567	42.716	60.936

Post hoc analysis of the differences between the three anxiety groups has demonstrated that the difference is statistically significant between matched and mismatched anxious users, with the control group scoring in between.

Table 3. Differences of mean scores in the matched and mismatched condition with regards to users' VWMS

Dependent Variable: Score %

Match_VWMS	Mean	Std. Error	95% Confidence Interval	
			Lower Bound	Upper Bound
matched	55.372	2.016	51.351	59.393
mismatched	45.417	4.237	36.963	53.780

The relatively small sample of the second experiment necessary limits the level of analysis that can be applied. However, it is certainly encouraging the fact that there were found significant differences in learners' scores that can be attributed to the importance of taking into account factors such as those included in our approach; it seems that designing educational hypermedia with such factors left at chance level may hamper the performance of users.

The finding that cognitive processing efficiency didn't affect users' performance may be explained by the fact that there were no real-time tasks involved in our online course; therefore, it would be difficult for this kind of individual differences to be revealed. It is also possible that a different approach to the personalization process or the experimental design could have provided different results.

Our methodology in this first endeavor to investigate the role of these human factors is of course not exhaustive. VWMS has been proven to be of importance as a parameter, and a certain effect of aesthetics has been demonstrated, but further empirical research is undoubtedly required.

5 Discussion and Conclusions

The results that are presented above may provide a good argument for incorporating human factors in educational adaptive hypermedia. More specifically, our research questions were answered as follows: (i) Matching the instructional style to users' cognitive style promotes performance, in the sense of more efficient information processing (ii) segmenting the simultaneously presented information according to learners' VWMS benefits their comprehension (iii) cognitive processing efficiency does not have an effect, nor is related to the amount of available time, and (iv) the aesthetical enhancement of the environment is correlated to the increase of performance of anxious learners.

These findings are quite consistent with the psychological theories that are refereed to in our framework, and it seems that the difficult task of translating these theories into adaptation rules was at some extent successful. The differences in scores are not extreme, but an aggregation of the added values that each human factor has for an educational environment may as well lead to a far more efficient learning procedure. Our next step is the provision of educational environments that are fully adapted or non-personalized (baseline), and the comparison of these two conditions. Our expectations, as demonstrated by the abovementioned findings, is that the differences will be far greater than marginal, also taking under consideration the results of the control groups that were used in some of the conditions of our experiments (see results section).

At this point we should mention that there are several limitations in our study. First of all, the second experiment was conducted with a limited sample. Though it is impressive that it yielded statistically significant results, we are aware that these findings must be repeatedly confirmed. We have already designed and conducted a replication study with a larger sample and we are in the process of analyzing our data- we may for the time being report that the role of VWMS seems to be prominent and highly important.

Secondly, our experiments were conducted within a specific adaptive system, which may as well not be considered as representative of all possible hypermedia applications. The integration of our theories seems to be viable in this specific educational hypermedia system, but it should be nevertheless tested in other e-learning procedures. We have clarified that our interest is on individual information processing differences, and the interaction of these human factors with other parameters (predominantly socially oriented) should be examined.

However, the feedback that this study has provided us is encouraging, and in our opinion there is quite some depth in personalization on individual differences. We certainly not consider our model as a rigorous construct, but as a framework that is driven by experimental research and methodology. The value of this approach for educational hypermedia designers is that the emphasis is placed upon the learner, exclusively on the level of a better understanding of the educational content. Since adaptive technologies offer the possibility of a highly personalized e-learning course, it would be rather obscure to not place users' intrinsic characteristics in the center of such an endeavor.

References

[1] Eklund, J., Sinclair, K.: An empirical appraisal of the effectiveness of adaptive interfaces of instructional systems. Educational Technology and Society 3(4), 165–177 (2000)

[2] Brusilovsky, P., Nejd, W.: Adaptive Hypermedia and Adaptive Web. In: Singh, M.P. (ed.) The Practical Handbook of Internet Computing, 1.1–1.14. Chapman & Hall/CRC, USA (2004)

[3] Cristea, A., Stewart, C., Brailsford, T., Cristea, P.: Adaptive Hypermedia System Interoperability: a 'real world' evaluation. Journal of Digital Information 8(3) (2007), http://journals.tdl.org/jodi/article/view/235/192

[4] Papanikolaou, K.A., Grigoriadou, M., Kornilakis, H., Magoulas, G.D.: Personalizing the Interaction in a Web-based Educational Hypermedia System: the case of INSPIRE. User-Modelling and User-Adapted Interaction 13(3), 213–267 (2003)

[5] Carver Jr., C.A., Howard, R.A., Lane, W.D.: Enhancing student learning through hypermedia courseware and incorporation of student learning styles. IEEE Transactions on Education 42(1), 33–38 (1999)

[6] Gilbert, J.E., Han, C.Y.: Arthur: A Personalized Instructional System. Journal of Computing in Higher Education 14(1), 113–129 (2002)

[7] Rezaei, A.R., Katz, R.: Evaluation of the reliability and validity of the cognitive styles analysis. Personality and Individual Differences 36(6), 1317–1327 (2004)

[8] Peterson, E.R., Deary, I.J., Austin, E.J.: The reliability of Riding's Cognitive Style Analysis test. Personality and Individual Differences 34(5), 881–891 (2003)

[9] Eysenck, M.W., Keane, M.T.: Cognitive Psychology, 5th edn. Psychology Press, New York (2005)

[10] Sternberg, R.J., Grigorenko, E.L.: Are Cognitive Styles Still in Style? American Psychologist 52(7), 700–712 (1997)

[11] Tsianos, N., Germanakos, P., Lekkas, Z., Mourlas, C., Samaras, G.: Evaluating the Significance of Cognitive and Emotional Parameters in e-Learning Adaptive Environments. In: Proceedings of the IADIS International Conference on Cognition and Exploratory Learning in Digital Age (CELDA 2007), Algarve, Portugal, December 7-9, 2007, pp. 93–98 (2007)

[12] Baddeley, A.: Working Memory. Science 255, 556–559 (1992)

[13] Demetriou, A., Efklides, A., Platsidou, M.: The architecture and dynamics of developing mind: Experiential structuralism as a frame for unifying cognitive development theories (Monographs of the Society for Research in Child Development). University of Chicago Press, USA (1993)

[14] Cassady, J.C., Jonhson, R.E.: Cognitive Test Anxiety and Academic Performance. Contemporary Educational Psychology 27(2), 270–295 (2002)

[15] Cassady, J.C.: The influence of cognitive test anxiety across the learning–testing cycle. Learning and Instruction 14(6), 569–592 (2004)

[16] Spielberger, C.D.: Manual for the State-Trait Anxiety Inventory (STAI). Consulting Psychologists Press, Palo Alto (1983)

[17] Germanakos, P., Tsianos, N., Lekkas, Z., Mourlas, C., Belk, M., Samaras, G.: An Adaptive Web System for Integrating Human Factors in Personalization of Web Content. In: Conati, C., McCoy, K., Paliouras, G. (eds.) UM 2007. LNCS (LNAI), vol. 4511, Springer, Heidelberg (2007)

[18] Germanakos, P., Tsianos, N., Lekkas, Z., Mourlas, C., Samaras, G.: Capturing Essential Intrinsic User Behaviour Values for the Design of Comprehensive Web-based Personalized Environments. Computers in Human Behavior (2007) doi:10.1016/j.chb.2007.07.010

[19] Rayner, S.: Cognitive Styles and Learning Styles. In: Smelser, N.J., Baltes, P.B. (eds.) International Encyclopedia of Social & Behavioral Sciences. Elsevier Science Ltd, UK (2001)

[20] Riding, R.J., Cheema, I.: Cognitive Styles – an overview and integration. Educational Psychology 11(3 & 4), 193–215 (1991)

[21] Baddeley, A.: The concept of working memory: A view of its current state and probable future development. Cognition 10(1-3), 17–23 (1981)

[22] Baddeley, A.: The episodic buffer: a new component of working memory? Trends in Cognitive Sciences 11(4), 417–423 (2000)

[23] Loggie, R.H., Zucco, G.N., Baddeley, A.D.: Interference with visual short-term memory. Acta Psychologica 75(1), 55–74 (1990)

[24] DeStefano, D., Lefevre, J.: Cognitive load in hypertext reading: A review. Computers in Human Behavior 23(3), 1616–1641 (2007)

[25] Demetriou, A., Kazi, S.: Unity and modularity in the mind and the self: Studies on the relationships between self-awareness, personality, and intellectual development from childhood to adolescence. Routdledge, London (2001)

[26] Picard, R.W.: Affective Computing. MIT Press, Cambridge (1997)

[27] Salovey, P., Mayer, J.D.: Emotional intelligence. Imagination, Cognition, and Personality 9, 185–211 (1990)

[28] Goleman, D.: Emotional Intelligence: why it can matter more than IQ. Bantam Books, New York (1995)

[29] Bandura, A.: Self-efficacy. In: Ramachaudran, V.S. (ed.) Encyclopedia of human behaviour, pp. 71–81. Academic Press, New York (1994)

[30] Halberstadt, A., Emotional, G.: experience and expression: An issue overview. Journal of Nonverbal Behavior 17(3), 139–143 (2005)

[31] Demetriou, A., Christou, C., Spanoudis, G., Platsidou, M.: The development of mental processing: Efficiency, working memory, and thinking. Monographs of the Society of Research in Child Development, 67, Serial Number 268 (2002)

Towards Computerized Adaptive Assessment Based on Structured Tasks

Jozef Tvarožek[1], Miloš Kravčík[2], and Mária Bieliková[1]

[1] Faculty of Informatics and Information Technologies,
Slovak University of Technology, Ilkovičova 3, 842 16 Bratislava, Slovakia
{jtvarozek,bielik}@fiit.stuba.sk
[2] Open University of The Netherlands,
Valkenburgerweg 177, 6419 AT Heerlen, The Netherlands
Milos.Kravcik@ou.nl

Abstract. In an attempt to support traditional classroom assessment processes with fully computerized methods, we have developed a method for adaptive assessment suitable for well structured domains with high emphasis on problem solving and capable of robust continuous assessment, potentially encouraging student's achievements, reflective thinking, and creativity. The method selects problems according to the student's demonstrated ability, structured task description schemes allow for a detailed analysis of student's errors, and on-demand generation of task instances facilitates independent student work. We evaluated the proposed method using a software system we had developed in the domain of middle school mathematics.

1 Introduction

Most classroom assessments today are carried out using traditional paper & pencil methods. Paper as a delivery medium allows the students to elaborate and justify their answers in a very liberal way. While linear and adaptive computerized tests are widely used in web-based education [1] and testing community [2], they do not provide sufficient freedom of expression required to assess student's progress in solution paths of the problems and thus are not a viable option for classroom assessment. Although not primarily designed for assessment, using an intelligent tutoring system (ITS) brings some hope. ITS obviously gives the student more expressiveness during the interaction on problems but since the authoring process is time-consuming and requires sophisticated analysis [3], the system usually contains only a limited set of questions.

Recently, the Assistments system [4] seems as a more suitable alternative for classroom use. Being a so-called pseudo-tutor, a simplification of the original ITS concept, the system provides a practice environment for students giving them the opportunity to learn while solving problems and reporting their progress on a scale representing a nation-wide test performance. The problems, also called assistments, are organized in sections and within a section the assistments are optionally presented in linear or random order. A single assistment is a tree

W. Nejdl et al. (Eds.): AH 2008, LNCS 5149, pp. 224–234, 2008.
© Springer-Verlag Berlin Heidelberg 2008

of scaffolding questions branched from the top-level question. While providing accurate predictions for the nation-wide MCAS test, the Assistments system in its present state does not account for issues with exposure of assistments, personalized sequencing, and open-ended student answers and therefore is usable only as an instructional assistance as originally intended.

In this paper, we present a novel method for adaptive assessment which has been proposed as a part of a broader effort to bring classroom assessment to its full potential by computerized methods utilizing adaptivity, suitable answer interfaces, automatic task generation, and collaborative approaches. The method is appropriate for well structured domains with high emphasis on problem solving such as middle school mathematics, high school and university level programming, data structures and algorithms courses.

The system we had developed based on the proposed method incorporates four major aspects we argue are important in any robust assessment system:

1. for an assessment task to identify the student's solution path,
2. personalized sequencing of tasks during examination,
3. suitable answer interfaces depending on the task type,
4. on-demand generation of new tasks.

Our assessment tasks are structured in the form of a tree comparable to the structure of an assistment. A node in the tree represents a solution path; multiple branches at a node can be defined modeling a possible error in the student's solution at the respective granularity. Tasks are described in schemes using a high-level object language facilitating on-demand task generation and effective judging of open-ended answers. Schemes are calibrated using a psychometric *Item Response Theory* (IRT) [5] model, and a standard *Computer Adaptive Testing* (CAT) [6] algorithm for adaptive selection is employed.

In the next section, we provide an overview of research on related problems. We describe the proposed method for adaptive assessment in detail in section 3. In the evaluation, in section 4, we explore the feasibility of the judging process, demonstrate the adaptive selection, and summarize the students' attitudes towards the assessment in the domain of middle school mathematics. Summarizing thoughts and proposals for future work are to be found in section 5.

2   Related Work

Based on an extensive survey of the research literature on assessment, the article [7] concluded that innovations which include strengthening the practice of formative assessment (evaluation carried out in the course of an activity in such a way that the information obtained is used to improve learning and/or instruction) produce significant, and often substantial, learning gains. The formative assessment experiments produce typical effect sizes between 0.4 and 0.7. Such effect sizes are larger than most of those found for educational interventions.

One of the assessment environments used today is SIETTE [8], a web-based tool in which teachers define tests, and students can take these tests on-line. SIETTE uses traditional multiple-choice questions while custom item formats can be implemented by a Java applet. To further enhance the system, possibilities of adding instructional support by adaptive hints are explored in [9].

Automatic item generation. Item pools in CATs need regular refreshing because even with a relatively few items compromised a substantial gain can be achieved [6]. Methods of automatic item generation are explored to lessen the costs of creating new items [10]. Items are usually generated from so-called item models, prototypes, or schemes, by instantiating parameters with random values. IRT parameters of the generated instances may be slightly different but provided that we preserve the item structure and calibrate the instances together as a single item no statistically significant differences in ability estimates have been observed [11,12]. A more sophisticated method, generating math word problems using frame semantics, is explored in [13].

Adaptive item selection. Selecting the next item in an adaptive test is a nontrivial task. The number of times an item is administered might differ significantly between items if we choose to select the most informative item only [6]. The often administered tasks are easily disclosed and may compromise the whole adaptive test. Therefore, methods for controlling the exposure of items, limiting items' usage, are employed. Normally, the simple method of randomly selecting one of the k most informative items is used. The sophisticated b-blocking-a-stratified method [14] stratifies available items into layers according to the discrimination parameter b. Balanced exposure is ensured by selecting less discriminating items early in the examination when the estimate is still inaccurate and using high discriminating items later when we need to pinpoint the estimate in a relatively narrow ability range.

3   Method for Adaptive Assessment

Let us describe the main parts of our assessment system which is divided up into several independent modules (see Figure 1). A task conceived by an expert is processed into a parametric task description scheme described using a high-level object library. Tasks are parametrized to provide sufficient abstraction for the generator module to create new task instances on-demand.

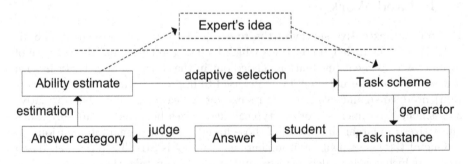

Fig. 1. Assessment system architecture

During the assessment phase, the system selects the task scheme that provides the most information for the current student's ability estimate. Using the selected task scheme, an unused task instance is generated and displayed to the student for answering. Students' answers are semi-automatically assigned to predefined categories. Having determined the category, the system either (1) asks the student a deeper question regarding her solution path, or (2) finishes the instance administration providing the task outcome which is subsequently used to update the ability estimate. Depending on the amount of error in the updated estimate, the selection module either (i) selects another task scheme at an appropriate level of ability to continue with, or (ii) finishes the assessment process providing the final ability estimate together with the amount of error.

Finally, estimates are transformed into grading levels required by the institution and the students are allowed to assert tasks' difficulties, confront their answers with the correct ones, and compare with their peers. Raw answers are further analyzed by domain experts to extract new patterns and solution paths not previously anticipated and to increase automatic judge efficiency.

3.1   Task Descriptions

Tasks are described in schemes consisting of:

1. *Static descriptions created during the authoring phase* - encompasses types and ranges of scheme parameters, set of constraints, and display templates of descriptions of subtasks and possible solution paths which are organized in the form of a tree (see Figure 2).
2. *Dynamic descriptions continuously maintained by the system* - psychometric parameters and usage indicators, both being required for the adaptive selection. Psychometric values correspond to the psychometric model used, while multiple models can be used simultaneously.

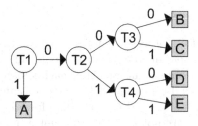

Fig. 2. Example of a scheme description tree having for each subtask only two possible answers. The task outcomes are represented by the leaf nodes A, B, C, D, and E.

Content authors specify scheme descriptions using an object language extended by a high-level library which provides them with abstract objects and operations. During the authoring process, the parameters and constraints are described by code fragments (see Example 1).

Example 1. Fibonacci sequence specification exported in XML. The author specified the sequence length and the generator code which is found in the CDATA section, resulting in a sequence of ten objects – numbers each having the value of the sum of the previous two:

```
<array name="fib" length="10">
 <singleton type="Integer" generator="code"><![CDATA[
   if (fib.Index <= 1) return Number.Integer (1);
   return Number.Integer (fib[fib.Index-2].Value+fib[fib.Index-1].Value);
 ]]></singleton>
</array>
```

Descriptions of subtasks and possible solution paths are specified using the XHTML markup language extended by a custom rendering element to allow the content authors to include a suitable rendering of the selected parameters.

Task instance generation process accounts for both procedural and declarative nature of scheme specifications. Using a pruned backtracking method, generation module instantiates the parameters in the order of appearance in the specification. If a parameter cannot be successfully constructed within k attempts during this process the instantiation process returns back to the previous parameter and tries another value. Increasing the value of k – while slowing the process – gives opportunity to produce more instances. We have found the value k=10 sufficient for high performance instance generation even in the presence of tens of parameters and constraints if they were specified efficiently. Slow instance generation at this value hinted at an ineffective code or parameter ordering.

Descriptions are fixed once the parameters in the schemes are instantiated, producing a task instance. Parameters in display templates are rendered for web delivery using MathML and SVG formats. Parametrization allows for not only a simple numerical variations between different instances but word and entity variations were employed along with preserving the structure of wording.

3.2   Assessment Process

The adaptive examination process requires a set of task schemes with precalibrated psychometric parameters. For the first run, parameters are determined manually by the content author. After each subsequent examination the parameters are recalibrated using all available student answers.

The 2PL IRT model [15] is used as a baseline for adaptive selection as long as more student answers are not available to grant a more sophisticated multidimensional IRT model. The structuring of tasks into trees does not allow for a straightforward use of a dichotomic model. As a helper, the system uses the 50% criterion, by which the student is awarded a correct answer for the current task if and only if he succeeds in answering at least half of the presented subtasks correctly (see Figure 3 for an example of a wrong task answer).

The adaptive selection of task schemes is initialized with an initial ability estimate of 0. To select the next task, the adaptation process considers all unused task schemes and identifies the maximum information value M that can be attained by the most informative scheme at the current ability estimate. To balance the scheme exposure, a small set of task schemes having the information value close to the value of M is picked and a random scheme from this set is selected for administration. The adaptive selection of task scheme occurs at the beginning of the examination and each time the student reaches a leaf node in the solution tree of current task instance.

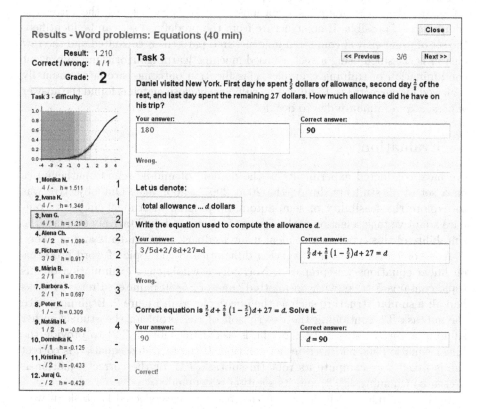

Fig. 3. After the examination is finished, students examine tasks' difficulties and compare answers with the correct ones. The student in the figure received a score of 1.210 by answering 4 tasks correctly and 1 task incorrectly (on display).

The examination finishes after a predefined test information value has been attained or none of the available schemes provides at least a threshold value of information. Consequently, grades are awarded only to students whose examination process resulted in at least a given test information value (see Figure 3). This threshold value is determined operatively by the teachers.

For a scheduled examination, students sign in to the system before the actual examination takes place for the assessments of all students in the class to commence simultaneously. Tasks are presented to the students one by one, each task is given a dedicated web page on which new subtasks appear as the student progresses in the solution tree. Students provide their answers in an open-ended format depending on the task type – free-text answer, drawing applet, etc.

For structured answer formats such as the geometry drawing applet, the answer is already specified in the domain's object model and the correctness of the automatic judge comparison procedure is thus straightforward.

For unstructured answer format such as the free-text answer, we at first try to transform the supplied answer into predefined answers described by structured templates of objects (numbers, equations, etc.) and proceed with the automatic comparison if possible. If no structure from the predefined set can be identified, the set of previously encountered unstructured patterns is consulted and the raw answer is classified using a vector-based machine learning algorithm. To prevent contamination of training examples, classification outcomes are later manually reviewed for correctness. Finally, if no sufficiently close match is found the answer is passed to a human judge to decide.

4   Evaluation

We have conducted experiments in the domain of middle school mathematics on a set of 45 students during the 2006–2007 school year. Our objective was to explore the feasibility of semi-automatic judging of student answers, compare adaptive task selection with human teachers, and qualitatively evaluate the suitability of this type of assessment using feedback from students and teachers.

A set of 7 task schemes of varying difficulties in the topic of word problems on linear equations was prepared. Normally a whole class examination of this topic contains 5 tasks with an allotted time of 35–40 minutes. Prepared tasks had all a similar structure such as the one depicted in Figure 2. Beginning with the subtask T1 containing the description of the problem, the student either submits a correct answer (A), or she is asked (in subtask T2) to provide the linear equation she had used in her solution. If the provided equation is correct she is asked to recompute its root (in subtask T4), or the correct equation is presented (in subtask T3) and its solution is demanded.

In the examination which took 40 minutes, we have collected 174 task answers in total, with a mean value of 3.867 task per student, and a total of 393 subtask

Table 1. Breakdown of students' answer patterns and an estimate of successful recognition by a contemporary machine learning algorithms based automatic judge

Answer type	N	prob.	Automatic judge
Numerical	76	100%	76
Empty	60	100%	60
Identical string	12	100%	12
Equation object	77	100%	77
Unknown text	71	50%	35
Request for help	19	80%	15
Other numerical	90	80%	72
Total	**393**	**88%**	**347**

answers. Table 1 breaks down the types of encountered answer patterns. Structured answer types: Numerical, Empty, Identical string, and Equation object were judged automatically, while the unstructured: Unknown text, Request for help, and Other numerical (e.g. "My result is w=47.") were judged manually by a teaching assistant during the examination process. We argue that using contemporary machine learning algorithms it is viable to construct a classifier successfully classifying the unstructured answers with the estimated probabilities stated in Table 1. In any case, the workload of the teaching assistant was low during this process, receiving about 3 answers to judge per minute.

Table 2. IRT parameters of the task schemes in the experiment

Task	#1	#2	#3	#4	#5	#6	#7
difficulty	0.514	0.600	0.368	-1.628	0.665	2.202	2.038
discrimination	1.674	0.574	1.607	0.443	1.747	1.154	1.220

Tasks schemes were calibrated using the 2PL IRT model (see Table 2). We have 5 schemes with a good discrimination value in $[1.154, 1.747]$ interval. With #2 and #4 having discrimination values of 0.574 and 0.443 respectively, we are expecting these schemes to be selected scarcely. Note that we do not have any schemes at difficulty level value near 0 and below except the low discriminative #4. Therefore it is expected that no appropriate tasks will be selected for students at these difficulty levels (average and low ability profile).

The adaptive selection of tasks is demonstrated on three student profiles – high, average, and low achieving student (see Table 3). Let us first examine the high ability student answering every question correctly. As expected, the adaptation process selects progressively harder tasks with good information values, granting her a final ability estimate of 1.926. Note that the resulting estimate is not infinite since we employ the Bayesian EAP (expected a posteriori) estimation procedure [16] with prior normal distribution of student abilities.

For the average ability student, we selected a student from our sample that is able to answer tasks #3 and #4 correctly and thus has an ability value of 0.105. As the opening task, she "accidentally" receives the #3 providing a correct answer awarding her a high ability estimate in the first step. Afterwards however, she is not that lucky and gets all the other tasks wrong. Similarly with the low ability student. Note the low information values in the 4th and 5th step of average and low ability student selection process hindering a more precise measurement. In fact, a precise measurement was not possible because of the lack of tasks at appropriate difficulty levels [2].

Finally, teachers and students were interviewed to provide a qualitative feedback. Excluding some occasional negative feedback in the high end and positive feedback in the low end of the ability scale, the students' positive attitudes were proportional to the attained ability estimate. Worth mentioning, students of all ability levels especially liked the structured approach presenting them with easier questions after a wrong answer, giving them the opportunity to ultimately

Table 3. Adaptive selection for high, average, and low ability student

Step:	0	1	2	3	4	5
High ability student (with ability +inf)						
Task selected:		5	1	3	6	7
Task information:		0.554	0.662	0.454	0.257	0.350
Answer:		correct	correct	correct	correct	correct
Ability estimate:	0.000	0.798	1.128	1.304	1.639	**1.926**
Average ability student (with ability 0.105)						
Task selected:		3	5	1	6	7
Task information:		0.592	0.762	0.664	0.088	0.099
Answer:		correct	wrong	wrong	wrong	wrong
Ability estimate:	0.000	0.663	0.239	-0.20	-0.57	**-0.095**
Low ability student (with ability -inf)						
Task selected:		3	1	5	2	7
Task information:		0.592	0.391	0.252	0.070	0.040
Answer:		wrong	wrong	wrong	wrong	wrong
Ability estimate:	0.000	-0.442	-0.653	-0.771	-0.865	**-0.887**

feel success after the final, though possibly the easiest, question was answered correctly. Teachers valued that the proposed system assesses their students independently of any subjective input thus perceivably providing them with objective formative assessment throughout the year.

5   Conclusions and Future Work

In this paper, we presented an adaptive assessment method proposed in an effort to empower traditional classroom assessment processes with computerized methods. It adaptively selects tasks according to the student's ability. Higher achieving students receive harder and lower achieving students easier questions, giving each the opportunity to demonstrate her ability level.

The proposed structuring of tasks into parametric solution trees which are described in a high-level object language using a library of domain objects makes a detailed assessment of student's solution possible. After submitting a wrong answer, the student is asked a deeper question regarding the solution path taken. Employing appropriate (e.g. polytomous) IRT models allows all of the demonstrated performance, be it right or wrong, to be included in the final ability estimate. In addition, structured parametric task descriptions facilitate automatic on-demand task generation and effective judging of open-ended answers.

We have evaluated the proposed method using a software system we had developed in the domain of middle school mathematics. By not administering a rigid set of tasks students fail to employ simple surface approaches to learning. In our observation after the experimental session students did not identify common problems to talk about at first since as much as 174 different task instances were administered even though only 7 task schemes were employed. Afterwards, students recognized the common features of the different instances each of them received, promoting higher order thinking skills.

As the next step we explore both individual-level and group-level improvements. On the individual level, observing the time spent on tasks and other in-system behavior patterns of an individual student can reveal interesting assessment and instructional opportunities. On the group level, we explore possibilities of enhancing the method with collaborative activities. Having multiple students working on the same task or in the role of the judge may result in a meaningful activity and lessen the required workload of the judging procedure.

Acknowledgements

This work was partially supported by the Cultural and Educational Grant Agency of the Slovak Republic, grant No. KEGA 3/5187/07 and the TENCompetence Integrated Project that is funded by the European Commission's 6th Framework Programme, priority IST/Technology Enhanced Learning.

References

1. Brusilovsky, P., Miller, P.: Web-based testing for distance education. In: De Bra, P., Leggett, J. (eds.) Proceedings of WebNet 1999, pp. 149–154. AACE (1999)
2. Mills, C., Steffen, M.: The GRE Computer Adaptive Test: Operational Issues. Computerized Adaptive Testing: Theory and Practice (2000)
3. Aleven, V., McLaren, B., Sewall, J., Koedinger, K.: The Cognitive Tutor Authoring Tools (CTAT): Preliminary evaluation of efficiency gains. In: Ikeda, M., Ashley, K.D., Chan, T.-W. (eds.) ITS 2006. LNCS, vol. 4053, pp. 61–70. Springer, Heidelberg (2006)
4. Feng, M., Heffernan, N., Koedinger, K.: Addressing the Testing Challenge with a Web-based E-Assessment System that Tutors as it Assesses. In: Proceedings of the 15th international conference on World Wide Web, pp. 307–316 (2006)
5. Lord, F., Novick, M.: Statistical theories of mental test scores. Addison-Wesley, Reading (1968)
6. Wainer, H.: Computerized Adaptive Testing: A Primer. Lawrence Erlbaum Associates, Mahwah (2000)
7. Black, P., Wiliam, D.: Inside the Black Box: Raising Standards Through Classroom Assessment. Phi Delta Kappan 80(2), 139–148 (1998)
8. Conejo, R.: SIETTE: A Web-Based Tool for Adaptive Testing. International Journal of Artificial Intelligence in Education 14(1), 29–61 (2004)
9. Conejo, R., Guzmán, E., Pérez-de-la Cruz, J.L., Millán, E.: An Empirical Study About Calibration of Adaptive Hints in Web-Based Adaptive Testing Environments. In: Adaptive Hypermedia and Adaptive Web-Based Systems, pp. 71–80 (2006)
10. Irvine, S., Kyllonen, P.: Item Generation for Test Development. Lawrence Erlbaum Associates, Mahwah (2002)
11. Bejar, I., Lawless, R., Morley, M., Wagner, M., Bennett, R., Revuelta, J.: A Feasibility Study of On-the-Fly Item Generation in Adaptive Testing. Journal of Technology, Learning, and Assessment 2(3) (2003)

12. Sinharay, S., Johnson, M.: Analysis of Data From an Admissions Test With Item Models. Educational Testing Service (2005)
13. Deane, P., Sheehan, K.: Automatic Item Generation via Frame Semantics: Natural Language Generation of Math Word Problems. In: Annual meeting of the National Council on Measurement in Education, Chicago, IL (2003)
14. Chang, H., Qian, J., Ying, Z.: a-Stratified Multistage Computerized Adaptive Testing with b-Blocking. Applied Psych. Measurement 25(4), 333–341 (2001)
15. Birnbaum, A.: Efficient design and use of tests of a mental ability for various decision-making problems. In: Randolph Air Force Base. Air University, School of Aviation Medicine, Texas (1957)
16. Baker, F., Seock-Ho, K.: Item Response Theory: Parameter Estimation Techniques. CRC Press, Boca Raton (2004)

Adaptation of Elaborated Feedback in e-Learning

Ekaterina Vasilyeva[1,2], Mykola Pechenizkiy[2], and Paul De Bra[2]

[1] Department of Computer Science and Information Systems, University of Jyväskylä,
P.O. Box 35, 40351 Jyväskylä, Finland
[2] Department of Mathematics and Computer Science, Eindhoven University of Technology,
P.O. Box 513, 5600MB Eindhoven, the Netherlands
{e.vasilyeva,m.pechenizkiy}@tue.nl, debra@win.tue.nl

Abstract. Design of feedback is a critical issue of online assessment development within Web-based Learning Systems (WBLSs). In our work we demonstrate the possibilities of tailoring the feedback to the students' learning style (LS), certitude in response and its correctness. We observe in the experimental studies that these factors have a significant influence on the feedback preferences of students and the effectiveness of elaborated feedback (EF), i.e. students' performance improvement during the test. These observations helped us to develop a simple EF recommendation approach. Our experimental study shows that (1) many students are eager to follow the recommendations on necessity to read certain EF in the majority of cases; (2) the students more often find the recommended EF to be useful, and (3) the recommended EF helped to answer related questions better.

Keywords: feedback authoring, feedback personalization, online assessment.

1 Introduction

Online assessment is an important component of modern education. Nowadays it is used not only in e-learning for (self-)evaluation, but also tends to replace or complement traditional methods of formal evaluation of the student's performance in blended learning.

Feedback is usually a significant part of the assessment as students need to be informed about the results of their (current and/or overall) performance. The existing great variety of the feedback functions and types that the WBLS can actually support make the authoring and design of the feedback in e-learning rather complicated [13]. An important issue is that different types of feedback can have a different effect (positive or negative) on the learning and interaction processes [2]. Badly designed feedback (and/or the lack of feedback) could distract the student from learning, it could provoke the students to stop using the e-learning system or even to drop the course (even in blended learning). Well-designed and adapted or tailored feedback can help the learning process, as we show in this paper.

Feedback personalization becomes a challenging perspective for the development of feedback in the assessment components of WBLSs as it is aimed to provide a student with the feedback that is most suitable and useful for his/her personality, the performed

W. Nejdl et al. (Eds.): AH 2008, LNCS 5149, pp. 235–244, 2008.

task and environment. The development of the personalized feedback requires having the answers to at least the following questions: (1) what can be personalized in the feedback; and (2) to which user or performance characteristics feedback should be personalized. Some answers to these fundamental issues can be found in [13].

In our earlier pilot experiment [14, 15] and more recently a series of real online assessment studies in [11, 12] we have been able to confirm that factors like the students' LS, certitude in response and its correctness, have a significant influence on (1) the feedback preferences of students and (2) the effectiveness of elaborated feedback (EF), i.e. improving students' performance during the test. These encouraging results motivated us to develop a feedback adaptation/recommendation approach for tailoring immediate EF for students' needs.

In this paper we present the result of our two most recent experimental field studies where we tested our approach in real settings during the online assessment of students through multiple-choice quizzes within the (slightly altered) *Moodle* WBLS. In each of the multiple-choice quizzes, students had to select their confidence (certitude) level and were able to receive different (adaptively selected and recommended) kinds of immediate EF for the answered questions.

The analysis of our assessment results and students' behavior demonstrate that (1) many students are eager to follow the recommendations on necessity or usefulness to read certain EF in the majority of cases, (2) after following the recommendations some students were willing to state explicitly whether particular EF indeed was useful to understand the subject matter better or not (and in most of the cases it was found helpful), and (3) recommended EF helped to answer related questions better.

The remainder of this paper is structured as follows. We briefly review functions and types of feedback that can be provided by WBLSs in Section 2. Section 3 discusses the issues of authoring and tailoring of feedback in WBLSs focusing on the problem of tailoring feedback to response certitude and correctness, and to students' LS. In Section 4 we first consider a very simple feedback personalization mechanism that displays the most suitable feedback (and/or provides ranked recommendations) to the students according to their knowledge of subject matter, correctness and certitude of response; then we describe the organization of and the results of our experiments. We briefly conclude with a summary and discussion of further research in Section 5.

2   Feedback in Online Assessment in Web Based Learning Systems

Feedback is usually a significant part of the assessment as students need to be informed about their (current and/or overall) performance. Feedback could play different functions in WBLS according to its learning effect: feedback can (1) inform the student about the correctness of his responses, (2) it can "fill the gaps" in the student's knowledge by presenting information the student appears not to know, and (3) it can "patch the student's knowledge" by trying to overcome misconceptions the student may have.

In traditional distance learning (external, but not computer-based learning) feedback has been examined from a number of different perspectives [3]. The studies have shown that students especially wanted detailed feedback and comments. The feedback was expected to provide positive comments on strengths, not vague generalizations. It is recommended that criticism in feedback be constructive and that students should have a chance to respond to comments [3].

In WBLS the main functions of the testing component are to evaluate the students, to give the students information about their performance, to motivate the students, and to focus the students' attention on further interaction with the system. Feedback differs from evaluation, where the main goal is simply to grade and record the result of the testing for the purpose of assessing the student.

The functions of the feedback imply the complexity of information that can be presented in immediate feedback: verification and elaborated feedback (EF) [4]. Verification can be given in the form of knowledge of response (indication of whether the answer was received and accepted by the system), knowledge of results (KR) (information about correctness or incorrectness of the response), or knowledge-of-correct response (KCR) (presentation of the correct answers) feedback. EF can address the topic and/or the response, discuss the particular errors, provide examples or give gentle guidance [10]. With EF the system presents not only the correct answer, but also additional information – corresponding learning materials, explanations, parts of problem-solutions etc.

Different types of feedback carry out different functions and thus they can be differently effective in terms of learning and interaction and can even be disturbing or annoying to the student and have negative influence on the learning and interaction processes [2]. An important issue in designing feedback is that it can draw attention away from the tasks, thereby increasing the time required to execute them. According to Oulasvirta and Saariluoma [9] interrupting messages such as feedback in human-computer interaction influence the extent and type of errors in remembering.

The effectiveness of different types of feedback in WBLS has been experimentally studied by Mandernach [5], who evaluated the educational impact of presenting various levels of computer-based, online feedback (no-feedback, knowledge-of-response, knowledge-of-correct-response, topic-contingent, and response-contingent). The results of this study have shown that the type of computer-based feedback did not have any influence on students' learning, but at the same time the students reported distinct preferences for knowledge-of-response and response-contingent computer-based feedback. This allowed concluding that the students prefer feedback that is direct and clearly addresses the correctness of their response.

Another problem of feedback is the time of its presentation. In [6] Mathan discussed the trade-off between the benefits of immediate and delayed feedback: whereas immediate feedback is more effective during the test, delayed feedback supports better transfer and retention. The advantages and disadvantages of immediate and delayed feedback can change with different learning goals and settings.

All these observations emphasize the necessity of careful design of feedback in WBLS. Our recent studies [11, 12, 13, 14] were aimed at demonstrating that the problems of feedback mentioned above could be partially solved by adaptation of feedback to the tasks and to the characteristics of an individual student. Feedback adaptation in WBLS can provide a student with feedback that is most appropriate for his or her personal characteristics, actual mood, behavior, and attentiveness.

3 Tailoring Feedback to LS, Response Certitude and Correctness

Design of feedback assumes that the following questions can/must be answered: (1) when should the feedback be presented; (2) what functions should it fulfil; (3) what kind of information should it include; (4) for which students and in which situations would it be most effective. The variety of possible answers to these questions makes authoring and design of feedback rather complicated, especially in WBLSs.

Personalization of feedback to the student's personality, performance, and involved contexts (currently performed task(s), environment, etc.) may be a solution for the design of effective feedback in WBLSs. It is essential to know what can be personalized in the feedback and to which characteristics should feedback be personalized. Here, we will focus on the student's LS and response characteristics.

Response certitude (also called response *confidence* or response *certainty*) specifies the student's certainty in the answer and helps in understanding the learning behavior. The traditional scheme of multiple-choice tests evaluation, where the responses are being treated as absolutely correct or absolutely wrong, ignores the obvious situations when the correct response can be the result of a random or an intuitive guess and luck, and an incorrect answer can be given due to a careless mistake or due to some misconceptions the student may have.

Such mistakes are especially crucial in the online assessment, where the evaluation of students' real knowledge and determining students' misconceptions become an even more difficult task for the teacher than in traditional in-class settings. Our results demonstrate that not allowing for discrimination of these situations may diminish the effects of personalized assessment.

The use of feedback in certitude-based assessment in traditional education has been researched for over 30 years; see for example [4, 7, 8] for the detailed reviews. The researchers examined the student's level of confidence in each of the answers and analyzed (1) the differences in performance of students with/without receiving immediate/delayed feedback; (2) how much time the student spent on processing corrective feedback information; (3) efficiency of feedback in confidence based assessment. In spite of the intensive research, the methods and guidelines for designing and implementing feedback in confidence-based assessment remain scarce so far. It is especially important for the design of feedback in WBLSs, where "teachers" could not be as flexible as in the traditional learning.

Our studies [11, 12] demonstrated that knowledge of response certitude together with response correctness allows to determine what kind of feedback is more preferable and more effective for the students, and EF may sufficiently improve the performance of students within the online tests.

Individual LS are one of the important characteristics of the student that characterize the ways in which the student perceives information, acquires knowledge, and communicates with the teacher and with other students. Incorporating LS in WBLSs has been one of the topical problems of WBLS design during recent years. There are currently several WBLSs that support adaptation to the individual LS (AHA!, CS383, IDEAL, MAS-PLANG, INSPIRE). However, according to our knowledge, there is no system or reported research (in the e-learning context) that addressed the issue aimed at providing feedback tailored to the LS of the student except our own recent study [11].

4 Immediate Elaborated Feedback (EF) Adaptation

4.1 Generic Feedback Adaptation Framework

Figure 1 presents a generic view of feedback adaptation in a WBLS. The *Student* is identified by the system and associated with his/her profile from the repository. During the interaction with the system the student receives a *Task* (or question) from the *Tasks Repository* and provides an *Answer*. The answer is compared with an expected 'correct' answer to this *Task* by the *Evaluation Module*. The result of the evaluation as well as the user model (information about the user from the *Student Profiles Repository* and *Performance Statistic Repository*) is the input to the *Feedback Adaptation Unit*. Feedback adaptation unit includes a knowledge base containing the adaptation rules that associate user (task, environment) characteristics with certain feedback parameters from the *Feedback Repository*. In the feedback adaptation unit the most convenient form and time of feedback presentation is inferred according to the (long-term and/or short term) characteristics of the student (task, environment). The user model (*Student Profile* and *Performance Statistic Repositories*) is updated with the information obtained by the *Evaluation Module*.

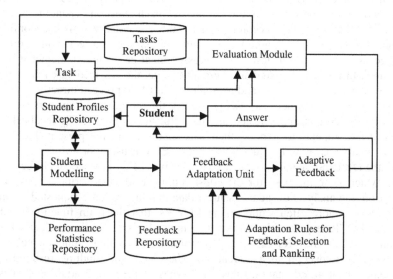

Fig. 1. A generic view on feedback adaptation in a WBLS

4.2   Authoring Adaptive EF and Overall Online Assessment Design

For our study we used a simple user model (UM) that includes information about knowledge of concepts (self-evaluated/estimated by the students[1]), and certitude and correctness of the current response (which constitute two dimensions of possible cases; high-confidence correct responses (HCCRs), high-confidence wrong response (HCWR), low-confidence correct responses (LCCRs), low-confidence wrong response (LCWR)). Other individual characteristics can be added easily of course,

---

[1] When the tasks/tests are part of a complete e-learning environment where the system can monitor the student's reading and learning activities the system may derive knowledge estimates itself, as is done for instance in typical AHA! applications. (See http://aha.win.tue.nl/ for more details, papers, software download, etc.) In our experiments the tests were done in a mostly traditional learning setting (with lectures and practice sessions), and we simply asked the students to estimate their own knowledge level.

however we tried to focus our study on a particular set of characteristics that allows us to verify our findings from previous experiments as well as to verify the feasibility of the EF adaptation approach and to make some new observations.

The study of EF adaptation was conducted within two tests with the students of a Databases (DB) course (30 students) and an Information Retrieval (IR) course (19 students) at the Eindhoven University of Technology during the fall semester of 2007. Before the tests the students were asked to answer a subset of the most representative (5 for each dimension) questions [16] of Felder-Silverman's index of LS quiz [1].

The tests themselves consisted of 15 multiple-choice questions. The questions were aimed at assessing the knowledge of the concepts and the development of the necessary skills (like computing a canonical cover or translating between English and SQL in the DB test and like reproducing decision tree learning or association rule mining in the machine learning (ML) part of the IR course). It was estimated that the students would need between 2 and 6 minutes for each question depending of its difficulty[2]. Each question was accompanied by the compulsory response confidence question: "Please evaluate your certainty about your answer (it affects your score)".

The general approach for designing the assessment procedures is depicted in Figure 2 below. In DB test, the students were able to get the KR feedback first and than to choose between theory-based and example-based EF or proceed directly to the next question. On the page, where EF was presented, the question and answers were presented with the correct and selected alternative(s) highlighted (KCR feedback). We also asked the students to express their satisfaction about the presented EF. They could optionally answer to the questions whether EF was useful or not.

With the DB experiment we were able to discover EF preference and effectiveness patterns which were the base for the construction of adaptation rules. Thus, it was evident from the analysis of the assessment data that the students requested example-based feedback more often while giving LCWRs, that the main function feedback plays after LCCR responses is "filling the knowledge gap" in the student's knowledge, and that for HCWRs EF should perform the "patching" function helping to overcome the misconceptions a student has. These and other findings resulted in the implementation of 48 adaptation rules for 3 types of EF with 2 additional rules for handling exceptional cases.

With the IR test we conducted the actual EF adaptation study aimed at confirming the feasibility of our approach. The main differences in the IR test is that the most suitable EF is adaptively selected (leaving possibilities of further study of other available EF types) and that KR was not provided separately, but had to be inferred from the EF instead. That is, students had to read the explanations of the EF to understand whether their answer was correct or not. The results of the DB test suggested that it is logical to place KR into EF to increase the overall effect of EF on the learning process during the assessment. This also made our study with the IR test more interesting since we got more EF requests (and EF was now requested for different reasons: extracting KR and learning from EF)[3].

---

[2] Tests were reasonably difficult given the amount of time to pass the test. About 40-70% of questions were answered correctly on average for different tests.

[3] Some further information, a reader may find essential regarding the implementation and organization of the experimental study, can be found in a compact Appendix on http://wwwis.win.tue.nl/~debra/ah08/

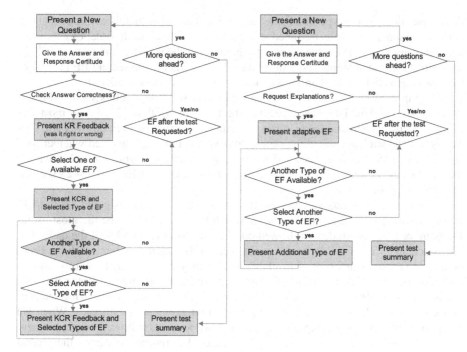

Fig. 2. Assessment process in DB (left) and IR (right) tests

4.3 Obtained Results

We evaluated the effectiveness of adaptive selection and recommendation by means of (1) the number of requests for the EF (only in the cases where the EF was not already directly shown as a result of the adaptation rules), (2) the time students spent for studying the adaptively selected or recommended EF, (3) usefulness of the EF according the students' feedback rating they have provided.[4]

Analysis of EF requests. We analyze only students' responses for which immediate EF was requested, that is 72.6% of all the responses. According to the mechanism of personalization (based on concept certitude, response certitude and correctness) the EF was provided either directly, or a student could request the explanations, selecting it from the available recommendations, which were example-based or theory-based EF. Students received both available types of EF directly in 25% of the cases, one type of EF in 54,1% of the cases, and, no EF in 20,9%. The average time the students spent on the directly received EF was 26 sec when only one type of EF was shown and 34 sec for two types of EF.

When the students received directly one of the available types of EF they could request the second available type (also with a highlighted level of importance) if they wanted. In our experiments the students did this only in 9.4% of the cases and in all

---

[4] The results of earlier experiments already demonstrated that EF sufficiently *improves* the students' performance during the test. Here we analyze the students' *perception* of the EF usefulness.

these cases that second type of EF was also recommended (which is evidence that our personalization rules were designed correctly). In 70% of such situations they requested example-based explanations after getting the theory-based immediate EF. In such situations the students spent more than 10 seconds for the second EF in 90% of the cases (as well as more than 10 seconds for the first EF they received).

Only in 27% of the cases when one type of EF was adaptively selected, the students spent less than 10 seconds reading the EF. Among those 27 %, the most frequently occurring situation was when the students answered correctly (81%). This means that the students quickly reviewed the explanations and analyzed whether they answered correctly or not. They did not want to spend much time for really reading the EF. For the correct responses the average time of reading EF was 15–25 sec, for incorrect responses it was 30–40 sec.

When no EF was adaptively presented automatically, students could request EF, either following our recommendation for which type of EF might be the most useful for them, or not. The students followed our recommendation in 54% of the cases, but this is actually 75% if we do not take into account the situation when we did not recommend to examine any type of available EF, but they were willing to do this anyway (in order to extract KR from EF). The first type of EF the students selected was theory-based EF in 89% of the cases overall and in 72% of cases by following our recommendations (otherwise, selecting example-based explanations instead). When we recommended studying example-based EF first, the students followed our recommendations in 100% of the cases. Only in 12% cases the students requested the second available EF after reading the first one.

In situations when the EF was selected by the students (and was not automatically shown already), they spent less time for examining it (16 sec on average), equally the same time for theory-based EF and example-based EF. This is also one of the confirmations that personalization worked correctly and those students indeed did not need EF in their situation.

Usefulness of EF. Students were willing to give both positive (73%) and negative (27%) responses regarding the perceived usefulness of the EF; in 68% of the cases for the theory-based EF and 32% for example-based EF. Among the responses about theory-based EF 20% were "not useful", and regarding example-based EF - 35%. Only in a very few cases, when one type of the EF was directly shown to the students, they found it not to be useful (and requested the second type of the explanations instead). Interestingly, most of the students who found feedback not useful were the students who gave HCWR (this once again confirms that during the test it is more difficult for the students to analyze and to amend their misconceptions than it is to fill a knowledge gap). There was one extreme case, when a student spent more than 2 minutes for studying directly received EF (HCWR) and marked both of types of feedback he got as not useful.

Summary. The results of the study demonstrate the feasibility and effectiveness of EF adaptation. In particular, the students (1) followed our recommendations of the type of EF they could select in most of the cases; (2) only occasionally selected another type of EF when the first was selected automatically; (3) spent more time for the feedback when it was directly shown for them than for the feedback which they had to choose; (4) gave sufficiently more positive than negative responses about the EF that was shown directly or recommended to them. Besides, the analysis of assessment data confirms the generality of EF patterns and corresponding adaptation rules at least within two completely independent experiments.

5 Conclusions and Further Work

Designing and authoring feedback and tailoring it to students is an important problem of online learning assessment. We have studied this problem through a series of experiments in the form of seven online tests organized as part of (three) TU/e courses with traditional in-class lectures and instructions.

In this paper we presented a part of our study focused on the EF adaptation by means of adaptive selection and/or recommendation of the appropriate type of EF to students. Adaptation rules that take into account students' response certitude and response correctness, and level of their knowledge of the subject were designed according to the EF effectiveness and students' preference patterns observed during the preceding studies. The results of the assessment data analysis and well as feedback from the students provide enough evidence that our EF adaptation approach is feasible.

Our current and ongoing work includes preparation of an extended report that includes a more detailed description of the experimental settings and design, and corresponding results including the effectiveness of EF with regard to "patching" vs. "filling the knowledge gap", and "awareness" functions, and organization of further studies with different scenarios of feedback recommendations and personalization. In particular, the results obtained in our studies strongly advocate the benefits and necessity of taking into account LS for providing different types of feedback during the online assessment, and reveal the additional possibilities of feedback personalization [11]. There is no space in this paper for presenting our initial findings regarding the importance of taking the LS into account in feedback adaptation. These findings have be validated through experiments we performed with TU/e students in the spring of 2008, and will be presented in a forthcoming paper.

Acknowledgments. This research is partly supported by the COMAS Graduate School of the University of Jyväskylä, Finland. We are thankful to the students who participated in the courses and provided their valuable comments regarding the organization of the online tests and, particularly, the feedback usefulness.

References

1. Felder, R.M., Silverman, L.K.: Learning and teaching styles in engineering education. J. of Engineering Education 78(7), 674–681 (1988)
2. Hatie, J., Timperley, H.: The power of feedback. J. Review of Educational Research 87(1), 81–112 (2007)
3. Hyland, F.: Providing effective support: investigating feedback to distance language learners. Open Learning 16(3), 233–247 (2001)
4. Kulhavy, R.W., Stock, W.A.: Feedback in written instruction: The place of response certitude. Educational Psychology Review 1(4), 279–308 (1989)

5. Mandernach, B.J.: Relative Effectiveness of Computer-based and Human Feedback for Enhancing Student Learning. J. of Educators Online 2(1) (2005)

6. Mathan, S.: Recasting the Feedback Debate: Benefits of Tutoring Error Detection and Correction Skills, PhD Thesis, Carnegie Melon University, Pittsburgh (2003)

7. Mory, E.H.: Feedback research revisited. In: Jonassen, D. (ed.) Handbook of research on educational communications and technology, pp. 745–783. Erlbaum Associates, Mahwah (2004)

8. Mory, E.H.: The use of response certitude in adaptive feedback: Effects on student performance, feedback study time, and efficiency. J. of Educational Computing Research and Development 40(3), 5–20 (1994)

9. Oulasvirta, A., Saariluoma, P.: Long-term working memory and interrupting messages in human-computer interaction. Behaviour and Information Technology 23(1), 53–64 (2004)

10. Shute, V.J.: Focus on formative feedback, Research Report (2007)(Retrieved January 15, 2008), http://www.ets.org/Media/Research/pdf/RR-07-11.pdf

11. Vasilyeva, E., De Bra, P., Pechenizkiy, M., Puuronen, S.: Tailoring feedback in online assessment: influence of learning styles on the feedback preferences and elaborated feedback effectiveness. In: Proc. of Int. Conf. on Advance Learning Technologies, ICALT 2008. IEEE CS Press, Los Alamitos (to appear, 2008)

12. Vasilyeva, E., Pechenizkiy, M., De Bra, P.: Tailoring of feedback in web-based learning: the role of response certitude in the assessment. In: Proc. of 9th International Conference on Intelligent Tutoring Systems, ITS 2008 (to appear, 2008), http://wwwis.win.tue.nl/~debra/its08/

13. Vasilyeva, E., Puuronen, S., Pechenizkiy, M., Räsänen, P.: Feedback adaptation in web-based learning systems. Special Issue of Int. J. of Continuing Engineering Education and Life-Long Learning 17(4-5), 337–357 (2007)

14. Vasilyeva, E., Pechenizkiy, M., De Bra, P.: Adaptation of Feedback in e-learning System at Individual and Group Level, In: Proc. of PING 2007 Int. Workshop on Personalization in E-Learning Environments at Individual and Group Level (UM 2007 Conf.), pp. 49-56 (2007)

15. Vasilyeva, E., Pechenizkiy, M., Gavrilova, T., Puuronen, S.: Personalization of Immediate Feedback to Learning Styles. In: Proc. of 7th IEEE Int. Conf. on Advanced Learning Technologies, pp. 622–624 (2007)

16. Viola, S.R., Graf, S., Kinshuk, Leo, T.: Analysis of Felder-Silverman Index of Learning Styles by a Data-driven Statistical Approach. In: Proc. of the 8th IEEE Int. Symposium on Multimedia, pp. 959–964 (2006)

Adaptive Link Annotation in Distributed Hypermedia Systems: The Evaluation of a Service-Based Approach

Michael Yudelson and Peter Brusilovsky

University of Pittsburgh, School of Information Sciences
135 North Bellefield Avenue, Pittsburgh, PA 15232, USA
{mvy3,peterb}@pitt.edu

Abstract. A service-based approach to link annotation expands the applicability of adaptive navigation support functionality beyond the limits of traditional adaptive hypermedia systems. With this approach, the decision-making functionality is separated from the application systems and encapsulated in a personalization service. This paper attempts to evaluate the feasibility of using this approach in the real world. After a brief overview of current efforts to develop service-based approaches to adaptive hypermedia, we describe our specific implementation of this approach as personalization architecture and report the results of an extensive performance evaluation of this architecture.

Keywords: Adaptive navigation support, adaptive annotation, personalization, service, distributed architecture.

1 Introduction

Adaptive link annotation is one of the most popular adaptive hypermedia (AH) technologies [1]. A number of AH systems have demonstrated the various benefits of adaptive link annotation. For example, in the educational context, adaptive link annotation is known to increase student progress and motivation to work, while decreasing the navigational overhead [2]. This paper addresses the challenges of implementing adaptive link annotation in the context of modern open corpus hypermedia systems [4]. In this context, which is becoming more and more popular, information resources are separated from their application in hypermedia. The resources reside in various web sites, repositories, and digital libraries, while application systems have emerged from being mere *collections* of these resources to being *portals* for accessing multiple resources. This modern distributed approach for developing hypermedia systems is very attractive to both system developers and content providers because it allows them to reuse high quality content in multiple application systems. On the other hand, the distributed nature of these hypermedia systems presents a real challenge for researchers and practitioners who want to implement AH techniques, such as adaptive link annotation, in this new, open corpus context. To produce adaptive link annotations, classic AH systems rely on resource metadata and adaptation algorithms which have been developed to handle the various kinds of resources available in that particular system. To expand this approach to the distributed context, a portal is needed that contains metadata for all these resources, as well as adaptation algorithms. Not only does that contradict the very idea of

W. Nejdl et al. (Eds.): AH 2008, LNCS 5149, pp. 245–254, 2008.
© Springer-Verlag Berlin Heidelberg 2008

separating content from application portals, it is simply not feasible, due to the large volume and diverse nature of reusable content.

A promising approach to overcome this problem is to encapsulate adaptation functionality by embedding it in a classical AH system, as a *personalization service*. For example, a distributed educational hypermedia system which uses visual cues to adaptively annotate educational resource links may no longer need its own decision-making algorithm to decide whether a specific resource is ready for a given user. Instead, the application could simply call a personalization service, pass references to both the user and the resource under consideration and receive the adaptation decision in the form an icon, shown next to the resource link. This approach, originally suggested by a research team from the University of Hannover [9; 11], offers a number of benefits. It makes the adaptation functionality itself highly reusable. It also decreases the level of AH expertise required from the developers of an adaptive application. Also, it allows personalization to be deployed on even lightweight portals, such as learning management systems.

Despite its conceptual attractiveness, the practical feasibility of this approach has not been proven. While successful implementations of personalization services have been reported [10], none of them have undergone performance evaluations. Distributed functionality comes at a price: every personalization effect, such as a visual cue shown next to a link, now requires considerable information exchange between various components of a distributed adaptive system (i.e., a portal, a personalization service, a user model server, etc).

In this paper we attempt to answer the question of whether personalization services are feasible in distributed AH systems. We first attempt this on a relatively small scale – in a classroom study which has a small number of users. Then, we use the observed performance of the limited scale personalization services to predict what will happen when the personalization task is scaled up.

After a brief overview of current efforts to develop a service-based approach to AH, we describe our practical implementation of the service-based personalization architecture and report the results of its extensive performance evaluation.

2 Related Work

The work on open corpus distributed AH began with an attempt to reuse external Web pages in the context of a regular closed corpus AH system. The first idea to explore was relatively simple: integrate external content by adding external references along with their connections (index) to the with domain model concepts of the host system. With this approach, which was successfully applied in KBS-Hyperbook [12] and SIGUE [6], the adaptive functionality still resides in the original adaptive system.

However, when the external reusable content becomes more sophisticated than simple Web pages, an AH system emerges into a truly distributed environment consisting of several interactive components and a hypermedia portal, which ties these components together and provides centralized access to them. We can distinguish several approaches that can offer personalization in this distributed context. One approach is to keep the content integrator (portal) simple while developing adaptive intermediary services, which reside between the portal and the interactive content, which will offer personalized access to this content [5; 14]. An advantage of this approach is that it provides personalization for very light portals, such as learning management systems. The negative side is that for every pool of new resources, a new intermediary service has to be devised. The opposite method is to create a smart content integrator (portal) that is aware of the local and/or remote resources and makes use of one or several personalization techniques available to it [13]. The advantage of a smart portal is that minimal or no effort is necessary to adapt a localized resource. A strong disadvantage is the high cost of such localization.

A third way also exists: outsource the adaptive functionality to a separate system— a personalization engine— that would provide adaptive value upon request. The idea of separating adaptation functionality into a stand-alone system has existed for some time. One of the first examples of this was the APeLS system [7]. Later, the authors of the Personal-Reader framework [8] created a very sophisticated and advanced architecture in which personalization services play the central role. A clear advantage to this third approach is the ubiquitous nature of personalization services that can be utilized by multiple systems in multiple contexts. The question, of course, is whether service-based approaches are feasible, given the overhead created by the distributed nature of AH systems. This is the question that we attempt to answer in this paper.

3 Personalization Services in ADAPT^2 Architecture

To evaluate the feasibility of personalization services, one needs to have a distributed framework where personalization functionality can be applied. An example of such a framework is ADAPT^2 (read adapt-square) - an advanced distributed architecture for personalized teaching and training, which was developed by our research team. In ADAPT^2 a portal – such as our KnowledgeTree portal – is a simple link aggregator without any embedded navigation support. The only way to provide personalization in this context is to use external personalization services, which is why it provides a very attractive platform to explore the feasibility of the service-based approach to personalization. The first personalization service deployed for our portal is an adaptive social navigation service [3]. We chose this type of adaptive navigation due to the simplicity of its implementation and its inherent cross-domain nature.

Fig. 1 shows an environment in which the ADAPT^2 personalization services work. The primary client of personalization services engine is the content aggregator. In our case it is the portal. A portal is a collection of resources that need personalization. In Fig. 1, a sample of the portal page is shown. On this page, a set of links from several sources are shown, including book readings, code examples, and lecture recordings. To obtain personalization for this set of resources, the portal sends a request to a specific service in the personalization engine. In our case it is a social navigation service. A social navigation service has the option to consult an external oracle. In the ADAPT^2 architecture user modeling server is such an oracle. Information about user and group navigation is obtained from the oracle. Finally, a personalization service generates navigation cues and sends them back to the portal. A portal displays cues to links obtained from the personalization service next to these links.

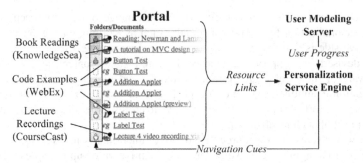

Fig. 1. The ADAPT2 personalization services engine environment and data flow

4 Experimental Evaluation

The question of whether adaptive navigation will work successfully as an interface technique has been studied extensively. It is not clear, however, whether the adaptation will work efficiently once the personalization functionality is outsourced to an external system and implemented as a service. A similar question has been studied regarding performance of the user modeling service in a distributed adaptive system [15]. This study has shown that there are, in fact, limitations to the performance of user modeling services. Since our personalization services depend on a user modeling component, the distribution factor of the adaptive system grows, which means that the answer to the question of efficiency of a distributed AH system is not obvious.

That is why we have decided to conduct a series of tests of our personalization service engine. First, we conducted a pilot study of one of the personalization services by deploying it in classroom. The point of the study was to test the general feasibility of personalization services. Results of this pilot study were then used to set up extensive performance evaluation experiment of our personalization services under a range of loads. We were interested in determining the limits of this approach: the critical loads our personalization service engine could handle and the number of users it could support.

4.1 Pilot Study

Our engine implements several adaptation techniques. One of the first and most desired was the social navigation personalization service. Upon the arrival of a request that has a set of resources, a user identity and a group identity, the service queries the user model for individual user progress with resources as well as average group average progress values. A personalization service would then connect the information from the user model with the requested resources by adding navigational cues to resources in the RDF format.

To pilot-test performance of this implementation and to deploy a social navigation personalization service, we conducted a classroom study in an undergraduate database course at the School of Information Sciences, University of Pittsburgh during the Fall 2007 semester. The class had 37 students. The resources available via social navigation personalization service were grouped into several thematic folders which included dissected SQL code examples and parameterized quizzes.

This course was very intensive and, as a result, the amount of student work exceeded our expectations. The load our adaptive tools had to cope with was quite high. There were nearly 5,300 clicks on lines of annotated SQL code examples, a little over 4,500 answers to the parameterized quizzes and approximately 2,000 accesses to the folders for which social navigation personalization service was deployed during the semester. Thus each student accessed these folders over 50 times. The maximum number of accesses per minute was 15, the median was 1, and the 95th percentile was 7. Every call to the personalization service contained about 20 resources awaiting personalization. It required the personalization service engine to construct models of 103.5±0.86 RDF triples. Each such call took personalization service engine 43.5 ms, on average, to complete. This means that the personalization overhead was .42 ms per RDF triple or a little more than 2 ms per resource.

4.2 Experimental Setup

The results of the pilot evaluation have shown that even though the active usage of adaptive tools created a very adaptation-intensive environment, this did not challenge our personalization service engine enough. Therefore, we decided to conduct a series of much more intensive experiments to test the effectiveness of the personalization service engine under heavy loads and determine the loads critical to its performance.

To accomplish this, we used a technique previously employed by us and described in [16]. We set up two machines: one with the personalization service engine, and the other with a special "flooder" installed. The role of the "flooder" was to imitate the personalization service client, subject the personalization engine machine to various types of load, and record the observed parameters.

To simplify the experiment, we decided to use discrete values for the load. The parameters of the load were the following.

- **Complexity of the request.** The majority of our portal lecture folders had roughly 20 resource links to personalize (this includes lecture folders of the pilot course described in section 4.1. and several other courses that are deployed on the portal). In addition to that we used two more values for complexity: 5 resources, to represent a "lightweight" folder, and 50 to signify a folder "overloaded" with resources. Thus we had 3 values: 5, 20, and 50 resources per request (35, 125, and 305 RDF triples respectively).
- **Request delivery rate** – delay between consecutive requests. From our experience with user modeling services [15], [16] and initial experiments with a personalization service engine, we had already learned that a delay of 10ms between requests is critical for our hardware/software configuration. In addition, delays between requests of 160ms and more did not present any challenge. Hence, we varied the request delivery rate parameter between 10 ms and 160 ms. Rates between boundaries were doubles of the previous value, giving us 5 loads: 10, 20, 40, 80, and 160 ms.
- **Duration of the load.** From prior experimentation we knew that the duration did not really matter, unless it was a peak load of 10ms or 20ms between requests. During these peak loads, the personalization server would stop responding to any requests at all after 30 seconds. We decided to keep the load sessions fairly short – a little less than 4 seconds (3,840ms, divisible by all delivery rates).

To obtain more data we repeated the flooding sessions 5 times for each of the three request complexities and each of the five request delivery rates, giving us 3 x 5 = 15 different settings. During these sessions we observed the following parameters:

- **Mean response delay**—the average amount of time it takes to complete a request.
- **Request success rate**—denoting the fraction of requests that completed successfully. For the least demanding load of 160 ms between requests, the amount of requests sent per each flooding session was 3,840/160=24. For the highest load of 10 ms between requests, it was 3,840/10=384.

The personalization service engine was run on a machine with Pentium 4 dual core 2.8 Mhz processor and 1Gb RAM. The user modeling server that the personalization service engine depended on was running on the same machine. To compensate for the high speed of the school's wired network, we used a WiFi network to communicate with the personalization engine. It also provided a realistic scenario for students who would be accessing adaptive content outside their fast university campus LAN.

4.3 Results

Fig. 2 shows a summary of the personalization service engine performance results. Charts in the left column are the percentile plots. Each curve there corresponds to one of the five request delivery rates. Each point on a percentile plot indicates the maximum response delay (x-axis) for the given percentile of requests (y-axis).

The right column of charts denotes request success. For each of the request delay rates, we show only the total number of requests sent, the number of requests responded – both successfully completed and "gracefully failed" (had an empty response or an error message), and the number of successfully completed requests. Each row within the charts corresponds to a different request complexity: the top was 5 resources (35 RDF triples) per request, the middle, 20 (125 RDF triples), and the bottom was 50 (305 RDF triples).

As we can see from Fig. 2 (a-1, a-2) – low request complexity – for almost all loads, 95% of the requests finished in about 25 ms. Only the peak load of 10 ms between requests slowed the personalization service engine considerably, with the 95th percentile being off the chart at 4,150 ms. This resulted in (3,840-3,488)/3,840 (9%) of the requests returning error messages.

In the case of medium request complexity, (Fig. 2 b-1, b-2) there were two peak loads of 10 and 20 ms between requests that result in deteriorated personalization service engine performance. The 95th percentiles for them are both off the chart at 12,530 and 6,300 ms for 10 and 20 ms rates respectively. While all other loads had 95% of their requests finishing in about 50 ms, around 38% ([3840-2388]/3840) of requests at 10ms resulted in errors. On the other hand, despite large delays, all requests under 20ms load completed successfully.

In the case of high request complexity (Fig. 2 c-1, c-2) three loads of 10, 20 and 40 ms between requests worsened the personalization service engine performance. The 95th percentiles for them were well off the chart at 24,230, 16,000 and 6,750 ms, for 10, 20, and 40 ms rates, respectively. For all other loads, 95% of the requests finished in about 200 ms. Also, instead of going almost vertically until the 95th percentile

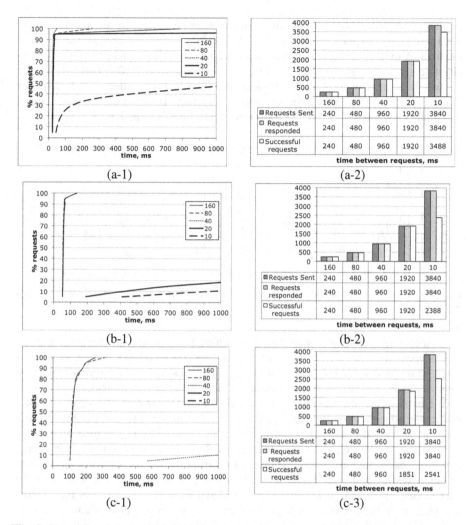

(a-1)   (a-2)

(b-1)   (b-2)

(c-1)   (c-3)

Fig. 2. Percentile plots (column 1) and request success charts (column 2) for three request complexities: a) 5 resources per request (top row), b) 20 resources per request (middle row), and c) 50 resources per request (bottom row)

(for low and medium request complexity), curves bend in the direction of delay increment. About 34% ([3,840-2,541]/3,840) of the requests at a 10ms load resulted in errors. Only 4% ([1,920 -1,851]/1,920) of requests at 20ms load return errors. All other loads (even 40ms load) do not result in errors.

Let us go from a discussion of delays and percentiles to focusing on how many students could be effectively served by the personalization service engine. We have based our estimation on the pilot course mentioned in the beginning of section 4. As previously stated, there were 37 students. Whenever they worked with the personalization services, they spent 95% of their time, collectively, making no more than 7 requests per minute. Since the typical request contained roughly 20 resources that needed personalization, we based the estimation on the results for the medium complexity requests obtained above. Loads of 10 and 20 ms between requests were clearly too high. A load of 40 ms between requests seemed to be quite plausible for a personalization service engine to handle. 40ms between requests is 60,000 / 40 = 1,500 per minute. In a class of 37 students, 95% of the time had a maximum 7 requests per minute, whenever they were working with the system. To reach the allowed request maximum of 1,500, (37*1500 / 7) ≈ 8,000 students have to be *actively* involved.

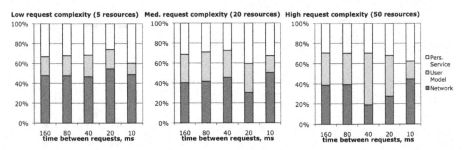

Fig. 3. Relative time distribution between network communication, user modeling server and the personalization engine

As mentioned before, we based our estimation on a class where students were working with adaptive tools intensively. For a less demanding course, a larger number of students could be supported. Also, at this point, no special techniques or software/hardware configurations were used to boost the performance of the personalization engine.

We have shown the feasibility of deploying a personalization service engine in a distributed adaptive environment, but due to the distributed nature of personalization, the adaptation delays cannot be attributed to the personalization engine alone. The personalization service had to consult an external oracle (user modeling server) which consumes more time. Network communication from the client (portal) to the personalization service and back again, as well as from the personalization service to the user model server and back – must be considered as well. Fig. 3 shows the relative distribution of the request delays. As we can see, the pure personalization time is comparable to the processing time of the user model and network communication time. Across all request complexities and loads, the breakdown is roughly 1/3 in each category.

5   Discussion and Future Work

This paper explored the feasibility of a service-based approach to personalization in distributed AH systems on both a small and large scale. We implemented a service-based personalization approach in the context of our distributed e-learning architecture and ran an extensive performance evaluation of this approach under different loads. The results of our study demonstrated that this approach is highly feasible, given modern networking and processing capacity. A regular desktop PC hosting a personalization service could easily support several thousand students working with the system. Moreover, the delay caused by the application of a personalization service is comparable to the delay caused by the user modeling server and the network itself, i.e., a personalization service is not really a stumbling point on the way to distributed personalization. Note that in our study we were using a slower WiFi network as opposed to the faster school LAN, when sending requests to the personalization engine. We did this on purpose to simulate realistic scenarios of students working from locations other than campus. Personalization request delays would be lower and supported user-base capacity of the personalization engine would be higher when faster networks are used.

The next step in our evaluation agenda is to check how the distributed personalization approach may be scaled to more sophisticated services. In our study we evaluated a social navigation support service, which is not computationally intensive and only requires a UM lookup. Currently, we are developing more complicated personalization services, which require a more sophisticated aggregation and transformation of the user modeling values. We plan a similar study to evaluate the performance of these personalization services.

References

1. Brusilovsky, P.: Adaptive hypermedia. User Modeling and User Adapted Interaction 11(1/2), 87–110 (2001)
2. Brusilovsky, P.: Adaptive navigation support in educational hypermedia: the role of student knowledge level and the case for meta-adaptation. British Journal of Educational Technology 34(4), 487–497 (2003)
3. Brusilovsky, P., Chavan, G., Farzan, R.: Social adaptive navigation support for open corpus electronic textbooks. In: De Bra, P., Nejdl, W. (eds.) AH 2004. LNCS, vol. 3137, pp. 24–33. Springer, Heidelberg (2004)
4. Brusilovsky, P., Henze, N.: Open corpus adaptive educational hypermedia. In: Brusilovsky, P., Kobsa, A., Nejdl, W. (eds.) Adaptive Web 2007. LNCS, vol. 4321, pp. 671–696. Springer, Heidelberg (2007)
5. Brusilovsky, P., Sosnovsky, S.: Individualized Exercises for Self-Assessment of Programming Knowledge: An Evaluation of QuizPACK. ACM Journal on Educational Resources in Computing 5 (3), Article No. 6 (2005)
6. Carmona, C., Bueno, D., Guzmán, E., Conejo, R.: SIGUE: Making Web Courses Adaptive. In: De Bra, P., Brusilovsky, P., Conejo, R. (eds.) AH 2002. LNCS, vol. 2347, pp. 376–379. Springer, Heidelberg (2002)
7. Conlan, O., Wade, V.P.: Evaluation of APeLS - an adaptive eLearning service based on multi-model, metadata-driven approach. In: De Bra, P., Nejdl, W. (eds.) AH 2004. LNCS, vol. 3137, pp. 291–295. Springer, Heidelberg (2004)
8. Dolog, P., Henze, N., Neidl, W., Sintek, M.: The personal reader: Personalizing and enriching learning resources using semantic web technologies. In: De Bra, P., Nejdl, W. (eds.) AH 2004. LNCS, vol. 3137, pp. 85–94. Springer, Heidelberg (2004)
9. Dolog, P., Henze, N., Nejdl, W., Sintek, M.: Personalization in distributed e-learning environments. In: Proc. of The Thirteenth International World Wide Web Conference, WWW 2004, pp. 161–169. ACM Press, New York (2004)
10. Henze, N.: Personal Readers: Personalized Learning Object Readers for the Semantic Web. In: Looi, C.-K., McCalla, G., Bredeweg, B., Breuker, J. (eds.) Proc. of 12th International Conference on Artificial Intelligence in Education, AIED 2005, pp. 274–281. IOS Press, Amsterdam (2005)

11. Henze, N.: Personalization Services for e-Learning in the Semantic Web. In: Proc. of Workshop on Adaptive Systems for Web-based Education at 12th International Conference on Artificial Intelligence in Education, AIED 2005, pp. 55–58. IOS Press, Amsterdam (2005)
12. Henze, N., Nejdl, W.: Adaptation in open corpus hypermedia. International Journal of Artificial Intelligence in Education 12(4), 325–350 (2001)
13. Trella, M., Carmona, C., Conejo, R.: MEDEA: an Open Service-Based Learning Platform for Developing Intelligent Educational Systems for the Web. In: Proc. of Workshop on Adaptive Systems for Web-based Education at 12th International Conference on Artificial Intelligence in Education, pp. 27–34 (2005)
14. Yudelson, M., Brusilovsky, P.: NavEx: Providing Navigation Support for Adaptive Browsing of Annotated Code Examples. In: Looi, C.-K., McCalla, G., Bredeweg, B., Breuker, J. (eds.) Proc. of 12th International Conference on Artificial Intelligence in Education, AI-Ed 2005, pp. 710–717. IOS Press, Amsterdam (2005)
15. Yudelson, M., Brusilovsky, P., Zadorozhny, V.: A User Modeling Server for Contemporary Adaptive Hypermedia: An Evaluation of Push Approach to Evidence Propagation. In: Conati, C., McCoy, K., Paliouras, G. (eds.) UM 2007. LNCS (LNAI), vol. 4511, pp. 27–36. Springer, Heidelberg (2007)
16. Zadorozhny, V., Yudelson, M., Brusilovsky, P.: A Framework for Performance Evaluation of User Modeling Servers for Web Applications. Web Intelligence and Agent Systems 5 (in press) (2008)

Do Students Trust Their Open Learner Models?

Norasnita Ahmad and Susan Bull

Electronic, Electrical and Computer Engineering
University of Birmingham, Edgbaston, Birmingham, B15 2TT, UK
{nxa707,s.bull}@bham.ac.uk

Abstract. Open learner models (OLM) enable users to access their learner model to view information about their understanding. Opening the learner model to the learner may increase their perceptions of how a system evaluates their knowledge and updates the model. This raises questions of trust relating to whether the learner believes the evaluations are correct, and whether they trust the system as a whole. We investigate learner trust in various OLM features: the complexity of the model presentation; the level of learner control over the model contents; and the facility to release one's own model for peer viewing.

1 Introduction

Student self-knowledge is essential for self-directed learning [1]. Opening the learner model (LM) to the user provides opportunities to encourage reflection, independent learning and formative assessment/monitoring [2]. In this paper we consider three features of open learner models (OLMs): (i) complexity of model presentation; (ii) learner control over the learner model; (iii) releasing the learner model to other users.

(i) LMs can be externalised using simple or detailed representations of knowledge. Simple displays often show the LM using skill meters. OLMlets is an example of a simple OLM with five views of the learner model, including skill meters [2] (see Fig. 1). The second example, Flexi-OLM, is an OLM that includes complex model presentations in seven formats [3]. Fig. 1 illustrates the structure of the concept map and hierarchical tree. Both OLMlets and Flexi-OLM use colour to indicate knowledge levels, problematic areas and misconceptions; and misconceptions are stated textually (e.g. "you may believe that the '=' operator can be used for comparison").

(ii) OLMlets and Flexi-OLM offer different levels of learner control over the LM. In OLMlets it can be viewed, but the learner cannot change the LM contents. Flexi-OLM allows students to edit or try to persuade it if they disagree with its representations [3]. Students can edit their LM by changing the knowledge to the desired level. Persuading the LM requires students to convince the system (about their skill) before the representations will be altered. In both cases Flexi-OLM offers evidence for its beliefs, but in persuasion, the learner has to demonstrate their belief in a short test.

(iii) OLMlets allows students to release their LM (named or anonymously) to instructors and peers [4]. All peer models accessible to a user can be viewed together. Students can also access data on the group's knowledge of each topic, and how their LM compares to instructor expectations for that stage of the course (see [2]).

W. Nejdl et al. (Eds.): AH 2008, LNCS 5149, pp. 255–258, 2008.
© Springer-Verlag Berlin Heidelberg 2008

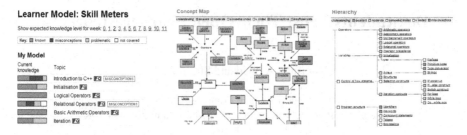

Fig. 1. OLMlets simple skill meter [2]; Flexi-OLM detailed concept map and tree structure [3]

OLMs raise questions of user trust that may not arise as strongly in other environments, as students do not usually see inferences about their knowledge. Trust is an important issue when there may be potential risks [5], and the topic has been of interest in many fields [5],[6],[7]. In human-computer interaction, a key question is the extent to which a user has sufficient confidence in a system's actions, decisions or recommendations, in order to act on these [8]. Minimum system performance is necessary for the development of trust; and the level of trust in a system may affect user decisions (manual or automated control) and whether they follow the system's advice [9]. In OLMs, risks could result from learner control over their model. For example, the learner may under/overestimate their knowledge in a self-assessment, and so provide incorrect information to their LM [10]. The validity of the model can be affected by model tampering [11]. However, it has been suggested that students may be less comfortable with editing the model: they may prefer an OLM that offers less direct control [3]. It seems that some learners may trust a system to infer their knowledge more than they trust themselves to assess it. We suggest, therefore, that persuading the LM may be a more 'trustable' feature than direct editing of it. With inspectable LMs, students can view the information (without altering it). Trust in the accuracy of the LM may be even more important if learners have no control over its contents. A different aspect of trust is relevant when considering whether users may be likely to release their LM to others. Here, trust not only concerns the representations in the LM, but also the manner in which other people might use this information.

We define trust in the learner model as *the individual user's belief in, and acceptance of the system's inferences; their feelings of attachment to their model; and their confidence to act appropriately according to the model inferences.* This paper describes an initial questionnaire investigation into features of an OLM that might make a system more 'trustable', as a starting point for future work on trust in OLMs.

2   Students' Trust in Open Learner Models

18 users (9 Masters, 9 beginning PhD) were instructed to answer questions, explore the LM views and system-specific features in the two OLMs, then continue to use them as best suits their approach to learning. Questionnaire responses are in Table 1.

(i) Two thirds of learners claimed to understand the detailed views, but only half stated they understood the overviews. Given that learners may have different preferences for model presentations [3], it is perhaps not surprising that not all rated the

Table 1. Learner trust in open learner models

		Agree	Neutral	Disagree
Complexity of Presentation	Understand simple overview of knowledge level	9	9	0
	Believe simple overview to be accurate	9	5	4
	Trust simple overview model information	14	4	0
	Understand detailed model information	12	5	1
	Believe detailed model to be accurate	14	3	1
	Trust detailed model information	10	7	1
Learner Control	Trust because can edit model	4	7	7
	Edited attributes believed to be correct	8	4	6
	Edited attributes believed to be incorrect	3	5	10
	Trust because can try to persuade model to change	10	4	4
	Tried to persuade attributes believed to be correct	9	5	4
	Tried to persuade attributes believed to be incorrect	6	7	5
Peer Models	Trust because can compare to peers	9	8	1
	Trust because can compare to instructor expectations	11	6	1
	Believe model to be correct and opened it to peers	12	6	0
	Believe model to be correct and opened it to instructor	12	4	1
	Believe model to be incorrect and opened it to peers	7	5	5
	Believe model to be incorrect and opened it to instructor	6	5	6

OLMs understandable in general - they may have used a subset of views, but felt less comfortable with the others. This is worth further investigation. However, more surprising, given previous findings regarding usage levels [2],[4], is that the simple views of OLMlets were rated harder to understand. This may be because users can more easily see the model update in simple views. As OLMlets models knowledge over the last five responses on a topic, with heavier weighting on the most recent, the views change in noticeable ways. Therefore it may be that users did understand that a 'more filled' skill meter (or equivalent) represented greater understanding of a topic, but did not realise that the recency of responses affected weightings in the model. Perhaps the complexity of the detailed views of Flexi-OLM, although fostering confidence in the model, made it harder to actually *use* than the simple views, and therefore trust in the utility for supporting one's own learning might be reduced.

(ii) Congruent with previous findings [3], learners do not simply trust their own amendments to the LM, but appear to have greater trust in a method requiring them to demonstrate their skill before the model is changed. Particularly interesting is that users edited and attempted to persuade attributes they considered correct, more than those they believed incorrect. This may have been in part due to curiosity in this experimental setting. However, it may instead be because students thought there was little point in interacting about their LM if it was inaccurate: perhaps they considered it a waste of time to try to change the model if the system was likely to continue making what they perceived as incorrect inferences. Indeed, users may have gained trust in the persuade feature by observing that Flexi-OLM would not change an accurate representation to an inaccurate one. Interesting further work could be undertaken here.

(iii) Half the users claimed to gain trust in the LM by being able to compare it to peer models. Perhaps this is because they could identify their position in the group matched with their expectations. Previous users have used peer models extensively

[4], but some prefer not to consult this information. It is unlikely that the latter would consider the ability to use peer models as increasing their trust in the system. The figure for the facility to compare to instructor expectations was a little higher. It would be interesting to discover whether this generally gave users a greater sense of where they should be, and trust was related to this feeling of understanding what their progress meant (e.g. defined as milestones). Most learners were willing to open their LM to other users if they believed the model was accurate, and some released what they considered an inaccurate model (as they could release their LM anonymously). Perceived inaccuracies in the modelling process may affect use of peer models for initiating or supporting collaboration. Trust in what colleagues might do with information about an individual is also particularly important in this kind of context.

3 Summary

This paper has undertaken an initial investigation of trust in OLMs, focusing on complexity of LM presentation, level of learner control over the LM, and the facility to release the LM to others. Many questions remain, but initial results suggest different users may find different features of OLMs important for developing trust. A key question, therefore, is how to design an OLM that might be trustable for a variety of users.

Acknowledgement. We thank Andrew Mabbott for providing Flexi-OLM.

References

1. Kay, J.: Learner Know Thyself: Student Models to Give Learner Control and Responsibility. In: International Conference on Computers in Education, AACE, pp. 17–24 (1997)
2. Bull, S., Quigley, S., Mabbott, A.: Computer-Based Formative Assessment to Promote Reflection and Learner Autonomy. Engineering Education 1, 8–18 (2006)
3. Mabbott, A., Bull, S.: Student Preferences for Editing, Persuading and Negotiating the Open Learner Model. In: Intelligent Tutoring Systems, pp. 481–490. Springer, Heidelberg (2006)
4. Bull, S., Britland, M.: Group Interaction Prompted by a Simple Assessed Open Learner Model that can be Optionally Released to Peers. In: PING Workshop, User Modeling (2007)
5. Mayer, R.C., Davis, J.H., Schoorman, F.D.: An Integrative Model of Organizational Trust. The Academy of Management Review 20, 709–734 (1995)
6. Lewis, J.D., Weigert, A.: Trust as Social Reality. J. Social Forces 63, 967–985 (1985)
7. McKnight, D.H., Chervany, N.L.: What Trust Means in E-commerce Customer Relationships: an interdisciplinary conceptual typology. Int. J. Electronic Commerce 6, 35–59 (2002)
8. Madsen, M., Gregor, S.: Measuring Human-Computer Trust. In: Gable, G., Viatle, M. (eds.) 11th Australasian Conference on Information Systems, p. 53 (2000)
9. Muir, B.M.: Trust between Humans and Machines and the Design of Decision Aids. J. Man-Machine Studies 27, 527–539 (1987); Fox, J.E.: The Effects of Information Accuracy on User Trust and Compliance. In: Conference on Human Factors in Computing Systems, pp. 35–36. New York (1996)
10. Kay, J.: Learner Control. User Modeling and User-Adapted Interaction 11, 111–127 (2001)
11. Tanimoto, S.: Dimensions of Transparency in Open Learner Models. In: LeMoRe Workshop, AIED 2005, pp. 100–106 (2005)

A Framework for the Development of Distributed, Context-Aware Adaptive Hypermedia Applications

Liliana Ardissono, Anna Goy, and Giovanna Petrone

Dipartimento di Informatica - Università di Torino
Corso Svizzera 185, 10149 Torino - Italy
{liliana,goy,giovanna}@di.unito.it
http://www.di.unito.it

Abstract. The CAWE framework supports the development of context-aware, Service Oriented applications which integrate heterogeneous services and customize the cooperation among multiple users. We present the techniques adopted in the framework to manage a context-sensitive interaction with the users.

1 Introduction

Service Oriented Architectures (SOA) [1] offer an excellent opportunity to develop distributed Adaptive Hypermedia applications but the composition model proposed in SOA does not explicitly deal with personalization. In order to address this issue, we have developed the CAWE (Context Aware Workflow Execution) conceptual framework, which extends standard Web Service composition with the management of context-aware processes and of Intelligent User Interface components. Being based on a workflow model, our approach advances the state of the art in Adaptive Hypermedia by supporting the following types of interaction with the user: a) the coordination of users playing different roles in the execution of a complex process; b) long lasting interaction sessions supporting the completion of operations which are not instantaneous; c) the management of interruptions in the execution of activities.

This paper presents the techniques adopted in the CAWE framework to handle context information (Section 2) and to adapt the interaction with the user accordingly (Section 3). In [2], we described the CAWE architecture and the context-aware management of the business logic of applications.

2 Context Information Management

The architecture of the CAWE framework, described in [2], includes a *Context Manager Web Service (CtxMgr WS)*, which manages the information about the users of the application, their environment and the execution context. In an application based on CAWE, the CtxMgr WS handles a Context including a Role

W. Nejdl et al. (Eds.): AH 2008, LNCS 5149, pp. 259–262, 2008.

```
Role Model (RM):
  ID: String (RM identifier)
  currentUM: String (reference to the UM of the role filler in focus)
  UMList: list of IDs (references of the UMs of -all- the role fillers)
  FeatureList: (possibly void) sequence of FeatureType elements
  PermissionList: (possibly void) sequence of FeatureType elements
User Model (UM):
  ID: String (UM identifier)
  CMRef: String (reference to the CM associated to the UM)
  RMList: list of IDs (references of the RMs filled by the user)
  FeatureList: sequence of FeatureType elements
Context Model (CM):
  ID: String (CM identifier)
  UMRef: ID (reference to the UM of the user)
  FeatureList: sequence of FeatureType elements
FeatureType:
  featureName: String
  featureVal: String
```

Fig. 1. Structure of the RMs, UMs and CMs

Model for each role to be handled in the workflow, as well as a User Model and a Context Model for each person actively or passively involved in the interaction. Notice that a role may be filled by multiple interchangeable users, and a user may fill more than one role. Figure 1 shows the structure of the models, which are represented as XML documents.

- The Role Model (RM) stores the references of the User Models of the human actors filling the role. Moreover, it stores domain-dependent, default information about the role. The RM is utilized to assign workflow tasks to the human actors involved in the task execution, or indirectly influencing the business logic of the application. E.g., the patient plays an important role in an e-Health application, which must be tailored to her health status.
- The User Model (UM) stores information about an individual user filling one or more roles (e.g., the patient role). User Models include information such as expertise, preferences, and individual capabilities; e.g., physical and mental capabilities.
- The Context Model (CM) stores information about the environment in which the user operates (e.g., light conditions), the device she utilizes during the interaction and other information such as the network bandwidth.

For generality purposes, the CAWE framework does not prescribe the introduction of specific features in the UMs, RMs and CMs; the application developer is free to define the information items relevant to a specific application.

During the execution of an instance of the application, serving a particular set of cooperating users, the CtxMgr WS instantiates the Role Models. Moreover, it updates the corresponding User Models and the Context Models with information collected by interacting with the users via the User Interface of the application; e.g., clickstream data, user information input by means of a form, and the device utilized by the user. The Context Models might also be updated with data collected by other information sources, such as sensors.

Notice that the CtxMgr WS is designed as a Web Service in order to decouple it from the other components of the framework. In this way, the framework enables the application developer to embed in the module, or to invoke, the user modeling and context management components most suitable to the application.

3   Context-Aware Interaction Management

The architecture of the CAWE conceptual framework also includes a *Context-Aware Workflow Manager*, which adapts to the context the interaction with the user and the business logic of the application. As described in [3], the business logic is a hierarchical workflow specifying context-dependent courses of action, which are selected at execution time depending on context information.

In a workflow, the interaction with the user is specified by means of a *task* assigned to the user role. The task specifies the information to be asked/presented as a list of input/output parameters. When the workflow engine selects a task for execution, it delegates a Task Manager for its management. The Task Manager operates asynchronously: when the user connects to the application, it generates the User Interface (UI) pages presenting the input/output parameters.

In the CAWE framework, a *Dialog Manager* module extends the default Task Manager by applying personalization rules aimed at generating context-dependent UI pages. The Dialog Manager interacts with the CtxMgr WS in order to retrieve the context information and the values of input parameters that are available in the user's UM and CM, and can be visualized as default values. Then, the Dialog Manager generates one or more UI pages displaying the information specified in the task; the module generates the pages as follows:

1. It selects the stylesheet (XSL) to be applied, depending on the user features and preferences, and on the characteristics of her device. The stylesheet specifies the layout properties; e.g., font size and background color.
2. It groups the information items to be displayed in subsets, in order to fit the size of the screen and the user's features.
3. For each subset, it fills in an XML page template with the content to be displayed. Then, it applies the stylesheet to the filled template. For each displayed parameter, it is possible to include a "more info" button linking a textual description of the data item. Notice that the splitting of contents and the stylesheet selection are tailored to the target user; therefore, the pages can be customized to each of the users cooperating to the service execution.
4. The Dialog Manager cycles sending the generated pages to the user's device and retrieving the responses, until all the input and output parameters specifyed in the task have been elicited/displayed.
5. Finally, the Dialog Manager returns the collected information to the Workflow Engine, which continues the workflow execution.

Our framework manages persistent and loosely coupled interactions with the users; in fact, the tasks are suspended until the users connect to the application. Moreover, the interaction with the user (within a task) can be suspended in order to handle interruptions, by saving the user session for later resumption.

4   Discussion

In this paper, we proposed the adoption of Service Oriented Architectures for the development of distributed AH applications integrating heterogeneous services and information sources. Moreover, we presented the adaptation features offered by CAWE framework in order to handle personalized interactions with the users.

The CAWE prototype [2] is implemented in the jBPM environment [4], which offers a workflow representation language based on the Petri Net process model. In order to test the framework, we instantiated the CAWE prototype on an application supporting the management of a clinical guideline. The application may be accessed by using a PC or a Smart Phone client. The development of our application showed that the workflow-based management of the interaction with the user does not support the flexibility of goal-based dialog systems. However, it suits the requirements of page-based interaction, as it supports the dynamic generation of device-dependent pages, whose contents are tailored to the interacting users, on the basis of their features and of the process activities.

Being based on workflow management, our work overcomes the limitations of planning technology, which does not support asynchronous, persistent interactions with the user. Moreover, our work advances the state of the art in context-aware workflows, which is mainly focused on Quality of Service (QoS) and on the adaptation to the user's device; e.g., see [5]. In fact, the CAWE framework supports the adaptation to multiple users who cooperate to the service execution, taking into account their preferences, requirements (e.g., QoS), and context features such as the physical environment or the available resources. Our work also differs from other workflow-based adaptive systems (e.g., [6]) in the following aspects: first, it handles the adaptation to multiple users cooperating to the service execution, including the indirect service recipients. Second, it personalizes the workflow to the users and their context, while in [6] the workflow underlying the system behavior is the same for all the users and contexts.

Acknowledgement. This work was funded by projects WS-Diamond (IST-516933) and QuaDRAnTIS (MUR).

References

1. Papazoglou, M., Georgakopoulos, D. (eds.): Service-Oriented Computing. Communications of the ACM 46 (2003)
2. Ardissono, L., Furnari, R., Goy, A., Petrone, G., Segnan, M.: A framework for the management of context-aware workflow systems. In: Proc. of WEBIST 2007, Barcelona, Spain, pp. 80–87 (2007)
3. Ardissono, L., Furnari, R., Goy, A., Petrone, G., Segnan, M.: Context-aware workflow management. In: Baresi, L., Fraternali, P., Houben, G.-J. (eds.) ICWE 2007. LNCS, vol. 4607, pp. 47–52. Springer, Heidelberg (2007)
4. Koenig, J.: JBoss jBPM white paper (2004),
   http://www.jboss.com/pdf/jbpm_whitepaper.pdf
5. Benlismane, D., Maamar, Z., Ghedira, C.: A view-based approach for tracking composite Web Services. In: Proc. of ECOWS 2005, Växjö, Sweden, pp. 170–179 (2005)
6. Holden, S., Kay, J., Poon, J., Yacef, K.: Workflow-based personalized document delivery. International Journal on E-Learning 4, 131–148 (2005)

Collection Browsing through Automatic Hierarchical Tagging

Korinna Bade and Marcel Hermkes

Otto-von-Guericke-University, D-39106 Magdeburg, Germany
korinna.bade@ovgu.de, marcel.hermkes@googlemail.com

Abstract. In order to navigate huge document collections efficiently, tagged hierarchical structures can be used. For users, it is important to correctly interpret tag combinations. In this paper, we propose the usage of tag groups for addressing this issue and an algorithm that is able to extract these automatically for text documents. The approach is based on the diversity of content in a document collection. For evaluation, we use methods from ontology evaluation and showed the validity of our approach on a benchmark dataset.

1 How to Tag

When searching for information, structured access to data, e.g., as given by web directories or social tagging systems like del.icio.us can be very helpful. The goal of our work is to automatically provide such structure for unstructured collections. For this, we automatically tag text documents based on their content. We do not tag resources individually, but compute the tags collection based. By this, we can directly aim at supporting efficient browsing by adapting presented tags to a dynamically created collection, which, e.g., can be the result set of a query based search. Our approach first structures the collection by a hierarchical clustering algorithm and then tags clusters in the hierarchy. This results in a set of tags combined with hierarchical relations. The cluster tags are then assigned to the documents that belong to this cluster. In this paper, we focus on the extraction of tags once the cluster hierarchy was built. Information on the clustering process can be found in [1].

In todays tagging systems, resources are tagged with one or more single words to describe them. Access to resources is usually provided by tag clouds, which can be used to browse the existing tags. Between tags, no relations are usually assumed (an exception are hierarchical relations from bundle tags). However, a user might use multiple tags for two different reasons. First, he wants to provide synonyms such that more people find his resource. Second, he wants to show that this resource actually belongs to an overlap of several topics. While browsing with a single tag is sufficient for finding a resource of the first type, the second case requires combining more tags in the search. For cluster tags, it is even more important to know how different tags shall be interpreted. Two tags of a cluster could correspond either to the same document or to different documents. This

W. Nejdl et al. (Eds.): AH 2008, LNCS 5149, pp. 263–266, 2008.

means that documents in the cluster could either belong to the intersection of two topics or that some documents in the cluster belong more to one topic and the others more to the other topic. As an example consider a cluster tagged with *Banking* and *Programming*. This can either mean that the cluster contains documents about banking software or that the cluster contains documents that deal with *Banking* and others that deal with *Programming*. To help in the interpretation of tags, our approach tries to group tags based on their relevance for documents. A group of tags means that all tags therein belong together in describing a document of this cluster. Such a group, therefore, contains synonyms as well as combined topics. Furthermore, tags in different groups are supposed to relate to different documents in the cluster. In the following, we write such a cluster tag as a set of tag groups, where each tag group is a set of tags. For the example above, we would have either the cluster tag $\{\{Banking, Programming\}\}$ or the cluster tag $\{\{Banking\}, \{Programming\}\}$.

2   An Algorithm for Automatic Hierarchical Tagging

Tagging is accomplished in three steps, i.e. candidate ranking, grouping, and refinement. In the **candidate ranking** step, terms are weighted for each cluster based on their descriptiveness (i.e. their value in describing the cluster) to identify the best tags. A good tag should not only describe the cluster but also distinguish a cluster from others. In a hierarchy, a tag must be able to distinguish a cluster from its sibling clusters as well as show the differences between the cluster and its parent cluster. These ideas are integrated in our own descriptive score DS_w (see also [4] for related ideas). This score is compared to pure document frequency df and modified information gain IG_{mod} [3]. In specific, the descriptiveness DS_w of a term t in node n is computed by

$$DS_w(t, n) = \log_2\left(\frac{rank_{df}(t, n_p)}{rank_{df}(t, n)}\right) \cdot \frac{1 - SI(t, n) + SI(t, n_p)}{2} \cdot \left(\frac{df_{t,n}}{|n|}\right)^w$$

$$SI(t, n) = \begin{cases} 1 & \text{if } ch(n) = \emptyset \\ \left(\sum_{n_c \in ch(n)} \frac{df_{t,n_c}}{df_{t,n}} \log_2 \frac{df_{t,n_c} \cdot |n|}{df_{t,n} \cdot |n_c|}\right) / \log_2 \frac{|n|}{min_{n_c \in ch(n)}|n_c|} & \text{else} \end{cases}$$

with $rank_{df}(t, n)$ being the rank of t in n if terms are ordered by their document frequency in n, $df_{t,n}$ the document frequency of t in n, n_p the parent node of n, and $ch(n)$ the set of child nodes of n. The score combines three factors. The first measures the boost of document frequency ranking in comparison to the parent. This assures that terms get higher scores that were not already good descriptors for the parent and are therefore too general for the current cluster. The second factor considers information on how the term is distributed in sibling and child nodes. SI is based on the KL-Divergence between the distribution of document frequency and the distribution of node size, normalized to stay in the interval $[0; 1]$. This means that SI becomes zero, if t is distributed in the child nodes with the same distribution as the documents, i.e. if $\frac{df_{t,n_c}}{df_{t,n}} = \frac{|n_c|}{|n|}$ for all child nodes.

On the other hand, SI reaches the maximum of 1, if t occurs only in the smallest child node. Therefore, the second factor favors terms that occur in several child clusters and penalizes terms that could be also descriptors in sibling nodes. The last factor considers the document frequency as a relatively high frequency is necessary however not sufficient for a good term. How strong the influence of the frequency should be on the final score is controlled by w. Our experiments showed that 0.33 is a good value for w (at least for the considered dataset).

In the **grouping** step, the ranked term list is handled sequentially to create tag groups. The first term forms the first tag group. For every following term, it is decided whether it forms a new tag group or belongs to an existing one. A tag group is hereby represented as a coverage vector over the documents in the collection. A document is covered by a term, if the term occurs in it. The coverage of a tag group is a summation of the individual term coverages, whereby the impact of each term is weighted by its rank in the tag group (exponentially decreasing by $e^{-0.5 \cdot (rank(t)-1)}$). Similarity between a term and a tag group (or two tag groups) is computed by the Dice coefficient between the coverage vectors $(\text{sim}(x,y) = \frac{2 \cdot x \cdot y}{||x||+||y||})$. A term is merged to the tag group with highest similarity, if it is above a threshold. Once all terms have been used, tag groups are merged as long as similarity between two tag groups is still above the threshold. From the remaining tag groups, all are removed that are a specialization from another tag group (which is determined by $\text{incl}(x,y) = (\sum_i \min(x_i, y_i))/\sum_i y_i$).

In the **refinement** step, more specific tag groups from deeper hierarchy levels are propagated up in the hierarchy, if the coverage of non-leaf cluster tags is not high enough. Tag groups from child nodes are added to the parent tag, if they sufficiently increase the cluster coverage. Tag groups with the highest increase in coverage are added first.

Table 1. Results with three f-score measures on three datasets

SETTING	RM	ORIGINAL			NOISE			BINARY		
		tb	rb	db	tb	rb	db	tb	rb	db
(1)	df	0.5000	0.5377	0.9794	0.4905	0.4751	0.8923	0.3745	0.4593	0.9464
	IG_{mod}	0.8214	0.6920	0.9467	0.7757	0.5992	0.8672	0.7249	0.7404	0.9204
	$DS_{0.33}$	0.7857	0.8003	0.9530	0.7035	0.6458	0.8684	0.6832	0.7556	0.9226
(2)	IG_{mod}	0.7775	0.6561	0.9316	0.7959	0.5953	0.8873	0.7233	0.7384	0.9099
	$DS_{0.33}$	0.7932	0.7962	0.9340	0.7762	0.7240	0.9043	0.6658	0.7791	0.8912

3 Evaluation and Conclusion

We evaluated our approach with the banksearch dataset [5]. We used three different hierarchies, the original one, a binary version of the original one, and a noisy one, in which groups of documents are moved to other clusters. While the first one requires the extraction of a single tag group per class, the other two include multiple tag groups. Our evaluation measures are borrowed and adapted from gold standard evaluation in ontology learning [2]. We present in Table 1 the f-score combining average precision and recall. For each class, precision and recall

are computed between the learned tag groups G_l and the reference tag groups G_r
by $precision(G_l, G_r) = |G_l|^{-1} \sum_{g_l \in G_l} \max_{g_r \in G_r} sim(g_l, g_r)$ and $recall(G_l, G_r) =$
$|G_r|^{-1} \sum_{g_r \in G_r} \max_{g_l \in G_l} sim(g_l, g_r)$. We use three similarity measures, which are
term-based (tb), rank-based (rb), and document-based (db). sim_{tb} measures
whether exactly the same terms were chosen in the 5 highest ranked terms, while
sim_{rb} takes into account the actual ranking in the tag group. sim_{db} compares the
covered documents of two tag groups while ignoring the actual terms. These measures allow to evaluate different granularities, i.e. whether the right documents
were assigned to the same tag group and whether correct tags could be extracted.
sim_{tb} and sim_{rb} are computed as follows while sim_{db} is the Dice coefficient (see
Section 2):

$$sim_{tb}(g_l, g_r) = \frac{\sum_{t \in g_r} \left\{ \begin{array}{l} 1 \text{ if } t \in g_l \\ 0 \text{ else} \end{array} \right\}}{|g_r|} \qquad sim_{rb}(g_l, g_r) = \frac{\sum_{t \in g_r} \left\{ \begin{array}{l} \frac{1}{rank(t, g_l)} \text{ if } t \in g_l \\ 0 \qquad \text{else} \end{array} \right\}}{1/1 + \cdots + 1/|g_r|}$$

Furthermore, we compared two settings, (1) the standard approach of using a
single tag group and (2) multiple tag groups. Table 1 only shows results for
the best parameter setup found for each measure and setting. Comparing the
three ranking measures, it can be seen that all three of them group the right
documents together (db measure). However, df fails to rank the good terms
high. While IG_{mod} is better in the first 5 terms (tb measure), our DS_w usually
ranks the important terms higher (rb measure). Furthermore, it can be seen that
performance drops in setting (1), if the clusters naturally consist of more than
one tag group. Our group method is capable of increasing the performance for
these datasets, especially in combination with DS_w.

Concluding the paper, we want to point out that we propose in this paper
to improve the effectiveness of tagging by integrating relations between tags in
form of tag groups. We developed a method that is capable of extracting such
tag groups automatically and evaluated it with a dataset. In future work, we
want to modify the descriptive score to better reflect multiple tag groups.

References

1. Bade, K., Hermkes, M., Nürnberger, A.: User oriented hierarchical information organization and retrieval. In: Kok, J.N., Koronacki, J., Lopez de Mantaras, R., Matwin,
   S., Mladenič, D., Skowron, A. (eds.) ECML 2007. LNCS (LNAI), vol. 4701, pp. 518–
   526. Springer, Heidelberg (2007)
2. Dellschaft, K., Staab, S.: On how to perform a gold standard based evaluation of
   ontology learning. In: Proc. of 5th Int. Semantic Web Conference, pp. 228–241 (2006)
3. Geraci, F., Pellegrini, M., Margini, M., Sebastiani, F.: Cluster generation and cluster
   labeling for web snippets. In: Proc. of the 13th Symposium on String Processing and
   Information Retrieval, pp. 25–36 (2006)
4. Glover, E., Pennock, D., Lawrence, S.: Inferring hierarchical descriptions. In: Proc. of
   11th Int. Conference on Information and Knowledge Management, pp. 507–514 (2002)
5. Sinka, M., Corne, D.: A large benchmark dataset for web document clustering.
   In: Soft Computing Systems: Design, Management and Applications. Frontiers in
   Artificial Intelligence and Applications, vol. 87, pp. 881–890 (2002)

Aspect-Based Personalized Text Summarization

Shlomo Berkovsky[1], Timothy Baldwin[1], and Ingrid Zukerman[2]

[1] University of Melbourne, Australia
{shlomo,tim}@csse.unimelb.edu.au
[2] Monash University, Australia
ingrid@csse.monash.edu.au

Abstract. This work investigates user attitudes towards personalized summaries generated from a coarse-grained user model based on document aspects. We explore user preferences for summaries at differing degrees of fit with their stated interests, the impact of length on user ratings, and the faithfulness of personalized and general summaries.

1 Introduction

Exponential growth in information availability has increased the need for intelligent filtering and efficient presentation methods. *Personalized* summarization [1] presents users with document extracts that are of interest to them, as defined by a user model [2] (c.f. general summarization, which is oblivious to user interests).

This research is novel in evaluating user attitudes towards personalized summarization of aspect-based documents, i.e., documents that can be partitioned into mutually-exclusive sub-documents that relate to different subject areas. In contrast, past research on personalized summarization has relied on an intrinsic representation of user interests via keywords or document categories [1].

Our results show that: (1) users prefer personalized summaries which accurately reflect their interests, supporting the findings of [1]; (2) users have a preferred summary length, and disprefer over-long or over-short summaries; and (3) users perceive the faithfulness to the original document of personalized and general summaries to be roughly equivalent.

2 Data Representation and Personalized Summarization

The domain for this research is natural science, to fit in with the scope of the Kubadji project (http://www.kubadji.org), which is focused on personalization in museums. For example, consider the following document d about blue whales, extracted and pre-processed from a longer Wikipedia article into coherent logical aspects as follows.

d_1	*The blue whale is a marine mammal belonging to the family of baleen whales. This family also includes the Humpback, Fin, and Minke Whales. Due to its yellow underparts, the blue whale is often called the sulphur-bottom.*

W. Nejdl et al. (Eds.): AH 2008, LNCS 5149, pp. 267–270, 2008.
© Springer-Verlag Berlin Heidelberg 2008

d_2	Blue whales are believed to be the largest animals to have ever lived. They reach 33 meters in length and 200 tonnes in weight. When breathing, they emit a spectacular vertical column blow of up to 12 meters.
d_3	The London Natural History Museum contains a life-size model of a blue whale. Living whales may be encountered in Saint Lawrence Gulf. It was represented as symbol of size and strength in the movie Doctor Dolittle.

Each of the sub-documents d_1, d_2, d_3 represents a different aspect or subject area, viz biological taxonomy, physical dimensions and popular culture, respectively. Assuming a relatively homogeneous document collection (as is the case with curated data) and a coarse-grained set of aspects, we can expect to be able to partition other documents about marine animals according to a single set of aspects (we considered the above three aspects, plus reproduction and life and threats and dangers).

The same set of aspects was also used as the basis of a content-based user model [3], where a user's interests are represented by a vector of domain aspects. Our representation was based on the following 4-point scale of interest in aspects: 0=*no interest*, 1=*low*, 2=*moderate*, and 3=*high*. For example, a user with moderate interest in biological taxonomy, high interest in physical dimensions and low interest in popular culture would be represented by $UM = \{LI_i\} = \{2, 3, 1\}$, where LI_i denotes the level of interest in aspect i.

The aspect-based representation of the user models facilitates the generation of personalized summaries, where the amount of text for a given aspect is proportional to the user's interest in it. For our experiments, we prepared a ranked list of n sentences for each aspect i, and included in the summary the first m sentences for a given aspect, where $\frac{m}{n}$ is proportional to LI_i. For example, a personalized summary of d based on the above model $UM = \{2, 3, 1\}$ is:

> The blue whale is a marine mammal belonging to the family of baleen whales. This family also includes the Humpback, Fin, and Minke Whales.
> Blue whales are believed to be the largest animals to have ever lived. They reach 33 meters in length and 200 tonnes in weight. When breathing, they emit a spectacular vertical column blow of up to 12 meters.
> The London Natural History Museum contains a life-size model of a blue whale.

3   User Study

We conducted three experiments to assess different aspects of users' attitudes towards personalized document summarization.

Experiment 1 evaluated whether the personalization of summaries has the desired effect, i.e., whether personalized summaries adjusted to actual user interests are preferable to those adjusted to other interests. Four summaries were composed for each of four documents, each of which contained the above mentioned five aspects. Each summary was adjusted to one of 16 pre-determined pseudo-models UM_{ps}. These pseudo-models were derived using fractional factorial design [4], such that they uniformly cover the search space of possible pseudo-models (4^5 states). A total of 19 users provided a rating *eval* (from 1=*bad* to 5=*good*) for each of the 16 summaries. After rating the 16 summaries, the users were asked to explicitly provide ratings for their interest in each of the five

Table 1. Average user evaluation at differing levels of user model fit

$sim(UM_r, UM_{ps})$	$(-1, -\frac{2}{3})$	$[-\frac{2}{3}, -\frac{1}{3})$	$[-\frac{1}{3}, 0)$	$[0, \frac{1}{3})$	$[\frac{1}{3}, \frac{2}{3})$	$[\frac{2}{3}, 1)$
$\overline{eval}$	2.29	2.59	2.63	2.77	2.85	3.11

aspects. This was taken to be the real user model UM_r, acknowledging that a user's self-perception may differ from actuality.

Given the user model UM_r and each pseudo-model UM_{ps}, we calculated their similarity $sim(UM_r, UM_{ps})$ using Pearson's Correlation. This allows us to measure the relative fit between the two models, and hence analyze the correlation between the rating $eval$ of the summaries and the faithfulness of the personalization to the actual user interests. In this analysis, we discretized the similarity values into six equal-width bins over the range of the Pearson Correlation Coefficient $[-1, 1]$, and calculated the average user rating $\overline{eval}$ in each bin.

Table 1 shows the average user rating ($\overline{eval}$) at each level of fit between the pseudo-model and the real user model ($sim(UM_r, UM_{ps})$).[1] The ratings of personalized summaries increase monotonically as the level of fit increases. This demonstrates that, as expected, users preferred summaries matching their actual interests. This finding was separately validated via a linear regression analysis of the ratings at the different levels of Pearson's Correlation (without discretization), which returned a right-increasing function.

Experiment 2 assessed the impact of compression on the ratings given by users. This experiment was conducted after the first experiment, i.e., after eliciting the real user model UM_r. We generated three personalized summaries at different compression levels: (1) an original-length summary adjusted to $UM_r = \{LI_i\}$, (2) a *lengthened* summary adjusted to $UM_l = \{\alpha LI_i\}$, and (3) a *shortened* summary adjusted to $UM_s = \{(1/\alpha)LI_i\}$; α was set to 1.5.

19 users were shown three randomly-ordered summaries (at the three levels of compression) for each of two previously unseen documents, and were asked to rate each summary. We obtained a total of 114 ratings — 38 for each type of summary. The average rating $\overline{eval}$ was 3.32 for the original length, 2.95 for the lengthened, and 2.37 for the shortened summaries (all differences statistically significant: $p = 2.0 \times 10^{-2}$ for lengthened and $p = 9.3 \times 10^{-7}$ for shortened). This shows that users disliked personalized summaries that were too long or too short, although they were less averse to overly-long summaries.[2]

Experiment 3 evaluated the perceived faithfulness of the personalized summaries to the original documents. We generated two summaries: (1) a personalized summary adjusted to UM_r — the user model elicited in the first experiment; and (2) a general summary adjusted to a model with equal interest levels in all aspects.

---

[1] These results do not include the ratings for 4 users with a uniform user model UM_r, due to a divide-by-zero error for Pearson's correlation.

[2] Noting that users were primed for summary length in the first experiment, where the average summary length was 12.5 sentences.

19 users were shown two original (previously unseen) documents, and a general and personalised summary for each. They were asked to rate the faithfulness rel of the summaries to the original document ($1 \leq rel \leq 5$). We obtained a total of 76 ratings — 38 for each type of summary. The average faithfulness $\overline{rel}$ was 3.11 for the personalized and 3.21 for the general summaries.[3] Although the faithfulness of the general summaries was slightly higher, the results were not statistically significant, i.e., the two types of summaries are comparable in terms of faithfulness to the original document.

4   Conclusions and Future Research

We have conducted three studies to evaluate users' attitudes towards aspect-based, personalized document summaries. The results of our studies show that the better the fit between the real user model and the user model on which a summary is based, the higher the user's rating for this summary; and that there is a preferred length for personalized summaries. Evaluating the perceived faithfulness of a summary to the original document did not show a significant difference between personalized and general summaries. This leads to the conclusion that personalized summaries are both appropriate and liked by users.

This conclusion motivates further research in the Kubadji project, where we intend to harness user models of museum visitors [5] to dynamically generate personalized exhibit summaries.

Acknowledgments

This research was supported in part by Discovery grant DP0770931 from the Australian Research Council. We would like to thank Willy for help in setting up the web experiment.

References

1. Díaz, A., Gervás, P.: User-model based personalized summarization. Information Processing and Management 43(6), 1715–1734 (2007)
2. Brusilovsky, P., Millán, E.: User models for adaptive hypermedia and adaptive educational systems. In: Brusilovsky, P., Kobsa, A., Nejdl, W. (eds.) The Adaptive Web: Methods and Strategies of Web Personalization, pp. 3–53. Springer, Heidelberg (2007)
3. Pazzani, M.J., Billsus, D.: Content-based recommendation systems. In: Brusilovsky, P., Kobsa, A., Nejdl, W. (eds.) The Adaptive Web: Methods and Strategies of Web Personalization, pp. 325–341. Springer, Heidelberg (2007)
4. Box, G.E.P., Hunter, J.S., Hunter, W.G.: Statistics for Experimenters: Design, Innovation, and Discovery. Wiley, Chichester (2005)
5. Bohnert, F., Zukerman, I., Berkovsky, S., Baldwin, T., Sonenberg, L.: Using collaborative models to adaptively predict visitor locations in museums. In: Proceedings of Adaptive Hypermedia 2008, Hannover, Germany (2008)

---

[3] The average sentence overlap between the personalized and general summaries was high at 0.83.

What Can I Watch on TV Tonight?[*]

David Bueno[1], Ricardo Conejo[1], David Martín[1], Jorge León[1], and Javier G. Recuenco[2]

[1] Departamento de Lenguajes y Ciencias de la Computación. Universidad de Málaga
bueno@lcc.uma.es, conejo@lcc.uma.es, jleon@lcc.uma.es,
dmartin@lcc.uma.es
[2] AbyPersonalize
javier.recuenco@abypersonalize.com

Abstract. This paper presents the methods used in a TV Recommender System that helps users in the difficult task of finding an interesting TV program from among the hundreds of channels that we can find nowadays on TV. Our aim is to cover not only user preferences but also user restrictions while watching TV. The recommendations use a hybrid method, combining content based and folksonomy (collaborative and social recommendations). We also present interesting initial results of some experiments that try to show the accuracy of the users recommendations.

1 Introduction

Everything related to television is evolving very fast. New channels are constantly being created, adding to the already considerable range on offer either via traditional means, or through relatively new media like the Internet and Digital television (DTV). Due to the huge increase in what is on offer, viewers sometimes spend more time on choosing a channel than actually watching it.

Our recommendation technique is a hybrid method, which combines content based recommendation and 'folksonomy' (collaborative and social recommendations). The architecture of the system is available in [1]. In this article we will focus on the algorithms and some experiments with real users.

Recommender Systems simplify the vast amount of information available to the public. Profiles are created based on user interactions and this data subsequently helps the user to select and discover things that may be of interest to them. An example of this is METIORE [2] a publications recommender; or AVATAR [3] a TV recommender based on ontologies. Ideally, the best results come from combining the approaches of different systems [4]. Amazon.com or Barnes&Noble both recommend books to purchase, and offer recommendations based on collaborative filtering [5]: if a customer purchases an item that has been purchased by a number of users coinciding with his/her profile, then other items common to those users will be recommended by the system to the original user.

---

[*] This research is being funded by the Company QueTVeo.

W. Nejdl et al. (Eds.): AH 2008, LNCS 5149, pp. 271–274, 2008.

2 Recommenders

The most interesting part of this project is the actual system recommender and there-fore, in this section we present the techniques we use to implement it. This system is a hybrid recommender which is mainly composed of the following parts:

- Collaborative recommender
- Content based recommender
- Social recommender

Collaborative recommender. The collaborative feature is a method used by recom-mender systems to combine different users' favorite items in order to obtain personal-ized recommendations. Slope One [6] is a group of algorithms used for collaborative filtering. This is possibly the simplest method of non-trivial item-based collaborative filtering based on points. In spite of the simplicity of the method which can be im-plemented easily and efficiently, its accuracy is often similar to more complex and expensive algorithms.

Content based recommender. From each program, the most relevant words from the title, category, description, main actors ... are extracted. All this information is stored in the database linking each keyword of the program and its frequency of appearance.
Each user will have the opportunity to evaluate each program with four stars: ****
very good, *** *good*, ** *bad*, and * *very bad*. This is part of the short term model of the user because it is related to the recent evaluations. The user model is constantly updated so that the most recent evaluations are considered to be more important than the older ones. The user can also express his preferences, which are recorded in the long term model. The user can select his favourite channels, programs, genres, direc-tor, actors, watching times, or simply a list of keywords. This information is handled separately from the short term model.
    Each time a user searches for programs according to any criteria (time of the broadcast, channel, start and finishing times, etc.), the system calculates the similarity between the user model and the programs that are result of the query. The highest score indicates greater similarity and this data is used to rank the results. The imple-mentation of the score for content using a Bayesian approach [7] with the algorithm WNBM *(Weighted Naive Bayes Metiore)* improves our previous version NBM [2] which returns the probability that a program will be of interest to a particular user. The algorithm can be tuned with different weights for the different attributes of the programs.

Social recommender. To allow social navigation we propose a tag system that allows users to add additional information to each TV program. This approach is similar to the mechanism used in "youtube", "flickr", "gmail" or other recent systems. In order to reduce the number of similar tags, when a user wants to add a new one, an auto-completion text area helps him to see if the tag has already been added previously. This works in a similar way to the movielens tag system [8].

Hybrid recommender. The benefit of having multiple sources for recommendations avoids the cold start problem that appears in pure single source systems, and especially in purely collaborative recommenders. Summarizing, we have two content based recommenders, (a short term and a long term model), also an item-item collaborative recommendation and other based on tags. Each of these recommender approaches produces a list of programs and in order to calculate the relevance of each one for the user, we compute a weighted sum, where $\alpha+\beta+\varphi+\delta=1$ and this determines the importance that we give to any of the four recommenders. The parameters can change with the time and the user decision.

$$R(user, item) = \alpha R_{u,i}^{short} \; \beta R_{u,i}^{long} \; \varphi R_{u,i}^{collab.} \; \delta R_{u,i}^{tags}$$

3   Experimentation

One of the most interesting things to check with the system in order to evaluate its results is the correlation between the system recommendation and the user evaluation. In order to ascertain this, certain information was recorded: which user performed the action, the program, the recommendation of the differrent recommenders for this program, and the user evaluation (number of stars)., ie. (user12, program4, 67%, 60%,

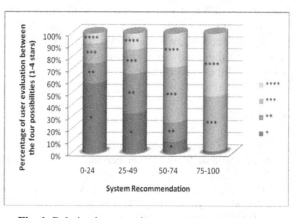

Fig. 1. Relation between the system recommendation and the user evaluation for different recommender method

**). The content recommendation and the collaborative recommendations (only those for this experiment) are used to rank a list of programs according to the user profile. Their values are between 0-100%. The possible user evaluations are between one and four stars as we explained above. In Figure 1 we represent this correlation, summarizing the information about all the evaluations of programs provided by the registered users. In order to see the results more clearly, we have divided the system recommendations seen in the X-axis into four groups. As illustrated in Figure 1, the results are very promising because there is a considerable correlation between the users' evaluations and the system recommendation. For example if we look at how many times the users evaluate a program with four stars (very good) we can see that the number of times increases when those programs were recommended as being of interest to the user. Likewise, the opposite occurs, i.e., when the user evaluates a program negatively, with only one star (very bad), this coincides with the system *not* recommending the program.

4 Conclusions and Future Work

In this document we have presented a hybrid recommender, which can be used for a TV Recommender System or indeed for any other field because it is a generic application. We have developed a hybrid recommender so that users will benefit from different existing recommender algorithms. It incorporates the content based approach proposing similar elements, in this case for viewing, because these elements are considered to be very similar to the information held on the user's personal taste. Using other users' evaluations, the collaborative approach proposes elements which are considered to be of interest to the system user.. Finally, we have also incorporated the social approach, which recommends to a user those elements that have been tagged by other users with common tags with him. We propose a way of using several techniques in parallel, with the objective of obtaining the best possible recommendation for users. We have shown in our experiments that exists a correlation between users evaluations and system recommendations. Our future ideas are: to apply other techniques to the different recommenders, with the objective of calculating which ones obtain the best performance. For example we are working on a Bayesian network that can take into account different preferences of the users (time to watch the TV, watch it alone, with the family or with friends...) in order to make a recommendation that can satisfy all the restrictions.

References

[1] Bueno, D., Conejo, R., Recuenco, J.G.: An architecture for a TV Recommender System. In: International Workshop on Personalization in iTV.Euro ITV 2007, Amsterdam, pp. 117–122 (2007)

[2] Bueno, D., David, A.A.: METIORE: A personalized information retrieval system. In: Bauer, M., Gmytrasiewicz, P.J., Vassileva, J. (eds.) UM 2001. LNCS (LNAI), vol. 2109, pp. 168–177. Springer, Heidelberg (2001)

[3] Fernandez, Y.B., Arias, J.J.P., Nores, M.L., Solla, A.G., Cabrer, M.R.: AVATAR: An improved solution for personalized TV based on semantic inference. Ieee Transactions on Consumer Electronics 52(1), 223–231 (2006)

[4] Szomszor, M., Cattuto, C., Alani, H., O'Hara, K., Baldassarri, A., Loreto, V., Servedio, V.D.P.: Folksonomies, the Semantic Web, and Movie Recommendation. In: 4th European Semantic Web Conference, Bridging the Gap between Semantic Web and Web 2.0 (2007)

[5] Linden, G., Smith, B., York, J.: Amazon.com recommendations: item-to-item collaborative filtering. IEEE Internet Computing 7(1), 76–80 (2003)

[6] Lemire, D., Maclachlan, A.: Slope One Predictors for Online Rating-Based Collaborative Filtering. In: SIAM Data Mining (SDM 2005), Newport Beach, California, April 21-23 (2005)

[7] Bueno, D.: Recomendación Personalizada de documentos en sistemas de recuperación de la información basada en objetivos. Ph.D. Universidad de Málaga (2003)

[8] Shilad, S., Shyong, K.L., Al, M.R., Dan, C., Dan, F., Jeremy, O., Maxwell, H., John, R.: Tagging, communities, vocabulary, evolution. In: Proceedings of the 2006 20th anniversary conference on Computer supported cooperative work, Banff, Alberta, pp. 181–190. ACM Press, Canada (2006)

Adaptive Navigation Support, Learner Control and Open Learner Models

S. Bull, N. Ahmad, M. Johnson, R. Johan, A. Mabbott, and A. Kerly

Electronic, Electrical and Computer Engineering, University of Birmingham, U.K.
{s.bull,nxa707,mdj384,rxj795,axm891,alk584}@bham.ac.uk

Abstract. We consider open learner models (OLM) with reference to adaptive navigation support and learner control. Our purpose is to assess the potential of a greater range of OLMs in adaptive educational hypermedia. We introduce five OLMs, discuss how these might be applied, and present learner reactions.

1 Introduction

Adaptive educational hypermedia (AEH) may take many forms. Traditional examples include adaptive presentation and adaptive link support [1],[2]. This may relate to selection or inclusion of content, or link highlighting/annotation to indicate currently recommended links [3]. User knowledge is held in a learner model (LM), typically inferred from browsing or test items, and used to personalise the interaction. Open learner models (OLM) 'open' the LM to the user. AEH sometimes releases some information about the learner's knowledge [4],[5], offering navigation support with link annotations as suggestions for appropriate pages according to the user's knowledge (e.g. a user can infer their knowledge of prerequisites for a topic from link annotations). Simple OLMs giving an overview of knowledge levels are also used [6]. OLMs may also have complex displays, e.g.: trees [7]; conceptual graphs [8]. Aims of OLMs include to: prompt reflection [9]; improve self-assessment [6]; provide accountability/responsibility in learning [7]. AEH already performs testing to inform the LM and offer guidance [5]. Linking other aspects of OLMs and AEH may provide additional navigation support while also prompting further reflection/self-assessment.

2 Open Learner Models and Adaptive Educational Hypermedia

We use 5 OLMs that allow learner control over the interaction, in common with the control users can typically take in AEH systems with adaptive navigation support [4].

Simple and detailed: OLMlets elicits learner knowledge using multiple choice questions. It has 5 simple views of the LM [10]. Fig. 1 shows two of these: the graph and skill meters. Users can use information about their knowledge level (medium shading) or misconceptions (dark shading) and misconception statements (e.g. "you may believe that you can leave factorisation with squared terms"), as a recommendation of where to navigate (here to questions/materials). Users can also see the knowledge they are currently expected to have, by comparing their LM to instructor expectations (shown in the skill meters). Some of these features are similar to navigation support in AEH.

W. Nejdl et al. (Eds.): AH 2008, LNCS 5149, pp. 275–278, 2008.
© Springer-Verlag Berlin Heidelberg 2008

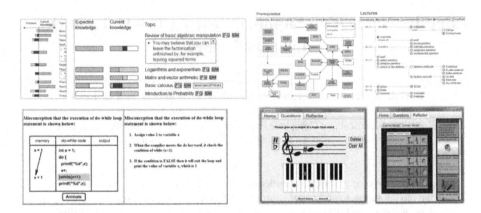

Fig. 1. *Upper left* simple OLM views - graph and skill meters; *upper right* complex OLM views - prerequisites and lecture structure; *lower left* an animated OLM - animation and text; *lower right* a music OLM - inputting musical notes; text, music notation and audio OLM views

Flexi-OLM shows more detailed LMs. It uses multiple choice and short answer questions, and provides 7 LM views [11]. Fig. 1 shows a map and hierarchical tree, which could be applied in AEH as such relationships are often defined.

Animated and audio: Some educational systems use materials in formats other than text or graphics, e.g. animation or audio [12],[13]. 2 other OLMs offering multiple views of the LM are AniMis, including animation; and musicaLM with audio. AniMis is built on top of OLMlets, so knowledge level is shown in the same way. Following 'misconceptions' links leads to misconceptions presented as text and animations (a programming example is in Fig. 1). In the animation, values are added to the left (memory) and right (output) columns as code is highlighted. Steps of a misconception are also given in text. Fig. 1 also shows how students input information in musicaLM: by music notation or keyboard. The LM is accessed in 3 forms: text description (e.g. "you may believe that whole tones are adjacent notes in the chromatic scale"); music notation, a natural way of referring to the music domain; audio, where the LM is presented by sound (notes). Domain and LM concepts (and misconceptions) recently accessed are displayed down the right side of the screen for easy comparison (text and music notation are shown; clicking on the sound icon replays audio).

Interactive: Some OLMs permit greater control over the LM such as allowing the user to scrutinise adaptations, increasing their understanding of the role of the model and enabling them to change their profile [14]. Learners may also edit their LM if it is inaccurate [5]. Although Flexi-OLM provides evidence for its beliefs, users can ignore this information and still change the LM if they wish. Editing the LM offers a quick way of updating it if the user can provide data that could not be predicted (e.g. recent learning from reading or a lecture). They may use links ignoring recommendations that no longer fit; or they may quickly update the LM allowing rapid re-adaptation. Editing the LM increases the user control that is important in many AEH applications, beyond the freedom to follow any link.

While learner control is considered important, it is suggested that if control of the LM is with learners, they may inaccurately assess their knowledge [15]. Although users may give information for modelling, they may be less comfortable with having full control [11]. More balanced control is offered by negotiated LMs: student and system agree on the LM contents through discussion - e.g. the user may challenge their LM. The system may provide evidence to support its views; it may offer a short test if the user does not accept the evidence; it may allow the user to give explanations (e.g. "I've forgotten"); etc. [8],[9]. Recent work has used a chatbot for negotiating the LM in CALMsystem [16], the final system used here. In an environment with an approach such as adaptive link support, where control is with the user, negotiating the LM or even simply discussing it, may be beneficial when the user does not understand why a link is recommended, or if they are unsure whether the LM is accurate.

Table 1. Open learner model preferences

		Agree		Neutral		Disagree	
1. Types of OLM students would use							
OLM to support navigation	(n=181)	78.5 %		20.5 %		1 %	
OLM to increase awareness of knowledge	(n=181)	82.5 %		17 %		0.5 %	
OLM to gain control over learning	(n=181)	53 %		40 %		7 %	
Overview presentation only	(n=181)	17 %		32 %		51 %	
Detailed presentation only	(n=181)	40 %		20 %		40 %	
Both overview and detailed presentation	(n=181)	64 %		32 %		4 %	
2. Understood OLM representations / trusted OLM							
OLMlets (understood / trusted)	(n=11)	10	9	1	1		1
Flexi-OLM (understood / trusted)	(n=9)	7	7	2	2		
AniMis (understood / trusted)	(n=10)	9	10	1			
musicaLM (understood / trusted)	(n=10)	10	8		2		
CALMsystem (understood / trusted)	(n=8)	8	6		1		2

181 university students who had used 2-5 OLMs, at least one throughout a term, completed a questionnaire. 8-11 used our 5 OLMs, interactions with each OLM lasting 90 mins. Table 1 shows that most of the 181 students wanted an OLM to support navigation. AEH often provides navigation support with link annotation. We suggest it may be useful if link adaptations also allow users to gauge their knowledge (in addition to the relevance of a link). This is achieved in ELM-ART, with a combination of link annotations indicating readiness to visit sections, and skill meters to show knowledge [5]. A little over 1/2 stated they would like greater control over learning, with only 7% responding negatively. While learner control and independence are seen as important by educators, not all students view it as critical. An advantage of adaptive navigation support is that control *is* with the user. For those who consider control over their learning to be important, additional features in the OLM may be a useful way of not only supporting decision-making, but also prompting reflection. This may also benefit those who had not considered their active role in learning. Learner control can also be achieved by interactive modelling. It may be worth considering allowing LM editing or negotiation: those who wish to inspect the model only, may still do so. AEH often has relatively simple indications of learner knowledge. Some users may find this less useful than detailed LM data, and many would prefer a combination. As

most users of our 5 OLMs understood and trusted the LMs, there seem little grounds at this stage to argue for any one approach (though some features may be useful in specific contexts). Of course, an attractive feature of AEH is its clarity. More complex OLMs may hamper this. Nevertheless, some combination of AEH and a range of OLM features seems worth considering, in particular: combining navigation support/knowledge awareness; sufficiently detailed LM data; and challenging LM representations. Investigations with a greater number of users will help to clarify this.

3 Summary

We have presented 5 OLMs to consider a greater range of OLMs in AEH - in particular for adaptive navigation support and learner control. We suggest various OLM features may be useful, especially a means of identifying knowledge; provision of more detailed information about the LM data; and a way to challenge the model.

References

1. Brusilovsky, P.: Adaptive Hypermedia. UMUAI 11(1-2), 87–110 (2001)
2. De Bra, P., Brusilovsky, P., Houben, G.-J.: Adaptive Hypermedia: From Systems to Framework. ACM Computing Surveys 31(4) (1999)
3. De Bra, P.: Adaptive Educational Hypermedia on the Web. Communications of the ACM 45(5), 60–61 (2002)
4. Brusilovsky, P., Eklund, J., Schwarz, E.: Web-Based Education for All: A Tool for Development Adaptive Courseware. Comp. Networks & ISDN Systems 30, 291–300 (1998)
5. Weber, G., Brusilovsky, P.: ELM-ART: An Adaptive Versatile System for Web-based Instruction. IJAIED 12, 351–384 (2001)
6. Mitrovic, A., Martin, B.: Evaluating the Effect of Open Student Models on Self-Assessment. Int. Journal of Artificial Intelligence in Education 17(2), 121–144 (2007)
7. Kay, J.: Learner Know Thyself: Student Models to Give Learner Control and Responsibility. In: Int. Conference on Computers in Education, AACE, pp. 17–24 (1997)
8. Dimitrova, V.: STyLE-OLM: Interactive Open Learner Modelling, IJAIED 13 (2003)
9. Bull, S., Pain, H.: Did I say what I think I said, and do you agree with me? In: Inspecting and Questioning the Student Model, World Conf. on AIED, AACE, pp. 501–508 (1995)
10. Bull, S., Quigley, S., Mabbott, A.: A Computer-Based Formative Assessment to Promote Reflection and Learner Autonomy. Engineering Education 1(1), 8–18 (2006)
11. Mabbott, A., Bull, S.: Student Preferences for Editing, Persuading and Negotiating the Open Learner Model. Intelligent Tutoring Systems, 481–490 (2006)
12. Carver, C.A., Howard, R.A., Lane, W.D.: Enhancing Student Learning Through Hypermedia Courseware and Incorporation of Student Learning Styles. IEEE Transactions on Education 42(1), 33–38 (1999)
13. Wolf, C.: iWeaver: Towards 'Learning Style'-Based E-Learning in Computer Science Education. In: Australasian Computing Education Conference, ACS Inc., pp. 273–279 (2003)
14. Czarkowski, M., Kay, J., Potts, S.: Web Framework for Scrutable Adaptation. In: Workshop on Learner Modelling for Reflection. AI in Education, pp. 11–18 (2005)
15. Kay, J.: Learner Control. UMUAI 11, 111–127 (2001)
16. Kerly, A., Ellis, R., Bull, S.: CALMsystem: A Conversational Agent for Learner Modelling. Knowledge Based Systems 21(3), 238–246 (2008)

News@hand: A Semantic Web Approach to Recommending News

Iván Cantador, Alejandro Bellogín, and Pablo Castells

Escuela Politécnica Superior, Universidad Autónoma de Madrid
Campus de Cantoblanco, 28049 Madrid, Spain
{ivan.cantador,alejandro.bellogin,pablo.castells}@uam.es

Abstract. We present News@hand, a news recommender system which applies semantic-based technologies to describe and relate news contents and user preferences in order to produce enhanced recommendations. The exploitation of conceptual information describing contents and user profiles, along with the capability of inferring knowledge from the semantic relations defined in the ontologies, enabling different content-based collaborative recommendation models, are the key distinctive aspects of the system. The multi-domain portability, the multi-media source applicability, and addressing of some limitations of current recommender systems are the main benefits of our proposed approach.

Keywords: recommender systems, ontologies, personalisation, user modelling, group modelling, semantic web.

1 Introduction

With the advent of the World Wide Web, people nowadays not only have access to more worldwide news information than ever before, but they can also obtain it in a more timely manner. Online newspapers present breaking news on their websites in real time, and users can receive automatic notifications about them via RSS feeds. RSS is indeed a convenient way to promote a site without the need to advertise or create complicated content sharing partnerships, and an easy mechanism for the users to be informed of the latest news or web contents. Even with such facilities, further issues remain nonetheless to be addressed. For one, the increasing volume, growth rate, ubiquity of access, and the unstructured nature of content challenge the limits of human processing capabilities. It is in such scenario where recommender systems can do their most, by scanning the space of choices, and predicting the potential usefulness of news for each particular user, without explicitly specifying needs or querying for items whose existence is unknown beforehand.

However, general common problems have not been fully solved yet, and further investigation is needed. For example, typical approaches are domain dependent. Their models are generated from information gathered within a specific domain, and cannot be easily extended and/or incorporated to other systems. Moreover, the need for further flexibility in the form of query-driven or group-oriented recommendations, and the consideration of contextual features during the recommendation processes are also unfulfilled requirements in most systems.

W. Nejdl et al. (Eds.): AH 2008, LNCS 5149, pp. 279–283, 2008.
© Springer-Verlag Berlin Heidelberg 2008

In this work, we present News@hand, a system that makes use of semantic-based technologies to recommend news. The system supports different recommendation models for single and multiple users which address several recommender systems limitations. The exploitation of meta-information in the form of ontologies that describe items and user profiles in a general, portable way, along with the capability of inferring knowledge from the semantic relations defined in the ontologies, are the key aspects of the system.

2 News@hand

News@hand combines textual features and collaborative information to make news suggestions. However, contrary to previous systems, it uses a controlled and structured vocabulary to describe the news contents and user preferences [7]. For this purpose, it makes use of semantic-based technologies. News items and user profiles are represented in terms of concepts appearing in domain ontologies, and semantic relations among those concepts are exploited to enrich the above representations, and enhance recommendations.

Figure 1 depicts how ontology-based item descriptions and user profiles are created in News@hand. Like in other systems [1,10,13], news are automatically and periodically retrieved from several on-line news services via RSS feeds. The title and summary of the retrieved news are then annotated with concepts (classes and instances) of the domain ontologies available to the system. Similarly to other approaches [1,2], a TF-IDF technique is applied to assign weights to the annotated concepts. A total of 17 ontologies have been used for the first version of the system. They are adaptations of the IPTC ontology (see http://nets.ii.uam.es/~mesh/datasets/newsathand/news-at-hand_iptc-kb.zip), which contains concepts of multiple domains such as education, culture, politics, religion, science, technology, business, health, entertainment, sports, etc.

News@hand has a client/server architecture, where users interact with the system through a web interface where they receive on-line news recommendations, and update their preferences. Thanks to the novel AJAX technology, a dynamic graphical

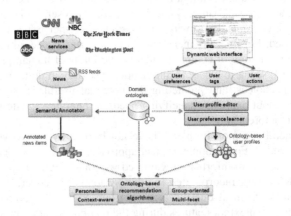

Fig. 1. Item descriptions and user profiles acquisition in News@hand

interface allows the system to automatically store all the users' inputs, analyse their behaviour with the system, update their preferences, and adjust the news recommendations in real time. As done in [8], explicit and implicit user preferences are taken into account, via manual preferences, tags and ratings, and via automatic learning from the users' actions.

Drawing benefit from the semantically annotated news items, the defined ontology-based user profiles, and the knowledge represented by the domain ontologies, a set of recommendation algorithms are executed. Specifically, News@hand provides personalised, context-aware [14], group-oriented [6], and multi-facet [4,5] recommendations.

Figure 2 shows a screenshot of a typical news page in News@hand. The news items are classified in 8 different sections: headlines, world, business, technology, science, health, sports and entertainment. When the user is not logged in the system, she can browse any of the previous sections, but the news items are listed without any personalisation criterion. She can only sort them by their publication date, source or level of popularity. On the other hand, when the user is logged in the system, recommendation and profile edition functionalities are enabled, and the user can browse the news according to her and others' semantic preferences in different ways. Like in other approaches [1,2,3], short and long term preferences are considered. As done in [9], click history is used to define the short term concepts, and similarly to [13], the resulting ranks can be adapted to the current context of interest.

At the centre of the screen, aside from its title, source, date, summary, images, and link to the full article, additional information is shown for each news item. The specific terms in the item text that are associated to either semantic annotations, or the user profile, or the current context are highlighted with different colours. A global rating is shown on a 5-star scale, and two coloured bars indicate the relevance of the news item for the user profile and the context. The user has the possibility to view and add comments, tags and ratings to the article, following the ideas presented in [11,12]. On the left side of the screen, the user can set the parameters she wants for single or group-oriented recommendations: the consideration of preferences of her profile, of her contacts, or of all the users, the degree of relevance that the concepts of the profile and the context should have, and multi-criteria conditions to be fulfilled by the user

Fig. 2. Screenshot of news recommendations in News@hand

evaluations. Finally, on the right side of the screen, general social information such as the most popular news, the most popular tags and the most active users is shown.

3   Benefits of the Approach

News@hand supports multiple recommendation functionalities, and addresses some of the limitations in current recommender systems, such as:

- *Domain dependency*. The use of ontologies and Semantic Web standards to represent user profiles and news items makes it possible to easily incorporate new domains into the system, and export the obtained knowledge to other applications.
- *Restricted content analysis*. Our annotation mechanism allows the distribution and exploitation of metadata from different multimedia sources, such as texts, videos, or audios.
- *Content overspecialisation, cold-start, portfolio* and *sparsity*. The extension of user preferences and item features through ontology properties enable the detection of further co-occurrences of interests between users, and finds new interests, available for recommendations.
- *Gray sheep*. The proposed hybrid models compare user profiles at different semantic interest layers, enabling further possibilities to find relations between users.
- *Group-oriented recommendations*. The vector-based preference description facilitates the combination of multiple profiles to generate a shared profile for groups of users.
- *Context-aware recommendations*. Under the ontology-based knowledge representation, we define the notion of semantic runtime context, which we apply to provide recommendations according to the live (complementarily to long-term) user interests.

Acknowledgments

This research was supported by the European Commission (FP6-027685-MESH) and the Spanish Ministry of Science and Education (TIN2005-06885). The expressed content is the view of the authors but not necessarily the view of the MESH project as a whole.

References

1. Ahn, J., Brusilovsky, P., Grady, J., He, D., Syn, S.Y.: Open User Profiles for Adaptive News Systems: Help or Harm? In: Proceedings of the 16th International Conference on World Wide Web (WWW 2007), Banff, Alberta, Canada, pp. 11–20 (2007)
2. Billsus, D.: A Personal News Agent that Talks, Learns and Explains. In: Proc. of the 3rd International Conference on Autonomous Agents (Agents 1999), Seattle, WA, USA, pp. 268–275 (1999)
3. Billsus, D., Pazzani, M.J.: User Modeling for Adaptive News Access. User Modeling and User-Adapted Interaction 10, 147–180 (2000)

4. Cantador, I., Bellogín, A., Castells, P.: Modelling Ontology-based Multilayered Communities of Interest for Hybrid Recommendations. In: Proceedings of the 1st Int. Workshop on Adaptation and Personalisation in Social Systems: Groups, Teams, Communities (SociUM 2007), at the 11th International Conference on User Modeling (UM 2007), Corfu, Greece (2007)

5. Cantador, I., Castells, P.: Multilayered Semantic Social Networks Modelling by Ontology-based User Profiles Clustering: Application to Collaborative Filtering. In: Proceedings of the 15th International Conference on Knowledge Engineering and Knowledge Management (EKAW 2006), Podebrady, Czech Republic, pp. 334–349 (2006)

6. Cantador, I., Castells, P., Vallet, D.: Enriching Group Profiles with Ontologies for Knowledge-Driven Collaborative Content Retrieval. In: Proc. of the 1st International Workshop on Semantic Technologies in Collaborative Applications (STICA 2006), Manchester, UK, pp. 358–363 (2006)

7. Castells, P., Fernández, M., Vallet, D.: An Adaptation of the Vector-Space Model for Ontology-based Information Retrieval. IEEE Transactions on Knowledge and Data Engineering 19(2), 261–272 (2007)

8. Claypool, M., Gokhale, A., Miranda, T., Murnikov, P., Netes, D., Sartin, M.: Combining Content-Based and Collaborative Filters in an Online Newspaper. In: Proceedings of the ACM SIGIR 1999 Workshop on Recommender Systems, Berkeley, CA, USA (1999)

9. Das, A., Datar, M., Garg, A., Rajaram, S.: Google News Personalisation: Scalable Online Collaborative Filtering. In: Proceedings of the 16th International Conference on World Wide Web (WWW 2007), Banff, AB, Canada, pp. 11–20 (2007)

10. Jones, G.J.F., Quested, D.J., Thomson, K.E.: Personalised Delivery of News Articles from Multiple Sources. In: Borbinha, J.L., Baker, T. (eds.) ECDL 2000. LNCS, vol. 1923, pp. 340–343. Springer, Heidelberg (2000)

11. Lang, K.: NewsWeeder: Learning to filter Netnews. In: Proceedings of the 12th International Conference on Machine Learning, pp. 331–339 (1995)

12. Maes, P.: Agents that Reduce Work and Information Overload. Communications of the ACM 37(7), 31–40 (1994)

13. Nadjarbashi-Noghani, M., Zhang, J., Sadat, H., Ghorbani, A.A.: PENS: A Personalised Electronic News System. In: Proceedings of the 3rd Annual Communication Networks and Services Research Conference (CNSR 2005), pp. 31–38 (2005)

14. Vallet, D., Castells, P., Fernández, M., Mylonas, P., Avrithis, Y.: Personalised Content Retrieval in Context Using Ontological Knowledge. IEEE Transactions on Circuits and Systems for Video Technology 17(3), 336–346 (2007)

A SOA-Based Framework to Support User Model Interoperability

Federica Cena and Roberto Furnari

Dipartimento di Informatica, Università di Torino
Corso Svizzera 185, Torino, Italy
{cena,furnari}@di.unito.it

Abstract. This paper presents an approach to achieve User Model (UM) interoperability exploiting Web Service technologies for syntactic interoperability, and Semantic Web languages for semantic interoperability, together with negotiation techniques based on dialogue. We propose a SOA-based framework where a central UDDI registry, enhanced with UM specific capabilities, is used to support and promote the cooperation between UM-based applications.

1 Introduction

Interoperability of User Model (UM) knowledge plays a crucial role when service access takes place in an open and dynamic environment as the Web. In reaching interoperability, a primary issue is how a system can find other systems available to cooperate (*discovery* issue). Once a partner has been found, interoperability implies the ability to i) exchange information, which requires to agree on the communication protocol (*syntactic interoperability*) and ii) to use such knowledge, which requires to correctly interpret the data (*semantic interoperability*). If the knowledge model is shared, and thus the involved services agree on the meaning of terms, it is possible to exploit simple *atomic communication* (where a system merely asks for the value of a property and the other system provides it) by means of a standard *request/response* invocation. Instead, when the systems do not share the same knowledge models, they may need to clarify the requested user feature, or to negotiate the response when the exact one is not available or is not considered satisfying by the requestor. In these situations, some form of *conversation*[1] could be used. The paper proposes a complete solution to support the UM interoperability process (discovery, semantic and syntactic interoperability issues) on the Web by means of a framework based on Service Oriented Architecture (SOA) (Section 2) exploiting Web Service and Semantic Web technologies, and offering a conversation support (Section 2.1).

2 The SOA Framework

In our vision a framework supporting UM interoperability has to offer facilities to: i) support the discovery of systems offering the desired information; ii) provide shared

---

[1] A conversation is a complex interaction among two parties, that may evolve in different ways, depending on the state and the needs of the two participants.

W. Nejdl et al. (Eds.): AH 2008, LNCS 5149, pp. 284–287, 2008.

ways to describe the different interoperability capabilities of applications (both syntactically and semantically); iii) support *atomic communication* and *conversation*.

The framework we propose is based on Web Services and Semantic Web standards and it provides a centralized and shared definition of the tools supporting communication. It uses an UDDI [2] registry in which each service provides its description and declares the supported syntactic and semantic communication tools. The central registry is enhanced with discovery functionalities (based on the *publish/subscribe* pattern) which can be exploited by systems for finding available services to interoperate with.

To take part in the framework, applications must: i) use Web Service standards as a basic communication protocol[3] and provide a publish/subscribe interface; ii) refer at least conceptually to a public ontology, regardless of the inner knowledge representation; iii) use a mechanism like OpenId (http://openid.net) to provide a common user identification.

2.1   Conversation Model

A novelty of the framework is the ability to support complex interactions in form of conversation. In this paper we exploit the dialogue model presented in [1]. The basic dialogue primitive in the model is the *Speech Act* [4]. It is represented as a couple *<move, statement>*. A *move* is a domain-dependent verb expressing the system intention (e.g. to inquire, to deny, to accept, to inform, etc). A *statement* about the UM is represented as a triple *<property,value,belief>*: for example, *<interestArt,0.8,0.2>* means that the value of the property *interest in art* is high with low certainty. The building blocks of the model are the *dialogue games*: templates describing the communication behaviour the systems can follow to reach a particular goal. A dialogue game is defined by the combination of: i) *conversation protocol*: conversation expressed in terms of messages exchanged between two roles; ii) *focus strategies*: strategies to collect the concepts that can be discussed in a conversation; iii) *scope strategies*: strategies to select from the focus the concepts to be used as statements. The model was instantiated in the UM interoperability context in [1], where three main dialogue games were identified: i) *Clarification Game*, to clarify the request (using concept properties to disambiguate the meaning of the requested UM feature); ii) *Explorative Game*, to approximate the response when an exact one is not available (if there is not the value of the requested concept, the values of related concepts can be used instead.); iii) *Explicative Game*, to explain the response (refer to [1] for more details).

2.2   Overview of the Framework Architecture

Each UM-based application running in our framework is a *Web Service* (see fig. 1) and has to provide the basic WSDL operation to support atomic communication to share UM knowledge (*getValueOf(property,..)*), and the interface to correctly interact with a central registry, *Enhanced User Model UDDI Registry* (*EUMUR*). This is a an UDDI registry (used as a standard discovery tool) adapted and enhanced according to the peculiarity of the UM context. Beside the declaration of all the services cooperating

---

[2] http://uddi.org/pubs/uddi-v3.0.2-20041019.htm
[3] A Web Service wrapper can be used to provide WSDL interface to existing applications.

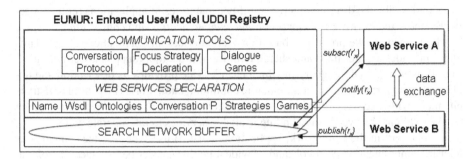

Fig. 1. Framework Architecture

in the framework, here we can find the definition of all the tools that can be used as model for the communication between services. EUMUR has three main components:

- *Communication Tools*, which contains the list of supported mechanisms for enable different kinds of enriched interactions; the description of the *Conversation Protocol*s used in the framework, the *Focus Strategy Declaration*s to browse through ontology concepts (described as semantics-based query over the ontology), the schemes of *Dialogue Game*.
- *Services Declaration*, which contains the list of Web Services available in the framework associated with the declaration of the *Ontologies* used and the *Communication tools* supported by each service;
- *Search Network Buffer* (SNB), which is a shared network space able to automatically match service requestors with service providers of specific UM knowledge. The interaction model is managed according to the *publish/subscribe* pattern and the data exchanged in this space represents *requests* of user features and *responses* of availability of values for the requested features. In particular: i) all the services *subscribe* to the SNB asking to be notified (as a provider) when a certain kind of request arrives; ii) when a service (acting as a requestor) looks for some user information, it *publishes* a request to the buffer[4]; iii) all the notified services reply to the SNB, declaring their availability; iv) the requestor service, reading the answers on the SNB, can directly contacts each provider to ask for the desired values.

In the SNB neither UM *dimensions* nor *values* are shared, since the buffer just hosts requests (and answers) of collaboration. The exchange of UM data will take place in a peer-to-peer way: the requestor service is free to select which tools to use for the interaction (according to the *Services Declaration* and to its internal policies), while the provider can apply its own privacy policies for data access.

---

[4] The format of a SNB request is: *(Sender, Action, Kind, Ontology, Focus, Object, User)*, where *Sender* is the name of the requestor, *Action* is the constant *inquiry*, *Kind* is the typology of the request: *byUri* (if it refers to a specific ontology) or *byLabel* (if expressed by means of a label); *Ontology* keeps a reference to the ontology; *Object* is the *Uri* of the requested concept (*byUri*) or its label (*byLabel*); *Focus* contains the focus strategy the requestor asks to use; *User* refers to the user the request is referring to.

As example we can consider two scenarios, where the required concept i) belongs to a shared ontology, ii) does not belong to a shared ontology. When the application *A1* needs information about the concept *c#134* (referring to the ontology *TO*) about its user *us4*, it invokes the following operation on the SNB: *publish(A1, inquiry, byUri, TO, null, c#134, us4)*. The application *A2*, previously subscribed by means of the operation *subscribe(A2, inquiry, byUri, TO)* will be notified by the SNB and answers to the call, since it stores the required value. Thus, *A1* can use *atomic communication* to get the desired value from *A2*.

In the case of request of the interest in a concept (labeled as *church*) not belonging to a shared ontology, *A1* can publish a request like: *publish(UM1, inquiry, byLabel, null, null, church, us4)*. In this case, A2 has the label in its ontology *Art* but it refers to two different concepts: a place for religious celebration or place to visit. To disambiguate the term, looking at the *Service Declaration*, *A1* can start a *Clarification Game* (see 2.1) with A2 (and thus ask for the values of concept properties) to refine the request. For instance, it could produce the Speech Act *<A1, A2, inquiry, celebration_time>* since *celebration_time* is a discriminating feature for religious places.

3   Conclusion

Two main solutions have been proposed to deal with UM interoperability: centralized [6] and decentralized [5]. Our solution exploits the advantages of the distributed approaches (such as flexibility in managing privacy) providing at the same time a central shared point used as a warranted reference to cooperation. We propose a mixed solution where the publish/subscribe pattern is just used as a central point for automatic user feature discovery, and where there is not a shared UM description and the exchange of user knowledge takes place in a P2P way. A similar model to our discovery mechanism has been proposed in [2] in order to share UM fragments by means of a central repository. Regarding solutions for semantic interoperability, [3] exploits facilities offered to applications for the ontologies mapping. Instead in our approach, conversations are used for reaching an agreement over not shared concepts. However, a similar form of semantic agreement can be implemented in our framework, integrating an ontology-mapper WS by means of the publish/subscribe mechanism.

References

1. Cena, F., Aroyo, L.: A semantics-based dialogue for interoperability of user-adaptive systems in a ubiquitous environment. In: Conati, C., McCoy, K., Paliouras, G. (eds.) UM 2007. LNCS (LNAI), vol. 4511. Springer, Heidelberg (2007)
2. Chepegin, V., Aroyo, L., De Bra, P.: Broker-based discovery service for user models in a multi-application context. In: ICALT 2005 (July 2005)
3. Houben, G.J., van der Sluijs, K.: Towards a generic user model component. In: UM 2005 (2005)
4. Searle, J.: What is a speech act. Language and Social Context (1972)
5. Vassileva, J.: Distributed user modelling for universal information access. Universal Access in Human - Computer Interaction 3, 122–126 (2001)
6. Yimam, D., Kobsa, A.: Centralization vs. decentralization issues in internet-based knowledge management systems:experiences from expert recommender systems. In: TWIST 2000 (2000)

Integrated Speaker Classification for Mobile Shopping Applications

Michael Feld and Gerrit Kahl

German Research Center for Artificial Intelligence, DFKI
{Michael.Feld,Gerrit.Kahl}@dfki.de

Abstract. This paper presents an approach to how speaker classification can be used to enable new ways for recommender systems in a mobile shopping environment to bootstrap user models and avoid common problems such as the "early rater". In a concrete shopping scenario, we introduce the speech-controlled Mobile ShopAssist demonstrator that allows a new customer to more quickly find a product that fulfills his or her demographic group's specific requirements by exploiting features extracted from speech using the AGENDER speaker classification system. We propose a method for computing preference scores based on the user's profile and demonstrate how the application's GUI can be adapted to deliver the recommendations to the user.

1 Introduction

In previous work [1,2], we have described an approach to speaker classification that enables us to classify a recorded voice according to various characteristics of the speaker, such as age and gender, and which is a great way to support user modelling in situations where no or little explicit information about the user is available. Another item of previous work is the MOBILE SHOPASSIST (MSA) [3]. It is implemented as a PDA-based application that is designed for use in a physical store to support the user in finding the appropriate product.

Our goal is to improve the MSA's modalities to support the user in making informed decisions about products offered in a shop by dynamically integrating knowledge about the user in the information filtering process. Consider the following scenario: A 43 year old customer enters a mobile phone store with the intention to buy a new phone. Looking at the products on display, he is presented with an overwhelming number of articles. He finds it hard to choose from them by just looking at the outer packaging, especially since many of the advertised features such as games and ringtones are rather aimed at teenagers. Using the MSA on his PDA, he can scan through the core information for each phone more quickly, but the comparison is still time-consuming and involves a lot of manual filtering. This paper outlines how AGENDER technology can be used to provide the necessary information about a user for whom no profile data is available, and it shows how this information is then used in the MSA application to adapt the displayed information according to the user profile obtained from AGENDER.

W. Nejdl et al. (Eds.): AH 2008, LNCS 5149, pp. 288–291, 2008.

2   The Agender Approach

A person's voice contains a lot of information about the speaker. This includes properties such as *language*, *accent*, *cognitive load*, *emotion* and *height*. In our shopping scenario, we focus on *age* and *gender*.

In a first step to determine the phonological attributes of these features in speech, data collection of several large corpora of labelled speakers and their empirical analysis have been performed by Müller [1]. Through these studies, several prosodic features such as *pitch*, *jitter*, *shimmer* and *harmonics-to-noise ratio* have been found which convey sufficient information to distinguish between genders and age groups. The current version uses four age classes: *children* (up to 12 years), *teenagers* (13-20 years), *young adults* (21-64 years) and *seniors* (65 years and older). The choice of these boundaries can be primarily attributed to the biological changes that typically occur to the human anatomy – especially the vocal tract – around these ages, and that affect the characteristics of speech.

Using methods from signal processing implemented in the tool *Praat*[1], common statistics based on these features were extracted on the available corpus data. The resulting data was used to train models for each of the speaker classes. Several machine learning methods have been investigated, in particular GMMs, kNN, Decision Trees, SVMs and Artificial Neural Networks. The results from multiple classifiers can be combined using a Dynamic Bayesian Network.

The AGENDER implementation used in this work is a refined version of what was developed in [2]. Using the framework tools, classifiers are trained for the required classes and are compiled into an embedded classification module. Using the DLL library interface, it can be directly integrated into any kind of application, which can then request a classification of the raw audio data it provides.

3   The Mobile ShopAssist

The Mobile ShopAssist (MSA) is a PDA-based multilingual multimodal shopping assistant [3]. The relevant input and output modalities are: speech, handwriting/text and gesture. With the MSA demonstrator, it is easy to get the specific information about the different products. For this purpose the user can write the name of the product and/or the requested feature on the touch-sensitive display of the PDA. Clicking on the product image represents another input mode. For the gesture input of the feature, the user can click on the corresponding expression in a scrolling text bar. The third alternative for input is speech, which is recognized using IBM Embedded ViaVoice[2]. After processing the input, the system outputs the value of the requested feature. Furthermore, this assistant facilitates the comparison of two products by contrasting their features.

The MSA was designed as a client-server architecture. After the user has logged in, the system loads his or her specific profile from the user model managing system called UBISWORLD [4]. In the previous version, there was only a

---

[1] http://www.praat.org

[2] http://www.ibm.com/software/pervasive/products/voice/vv_enterprise.shtml

standard profile for users who had no UBISWORLD login. According to the approach presented in this paper, this standard profile can be adapted dynamically to the current user.

Table 1. Selected mobile phone features and phones that may exhibit statistically significant influence on purchase decisions for certain audiences

Feature	Style/color	Weight	UMTS	Display size	Digital camera
Suggested Relevance	custom, per product	lower weight preferred by women	mostly requested by adults	large displays preferred by seniors	good cameras important for teenagers
Samsung SGH U600	classic	81g	no	5.59cm	3.2 megapixels
SecuPoint Secu-B	somewhat old-fashioned	130g	no	large text-only	none
Siemens SXG 75	classic	134g	yes	5.5cm	2 megapixels

4   Recommendations and Score Computation

For our scenario, we have created a product assortment for a fictitious mobile phone store. Mobile phones are one category of products on the choice of which the speaker characteristics presented here have quite a large impact. We chose *teenagers*, *young adults*, and *seniors* as target age groups for this application.

The content for the basic recommender system we have implemented in our prototype is provided by product data annotations. For each mobile phone feature, we can specify recommendation ratings. A rating can be created for every subset of user classes and indicates whether that feature is often requested and typically important for this audience w.r.t. the feature's setting. For example, WLAN functionality may receive an increased rating for the *adults* group, while ringtones and gaming capabilities (*Java*) are rated high for the *teenagers* group. In the same way, features that make the mobile phone more accessible to elderly people, like readability, can be promoted. Table 1 lists some of the features we incorporated in this application. To obtain a recommendation score for a product, all ratings matching the current user's profile are added together. It should be pointed out that the choice of the actual parameters needs to be subject to adequate market research in the chosen product category.

5   Adaptation of the User Interface

The speech that is used to control the MSA is also the input for the classifier. By calling a function in the Agender Client DLL, the speech data is transferred to the server running Agender over WLAN and classified. The application can then request an updated user profile from the server. Using this model, we provided two means of GUI adaptation: (1) The user-adaptive product list is sorted according to the product's score and (2) the detail page highlights features of special relevance (i.e. score) of both supporting and prohibiting type (Fig. 1), e.g. the price of a mobile phone is less important for adults than for teenagers.

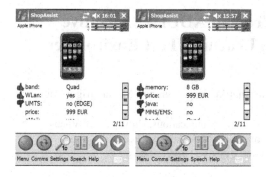

	Tf	Tm	Af	Am	Sf	Sm
Tf	75.5	0.9	19.3	0.3	3.6	0.4
Tm	3.6	43.6	5.6	39.0	2.7	5.6
Af	27.9	1.5	60.0	1.7	7.3	1.6
Am	0.8	22.6	1.8	61.2	2.6	11.0
Sf	9.4	1.5	7.3	3.5	64.8	13.4
Sm	0.7	8.1	2.1	23.1	12.4	53.5

Fig. 1. Screenshots of the MSA: The left image shows the specific order of the *iPhone*'s features for an *adult* user whereas the right image shows the product's feature ordering for a *teenager*

Fig. 2. Confusion matrix. Rows show reference classes, columns the predicted class, and each cell the percentage of class instances.

6 Results and Future Work

Fig. 2 shows the confusion matrix of the evaluation results obtained with the AGENDER classifier for the six-class configuration described earlier. This classifier is a 20-node ANN trained with ~10,000 utterances stemming from *GlobalPhone*, *Timit* [5] and *Scansoft* corpora, each in 8 kHz 16 bit mono format. Evaluation has been performed using a ten-fold cross validation approach. The total accuracy is 59.8% at a chance level of 17%, with a precision of 0.6.

Our research suggests several areas for possible future work and improvements. One main focus should be the integration of a collaborative recommender system as described in [6] and to evaluate the effectiveness of the combination of both systems. Further, by exploiting classifier scores, we want to move from a discrete approach to a speaker model that represents beliefs in each of its classes.

References

1. Müller, C.: Zweistufige kontextsensitive Sprecherklassifikation am Beispiel von Alter und Geschlecht. PhD thesis, Computer Science Institute, Saarland University, Germany (2005)
2. Feld, M.: Erzeugung von Sprecherklassifikationsmodulen für multiple Plattformen. Master's thesis, Computer Science Institute, Saarland University, Germany (2006)
3. Wasinger, R.: Multimodal Interaction with Mobile Devices: Fusing a Broad Spectrum of Modality Combinations. PhD thesis, Saarland University, Department of Computer Science (2006)
4. Heckmann, D.: Ubiquitous User Modeling. PhD thesis, Department of Computer Science, Saarland University (2005)
5. Garofolo, J.e.A.: DARPA TIMIT CD-ROM: An Acoustic Phonetic Continous Speech Database. National Institute of Standards and Technology, Gaithersburg, MD, USA (1998)
6. Burke, R.: Hybrid recommender systems: Survey and experiments. User Modeling and User-Adapted Interaction 12(4), 331–370 (2002)

The Authoring Tool of ADULT: Adaptive Understanding and Learning Text Environment

Alexandra Gasparinatou, Grammatiki Tsaganou, and Maria Grigoriadou

Department of Informatics and Telecommunications, University of Athens
Panepistimioupolis, GR-15784 Athens, Greece
{alegas,gram,gregor}@di.uoa.gr

Abstract. Previous research in the domain of text comprehension in Informatics has demonstrated that readers with little knowledge in this domain benefit from a coherent text, whereas high-knowledge readers benefit from a minimally coherent text. With respect to educational applications, these findings suggest constructing several versions of a text in order to adapt to varying levels of knowledge among readers. In this paper we present the design of the authoring tool of the learning environment ADULT (Adaptive Understanding and Learning from Texts), capable of supporting authors while constructing texts of different coherence in the domain of Informatics, accompanied by questions or tasks designed to access students' comprehension on line. This way students will be activated to use their background knowledge while reading and more students will have the opportunity to achieve better learning results in learning from Informatics texts than reading a single textbook in Informatics targeted at an average reader.

Keywords: Adaptive environment, Authoring tool supporting adaptive environment, Understanding and learning from texts, Background knowledge.

1 Introduction

In this paper we present the design of the authoring tool of the learning environment ADULT (Adaptive Understanding and Learning from Texts) [1]. ADULT is based on Kintsch's Construction-Integration model for text comprehension and takes into account the learner's background knowledge in order to suggest to him the text of appropriate coherence [2,3,4,5]. The design of our system includes the following activities: (1) Sorting Task, (2) Background Knowledge Questions, (3) Text, (4) Text Recall, (4) Assessment Questions. The system suggests a specific learning sequence however the student can set his own sequence.

The paper is organized as follows: In the first section we present the learning design of the authoring tool of the ADULT authoring tool. Subsequently, the learner model of the system is discussed. The paper concludes with suggestions in relation to improving the currently used authoring tool in order to achieve more personalized learning.

2 The ADULT Authoring Tool

The objective of ADULT Authoring tool is to support authors while constructing texts of different coherence in the domain of Informatics, accompanied by questions or tasks

W. Nejdl et al. (Eds.): AH 2008, LNCS 5149, pp. 292–295, 2008.

designed to assess students' comprehension on line. An instructional Informatics text can then be presented at the level of coherence that is adapted to the students' current level of understanding. This way, students are activated to use their background knowledge while reading and have the possibility to achieve better learning results in learning from Informatics texts than reading a single textbook in Informatics targeted at an average reader. Using the authoring tool ADULT, authors can define an adaptive learning design that includes the following texts and activities [4,5]:

- **Texts:**

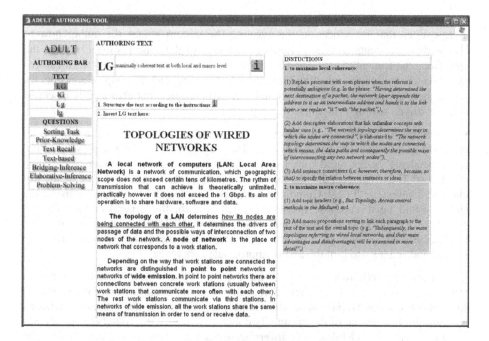

Fig. 1. The system leads the author to construct the four text versions

For each topic of interest the author constructs four versions of a text (Fig. 1): a) A minimally coherent text at both the local and the macro level (lg), b) a text minimally coherent at the local level and maximally coherent at the macro level (l G), c) a text maximally coherent at the local level and minimally coherent at the macro level (Lg), d) a maximally coherent text at both the local and the macro level (LG). The system gives directions to the author how to construct these versions. Therefore, the system gives the following three types of rules to the author used to maximize local coherence: (1) Replacing pronouns with noun phrases when the referent is potentially ambiguous (e.g. In the phrase: *"Having determined the next destination of a packet, the network layer appends this address to it as an intermediate address and hands it to the link layer."* we replace *"it"* with *"the packet".*), (2) Adding descriptive elaborations that link unfamiliar concepts with familiar ones (e.g., *"The network topology determines the way in which the nodes are connected"*, is elaborated to: *"The network topology determines the way in which the nodes are connected, which means, the data paths and consequently the possible ways of interconnecting any two network nodes"*), (3) Adding sentence connectives (i.e. *however, therefore, because, so that*) to specify the relation between sentences or ideas. The system also gives the following rules to the author used to maximize macro coherence: (1) Adding topic headers (e.g., *Bus Topology, Access control methods in the Medium*) and (2) Adding macro propositions serving to link each paragraph to the rest of the text and the overall topic (e.g., *"Subsequently, the main topologies referring to wired local networks, and their main advantages and disadvantages, will be examined in more detail".)*

- **Sorting task:** For each topic the author has to compose a set of concepts and a set of categories that introduces to the system. The system guides the author how to choose these concepts and categories (e.g. the most of the concepts must be from the text which the student reads). The student has to sort them into the predefined categories. The motivation for selecting these concepts is to provide a group of concepts for which there are not only several rational sorting principles, but also clearly discernible, text-driven sorting principles.

- **Background knowledge questions:** The system leads the author to compose a set of questions that introduces to the system. The purpose of these questions is the detection of students' background knowledge and concerns the general domain of the topic of interest. The system guides the author to construct these questions (e.g. if the domain of interest is "Local Computer Network Topologies" the instructions to the author would be to compose questions which concern the general domain of networks, i.e. *"Why do we use communication networks?"* The student has to complete the background knowledge questionnaire. After that, the system characterizes the student and suggests to him the text of appropriate coherence.

- **Assessment activities:** For each topic the author has to introduce to the system four types of questions The system guides the author to construct these questions (1) **Text-based questions:** The necessary information to answer the question contained within a single sentence of the minimally coherent lg text (e.g., *"What is a local computer network"?)*, (2) **Elaborative-inference questions:** Linking text information and information from outside knowledge is required in order to answer the question (e.g., *"What is the distinction between a local network and an internet?"),* (3) **Bridging-inference questions:** The information is contained in the text but requires linking two or more sentences to answer the question (e.g., *"What is the difference between using CSMA protocol and CSMA/CD protocol in a bus topology;"),* (4) **Problem-solving questions:** Linking information from separate sentences within the text and applying this information to a novel situation is required (e.g., *"Let us assume a bus network with 1-persistent CSMA. What is the process that a node follows in order to send a packet? What happens: (1) if the medium of transmission is occupied?(2) if the medium of transmission is free?")*

3 Learner Model

The learner model keeps information about: (1) learner's background knowledge level with respect to the learning goals/text version/ activities that s/he has worked on, and (2) learner's behavior during his/her interaction with the environment in terms of the learning sequence s/he has chosen, the number of times that feedback was asked, time spent on reading the text, time spent on an activity, etc. The learner model also keeps general information about the learner such as username, profession, and learner's preferences on feedback types, last time/date the learner logged on/off. The learner model is dynamically updated during learner's interaction with the system in order to keep track of the learner's "current state". During interaction, learners may access their model and see the information held concerning their progress and interaction behavior [6].

4 Conclusions and Future Work

The ADULT Authoring tool, presented in this article, supports authors while constructing texts of different coherence in the domain of Informatics to provide readers with the appropriate level of coherence according to their background knowledge. Texts, accompanied by activities or tasks, are designed to assess a student's comprehension on line. Our future plans include the consideration of students' background knowledge and learning style in order to suggest them specific learning activities and support group formation. We also intend to evaluate ADULT with the participation of students and experts.

References

1. Gasparinatou, A., Tsaganou, G., Grigoriadou, M.: Adaptive Environment Supporting Understanding and Learning from Texts in Informatics (ADULT). In: The 8th IEEE International Conference on Advanced Learning Technologies, Santander, Cantabria, Spain, July 1st-July 5th (2008) (under publication)
2. Kintsch, W.: The use of knowledge in discourse processing: A construction-integration model. Psychological Review 95, 163–182 (1988)
3. Kintsch, W.: Text comprehension, memory and learning. American Psychologist 49, 292–303 (1994)
4. McNamara, D.S., Kintsch, E., Songer, N.B., Kintsch, W.: Are good texts always better? Text coherence, background knowledge, and levels of understanding in learning from text. Cognition and Instruction 14, 1–43 (1996)
5. Gasparinatou, A., Tsaganou, G., Grigoriadou, M.: Effects of Background Knowledge and Text Coherence on Learning from Texts in Informatics. In: Proceedings of the IADIS International Conference "Cognition and Exploratory Learning in Digital Age" (CELDA 2007), Algarve, Portugal, December 7-9 (2007) (under publication)
6. Brusilovsky, P.: Methods and Techniques of Adaptive Hypermedia. User Modeling and User-Adapted Interaction 6, 87–129 (1996)

Interoperability between MOT and Learning Management Systems: Converting CAF to IMS QTI and IMS CP

Fawaz Ghali and Alexandra I. Cristea

Department of Computer Science, University of Warwick,
Coventry, CV4 7AL, United Kingdom
{F.Ghali,A.I.Cristea}@warwick.ac.uk

Abstract. The chain of applying adaptivity to Learning Management Systems (LMS) is still deficient; there is a gap between authoring adaptive materials and delivering them in LMS. In this paper, we extend My Online Teacher (MOT), an adaptive authoring system, by adding compatibility with IMS Question & Test Interoperability (QTI) and IMS Content Packaging (CP). Thus, the authors can *utilize the authored materials for learning process adaptation on any standards-compatible LMS.* From a technical perspective, we initialize the creation of adaptive LMS by converting Common Adaptation Format (CAF), XML representation of MOT database, into IMS QTI and IMS CP, to ensure a wider uptake and use of adaptive learning systems. Finally, this work represents a significant step towards the little explored avenue of *adaptive collaborative systems* based on extant learning standards and popular LMS.

Keywords: Adaptive authoring, MOT, LMS, IMS QTI, IMS CP.

1 Introduction

Authoring of adaptive material is, generally speaking, a challenging arena. A clear weakness appears specifically when it comes to delivering these materials to students using regular Learning Management Systems (LMS). While [4] considers adaptive authoring a *"serious problem"*, it also provides two applicable approaches to solve it: 1) a *common language*, a lingua franca, used by all authors of Adaptive Educational Hypermedia (AEH); and 2) usage of *converters* between AEH systems. Thus, in our work, we follow a combined approach, by developing promising *converters*, which use adaptation materials as input and produce *standardized* material (the most widely accepted lingua franca) as output. Thus, we move one step forward from previous research, by limiting the lingua franca, to the degree it is possible, to existing standards. A large body of research states that standards cannot incorporate all requirements of an adaptive hypermedia [6]. However, as standards progress, it is unwise to ignore them. LMS rely heavily on standards, and are very popular. Therefore, if adaptive hypermedia is to move into the large-scale use and commercial market, it has to be able to interface with – or extend – existing LMS.

W. Nejdl et al. (Eds.): AH 2008, LNCS 5149, pp. 296–299, 2008.

1.1 MOT and CAF

MOT is an adaptation authoring system based on the LAOS (*Layered WWW AHS Authoring Model and their corresponding Algebraic Operators*) framework [3]. The Common Adaptation Format (CAF) reflects the content-related data structure of the MOT database; however, it uses XML representation, which is more suitable for web conversions. Thus, a CAF XML file has: 1) *Domain model*: containing a hierarchy of concept(s); as well as a collection of attribute(s) that describe related concept data. A concept may have sub-concept(s) that represent associations to other concepts. An attribute has a name and contents. 2) *Goal model*: The goal model represents the actual lesson, which may have a set of sub-lesson(s). Each lesson is composed of a set of link(s) where each link points to an attribute in the domain model. The link has two attributes: weight and label, which are used to determine the adaptive requirements via adaptation strategies (not detailed here due to lack of space).

2 Converting CAF to IMS QTI and IMS CP

We present a unique and novel initial step towards applying adaptation in LMS. This is a two step process: firstly, we convert CAF to IMS QTI and IMS CP; secondly, we import the converted results into a popular LMS, e.g., Sakai. To tackle the difficulties and challenges found in our work we use the Java Architecture for XML Binding (JAXB), as CAF, IMS QTI and IMS CP are based on XML and can be thus processed (see URL at: http://als.dcs.warwick.ac.uk/mot/).

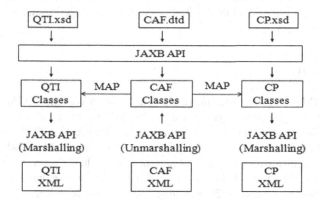

Fig. 1. JAXB facilitate converting CAF to IMS QTI and IMS CP

2.1 The Utilization of JAXB

As is illustrated in Figure 1: firstly, we generate Java classes for CAF.dtd, QTI.xsd and CP.xsd; secondly we parse (i.e., *unmarshalling*) the CAF XML file and generate Java objects; thirdly we map the results onto IMS QTI and IMS CP classes accordingly; finally we generate (i.e., *marshalling*) IMS QTI and IMS CP.

2.2 Converting CAF to IMS QTI

The IMS Question & Test Interoperability (QTI) is a data model and *de facto* standard for the representation of questionnaires and quizzes. Compared to the structure of CAF, we map the main lesson of the goal model into one 'assessment'; and the domain model into one 'section'. Each attribute in CAF is mapped to one item in IMS QTI. CAF has a hierarchical structure; however, IMS QTI has a flat one. Therefore, the hierarchical structure is flattened. As JAXB facilitates the mapping process, our algorithm *unmarshalls* the CAF file, and finds the concepts which contain "question" and "answer" as attributes, then it *marshals* the generated IMS QTI file with the "question" and the "answer". The question-answer pairs in the concept are retrieved from the goal model rather than from the domain model, which reflects the effective use of the authoring in MOT.

2.3 Converting CAF to IMS CP

The IMS Content Packaging (CP) is a *de facto* standard, which describes data structures that are used to provide interoperability for the contents of Learning Management Systems (LMS). Therefore, IMS CP provides standardized data structures that can be used to exchange content. The structure of IMS CP consists mainly of: 1) *Manifest XML file*: describing the contents' hierarchy, and pointers to the actual contents (physical files), and 2) the actual *physical files* (resources). IMS CP has more flexibility than IMS QTI, amongst which, the fact that it also supports hierarchical structures (same as CAF). Therefore, each attribute of each concept in CAF is mapped to one item in IMS CP with the preservation of the hierarchy. The attribute's *name* is converted to *title* of item and the attribute's *content* is mapped to the actual resource that matches the item.

3 Discussion

The CAF to IMS QTI converter manipulates adaptation content in CAF format and generates the matched assessment in IMS QTI; here we have two benefits from an adaptation point of view: 1) utilizing the adaptive parameters in CAF, and 2) enrich the generated assessment with new adaptive concepts using LOM in IMS QTI. Using assessments together with personalized learning access has a positive impact on the learning process, because it helps in: 1) checking if the learners have understood the materials correctly or not, and 2) providing feedback for both learners and teachers. Therefore, adding assessment potentials to AHES will enhance the learning process and give the students the chance of tracing their learning progress [1].

On the other hand, creating adaptive content is considered costly and time-consuming [2]. Therefore, reusing already created content is valuable, and this can be done by providing facilities to export the adaptive content into standardised format, such as IMS CP. The CAF to IMS CP converter performs this by partitioning the adaptive content into unique granularly items that can be reused for different learners. Moreover, those items can be enriched with metadata that follow the LOM standard to give a new dimension to applying adaptivity in LMS that support IMS CP.

4 Conclusion and Future Work

The majority of adaptive learning systems focus on personalizing the delivery of course materials to individual learners. However, little work has been done on applying adaptivity on collaborative learning systems. Converting adaptive content into learning standards can supply a dynamic learning process which is compatible with all systems that support these standards. In this paper we present the interoperability between adaptive authoring and Learning Management Systems by converting CAF into IMS QTI and IMS CP. Thus, the authored adaptive materials in MOT can be imported to well-known LMS such as Sakai. This is a first step towards the novel endeavour of bringing adaptation into collaborative LMS. For future work, we intend to apply adaptation on IMS QTI and IMS CP by using LOM (Learning Object Metadata) [5] – which is supported by IMS QTI and IMS CP - by enriching materials with further adaptation metadata.

Acknowledgments. The work accomplished in this paper is supported by the EU *ALS* Minerva STREP, the EU FP7 *GRAPPLE* STREP, and was based on the *PROLEARN* Network of Excellence.

References

1. Cheniti-Belcadhi, L., Braham, R., Henze, N., Nejdl, W.: A Generic Framework for Assessment in Adaptive Educational Hypermedia. In: Proceedings of the IADIS International Conference WWW/Internet, Madrid, Spain, vol. 2 (2004) ISBN: 972-99353-0-0
2. Conlan, O., Dagger, D., Wade, V.: Towards a Standards-based Approach to e-Learning Personalization using Reusable Learning Objects. In: E-Learn 2002, World Conference on E-Learning in Corporate, Government, Healthcare and Higher Education, Montreal (2002)
3. Cristea, A., De Mooij, A.: LAOS: Layered WWW AHS Authoring Model and its corresponding Algebraic Operators. In: Proceedings of WWW 2003, Alternate Education track, Budapest (2003)
4. Cristea, A., Smits, D., De Bra, P.: Towards a generic adaptive hypermedia platform: a conversion case study. Journal of Digital Information (JoDI) Special Issue on Personalisation of Computing & Services 8(3) (2007)
5. IEEE Learning Technology Standards Committee: 1484.12.1-2002 IEEE standard for Learning Object Metadata (2002)
6. Stash, N., Cristea, A.I., De Bra, P.: Explicit Intelligence in Adaptive Hypermedia: Generic Adaptation Languages for Learning Preferences and Styles. In: Int. Workshop on Combining Intelligent and Adaptive Hypermedia Methods/Techniques in Web-Based Education Systems, HT 2005, Salzburg, Austria, September 6-9, 2005. ACM, New York (2005)

Proactively Adapting Interfaces to Individual Users for Mobile Devices

Melanie Hartmann and Daniel Schreiber

Telecooperation Group, Technische Universität Darmstadt
Hochschulstraße 10, D-64289 Darmstadt, Germany
{melanie,schreiber}@tk.informatik.tu-darmstadt.de

Abstract. The amount of functionality offered by nowadays applications is constantly growing, mostly leading to more and more complex user interfaces. This often decreases their usability, especially in mobile settings where we have to deal with limited input and output capabilities. We state that adapting the interface to the available devices as well as to the user's current needs is the key to improving usability. In this paper, we present the AUGUR system that can automatically generate user- and device-adapted interfaces. We thereby focus on the FxL* algorithm that determines which user interface elements are currently relevant for a user. We show that it clearly outperforms algorithms that do not take the user or her situation into account.

1   Introduction

Mobile web access is supported by most modern portable devices. However, these devices are restricted in size and thus have limited input and output capabilities. For desktop settings Gajos [1] showed that correctly applied automatic personalization can increase the usability. As we have to deal with even higher interaction costs for mobile applications, we assume that adapting the user interface (UI) to the user's needs is one of the key issues for increasing their usability. Further, the UI has to be adapted to device constraints like the available screen space. However, existing approaches only take either the device or the user into account. AUGUR combines these two approaches and uses a new strategy for adapting the UI to the individual user's needs. AUGUR is built as a proxy architecture and can thus automatically adapt arbitrary form-based web applications. Figure 1 shows the result of AUGUR adapting the Deutsche Bahn website (German railways www.bahn.de). Almost all information required for the adaptation is learned from observation. However, it is difficult to automatically determine the relevant non-interactive elements on a web page, e.g. the departure times of trains, thus this information has to be annotated by the user or the application developer in the corresponding task model [2]. In this paper, we focus on the algorithm needed to determine the interaction elements that are most relevant for a specific user in a given situation and that can also take the available screen space into account.

One possibility for adapting UIs to small screen devices is using model driven approaches [3,4]. They instantiate a device independent model of the UI to a device specific model, which is then rendered on the device. Thereby, the rendering process does not take specific user features into account, and thus optimizes the UI for the average user. A UI

W. Nejdl et al. (Eds.): AH 2008, LNCS 5149, pp. 300–303, 2008.

| **(a)** Mobile | **(b)** Desktop | **(c)** Mobile | **(d)** Desktop |

Fig. 1. Unadapted (a and b) and adapted (c and d) user interface

system for small screen devices that adapts to the individual user has been proposed by
[5], where cards in a WAP deck are reordered to match navigational patterns. In contrast,
AUGUR can reorder at the level of single interaction elements. Another user-adapted approach is taken by [6]. However, it is restricted to hierarchically organized applications,
where every interface element can only be reached in a single way.

2 Prediction Algorithm

We apply a sequence prediction algorithm (SPA) to predict the currently most relevant
interaction elements for a user. A SPA returns for a given sequence $a_1...a_i$ the probability distribution P over all interaction elements whether it will occur next. We found that
the SPA most suitable for mobile use due to its low resource consumption is the FxL
algorithm [7]. However, it predicts only the most probable next interaction element.
Therefore, we augment FxL to FxL* that determines the next n elements the user will
most probably use. Thereby, n depends on the available display size and on how much
additional information is presented, i.e. it represents how many interaction elements can
be displayed. FxL* works as follows (the corresponding pseudo-code can be found in
Algorithm 1): For the most probable interaction elements $x_1, ..., x_n$ returned by FxL for
the recent interaction history $a_1..a_i$, we apply FxL again on every sequence $a_1...a_i x_j$.
The resulting probabilities are multiplied by the formerly computed probabilities for x_j

---

Algorithm 1. FxL*

Require: $a_1...a_i$ Sequence of most recent actions, p parent probability (initialized with 1)
$\quad\quad$ n amount of elements to be displayed, R global hash
Ensure: R contains probabilities for all actions that they will be needed in next n user actions

```
1: P(x|a₁ ... aⱼ) = FxL(a₁...aⱼ)
2: for all x do
3:      q(x) = P(x|a₁...aⱼ) · p
4:      R(x) = Max(R(x), q(x))
5:      if n > 0 then
6:          FxL*(a₁...aⱼx, q(x), n − 1)
7:      end if
8: end for
```

succeeding $a_1...a_i$, as the probability of an action cannot exceed the probability of its preceding action. Further, the resulting probabilities are merged with the probabilities calculated so far. This process is repeated until the most probable n elements are found (for simplification purposes, we only consider the next n steps in the pseudo-code for that purpose). These n actions are then presented to the user in the adapted UI, ordered by the sequences in which the user will most probably use them in order to have a familiar appearance for the user.

3   Evaluation

For evaluating the benefit of FxL*, we compared it to other adaptation strategies, which do not adapt to individual users or to their current situation. We applied every strategy to three sets of real usage data: The Greenberg dataset [8] containing UNIX commands, the CrossDesktop log data[1] and the Word dataset with logs of MS Word usage[2]. Device constraints were modeled by varying the amount of elements n that can be displayed at the same time. As dependent variable we measured the hit ratio how often the action that was actually performed next given by the usage log, was found among the elements that were displayed according to the adaptation strategy applied. The elements that are displayed were recalculated whenever an action was requested that was not present among the current elements.

As baseline. we used the strategy *static* which presents the interaction elements most frequently used averaged over all users. We chose this strategy because it represents the best result reachable by a non user-adaptive interface, as this has to optimize for the average user for all situations. The second strategy *user-adapted* takes the individual user into account, presenting the actions the user has used most often so far. However, the user's current situation reflected by the immediate interaction history is not considered. In contrast, the third strategy *situation-adapted* considers all interaction histories ignoring the individual user. In this strategy, we compute a single interaction model for all users and apply the FxL* algorithm to predict the next actions for each user. Finally, the strategy *FxL** combines user- and situation-awareness by applying FxL* on the interaction model learned for each individual user. All strategies operate incrementally and update their user model after each observed action.

Due to space limitations we only present here the results for the Word dataset. In Figure 2 the average results over all user traces from the Word dataset are shown. The *static* strategy performs only slightly worse than the *user-adapted* and *situation-adapted* strategy, in the other two datasets even no difference could be detected. This indicates that the frequently used actions for the given datasets are the same for most users and that there are no global usage patterns over all users. However, the user- and situation-adapted *FxL** strategy clearly outperforms the three other strategies (the difference in the hit ratio ranges for $n \in [2, 10]$ from 6.0% to 27.1% for the Word dataset, 25.3% to 30.2% for the Greenberg dataset and 3.2% to 15.2% for the CrossDesktop dataset). This shows that it is important to take the user and her recent interactions into account to be able to provide a useful interface adaptation.

---

[1] Web application for managing files and emails http://www.crossdesktop.com
[2] http://www.cs.rutgers.edu/ml4um/datasets/

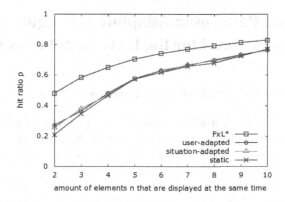

Fig. 2. Evaluation results for Word dataset. The y-axis represents how often the next user action was displayed on the adapted UI when applying one of the four adaptation strategies.

4   Conclusion

In this paper, we presented the AUGUR system that is to our knowledge the first system for adaptive UIs that combines device adaptation and dynamic adaptation to the user and her situation. The main contribution of this paper is the FxL* algorithm for determining the most relevant interaction elements depending on the user's past interactions and the number of interaction elements that can be displayed on the screen of the device used. We showed that this adaptation strategy is superior to strategies that do not take the user or her current situation into account.

Acknowledgments. We would like to thank SAP Research Darmstadt for supporting our research in the AUGUR project.

References

1. Gajos, K.Z., Czerwinski, M., Tan, D.S., Weld, D.S.: Exploring the design space for adaptive graphical user interfaces. In: Proceedings of AVI 2006, pp. 201–208. ACM Press, New York (2006)
2. Hartmann, M., Schreiber, D., Kaiser, M.: Task Models for Proactive Web Applications. In: Proceedings of WEBIST 2007, March 2007, pp. 150–155. INSTICC Press (2007)
3. Eisenstein, J., Vanderdonckt, J., Puerta, A.R.: Applying model-based techniques to the development of uis for mobile computers. In: Proceedings of IUI 2001, pp. 69–76 (2001)
4. Paterno, F., Mancini, C., Meniconi, S.: Engineering task models. In: Proceedings of ICECCS 1997, Washington, DC, USA, p. 69. IEEE Computer Society Press, Los Alamitos (1997)
5. Anderson, C.R., Domingos, P., Weld, D.S.: Adaptive web navigation for wireless devices. In: IJCAI, pp. 879–884 (2001)
6. Smyth, B., Cotter, P.: The plight of the navigator: Solving the navigation problem for wireless portals. In: De Bra, P., Brusilovsky, P., Conejo, R. (eds.) AH 2002. LNCS, vol. 2347, pp. 328–337. Springer, Heidelberg (2002)
7. Hartmann, M., Schreiber, D.: Prediction algorithms for user actions. In: Proceedings of ABIS 2007, September 2007, pp. 349–354 (2007)
8. Greenberg, S.: Using unix: collected traces of 168 users. Research report 88/333/45 (1988)

Reuse Patterns in Adaptation Languages: Creating a Meta-level for the LAG Adaptation Language

Maurice Hendrix and Alexandra I. Cristea

The University of Warwick, Department of Computer Science
Gibbet Hill Road, CV4 7AL, Coventry United Kingdom
{maurice, acristea}@dcs.warwick.ac.uk

Abstract. A growing body of research targets authoring of content and adaptation strategies for adaptive systems. The driving force behind it is *semantics-based reuse*: the same strategy can be used for various domains, and vice versa. Whilst using an *adaptation language* (LAG e.g.) to express reusable adaptation strategies, we noticed, however, that: a) the created strategies have common patterns that, themselves, could be reused; b) templates based on these patterns could reduce the designers' work; c) there is a strong preference towards XML-based processing and interfacing. This has leaded us to define a new meta-language for LAG, extracting common design patterns. This paper provides more insight into some of the limitations of Adaptation Languages like LAG, as well as describes our meta-language, and shows how introducing the meta-level can overcome some redundancy issues.

Keywords: LAG, AHA!, Adaptive Hypermedia, Adaptation Engine.

1 Introduction

The use of adaptive systems [2] is increasingly popular, as it can provide a richer personalised learning experience. Commercial systems on the web (e.g., Amazon) or beyond (PDA device software) present at least a rudimentary type of adaptation. However, adaptation specification cannot be fully expressed by standards[1] yet, and most commercial and non-commercial systems rely on proprietary, custom designed, system specific, non-portable, and non-interoperable adaptation. An intermediary solution, until standards emerge, is the creation of *Adaptation Languages*, which, with their power of semantics-based reuse, appear as a reliable future vehicle [3, 4]. Once written, the same adaptation strategy can be used for various domains and vice versa. However, there are a number of limitations regarding adaptation engines, which ultimately influence the efficient authoring of adaptation strategies.

In Section 2 we define what we see as the main limitations. Moreover, we propose a *meta-language*, as a supplement to Adaptation Languages like LAG, showing how introducing it can overcome such limitations. This solution is compatible with *extant* adaptation engines, instead of requiring the creation of new engines.

---

[1] SCORM Simple sequencing allows basic adaptation. IMS-LD promises more for the future.

W. Nejdl et al. (Eds.): AH 2008, LNCS 5149, pp. 304–307, 2008.

2 Adaptation Engine Issues and Limitations

The following are issues and limitations identified as influencing the authoring flexibility of adaptive hypermedia (AH) systems:

L1. Most adaptive hypermedia delivery systems determine the *adaptation on a per-concept base* [1]. A broad knowledge of the whole content at every adaptation step is (usually) unavailable, mainly due to run-time complexity limitations. Thus, adaptation strategies cannot specify complex inter-concept rules; e.g., a strategy with an arbitrary set of labels denoting topics of interest, displaying to the user concepts related to his topic, without limiting the possible topics at design-time.

L2. Adaptation engines don't (usually) allow for *non-instantiated program variables* [1]. Thus, authoring strategies which involve an unknown number of types, categories, etc., are currently not permitted. All domain-related variables need to be instantiated in the authoring stage.

L3. There are extreme difficulties arising when *combining multiple strategies* [1], which would facilitate authors to create their own behaviour by composing strategies. Adaptation engines update sets of variables based on some triggering rules, without knowing which high-level adaptation strategies these variables represent. An example of a combined strategy currently difficult to implement is one where the system checks whether the user prefers text or images, and then displays the preferred type of content, filtered via a beginner-intermediate-advanced strategy, where concepts are shown based on the user's knowledge.

3 Solutions to Adaptation Engines Issues and Limitations

A straightforward way of defeating limitations L1 and L2 would be to build new adaptation engines. The first scenario could be achieved by establishing which labels exist, in the *initialization* step. The second issue could be overcome by either allowing arrays of labels, or otherwise allowing multiple data to be stored in the label. However, in order to function with current systems, these issues should be solved in the authoring stage. For the third limitation (L3), the difficulty in application of multiple strategies, there are some efforts already to deal with this. The MOT to AHA! [1] converter, e.g., has already implemented an elegant solution (unique to our knowledge so far), in that it can apply multiple LAG files, with different adaptation strategies, with the order of execution set by priorities of the respective strategies (1: highest priority; any following number: lower priority).

Nevertheless, this method could override previous variables, thus, a unitary strategy merge, based on multiple labels for domain-related concepts and attributes, is preferable. Moreover, only simple types are currently allowed by most Adaptation Languages, for example arrays, due to lack of adaptation engine support. For example arrays or lists are not allowed.

However, we have noticed that a) strategies have common patterns that could be reused; b) templates based on these patterns could reduce the designers' work; c) a strong preference exists for XML-based processing and interfacing.

For the creation of Adaptation Language strategies explicit knowledge about the content is needed. In a template version, this can be described and a pre-processor can then take both the content and the template strategy to create the concrete strategy for adapting the content. In the next section our solution will be described, it is based upon the LAG adaptation language and uses an XML-based template LAG language as Adaptation Language.

4 Meta-level Addition to LAG

To solve the limitations mentioned in section 2, we add a pre-processing step to the whole authoring process. This step takes a LAG template and the content, in the form of a CAF (Common Adaptation Format) file, and generates a new LAG file which extends the strategy sketched by the LAG template for the specific content described in the CAF file. For reusability, maintainability and to accommodate for future changes, we propose an XML-based notation for the template LAG files. Since CAF is already written in an XML-based notation, both documents can be used as input for an XSLT transformation which generates the resulting LAG file. Below we give the DTD (document type definition) for the template LAG file.

```
<!ELEMENT TLAG ((LAGfragment*, LIKE*)*)>
<!ELEMENT LIKE attribute CDATA value CDATA
LAGfragment, MATCH, LAGfragment, (LAGfragment*, LABEL,
LAGfragment*)*) >
<!ELEMENT LAGfragment (#PCDATA)>
<!ELEMENT MATCH EMPTY>
<!ELEMENT LABEL EMPTY>
```

A template LAG file consists of a number of blocks of the following kind: a number of LAG fragments followed by a LIKE element. The fragments contain LAG adaptation snippets. The LIKE elements consist of an attribute and a regular expression against which it is matched, followed by a fragment of LAG program. The word MATCH represents the place where the LABEL needs to match the regular expression.

L1. *Problem: adaptation on a per-concept base*; a broad knowledge of the whole content at every step of the adaptation is (usually) unavailable.
    Solution: such knowledge is not necessary in the adaptation engine. It is accept- able that this type of knowledge can be acquired as a one-off, at authoring time, as it is not to be expected that content labels will change at execution time. There- fore, the authoring strategy should contain this knowledge. As for an author it is difficult to manually extract all the pedagogical label types existent in a course, templates such as the DTD of the template LAG above can help in dealing with groups of labels (such as all labels containing 'beginner', i.e., '*beginner*'). An author can then generate the appropriate adaptation strategy (of which a snippet is shown above) in an easy and quick manner, making use of existing patterns in the authoring strategy itself.
L2. *Problem:* adaptation engines don't usually allow *non-instantiated variables*.
    Solution: Unknown domain-related variables can be instantiated in the authoring stage, with the help of patterns specified via the LAG template language based on the above DTD. It is not necessary for an author to perform these searches manu- ally; the two-step authoring system can extract unknown variables for him.

L3. *Problem:* extreme difficulties arise when *combining strategies.*

Solution: similar pattern extraction mechanisms have to be used in order to merge adaptation strategies. In (nearly) every system there is a limited number of weights and labels; this causes problems in combining a number of strategies greater than the number of weights and labels available. A solution to this can be to apply pattern matching on labels in order to be able to encode multiple strategies, by using the same label field. This thus enhances simple prioritization of strategies, as it allows the combination of multiple strategies which each requires specific labels.

5 Conclusions and Further Work

In this paper we have analyzed adaptation problems inherent in current adaptation engines, which reduce the power and generality of Adaptation Languages. We described and exemplified these issues with the help of the *LAG language*, currently one of the only exchange formats of adaptation language specification between systems. Moreover, we have moved one step further, by proposing improvements that can overcome run-time issues of adaptation engines, by solving them at the authoring stage. More specifically, templates can be used to create adaptation strategies, customized for the given domain models and pedagogical labels. For this purpose, we have proposed the *template LAG language.* The process is technically implemented by adding a pre-processor to the system setup, which has access to content at compile-time, which is not available at run-time. In such a way, more powerful adaptation strategies can be created for *existing* adaptation engines. The next step is to implement the pre-processor for LAG, merging efforts with new versions of AHA!

Acknowledgments. This research has been performed with the help of the EU *ALS* Minerva STREP, the EU FP7 *GRAPPLE* STREP, and was based on the *PROLEARN* Network of Excellence.

References

1. AHA! Adaptive Hypermedia For All, http://aha.win.tue.nl
2. Brusilovsky, P.: Adaptive hypermedia, User Modelling and User Adapted Interaction. Ten Year Anniversary Issue, A. Kobsa (ed.) 11(1/2), 87–110 (2001)
3. Cristea, A.I., Calvi, L.: The three Layers of Adaptation Granularity. In: Brusilovsky, P., Corbett, A.T., de Rosis, F. (eds.) UM 2003. LNCS, vol. 2702. Springer, Heidelberg (2003)
4. Stash, N., Cristea, A.I., De Bra, P.: Adaptation languages as vehicles of explicit intelligence in Adaptive Hypermedia. International Journal on Continuing Engineering Education and Life-Long Learning 17(4/5), 319–336 (2007)

Implementing a Multimodal Interface to a DITA User Assistance Repository

Aidan Kehoe and Ian Pitt

University College Cork, Ireland
{ak2,i.pitt}@cs.ucc.ie

Abstract. User assistance systems can be extended to enable multimodal access to user assistance material. Implementing multimodal user assistance introduces new considerations with respect to authoring and storage of assistance material, transformation of assistance material for effective presentation on a range of devices, and user interaction issues. We describe an implementation of a multimodal interface to enable access to a DITA user assistance repository.

Keywords: User Assistance, DITA, Multimodal Interface.

1 Introduction

Developers are striving to create applications and services that are usable on a broad range of devices, and in a variety of contexts. Despite the best efforts of product designers to design for usability, there are still situations in which users need help. In such situations, ubiquitous online user assistance (UA) should be the norm.

Several recently-developed user assistance infrastructures (e.g., DITA Open Toolkit [1], Eclipse Help, etc.) support the concept of a single source repository for technical documentation. We are enabling access to DITA-based UA material through a number of additional channels including small portable displays (Windows Side-Show-compatible devices [2]) and speech interfaces utilizing Microsoft Speech Applications Programming Interface (SAPI). In our application we need to transform the material from the single source repository in such a way that the UA material is accessible via a number of different devices and modalities. Specifically, we must transform DITA material to SSML (Speech Synthesis Markup Language) to enable auditory access; and transform to Microsoft Windows SCF (Simple Content Format) for use on SideShow-compatible devices [3].

Our aim is to extend and complement existing user assistance systems, and work within the constraints of commercially available speech and auxiliary-display technologies. Implementing multimodal user assistance introduces new considerations with respect to authoring and storage of assistance material, transformation of assistance material for effective presentation on a range of devices, and user interaction issues.

2 Multimodal Interface to a DITA User Assistance Repository

Utilizing speech interaction in conjunction with SideShow-compatible devices allows for a wide variety of possible UA system configurations; but for this paper we limit

W. Nejdl et al. (Eds.): AH 2008, LNCS 5149, pp. 308–311, 2008.

most of the discussion to the configuration shown in Figure 1. In this usage scenario, both the user's hands are occupied with mouse and keyboard activities while using a display-greedy application on a desktop computer, e.g., an application such as a computer game or CAD package uses virtually all of the available display space leaving no room for display of traditional text-based help windows. The UA material is accessible via a speech interface, and the speech interaction is supported by the use of a small SideShow-compatible auxiliary display integrated into a keyboard, e.g., [4].

In 2004 many of the leading researchers in the area of multimodal interaction design co-authored an article that described six major categories of guidelines in a "preliminary attempt to establish principles for multimodal interaction design" [5]. Below we describe some of the issues encountered and associated solutions, while implementing a multimodal UA interface to a DITA repository which conforms to the guidelines outlined in the "Guidelines for Multimodal Interface Design" article [5].

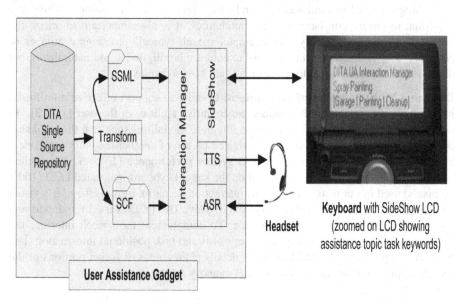

Fig. 1. Multimodal UA Software using Speech and SideShow Keyboard LCD

Error Prevention/Handling. In an attempt to minimize potential for speech recognition errors the software uses a very simple command-and-control style vocabulary. Active vocabulary words can also be displayed on the LCD; this is useful when users initially become familiar with the speech interface.

Adaptivity. It is important to adapt the type and quantity of the assistance information to match the capabilities of devices [6, 7]. However, in our UA application the information displayed on the LCD is not, in the majority of cases, simply a replication of the information that is already presented using speech. Assistance topic title information is directly replicated on the LCD. However, due to LCD size limitations only topic keywords are displayed. Also, associated topic metadata which is not presented at all using speech is displayed on the LCD, e.g., the total number of steps in the task and the current step number.

Feedback. UA material is typically stored in a hierarchical structure, e.g., UA books contain chapters, sub-chapters and pages. Such location information is difficult to effectively present using speech, and it is time-consuming to listen to. The LCD is used to display this location information, i.e., the user can glance at the LCD to review this information as needed. Visual feedback is provided on the speech recognition status, and speaker volume level, since this can be an important factor in inhibiting the Lombard effect [8, 9]. Our DITA-to-SSML transform also adds a number of structural "mark" elements to the generated SSML. When the speech synthesis engine renders the UA topic speech output, these "mark" elements generate events; the UA software monitors these events in real-time and ensures that the LCD output is updated synchronously with the speech output.

Consistency. Care must be taken in authoring UA topics to ensure that consistent terminology is used in both auditory and visual presentation modalities. While it is important to ensure consistency across modalities, it is also important to utilize the norms of a specific modality. For example, speech typically contains a number of elements such as discourse markers [10] to enhance intelligibility and naturalness, but these would consume valuable space on a small screen display.

Designing Multimodal Input and Output. In order to support effective multimedia interactions, it is important to consider the cognitive abilities of the user [11, 12]. In our design, we looked for possibilities to integrate modalities such that the weakness of one modality (or device) might be mitigated by use of another modality (or device) in such a way as to improve the overall system performance [13]. A very limited amount of information can be displayed on the small keyboard-integrated LCD (160 x 43 pixels) used in our tests. Also, in this interaction scenario, most of the user's visual attention is focused on the primary system display. The LCD is used to support and complement the primary speech interface. To complement the speech interface the keyboard LCD is used to display topic keywords and task positional information (i.e., the user can glance at the LCD to check details if they miss or forget portions of the speech output) and thus acts as an external memory for the user.

3 Summary

Traditionally, user assistance material has been available in the form of browsable online content or in print. However, user assistance is now required to support a variety of applications and services that are usable across a broad range of devices, and in a variety of contexts, and using different modes. The use of an auxiliary display device technology, such as SideShow, to provide access to user assistance material could mitigate some of the problems associated with context switching, limited space on the primary display, and remote access [14]. Speech technology, in conjunction with SideShow-compatible devices, can be used as elements in a multimodal interface to a DITA UA repository.

Our initial pilot study demonstrated that the completion rates for short, task-oriented UA topics presented using speech is comparable with rates achieved when accessing such material visually [14]. Our subsequent experiments will determine if the use of an auxiliary display device, used to complement a speech interface, results in improved performance, e.g., less repeat listens to topics, faster task completion times and improved successful task completion.

References

1. DITA Open Tookit, January 20 (2008),
   http://sourceforge.net/projects/dita-ot/
2. Windows SideShow, January 20 (2008),
   http://www.microsoft.com/windows/products/windowsvista/
   features/details/sideshow.mspx
3. DITA to SSML Transform Files, http://www.cabhair-cainte.com/dita
4. Logitech G15 Keyboard, January 20 (2008),
   http://www.logitech.com/index.cfm/keyboards/keyboard/devices/
   3498&cl=us,en
5. Reeves, L.M., et al.: Guidelines for multimodal user interface design. Comm. of the ACM 47(1) (2004)
6. González-Castaño, F.J., et al.: A New Transcoding Technique for PDA Browsers, Based on Content Hierarchy. In: 4th Conf. on Mobile Human-Computer Interaction, pp. 69–80 (2002)
7. Shao, Z., Capra, R.G., Pérez-Quiñones, M.A.: Transcoding HTML to VoiceXML Using Annotation. In: Proc. 15th IEEE Conference on Tools with Artificial Intelligence, vol. 249 (2003)
8. Lane, H., Tranel, B.: The Lombard sign and the role of hearing in speech. J. of Speech and Hearing Research 14, 677–709 (1971)
9. Pick, H., Siegel, J., Fox, P., Garber, S., Kearney, J.: Inhibiting the Lombard effect. Journal of Acoustical Society of America 85(2), 894–900 (1989)
10. Redeker, G.: Ideational and pragmatic markers of discourse structure. Journal of Pragmatics 14, 367–381 (1990)
11. European Telecommunications Standards Institute. Guidelines on the multimodality of icons, symbols, and pictograms, Report No. ETSI EG 202 048 v 1.1.1 (2002)
12. Kalyuga, S., Chandler, P., Sweller, J.: Managing split-attention and redundancy in multimedia instruction. Applied Cognitive Psychology 13, 351–371 (1999)
13. Oviatt, S.: Advances in the robust processing of multimodal speech and pen systems. In: Multimodal Interfaces for Human Machine Communication, pp. 203–218 (2001)
14. Kehoe, A., Neff, F., Pitt, I., Russell, G.: Modifications to a Speech-Enabled User Assistance System Based on a Pilot Study. In: Proceedings ACM SIGDOC 2007 Conference, pp. 42–47 (2007)

Analysing High-Level Help-Seeking Behaviour in ITSs

Moffat Mathews, Tanja Mitrović, and David Thomson

Computer Science & Software Engineering,
University of Canterbury, New Zealand
{moffat,tanja,djt88}@cosc.canterbury.ac.nz

Abstract. In this paper, we look at initial results of data mining students' help-seeking behaviour in two ITSs: SQL-Tutor and EER-Tutor. We categorised help given by these tutors into high-level (HLH) and low-level help (LLH), depending on the amount of help given. Each student was grouped into one of ten groups based on the frequency with which they used HLH. Learning curves were then plotted for each group. We asked the question, *"Does a student's help-seeking behaviour (especially the frequency with which they use HLH) affect learning?"* We noticed similarities between results for both tutors. Students who were very frequent users of HLH showed the lowest learning, both in learning rates and depth of knowledge. Students who were low to medium users of HLH showed the highest learning rates. Least frequent users of HLH had lower learning rates but showed higher depth of knowledge and a lower initial error rate, suggesting higher initial expertise. These initial results could suggest favouring pedagogical strategies that provide low to medium HLH to certain students.

A primary aspect of researching and developing adaptive systems is to try and understand the behaviour of those using the system. Being able to comprehend various types of behaviour gives us the basis to form strategies to adequately, effectively, and even adaptively aid users of the system. This is particularly the case in Intelligent Tutoring Systems (ITSs), where understanding each student's behaviour is critical to creating and implementing suitable pedagogical strategies to appropriately guide each student adaptively through their learning tasks in order to maximise their learning. One such type of behaviour is the way in which a student requests and utilises help. Help-seeking behaviour has been studied in various contexts; from traditional teaching methods in the classroom to e-learning applications. It has long been noted in education literature that seeking help and way in which it is sought affects learning [1]. Certain aspects of help-seeking behaviour (such as gaming [2]) have been researched in the context of ITSs [3]. In an adaptive system, one method of studying users' behaviour is by mining data collected from users (e.g. user models and logs).

In this paper, we discuss the initial results of data mining student logs and user models for help-seeking behaviour in two ITSs, namely SQL-Tutor [4] and EER-Tutor [5]. We grouped students by the frequency with which they used help

W. Nejdl et al. (Eds.): AH 2008, LNCS 5149, pp. 312–315, 2008.

and tried to determine if there were differences in learning between the groups of students. We did this by plotting learning curves for each group and seeing if any trends existed, and if these trends were similar between the two ITSs.

SQL-Tutor is a constraint-based modelling (CBM) ITS that provides intelligent and adaptive guidance in the domain of SQL database querying. SQL-Tutor has been used since 1998 in tertiary undergraduate database courses. The student spends the majority of time solving problems in the task environment. The task environment contains the problem text, solution workspace, feedback pane, and problem context information (e.g. information about the schema). On submission of their solution, a student can receive help from six levels of problem-related feedback. These levels increase in the amount of help, and are 1. Simple Feedback, 2. Error Flag, 3. Hint, 4. Partial Solution, 5. List All Errors, and 6. Complete Solution. On each incorrect submission, the help level automatically increments to a maximum of 3 (i.e. hint). Help levels are selected via a combo box and the student has the ability to override the current selection at any time by selecting a different level. We divided the help into two categories depending on the amount of help given: low-level help (LLH) for the first three help levels and high-level help (HLH) for levels four, five, and six. Furthermore, LLH automatically increments on incorrect submissions whereas HLH has to be selected by the student.

EER-Tutor (Enhanced-Entity Relationship Tutor) is a CBM ITS that teaches conceptual database design using the Enhanced Entity Relationship Model, and provides students with problems to practise their entity relationship modelling skills in a coached environment. Developed initially as KERMIT (Knowledge-based Entity Relationship Modelling Intelligent Tutor) then ER-Tutor (Entity-Relationship Tutor) and now EER-Tutor, this ITS has also had many years of successful use with students in tertiary undergraduate database courses. The help-levels in EER-Tutor are similar to SQL-Tutor and thus make it easy for comparison. As with SQL-Tutor, we divided help into LLH and HLH.

Although these two ITSs deal with database related areas, each domain is very different, Furthermore, the method of solving problems (even to the point of *text* versus *diagrammatic*) is considerably different.

1   Method

In both datasets, data for students who made less than five attempts was omitted from the analysis. The SQL-Tutor dataset consisted of 1,803 students who made a total of 100,781 attempts, and spent just over a total of 1,959 active hours on the system. EER-Tutor dataset consisted of 936 students who made a total of 43,485 attempts, and spent just over 2,830 active hours on the system.

To enable us to compare the frequency of HLH use among students, we calculated an HLH-Ratio ($\frac{\text{Number of HLH attempts}}{\text{total number of attempts}}$) for each individual. For example, a student with an HLH ratio of one used HLH on every attempt; in contrast a student with an HLH ratio of zero never used HLH. For comparison between groups of users with similar HLH, ten groups ($A1 - A10$) were formed, each with an HLH ratio range of 0.1. Students were placed into groups depending on their

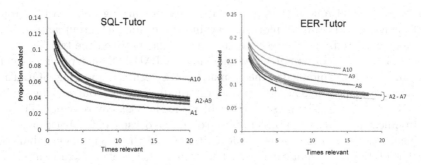

Fig. 1. Learning curves for the HLH groups (A1-A10) for SQL-Tutor and EER-Tutor

HLH ratio, such that students in group A10 (who used HLH 90–100% of the time) were the most frequent users of HLH while the least frequent HLH users were in group $A1$. Learning curves were then plotted for each group (Figure 1).

Table 1. Power curve equations and fits (R^2) for the ten HLH groups $(A1 - A10)$ in SQL-Tutor and EER-Tutor

			SQL-Tutor			EER-Tutor	
Group	HLH ratio	Users	Curve equation	R^2 (Fit)	Users	Curve equation	R^2 (Fit)
A1	0.0 - 0.1	222	$y = 0.061x^{-0.30}$	0.844	210	$y = 0.156x^{-0.28}$	0.959
A2	0.1 - 0.2	214	$y = 0.084x^{-0.31}$	0.956	186	$y = 0.162x^{-0.25}$	0.963
A3	0.2 - 0.3	248	$y = 0.101x^{-0.38}$	0.955	120	$y = 0.169x^{-0.26}$	0.963
A4	0.3 - 0.4	315	$y = 0.109x^{-0.37}$	0.956	103	$y = 0.185x^{-0.33}$	0.938
A5	0.4 - 0.5	295	$y = 0.110x^{-0.36}$	0.965	89	$y = 0.181x^{-0.28}$	0.967
A6	0.5 - 0.6	211	$y = 0.123x^{-0.39}$	0.961	57	$y = 0.183x^{-0.28}$	0.947
A7	0.6 - 0.7	122	$y = 0.122x^{-0.36}$	0.953	51	$y = 0.184x^{-0.33}$	0.978
A8	0.7 - 0.8	88	$y = 0.115x^{-0.35}$	0.953	51	$y = 0.189x^{-0.23}$	0.954
A9	0.8 - 0.8	44	$y = 0.118x^{-0.36}$	0.912	34	$y = 0.190x^{-0.16}$	0.858
A10	0.9 - 1.0	44	$y = 0.123x^{-0.22}$	0.956	35	$y = 0.204x^{-0.15}$	0.878

2   Results and Discussion

The power curve equations and fits are shown in Table 1. The results discussed are similar for both tutors.

All learning curves have a very good fit (R^2), with the lowest fit being just 0.844. The degree of fit usually indicates level of transferability of the skills that were learned. For example, a low fit indicates high variability in the error rates (i.e. high deviation of points from the power curve) indicating that error rates still vary each time a particular concept is encountered (i.e. low transferability). This result indicates that whatever skills students are learning are also transferable. This does not indicate that all students are learning the same skills.

The exponent in the equation indicates the learning rate. As can be seen from Table 1, the learning rates are highest for students who are low to medium users of HLH. Students that are extremely high users of HLH (e.g. A10) have the lowest learning rates. These students also display shallow learning. This can be seen from the point at which the slope of the learning curves approximates zero. For extremely high HLH users, this point still shows a high error rate, indicating that the concept has not been learned to any great depth. This could be because students that rely heavily on HLH do not actively think for themselves or engage in deliberate practice, and therefore do not get the opportunity to learn from their mistakes.

The coefficient of x (known as χ) shows the initial error rate. Low χ usually means the presence of expertise or previous experience and vice-versa. The χ value for group $A1$ in SQL-Tutor shows this expertise or prior knowledge. Manual inspection of logs indicated the presence of students with higher expertise in this group. As a consequence, students who have a higher χ find the domain more difficult than those with lower χ values. From Figure 1, we can see that the students who used the least help had the least χ, whereas students who used the most help had the highest χ and therefore found the domain more difficult.

Although these initial results provide a good basis for understanding one aspect of help-seeking behaviour, and thus aids in creating pedagogical strategies, it cannot be construed from these results that providing low to medium help to students will automatically increase learning. Other factors such as the meta-cognitive ability (e.g. help-seeking skills) of students, their upbringing, and even their cultural influences also need to be considered. It could also be that students who are slower to learn are less confident and therefore seek HLH more often.

In the near future, we intend to analyse the effect of other variables such as time spent on attempts, number of problems solved, and difficulty of problems solved on these groups of students.

References

1. Gall, S.N.: Help-Seeking Behaviour in Learning. Review of Research in Education 12, 55–90 (1985)
2. Baker, R., Corbett, A., Koedinger, K., Roll, I.: Detecting When Students Game the System, Across Tutor Subjects and Classroom Cohorts. In: Ardissono, L., Brna, P., Mitrović, A. (eds.) UM 2005. LNCS (LNAI), vol. 3538, pp. 220–224. Springer, Heidelberg (2005)
3. Aleven, V., Koedinger, K.: Limitations of Student Control: Do Students Know when They Need Help? In: Gauthier, G., VanLehn, K., Frasson, C. (eds.) ITS 2000. LNCS, vol. 1839, pp. 292–303. Springer, Berlin (2000)
4. Mitrović, T.: An Intelligent SQL Tutor on the Web. IJAIED 13, 173–197 (2003)
5. Suraweera, P., Mitrović, T.: An Intelligent Tutoring System for Entity Relationship Modelling. JIJAIED 14, 375–417 (2004)

Data-Driven Prediction of the Necessity of Help Requests in ILEs

Manolis Mavrikis

London Knowledge Lab*,
23-29 Emerald Street, London, WC1N 3QS
m.mavrikis@lkl.ac.uk

Abstract. This paper discusses the data-driven development of a model which predicts whether a student could answer a question correctly without requesting help. This model contributes to a broader piece of research, the primary goal of which was to predict affective characteristics of students working in ILEs. The paper presents the bayesian network which provides adequate predictions, and discusses how its accuracy is taken into account when the model is integrated in an ILE. Future steps to improve the results are briefly discussed.

1 Introduction

Towards developing a component, which predicts students' affective characteristics while they are interacting with an Interactive Learning Environment (ILE), previous research established (a) part of the evidence that human tutors employ, in order to diagnose students' affective characteristics (e.g. confidence, effort), comes from students' help-seeking behaviour [1] and particularly during the interaction with questions where help seems superfluous [2]. The above, and relevant literature in motivational psychology (e.g. [3]) which suggests that the cause of the need for help is one of the most important determinants on the decision to help a student, inspired the development of a model which predicts whether a student could answer questions without any help.

Predicting whether a student needs help or not in a given educational situation is quite complex. In the context of Intelligent Tutoring Systems (ITS) this information is particularly crucial, and definitely not a unique requirement of the current research. Due to the complexity of the problem, different researchers address it in different ways depending on the special characteristics of the system and the overall context. For example, in the CMU tutors the problem is approached as an attempt to estimate the probability of knowledge that a skill has been mastered (*knowledge tracing* [4]). Similarly, Bayesian networks are often used (e.g. [5]) to predict students' knowledge. The approach presented here differs in that the model predicts whether students' help requests are necessary given their previous interaction with the system rather than their skills or knowledge. Moreover, the model is learned based on data of all students' interactions with the ILE WaLLiS [6] during its previous applications in the classroom.

---

* The work presented here is part of the author's PhD thesis and was partially funded by the School of Mathematics of The University of Edinburgh.

W. Nejdl et al. (Eds.): AH 2008, LNCS 5149, pp. 316–319, 2008.

The data collection was possible thanks to the iterative design methodology behind the WaLLiS project and the integration of the ILE in the teaching and learning of a second year module called 'Geometry Iteration and Convergence' (GIC) undertaken by honour students. Materials were built for one of the last concepts taught in this module; *conic sections*. One of the reasons for choosing this particular course was that the materials were unknown to the students and they involve rather individual parts that are not covered in the course textbook. Since this particular part of the course was delivered solely through the ILE, it does not seem too bold to assume that students who do not ask for help and answer a question correctly with the first attempt have learnt either from carefully reading the materials in the system or from the interaction with related items. In other words, all other characteristics of a student being equal, similar interactions should have given the student the opportunity to answer without the need for help. The opposite, of course, is not necessarily true.

2 Machine Learning

The machine learning performed relies on two datasets GIC03 and GIC04 with 126 and 133 students out of the 153 and 165 who attended the course respectively. The data pre-processing reduced the dataset to 106 and 126 students due to noise, lack of students' consent, or absence during the familiarisation session. Initial investigations with the GIC03 dataset as a learning set and the GIC04 as a testset, supported the claim that a machine learning algorithm (such as bayesian networks) could be used to automatically predict with reasonable accuracy the necessity of a student's help request. It was decided to focus the prediction only on help requests prior to the first attempt to answer a question. Further attempts are quite complex and depend on students' understanding of the feedback and several other factors, which add noise to the prediction task.

In order to learn a more accurate model from the data both the GIC03 and GIC04 datasets were used as a training set. In an attempt to have a simple model and a method that could be generalised to other courses of our ILE or other ILEs, only few aspects of the interaction were considered as features for the learning task. These should be available across courses in WaLLiS and are quite common in ILEs. Accordingly, vectors were constructed that contain the following variables: (a) time spent on related page (*trp*) (b) time spent on attempt (*tsa*) (c) student previous performance in the course (*prev*) (d) a rule-based measurement of the degree of 'completeness' of the goals of interactions on related skills (*rel*) (e) difficulty of the item (*diff*) and (f) the type of the answer required (mcq, blank, matrix, checkbox) (*answertype*). The boolean class learned represents whether the student seems to be able to answer correctly without any help. Its value therefore, is FALSE when students provided completely wrong answers, or answered wrongly very quickly[1] demonstrating, in a sense, that they only answer to 'game the system' [7]. The value of the class is TRUE when a student's answer was correct or partially correct (according to a list of common misconceptions). Students who asked for help without

---

[1] The breakpoint for 'very quickly' when discretizing data was $z <= -1.28$.

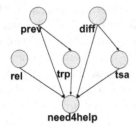

	BayesNet		J4.8	
	Cross	Test	Cross	Test
accuracy	67.64	66.52	65.84	64.05
Kappa	0.32	0.32	0.30	0.23
recall True	0.74	0.77	0.71	0.72
recall False	0.61	0.56	0.59	0.50

Fig. 1. Bayesian network for predicting need for help

Fig. 2. Accuracy, Kappa statistic and recall values for two different techniques

an attempt are not included since there are many explanations behind this request and including these data would not necessarily provide instances that demonstrate whether a student really needed help or not. All the above restrictions resulted in a set of 1230 attempts (the class of 429 of which was unsuccessful).

The next step was to choose the exact modelling approach. Preliminary investigations with cross-fold validation with the combined GIC03-04 dataset suggested that from all the approaches attempted (decision trees, Bayesian network, classification via regression) the Bayesian network and the decision tree were the most accurate ones and very close to each other. The Bayesian network was therefore preferred mainly because of the uncertain nature of the prediction. In particular, conditional independence test based learning methods were preferred as they stem from the need to uncover causal structure in the data [8]. Although directed edges in a network do not necessarily represent causal effects, the ICS algorithm [9] as implemented in WEKA[2] starts from a complete undirected graph and tries to find conditional independencies in the data.

The conditional independence tests of ICS left out the variable answertype from the model as irrelevant. Feature selection (FCBF [10]) also confirmed the relevance of all variables apart from answertype. The final model learned appears in Figure 1. To evaluate the result another dataset (GIC05) (with 99 students and 590 instances) was employed (see accuracy report in Figure 2). Further steps to improve the results are discussed in the next Section.

3   Discussion

The results suggest that this model can be used adequately for predicting whether a student needs help. The benefits of such a prediction in an ILE such as WaL-LiS are multi-fold. However, due to the uncertainty of the prediction one has to consider pedagogical implications. For example, based on the prediction, students could have been denied help which could be frustrating and pedagogically harmful in almost 30% of the time. Therefore, it was decided to follow a suggestive rather than a preventative approach (see [7] for similar concerns). Accordingly, the prediction is used directly to provide other types of feedback (e.g. suggestions to

---

[2] See http://www.cs.waikato.ac.nz/ml/weka/

attempt an item again, or to ask for help when it seems that they may benefit from it) and is taken indirectly into account in another model that predicts the quality of their interaction [2]. In addition, it was used as a variable for the development of machine-learned decision trees for affective diagnosis [2,1].

Further investigation showed that considering a different model for every item in the ILE improves the results substantially (an average of 68.37% accuracy for all items). The main reason behind this, is the fact that not all variables play the same role for every item (for example, the influence of a related item is not always the same on subsequent items) and therefore, one model cannot accommodate all the items. This process simplified the models considerably and therefore, the separate models were preferred for the actual implementation. It is worth noting that, further investigation with the data showed that logistic regression is slightly more accurate in certain cases (on average it has accuracy 68.92% against the testset and for the model that combines all items 69.89%). Future work will investigate this issue further.

The separation of the model by item seems to be against the long-term goal of coming up with one model that could be used in other lessons. However, the methodology for building the models can be used in other lessons and ILEs. In addition, the descibed approach does not require human intervention and could be automated allowing the system to learn and improve itself while it is used.

References

1. Porayska-Pomsta, K., Mavrikis, M., Pain, H.: Diagnosing and acting on student affect: the tutor's perspective. UMUAI 18(1-2) (2008)
2. Mavrikis, M.: Modelling Students' Behaviour and Affective States in ILEs through Educational Data Mining. PhD thesis, The University of Edinburgh (2008)
3. Weiner, B.: Human motivation: Metaphors, theories, and research. Sage, Thousand Oaks (1992)
4. Corbett, A., Anderson, J.: Student modeling and mastery learning in a computer-based programming tutor (1992)
5. Conati, C., Gertner, A., VanLehn, K., Druzdzel, M.: On-line student modeling for coached problem solving using bayesian networks. In: Jameson, A., Paris, C., Tasso, C. (eds.) UM: Proceedings of the Sixth International conference (1997)
6. Mavrikis, M., Maciocia, A.: WaLLiS: a web-based ILE for science and engineering students studying mathematics. In: AIED 2003, Workshop on Advanced Technologies for Mathematics Education, vol. VIII, pp. 505–513 (2003)
7. Baker, R.S., Corbett, A., Koedinger, K., Wagner, A.: Off-task behavior in the cognitive tutor classroom: When students "game the system". In: Proceedings of ACM CHI 2004 Conference on Human Factors in Computing Systems, April 24-29, 2004, pp. 383–390. ACM Press, New York (2004)
8. Bouckaert, R.: Bayesian networks in Weka. Technical report, Computer Science Department University of Waikato (2004)
9. Verma, T., Pearl, J.: An algorithm for deciding if a set of observed independencies has a causal explanation. In: Proceedings of the Eighth Conference on Uncertainty in Artificial Intelligence, pp. 323–330 (1992)
10. Yu, L., Huan, L.: Feature selection for high-dimensional data: A fast correlation-based filter solution. In: International Conference on Machine Learning (2003)

A Dynamic Content Generator for Adaptation in Hypermedia Systems

David Mérida, Ramón Fabregat, Xavier Prat, David Huerva, and Jeimy Velez

University of Girona, Campus de Montilivi
17071 Girona, Spain
{david.merida,ramon.fabregat,david.huerva,jeimy.velez}@udg.edu

Abstract. The heterogeneity problem (in terms of different types of access devices, network bandwidth, preferences/characteristics of the user, etc.) has become a major problem for the Internet. Different alternatives have been developed to allow universal access to any type of content. Adaptive Hypermedia Systems (AHS) have emerged as a solution for this. In previous works we proposed the SHAAD[1] model, which includes the concepts of adaptability, adaptivity and dynamism to adapt web contents. Based on this model we implemented MAS-SHAAD, a multiagent system implementation of SHAAD. In this work we present the design and development of a **dynamic content generator** that can be added to any JAVA AHS implementation, such as MAS-SHAAD. The structure of the generator is defined by an ontology; therefore, a standard behavior can be obtained for any object included in the web pages generated and stored in the content repository.

Keywords: Adaptive hypermedia systems, multiagent systems, user modeling, device independency, heterogeneity, decision engine.

1 Introduction

The growing heterogeneity of the Internet in terms of user devices, network access links, preferences and user characteristics, and the increasing amount of multimedia content in web pages are important problems these days. One way of solving the problem of presenting contents to different types of devices is replicating the websites for each type. However, web servers usually do not consider this heterogeneity, which creates problems such as slow content delivery or even making it impossible to visualize some pages. Adaptation has been widely researched in the field of hypermedia systems [1-4] and several kinds of applications have been proposed.

In this work we design and implement a **dynamic content generator** based on the SHAAD model [5]. Its objective is to select the atomic elements that make up a web page in real time from a repository.

The design includes two parts: a *content repository*, which stores the atomic elements; and the *content assembler* uses CSS (Cascading Style Sheets) to assemble the

---

[1] SHAAD is the Spanish acronym for "Adaptable, Adaptive and Dynamic Hypermedia System".

W. Nejdl et al. (Eds.): AH 2008, LNCS 5149, pp. 320–323, 2008.

contents according to the adaptation variables that characterize the user preferences and technology. The dynamic content generator is integrated into the multiagent system MAS-SHAAD [6] for web content adaptation. This implementation is based on the proposed SHAAD model.

MAS-SHAAD is a multi-agent application of the SHAAD model using the JADE platform [7]. To implement the system, MAS-SHAAD uses CC/PP (Composite Capabilities / Preference Profiles) [8] to store the characteristics of the access device in the user model.

2   The Content Adaptation Process

The mechanisms used by the generator to adapt the contents from the adaptation variables are shown in Figure 1. Each of the modules performs the following functions:

1. *User preferences and device characteristics.* These are what we call the *adaptation variables* and are represented by a list of properties with assigned values that describes the preferences and characteristics.
2. The *constructor generator* and *constructor object.* The decision engine, which we represent by the *constructor generator*, creates a *constructor object*. This object contains a list with the **object types** that form the web page and that are requested from the content repository.
3. *Content Selection.* The *constructor object* is delivered to the *assembler* (the *builder agent*), which retrieves the object types from the repository according to the list of object types specified by the constructor object.
4. *Web building from the contents.* Once the appropriate contents are selected and obtained the assembler converts them to XHTML.

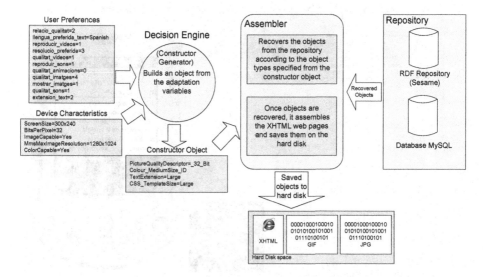

Fig. 1. Mechanisms of the dynamic content generator for adapting content

3 Integrating the Generator into the MAS-SHAAD Platform

The dynamic content generator has been integrated into the existing multiagent system MAS-SHAAD. The required agents are created from the existing agents in this system in order to incorporate the generator.

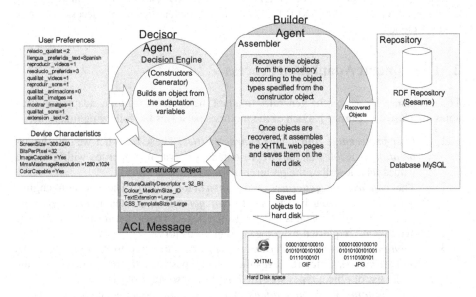

Fig. 2. Content Generator Modules in MAS-SHAAD

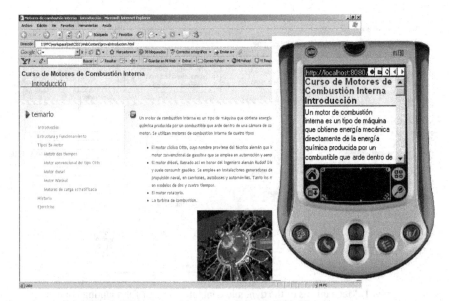

Fig. 3. Web page adapted to desktop and PDA browsers

The final system works exactly as the previous one (Figure 2), since the elements behave in the same way. Therefore, we have achieved total compatibility of the content generator with the MAS-SHAAD system.

Figure 3 shows two adaptation examples obtained with the content generator integrated into MAS-SHAAD. The images are web pages delivered to desktop and PDA browsers.

4 Conclusions

In this work we have presented a dynamic content generator for adaptation in hypermedia systems. It was designed using a modular structure that can be scaled easily to consider other adaptation variables. We have only considered the user preferences and the characteristics of the access devices for the tests.

Moreover, the structure of the objects that form the web page has been defined using an ontology, specifically for an educational context, based on the SCORM standard.

The entire implementation was later integrated into the multiagent system MAS-SHAAD, which shows its modularity and that it is easily integrated into these kinds of platforms designed using Java technology. Finally, in the future we plan to add other adaptation variables, which will allow the adaptation to be extended to all kinds of variables that are considered in the SHAAD model.

Acknowledgments. To the Spanish Ministry of Education and Science (TIN2005-08945-C06-03), and the Government of Catalonia (SGR 00296).

References

[1] Brusilovsky, P., Maybury, M.: The Adaptive Web. Communications of the ACM 45(5) (2002)
[2] De Bra, P.: Design Issues in Adaptive Web-Site Development. In: Proceedings of the 2nd Workshop on Adaptive Systems and User Modelling on the WWW (1999)
[3] Brusilovsky, P.: Methods and Techniques of Adaptive Hypermedia: User Modeling and User-Adapted Interaction, vol. 6, pp. 87–129. Kluwer academic publishers, Dordrecht (1996)
[4] Rosaci, D., Sarné, G.M.L.: MASHA: A Multi Agent System Handling User and Device Adaptivity of Web Sites. User Modeling and User-Adapted Interaction: The Journal of Personalization Research 16(5) (2006)
[5] Mérida, D., Fabregat, R., Marzo, J.L.: SHAAD: Adaptable, Adaptive and Dynamic Hypermedia System for content delivery. In: Workshop on Adaptive Systems for Web Based Education. WASWE 2002, Málaga España (2002)
[6] Mérida, D., Cannataro, M., Fabregat, R., Arteaga, C.: MAS-SHAAD a Multiagent System Proposal for an Adaptive Hypermedia System. Proceedings of IJCEELL journal Special issue: Adaptivity in Web and Mobile Learning Services (2004)
[7] JADE, http://jade.tilab.com/
[8] CC/PP Information Page, http://www.w3.org/Mobile/CCPP/

Automatic Generation of User Adapted Learning Designs: An AI-Planning Proposal

Lluvia Morales, Luis Castillo, Juan Fernandez-Olivares,
and Arturo Gonzalez-Ferrer

Univeristy of Granada, Spain
lluviamorales@ugr.es, {L.Castillo,faro}@decsai.ugr.es, arturogf@ugr.es

Abstract. A Learning Design(LD) definition under the IMS-LD standard is a complex task for the instructor because it requires a lot of time, effort and previous knowledge of the students group over which will be defined the knowledge objectives. That is why, taking advantage from diffusion of learning objects(LO) labeling using IMS-MD standard, we have proposed to realize a knowledge engineering process, represented as an algorithm, over LO labels and user profiles to automaticaly define a domain that will be used by an intelligent planner to build a LD. This LD will be finally implemented in the ILIAS Learning Management System(LMS).

Keywords: Planning and Scheduling, e-learning, IMS standars, Automatic Generation of Planning Domains.

1 Introduction and Previous Work

Since the appearance in 2003 of the IMS-LD v.1 endorsed by IMS Global Consortium[6], lot of educators have tried to implement it within on-line LMS's they use. However, this implementation is not an easy work because LO's have to be completely labeled[1] and it is necessary to detail the process to use them in order to achieve each student objectives, that is, specify a LD. For this reason, researchers have actually being looking for techniques to facilitate and even skip the LD construction step that commonly is assigned to the tutor.

To date reaserchers have been working with ontologies and knowledge databases[7] to do the knowledge extraction process over LO's, as it is a semi-automatic procedure to obtain the knowledge since the beginning of the course in order to create a LD. Also, other researchers have attempted to obtain information about the user through the course and, taking advantage of his interaction with the Intelligent Tutoring System(ITS), have tried to design several plans by using an intelligent planner[2] but, this process constantly showing to the student different learning routes to follow. Approaches such as these or similar had begun to be proposed since 1986[11] who is actually investigating about the advance we are addresing in this paper, working with IMS standards and its integration in LMS's[9].

W. Nejdl et al. (Eds.): AH 2008, LNCS 5149, pp. 324–328, 2008.

2   The Adaptive LD Construction Problem

In IMS-LD standard three representation levels of a LD are described. *Level B* works over the definition of personalized learning units according to different pedagogies. This take into account the reusability of LO's, the previous knowledge of each student and his preferences.

The job of exhaustively analyze the student characteristics and, after that, to define the better personalized learning unit for each one was initialy assigned to tutors and, after the integration of intelligent planning in ITS's, to planning experts. But, in order to automate this process and to save time and costs, we have proposed a knowledge engeenering algorithm explained in next section besides its required environment and practical application.

3   LD Automatic Construction Using AI Planning

3.1   Required Information

In order to be able to start with the LD generation process is essential to extract mandatory information about LO's of the subject using its metadatas(MD) and the user models of each one of the students registered.

From LO's we can extract two kinds of metadatas.

Hierarchy Relations Metadatas. Is-Part-Of. It describes a hierarchical compositional structure between LO's through the course as is shown in figure 1. **Is-Based-On**, provides ordering relations between primitive objects(PO) or compound objects(CO). **Requires.** Reports content dependencies between CO's.

Objects Attributes Metadatas. Language. Object required language i.e. spanish, english, etc. **Learning Resource Type.** Describes what kind of learning resource we are working on, i.e. lecture, simulation, exercise, etc. **Other Platform Requirements.** Describes if there are special hardware or software requirements to use the LO. **Difficulty.** Defines the performance level required by the student for this object to be in his plan.

In order to personalize the LD, our algorithm use the next *student profile* options from our LMS: **English Level.** To determine if he could take a high

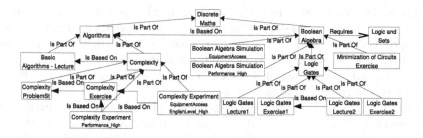

Fig. 1. Hierarchy Relations in a Subject

level english object. **Equipment**. Defines software and hardware availability of the student like java environment, bandwidth, etc. **Previous Courses Level**. Score in a related course. **Performance Level**. Performance level of the student. **Learning Style**. To offer each user a set of LO's with a temporal sequence that best fits his/her learning style. This style is defined by a psicological test, in this case the Honey-Alonso[4], that is answered by the student in his/her first visit to the LMS.

3.2   The Automatic Construction Process

In this section we show a brief description of the basic elements and steps followed by our algorithm to construct the planner domain and problem in the Planning Domain Definition Language[8], but a description of the basis of this documents is briefly explained in the next pharagraph, first.

LPG-td planner is a state-based intelligent planner based on local search and planning graphs methods that handles PDDL2.2 domains[3]; this is the planner that help us to create the LD. To date, we have to consider the following assumptions to define its problem and domain definition: *First*, the initial state of the planning problem is based on the contextual information extracted from LMS databases like user profiles and academic history. *Second*, the goal of the planning problem is translated from the learning objectives of a given course, in this case, the last LO's needed to complete the subject. *Third*, the set of the available actions in the domain is built from the LO's repository, so that every primitive object is translated into an action whose preconditions and effects are inherited from the information expressed in its MD.

The Domain Generation Algorithm. The planning domain generation algorithm is responsible of specifying required preconditions for every LO. These LO's are defined and labeled by the instructor in order to be used by the student in the better way according to the LO's attributes and his/her **Learning Style**.

The algorithm first analyze attributes and relations from each object; attributes give us state preconditions of PO's (actions in PDDL). Secondly, the algorithm defines order preconditions for PO's according to the requirements given by hierarchy relations. This second step is really arduous because it implies to check a subject graph from PO's, forming groups linearly arranged (even in a parallel way because of objects with the same name, but different attributes as *Complexity Experiment* in 1). These groups(called primitive groups) are ordered according to the **Is-Based-On** relation or the **Learning Style**, and subsequently we rise to each one of the hierarchical levels occupied by CO's(tasks in PDDL) and inheriting its relations to the first PO of the primitive group previously formed that is part of this CO. With this inheritance relations we can reorder those groups and form new ones.

The process described in the previous paragraph is done till cover every order relation from CO's which are part of a root compound object(*Discrete Maths* in figure 1 is and example) and finally we have to connect this root objects according to **Requires** relations.

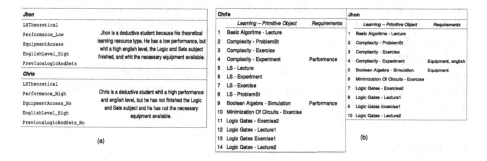

Fig. 2. Two Studied Students - (a) Problem Definition (b) Obtained LD's

Using this process is possible to generate a planning domain in PDDL with the same expressive capacity than the IMS-MD repository.

Problem Generation. The problem file is extracted in an automated manner from each student profile mentioned in section 3.1, which are translated to predicates that the domain will be able to evaluate as in Figure 2-(a) where two expamles are showed.

LD Generation by LPG. Once domain and problem PDDL files are generated, the LPG planner creates the user profile adaptive LD's to the subject we are making the domain as in Figure 2-(b) examples of automatically generated LD's to the student models described in (a). Those LD's are adapted to each student, i.e. Chris has a `theoretical` LD, his LO's can be difficult resources, but can not take objects with `equipment` needs and he `requires` to take Logic and Sets PO's(Lecture, ProblemSt, Exercise and Experiment); while Jhon has a `theoretical` ordered plan too, but he needs easier LO's in his LD because of his low `performance`.

LD Integration in ILIAS. The procedure described along this paper has been fully integrated in the ILIAS LMS, which embeds a SOAP (Simple Object Access Protocol) server which recives the LD plan generated by LPG. ILIAS does not support IMS-LD specification yet, but we have translated the plan into a follow up guideline that appears over the student' ILIAS desktop.

4   Concluding Remarks and Future Work

It is important to point out three merits of this paper. First, that the labeling extraction from the IMS-MD can be carried out independently of the course over which our LD(in its abstraction level B) is going to be created. Second, that the knowledge extraction process is carried out by an algorithm (designed by our research team) that does not require the participation of any planning expert or tutor. However, the final product after this process, the LD, must be supervised by the instructor to make the considered modifications, in case it is needed. Finally, that this advance has been implemented on an IMS.

Althought, we thought that should be designed a domain representation that works out the common characteristics of a user group to be able to generate a collaborative LD. And, we must to identify the way to work with different kinds of LO's (i.e. optionals) and to represent global and partial deadlines that can be managed by a state-based planner.

References

1. IEEE Standard for Learning Objects Metadata, http://ltsc.ieee.org/wg12/
2. Camacho, D., R-Moreno, M.D., Obieta, U.: CAMOU: A Simple Integrated eLearning and Planning Techniques Tool. In: 4th International Workshop on Constraints and Language Processing (August 2007)
3. Gerevini, A., Serina, I.: LPG: A Planner Based on Local Search for Planning Graphs. In: Proceedings of AIPS 2002. AAAI Press, Toulouse (2002)
4. Honey Alonso Learning Style, http://www.estilosdeaprendizaje.es/chaea/chaea.htm
5. ILIAS Learning Management System, http://www.ilias.de/ios/index-e.html
6. IMS-GLC IMS Global consortium, http://www.imsglobal.org/
7. Kontopoulos, E., Vrakas, D., et al.: An Ontology-based Planning System for e-course Generation. In: Expert Systems with Applications, vol. 37 (1). Elsevier, Amsterdam
8. Long, D., Fox, M.: PDDL 2.1: An Extension to PDDL for Expressing Temporal Planning Domains. Journal of Artificial Intelligence Research 20, 24–61 (2003)
9. Mohan, P., Greer, J., McCalla, G.: Instructional Planning with Learning Objects. In: Baumgartner, K.M., Cairns (eds.) IJCAI 2003 Workshop Knowledge Representation and Automated Reasoning for E-Learning Systems (2003)
10. Myers, K.L.: Towards a Framework for Continuous Planning and Execution. In: Proceedings of the AAAI Fall Symposium on Distributed Continual Planning (1998)
11. Peachey, D.R., McCalla, G.I.: Using Planning Techniques in Intelligent Tutoring Systems. International Journal of Man-Machine Studies 24, 77–98 (1986)

Guaranteeing the Correctness of an Adaptive Tutoring System*

Pilar Prieto-Linillos[1], Sergio Gutiérrez[2], Abelardo Pardo[1], and Carlos Delgado Kloos[1]

[1] Carlos III University of Madrid
[2] London Knowledge Lab
Birkbeck College, University of London
sergut@dcs.bbk.ac.uk, {plinillos,abel,cdk}@it.uc3m.es

Abstract. This paper presents an approach to create adaptive web-based educative systems that can be automatically audited by means of standard web testing tools. The auditing tool takes the role of a learner interacting with the system, checking that no errors are present. The tool can communicate with the exercises to know the correct answers to them; a configurable ratio of correct to incorrect answers allows the tool to behave as a range of different students. More complex checking techniques will be tested in the future using this architecture.

1 Introduction

Authoring an educational adaptive hypermedia system is a difficult task [1] that usually involves a multidisciplinary team of people (e.g. learning scientists, computer scientists and domain experts). However, the authoring process is vulnerable to errors. Therefore, having techniques that guarantee the correctness of the system (even partially) becomes extremely important. Checking the correctness of all the possible variants is something beyond the reach of a few tests by a human. As a solution, some authors have proposed the use of automatic monitoring [2] or off-line automatic auditing [3].

This paper presents an approach for designing an educational adaptive system in a way that it can be audited using automatic tools. This approach has been applied during the creation and maintenance of a web-based ITS, that is being used at a higher level educational institution as support for the normal classes. The system is composed of a series of learning activities comprising pages that explain certain concepts and parametric exercises. These activities are presented to the students in a sequence that is adapted to them, according to their user model and results obtained in previous activities. The interaction between the users and the tutor is done entirely through a web browser.

When additional exercises are added to the tutor, or when the sequencing strategy is changed (e.g. new transitions or conditions between exercises exercises), the system can be checked again automatically to verify its correctness. Similar techniques are extensively used in other research areas such as digital circuit verification [4] or software design [5]. The premises of the abstract problem, though, are quite similar. The behavior of a system is represented by a large number of transitions between states that are part of an unusually large state space.

---

* Work partially funded by Programa Nacional de Tecnologías de la Información y de las Comunicaciones, project TSI2005-08225-C07-01/2.

W. Nejdl et al. (Eds.): AH 2008, LNCS 5149, pp. 329–332, 2008.

2   Description of the System

In the proposed strategy the system is created in two steps. The first one is the creation of the learning activities, specifying for each of them what inputs they expect and what output they can provide in order to influence the sequencing (this can be viewed as the interface of the activity). The information created in this step will be needed by the auditing tool later. The second step is the definition of the sequences that the system will supply according to the learner's actions and the user model. Sequencing graphs have been used for this work, but other techniques like UML diagrams [6] or stochastic graphs [7] are also possible.

In order to check for the desired consistency in the exercise sequence, it is necessary to design a auditing program capable of exchanging questions and answers with the system. For that purpose, a Java program was designed based on the JWebUnit toolkit to simulate the presence of a user. Figure 1 shows the architecture used for the test bench.

First, an instance of the tutor is installed in a remote server. Such tutor has access to all the parametric exercises and is able to sequence them based on the heuristic used. On the client side, a specially designed test engine is comprised of a layer to exchange HTTP data with the server, a set of testing scripts and a location where the received HTML page is manipulated. The JWebUnit layer performs two tasks. Upon reception of an HTTP answer from the server, it stores its content internally and offers an object through which the structure of the web page is fully available to the test engine. The API offered by JWebUnit allows to perform operations similar to those that would perform a regular user when using a browser: clicking in a link, setting values in form fields and pushing form buttons.

But the difficulty of using a fully automatic approach is that the answers to the exercises need to be produced as to simulate the ones obtained from a real student. An initial brute-force approach of randomly assigning answer values to every question would provide an extremely poor simulation. In order to replicate a real situation accurately, the automatic testing paradigm needs to insert, at least in some cases, the correct answers to the questions.

Therefore, a change in the design of each exercise was introduced. A new parameter specially conceived for testing purposes was created in each exercise. Whenever this parameter is set to true, the exercise would include, aside from the exercise text, a table containing the values that would make all values correct; so the auditing engine, using conventional XML parsing techniques, can store it.

Unique identifiers were also included in various fragments of the HTML code produced by the tutor. The role of such identifiers was to allow the testing engine to check

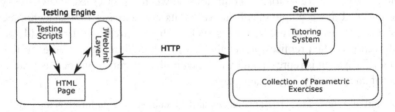

Fig. 1. Architecture of the testing engine

that the exercises were properly instantiated by the tutor. For example, when checking for the proper feedback, the testing engine compares the expected feedback with the text returned by the tutor with the proper identifier.

The testing suite was organized for each of the modules in the tutor around three tests. The first one is to guarantee that the tutor has the expected behavior when all the answers are incorrect. This sequence is a extreme case, but empirical observations showed it to be useful at detecting anomalies.

The second one is based on all the answers being correct. This case is useful to detect exercise sequences incorrectly defined. The reason is that a student answering correctly all the exercises should have to traverse a short sequence of exercises. The script to test this case executes a loop with a predefined length equal to the maximum expected sequence. It then starts processing the exercises and setting all the correct values. If the loop terminates without detecting a termination page has been sent by the tutor, the run is considered incorrect.

Finally, a third case is situated between these two extreme cases. After the correct answers contained in the exercise have been obtained, a randomly selected subset of them is modified to produce incorrect answers, and the new values are submitted to the tutor. A special case needs to be considered when answers are correlated. For example, if a problem expects as answer a sequence of numbers, a correct answer is when all of them have the right value. In other words, the testing engine should either change one of the numbers or maintain all of them to the correct values in order to truly randomize the answers.

This problem was solved by increasing the information offered by the parametric exercises and providing the answers in groups. When a set of values are all part of a single answer, they are included in a group. The decision by the testing engine of providing a correct or incorrect value is done at the group level.

Once the system is deployed, the auditing application logs into the system and behaves as a regular user. Multiple instances of this application are used simultaneously to check the robustness for the case of several concurrent users; additionally, this can be used to verify sequencing techniques based on group modeling [8]. In order to maximize the number of possible sequences explored by the testing engine, several executions of the three types of test were done with different values for the percentage of correct answers submitted per exercise.

These tests were executed automatically before the deployment of a new instance of the tutor, and whenever a new set of parametric exercises were added to the sequencing graph. The presented paradigm has helped to achieve the two objectives: detect errors that would rule it unusable by regular users before the final deployment, and guarantee a level of robustness when the sequencing subsystem was modified.

3   Conclusions and Future Work

This paper has described a strategy for automatically checking if an educational web-based system is consistent. The strategy is based on two tools: parametric exercises, for the creation of multiple variations of the same problem; and sequencing graphs, used to define sequencings (i.e. families of possible sequences) that are adapted to the student.

An auditing tool interacts with the system in the role of a student, giving right or wrong answers to the exercises when asked, with the goal of checking every possible combination of learning activities over time. Three techniques have been used with this tool: giving always correct answers, always incorrect, and a fixed ratio of correct answers, but more complex strategies for correction checking can be studied. First, some could be inspired by those used in software design (see [9] for a survey), for checking the system from the point of view of reliability. Additionally, other strategies with a pedagogical foundation, that simulate students based on user modelling techniques [10], could allow to check the correcness of the system from the point of view of its learning design. This is the main line of future development of the system.

The main advantage of the proposed approach is that it distributes the workload of checking the whole system over the individual elements. When a new exercise is added to the system, it only has to define the questions that it expects to be answered, and what are the correct answers for them. Its main limitation is the fact that, in order to perform any non-trivial checking, exercises have to provide a secure way to know the correct answers to the system.

References

1. Cristea, A.: Authoring of adaptive and adaptable educational hypermedia: where are we now and where are we going? In: Web-based Education (February 2004)
2. Camacho, D., Rodriguez-Moreno, M.D.: Towards an automatic monitoring for higher education learning design. International Journal of Metadata, Semantics and Ontologies 2, 1–10 (2007)
3. Gutiérrez, S., Valigiani, G., Jamont, Y., Collet, P., Delgado Kloos, C.: A swarm approach for automatic auditing of pedagogical planning. In: IEEE Int. Conference on Advanced Learning Technologies, pp. 136–138 (2007)
4. Kurshan, R.P.: Computer-Aided Verification of Coordinating Processes. Princeton University Press, Princeton (1994)
5. Mili, A., Desharnais, J.: A system for classifying program verification methods: Assigning meanings to program verification methods. In: Proc. of the 7th Int. Conf. on Software engineering, pp. 499–509. IEEE Press, Los Alamitos (1984)
6. Retalis, S., Papasalouros, A.: Designing and automatically generating educational adaptive hypermedia applications. Educational Technology and Society 8, 26–35 (2005)
7. Semet, Y., Lutton, E., Collet, P.: Ant colony optimisation for e-learning: Observing the emergence of pe dagogical suggestions. In: IEEE Swarm Intelligence Symposium (2003)
8. Wessner, M., Pfister, H.R.: Group formation in computer-supported collaborative learning. In: Proceedings of the 2001 Int. ACM SIGGROUP Conference on Supporting Group Work, pp. 24–31. ACM, New York (2001)
9. Rabejac, C., Blanquart, J.P., Queille, J.P.: Executable assertions and timed traces for on-line software error detection. In: FTCS 1996: Proc. of the The 26th Int. Symposium on Fault-Tolerant Computing (FTCS 1996). IEEE Computer Society, Los Alamitos (1996)
10. Matsuda, N., Cohen, W.W., Sewall, J., Lacerda, G., Koedinger, K.R.: Evaluating a simulated student using real students data for training and testing. In: Proceedings of User Modelling (June 2007)

Designing a Personalized Semantic Web Browser

Melike Şah, Wendy Hall, and David C. De Roure

IAM Group, School of Electronics and Computer Science, University of Southampton
{ms305r,wh,dder}@ecs.soton.ac.uk

Abstract. Web browsing is a complex activity and in general, users are not guided during browsing. Our hypothesis is that by using Semantic Web technologies and personalization methods, browsing can be supported better. However, existing personalization mechanisms on the Web are obstructive; users need to log in to multiple websites and enter their personal information and preferences, and the profiles are different for each site. There is a need for generic user profiles, which can also support the user's browsing. In this paper, we propose a novel Semantic Web browser using an ontology-driven user modeling architecture to enable semantic and adaptive links. We also introduce a new behavior-based user model. With our approach, users need to log in to their Web browser only and personalization is achieved on different websites.

Keywords: Semantic Web Browser, Semantic Web, User Modeling, Ontology, Personalization.

1 Introduction

Searching and browsing are two important information filtering activities on the Web. Usually, users use search engines for finding Web resources but this is only half of the story. When users follow a link from search results, they have to read and understand page content and in general they are not guided during browsing. Browsing is a complex activity and its nature is not understood well. According to Bawden [1], the activity of browsing can be categorized into three groups: purposive browsing (looking for a definite piece of information), capricious browsing (randomly examining material without a defined goal) and exploratory browsing (deliberately searching for inspiration). Cove and Walsh [2] also divide browsing into three categories: search browsing (searching for defined information), general purpose browsing (looking for items of interest) and serendipity browsing (random). Based on these definitions, we can say that browsing tends to be used in three broad senses: a purposeful activity (directed), searching for inspiration (semi-directed) and capricious behavior (undirected). In our opinion, user profiles should contain such information.

Nowadays, personalization is supported by many websites on the Web (e.g. Amazon, Google). However, they require users to log in to multiple websites and the user profiles change from site to site. There is a need for generic user profiles and personalization architectures, which can achieve adaptive hypermedia on diverse websites. Our hypothesis is that Semantic Web technologies can offer the solution to these problems. Semantic metadata can be used for finding related information during browsing. Additionally, ontology-based user profiles are interoperable, and they can be easily extended and combined with semantic metadata on the Web.

W. Nejdl et al. (Eds.): AH 2008, LNCS 5149, pp. 333–336, 2008.
© Springer-Verlag Berlin Heidelberg 2008

COHSE [3] and Magpie [4] are two semantic-enabled systems that aim to provide useful browsing hyperlinks using semantic metadata. However, they paid little attention to the user's role and they do not supply adaptive links or contents. In addition, they both use back-end databases for semantic linking.

In user modeling, there have been several studies. IMS LIP and IEEE PAPI are well known user modeling standards. Although these standards can be applied to any domain, they mainly developed for learners in educational hypermedia. The Onto-logging project [5] develops a user ontology in the context of knowledge management systems. However, the user model is specific to a certain domain. In [6], a general meta-ontology is developed for modeling user and adaptive hypermedia methods.

In this paper, we propose a novel personalized Semantic Web browser architecture, which we named SemWeB. SemWeB is able to annotate Web pages with semantic metadata using ontologies and provides adaptive and semantic hyperlinks on different websites. For semantic linking, we use Web as source for linking (no back-end database is used). A new behavior-based and an ontology-driven user modeling architecture is also integrated into SemWeB and user profiles can be implicitly and explicitly updated with semantic metadata. This paper presents our user ontology, user modeling approach and ongoing work on the Semantic Web browser.

2 Architecture of SemWeB

SemWeB is a browser extension of the Mozilla Firefox Web browser (Fig. 1). SemWeB extends the Web browser with a vertical sidebar. The sidebar has two tabs: the navigation tab and the personalization tab. The navigation tab is used for highlighting ontological concepts found on the page and adding semantic and adaptive links. The personalization tab is used for updating user profiles. SemWeB annotates Web pages using ontologies and an ontology-driven lexicon based on a modified GATE framework [7]. GATE is a general text engineering architecture for extracting named entities from text. We are using rules and gazetteers for IE. Also, we extend GATE with a lookup service and annotation storage unit. Lookup service returns the URIs of found concept instances and annotation storage unit creates and stores semantic annotations as XML files at server-side. Because IE requires some pre-processing (creating lexicons, etc.), SemWeB uses predefined ontologies, particularly ECS ontology [8]. SemWeB can also be adapted to different ontologies.

Semantic links are inserted, when the user highlights a concept from the navigation tab. SemWeB embeds icons next to recognized instances on the Web page. Then, user is required to click the icon. Once user clicks, URI of the instance is sent to the server. First, server dereferences URI using HTTP content negotiation and finds possible link anchors and targets. More URI dereferencing performed and related URIs on the Web is searched. Finally, semantic links are presented in a new Web page at the browser.

To benefit personalization, users need to register and log in to SemWeB from the personalization tab. User profiles are kept at a server-side triple store. Additionally, we created a profile editor. By using this editor, users can explicitly add, remove, change information to their profiles from the personalization tab. As well as, users can be explicitly assigned to expertise, interests and goals from the interface of SemWeB. Implicit user characteristics, such as browsing level and browsing type are automatically updated by SemWeb.

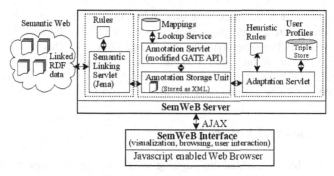

Fig. 1. The architecture of SemWeB

3   The Proposed User Model

In user modeling, IMS LIP and IEEE PAPI are well known standards. Although these standards can be applied to any domain, they do not contain information about browsing behaviors. Thus, we developed a new behavior-based user model, which can also be applied to different domains. In our model, currently we use seven categories: identification, preference, security, *browsing goal, interest, expertise* and *browsing behavior* (our main contributions are in italic). In future work, the user model can be extended with more information, such as portfolio. The identification category contains personal information about users. The preference is layout, color scheme and language preferences. The security contains username and password.

The browsing goal concept represents browsing aims of users and it is divided into two sub-concepts: short-term browsing goal and persistent browsing goal. The short-term browsing goal indicates the current information needs of the user. The persistent browsing goals are long-term goals of the user, which are motivated from long-term interests. Such as, a user interested in politics, probably likes politic related pages. In our ongoing work, browsing goals are automatically defined based on the semantic context found on the page. Users are only required to select appropriate browsing goal from their browsers. The interest category represents browsing interests of users that can be understood from bookmarked pages and accessed semantic hyperlinks. Thus, the interest category is divided into bookmark (interest to a webpage) and browsing interest (interest to a semantic concept). Users can explicitly enter interest values to recognized semantic instances from their browsers. The expertise category represents expertise of users for a semantic instance. Users can explicitly enter expertise values to the semantic instances recognized on the Web page.

Additionally, in order to implicitly understand the activities of users, we introduce the Browsing Behavior concept. The browsing behavior has browsing_level and browsing_type properties. Browsing_level (*very active, active, passive, inactive*) is the number of clicks made by a user in a browsing session. According to Cove and Walsh [1], and Bawden [2], different browsing strategies exists and we use browsing_type (*directed, semi-directed, un-directed*) to represent this. In our model, browsing strategy of the user is implicitly understood from their interactions with SemWeB. When the user has a short-term browsing goal, it is assumed that user is looking for a defined piece of information and browsing_type is set to "*directed*". This probably accounts for perception of search browsing. When the user has a browsing interest or has bookmarked current Web page, then it is assumed that the user is looking for items of interest and browsing_type is set to *"semi-directed"*. This probably accounts for perception of general purpose browsing. When the user does not have short-term browsing goals or browsing interests, browsing_type is set to *"undirected"*. This probably accounts for perception of serendipity browsing.

4 Conclsusions and Future Work

In this paper, we have presented our ongoing work for the novel personalized Semantic Web Browser (SemWeB). Our main contribution is the integration of a new behavior-based and an ontology-driven user modeling architecture into the Semantic Web browser. As a result, SemWeB provides semantic and adaptive hyperlinks on different web sites and user profiles can be easily extended with semantic metadata coming from browser. We have also introduced a new user model, which uses the user's browsing behaviors for adaptation and it can be applied to different domains.

In our ongoing work, adaptive hypermedia is achieved on the recommended semantic links based on the user model and found concept instances on the page. In addition, based on different browsing types and expertise, we are planning to provide adaptive links. For instance, if it is directed browsing, show related links according to short-term browsing goals. If it is semi-directed browsing, use most recently added interests to supply related links. If it is un-directed browsing, make use of semantics. When a link is requested by a novice user, provide links to Wikipedia pages. When the user is an expert, provide detailed semantic links. Also, link sorting and link annotation can be done based on interest ratings, goal priorities, and browsing levels.

References

1. Bawden, D.: Information Systems and the Stimulation of Creativity. J. of Information Science 12, 203–216 (1986)
2. Cove, J., Walsh, B.: Online Text Retrieval via Browsing. Information Processing and Management 24, 31–37 (1988)
3. Carr, L., Hall, W., Bechhofer, S., Goble, C.: Conceptual Linking: Ontology-based Open Hypermedia. In: International World Wide Web Conference, pp. 334–342 (2001)
4. Dzbor, M., Domingue, J., Motta, E.: Magpie – towards a semantic web browser. In: Fensel, D., Sycara, K.P., Mylopoulos, J. (eds.) ISWC 2003. LNCS, vol. 2870. Springer, Heidelberg (2003)
5. Razmerita, L., Angehrn, A., Maedche, A.: Ontology-based User Modeling for Knowledge Management Systems. In: International Conference on User Modeling, pp. 213–217 (2003)
6. Yudelson, M., Gavrilova, T., Brusilovsky, P.: Towards User Modeling Meta-Ontology. In: Ardissono, L., Brna, P., Mitrović, A. (eds.) UM 2005. LNCS (LNAI), vol. 3538. Springer, Heidelberg (2005)
7. Cunningham, H., Maynard, D., Bontcheva, K., Tablan, V.: GATE: A Framework and Graphical Development Environment for Robust NLP Tools and Applications. In: Proceedings of 40th Anniversary Meeting of the Association for Computational Linguistics (2002)
8. ECS Ontology, http://id.ecs.soton.ac.uk/docs/

Towards Inferring Sequential-Global Dimension of Learning Styles from Mouse Movement Patterns[*]

Danilo Spada, Manuel Sánchez-Montañés, Pedro Paredes, and Rosa M. Carro

Escuela Politécnica Superior, Universidad Autónoma de Madrid
28049 Madrid, Spain
{danilo.spada,manuel.smontanes,pedro.paredes,
rosa.carro}@uam.es

Abstract. One of the main concerns of user modelling for adaptive hypermedia deals with automatic user profile acquisition. In this paper we present a new approach to predict sequential/global dimension of Felder-Silverman's learning style model that only makes use of mouse movement patterns. The results obtained in a case study with 18 students are very promising. We found a strong correlation between maximum vertical speed and sequential/global dimension score. Moreover, it was possible to predict whether students' learning styles are global or sequential with high accuracy (94.4%). This suggests that mouse movement patterns can be a powerful source of information about certain user features.

1 Introduction

Adaptive hypermedia based systems take advantage of knowledge about users interacting with them in order to provide contents and links adapted to each individual, taking into consideration his particular needs, interests, behavior, personality, context, and many more features. In order to provide adaptation it is necessary to store and maintain information about the user, which constitutes the user model [11].

Before a user model can be used it has to be constructed. The initialization of a user model represents the process of gathering information about the user and transferring this information into the model. Many systems use questionnaires for detecting users' features while others try to infer them from user interactions with the system.

In the area of education, one of the student features to be modeled and used with adaptation purposes is learning style. Felder and Silverman created a learning style model (FS-LSM) [5] that has been widely used. It describes learning styles distinguishing between preferences on four dimensions (active/reflective, sensing/intuitive, visual/verbal, and sequential/global). Focusing on the last one, sequential learners tend to gain understanding in small incremental linear steps, each step following logically to the previous one. Global learners tend to learn in large jumps, absorbing and

---

[*] This work is supported by the Spanish Ministry of Science and Education, projects TIN2007-64718, TEC2006-13141-C03-03 and BFU2006-07902/BFI. We are also grateful to GHIA and ATVS groups of Escuela Politécnica Superior (UAM) for their comments.

W. Nejdl et al. (Eds.): AH 2008, LNCS 5149, pp. 337–340, 2008.

learning materials almost randomly without seeing connections, and then suddenly getting the whole picture. Information about these preferences can be extracted from the corresponding questionnaire (ILS) [6], which contains 44 questions. We have used Felder's model and questionnaire in previous works [1] [12] [13].

The use of questionnaires, although usually provides accurate information, can be very time-consuming. Some works have investigated the use of Bayesian networks [9], behavior patterns [10] and feed-forward neural networks [14] to detect learning styles starting from information of user behavior in educational websites (tasks done, time spent, scores obtained). To our knowledge, only in [2] information about user-mouse interaction, specifically mouse distance in the Y axis, along with other parameters (such as scrolling or time spent in pages) has been used to try to predict sequential/global learning style dimension, achieving an accuracy of 57% in this dimension.

In this work we explore whether sequential/global learning style dimension can be satisfactorily inferred by using only information about mouse movements of learners when interacting with an e-learning environment.

2 Methods

An educational website for the course on Neurocomputing of Computer Science studies (Escuela Politécnica Superior, Universidad Autónoma de Madrid) was designed. The website has a total of 12 pages (with a good balance between images and text, examples and theory), and no scrollbars. An acquisition module was developed to record mouse coordinates and the instant in which mouse is moved and, therefore, coordinates change. This module performs like a transparent shell with respect to the web pages. To enter the site, students had to login with their username and password. They were required to fill in the ILS questionnaire, also integrated in the site.

After one week, the data stored in the server were extracted and verified, so that only data from students who completely filled in the questionnaire were considered. Focusing on sequential-global dimension of FS-LSM, the score obtained by students in the ILS questionnaire was considered along with information about their mouse movements in order to detect any correlation between them. Scores can range from -11 (extreme global style) to +11 (extreme sequential style). This dataset was analysed in MatLab to find out whether scores can be inferred from features extracted from mouse movements such as statistics of mouse speed, acceleration, etc.

3 Results

The number of students that filled the whole questionnaire was 18. We found that the maximum vertical speed of the mouse was highly correlated with the score obtained for sequential/global dimension. Specifically, the correlation coefficient was found to be $r = -0.8$, implying that students with smaller maximum vertical speed tend to be more sequential, while students with higher maximum vertical speed tend to be more global, as it can be seen in figure 1. This is clearer if we represent the sign of the score for the sequential/global dimension (figure 2). 61% percent of the scores obtained by the students are positive (more sequential than global), while 39% are negative (more

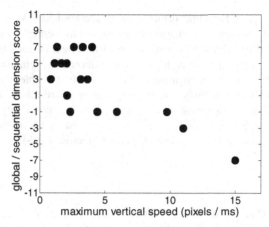

Fig. 1. Maximum vertical speed versus global/sequential dimension score

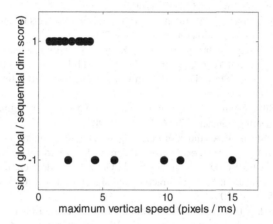

Fig. 2. Maximum vertical speed versus sign of sequential/global dimension score

global than sequential). We used leave-one-out cross-validation [4] to estimate the accuracy of a rule of the type "predict sign as positive when the maximum value of vertical speed is smaller than a threshold, otherwise predict it as negative", obtaining an estimated prediction error of only 5.6% (94.4% accuracy).

4 Discussion

In this work we have presented a new approach to predict sequential/global dimension of learning styles that only makes use of mouse movement patterns in a website. The results of this case study are very promising since the prediction accuracy obtained is very high (94.4%). We will extend our study collecting and analyzing data from groups of students interacting with different websites already developed. In addition, we are planning a similar analysis to throw more light upon the possibility of automatically predicting the other dimensions of the FS-LSM. With this in mind, we plan to eventually combine information from mouse movements with that related to the type of information selected, activities done, time spent on each one, and so on.

The software we developed to collect data from mouse movements can be easily integrated within different web applications. Thus, it will be possible to check whether the conclusions obtained in this study and the ongoing ones are related to the application domain. Our challenge is to bring more insight about the possibility of automatically detecting learning styles, which we think can be interesting for research areas such as user modeling [11], adaptive hypermedia [3] and biometrics [7][8].

References

1. Alfonseca, E., Carro, R.M., Martín, E., Ortigosa, A., Paredes, P.: The Impact of Learning Styles on Student Grouping for Collaborative Learning: A Case Study. User Modeling and User Adapted Interaction, special issue on User Modeling to Support Groups, Communities and Collaboration 16(3-4), 377–401 (2006)
2. Bergasa-Suso, J., Sanders, D.A.: Intelligent browser-based systems to assist Internet users. IEEE Transactions on Education 48(4), 580–585 (2005)
3. Brusilovsky, P.: Adaptive hypermedia. In: Kobsa, A. (ed.) User Modeling and User Adapted Interaction, Ten Year Anniversary Issue, vol. 11(1/2), pp. 87–110 (2001)
4. Duda, R.O., Hart, P.E., Stork, D.G.: Pattern Classification, 2nd edn. John Wiley & Sons, Chichester (2001)
5. Felder, R.M., Silvermann, L.K.: Learning and teaching styles in engineering education. Journal of Engineering Education 78, 674–681 (1988)
6. Felder, R.M., Soloman, B.A.: Index of Learning Styles Questionnaire, http://www.engr.ncsu.edu/learningstyles/ilsweb.html
7. Fierrez, J., Ramos-Castro, D., Ortega-Garcia, J., Gonzalez-Rodriguez, J.: HMM-based on-line signature verification: feature extraction and signature modeling. Pattern Recognition Letters 28, 2325–2334 (2007)
8. Gamboa, H., Fred, A.L.N., Jain, A.K.: Webbiometrics: User Verification Via Web Interaction. In: Proceedings of Biometric Symposium, Biometric Consortium Conference (2007)
9. García, P., Schiaffino, S., Amandi, A.: An enhanced Bayesian model to detect students' learning styles in Web-based courses. Journal of Computer Assisted Learning (OnlineEarly Articles), doi:10.1111/j.1365-2729.2007.00262.x
10. Graf, S., Kinshuk: An Approach for Detecting Learning Styles in Learning Management Systems. In: Sixth International Conference on Advanced Learning Technologies (ICALT), pp. 161–163 (2006)
11. Kobsa, A.: Generic User Modeling Systems. User Modeling and User-Adapted Interaction: The Journal of Personalization Research 11, 49–63 (2001)
12. Paredes, P., Rodríguez, P.: A Mixed Approach to Modelling Learning Styles in Adaptive Educational Hypermedia. Advanced Technology for Learning 1(4), 210–215 (2004)
13. Sánchez Hórreo, V., Carro, R.M.: Studying the Impact of Personality and Group Formation on Learner Performance. In: Haake, J.M., Ochoa, S.F., Cechich, A. (eds.) CRIWG 2007. LNCS, vol. 4715, pp. 287–294. Springer, Heidelberg (2007)
14. Villaverde, J., Godoy, D., Amandi, A.: Learning styles' recognition in e-learning environments with feed-forward neural networks. Journal of Computer Assisted Learning 22, 197–206 (2006)

VUMA: A Visual User Modelling Approach for the Personalisation of Adaptive Systems

Melanie B. Späth and Owen Conlan

School of Computer Science and Statistics
Trinity College, Dublin, Ireland
{mspaeth, Owen.Conlan}@cs.tcd.ie
http://kdeg.cs.tcd.ie/

Abstract. Current approaches to explicit user modelling are generally time consuming and tedious for the user. Oftentimes poor usability and overly long questionnaires deter the end user from reusing such modelling tools, thus only facilitating explicit personalisation once as they enter the system. This paper proposes a visual approach to user modelling resulting in the VUMA (Visual User Modelling Approach) tool that can be used in a playful and dynamic manner repeatedly during a user's engagement with a personalisation system. This work proposes and evaluates a visually empowering, usable, highly configurable and playful user modelling interface that is utilised to elicit user interests and preferences in a chosen knowledge domain.

Keywords: visual user modelling, user profiling, user interface, personalisation.

1 Introduction

Appropriate user models are fundamental to the provision of personalisation in Adaptive Systems. A user model contains modelled assumptions that represent the characteristics of the user which have been deemed relevant to the system [5]. The validity of the assumptions is determined by the technique used to acquire the relevant information. Explicit modelling asks the user for information through direct questionnaires and tests [7]. Implicit approaches observe the user's interaction with the system and analyse the information which they request from a database or repository [6] while they are using it in order to build a user model. Both approaches have their draw-backs and may lead to user frustration. Explicit approaches may involve the user spending a lot of time modelling their interests before using the system, whereas all implicit approaches are ultimately predicated on intelligent guesses [4] with inaccurate guesses potentially causing frustration.

In this paper an approach is proposed that targets the limitations of explicit modelling by designing an intuitive visual user modelling approach, embodied by the VUMA tool, that users can use in a playful manner to specify their interests and preferences. As a proof of concept, the VUMA tool has been adapted to a

W. Nejdl et al. (Eds.): AH 2008, LNCS 5149, pp. 341–344, 2008.

sightseeing itinerary planner where the system's purpose is to assist a tourist in planning their own personalised sightseeing day.

2   Design and Architecture

There are many text-based questionnaire approaches to modelling user interests, e.g. [1], but these approaches lack the potential for the user to play with their modelled information, i.e. make speculative changes to their model in order to see what the resulting personalizations might be. Several approaches also utilise concept maps as a means to construct user models, e.g. [2]. These approaches tend to built on ontology and topic map building tools, but do not generally represent, in a visual way, the goal of the modelling. As such, even though the modelling approach is explicit the goal is often implicit. These visual approaches definitely offer more playful potential. Approaches such as VIUM [8] offer the possibility for users to inspect large user models. Again the goal of the user model is implied, but the potential for scrutability is increased.

The approach proposed in this paper assumes that the model being produced is centred around a single simple goal and that this goal will provide the focal reference point of the visual design. This design should enable the presentation of multiple options in a manner that allows the user to easily locate the desired information, and should allow the user to dynamically assign an interest and qualitative preferences to these choices in a playful and enjoyable way and should visually and intuitively reflect the choices being taken. Similarly, the limiting constraint, e.g. time, should also be represented visually.

The realisation of the Visual User Modelling Approach tool has been achieved through intensive user-centric engagement at several stages of development. As part of VUMA individual items, both specific and abstract are represented as circles. In order to reduce visual clutter and information overload, a hierarchical concept of going from abstract to specific has been employed (Fig. 1a). Specific items can be retrieved through abstract items, i.e. by clicking on the circle that represents an abstract category. This would expand it to display a set of more specific items or sub-categories which could be further expanded and so forth. Abstract and specific items may be visually distinguished by background or colour. The area of the circles serves as an approximation for a constraint, such as money or time, i.e. the bigger the circle, the more of the constraint is available or consumed or desired, depending on the situation (Fig. 1b). The items can be configured to be resizable.

The distance of a particular circle from a static reference point is used to represent an interest in that item (Fig. 1c). Once a circle is dragged past a boundary a level of interest will be associated with the item that is inversely proportional to its distance from the reference point, i.e. the nearer the item to the reference point, the higher the interest. Items outside this boundary have an interest of zero. The user can playfully register their interest and preference in any of the available items by dragging items nearer to or farther from the reference point. The reference point was chosen to be in the middle of the visualization, and

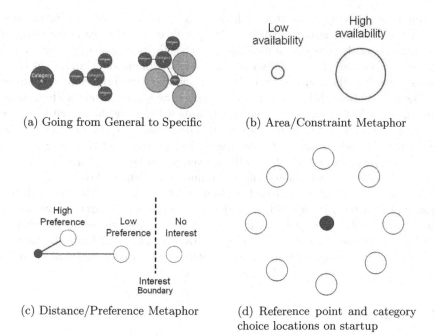

(a) Going from General to Specific

(b) Area/Constraint Metaphor

(c) Distance/Preference Metaphor

(d) Reference point and category choice locations on startup

Fig. 1. Visual Concepts and Metaphors

the potential choices are initially placed on an invisible circumference around this central reference point (Fig. 1d). The more items that are pulled towards the central reference point, the more crowded the area becomes, reflecting that more and more of the available constraint is being used up. When two or more circles within the interest boundary touch while one of them is being dragged, the touched circle(s) are pushed out of the way at the same distance from the reference point, or, when the area is too crowded, the least interesting touching item is pushed away from the reference point, thereby reducing its interest level and making space for the dragged incoming circle.

The VUMA tool employs a client/server architecture based on XML data models passed between a Java Servlet based back end and an Adobe Flash and ActionScript front end. The Flash movie, integrated into a website, enables the user to manipulate their model in accordance with the visual metaphor described above and the changes are sent to a Java-based planner on the back end. The resultant plan is returned to the front end immediately giving the user feedback. The Google Map API is also employed to generate a Google Map output of the personalised sightseeing itinerary.

3   Use Case and Future Work

When using the VUMA tool a user is initially presented with a view, similar to that seen in Fig. 1d, of the categories of tourist activities such as Museums, Art,

Shopping etc. The user can browse through these categories by clicking on them and expanding them into sub-categories or specific items. They can then assign an interest in a whole category, sub-category or specific item by dragging it towards the reference point. If the user would like to delete an option from his selection, they simply drag the item out of the interest boundary until the connecting interest line breaks. In addition, the user can change the size of the circles to indicate that they would like to allow more or less time for the specific activity. On any change in their interest configuration or time preferences, the planner will update automatically and reschedule the tourist's itinerary to reflect these changes. Finally, their personalised itinerary will be overlaid on Google Maps. The tourist can tweak and play with the interface to refine their planned day.

To date a favourable trial and evaluation of the current tourism oriented prototype has been conducted. In order to provide a comparative evaluation, the VUMA tool is currently being adapted as the user modeling interface to a long-running personalized eLearning course [3]. This will form the basis of a trial that will comparatively analyse both a text-based questionnaire and a visual approach to modelling learner interests.

References

1. Ardissono, L., Goy, A., Petrone, G., Segnan, M., Torasso, P.: INTRIGUE: Personalized Recommendations of tourist attractions for desktop and handset Devices. In Applied Artificial Intelligence: Special Issue on Artificial Intelligence for Cultural Heritage and Digital Libraries 17(8-9), 687–714 (2003)
2. Carmichael, D.J., Kay, J., Kummerfeld, R.J.: Personal Ontologies for feature selection in Intelligent Environment visualisations. In: Baus, J., Kray, C., Porzel, R. (eds.) AIMS 2004 - Artificial Intelligence in Mobile System, pp. 44–51 (2004)
3. Conlan, O., Wade, V.: Evaluation of APeLSAn Adaptive eLearning Service Based on the Multi-Model, Metadata-Driven Approach. In: De Bra, P.M.E., Nejdl, W. (eds.) AH 2004. LNCS, vol. 3137, pp. 291–295. Springer, Heidelberg (2004)
4. Espinoza, F., Hook, K.: An Interactive interface to an Adaptive Information System. In: Proceedings of the User Modelling for Information on the World Wide Web, a mini-workshop at the Fifth International Conference on User Modelling (1995)
5. Fink, J., Kobsa, A., Nill, A.: User-Oriented Adaptivity and Adaptability in the AVANTI project. In: Designing for the Web: Empirical Studies, Microsoft Usability Group, Redmond (WA) (1996)
6. Kass, R., Stadnyk, I.: Using User Models to Improve Organizational Information. In: Proceedings of the 3rd International Workshop on User Modeling, Dagstuhl, Germany (1992)
7. Kobsa, A.: User modeling: Recent Work, Prospects and Hazards. In: Schneider-Hufschmidt, M., Kühme, T., Malinowski, U. (eds.) Adaptive User Interfaces: Principles and Practice, pp. 111–128. North-Holland, Amsterdam (1993)
8. Uther, J., Kay, J.: VIUM, a web-based visualisation of large user models. In: Brusilovsky, P., et al. (eds.) UM 2003. LNCS, vol. 2702, pp. 198–202. Springer, Heidelberg (2003)

Bookmark Category Web Page Classification Using Four Indexing and Clustering Approaches

Chris Staff

University of Malta, Department of Artificial Intelligence, Malta
`chris.staff@um.edu.mt`

Abstract. Web browser bookmark files store records of web pages that the user would like to revisit. We use four methods to index and automatically classify documents referred to in 80 bookmark files, based on document title-only and full-text indexing and two clustering approaches. We evaluate the approaches by selecting a bookmark entry to classify from a bookmark file, re-creating a snapshot of the bookmark file to contain only entries created before the selected bookmark entry. The baseline algorithm is 39% accurate at rank 1 when the target category contains 7 entries. By fusing the recommendations of the 4 approaches, we reach 78.7% accuracy on average, recommending at most 3 categories.

1 Motivation

Web browsing software, such as Mozilla Firefox, includes a 'bookmark' or 'favorites' facility, for users to keep a record of web pages they are likely to want to revisit. These bookmark entries can be organised into related collections called 'folders' or categories. If bookmark files are organised, they can be an indication of a user's long-term and short-term interests. Bookmark files require user effort to keep organised, so they may become disorganised over time [1]. HyperBK2 assists users to keep bookmarks organised by recommending the category in which to store the entry for a web page being bookmarked. In section 2 we discuss similar systems. Our indexing and classification approach is discussed in section 3. The evaluation approach is described in section 5. Results are presented and discussed in section 6. Section 7 outlines our future work and conclusions.

2 Background and Similar Systems

Web pages are classified to automatically create web directories [4], and to assist users in bookmarking favourite web pages [2]. Bookmarking is a popular way to store and organise information for later use [1]. Bookmark managers support users to create and maintain bookmarks' lists, storing information locally, such as Conceptual Navigator[1], or centrally, such as Caribo [2]. Web pages are classified using supervised [3] or partially supervised [4] learning techniques.

---

[1] `http://www.abscindere.com/`

W. Nejdl et al. (Eds.): AH 2008, LNCS 5149, pp. 345–348, 2008.

3   HyperBK2's Indexing and Classification Approach

We take a partially supervised approach to clustering with web page entries in a user's bookmark categories acting as positive examples. We examine four approaches to indexing bookmark files and classifying web pages into bookmark categories. TITLE-ONLY is used as a baseline and we use TFIDF to create a forward index using the document title only. The forward indices for the other approaches, FULL-TEXT, CLUSTER, and SINGLETON, are built using the full-text. Next, we create the centroid(s) for each category. TITLE-ONLY and FULL-TEXT take the forward index of each category entry and merge them to create one centroid, calculating a term weight by summing the term frequencies (TF) of each term j_1 to j_k in each document, and multiplying it by the Normalised Document Frequency ($NDF_j = DF_j/\text{N}$), $\sum_{d=1}^{N} TF_{j_i,d} \times NDF_{j_i}$, where N is the number of documents in the category. This reduces the weight of terms that occur in few documents and maximises the weight of terms that occur in many. SINGLETON treats each document in a category as a centroid. For CLUSTER, we examine each bookmark entry in the order it was added to the category, adding it to an existing cluster within the category if it is similar enough (threshold arbitrarily set to 0.2), or creating a new cluster with it. We then create a centroid for each cluster in the category, where N is the number of documents in the cluster. A web page to be bookmarked is indexed using its title-only and the full-text and is classified according to its similarity to each of the category centroids. In both SINGLETON and CLUSTER, the category recommended for a page is the category containing the centroid to which it is most similar.

4   Bookmark File Properties and Bookmark Entries Selected for Classification

On average, the 80 anonymously collected bookmark files used in the evaluation have 23 categories, with a minimum of 1 and a maximum of 229. 8 files (10%) contain only one category. 28 files (35%) contain between 2 and 5 categories, 13 (16.25%) contain 11–20, 9 (11.25%) contain 21–50, 8 (10%) contain 51–100, and 4 (5%) files contain 101 or more categories.

5   Evaluation Approach

Each bookmark file is in the Netscape bookmark file format[2]. We use the bookmark entry creation date to re-create a snapshot of the file's state just prior to the addition of the bookmark to be classified. Bookmark entries are selected according to some criteria (see below), and we measure the classification accuracy to recommend their original category. The presence of the target category in ranks 1 to 5 is the accuracy at each rank. We select bookmark entries for

---

[2] http://msdn2.microsoft.com/en-us/library/Aa753582.aspx

Table 1. No. of bookmark entries classified

Run	1	2	3	4	5	6	7	8
ENTRY-TO-TAKE	2	4	6	7	8	8	9	11
NO-OF-CATEGORIES	5	5	5	5	5	1	5	5
Total Eligible Entries	1064	567	372	310	253	255	204	144

classification according to ENTRY-TO-TAKE, which is the nth entry in a category to be selected for classification, and NO-OF-CATEGORIES, which is the number of categories that must exist in a bookmark file snapshot for it to participate in the evaluation (normally 5). Table 1 gives the parameters for each run, and the number of bookmark entries selected for classification in each run (Total Eligible Entries).

6 Results

As expected, the baseline TITLE-ONLY approach gives poor results, with accuracy ranging from 26% at rank 1 to 34% at rank 5 on run 1, and rising to 40% accuracy at rank 1 and 55% accuracy at rank 5 on run 8. The FULL-TEXT approach has slightly better, but still poor, accuracy. However, we noted that the recommendations made by each approach tended to differ, and fusing the recommendations gives better results (table 2), although we would need to show the user on average seven recommended categories instead of five. The CLUSTER and SINGLETON approaches behaved similarly, so we experimented with fusing the recommendations of all four approaches, at rank 1, for run 5 only.

Table 2. Accuracy achieved by fusing FULL-TEXT and TITLE-ONLY recommendations (percent)

Run	1	2	3	4	5	6	7	8
Rank 1	37	43	52	56	59	59	53	53
Rank 2-5	...	...	...	...	...	...	...	...
Rank 5	58	66	75	79	80	80	76	76

6.1 Fusing Recommendations at Rank 1

We want a mechanism that has a good chance of recommending the correct category, without giving the user too many choices of category. We measure the frequency with which the different approaches recommend the same category at rank 1, and the recommendation accuracy when there is agreement between the different approaches, and compare the results obtained for run 5 (table 3). The following arrangements of agreement between the different approaches are possible: all four approaches give the same result (4-of-a-kind); three (three-of-a-kind) or two (two-of-a-kind) of the approaches make the same recommendation;

Table 3. Comparing merged recommendations at rank 1 with the baseline at rank 5

	4-of-a-kind	3-of-a-kind	2-of-a-kind	1-of-a-kind
Probability of observation:	30.6%	38.4%	21.4%	9.6%
Accuracy:	81.4%	64.2%	95.8%	40.6%
No. of recommended categories:	1	2	2 or 3	4
% improvement over baseline (52% accuracy @ rank 5):	+56.7%	+23.5%	+84.2%	−21.9%

or each approach makes a different recommendation (1-of-a-kind). Table 3 gives the different combinations, the frequency of observing them, their accuracy, the number of categories that would need to be shown to users, and the percentage improvement of the accuracy over the TITLE-ONLY baseline (at rank 5). When the approaches agree on 2 or more recommendations, it is correct on average 78.7% of the time, and HyperBK2 needs to recommend only 1, 2, or 3 categories. The approaches disagree totally 9.6% of the time, when accuracy is 40%.

7   Future Work and Conclusions

Fusing the recommendations of the four indexing and clustering approaches at rank 1 gives 78.7% accuracy, and we can show users just 1, 2, or 3 recommended categories 90.4% of the time. Our results are an improvement on CariBo's: a collaborative bookmark category recommendation system evaluated on the bookmark files of 15 users that has 60% accuracy at rank 5 [2]. In future work we will automatically generate a query from the category centroids to automatically find unseen documents that users consider relevant and worth bookmarking.

References

1. Abrams, D., Baecker, R., Chignell, M.: Information archiving with bookmarks: personal web space construction and organization. In: CHI 1998: Proceedings of the SIGCHI conference on Human factors in computing systems, pp. 41–48. ACM Press/Addison-Wesley Publishing Co, New York (1998)
2. Benz, D., Tso, K.H.L., Schmidt-Thieme, L.: Automatic bookmark classification - a collaborative approach. In: Proceedings of the 2nd Workshop in Innovations in Web Infrastructure (IWI2) at WWW 2006, Edinburgh, Scotland (May 2006)
3. Tsukada, M., Washio, T., Motoda, H.: Automatic web-page classification by using machine learning methods. In: Zhong, N., Yao, Y., Ohsuga, S., Liu, J. (eds.) WI 2001. LNCS (LNAI), vol. 2198, pp. 303–313. Springer, Heidelberg (2001)
4. Yu, H., Han, J., Chang, K.C.-C.: Pebl: Web page classification without negative examples. IEEE Transactions on Knowledge and Data Engineering 16(1), 70–81 (2004)

Personalization Using Ontologies and Rules

Thanh Tran[1], Haofen Wang[2], Steffen Lamparter[1], and Philipp Cimiano[1]

[1] Institute AIFB, Universität Karlsruhe, Germany
{dtr,sla,pci}@aifb.uni-karlsruhe.de
[2] Department of Computer Science & Engineering
Shanghai Jiao Tong University, Shanghai, 200240, China
{whfcarter}@apex.sjtu.edu.cn

Abstract. Adaptive hypermedia systems can alleviate information overload on the Web by personalising the delivery of resources to the user. These systems are however afflicted with difficulties in the acquisition of user data as well as the general lack of user control on and transparency of the systems' adaptive behavior. In this paper, we argue that the use of rules on top of ontologies can enable adaptive functionality that is both transparent and controllable for users. To this end, we sketch ODAS, a domain ontology for adaptive hypermedia systems, and a model for the specification of adaptation rules.

1 Introduction

The vast amount of available information leads to confusion for the average user, manifested by "comprehension and orientation problems" and a general "loss in information space" [8]. Targeting at this problem, there are *adaptable* systems that allow users to manually configure the resource provision. More advanced *adaptive* systems automatically identify the information that is relevant to the user.

This adaptive behaviour is typically realised in commercial systems by collaborative [4] and content-based filtering [5]. These filtering-based systems employ either a user or a content model to recommend relevant information. The main drawbacks of filtering-based approaches are well-known and have been discussed extensively in literatures [9]. Content-based approaches lead to *overspecialization*, resulting in too much recommendations of items of one specific type. In collaborative filtering, it is not possible to recommend a *new item* not yet rated by users. So, when there are *few user ratings*, only a small set of items can be considered by the system for recommendation.

However, these drawbacks can be addressed when combining user with content related data [1]. In the same line, further data such as the user task, the environment and the system have been incorporated. This extensive usage of contextual information as well as the adoption of advanced machine learning techniques can improve adaptive functionalities. However, apart from the inherent difficulties in *collecting contextual information*, adaptive systems are seen by the user as *black-boxes*, which give advices but cannot be questioned. The underlying algorithms are built on latent factors and heuristics that cannot be directly translated to explanations to facilitate the user in understanding the adaptive behavior.

In this paper, we propose ODAS as a domain ontology that improves the reuse and exchange of context information (Section 2). ODAS allows to capture different aspects

W. Nejdl et al. (Eds.): AH 2008, LNCS 5149, pp. 349–352, 2008.

of the adaptation context such as the user, the task, the system, the environment, and various aspects of the content—all contextual information that has been successfully used to achieve sophisticated adaptive behaviour. In addition, we propose a model for the specification of adaptation rules based on ODAS (Section 3). These rules capture the logic of the adaptive behavior in a declaratively manner and hence, facilitate the inspection and modification of the underlying adaptation model.

2   Towards a Domain Ontology for Adaptive Hypermedia Systems

In adaptive hypermedia systems, the use of contextual information of different types is crucial to achieve effective adaptive behavior. We have identified different aspects of the context, and incorporated into ODAS, an ontology we propose for the domain of adaptive hypermedia systems. It contains 138 subclass definitions, and a total of 504 axioms. They have been specified using the standard Ontology Web Language (OWL) recommended by the W3C. Figure 1 shows a portion of the ODAS concept hierarchy (black arrows indicate that some concepts have been omitted). ODAS extends the well-known top-level Suggested Upper Merged Ontology (SUMO). Also, ODAS has been aligned with related domain ontologies and taxonomies, namely the Public and Private Information (PAPI) [2], the IMS Learner Information Package (LIP), the Dublin Core metadata scheme, its extension Learning Object Metadata scheme (LOM) [7] and the MPEG-7 ontology [3]. We consider this adoption of existing standards as crucial to achieve acceptance by the community and interoperability for the domain. We will now focus on the main ODAS concepts that have been introduced to represent the context. They are highlighted by rectangles in Fig. 1 and, henceforth, will be referred to as *models*.

   Central to the representation of the adaptation context is the concept Application Interaction. Basically, an instance of this concept establishes a context by connecting different models. It tells the system that in an Application Environment (*environment model*) a particular Cognitive Agent (*user model*) is currently interacting with a Content embodied in a Content Bearing Object (*resource model*) of the Application (*system model*) to accomplish a task (*task model*). A task

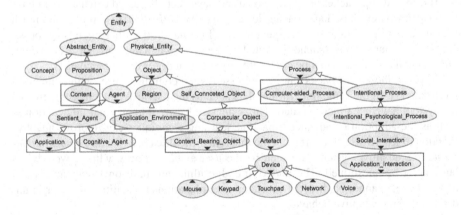

Fig. 1. ODAS Concept Hierarchy

that is supported by the system can be modelled as a `Computer-aided Process` which is a subconcept of `Composite Process`.

For the resource model, we have incorporated the DC metadata scheme, its extension LOM and the MPEG-7 ontology. Metadata and concepts defined in these standards have been adopted and formalized as ODAS concepts and properties.

The user model is reflected in the `User` concept. `Has credential`, `has read`, `knows`, `has interest` or `is able to` are some example properties that capture user characteristics. When developing this model, we have aligned the naming of the introduced concepts and properties with PAPI and LIP, which contain a large number of vocabulary for the representation of user data.

More details on the user and the resource model can be found in the adopted standards. The formal description of all the models discussed above can be found in the ontology available at `http://ontoware.org/projects/odas/`. We continue to elaborate on an adaptation model that exploits the formal semantics of these different models to achieve adaptive behaviour.

3   A Declarative Adaptation Model Based on Rules

This section demonstrates that the logic underlying the adaptive behavior can be explicitly captured by an adaptation model based on rules. We begin with a formalization of the adaptation model. Then, we discuss a concrete instantiation based on DL-safe rules.

Let $cc_i \in CC$ be the context conditions, $ac_i \in AC$ the adaptation conditions, $uc_i \in UC$ the user conditions, $ec_i \in EC$ the environment conditions and $r_i \in R$ the recommendations; CC, AC, UC, EC and R are pairwise disjoint; let $V = (EC \cup UC \cup AC \cup CC) \cup R$ be the set of all conditions and recommendations. An adaptation model is defined as a finite set of adaptation rules of the following form, where r_i^+ are positive head atoms, ec_i^+, uc_i^+, ac_i^+, cc_i^+ are positive body atoms and $\neg ec_i^-$, $\neg uc_i^-$, $\neg ac_i^-$ and $\neg cc_i^-$ are negative body atoms and $\oplus \in \{\vee, \wedge\}$:

$$
\begin{aligned}
(r_1^+ \wedge \ldots \wedge r_n^+) \leftarrow\ & [ec_1^+ \oplus \ldots \oplus ec_m^+ \wedge \neg ec_1^- \oplus \ldots \oplus \neg ec_l^-] \wedge \\
& [uc_1^+ \oplus \ldots \oplus uc_k^+ \wedge \neg uc_1^- \oplus \ldots \oplus \neg uc_x^-] \wedge \\
& [ac_1^+ \oplus \ldots \oplus ac_x^+ \wedge \neg ac_1^- \oplus \ldots \oplus \neg ac_z^-] \wedge \\
& [cc_1^+ \oplus \ldots \oplus cc_v^+ \wedge \neg cc_1^- \oplus \ldots \oplus \neg cc_w^-]
\end{aligned}
\tag{1}
$$

The rule head is a conjunction of recommendations. The rule body is a conjunction of atoms, which consists of an arbitrary combination (disjunction or conjunction) of positive and negative conditions. This formalization is independent of a concrete logical formalism. The actual semantics of the rules depends on the concrete formalism that is used to specify a particular adaptation model. We now elaborate on such a concrete adaptation model on the basis of DL-safe rules [6].

The example adaption rule (2) illustrates how ODAS concepts and properties can be used as conditions on recommendations. The context part is defined by the `Application Interaction` and its relations to other ontology entities. In our example, the current context is defined by the current interaction p (an instance of Reading that is a subconcept of `Application Interaction`), the current user u, and the content c the that user interacts with using v. These entities are tracked by the system and the concrete rule is constructed by inserting these entities into a rule template of the same form. The adaptation logic specified in the second part is based on the content. In the processing of the rule, the system computes possible bindings for the variables. It results in a set of recommended resources $?z$ of the type CBO. Their content are about an entity $?e$ that is also the subject of the current content c. The next parts might contain conditions related to the User and the Environment. They act as constraints on the recommendations produced by the adaptation part to ensure that they are indeed relevant. In the example, these constraints are related to the user: recommended resources must not have been read by the user and can be consumed because of the credentials the user owns.

$$
\begin{aligned}
needs(u, ?z) \leftarrow \ & [Reading(p) \wedge CognitiveAgent(u) \wedge agent(p, u) \wedge \\
& ContentAboutEntity(c1) \wedge resource(p, c1) \wedge] \\
& [ContentAboutRelation(?c2) \wedge CBO(?z) \wedge Entity(?e) \wedge \\
& hasSubject(c1, ?e) \wedge hasSubject(?c2, ?e) \wedge contain(?z, ?c2) \wedge] \\
& [Credential(?h) \wedge requiresCredential(?z, ?h) \wedge \\
& hasCredential(u, ?h) \wedge \neg hasRead(u, ?c2) \wedge]
\end{aligned}
\tag{2}
$$

Of course, adaption rules can be defined based on content, tasks and other additional constraints. However, a detailed discussion of these approaches is beyond the scope of this paper.

4   Conclusion

We have proposed ODAS as a domain ontology that can be used for the representation, exchange and reuse of contextual information. Based on ODAS, we have introduced an adaptation model, formalized in an abstract, formalism-independent way. A concrete model based on DL-safe rules have been shortly sketched. The system has been implemented and first evaluations suggest that the use of rules can result in effective adaptive behaviour, amendable to user assessment and manipulation.

References

1. Balabanovic, M., Shoham, Y.: Content-based, collaborative recommendation. Communications of the ACM 40(3), 66–72 (1997)
2. Farance, F.: PAPI Specification Version 5 – Learning Technology: Public and Private Information. Specification (November 1999)
3. Hunter, J.: Adding multimedia to the semantic web - building an mpeg-7 ontology. In: Proceedings of the First Semantic Web Working Symposium, Stanford, CA, USA (2001)
4. Konstan, J., Miller, B., Maltz, D., Herlocker, J., Gordon, L., Riedl, J.: GroupLens: applying collaborative filtering to Usenet news. Communications of the ACM 40(3), 77–87 (1997)
5. Lang, K.: NewsWeeder: learning to filter netnews. In: Proceedings of the 12th Int. Conf. on Machine Learning (ICML), Tahoe City, CA, USA, pp. 331–339 (1995)
6. Motik, B., Sattler, U., Studer, R.: Query Answering for OWL-DL with Rules. Journal of Web Semantics: Science, Services and Agents on the World Wide Web 3(1), 41–60 (2005)
7. Neven, F., Duval, E.: Reusable learning objects: a survey of LOM-based repositories. In: Proc. of the 10th ACM International Conf. on Multimedia, Juan-les-Pins, France (2002)
8. Nielsen, J., Lyngbaek, U.: Two field studies of hypermedia usability. In: McAleese, R., Green, C. (eds.) Hypertext: State of the Art, pp. 64–72 (1989)
9. Terveen, L., Hill, W.: Beyond Recommender Systems: Helping People Help Each Other. In: Carroll, J. (ed.) HCI In The New Millenium. Addison-Wesley, Reading (2001)

RSS-Based Interoperability for User Adaptive Systems

Yiwen Wang[2], Federica Cena[1], Francesca Carmagnola[1], Omar Cortassa[1],
Cristina Gena[1], Natalia Stash[2], and Lora Aroyo[2,3]

[1] Dipartimento di Informatica, Università di Torino
Corso Svizzera 185, Torino, Italy
{carmagnola, cena, cgena}@di.unito.it
[2] Eindhoven University of Technology, Computer Science
{n.v.stash, y.wang}@tue.nl
[3] VU University Amsterdam, Computer Science
l.m.aroyo@cs.vu.nl

Abstract. This paper presents an approach to exploit widely used tag
annotations to address two important issues in user-adaptive systems:
the cold-start problem and the integration of distributed user models.
The paper provides an example of re-use of user interaction data (tags)
generated by one application into another one in similar domains for
providing cross-system recommendations.

1 Introduction

The *Web 2.0* phenomenon introduced various social applications enabling online collaboration and encouraging the participation and contribution of spontaneous social networks. Users are increasingly involved in multiple Web 2.0
environments, such as Facebook.com, Flickr.com, Del.icio.us, etc. However these
applications are still "digital islands" in terms of personalized experience - not
truly interconnected in a way which allows users to capitalize on the full potential
of a distributed multi-application environment. Most of those services maintain
a different identity, e.g. login information, preferences or profile of users with a
limited integration of these data between different applications. However, tags
inserted by users could be extremely useful for adaptive web applications [2], e.g.
to enrich and extend the user model. User usually tags to highlight and organize
the items she is interested in, in order to retrieve them later. Thus the action
of tagging can be be analyzed in order to make interesting inferences on the
user model [3]. The exploitation of tags for improving the user model, requires
that systems could understand the semantics of the tags (e.g., applying suitable
strategies borrowed from automatic Word Senses Disambiguation).

The focus of this paper is to illustrate how existing fragments of user data in
the form of tags can be brought together with the help of explicit semantics, and
in this way allow for an adequate personalized experience across the boundaries
of particular applications. This poses a considerable number of technological
demands. Working in a distributed setting implies that personalization considers

W. Nejdl et al. (Eds.): AH 2008, LNCS 5149, pp. 353–356, 2008.

both *data-integration issues*, i.e. how the information from different applications
is related, as well as *context-modeling issues*, i.e. in which space/time/mode the
statements about a user are valid. In this paper we look at the data-integration
issue.Concretely, we provide a method for extracting, conceptualizing and linking
user tags contained in public RSS files generated in the interaction of users with
a social recommender system iCITY [3]. The tags are mapped to art-related
concepts used in the personalized museum applications CHIP [1].

The paper is structured as follows: Section 2 describes the architectural
specifics of iCITY and CHIP. These are further elaborated in Section 3 wherein
we present the conceptualization of iCITY tags, and the mapping of such tags
into CHIP user model. Finally, in section 4 we draw conclusions and future work
trends.

2   iCITY - CHIP User Interoperability Architecture

iCITY   is a social web-based, multi-device recommender system. It provides
suggestions on cultural events in the city of Turin, and allows users to insert
new events, comments and tags. Recommendations are based on the user model
enriched with tags, exploited to infer user features (see for details [3]). iCITY
has a modular architecture for extracting, maintaining, reasoning and exporting
user tags, which can be shared with other applications via a RSS feed. The main
components for interoperability are:

The *Importer Module* which is responsible for the extracting the tags, available
in form of RSS files, from external sources, e.g. web community like flickr.com and
del.icio.us. Once all the user tags have been extracted, they are used to obtain
useful information about user's interest and knowledge. In order to understand
their meaning, the system looks for correspondences between the tags and the
synsets and the *domains* of the MultiWordet database.

The *Exporter Module* which generates, for every user, a RSS file containing the
list of the events tagged by the user. For every event, the RSS file stores: the title,
the URL, the description, the reference to the event category and subcategory
in the iCITY event ontology, the reference to the Wordnet synsets and domains
linked to the subcategory, and finally the list of the tags associated by the user to
the event. In this way, a recipient system can import this RSS file containing the
tags and reason about them. The recipient can try to disambiguate the meaning
of tags thanks to the information, provided in the RSS file, about the event
subclass they belong to and the references to WordNet domain and synset.

The **CHIP** sytem[1] illustrates a personalization infrastructure for semantically
enriched museum collections. We use the digital database of the Rijksmuseum
ARIA[2] (750 master pieces) and its mappings to external vocabularies [1], namely
the three Getty vocabularies[3], as well as the subject classification Iconclass[4]. The

---

[1] http://www.chip-project.org/demo
[2] http://rijksmuseum.nl/aria/
[3] http://www.getty.edu/research/conducting research/vocabularies
[4] http://www.iconclass.nl/libertas/ic?style=index.xsl

use of common vocabularies provides the new data repository a relational and hierarchical structure for reasoning and making recommendations. Based on this semantics-enriched data model, we have implemented a set of Web-based tools [1], e.g. Artwork Recommender and Online Tour Wizard, and a PDA-based Mobile Tour Guide to collect user input both in the virtual museum space on the Web and in the corresponding physical museum. All user interactions in each of the tools are stored in a user profile, categorized in four clusters: *personal* characteristics, e.g. name, age, gender, which could be initialized by either importing an existing FOAF RDF profile or via an OpenID channel linking the CHIP login data to an existing login information of third party Web application; *social* information initialized by FOAF properties, e.g knows, openid, organization, OnlineAccount, user *ratings* of artworks and topics in terms of VRA Core properties[5], e.g. work, creator, title, creationDate, creationSite, subject; and user *iteraction* with, e.g. virtualTours.

3   iCITY-CHIP User Tag Interoperability

In this interoperability use case, an open API is adopted to request and link user data. Once the user personal (login) information is aligned between CHIP and iCITY, based on the RSS feed we maintain a dynamic mapping of iCITY user tags to the CHIP vocabulaty set (ARIA shared with Getty and IconClass) and general purpose lexical data such as WordNet. This will populates users' profiles (especially first-time users) in CHIP and enable instantly generate recommendations in the Rijksmuseum collection.

The mapping is realized in two steps: (i) to identify the type (e.g. creator, place, material, etc.) of iCity tags as a simple restriction; (ii) to map tags to CHIP art concepts by using the Simple Knowledge Organization System (SKOS) Core Mapping Vocabulary Specifications[6]. For the first stage alignment, the mappings are still based on the lexical match of tags. With a few additional simple restrictions by applying the type of tags, a lexical match gives more confidence to generate a strong semantic match [4]. For example, the semantic equivalence between iCITY tag "Amsterdam" and Getty Thesaurus of Geographic Names (TGN) creationSite "Amsterdam" is expressed with *skos:equivalentConcept* for the type of place. And *skos:narrower* for the type material points from tag "photo" to concepts "Photo collotype", "Photo Gelatin silver print" and "Photo Bromide print" in the Rijksmuseum ARIA hierarchical specialization.

4   Conclusion and Future Work

In this paper we have presented an approach to exploit widely used tag annotations to address two important issues in user-adaptive systems in the cultural heritage domain: the cold-start problem and the integration of distributed user

---

[5] http://www.vraweb.org/projects/vracore4/index.html
[6] http://www.w3.org/2004/02/skos/

profiles. We have sketched a scenario, in which user tagging about cultural events gathered by iCITY is used to enrich the user profile for generating personalized recommendations of artworks and topics in CHIP. To realize the tagging interoperability, first we have investigated the problems that arise in mapping user tags to shared vocabularies (ontologies). With the help of SKOS matching operators we propose an approach to deal with the possible misalignment of tags and domain-specific ontologies. Further, we need to address the mapping of user tags to event ontologies (iCITY) and possibly to multiple concepts in the domain-specific ontologies. Further, we need to close the loop by allowing import of the CHIP user profile into iCITY and in this way to refine the iCITY user model.

References

1. Aroyo, L., Stash, N., Wang, Y., Gorgels, P., Rutledge, L.: Chip demonstrator: Semantics-driven recommendations and museum tour generation. In: Aberer, K., Choi, K.-S., Noy, N., Allemang, D., Lee, K.-I., Nixon, L., Golbeck, J., Mika, P., Maynard, D., Mizoguchi, R., Schreiber, G., Cudré-Mauroux, P. (eds.) ISWC 2007. LNCS, vol. 4825, pp. 879–886. Springer, Heidelberg (2007)
2. Brusilovsky, P., Kobsa, A., Nejdl, W. (eds.): The Adaptive Web, Methods and Strategies of Web Personalization. LNCS, vol. 4321. Springer, Heidelberg (2007)
3. Carmagnola, F., Cena, F., Cortassa, O., Gena, C., Torre, I.: Towards a tag-based user model: How can user model benefit from tags? In: Conati, C., McCoy, K., Paliouras, G. (eds.) UM 2007. LNCS (LNAI), vol. 4511, pp. 445–449. Springer, Heidelberg (2007)
4. Omelayenko, B., Tordai, A., Schreiber, G.: Thesaurus and metadata alignment for a semantic e-culture application. In: Semantic Authoring, Annotation and Knowledge Markup Workshop (2007)

Assisting in Reuse of Adaptive Hypermedia Creator's Models

Nadjet Zemirline[1], Yolaine Bourda[1], Chantal Reynaud[2], and Fabrice Popineau[3]

[1] SUPELEC/Department of Computer Science, Plateau de Moulon, 3 rue Joliot-Curie,
91192 Gif sur yvette Cedex, France
{Nadjet.Zemirline,Yolaine.Bourda}@supelec.fr
[2] Université Paris-Sud XI, CNRS (LRI) & INRIA - Saclay Île-de-France / Projet Gemo,
Bât. G, 4 rue Jacques Monod, Parc Orsay Université, 91893 Orsay Cedex, France
chantal.reynaud@lri.fr
[3] SUPELEC/Metz Campus, 2 rue Édouard Belin 57070 Metz, France
Fabrice.Popineau@supelec.fr

Abstract. The design of Adaptive Hypermedia is a difficult task which can be made easier if generic systems and AH creators' models are reused. We address this design problem in the setting of the GLAM platform only made up of generic components. We present a rule-based approach helping an AH creator in reusing its user and domain models to create a specific adaptive hypermedia. This semi-automatic approach takes the creator's models as specialisations of GLAM generic models and requires the creator to express a minimum set of mappings between his models and the generic ones. The process results in a merged model consisting of the generic and the corresponding specific model. This merged model can be used by the adaptation model.

Keywords: adaptive hypermedia, assisting tools, user and domain modelling.

1 Introduction

Although adaptive hypermedia have proved their benefits, particularly in the educational domain [1], authoring an adaptive hypermedia for a particular need is still a difficult task [2]. Some freely available adaptive hypermedia systems, which are, in fact adaptive educational hypermedia systems, like AHA![1], come with an authoring tool but they required to learn how to use the system and it is necessary to adapt the resources to the format used by the system. Some systems [3,4] can translate resources from one particular adaptive system to another one. But, all those systems have developed "ad-hoc" solutions closed to the adaptive systems used and are not applicable to other adaptive systems. If a user wants to use a specific AH system, he needs to translate his models into the specific format understood by the system and to use the vocabulary specific to that system. Furthermore, he also needs to translate all the instantiations of his models (i.e. the resources and their metadata). We think that this task is tedious and time-consuming and we want to avoid it. Our objective is to

---

[1] http://aha.win.tue.nl/

W. Nejdl et al. (Eds.): AH 2008, LNCS 5149, pp. 357–360, 2008.
© Springer-Verlag Berlin Heidelberg 2008

allow the creator of an adaptive hypermedia to reuse his models (his vocabulary) and his models' instantiations without any change of format or vocabulary.

We are currently working on the GLAM platform [5] defined for an entire class of adaptive hypermedia systems. The platform is made of a generic adaptation model relying on generic user and domain models. Specific systems can be obtained by specializing the GLAM generic user and domain models. The main steps of the approach that we propose are the following: (1) Specification, by the AH creator, of equivalence and specialization mappings between classes of the generic and the specific models, merging the whole generic GLAM model and the mapped classes of the specific model (together with the associated mapping links) in order to obtain a new model. (2) Automatic computation of additional mappings between the classes. (3) Automatic computation of mappings between relations and properties. (4) Validation by the AH creator of the deductions made by the system.

In this paper, we focus on step 3, steps 1, 2 and 4 are detailed in [6]. In section 2, we describe the structural knowledge applicable to whatever the model is (user or domain model) to deduce automatically mappings between relation and properties. As the models are expressed in OWL[2], structural knowledge has been modelled in a meta-model [6] based on the OWL meta-model. In section 3, we describe inferences made on the knowledge modelled in our meta-model.

2 Structural Knowledge

The exploitation of structural knowledge aims at defining the nature of mapping links between OWL properties which are referred to in this paper by relations because relations (in its usual meaning) and attributes are both represented by properties in OWL. In our approach, the deduction of mappings between relations is inferred from information characterizing the compatibility of the relations. A mapping between two relations is possible only when the relations are compatible. A mapping may be either a potential or a probable link according to the compatibility information (inferred from mappings between classes and from properties restrictions) associated to the mapped relations. We will note $R_{m,d,j}$ to represent the relation j with the domain d in the model m.

Definition 1. Two relations $R_{s,i,j}$ and $R_{g,k,l}$ are linked by a *potential link* if a mapping is defined between their domain and between their range.

Definition 2. Restrictions relative to two relations $R_{s,i,j}$ and $R_{g,k,l}$ are *compatible* if those relations are linked by a potential link and if:

1. $(\text{Cardinality}_{max}(R_{s,i,j}) \leq \text{Cardinality}_{max}(R_{g,k,l})$
   and $\text{Cardinality}_{min}(R_{s,i,j}) \geq \text{Cardinality}_{min}(R_{g,k,l}))$
   or $\text{Cardinality}_{value}(R_{s,i,j}) = \text{Cardinality}_{value}(R_{g,k,l})$.

   or

2. $R_{s,i,j}$ and $R_{g,k,l}$ are both functional or not (resp. inverse functional or not) or $R_{s,i,j}$ is functional (resp. inverse functional) and $R_{g,k,l}$ is not.

---

[2] http://www.w3.org/TR/owl-features/

Definition 3. Two relations $R_{s,i,j}$ and $R_{g,k,l}$ are linked by a *probable link* if they are linked by a potential link and if their restrictions are compatible.

Probable links can be either equivalence or specialization links according to the nature of mapping between the classes corresponding to the range and according to the restrictions associated to the relations.

Definition 4. A probable link between $R_{s,i,j}$ and $R_{g,k,l}$ is an *equivalence probable link* if the two ranges are linked by an equivalence relation and if they have the same restrictions.

Definition 5. A probable link between $R_{s,i,j}$ and $R_{g,k,l}$ is a *specialization probable link* if a mapping is defined between their range but the restrictions on $R_{s,i,j}$ are stronger than those on $R_{g,k,l}$ or if they have the same restrictions but the $R_{s,i,j}$ range is a subcategory of the $R_{g,k,l}$ range.

3 Deduction Rules

In this section, we give the rules, expressed in SWRL[3], to deduce mappings between relations of the generic and specific models. The rules derive from the definitions given in section 2 and are based on the proposed meta-model.

Deducing a potential mapping. The rule inferring a potential mapping derives directly from Definition 1. It uses mappings between a class of the generic model and one of the specific model.

Deducing compatible restrictions. We defined 9 rules which group all cases where a relation of the generic model Pg and one of the specific model Ps are linked by a potential link and have compatible restrictions. For example the rule deducing compatible functional properties is

```
potentialLinkedProperties(?Pg,?Ps) ^ functional(?Pg,false) ^
functional(?Ps,false) → sameFunctionality(?Pg,?Ps) ^
compatibleFunctionality(?Pg,?Ps)
```

Deducing a probable mapping. The rule inferring a probable mapping derives directly from Definition 3.

```
potentiallyLinkedProperties(?Pg,?Ps) ^
compatibleRestriction(?Pg,?Ps)
→probablyLinkedProperties(?Pg,?Ps)
```

Two kinds of probable mappings are distinguished. A rule arising directly from Definition 4 allows deducing an equivalence probable mapping link. The deduction of a specialization probable mapping link can be expressed by the following formula: *Probable link ∧ (Restrictive range ∨ restrictive functional ∨ restrictive inverse functional ∨ restrictive cardinality).* As the disjunction operator doesn't exist in SWRL, here is one of these four rules needed to deduce a specialization probable link:

```
probablyLinkedProperties(?Ps,?Pg) ^ range(?Pg,?Rg) ^
range(?Ps,?Rs) ^ mapping(?Rg,?Rs)
→probablySubProperties(?Pg,?Ps)
```

---

[3] http://www.w3.org/Submission/SWRL/

Deducing an inconsistent mapping. Inconsistencies relate to potential mappings and derive directly from restrictions. We defined 5 rules which group all cases where a relation of the generic model is more restrictive than the potential one mapped with.

4 Conclusion and Future Work

We have proposed a solution enabling the user to create an adaptive hypermedia with the GLAM system re-using his own models and consequently his own resources and their metadata. In this paper, we detailed the automatic deduction step of mappings and potential inconsistencies between relation and properties of the two models. This step is based on specified mappings between classes and on additional mappings automatically deduced. Then the AH creator has only to validate the system proposals. We have implemented a prototype using the Protégé platform and its plug in: OWL Protégé, SWRL Tab and SWRLJessTab, it has allowed us to make some experiments in which we have personally played the role of an AH creator.

We now intend to complete the implementation in integrating the developed components and to design an ergonomic IHM. It can also be interesting to consider the relations between the adaptation rules and the user and domain model. We envision an extension enabling AH creators to interact with the adaptation model. Finally, our solution is based on the use of OWL to express the models and it is not dependent on the use of GLAM, so we plan to apply it to other systems.

References

1. Brusilovsky, P.: Adaptive hypermedia. User Modeling and User Adapted Interaction 11(1-2), 87–110 (2001)
2. Celik, I., Stewart, C., Ashman, H.: Interoperability as an Aid to Authoring: Accessing User Models in Multiple AEH Systems. In: 4th Adaptive and Adaptable Educational Hypermedia workshop at AH, pp. 71–85. Springer, Heidelberg (2006)
3. Cristea, A.I., Smits, D., De Bra, P.: Writing MOT, Reading AHA! - converting between an authoring and a delivery system for adaptive educational hypermedia. In: A3EH workshop at AIED 2005, Amsterdam, The Netherlands (2005)
4. Cristea, A., Stewart, C.: Automatic Authoring of Adaptive Educational Hypermedia. In: Ma, Z. (ed.) Web-Based Intelligent e-Learning Systems: Technologies and Applications, pp. 24–55. Information Science Publishing (IDEA group) (2006)
5. Jacquiot, C., Bourda, Y., Popineau, F., Delteil, A., Reynaud., C.: GLAM: A generic layered adaptation model for adaptive hypermedia systems. In: Wade, V.P., Ashman, H., Smyth, B. (eds.) AH 2006. LNCS, vol. 4018, pp. 131–140. Springer, Heidelberg (2006)
6. Zemirline, N., Reynaud, C., Bourda, Y.: Aide à la conception d'un hypermédia adaptatif au sein de la plateforme GLAM, rapport interne, Supélec, France (2007)

Convergence of Web and TV Broadcast Data for Adaptive Content Access and Navigation

Pieter Bellekens, Kees van der Sluijs, Lora Aroyo*, and Geert-Jan Houben**

Technische Universiteit Eindhoven
P.O. Box 513, NL 5600 MB, Eindhoven, The Netherlands
{p.a.e.bellekens,k.a.m.sluijs,l.m.aroyo,g.j.houben}@tue.nl

Abstract. iFanzy is a personalized TV guide application aiming at offering users television content in a personalized and context-sensitive
way. It consists of a client-server system with multiple clients and devices such that the user can ubiquitously use TV set-top box, mobile
phone and Web-based applications to select and receive personalised TV
content. TV content and background data from various heterogeneous
sources is integrated to provide a transparent knowledge structure, which
allows the user to navigate and browse the vast content sets nowadays
available. Semantic Web techniques are applied for enriching and aligning Web data and (live) broadcast content. The resulting RDF/OWL
knowledge structure is the basis for iFanzy's main functionality, like semantic search of the broadcast content and execution of context-sensitive
recommendations.

1   Introduction

Current Web-based applications are characterized by the fact that users use
many different types of devices to access content. As a consequence, engineering
such applications has to respect the different environments and capabilities to
ensure that the application adapts to the circumstances. A big advantage for the
purpose of personalization is that the user spends more time with these devices
than with the PC alone which gives more information to assess and model the
user's situation. In the TV broadcasting domain the combination of multiple
devices such as mobile phone and TV with multiple applications accessible via
the Web shows how access to content will evolve [1].

At the same time we see the integration of background information that relates to TV content which can help the user in selecting and using this data.
Much of this information is available via the Web, which leads to the significant trend that television viewers use their PC for the larger part of the TV
content access process[2]. While advantageous this trend also implies an information overload that cries out for adaptation to the user's knowledge, preferences
and situation. Personalization in this setting can benefit from several different

---

* Also affiliated with Vrije Universiteit, Amsterdam, the Netherlands.
** Also affiliated with Vrije Universiteit Brussel, Brussels, Belgium.

W. Nejdl et al. (Eds.): AH 2008, LNCS 5149, pp. 361–365, 2008.

kinds of integration: friends or relatives watching TV content together, integrating (background) data from different connected applications and integrating temporal and spatial-specific viewpoints in context modeling.

In this paper we present iFanzy - a personalized TV guide application aiming at offering users television content in a personalized and context-sensitive way (developed in collaboration with Stoneroos Interactive TV, Ltd.[1]). It is currently available as a Web application and a TV set-top box front-end, while a mobile version is under development. In a client-server model, iFanzy acts as a client that uses a server framework called SenSee [3] as underlying data source. This takes care of content integration, user modeling and content recommendation.

Several other TV recommender systems exist, e.g. AVATAR [4] which has a focus on reasoning over TV content metadata and user preferences. iFanzy differs from AVATAR mainly because of our focus on combining and integrating the information from several large and live datasources. Many systems exist that focus on the recommendation part, for example the movie recommendation application MovieLens[2] that uses collaborative filtering. For an overview of different recommendation strategies e.g. refer to [5].

2   Semantics-Based Content Integration

The use of semantics is an important instrument in order to combine and integrate the content from different applications and in this way to enhance personalization. In this sense iFanzy represents a large class of multi-device applications with a high degree of interactivity where semantics is key to effective integration [3]. In our work we have applied a general strategy that supports this large class of semantics-based applications, illustrated here in terms of iFanzy.

Step 1: Making TV metadata available in RDF/OWL
As a first step we make the relevant metadata from various data sources available in RDF/OWL. In the current iFanzy demonstrator we use three live data sources, online TV guides in XMLTV format (e.g. 1.2M triples for the daily updated programs), online movie databases such as IMDB in custom XML format (e.g. 8M triples for 12K movies and trailers from Videodetective.com), and broadcast metadata available from BBC-backstage in TV-Anytime (http://www.tv-anytime.org/) format (e.g. 92K triples, daily updated). Next to the live data we also use the W3C OWL Time Ontology[3] to represent time information.

Step 2: Making relevant vocabularies available in RDF/OWL
Having the metadata available, it is also necessary to make relevant vocabularies available in RDF/OWL. In iFanzy we did this in a SKOS-based manner for the genre vocabularies (resulting in 5K triples), and for the TV-Anytime Genres, the XMLTV Genres, and the IMDB Genres. All these genres play a role in the

---

[1] http://www.stoneroos.nl/, http://ifanzy.nl/

[2] http://www.movielens.org/

[3] http://www.w3.org/TR/2006/WD-owl-time-20060927/

classification of the TV content and the user's likings (supporting the recommendation). We also used WordNet 2.0 (http://www.w3.org/2006/03/wn/wn20/) as published by W3C (2M triples) and the locations used in IMDB (60K triples).

Step 3: Aligning and enriching vocabularies/metadata
Here we did (1) alignment of Genre vocabularies, (2) semantic enrichment of the Genre vocabulary in TV-Anytime, and (3) semantic enrichment of TV metadata with IMDB movie metadata.

First, aligning the Genre vocabularies was a small semi-automated exercise in which several translations were specified towards the TV-Anytime vocabulary, such as the associations between `xmltv:documentaire` and `tva:documentary`, between `imdb:thriller` and `tva:thriller`, and between `imdb:sci-fi` and `tva:science_fiction`.

Second, for the semantic enrichment of the *Genre* vocabulary,

- based on the original XML Term hierarchy, `skos:narrower` relations are introduced, for example between `tva:news` and `tva:sport_news`.
- based on partial label matching, `skos:related` relations are defined, for example between `tva:sport_news` and `tva:sport`.
- background design knowledge has been the motivation for distinguishing `skos:related` relations between siblings, such as between `tva:rugby` and `tva:american_football`.

Third, in terms of semantic enrichment of the TV metadata (that can come from different grabbers in different languages) we use from IMDB the country AKA-titles to link each grabbed program to the associated concept in IMDB.

Step 4: Using the resulting RDF/OWL graph for recommendations
To recommend TV programs or movies, the resulting RDF/OWL graph is extended with the user model in a format such that the eventual RDF/OWL knowledge structure can be directly used for the recommendation. What happens is that when user rates a program P, implicitly program P is rated as well as all programs which are related in the knowledge structure. Moreover all programs with a genre that is related to a genre of P are rated, as well as the genres themselves via `skos:related` and `skos:narrower` relations. In `imdb:persons` all actors, directors and persons associated with P are rated. In this way, ratings are added to the user model, within the user's context.

3   iFanzy Architecture

An important requirement for iFanzy is to provide this service in a ubiquitous and responsive way, e.g. independent of the platform used or the current location of the user. Therefore we opted for a client-server architecture, where the user uses the iFanzy front-end with different devices connected to the SenSee server. All heavy computation work is done at the server side. This ensures that virtually any machine (including mobiles and set-top boxes) that can connect through the Internet can be linked to the system.

The server deals with very large data collections of browsable content - hundreds of thousands of programs from various sources, as well as knowledge structures used for recommendation and semantic search. Thus, SenSee should handle the concurrent use of hundreds of potential users per server. Although we see many data-intensive Semantic Web applications, scalability is still an important research issue for truly real-time Web-applications. In order to reach the desired scalability we performed many optimization steps [6].

The recommendation part depends heavily on the quality of the system's knowledge of the user. To cope with the cold start, we devised a statistical recommendation algorithm to find the most relevant programs based on a basic set of user registration data. Further, iFanzy's training algorithm allows to refine the user data from the user's behaviour and explicit feedback. The Web client, for instance, tracks the clicks made on specific content items and the search terms used. The set-top box on the other hand, monitors and stores the viewing behaviour. The user can also utter specific likings (explicit feedback) to inform the system what he/she appreciates.

4   Conclusion and Future Work

Different versions of the different clients and server systems have been implemented and successfully evaluated in collaboration with our commercial partner Stoneroos. As future work we are redesigning the iFanzy frontend and SenSee backend, based on our practical experiences, and we plan a next performance optimization step with parallel query evaluation and load-balancing strategies. Currently, an evaluation trial with 500 set-top boxes in Dutch households is prepared together with Stoneroos.

References

1. Bjorkman, M., Aroyo, L., Bellekens, P., Dekker, T., Loef, E., Pulles, R.: Personalised home media centre using semantically enriched tv-anytime content. In: EuroITV 2006 Conference, pp. 156–165 (2006)
2. Aroyo, L., Bellekens, P., Bjorkman, M., Houben, G.J.: Semantic-based framework for personalised ambient media. Multimedia Tools and Applications 36(1-2), 71–87 (2008)
3. Bellekens, P., van der Sluijs, K., Aroyo, L., Houben, G.J.: Engineering semantic-based interactive multi-device web applications. In: Baresi, L., Fraternali, P., Houben, G.-J. (eds.) ICWE 2007. LNCS, vol. 4607, pp. 328–342. Springer, Heidelberg (2007)
4. Blanco Fernández, Y., Pazos Arias, J.J., Gil Solla, A., Ramos Cabrer, M., López Nores, M.: Bringing together content-based methods, collaborative filtering and semantic inference to improve personalized tv. In: 4th European Conference on Interactive Television (EuroITV 2006) (May 2006)

5. van Setten, M.: Supporting people in finding information: Hybrid recommender systems and goal-based structuring. Telematica Instituut Fundamental Research Series, No.016 (TI/FRS/016). Universal Press (2005)
6. Bellekens, P., van der Sluijs, K., van Woensel, W., Casteleyn, S., Houben, G.J.: Achieving efficient access to large integrated sets of semantic data in web applications. In: Proceedings of the 8th International Conference on Web Engineering (ICWE 2008) (to be published, 2008)

Recommending Background Information and Related Content in Web 2.0 Portals

Andreas Nauerz[1], Birgitta König-Ries[2], and Martin Welsch[1,2]

[1] IBM Research and Development, Schönaicher Str. 220, 71032 Böblingen, Germany
{andreas.nauerz|martin.welsch}@de.ibm.com
[2] University Jena, Institute of Computer Science, 07743 Jena, Germany
koenig@informatik.uni-jena.de

Abstract. Modern Web 2.0 Portals have become highly collaborative participation platforms. Users do not only retrieve information, they even contribute content. Due to the large number of different users contributing, Web 2.0 sites grow quickly and, most often, in a more uncoordinated way than centrally controlled sites. Finding relevant information can hence become a tedious task. We will demonstrate a solution allowing for the in-place, in-context recommendation of background information with respect to a certain term or topic and for the recommendation of related content being available in the system. Our solution is based on the extraction of enriched units of information which we either gain automatically via unstructured data analysis or by analyzing user-applied annotations. Our main concepts have been embedded and evaluated within IBM's WebSphere Portal.

1 Introduction

Years ago the World Wide Web was basically a read-only media. Authors put their static documents onto web servers which users read via their browsers. In contrast, in today's Web 2.0 world content is created by entire user communities. Users do not only retrieve information anymore, they contribute content. Due to the large number of different users contributing, Web 2.0 sites grow quickly and, most often, in a more uncoordinated way than centrally controlled sites. Finding relevant information can hence become a tedious task.

We will present solutions allowing users to find relevant information, either background information w.r.t. a certain topic or related content being available in the system, easier.

Our system identifies units of information of certain types in text fragments usually residing inside portlets (fragments delivering content) and automatically wraps them into semantic tags. In our novel approach we connect the semantically tagged units of information to other (external) information sources to recommend interesting background information. For instance, a location might be connected to Google maps, a person to the company's employee directory etc. We further allow the tagged units of information to be annotated by users

W. Nejdl et al. (Eds.): AH 2008, LNCS 5149, pp. 366–369, 2008.
© Springer-Verlag Berlin Heidelberg 2008

manually to perform an even more fine-granular categorization of content. In addition to linking to background information, we use the information we obtain via automatic semantic annotation extraction and user-generated annotations to recommend related content.

2   Related Work

Providing background information or interlinking units of information is based on the ability to either allow users or programmatic, automated, annotators to annotate these units. We have described the first approach in [1] already. The second approach is based on information extraction from unstructured machine-readable documents. Although the approach to perform the extraction is often differing, most papers in this area regard information extraction as a proper way to automatically extract semantic annotations from web content. Many of these systems are based on machine learning techniques, e.g. [2].

3   Concepts

In the following we will first shortly explain how we extract units of information (usually textual fragments) such as persons, locations, etc. either automatically or by allowing users to perform annotations. We will afterwards outline how we use this information to recommend in-place, in-context background information and related content.

3.1   Extracting Enriched Units of Information

To extract enriched information about units of information, we allow for the usage of three different mechanisms:

Automated Tagging. Here the system analyzes markup generated by the Portal to find occurrences of identifiable units of information of certain types such as persons, locations, etc., and wraps these into semantic tags. We have integrated the UIMA framework [1] and written customized analysis engines able to identify such units.

Semi-automated Tagging. If the system cannot unambiguously identify the type of a unit of information it still allows users to mark it and tell the system of what type it is. We call this process semi-automated tagging. For instance, if we find a fragment "Paris H. was sighted leaving a Hotel in Paris" it becomes difficult for the system to determine whether *Paris* is a name or a location. The user can then mark the corresponding units and tell the system their type. The units are then wrapped into a semantic tag exactly as outlined before.

---

[1] http://www.research.ibm.com/UIMA/

Manual Annotating. Moreover, our system allows semantically tagged units of information to be annotated manually again. E.g., if the name of three persons *Alice, Bob,* and *Charly* often appear somewhere in the Portal system, e.g. in blog- or wiki portlets, our system automatically determines these fragments to be of type person, wraps them into semantic tags and allows for advanced interaction with these units of information. Our tag engine allows these enriched fragments to be annotated e.g. with the term *project-x* which indicates that all three persons are somehow related to this project. This means that the options for manual annotating allow for an even more fine-granular categorization of units of information.

3.2 Recommending Background Information

As said, in today's Web 2.0 world content is created by entire user communities. Different users use different terms to describe the same things. Some terms might be well-understood by most users, some might not. Thus, looking up terms is needed more frequently and becomes a tedious task. When reading web sites, users want background information at their fingertips. If they do not understand what an abbreviation or a term stands for, who a certain person actually is, or where a certain city is located, they want to be able to retrieve this information as easily and quickly as possible. They do not want to fire up a search engine to search for another site from which they could probably get the information they want, but rather be provided with that information directly, in-place. We provide an environment which unobtrusively enriches the units of information to allow for such look-ups throughout different information sources.

Fig. 1 shows our system in action: it illustrates how a fictious person name (*John Doe*), a location (*Stuttgart*), and a currency have been identified within a text fragment residing in a portlet and are visualized to the user. Pop-ups provide the users with background information.

3.3 Recommending Related Content

Analyzing occurrences of semantically tagged units of information also allows us to recommend related content. For instance, if the term *WebSphere Portal* is identified in a news portlet and hence semantically tagged as a product name our system would provide users with background information about WebSphere Portal probably by linking to the product site. But, within a Portal system, the same term might occur at many other places, e.g. in a wiki portlet where users have posted some best practices when working with this product, in a blog where users have commented on the product and so forth. We track all occurrences and recommend them as related content as soon as the user interacts with one single occurrence.

This can even be taken one step further. As mentioned above, we allow users to annotate already semantically tagged units of information. This way we can recommend related content not only by having identified "exactly matching" occurrences of semantically tagged units of information, but also by having identified similarly annotated units of information. E.g., *Alice, Bob,* and *Charly* might have

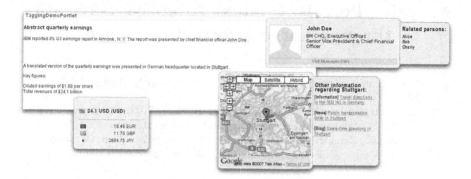

Fig. 1. Recommending background information and related content

been tagged as persons and manually annotated with the term *project-x* to express their relationship to this project. This allows us to recommend any two of these users as related "content" w.r.t. the third user, just because they all seem to be assigned to the same project. This can be useful if a user tries to contact a user who is currently unreachable as it allows us to recommend backups.

Fig. 1 shows how we can recommend related information for the detected unit of information *Stuttgart* and *John Doe* (other people probably working in the same team, on the same project etc.).

4   Demonstration

In our demonstration, we will present a typical Web Portal embedded in IBM's WebSphere Portal. We will demonstrate how the system automatically extracts units of information via unstructured data analysis and how users can annotate units of information that have not been recognized by the system. We will show how we connect these units to other information sources to provide users with in-place, in-context background information. We will also illustrate how we can recommend related content by tracking occurrences of exactly matching or similar annotations.

IBM and WebSphere are trademarks of International Business Machines Corporation in the United States, other countries or both. Other company, product and service names may be trademarks or service marks of others.

References

1. Nauerz, A., Welsch, M. (Context)Adaptive Navigation in Web Portals. In: Proc. of the Intl. IADIS WWW/Internet Conference 2007, Vila Real, Portugal (October 2007)
2. Dill, S., Eiron, N., Gibson, D., Gruhl, D., Guha, R.V., Jhingran, A., Kanungo, T., Rajagopalan, S., Tomkins, A., Tomlin, J.A., Zien, J.Y.: Semtag and seeker: bootstrapping the semantic web via automated semantic annotation. In: WWW, pp. 178–186 (2003)

Adaptive Portals: Context Adaptive Navigation through Large Information Spaces

Andreas Nauerz[1], Martin Welsch[1,2], and Birgitta König-Ries[2]

[1] IBM Research and Development, Schönaicher Str. 220, 71032 Böblingen, Germany
{andreas.nauerz,martin.welsch}@de.ibm.com
[2] University Jena, Institute of Computer Science, 07743 Jena, Germany
koenig@informatik.uni-jena.de

Abstract. Today, Portals provide users with a central point of access to companywide information. Initially they focused on presenting the most valuable and widely used information to users for efficient information access. But the amount of information accessible quickly grew and finding the right information can hence become a tedious task. We will demonstrate a solution for adapting the Portal's structure, especially its navigation and page structures. We allow for advanced adaptations that each user can perform manually as well as for automated adaptations based on user- and context models reflecting users' interests and preferences. Our main concepts have been embedded and evaluated within IBM's WebSphere Portal.

1 Introduction

Enterprise Information Portals have gained importance in many companies. As a single point of access they integrate various applications and processes into one homogeneous user interface. Today, typical Portals contain thousands of pages which in turn typically contain several portlets (fragments delivering content). This continuous growth makes access to really relevant information difficult. Users need to find task- and role-specific information quickly, but often face information overload. The huge amount of content available results in complex structures designed to satisfy the majority of users. However, those super-imposed structures defined by Portal authors and administrators are not necessarily compliant to the users' mental models and therefore result in long navigation paths and significant effort to find the information needed.

We will present options especially designed for their use within modern Portal systems to ease navigation through such large information spaces.

2 Concepts

In the following we will first shortly describe the restrictions to overcome and then present five approaches developed and implemented to overcome those.

The first restriction to deal with is that current Portals usually support only one single navigation (or page) structure for all users. Although certain pages (or

W. Nejdl et al. (Eds.): AH 2008, LNCS 5149, pp. 370–373, 2008.

portlets) may be blended out based on access control rules, the overall structure is defined by some administrator to satisfy the majority of all users.

The second restriction is that most of today's Portal structures are rather static. Since they do not learn from users, they do not adapt when their behavior changes. Such a change in behavior may be due to a new job role or only because the context changes, like time (weekend vs. working days) and location (office or travel).

To address both problems five solutions have been developed: The first extension allows for separate navigation models for each user. Specialized portlets enable users to adapt the navigation structure to their needs. The second extension, called *page-flow recorder*, allows users to record sequences of pages traversed often and recall them later. The third extension is based on user- and context models which we construct by observing users' behavior and which reflect their interests and preferences. We exploit these models to let the system **automatically** perform adaptations. Recognizing the aggressiveness of the previous solution, we developed, as a fourth extension, a recommendation engine. The engine issues recommendations based on the users' previous behavior and allows to follow short-cuts. We finally started analyzing users' tagging behavior to built navigation structures entirely based on semantic interrelations of tags that have been applied to system resources (i.e. pages, portlets, etc.).

The following sections explain the details of the solutions outlined above.

2.1 User-Adapted Structures

Normally, during runtime, the aggregation uses a (single) navigation structure stored in a database to render the navigation. To allow for user scoped navigations so called *transformations*, which can be regarded virtual views on existing structures, have been introduced.

We will demonstrate a specialized portlet that allows users to create their own virtual navigation structure on-demand. They can hide irrelevant pages and re-order pages being part of the navigation model in order to reach relevant pages more quickly. The virtual structure created is also kept (as *diff* to the original structure) in the database. The transformation accesses this stored model and generates a structure matching the user-created model.

2.2 User-Created Pageflows

The analysis of users' navigation behavior revealed that, when pursuing specific tasks, users often follow similar clickstreams (i.e. the same set of pages in the same order). Often different pages are part of different flows so that the simple manual reordering of the topology structure would improve some tasks but downgrade others.

We will therefore demonstrate a second specialized portlet to overcome this drawback. The *pageflow recorder* records paths (i.e. sequences of pages) traveled often. These recordings can be recalled later and navigated through by just clicking *previous* and *next* links. This eases completing tasks that have to be performed regularly as irrelevant pages do not have to be visited anymore. The recordings can even be exchanged with other Portal users which allows experts to record common paths for their colleagues.

2.3 System-Adapted Structures

In order to perform reasonable automated adaptations or to provide recommendations to users we need to understand users' interests and preferences. Therefore we construct user models reflecting their behavior. We use static information from users' profiles, as well as dynamical information which we retrieve via *web usage mining*. For the latter we analyze Portal logs which reveal information about several events, e.g. when pages (or portlets) are created, read, updated or deleted. Thus we get to know which pages (or portlets on pages) are of higher interest than others.

More generally, we apply techniques from the area of frequent set mining [1] to analyze the usage of pages and portlets. We use the Apriori algorithm [2] to determine items, such as pages and portlets that co-occur frequently. We apply the GSP algorithm [3] to determine sequences of items, such as pages and portlets, that co-occur frequently.

However, focusing on user models only, neglects the context users are acting in. A user who is in the process of planning a business trip will need resources that provide information about hotels, rental cars, and flights. When the same user returns to his tasks as a project manager, he will need a completely different set of resources. Of course his interests and preferences will be totally different in both roles and obviously he needs access to totally different resources (pages, portlets, etc.). Thus our solution allows single users to have several context *profiles* between which either the system switches automatically, based on context attributes being observed (date, time, location, etc.), or the user manually.

We use a structure reordering algorithm that continuously rearranges pages that are part of the navigation structure. More important pages are promoted to better navigational positions, less important ones demoted or even hidden. Continuous adaptation, based on the most current user models available, guarantees that the navigation structure permanently fits the users needs as best as possible. As soon as the users behavior changes the user model changes too and hence the navigation topology provided. We will also demonstrate that we are not only able to adapt navigation structures, but also pages structures by reordering portlets on single pages to increase their usability.

2.4 System-Created Recommendations

Especially users that navigate according to the aimed navigation paradigm [4] do not like permanent adaptations because of its aggressiveness. Automated provisioning of recommendations avoids permanent restructuring of the navigation structure providing users with the option to follow short-cuts.

We will demonstrate a solution where we blend-in recommendations into the Portal's theme. The recommendation engine provides users with an adaptive navigational aid besides the standard navigation. The short-cuts are dynamically generated depending on the current navigational position. We apply a MinPath algorithm [5] and try to predict short-cuts to pages that are far away from the current page but have a high probability to be navigated to [6,7].

2.5   Tag-Based Adaptation

Having realized the tremendous use of Web 2.0 techniques such as tagging, we have come up with a mechanism allowing us to construct navigation structures entirely based on users' tagging behavior. Based on cosine-similarity calculations we are able to calculate semantic distances between tags applied to resources (i.e. pages, portlets, etc.) and are thus able to calculate semantic relatedness between resources themselves.

3   Demonstration

We will demonstrate a typical, large, Sports Portal embedded into IBM's WebSphere Portal. We will illustrate the problems outlined before and demonstrate how each single solution can overcome certain drawbacks: We will start with demonstrating how we allow users to manually adapt the system using our extensions and end with a demonstration how the system can automatically adapt structures or issue recommendations.

IBM and WebSphere are trademarks of International Business Machines Corporation in the United States, other countries or both. Other company, product and service names may be trademarks or service marks of others.

References

1. Liu, B.: Web Data Mining: Exploring Hyperlinks, Contents, and Usage Data (Data-Centric Systems and Applications). Springer, Heidelberg (2006)
2. Agrawal, R., Srikant, R.: Fast Algorithms for Mining Association Rules. In: Proc. of the 20th Very Large Data Bases Conf., Santiago, Chile (1994)
3. Srikant, R., Agrawal, R.: Mining Sequential Patterns: Generalizations and Performance Improvements. In: Advances in Database Technology - EDBT 1996 (1996)
4. Robertson, G.G.: Navigation in Information Spaces. In: Submision to CHI 97 Workshop on Navigation in Electronic Worlds, March 23-24 (1997)
5. Anderson, C.R., Domingos, P., Weld, D.S.: Adaptive web navigation for wireless devices. In: IJCAI, pp. 879–884 (2001)
6. Anderson, C.R., Domingos, P., Weld, D.S.: Relational markov models and their application to adaptive web navigation. In: KDD, pp. 143–152 (2002)
7. Smyth, B., Cotter, P.: Intelligent Navigation for Mobile Internet Portals. In: Proc. of the 18th Intl. Joint Conf. on Artificial Intelligence, Acapulco, Mexico (2003)

Personalized Recommendations for the Web 3D

Bartek Ochab, Nicolas Neubauer, and Klaus Obermayer

Neural Information Processing Group, Technische Universität Berlin, Germany
{bauscho,neubauer,oby}@cs.tu-berlin.de

Abstract. We introduce the Second Life Location Recommender System (SLLoRS)[1]. This system lets users rate and tag locations within the 3D environment Second Life in order to provide personalized recommendations on a collaborative basis. We demonstrate the system as an in-world application and explore some of the general challenges of applying recommendation systems to 3D online environments, like the implementation of data-intensive applications facing restricted computational resources and the segmentation of recommendations in a continuous input space.

1 Introduction

Three-dimensional multi-user online worlds, in the last few years, have started to enable users to create and share content. The term "Web 3D" has been coined to distinguish such applications from more traditional, game-like online worlds: Instead of letting users consume predefined plots, they blur the border between users and authors of 3D content much like the WWW did for (hyper-)textual content. For the Web 3D, however, we face similar challenges as for the WWW: Without a central authority supervising the creation of content, the problem of finding interesting or relevant information becomes more difficult.

Our work is realized in Second Life, currently the most prominent Web 3D application. The conceptual scope of our work however lies beyond a single concrete application: Expecting increased establishment of 3D applications particularly for more every-day like tasks (technology consultants Gartner, e.g., expect that 80% of active internet users will be using 3D worlds by 2011 [1]), it is important to explore navigational tools which take into account the specific properties of user-generated 3D worlds. Search in Second Life, so far, mostly imports the text-based approaches known from the WWW, crawling textual descriptions and author-generated metadata. Our approach is to apply some of the user-centric techniques that have proven successful in the last years: Instead of facing the complicated challenge of extracting the meanings of three-dimensional structures (which seem largely socially constructed anyway), we let users rate and tag locations within Second Life, leading to a representation of its contents in a bottom-up fashion. This data is used to provide personalized recommendations on a collaborative basis.

---

[1] http://aldebaran.ni.cs.tu-berlin.de/SLLORS/

W. Nejdl et al. (Eds.): AH 2008, LNCS 5149, pp. 374–377, 2008.

2   Description of the System

Users within Second Life receive a so-called SLLoRS client. This little tool is attached on the top left of their screen and will offer them all available services of the system. Guided by an assistant, users can rate their current location, ask SLLoRS for a recommendation, or search among all stored locations. To rate a location users only need to click on the option offered by the SLLoRS-client and enter optional tags into the chat window of the Second Life client. Also when asking for a recommendation or searching for a location, users have the option to add a few tags to further specify his request. The result will then be shown by messages shown in the chat window of the Second Life client. The recommended locations are presented as interactive "SLURLs" (Second Life URLs). Clicking on these highlighted links opens an information window about the referred location and allows direct teleportation to this destination.

3   Technical Background: Challenges

Instead of giving a complete description of the system, we would like to shortly highlight some specific challenges and our solutions.

3.1   Data Storage and Mining

Web 3D applications basically by definition provide basic scripting facilities. However, are they powerful enough to provide a recommendation service, which requires persistent data storage and potentially heavy computation?

SLLoRS has been implemented as a web service consisting of a central server and independent clients. This keeps SLLoRS' demands on the scripting facilities minimal: it only requires support of HTTP communication with an external

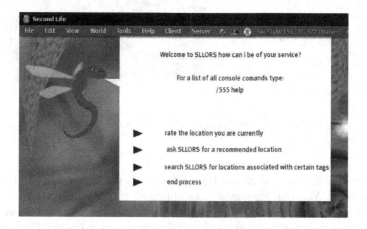

Fig. 1. Most recent SLLoRS client in Second Life

server. The Java-based server stores and processes the data and offers different services (like rating a location or asking for recommendations) via parametrised HTTP requests. The client has been implemented as a tool within Second Life as shown in Fig. 1. Its purpose is to allow users simple access to the offered services and to collect all information needed to represent the location the user is rating.

3.2 Segmenting Positions into Locations

We want users to share recommendations for locations within Second Life. However: What is a location? User ratings are attached to the user's current position, so there may never be two ratings referring to exactly the same coordinates. When should two ratings be regarded as referring to the same location? Simply grouping recommendations by a fixed-size grid, in our opinion, would be too static: Ratings may refer to densely populated areas, in which distinct locations are only meters away from each other, or to large spaces in which a logical location spans a whole region.

Our solution is to combine[2] different types of information into one representation of a single point: Euclidean coordinates, ownership information, and a list of descriptive, user-provided tags to catch the content of a location which largely depends on the visitors' perceptions. To discretize these noisily distributed, punctual user ratings to actual locations we use a clustering algorithm [3] to group subsets of ratings to distinct locations which the users supposedly meant when rating. This combined approach allows us to distinguish different locations in more detail than simply recommending entire Second Life regions.

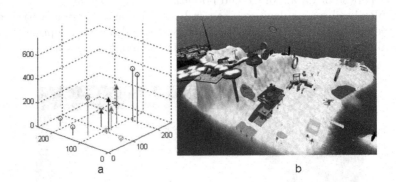

a   b

Fig. 2. "Vermin Isle"-region in rating space (a) – circles are ratings, triangles are cluster centers – and in Second Life (b)

Fig. 2a displays a recent clustering result of a Second Life region called "Vermin Isle". You can clearly see the different ratings illustrated by circular markings. The triangular marks represent locations as the pairwise clustering extracted out of the provided ratings. The different colors indicate different groups. If we compare this region-wide plot with a screenshot of the ground level of the same region as provided in Fig. 2 b, we can see how the algorithm merged all ratings concerning the sandbox into the green cluster and those concerning the club of the region into the blue cluster.

3.3 Generating Recommendations

Once there is a group of ratings for a set of discrete locations, the question remains how these ratings should be used to create a personalized recommendation for a given user. At this abstraction level, having distinct locations as items, we can apply one of many sophisticated recommendation algorithms. Currently we use a traditional memory based recommender, i.e. item based collaborative filtering[4]. In this algorithm, the prediction of the user opinion for a new item is calculated by the sum of all ratings of items the user has rated, weighted by the similarities between the new item and the rated ones.

4   Conclusion and Outlook

We introduced SLLoRS, the collaborative recommendation system for Second Life. We showed some of the challenges that appear when applying collaborative systems to 3D worlds and proposed some solutions using machine learning techniques and specialized representations of the item space.

As we have only recently released the system, our next steps will involve gathering data from users, evaluating the system's performance and adapting it accordingly. Beyond that, a major issue is how to deal with the dynamic nature of the virtual world: Whatever a user rated may be deconstructed a second later. So how can we keep track of a rating's validty? On a more long term scale, we want to explore which additional services can be provided beyond the recommendations, using the data given.

References

1. Gartner, I.: (2007) http://gartner.com/it/page.jsp?id=503861
2. Gärtner, T., Lloyd, J.W., Flach, P.A.: Kernels and distances for structured data. Machine Learning 57(3), 205–232 (2004)
3. Hofmann, T., Buhmann, J.M.: Pairwise data clustering by deterministic annealing. IEEE Transactions on Pattern Analysis and Machine Intelligence 19(1) (1997)
4. Wang, J., de Vries, A.P., Reinders, M.J.: Unifying user based and item based collaborative filtering approaches by similarity fusion. SESSION: Recommendation: use and abuse, 501–508 (2006)

Adaptive User Modelling and Recommendation in Constrained Physical Environments

Fabian Bohnert*

Faculty of Information Technology, Monash University
Clayton, Victoria 3800, Australia
fabian.bohnert@infotech.monash.edu.au

Abstract. Visitors to physical educational environments, such as museums, are often overwhelmed by the information available in the space they are exploring. They are confronted with the challenge of finding personally interesting items to view in the available time. Electronic mobile guides can provide guidance and point to relevant information by identifying and recommending items that match a visitor's interests. However, recommendation generation in physical spaces has challenges of its own. Factors such as the spatial layout of the environment and suggested order of item access must be taken into account, as they constrain the recommendation process. This research investigates adaptive user modelling and personalisation approaches that consider such and other constraints.

1   Introduction

Educational leisure environments, such as galleries, museums and zoos, offer enormous amounts of information. However, a visitor's receptivity and time are typically limited, confronting the visitor with the challenge of selecting interesting items to view within the available time. A personal human guide could support the visitor in this selection process, but the provision of personal guides is generally impractical. Advances in user modelling and mobile computing have made possible an alternative solution: personalised electronic handheld guides. Electronic guides have the potential to infer a visitor's interests by tracking his/her behaviour within the environment. However, to date, adaptable user models have often been employed, requiring visitors to explicitly state their interests in some form [1,2]. Adaptive user models, which do not require explicit user input, have usually been updated from a visitor's interactions with the system, with a focus on adapting content presentation [3], rather than predicting or recommending exhibits to be viewed. Moreover, most systems rely on knowledge-based user models, which require an explicit, a-priori built representation of the domain knowledge. In contrast, this research focuses on non-intrusive statistical user modelling techniques that do not require this explicit representation [4].

User modelling and recommendation in physical educational spaces have challenges of their own. As items have informational dependencies suggesting a certain order of access, careful thought is usually put into placing the items into the physical space to enable a coherent experience. Consequently, visitor behaviour is influenced by both the

* This research is supported in part by Discovery grant DP0770931 from the Australian Research Council. The author thanks his advisors Ingrid Zukerman and Liz Sonenberg, and also Shlomo Berkovsky for their valuable comments on this paper.

W. Nejdl et al. (Eds.): AH 2008, LNCS 5149, pp. 378–383, 2008.

suggested order of item access and the spatial layout of the environment. Hence, these factors must be considered when modelling a visitor from non-intrusive observations of his/her movements through the space, and when generating recommendations. Further, these recommendations must consider a visitor's position and time limitations. That is, the personalisation process is constrained by the spatial layout, informational dependencies between items (and imposed order of access), and time constraints. To date, these factors have not been considered sufficiently.

This research investigates non-intrusive statistical user modelling and recommendation techniques that take the above constraints into account. It aims to reduce information overload and to improve a visitor's experience by means of

... **Personalised guidance:** Lead the visitor through both the physical space and informational space by finding and pointing to content pro-actively, matching the visitor's interests and needs.
... **Coherence:** Select the items sensibly as a coherent whole, i. e., spatially and informationally coherent, considering also the educational objectives of the provider (e. g., by including highlight displays).

From these objectives, the following research questions were derived.

1. How do constraints such as the spatial layout, informational dependencies between items and time constraints affect a visitor's behaviour?
2. How can these constraints be effectively considered when predicting a visitor's interests and activities from non-intrusive observations of his/her movements through the environment?
3. How can these constraints be incorporated in the construction and recommendation of a suitable pathway for the continuation of a visit?

To date, we have focused on the prediction of a visitor's interests and future pathway from his/her behaviour, partially addressing the first two questions. In the future, we propose to address the third question. The adaptation of the content delivered for the recommended items is outside the scope of this research.

2 Approach and System Architecture

Recent developments in the area of positioning technology have made possible the non-intrusive indoor tracking of users equipped with a positioning device. Although a detailed assessment of such technologies is outside the scope of this work, the availability of techniques to infer a visitor's high-level activities from sensing data, e. g., [5], is crucial to this research. For our purposes, we assume to be given a visitor's pathway as a time-annotated sequence of visited items, i. e., each *observation* comprises the tuple (item, visit duration). These observations are the only input to our system GECKO for the current visitor.

Architecturally, GECKO consists of two main parts, reflecting the sequential nature of the recommendation process: a *modelling component* and a *personalisation component* (Figure 1). The modelling component is further subdivided into two modules: space models and user models, both of which make use of *external data sources (knowledge base)*. Visitor observations trigger updates within the *user models*, which capture

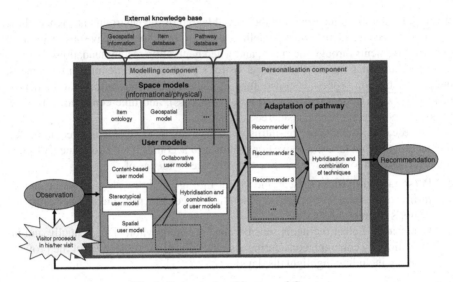

Fig. 1. Conceptual architecture of GECKO

the information required for predicting a visitor's activities and interests. We propose to combine different user modelling techniques, with the aim to overcome their respective drawbacks [6]. Our experiments include collaborative and content-based approaches to model a visitor's interests. Additionally, spatial user models capture the visitor's behaviour suggested by the space. For example, we employ transition models based on user transitions between items, and propose to use distance models based on the spatial arrangement of items. Further, we consider employing stereotypical user models to predict what type of visitor a user is (e. g., greedy or selective). The user models are consulted to predict a visitor's interests, movements, and visitor type. These predictions are then passed on to GECKO's personalisation component. However, as discussed above, spatial and informational constraints must be considered in the adaptation process. *Space models* capturing informational dependencies between items (item ontology) and spatial layout (geospatial model) constitute further input. Within the personalisation component, a suitable pathway satisfying the above constraints is constructed, before GECKO delivers a *recommendation* to the visitor.

Physical educational environments are spaces where the physical layout is used to structure information. For instance, a museum might be subdivided into galleries that are usually fairly heterogeneous with respect to the concepts presented, and these galleries might be further subdivided into exhibitions and collections of exhibits whose content is rather homogeneous. We call this hierarchical organisation *(physical) space taxonomy*. Different levels of the space taxonomy might require different prediction and recommendation mechanisms. In principle, this suggests the following research methodology, with the cell numbering 1 to 4 indicating the order of study.

Level of space taxonomy \ Step	**Prediction**	**Recommendation**
Micro (item, room)	1	3
Macro (subsection, section)	2	4

3   Prediction of Visitor Locations

To date, the focus of this research has been the prediction of a visitor's interests and locations at the item level (cell 1). The proposed framework (Figure 1) has been implemented and validated as far as our research has progressed. We developed two collaborative models of visitor behaviour (*Interest* and *Transition*), and a hybrid model that combines their predictions [7]. The collaborative *Interest Model* is built by calculating the *Relative Interest* for all combinations of visitors and items that occurred.[1] Missing relative interest values for the current visitor are predicted from these values collaboratively. In contrast, the *Transition Model* models a visitor's behaviour based on visitor movements between items, and hence implicitly captures the spatial layout. These models are employed to predict the next K items (we used $K = 1$ and $K = 3$), using two types of prediction approaches: set (unordered) and sequence (ordered). We evaluated the different model variants with a dataset collected at a rather homogeneous exhibition in Melbourne Museum. Our results show that the *Transition Model* outperforms the *Interest Model*, indicating that the layout of a physical space with homogeneous items is the main factor influencing visitor behaviour. However, the *Hybrid Model* yielded the best performance, which shows the importance of also considering a visitor's interests. Moreover, our results indicate that, when predicting the next three exhibits, a sequence-based model has a higher predictive accuracy than a model that predicts a set. Surprisingly, this is not the case when predicting a single item, where the performance of the simpler set-based model is comparable to the performance of the model that predicts the next item as the first item in a sequence.

Currently, we are extending this work by investigating a combination of collaborative user models with content-based models. We also intend to investigate stereotypical user models, which could be employed in the initial phase of a visit to address the cold-start problem of statistical user modelling techniques. The next challenge will be to transfer the prediction techniques discussed above to higher levels of the space taxonomy (cell 2), where the space is less prescribed and more heterogeneous. By evaluating the predictive accuracy of our algorithms at different taxonomy levels, we expect to gain insights about the influence of space prescriptiveness and item diversity on the performance of our models. For instance, we expect the relative performance of the *Interest Model* to improve in a less prescribed space with heterogeneous content. We are currently undertaking a manual data collection in Melbourne Museum covering the entire space, which will enable us to undertake this evaluation.

4   Recommendation of Pathway Continuation

As yet, we have focused on the prediction of a visitor's interests and future locations. Accurate predictions will enable us to make recommendations about items to visit. However, in our scenario, the transition from prediction to recommendation is not trivial. The second part of this thesis will investigate this step.

---

[1] We devised a measure of *Relative Interest* to transform observations into implicit ratings, based on the assumption that visitors are expected to spend more time on relevant information than on irrelevant information in an information-seeking context [8].

Recommendations that match a visitor's intentions build trust in the system. However, recommendations that are too detailed, or trivial recommendations, e. g., of items along a path prescribed by the spatial layout or predicted to be visited anyway, are likely to annoy a visitor. As this is likely to occur at the lower space taxonomy levels, we propose to refrain from recommendations at these levels where the space is homogeneous and prescribed (cell 3). However, at the higher levels of the space taxonomy, where the space is less prescribed and content is heterogeneous (cell 4), recommendation generation is reasonable. A number of competing factors must be considered in order to construct the pathway continuation that is most appropriate given a visitor's current situational context.

- **Content:** Include items matching a visitor's interests to enrich his/her knowledge of topics of interest (collaborative and content-based recommendations).
- **Serendipity and Surprise:** Surprise with out-of-the-box items which do not reflect a visitor's obvious interests (collaborative recommendations).
- **Intensity:** Choose the most appropriate number of items based on the user's visiting style (stereotypical recommendations).
- **Continuity and Coherence:** Take into account spatial layout, informational dependencies between items, and curator constraints such as must-see items.
- **Consistency and Detail:** Achieve consistency with previous recommendations, and consider consistency when determining the horizon and level of detail of a recommendation.
- **Time:** Take into account time constraints both of the visitor and the environment.

We propose to investigate utility-based recommendation generation strategies which balance these factors, e. g., Markov Decision Processes, which were recently proposed for decision-theoretic and user-adaptable planning in the shopping guide domain [9].

References

1. Cheverst, K., Mitchell, K., Davies, N.: The role of adaptive hypermedia in a context-aware tourist guide. Communications of the ACM 45(5), 47–51 (2002)
2. Aroyo, L., Stash, N., Wang, Y., Gorgels, P., Rutledge, L.: CHIP demonstrator: Semantics-driven recommendations and museum tour generation. In: Proc. of the Sixth Intl. Semantic Web Conf. (ISWC 2007), pp. 879–886 (2007)
3. Stock, O., Zancanaro, M., Busetta, P., Callaway, C., Krüger, A., Kruppa, M., Kuflik, T., Not, E., Rocchi, C.: Adaptive, intelligent presentation of information for the museum visitor in PEACH. User Modeling and User-Adapted Interaction 18(3), 257–304 (2007)
4. Zukerman, I., Albrecht, D.W.: Predictive statistical models for user modeling. User Modeling and User-Adapted Interaction 11(1-2), 5–18 (2001)
5. Liao, L., Fox, D., Kautz, H.: Extracting places and activities from GPS traces using hierarchical conditional random fields. Intl. Journal of Robotics Research 26(1), 119–134 (2007)
6. Burke, R.: Hybrid recommender systems: Survey and experiments. User Modeling and User-Adapted Interaction 12(4), 331–370 (2002)
7. Bohnert, F., Zukerman, I., Berkovsky, S., Baldwin, T., Sonenberg, L.: Using collaborative models to adaptively predict visitor locations in museums. In: Proc. of the Fifth Intl. Conf. on Adaptive Hypermedia and Adaptive Web-Based Systems (AH 2008), pp. 42–51 (2008)

8. Bohnert, F., Zukerman, I.: Using viewing time for theme prediction in cultural heritage spaces. In: Proc. of the 20th Australian Joint Conf. on Artificial Intelligence (AI 2007), pp. 367–376 (2007)
9. Bohnenberger, T., Jacobs, O., Jameson, A., Aslan, I.: Decision-theoretic planning meets user requirements: Enhancements and studies of an intelligent shopping guide. In: Proc. of the Third Intl. Conf. on Pervasive Computing (Pervasive 2005), pp. 279–296 (2005)

Learning Style as a Parameter in a Unified e-Learning System Architecture: The Adaptive Diagnosis

Sotirios Botsios and Dimitrios Georgiou

Department of Electrical & Computer Engineering
Democritus Univ. of Thrace, GR 671 00, Xanthi, Greece
smpotsio@ee.duth.gr

Abstract. Adaptation and personalization services in e-learning environments are considered the turning point of recent research efforts, as the "one-size-fits-all" approach has some important drawbacks, from the educational point of view. Adaptive Educational Hypermedia Systems in World Wide Web became a very active research field and the need for standardization arose, as the continually augmenting research efforts lacked the interoperability dimension. To this end, we propose an adaptive hypermedia educational system architecture strongly coupled to existing standards that overcomes the above mentioned weakness. Part of such architecture is the development of diagnostic tools capable to recognize certain learner's characteristics to the purpose of providing learning material tailored to the learner's specific needs in an asynchronous learning environment. This paper describes Learning Style diagnosis which can be approached either by the use of probabilistic expert systems or by the use of fuzzy systems.

Keywords: Learning Management Systems, Adaptive Educational Hypermedia Systems, Standards, Learning Style Diagnosis, Probabilistic Expert Systems, Bayesian Networks, Fuzzy Cognitive Maps.

1   Introduction

A recent research [1] demonstrated that both instructors and learners have very positive perceptions toward using e-learning as a teaching assisted tool. According to Brusilovsky and Miller [2] Adaptive and Intelligent Web-Based Educational Systems provide an alternative to the traditional 'just-put-it-on-the-Web' approach in the development of Web-based educational courseware. In their work Brusilovsky and Pyelo, [3] mention that Adaptive and Intelligent Web-Based Educational Systems attempt to be more adaptive by building a model of the goals, preferences and knowledge of each individual student and using this model throughout the interaction with the system in order to be more intelligent by incorporating and performing some activities traditionally executed by a human teacher – such as coaching students or diagnosing misconceptions.

There exist a wide variety of diverse Adaptive and Intelligent Web-Based Educational Systems. The 'rules' that are used to describe the creation of such systems are not yet fully standardized, and the criteria that need to be used pedagogically effective

W. Nejdl et al. (Eds.): AH 2008, LNCS 5149, pp. 384–388, 2008.

rule-sets (i.e. adaptation parameters) are, as yet, poorly mentioned [4]. Many experimental Adaptive Educational Hypermedia Systems have been created – each to their own unique specifications. As yet, however, no combined effort has been made to extract the common design paradigms from these systems [4].

The current research efforts of the authors are concentrated in providing a starting point for the development of a unified architecture for the retrieval of learning objects from disperse Learning Objects Repositories (LOR) to an e-learning environment. Rehak and Mason [5] consider Learning Object (LO) as a digitized entity which can be used, reused or referenced during technology supported learning. Practically, LOs acquisition is achieved by querying LOR distributed over the internet. This LO "journey" must comply with widely accepted standards. The LO query includes "filters" that refer to various adaptation parameters. Examples of LOR for use in education can be found in [6].

These parameters are strongly coupled with various aspects of the learner profile, i.e. cognitive style-cognitive abilities, learning style (LS), learning behavior-motivation, competency level-personal goals-course material difficulty [7]. The authors believe that the accurate estimation of some or all of these parameters in a standardized manner can boost the efficiency of the adaptive e-learning process. Therefore, part of the research conducted and main topic of this paper concerns the LS estimation. We describe two techniques for LS estimation that can provide some service to the previously mentioned architecture. Both of the techniques are based on the Kolb's Learning Style Inventory (KLSI) [8]. The first one consists of the Fault Implication Avoidance Algorithm (FIAA) and a Probabilistic Expert System. [9]. The second technique describes an adjustable tool that allows experts to reinforce the system's LS recognition ability. To this end, we developed a three layer Fuzzy Cognitive Map (FCM).

The rest of the paper is structured as follows. Section 2 provides a brief theoretical background of LS, while in section 3 the previously mentioned techniques are described.

2 Learning Style

Learning Theories diverge with respect to the fact that students learn and acquire knowledge in many different ways, which have been classified as LSs. There exists a great variety of models and theories in the literature regarding learning behavior and cognitive characteristics i.e. LSs or Cognitive Styles (CSs) [10]. According to Riding and Rayner, CS refers to an individual's method of processing information [11]. The building up of a repertoire of learning strategies that combine with cognitive style, contribute to an individual's LS. In particular, LSs are applied CSs, removed one more level from pure processing ability usually referring to learners' preferences on how they process information and not to actual ability, skill or processing tendency [12]. LSs classifications have been proposed by Kolb [8] and others [13], [14], [15]. Most of the authors categorize LSs and/or CSs into groups and propose certain inventories and methodologies capable of classifying learners accordingly.

The KLSI is considered as one of the most well known and widely used in research. According to the model students have a preference in the way they learn: a. Concrete Experience or Abstract Conceptualization and b. Active Experimentation or Reflective Observation. [16] The model is represented in a two dimensions graph. The preference is diagnosed by analysing subject's responses in given questions of a questionnaire.

3 Techniques for Adaptive LS Estimation

3.1 FIAA and Probabilistic Expert System

The first technique consists of the FIAA and a Probabilistic Expert System [9]. Taking into account the structure of KLSI, FIAA dynamically creates a descending shorting of learner's answerers per question, decreases the amount of necessary input for the diagnosis, which in turn can result to limitation of possible controversial answers. The applied Probabilistic Expert System, funded upon Bayesian Networks, analyzes information from responses supplied by the system's antecedent users (users that complete the questionnaire before the present user) to conclude to a LS diagnosis of the present user. One of the primary roles of a Bayesian model is to allow the model creator to use commonsense and real-world knowledge to eliminate needless complexity in the model. Evidence is provided that the effect of some factors, such as cultural environment and lucky guesses or slippery answers, that hinder an accurate estimation, is diminished. This technique produces a "clear" LS estimation (no "grey" estimation areas).

Let us consider the $BN=(V,A,P)$ where $V=\pi_v \cup M$ and $\pi_v=LS=\{C_1, C_2,..., C_v\}$ is the set of LSs. A learner is recognized as being of class C_i, $(i=1,2,...,v)$ according to his/her responses to a given set of m questions. Each question can be answered by yes or not. Let $Q=\{Q_1^{(k)},Q_2^{(k)},...,Q_m^{(k)}\}$ be the set of answers where k is a Boolean operator taking the values TRUE or FALSE whenever $Q_1^{(k)}$ represents the answer YES or NOT respectively. There are 2^m different sets of such responses to the questionnaire. Let us consider the index j, where $j \in \{1,2,...,2^m\}$. A learner's responses to the set of questions formulates an element

$$r_j = \bigcup_{l=1}^{m} Q_l^{(k)} \qquad (1)$$

where $r_j \subset M$ the set of BN leaves. Obviously, $r_i \neq r_j$ for any pair $(r_i, r_j) \subset M$, with $i \neq j$.

Let n be the number of learners who made use of the system, and n_{ri} be the number of those who responded to the questionnaire with r_i. The a priori probability that the $(n+1)^{th}$ user responded to the questionnaire with an element r_i is

$$P\left(r_i^{(n+1)}\right) = \frac{(n+1)_{r_i}}{n+1} \qquad (2)$$

In this case, the BN in use is a weighted and oriented $K_{2^m}^v$ graph, i.e. a weighted and oriented complete bipartite graph on n and 2^m nodes. At each edge of the network's graph we adjust the conditional probability $P(r_i^{(n)}/C_j^{(n)})$, i.e. a probability which dynamically changes as a new user enters the system. This probability expresses the ratio of users who responded to the questionnaire with the element r_i and were finally classified in C_j, in terms of the total number of r_i responses. Thus, the measure $P(C_j^{(n+1)})$ is the probability that the LS of the $(n+1)^{th}$ learner belongs to C_j. This probability is given by the relation

$$P\left(C_j^{(n+1)}\right) = \sum_{i=1}^{2^m} P\left(C_j^{(n)} / r_i^{(n)}\right) P\left(r_i^{(n+1)}\right), \quad j=1,2,...,v \qquad (3)$$

where

$$P\left(C_j^{(n)}/r_i^{(n)}\right) = \frac{P\left(r_i^{(n)}/C_j^{(n)}\right)P\left(C_j^{(n)}\right)}{\sum\limits_{k=1}^{v} P\left(r_i^{(n)}/C_k^{(n)}\right)P\left(C_k^{(n)}\right)}, \quad \forall (i,j) \in \{1,2,...,n\} \times \{1,2,...,2^m\} \tag{4}$$

Let $score_j^{(n+1)}$, $j=1,2,...,v$ be the score for the jth LS, that the $(n+1)^{th}$ student gets by responding to the revised inventory. Then, by the contribution of BN, the learner's j^{th} LS final score is given by

$$ls_j = P\left(C_j^{(n+1)}\right)\left(score_j^{(n+1)}\right) \tag{5}$$

Then the dominant LS is the maximum value of ls_j, $j=1,2,...,v$.

3.2 Fuzzy Cognitive Maps

The second technique describes an adjustable tool that allows experts to reinforce the system's LS recognition ability. To this end, we develop a three layer Fuzzy Cognitive Map (FCM). FCM is a soft computing tool which can be considered as a combination of fuzzy logic and neural networks techniques. FCM representation is as simple as an oriented and weighted compact graph consisting of nodes (concepts) and arcs (fuzzy relation between linked concepts). The inner layer contains LSs, the middle one contains Learning Activity Factors (LAFs) and the outer layer refers to the 48 statements one can find in the KLSI [8]. The list of LAFs and their relational links to the LSs are those indicated in Kolb's [16]. Each pair of layers (outer–middle, and middle–inner) consist a complete bipartite oriented and weighted graph. Student's responses to inventory reflect on certain LAFs according to relations which have been pointed out by experts. At a second step LAF reflect on LSs. Unlike the technique of LSs recognition which is based directly to student's response to LS inventory, the proposed schema allows the cognitive scientists or experienced educators to interfere, tuning up the system, in order to contribute on the accuracy of the recognition. For example, a teacher, having its own clear diagnosis on a learner's LAFs, can tune up the system's weights in order to adjust it in situation at hand.

Initially, every concept gets a hypothetic value and as the time proceeds (i.e. new learners use the system), the values of the concepts change, as they are under the influence of the adjacent concepts and their corresponding weights.

At the step n the value $V^n(C_i)$ of the concept C_i is determined by the relation [5]

$$V^{n+1}(C_i) = f\left(k_1 \sum w_{ji} V^n(C_j) + k_2 V^n(C_i)\right) \tag{6}$$

where $V^{n+1}(C_i)$ is the value of the concept C_i at the discrete time step $n+1$, w_{ji} the defuzzified value of the weight between concepts C_i and C_j. The coefficient $0 \leq k_1 \leq 1$ defines the concept's dependence of on its interconnected concepts, while the coefficient $0 \leq k_2 \leq 1$ represent the proportion of contribution of the previous value of the concept in the computation of the new value. In other words, k_2 is the effect of the knowledge the system has gained by the previous users. Function f is a predefined threshold function. We used the unipolar sigmoid function, as we want to restrict values of concepts between 0 and 1. The maximum value between four $V(C_i)$, which represent the four LSs, is considered as the dominant LS of the $(n+1)^{th}$ user.

Acknowledgments. This work is supported in the frame of Operational Programme "COMPETITIVENESS", 3rd Community Support Program, co financed: a) 75% by the public sector of the European Union – European Social Fund and b) 25% by the Greek Ministry of Development – General Secretariat of Research and Technology.

References

1. Liaw, S.S., Huang, H.M., Chen, G.D.: Surveying instructor and learner attitudes toward e-learning. Computers and Education 49, 1066–1080 (2007)
2. Brusilovsky, P., Miller, P.: Course Delivery Systems for the Virtual University. In: Della Senta, T., Tschang, T. (eds.) Access to Knowledge: New Information Technologies and the Emergence of the Virtual University, pp. 167–206. Elsevier Science, Amsterdam (2001)
3. Brusilovsky, P., Pyelo, C.: Adaptive and Intelligent Web-based Educational Systems. International Journal of Artificial Intelligence in Education 13, 159–172 (2003)
4. Brown, E., Cristea, A., Stewart, C., Brailsford, T.: Patterns in authoring of adaptive educational hypermedia: A taxonomy of learning styles. Educational Technology and Society 8, 77–90 (2005)
5. Rehak, D., Mason, R.: Keeping the learning in learning objects. In: Littlejohn, A. (ed.) Reusing Educational Resources for Networked Learning, Kogan, London (2003)
6. Nash, S.S.: Learning Objects, Learning Object Repositories, and Learning Theory: Preliminary Best Practices for Online Courses. Interdisciplinary Journal of Knowledge and Learning Objects 1, 217–228 (2005)
7. Brusilovsky, P.: Adaptive hypermedia. User Modelling and User-Adapted Interaction 11 (2001)
8. Kolb, D.A.: Experimental learning: Experience as the source of learning and development. Prentice Hall, Jersey (1984)
9. Botsios, S., Georgiou, D., Safouris, N.: Contributions to AEHS via on-line Learning Style Estimation. Journal of Educational Technology and Society (in press)
10. Sternberg, R.J., Zhang, L.F.: Perspectives on Thinking, Learning, and Cognitive Styles. The Educational Psychology Series 276 (2001)
11. Riding, R., Rayner, S.: Cognitive Styles and Learning Strategies. David Fulton Publishers, London (1998)
12. Jonassen, D.H., Wang, S.: Acquiring structural knowledge from semantically structured hypertext. Journal of Computer-Based Instruction 20, 1–8 (1993)
13. Honey, P., Mumford, A.: The Learning Styles Helper's Guide. Peter Honey Publications, Maidenhead (2000)
14. Dunn, R., Dunn, K.: Teaching elementary students through their individual learning styles. Allyn and Bacon, Boston (1992)
15. Felder, R.M., Silverman, L.K.: Learning and teaching styles in engineering education. Engineering Education 78, 674–681 (1988)
16. Kolb, D.A.: Learning Style Inventory - version 3: Technical Specifications. TRG Hay/McBer, Training Resources Group (1999)

Facilitating Collaboration in Virtual Environments

Diana Chihaia

National College of Ireland
Mayor Street, Dublin 1, Ireland
dchihaia@ncirl.ie

Abstract. The evolution of learning systems brought improvements to the functionality of their components by offering support and mediating learning, communication and collaboration. However, there are still existing barriers caused by the lack of face to face contact between users. Through our research we aim to provide novel means for supporting the social cohesion of the groups and personalize the e-learning spaces by offering adaptive support in group forming and collaboration processes. As a first step in designing a filtering tool for an adaptive system which recommends application and activities for collaboration within the group, we designed a series of experimental studies on different components of an e-learning system to find out what initiates, influences and increases the level of collaboration between learners.

Keywords: collaboration, adaptive support, team forming.

1 Introduction – Research Topic and Questions

In psychology and also in sciences of education, social constructivism offered a new perspective: the influence of social interaction in learning. There are several factors which influence learning and the final result of the educational process: the students' learning style, the learning content, motivation, the students' knowledge level and communication level.

A prerequisite for sharing information and collaboration is to establish trust between the parties involved, i.e., learners and teachers. Given that communication mediated through technology is a critical part [1] of the challenge of building trust on-line, it is very important to discover how users and all the facilities offered by technology, may influence trust. Especially for a virtual team, collaborative learning requires trust between learners and a balanced level of knowledge among the team members, to make the information which is going to be transmitted easy to understand by every learner. In an e-learning system, keeping the students in the zone of proximal development (ZPD) [2] requires not only adapting the information [3], but also finding how to select a group which will learn in collaborative atmosphere and will sustain every member in making the next step in learning.

Our aim is to determine what facilitates the initiation of collaboration between learners and sustain it along the learning process in virtual environment as this could be exploited in an adaptive system to support collaboration. Thus we are addressing the following research questions:

W. Nejdl et al. (Eds.): AH 2008, LNCS 5149, pp. 389–393, 2008.

1. Which are the factors that are influencing trust among users from an e-learning system?
2. Which is the best way to group automatically teams for efficient collaboration and information sharing?

The next sections describe previous work in the area, the implications of our research in offering adaptive support within e-learning systems, our research plan, the actual progress of the research to date, and how we are going to validate our findings.

2 Previous Work and the Importance of Our Research

In order to answer to above presented questions we designed our research based on a scenario with new users accessing an e-learning system. We assume that filling a user profile, learners start introducing themselves to the community/virtual class and become trustworthy users for their peers. Also, users with a filled profile can be considered potential collaborators by the other users and are more likely to be contacted by peers for solving a task.

Existing research on the topic of user profiles has been conducted mainly as a component of the wider area of Social Networking Sites (SNSs) and to a lesser extend in the area of e-learning systems. Collaborative on-line learning systems can be seen as small SNSs that provide internal social network functionality in order to facilitate interaction between learners, to form teams based on users' interest, skills, level of knowledge or preferences. Analysis of user profiles and users' preferences in choosing peers have been used for a variety of purposes: finding the impact of trust and internet privacy on using social networking [4], examining the relationship between use of a social networking site (e.g., Facebook) and the formation and maintenance of social capital [5], using lists of interests as an 'expressive arena for taste performance' [6], evaluation of self-presentation strategies in dating sites [7].

The history of SNSs begins in 1997 and it is save to say that the recent expansion of SNSs influenced the development of e-learning system components (e.g. presence of blogs, personal profiles).

Exploring what type of information in a profile influences learners in choosing potential collaborators will help us to design a profile template with prioritized fields. Also, the information available in the profiles could be used as a criterion for adaptive team forming. Thus, we will expand the perspective of forming groups based on common interests, to e-learning, using criteria related to the level of knowledge, skills and experience.

Assuming that not only the content of profiles is initiating trust which leads to collaboration, we proposed a second and complementary approach used in research on trust: sustaining personal conversation through communication tools within the system and telling stories as forms of discourse in communication (e.g. using personal blogs) will establish a culture of support among users [8].

3 Proposed Framework and Methodology

The research will follow two paths: detecting and improving the level of trust between users and forming balanced teams based on the profile content. In the context of our research, a balanced team has members with different levels of knowledge and skills, who reciprocally support their evolution. Two experimental studies with different settings have been developed. The focus will be on qualitative methods.

We presume that sharing the profile content and personal information through blogs, video-chat, audio-chat or simply through messages leads to trust (see Figure 1). Our hypothesis is that higher levels of trust will result in better collaboration. We also expect that balanced teams perform better.

Fig. 1. Improving the level of collaboration in e-learning systems

In order to find out what type of profile influences users in choosing collaborators, in the first experimental study 12 profiles with different levels of information were designed. To have a balance of the information offered in the profiles a categorization was applied. Three profiles contained personal details and ideas only (likes, dislikes, hobbies, I would like to, more contact data, a brief presentation). Three profiles contained professional details only (university, level of education, occupation, job, main skills, career goals, degree). Three full profiles contained balanced personal and professional information, and three profiles were left empty. Each of these four categories had one profile with photo, one profile with an image and one profile with a default image (4 levels x 3 photo conditions = 12 profiles).

The participants who were recruited in accordance with the task domain and who had a basic level of knowledge in programming languages had to select potential collaborators from the list of 12 profiles, in order to design a multimedia presentation of a programming language. The condition imposed was to select three most liked profiles (people with whom they would collaborate) and three least liked profiles (people with whom they would not collaborate). For both sections we assigned scores from 3 to 1 according to the first, second and third choice.

After selecting their potential collaborators, participants were asked to complete a questionnaire regarding their decision. In order to determine which aspects are important in sustaining and improving collaboration in learning process within an e-learning system, we used as evaluation criteria preference of characteristics from users' profile (personal details, professional details, and picture), willingness to share information.

The second experimental study is currently under way. The study will confirm if there is any influence of sharing personal information and communication using different channels from on-line environment, on the collaboration level between team members. An e-learning system with instruments that support communication is used by groups of students to initiate and finish a project related to the course. The evaluation criteria will be the time spent by teams in solving a task, the team cohesion [9], as well as the quality of results.

The participants will be encouraged to use blogs, audio-chat, video-chat and instant messaging to keep in touch with their team members, during the period imposed for finishing the project. We presume that keeping an on-line journal of the team, by describing periodically the role of each member and also, maintaining a permanent connection between team members would lead to trust and also to better collaboration among the team.

4 Research Progress and Preliminary Results

A total of 24 participants with an average age of 20 years, studying in the area of computing, selected their preferred profiles and answered the questionnaire. The results from the first experimental study indicate that the participants preferred the profiles containing more professional information. Professional profiles were preferred significantly over balanced and personal profiles ($X^2 = 61.6$; p<.001). As expected, blank profiles scored highest in the least preferred category, but the differences are not significant ($X^2 = 6.39$; p=.094). This led us to the conclusion that learners should be advised to complete their profiles with professional details because this increases the chances of being selected as a collaborator.

Under the condition of presence of photo in the profiles, we found no significant difference in the case of preferred profiles ($X2 = 0.69$; p=.709), and a significant difference in the case of least preferred profiles ($X2 = 12.792$; p<.001).

Trying to delineate a profile structure we designed the last question of the questionnaire in order to discover what is important for the participants in a profile and what they would share with other users. As expected, participants equally selected fields from both categories professional and personal which means that a profile in the e-learning system should contain fields requiring data form both areas but considering the previous results the professional data fields should be labelled as important.

In the second study, beside the instruments used in evaluating the level of trust and collaboration between learners, interviews and questionnaires will be used for assessing the influence of using communication tools.

At the end of the second study we expect to have a list of factors which induce trust between users or, if trust can not be induced, what influenced the users to collaborate.

5 Validation and Further Work

Using the results from both experimental studies in the process of implementation of new components within an e-learning platform in the context of Adaptive Learning Spaces (ALS) project is the way of testing the efficacy of our research plan. Considering that this is a pilot work, at the end of the studies we can not consider yet the idea of generalising the results but these results lead to further work in the area of adaptive systems. For validating the results a higher number of participants, different types of courses and tasks is needed.

In the next phase of the research, the priority is to set up an algorithm for a system which adapts its behaviour for a better collaboration within the groups of learners and to select the type of this system: a recommender one, a filtering one or a personal or social retriever one [10].

Acknowledgement. This research project is conducted in the context of the Adaptive Learning Spaces (ALS) project, partly supported by European Commission under the Minerva Program.

References

1. Stewart, K.: How hypertext Links Influence Consumer Perceptions to Build ans Degrade Trust Online. Journal of Management Information Systems 23(1), 183–210 (2006)
2. Vygotsky, L.S.: Mind and society: The development of higher psychological processes. Harvard University Press, Cambridge (1978)
3. Murray, T., Arroyo, I.: Toward Measuring and Maintaining the Zone of Proximal Development in Adaptive Instructional Systems. In: Proceedings of the 6th International Conference on Intelligent Tutoring Systems, pp. 749–758 (2002)
4. Dwyer, C., Hiltz, S.R., Passerini, K.: Trust and privacy concern within social networking sites: A comparison of Facebook and MySpace. In: Proceedings of AMCIS 2007, Keystone, CO (2007) Retrieved January 7, 2008,
   http://csis.pace.edu/~dwyer/research/DwyerAMCIS2007.pdf
5. Ellison, N., Steinfield, C., Lampe, C.: The benefits of Facebook friends: Exploring the relationship between college students' use of online social networks and social capital. Journal of Computer-Mediated Communication 12(3) (2007), Retrieved January 10, 2008,
   http://jcmc.indiana.edu/vol12/issue4/ellison.html
6. Liu, H.: Social network profiles as taste performances. Journal of Computer-Mediated Communication 13(1) (2007) Retrieved December 6, 2007,
   http://jcmc.indiana.edu/vol13/issue1/liu.html
7. Ellison, N., Heino, R., Gibbs, J.: Managing impressions online: Self-presentation processes in the online dating environment. Journal of Computer-Mediated Communication 11(2) (2006), Retrieved June 22, 2007,
   http://jcmc.indiana.edu/vol11/issue2/ellison.html
8. Holton, J.A.: Building trust and collaboration in a virtual team. Team Performance Management: An International Journal 7(3/4), 36–47 (2001)
9. Bendaly, L.: Strength in Numbers: Easy Steps to High Performance Teams. McGraw-Hill Ryerson, Toronto (1997)
10. Wærn, A.: User Involvement in Automatic Filtering: An Experimental Study. User Modeling and User-Adapted Interaction 14(2/3), 201–237 (2004)

Learner Modelling in Exploratory Learning for Mathematical Generalisation

Mihaela Cocea

London Knowledge Lab, Birkbeck College
23-29 Emerald St, WC1N 3QS London (UK)
mihaela@dcs.bbk.ac.uk

Abstract. Exploratory learning supports creative thinking, allowing learners to control their own learning process, whilst it provides them with help and guidance when necessary. This pedagogical approach emphasises learners' active involvement in authentic activities/tasks that simulate real world processes and has been applied to several domains. In this paper we propose a framework for learner modelling that reflects the incremental nature of knowledge construction as learners are engaged in learning mathematical generalisation. We also describe how such a model can potentially support feedback generation.

Keywords: learner modelling, exploratory learning, feedback generation, mathematical generalisation.

1 Introduction

Constructivism [11] sees learning as an active, constructive process in which knowledge is built and structured gradually. Exploratory/discovery learning supports this view of learning and has been argued to be particularly beneficial [2] in terms of providing opportunities for acquiring deep conceptual and structural knowledge. However pure discovery learning without any guidance and support is hardly beneficial [4]. The main challenge with this approach is to balance freedom with control: learners should be given enough freedom so that they can actively engage in constructing models and they should be offered enough guidance in order to assure that their constructions lead to useful knowledge [7].

Besides the clear and well-acknowledged challenge of balancing freedom with guidance, there are other issues that make the process of learner modelling in Exploratory Learning Environments (ELEs) demanding:

- *What to model?* Usually learner models relate to knowledge or skills. In the context of exploratory learning, the knowledge results from constructionist processes and there is a clearer indication of this knowledge at the *end* of these processes. Nevertheless, support is required both during knowledge construction and at the end of certain processing stages. Thus, a key question is what to model so that support can be provided during and at the end of knowledge construction.
- *Value of correct vs. incorrect actions.* In most e-Learning systems, feedback is related to correctness or incorrectness of answers/actions, while in ELEs learner's

W. Nejdl et al. (Eds.): AH 2008, LNCS 5149, pp. 394–399, 2008.

explorations are difficult to categorise into correct or incorrect. Moreover, even if such a classification would be possible, incorrect actions may be more valuable for learning than correct ones. Actually, one of the advantages of ELEs is that learners are given the opportunity to realise their own mistakes and learn from them; thus, rather then pointing out possible mistakes, the system should provide learners with feedback that would encourage reflection on their actions and help them realise that their knowledge construction is not entirely correct.

- *Relation between abstract knowledge and forms of (re)presentation in the system.* ELEs have different ways of (re)presenting and exploring models that should gradually help the learner build abstract knowledge. Each part of the model and each type of exploration (e.g. changing parameters, creating new models, testing models etc.) contributes to this process. Identification of relevant abstract knowledge is needed as well as its representation in the learner model.
- *Identification of underlying strategies* from actions or sequences of actions. Sometimes is neither realistic nor feasible to include all possible outcomes (correct or incorrect) and ways to achieve them when modelling an extensive knowledge domain. Thus, a different approach to what is included in the knowledge structure is required; rather than storing complete information about a task or expert knowledge, key information with informative educational value could be stored such as strategies for approaching the (sub)task and landmarks indicating a particular strategy or (lack of) knowledge about a particular aspect. The challenge is how to find this information and how to represent it in the knowledge structure.

Given the abovementioned challenges, a classical approach to learner modelling based on concepts would not fit the purposes of ELEs. The classic approach involves a particular scenario: learners are required to study materials about a concept and then their knowledge level is assessed through testing. On the contrary, ELEs involve knowledge discovery by means of constructive activities and the emphasis is on the process rather that the knowledge itself and thus, the learner modelling process should reflect this way of learning. The nature of this process places the focus on the interactions of the learner with the system rather than on their answers to tests. Thus, analysing interactions during knowledge construction and extracting relevant information is an essential part of the learner modelling process that together with knowledge about student's learning processes inferred from their models and their learning progression can play an important role in generating feedback and support.

In this paper, we propose a framework for learner modelling in ELEs that follows the principles of constructivism and supports provision of feedback in order to guide the learner towards useful and sound knowledge construction. The following section gives a brief overview of previous research in ELEs and introduces our research questions. In Section 3, our framework is presented together with the methodology and one example. Section 4 presents the expected contributions of our research.

2 Background and Research Questions

We briefly present here three approaches to support exploratory learning: (a) heuristics were used by [10] to guide the learning process for a physics domain; (b) Bayesian networks were used by [1] for the mathematical functions domain; (c) a neuro-fuzzy approach was proposed by [9] for student diagnosis for a physics domain.

The idea of intelligent support is tackled in the first approach using induction and deduction, whilst templates are used to generate feedback; no learner model is used. The second approach addresses "effective exploration" [1], but uses "standard" student modelling in the sense that essential cases for the problems to be explored are used as the equivalent of concepts in classical overlay models. Two of the challenges previously mentioned, i.e. what to model and the difficulty of determining the (in)correctness of an action, were also addressed. The third approach uses knowledge of experts in teaching physics encoded in the form of fuzzy sets and rules and applies training from practical examples when teachers' knowledge is not accurate or well-defined; the purpose was student diagnosis and no feedback is provided.

In contrast to previous attempts, here we advocate an approach that extends user modelling in ELEs by reflecting and supporting the constructionist learning process. Since the focus is on the process, interaction analysis [8] plays an essential part in learner modelling. Typically it starts with filtering raw data in order to extract some indicators related to the quality of the learning process. These indicators can be used for several purposes; in our case, the main purpose is the regulation of the learning process through feedback, while a secondary purpose is to inform teachers about students' learning process and progression. Thus, the research questions addressed in our research are the following: (a) What interactions are relevant and how can they be extracted them from the flow of raw data and transformed into indicators? (b) What should be stored in the learner model in order to represent the evolution of the learner's constructionist models and their corresponding cognitive processes? (c) How should the learner model be updated in order to reflect both the current knowledge and the evolution of knowledge? (d) Using the learner model, how can personalised feedback be provided to support the constructionist process and inform the teacher?

3 Proposed Framework and Methodology

In our framework the ELE includes two components (see Fig. 1): a domain and a task model. The domain model includes high level learning outcomes related to the domain and considers that each learning outcome can be achieved by exploring several tasks. The task model includes different types of information: (a) strategies of approaching the task which could be correct, incorrect or partially correct; (b) outcomes of the exploratory process and solutions to specific questions associated with each (sub) task; (c) landmarks, i.e. relevant aspects or critical events occurring during the exploratory process; (d) context, i.e. reference to this particular task.

In our approach, the structure of the learner model and the updating process follow the model of human memory often used in user modelling (e.g. [5]), and includes two components: a short-term model (STM) and a long-term model (LTM). The STM includes recent actions of the learner. The LTM contains information about the domain and the task and thus has two parts: the Task LTM that has the same structure as the task model, and the Domain LTM, which is an overlay model of the domain and maintains the knowledge of the learning outcomes associated with the learning process as inferred from the learner's constructions.

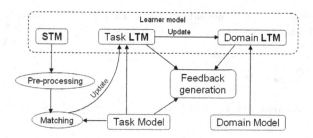

Fig. 1. Learner modelling process

The learner model update and feedback generation are illustrated in Fig. 1. Recent actions of the learner (raw data) are stored in the STM. They are *pre-processed* and the transformed data are *matched* to cases from the Task Model; any identified strategies together with landmarks (if any), outcomes and context are stored or updated in the Task LTM. Based on Task LTM, Task Model and Domain LTM feedback is generated. Finally, the degree of meeting the learning outcome that was explored through the (sub)task is *updated* in the Domain LTM. Thus, the modelling process reflects the constructionist approach of incremental knowledge acquisition.

The learner modelling process supports two types of feedback: during the exploration process and at the end of certain processing stages. The first one aims to guide the learner in gradually constructing the knowledge, while the second one is more related to outcomes of the exploration and specific solutions.

Our framework will be validated by incorporating it into an ELE for mathematical generalisation developed in the context of MiGen project[1] and testing in classrooms. To illustrate our approach we use an example from this domain and a task called 'pond tiling', which is common in the English school curriculum and expects learners to produce a general expression for finding out how many tiles are required for surrounding *any* rectangular pond. The high level learning outcome in the Domain Model is the students' ability to perform structural reasoning. In order to achieve this, subtasks can be explored, e.g. construct a pond of fixed dimensions, surround it with tiles and determine how many are required; generalise the structure using variables.

The Task Model (Fig. 2) could contain: (a) strategies, e.g. thinking in terms of width and height, thinking in terms of areas; (b) landmarks, e.g. creating a rectangle that has the height and width of the pond incremented by two as an indication of the 'areas strategy'; (c) outcomes (e.g. model built, numerical answer for a particular pond) and solution, i.e. a general algebraic expression (e.g. 'areas strategy': $(width+2)*(height+2) - width*height$); (d) context, i.e. reference to the task.

During the task, the actions of the learner are stored in the STM and pre-processed. This process aims to transform the raw data into intermediate level data that will be used to identify (match) the relevant strategies, landmarks, outcomes and solutions for a learner in the current task or subtask. Knowledge of the domain and teachers' expertise together with findings from pilot studies will be used to derive these aspects for every (sub) task and define a 'light-weight' model for mathematical generalisation. For pre-processing, a technique similar to *episodes identification and*

---

[1] The MiGen project is funded by ESRC/EPSRC (TLRP); project website: www.migen.org

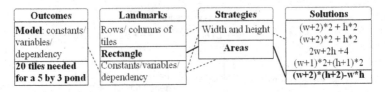

Fig. 2. Partial task model (slots connected by solid lines correspond to the example in the text)

association [6] can be used and comparisons will be made using *fuzzy similarity measures*. After matching, the Task LTM is updated. At the end of the "generalise the structure with variables" subtask, the knowledge associated with variables manipulation, which is considered an important step in the process of developing mathematical reasoning and generalisation ability, is updated in the Domain LTM.

During the (sub) task, feedback is provided based on the Task Model, Task LTM and Domain LTM; e.g. if the learner has surrounded the pond following a strategy that does not generalise well, the feedback can suggest resizing of the pond, which would result in "messing up" [3] the model, and encourage the learner to reflect on what is missing in order to make the solution general.

4 Concluding Remarks and Contribution

Exploratory learning operates on the principle that knowledge is built gradually as a result of active participation in learning. In this context, we proposed a framework for user modelling and briefly described how the model can be used for feedback generation in mathematical generalisation. The expected contributions of this research are: (a) a novel framework for learner modelling that reflects the constructionist learning approach; (b) a mechanism for updating such a model and (c) usage of the learner model for personalised feedback in an ELE and for informing teachers.

References

1. Bunt, A., Conati, C.: Probabilistic Student Modeling to Improve Exploratory Behaviour. Journal of User Modeling and User-Adapted Interaction 13(3), 269–309 (2003)
2. de Jong, T., van Joolingen, W.R.: Scientific discovery learning with computer simulations of conceptual domains. Review of Educational Research 68, 179–202 (1998)
3. Healy, L., Hoelzl, R., Hoyles, C., Noss, R.: Messing Up. Micromath 10(1), 14–16 (1994)
4. Kirschner, P.A., Sweller, J., Clark, R.E.: Why minimal guidance during instruction does not work: An analysis of the failure of constructivist, discovery, problem-based experiential and inquiry-based teaching. Educational Psychologist 41(2), 75–86 (2006)
5. Li, L., Yang, Z., Wang, B., Kitsuregawa, M.: Dynamic Adaptation Strategies for Long-Term and Short-Term User Profile to Personalize Search. APWeb/WAIM, 228–240 (2007)
6. Liu, J., Wong, C.K., Hui, K.K.: An Adaptive User Interface Based on Personalized Learning. IEEE Intelligent Systems 18(2), 52–57 (2003)

7. Mayer, R.: Should There Be a Three-Strikes Rule Against Pure Discovery Learning? The Case for Guided Methods of Instruction. American Psychologist 59(1), 14–19 (2004)
8. Papanikolaou, K., Grigoriadou, M.: Modelling and Externalising Learners' Interaction Behaviour. In: Proceedings of the LeMoRe 2005 workshop, AIED 2005, pp. 52–61 (2005)
9. Stathacopoulou, R., Magoulas, G.D., Grigoriadou, M., Samarakou, M.: Neuro-fuzzy knowledge processing in intelligent learning environments for improved student diagnosis. Information Sciences 170, 273–307 (2005)
10. Veermans, K.H.: Intelligent support for discovery learning, PhD thesis. University of Twente (2003)
11. Vygotsky, L.S.: Mind and society: The development of higher mental processes. Harvard University Press, Cambridge (1978)

GAF: Generic Adaptation Framework

Evgeny Knutov

Technische Universiteit Eindhoven
P.O. Box 513 5600 MB Eindhoven, The Netherlands
e.knutov@tue.nl

Abstract. The Generic Adaptation Framework research project aims to develop a new *reference model* for the adaptive information systems research field. The new model will extend the well known AHAM reference model, taking into account newly developed techniques and methodologies in this area as well as attempts to capture them in architecture models such as the Munich Reference Model [4], LAOS/LAG [2], [5] and the extension from pure adaptive *hypermedia* to adaptive *information systems*, as studied in the Hera research program for instance [6].

Keywords: AHAM, adaptation, generic framework.

1 Introduction

The research field of adaptive hypermedia and adaptive web-based information systems (called AHS for short) has been growing rapidly during the past ten years and this has resulted in new terms, concepts, models, prototypes and methodologies. The main existing reference model AHAM, developed in the beginning of this period, predates many of these new developments. In particular, *open corpus adaptation*, *ontologies*, *group adaptation*, and *data mining tools for adaptation* are not or at least insufficiently supported. Therefore, the GAF project aims at the research how these methodologies can fit into a new reference model of AHS (based on AHAM where possible), called "Generic Adaptation Framework" (or *GAF*), that provides a common reference in terms of both taxonomy and architecture. The new reference will be accompanied by an implementation of a modular generic adaptation framework that can be used for adaptive information systems (or AIS) research as well as for commercial adaptive applications. The implementation will be inspired by (and perhaps partly based on) the well known open source AHA! system [3].

In this paper the research background and research approach for the GAF project will be reviewed, concluded by an on-going work summary.

2 Research Background

The "Generic Adaptation Framework" (GAF) project will research the overall design and implementation of adaptive information systems, aiming at the analysis and definition of a new reference model based on and extending AHAM [7]. GAF is supposed to depict a generic adaptation structure as well as a taxonomy and architectural description

W. Nejdl et al. (Eds.): AH 2008, LNCS 5149, pp. 400–404, 2008.

that can be used for AIS development as well as for adaptive systems research. Research takes into consideration recent methodologies and techniques that took place since AHAM has been developed. Among them open corpus adaptation, ontologies, group adaptation and data mining:

Open corpus adaptation. Most AHS deal with a known set of information items, whether it is a single course, a "bookshelf" or a whole encyclopedia. In such applications a concept space can be mapped onto the document space by the author. However, adaptive applications increasingly consider open corpus adaptation, where resources come from search results in large and dynamic learning object repositories or from a Web search engine. In order to perform adaptation to an unknown document space, the mapping between concepts and documents can only be done at run-time, bringing the fields of hypermedia, databases and information retrieval together.

Ontologies. In many AHS authors create not only the information space but also the concept space for applications. In order to start combining the adaptation from different applications, taking advantage of what one AHS has learnt about the user in another AHS, the meaning of the concepts must be agreed upon. Therefore, instead of arbitrary conceptual structures adaptive applications are becoming based on ontologies. Combining the user models and the adaptation from different applications based on the same ontology is a feasible problem, but when different ontologies are used, the problem of ontology mapping must be tackled first, making the reasoning on the Semantic Web more challenging. Research into reasoning over different ontologies will become core AH research. AHAM can almost handle the single ontology case but has no provision for dealing with multiple ontologies, therefore it becomes a new challenge for GAF.

Group adaptation. With few exceptions AHS perform adaptation to individual users. However this process can be significantly extended by taking into account that adaptation has been performed for other users with a similar profile properties or belonging to the same group. Determining the best partitioning of users into groups and fit this within the generic adaptation framework is another challenge.

Data mining support. The behavior of user groups may provide information that can be used to improve the navigation structure of an application. Data mining is a valuable tool in this respect. For example, clustering users into groups based on their navigational patterns can be used to automatically suggest hyperlinks or products to a user or customer, based on the common interests of the members of the group. The application of data-mining in AH research has been started mostly in the area of e-learning, (see e.g. [11]) but through contacts with industry we have already been examining the need and potential benefits of data mining in other AH areas as well.

3 Research Goal and Approach

Research will focus on how previously mentioned (chapter 2) and other aspects can fit in a generic adaptive information system framework. Like with AHAM the goal is to describe the framework not as an abstract formal model but rather as an abstract description of a non-existent very generic adaptive information system architecture.

The GAF research consists of the following steps or phases:

1. Studying existing adaptive hypermedia systems, web-based information systems, intelligent tutoring systems, intelligent agent systems and other related fields, in order to create an inventory of methods and techniques used in such systems and applications.

2. The architecture consists of a number of components, including a part that deals with concepts, concept relationships and relationships in ontologies, a part that deals with individual user-modeling, a part that performs data mining to identify groups (and group properties), and a part that deals with the low-level adaptation rules. The global architecture will describe how the different modules or services work together.

3. Semantic-Web will be studied in order to learn how systems can reason over concept structures and will be used to define powerful search facilities that use concepts, not page contents, as the basis for searching. The types of relationships used may already be present in the ontologies used by the applications or may be defined as extensions to these ontologies.

4. The subject of data mining will be considered in order to identify user groups, and global navigation patterns. Part of this research is fairly standard sequence mining, but a novel aspect will be the combination of the knowledge of the available (possibly adaptive) navigation structure with the observed navigation patterns in order to determine which changes (adaptation) to the navigation structure is needed.

5. The global architecture will be used to describe the architecture and models of other research projects (AHAM [7], AIMS, CHIME [10], Hera [6], LAOS [5], LAG [2], MOT [8], CHIP [9]) and models and systems developed in other research groups.

6. A model as general as GAF is able to describe systems that exhibit undesirable properties, like having adaptation specifications that may result in infinite loops when executed. In the study of AHAM we already studied *termination* and *confluence* problems and developed a conservative analysis method for the AHAM adaptation rules. In GAF the properties of adaptation specifications will be studied formally as well, leading to the specification of analysis tools that help application developers determine important properties of their systems.

7. Interim results will be presented in papers and at workshops and conferences so as to get feedback from other adaptive hypermedia researchers, and change, adapt and extend the model to cover the important innovations in the field.

An essential part of the research approach is the close collaboration with the researchers working in the other projects in our group.

Validations of achievement and contribution of the research project will be demonstrated through system development. A reference model describing the functionality of adaptation framework will be implemented. In terms of implementation the GAF model needs to describe an abstract machine that could possibly be built. The AHAM reference model was partially implemented in AHA!. In order for GAF to be not just a model for describing and comparing systems, but also a guide for future development of AIS a partial implementation of GAF is needed. A complete implementation is not feasible within the boundaries of the GAF project and current research observations. Additional effort will be put into the development of general-purpose software system. The main goal of GAF in this area is to provide the architecture that needs to be implemented, to separate essential elements from optional and to define criteria distinguishing within these elements, to provide modular structure that can be used either separately or together, depending on the needs of the intended application, that can be developed over generic framework to satisfy different needs.

4 Ongoing Work

So far a high level study of existing methods was done to get a basic understanding of adaptive information systems. A comparison of major AHS systems was done to discover common parts and extract a generic modular structure of the systems. A few proposals have been made regarding usage of state machines and considering a versioning system similar to some aspects of adaptive systems. A high-level sketch of a first architecture proposal was drafted (see Fig.1), where 3 major areas like User/Group model, Content/Link and Domain models tightly connected are presented. A detailed study should be performed in this area to fit existing proposals and new ideas in the concept of GAF. The study of the Layers Adaptation Granularity (LAG) Grammar and LAOS layered WWW authoring model is ongoing to fit that model's adaptation language principles into GAF. Current challenges are to investigate the applicability of different approaches used within different implementations and methodologies like LAG, LAOS, Adaptive Personalized eLearning Service (APeLS), Grapple, as well as new developments in adaptive information systems like open corpus adaptation, ontologies, group adaptation and data mining support and how all these can meet GAF goals and fit architecture proposals.

Fig. 1. GAF high-level architecture proposal

Acknowledgements. This research is supported by NWO "GAF: Generic Adaptation Framework" project.

References

1. De Bra, P., Calvi, L.: AHA! An open Adaptive Hypermedia Architecture. The New Review of Hypermedia and Multimedia 4, 115–139 (1998)
2. Cristea, A., Verschoor, M.: The LAG Grammar for Authoring the Adaptive Web. In: Proceedings of the international Conference on information Technology, vol. 2, p. 382 (2004)
3. De Bra, P., Smits, D., Stash, N.: The Design of AHA! In: Proceedings of the ACM Hypertext 2006 Conference, pp. 133–134 (2006)
4. Koch, N., Wirsing, M.: The Munich Reference Model for Adaptive Hypermedia Application. In: Proceedings of the Second International Conference on Adaptive Hypermedia and Adaptive Web-Based Systems, pp. 213–222 (2002)
5. Cristea, A., De Mooij, A.: LAOS: Layered WWW AHS Authoring Model and their corresponding Algebraic Operators. In: The Twelfth International World Wide Web Conference, Alternate Track on Education (2003)
6. Houben, G.J., Van der Sluijs, K., Barna, P., Broekstra, J., Casteleyn, S., Fiala, Z., Frasincar, F.: Hera – book chapter: Web Engineering: Modeling and Implementing Web Applications. Human-Computer Interaction Series, pp. 263–301. Springer, Heidelberg (2008)
7. De Bra, P., Houben, G.J., Wu, H.: AHAM: A Dexter-based Reference Model for Adaptive Hypermedia. In: Proceedings of the ACM Conference on Hypertext and Hypermedia, pp. 147–156 (1999)
8. Cristea, A., De Mooij, A.: Evaluation of MOT, an AHS Authoring Tool. In: CATE 2003 (International Conference on Computers and Advanced Technology in Education), Greece, IASTED, pp. 241–246. ACTA Press (2003)
9. Aroyo, L., Stash, N., Wang, Y., Gorgels, P., Rutledge, L.: CHIP Demonstrator: Semantics-driven Recommendations and Museum Tour Generation. In: Proc. International Semantic Web Conference (2007)
10. De Bra, P., Aroyo, L., Chepegin, V.: The Next Big Thing: Adaptive Web-Based Systems. Journal of Digital Information 5(1), article 247 (2004)
11. Romero, C., Ventura, S., De Bra, P., De Castro, C.: Discovering Prediction Rules in AHA! Courses. In: Proceedings of the User Modeling Conference, pp. 35–44 (2003)

Engineering Information Systems towards Facilitating Scrutable and Configurable Adaptation

Kevin Koidl and Owen Conlan

Knowledge & Data Engineering Group, School of Computer Science and Statistics,
O'Reilly Institute, Trinity College Dublin, Ireland
{Kevin.Koidl, Owen.Conlan}@cs.tcd.ie

Abstract. End users of Adaptive Hypermedia Systems (AHS) receive an experience that has been tailored towards their specific needs. Several AHS have produced favourable results showing benefits to the user experience [2]. However, the nature of AHS is that they tend to operate across a focused and fixed domain with a single body of content that is known a priori. This approach limits the user's freedom to choose other information sources and restricts the potential impact an adaptive systems may have. To provide more flexibility several service orientated approaches extending traditional AHS architectures have been introduced. This Ph.D. work proposes the re-engineering of information systems in order to support the portability of adaptive services, thus enabling them to personalize any information system on behalf of the user. This approach espouses user empowerment through this mobility and through a highly scrutable and configurable approach to such service-oriented adaptation.

Keywords: Personalization, Adaptation systems and techniques, intelligent agents for personalization and adaptivity.

1 Introduction

Adaptive Hypermedia Systems (AHS) typically concentrate on adapting content and structure within a specific domain to a user's needs and preferences. They have achieved quite high degrees of success [2]. However, these attempts to overcome the 'one size fits all' issue are isolated, contextualized and highly domain specific. Most adaptive systems rely on a fixed and well known environment, consisting of a well described domain, adaptive logic and various other information models [10]. Although this approach can be effective within the defined domain, it mostly results in an inflexible and dependant architecture. Once designed, it is difficult and costly to alter. From a users perspective these approaches potentially minimize the 'lost in hyperspace' experience, but can lead to a loss of navigational freedom within the content and in the choice of content repositories. A user should have the choice of accessing different information sources without any assistance or, if using an adaptive system, being able to use it in a flexible and scrutable manner.

Recent approaches, such as APeLS [5] and KnowledgeTree [3] are heading in this direction by attempting to abstract the adaptation process from the adapted and personalized information. These service-oriented approaches have initially concentrated

W. Nejdl et al. (Eds.): AH 2008, LNCS 5149, pp. 405–409, 2008.

on the adaptation logic, but have not yet offered guidance on how the information system[1] they are adapting may be modified to best accept their recommendations.

This work concentrates on re-engineering information systems in order to best accept recommendations from adaptive services. For the adaptive service this approach leads to more flexibility in the choice of the information system and for the user it enables possibilities for a higher level of control and scrutiny in what has been adapted on his behalf.

Therefore the research introduced in this paper addresses the following challenges:

1. To enable more flexible and independent adaptive services.
2. To develop a reference model for designing information systems towards facilitating such flexible and independent adaptive services.
3. To design a holistic adaptive approach emphasising the needs of the user by providing appropriate possibilities for scrutiny in all adaptive processes.

This paper, which reflects the early stages of Ph.D. research, will give a brief overview of the State of the Art in the described subject area, followed by a simple Use Case and conclusion considering the proposed research challenges.

2 State of the Art

In the following, different traditional and service orientated approaches in the research area of AHS will be discussed.

The Adaptive Personalized eLearning Service (APeLS) [4] is service based, with a generic adaptive engine implementing a multi model approach. This approach provides the possibility of creating independent narratives representing the adaptive logic in a flexible way [5]. APeLS service orientated design, allows flexibility not only within the model approach, but also towards different information systems and platforms.

A different approach is followed by ELM-ART [12]. The two main adaptive features are *visual adaptive annotation of links* and *individual curriculum sequencing*. For adaptive annotation of links a multi-layered overlay model is used leading to a visual annotation of the links according to the learning state of the corresponding unit. The individual curriculum sequencing is based on an optimal path calculation using the current learning goal and all prerequisites necessary to reach that goal. In addition the learner can alter the adaptation logic indirectly by editing the learner model.

AHA! [6], as another example, provides *adaptive link hiding or link annotation* and *conditional inclusion of fragments* with a concept based overlay user model. Changes in the user model are defined by adaptation rules which can be created manually with a concept editor. Even though ELM-ART and AHA! provide powerful adaptive features and additional tools for the simple creation of adaptive courses they miss the flexibility of a web service driven architecture.

Most adaptive systems provide sound adaptive features, but it is still a complex undertaking to add a new domain area, user group or adaptive logic. In order to overcome this disadvantage some AHS are based on an underlying reference model.

---

[1] In this context an information system is seen as a semantically enriched content repository providing service orientated interfaces and structured web-based access.

The most fundamental reference model in hypermedia is the Dexter reference model [8] which inspired several extensions. In this context especially those with the focus on semantic interoperability of different components and links are of interest. For example, the AHAM reference model consists of user model integration, session independency and the enabling of plugging different adaptive techniques into the reference model [7]. Many of the AHA! features are inspired by the AHAM reference model [6]. A different, but also Dexter model based approach is followed by Albert and Hockemeyer [1]. They introduce an extension of the Dexter model connecting hypertext structures and knowledge space theory by using the concept of prerequisite links in dynamic hypertext to create individual learning paths. Wang on the other hand extends the Dexter model to support semantic relationships between nodes [11]. These concepts lead to the promising conclusion that designing adaptive approaches based on accepted reference models can lead the way into more flexible adaptive approaches.

These models, however, focus exclusively on the abstracted modelling of the system and do not make reference to the quality of the end-user experience. In order to provide a holistic adaptive approach it is seen as essential that the adaptive service provides the user with the possibility of scrutiny. This supports the user in examining what has been modified on their behalf and why it has been modified [9]. The goal is to provide transparent and scrutable access to both the user model and all adaptive processes. This in effect should potentially lead to a more involved experience of the adaptive service, thus facilitating the user in gaining better control over this experience.

3   Use Case / Example

In order to indicate the challenges of this research a simple Use Case, in the context of self-guided adaptive eLearning, is described.

In this Use Case a user, named Sean, wishes to learn more about car engines. Previously he has read about electric motors and he understands the basics of Newtonian physics. In Sean's previous learning he used a personal adaptive service that monitored and adapted the information systems that he engaged with, in order to improve his experience. This adaptive service is available at all times and 'hooks' into the information systems in order to tweak their operation and provide Sean with means to adjust his interests and goals. To achieve this, the adaptive service enables three types of adaptations – modification of content, scrutiny of all adaptive processes and a user modeling portlet. In continuing this Use Case the applicability of each of these adaptations will be highlighted.

Sean browses to a well know internet encyclopedia in order to begin his exploration of the car engine. This website, which may be seen as an information system, exposes a service interface that facilitates a connection to an adaptive service. When Sean logs into the encyclopedia his preferred adaptive service, recorded in his website preferences, is contacted. At this point a portlet, a discrete piece of dynamic web content, which represents his preferences and goals, is integrated into the encyclopedia page. This portlet, representing one of the three adaptation types mentioned earlier, is generated by the adaptive service and gives Sean direct and usable means of controlling what he is interested in. Sean specifies that he is interested in car engines. The adaptive service records this interest as a goal in his user model and uses it to inform and guide the encyclopedia.

As Sean has previously learned about electric motors and Newtonian Physics there are certain topics, in learning about the car engine, which he may skip. The adaptive service has an associated domain ontology that it uses to semantically guide selections in the information service. For example, when starting to read about the car engine, a topic such as 'torque' may be hidden, using simple presentation adaptation techniques. This adaptation has been requested by the adaptive service and is implemented within the encyclopedia website. This illustrates the content modification. It assumes that a common semantic understanding exists between the information system and the adaptive service, as well as, a reasonably fine grained mechanism for turning on and off certain pieces of content.

The final type of adaptation, espoused in this Use Case, is that of scrutiny. It may appear very similar to the content modification described earlier, but it relates to the choice Sean made in the user modeling portlet. The modifications made in the user model enact on his behalf. For example, if Sean is not satisfied with what is being displayed, he may turn on the scrutiny feature and view the positions where content was hidden. In this simple Use Case, it will be highlighted, coupled with the adaptive services rationale for hiding it.

If Sean now wishes to use another information system, such as a car manufacturer's website, the adaptive service will retain his previous preferences and a semantic understanding of what he browsed in order to inform and adapt his experience with this new information source.

4 Conclusion

The above Use Case highlights a very different paradigm for how users currently receive personalised information. It matches closely to the user's current browsing pattern, i.e. using many different sources, with the difference that the described enriched information systems now communicate and cooperate with a personal adaptive service, which has prior knowledge of the user and an understanding of their goals. This approach has significant implications on the design of the information system and exposes a different methodological approach for adaptation. Service oriented systems, such as APeLS and KnowledgeTree, provide a technological framework that may be suitable for the proposed approach. However, adaptation reference models, such as AHAM!, do not explicitly support this highly semantic interoperation. Central to the Use Case is to empower the user with a high level of control and feedback. As such, scrutiny is essential in order to ensure the adaptive service can be agile and responsive enough to meet the user's evolving needs.

This Ph.D., still in its early months, will address the engineering of information systems and the associated modifications necessary to service-oriented adaptation approaches. It will do so in the context of a semantically rich interchange of information and instructions between the information system and the adaptive service. This approach, which offers users an unprecedented level of mobility between different information systems, has the potential to bring the benefits of personalization to general web browsing activities.

References

[1] Albert, D., Hockemeyer, C.: Adaptive and Dynamic Hypertext Tutoring Systems Based on Knowledge Space Theory. Artificial Intelligence in Education: Knowledge and Media in Learning Systems 39, 553–555 (1997)

[2] Brusilovsky, P.: Adaptive and Intelligent Technologies for Web-based Education. Künstliche Intelligenz, Special Issue on Intelligent Systems and Teleteaching 4, 19–25 (1999)

[3] Brusilovsky, P.: KnowledgeTree: A Distributed Architecture for Adaptive E-Learning. In: International World Wide Web Conference, Proceedings of the 13th international World Wide Web conference, pp. 104–113 (2004)

[4] Conlan, C., Wade, W.: Evaluation of APeLS – An Adaptive eLearning Service based on the Multi-model, Metadata-driven Approach. In: De Bra, P.M.E., Nejdl, W. (eds.) AH 2004. LNCS, vol. 3137, pp. 291–295. Springer, Heidelberg (2004)

[5] Conlan, O., Wade, V., Bruen, C., Gargan, M.: Multi-model, Metadata Driven Approach to Adaptive Hypermedia Services for Personalized eLearning. In: De Bra, P., Brusilovsky, P., Conejo, R. (eds.) AH 2002. LNCS, vol. 2347, pp. 100–111. Springer, Heidelberg (2002)

[6] De Bra, P., Aerts, A., Berden, B., De Lange, B., Rousseau, B., Santic, T., Smith, D., Stash, N.: AHA! The Adaptive Hypermedia Architecture. In: Proceedings of the ACM Hypertext Conference (2003)

[7] De Bra, P., Houben, G.J., Wu, H.: AHAM: A Dexter-Based Reference Model for Adaptive Hypermedia. In: UK Conference on Hypertext, pp. 147–156 (1999)

[8] Halasz, F., Schwartz, M.: The Dexter Hypertext Reference Model. ACM Communications 37, 30–39 (1994)

[9] Kay, J.: Scrutable Adaptation: Because We Can and Must. In: Adaptive Hypermedia and Adaptive Web-based Systems. In: Wade, V.P., Ashman, H., Smyth, B. (eds.) AH 2006. LNCS, vol. 4018, pp. 11–19. Springer, Heidelberg (2006)

[10] Stash, N., Cristea, A.I., De Bra, P.: Adaptation languages as vehicles of explicit intelligence in Adaptive Hypermedia. International Journal of Continuing Engineering Education and Life-Long Learning 17(4/5), 319–336 (2007)

[11] Wang, B.: Extend Dexter model to capture more semantics of hypermedia. In: Quirchmayr, G., Bench-Capon, T.J.M., Schweighofer, E. (eds.) DEXA 1998. LNCS, vol. 1460, pp. 511–522. Springer, Heidelberg (1998)

[12] Weber, G., Brusilovsky, P.: ELM-ART: An adaptive versatile system for Web-based instruction. International Journal of Artificial Intelligence in Education 12, Special Issue on Adaptive and Intelligent Web-based Education Systems 4, 351–384 (2001)

Flexible Adaptivity in AEHS Using Policies

Arne W. Koesling[1,2], Daniel Krause[1], and Eelco Herder[1]

[1] L3S Research Center,
Appelstr. 9a, 30167 Hannover, Germany
[2] Peter L. Reichertz Institute for Medical Informatics,
University of Braunschweig-Institute of Technology and Hannover Medical School,
Muehlenpfordtstrasse 23, 38106 Braunschweig, Germany
{koesling,krause,herder}@L3S.de

Abstract. In this paper, we show how existing adaptive educational hypermedia systems can be enhanced by policies. In traditional systems, the adaptation is based on predefined user and domain models and fairly restricted adaptation rules. Policies allow for sophisticated and flexible adaptation rules, provided by multiple stakeholders. We present the benefits and feasibility of the approach with AHA! as a hands-on example.

Keywords: AHA, adaptive, hypermedia, trust management, policy.

1 Introduction and Problem Statement

Lifelong learning has become an essential element of our everyday working life. As lifelong learning is associated with a large diversity in interests, knowledge and backgrounds, the one-size-fits-all approach of conventional learning management systems may not cater all individual user needs. The field of Adaptive Educational Hypermedia Systems (AEHS) is an active research area and the community has become aware of the benefits of adaptivity. Nevertheless, in contrast to commercial (non-adaptive) systems, AEHS are often (prototypic) systems that are used by a small audience [10]. One of the reasons for this is the use of hand-tailored, application-specific models of the user and the domain, and a limited, predefined set of adaptation rules. Interoperability and flexible rules that allow for conflicting statements would allow adaptive systems to benefit from user profile information from other systems. Furthermore, authoring courses in adaptive systems can be a complex task for course designers. Policy languages, together with engines that interpret the policies, offer an easy-to-integrate solution for this problem. Depending on the language used, policies can be used for negotiations and for access control and explanations. This does not only allow for resolving conflicting statements, but also provides means for making a system scrutable. In this paper we describe our approach and discuss the benefits and feasibility. Section 2 shows a motivation scenario. In Section 3 we give a short overview of the features of policy languages. Section 4 shows the detailed benefits for AEHS and presents a hands-on example for AHA!. The paper ends with a section on related work and some concluding remarks.

W. Nejdl et al. (Eds.): AH 2008, LNCS 5149, pp. 410–415, 2008.

2   Motivation Scenario

In the following scenario we demonstrate how an adaptive system may benefit from policies. John is a student in economics, with a minor in German. John performed several courses at different universities, making use of several AEHS. John wants to subscribe to a course in 'Advanced Business German' at a different university than where he studies. The course designer has defined as a prerequisite that the learner has to have at least 'Fundamentals of German Grammar'. John's ePortfolio does not contain the required credential, but has instead the credential 'Intermediate German 2' from his home university, which is actually better than the required credential.

When John applies for the course, a negotiation process is started in the background. As John considers his learning knowledge sensitive, the AEHS uses policies for negotiating a certain level of trust between the learner and the system. John's computer sends credentials to proof that he is a student of the university and the server shows the university credentials and the university's privacy policy. Additionally, the server asks for the credential 'Fundamentals of German Grammar'. John's computer offers the credential 'Intermediate German 2'. The policy engine at the server requests an external competence map service that confirms that John's competence fullfils the minimum requirement. John is therefore able to join the course. As a certain level of trust has been established, John grants access to his ePortfolio, so the server is able to fetch John's learner preferences. A third-party server is used for translating John's university's proprietary ePortfolio format into an exchangeable format. These preference policies are used to negotiate the actual structure of the group course by matching it with his fellow students' profiles and the teacher's preferred mentoring style.

Policies can also contribute to the ongoing work on scrutability. *Explanations* allow for queries to the policy engine asking about details for certain decisions. At some point in the course, John notices that his peer students receive more contextual information. The system may explain that the text was omitted because of his high level knowledge in that field, as stated by his certificate. As a group discussion was planned on Friday afternoon, his second choice, he wants to know why the discussion has not been planned on Thursday morning. The system shows a trace of the reasoning on his own and his fellow learners' agendas.

3   Policies

A policy is generally understood as a statement that defines the behaviour of a system. Policies are intended to guide decisions and actions. In today's software systems, policies are primarily used for solving security and privacy concerns – such as controlling access to sensitive user data – and to model business rules. As an example, new customers of an online shop have to pay in advance, while regular costumers may be allowed to pay after delivery. In the scope of eLearning, similar policies would be possible, formulated in a logic-based format, that depends on the policy language used. Assuming that the course designer creates a 'beginner business german course' and wants to ensure, that each participant has sufficient knowledge, she may define a policy stating a prerequisite for the course that requires a certificate of 'german fundamental grammar' to be possessed by the learner requesting access. In the Protune policy language this may be written as:

$$(1) \quad isAllowedToSubscribe(LearnerName) \leftarrow$$
$$(2) \qquad credential(C),$$
$$(3) \qquad C.type : competence,$$
$$(4) \qquad C.owner : LearnerName,$$
$$(5) \qquad C.issuer : 'UK\ National\ Language\ Institute',$$
$$(6) \qquad C.attribute : LanguageCertificate,$$
$$(7) \qquad LanguageCertificate.name : 'Certificate\ Name',$$
$$(8) \qquad LanguageCertificate.value : 'German\ Fundamental\ Grammar'.$$

$$(9) \quad credential(\_) \rightarrow type : provisional.$$
$$(10) \quad credential(\_) \rightarrow actor : peer.$$
$$(11) \quad credential(C) \rightarrow explanation : ``Credential"\ \&\ C\ \&\ ``is\ sent".$$

Similar to logic programs, the predicate 'isAllowedToSubscribe' in line 1 holds, if each statement in the lines 2–8 hold. Lines 9–11 represent Metarules defining additional statements about the predicates used. Line 9 states the type of the predicate. In this case, we assume that 'credential' is defined further outside the policy and associated with the action to send a credential to the communicating party. Line 10 tells that the party that needs to perform the action is the other peer and line 11 states an explanation for 'credential' described below. In [4] we examined the applicability of policies in open infrastructures for lifelong learning in general. In this paper, we gave an overview of both policy languages and policy engines, which are used to evaluate policies. The declarative nature of policy languages enables users to define *what* the system should do, and do not require knowledge about *how* the system realizes it. Policy engines like Protune [11], which operate on a rule-based policy language, have a declarative nature. In general, policy languages also provide reasoning support. In addition, Protune offers the previously described explanations. Users have the possibility to specifically ask *why* a certain answer was deduced or a decision was taken.

A remarkable feature of (Protune) policies is that they also allow for integrating external (environmental) information into the decision making process. By performing negotiations, the user can be asked for particular preferences, credentials, etc. Furthermore, integration of policies into existing systems can be easy as some policy engines can be called in a service-oriented manner.

4   Implementation of Policies in AEHS

In this section, we show how policies can be integrated into the well-known adaptive educational hypermedia system AHA! [3]. A lower-level integration does not allow for all of the issues which were included in the above scenario, but it can be reached in a less complex way by integrating queries to the policy engine into the AHA! adaptation rule conditions. If a user follows an AHA! course and the AHA! engine evaluating its adaption rules hits such a policy engine query, it just has to pass the query to a connected policy engine.

The policy engine can be connected to any information source – from specific user models to generic resources on the Internet – and will evaluate the query and reason over the existing policies. The result is passed back to the AHA! engine. Such a query that is sent e.g. to the Protune Policy Engine is similar to a query to a Prolog engine. The result can be a boolean value. However, if the query contains variables, the result will return those variables, bound to values. As an example, such a query could utilize external sources to verify if the provided resume fulfills the prerequisites of a learning resource or to check for the user's learning style, as specified in some local user profile. This approach gives a powerful means to the course designers, as they allow for considering some aspects outside the system that AHA! currently can't provide itself.

Additionally, such a query is built in a simple manner, due to the fact that, in most cases, it mainly consists of a meaningful term, like a method call from programming, which hides a complex set of policies and reasoning mechanisms within the policy engine. The policy sets can be edited by a rule designer to provide course authors with both predefined queries for instant use and powerful advanced functionality. By separating the rule design from course authoring, course authors do not need to know in detail how the adaptation functionality is technically accomplished.

5 Related Work

There are already many systems with their own, proprietary rule frameworks. These frameworks allow for complex adaption rules that provide many of the features presented in this paper and in [4]. As these rule systems have different emphasis, they are limited in their functionality and are strongly coupled to their systems. We are not aware of other approaches that rely on using advanced policies like we do here. General learning management systems – such as Moodle or Sakai – have very simple rule systems and offer no or only rudimentary features regarding adaptivity. However, there are already some efforts to enhance generic LMS like Moodle with adaptive functionality (see [5]). In an ambitious research project like Alfanet [8], which aims to make use of multi-agent technologies, learner preferences can be used to steer the behaviour of agents. Managements of interaction between multiple agents is already an objective in policy research. To the best of our knowledge, the idea of adding policies to e-learning in general and especially to AEHS is a largely unexplored area.

6 Conclusions

In traditional systems, the adaptation is based on predefined user and domain models, and fairly restricted adaptation rules. In this paper, we showed how existing adaptive educational hypermedia systems can be enhanced by policies. In particular in the field of lifelong learning, with many stakeholders and potentially many conflicting requirements and preferences, there is a need for adaptive systems that employ flexible rules and conflict resolution mechanisms. We discussed how the approach can be used for integration into the well-known AHA!-system. As a next step, we will conduct a qualitative study, at an Hannover-based institute for higher education, on what implicit policies authors, teachers and learners currently employ – and to what extent this is supported by their current systems. We also plan to implement and evaluate the use of policies within the TENCompetence project.

Acknowledgments. We would like to thank Daniel Olmedilla and Fabian Abel for contributing with suggestions, remarks and feedback. The work reported in this paper is partially funded by the European Commission in the TENCompetence project (IST-2004-02787).

References

1. Hauger, D., Koeck, M.: State of the Art of Adaptivity in E-Learning Platforms. In: ABIS 2007 - 15th Workshop on Adaptivity and User Modeling in Interactive System, Halle, Germany, pp. 355–360 (2007)
2. De Bra, P., Aerts, A., Berden, B., de Lange, B., Rousseau, B., Santic, T., Smits, D., Stash, N.: AHA! The Adaptive Hypermedia Architecture. In: Conference on Hypertext and Hypermedia - Proceedings of the fourteenth ACM conference on Hypertext and Hypermedia, Nottingham, UK, pp. 81–84 (2003)
3. De Bra, P., Smits, D., Stash, N.: Creating and Delivering Adaptive Courses with AHA! In: Innovative Approaches for Learning and Knowledge Sharing - 1st European Conference on Technology Enhanced Learning, EC-TEL 2006, Crete, Greece, pp. 21–33 (2006)
4. De Coi, J.L., Kaerger, P., Koesling, A.W., Olmedilla, D.: Exploiting Policies in an Open Infrastructure for Lifelong Learning. In: Duval, E., Klamma, R., Wolpers, M. (eds.) EC-TEL 2007. LNCS, vol. 4753, pp. 26–40. Springer, Heidelberg (2007)
5. Tiarnaigh, M.: Adaptive Moodle. An Integration of Moodle (Modular Object Oriented Dynamic Learning Environment) with an AHS. Final Year Project. University of Dublin (May 2005)
6. Brusilovsky, P.: Developing adaptive educational hypermedia systems: From design models to authoring tools. In: Murray, T., Blessing, S., Ainsworth, S. (eds.) Authoring Tools for Advanced Technology Learning Environment, pp. 377–409. Kluwer Academic Publishers, Dordrecht
7. Brusilovsky, P., Farzan, R., Ahn, J.: Layered Evaluation of Adaptive Search. In: Proceedings of Workshop on Evaluating Exploratory Search Systems. At SIGIR 2006 (2006)
8. van Rosmalen, P., Brouns, F., Tattersall, C., Vogten, H., van Bruggen, J., Sloep, P., Koper, R.: Towards an open framework for adaptive, agent-supported e-learning. International Journal of Continuing Engineering Education and Life-Long Learning 15(3/4/5/6), 261–275 (2005)

9. Brusilovsky, P., Henze, N.: Open Corpus Adaptive Educational Hypermedia. In: The Adaptive Web 2007, pp. 671–696 (2007)
10. Paramythis, A., Loidl-Reisinger, S.: Adaptive Learning Environments and e-Learning Standards. Electronic J. of e-Learning 2(2) (2004) (paper 11)
11. Bonatti, P., Olmedilla, D.: Driving and monitoring provisional trust negotiation with metapolicies. In: 6th IEEE Policies for Distributed Systems and Networks (POLICY 2005), Stockholm, Sweden, June 2005, pp. 14–23. IEEE Computer Society, Los Alamitos (2005)

A Validation Framework for Formal Models in Adaptive Work-Integrated Learning

Barbara Kump

Inffeldgasse 21a, 8010 Graz
Knowledge Management Institute, TU Graz
bkump@tugraz.at

Abstract. The focus of my thesis is on the development of a multi-method framework for the validation of formal models (domain model, user model, and teaching model) for adaptive work-integrated learning. In order to test its general applicability, the framework will be applied in four different realistic work domains. In this article, specific challenges of traditional validating approaches in work-integrated learning are being discussed. Eventually, the core ideas and methods of the validation framework are outlined.

1 Formal Models for Adaptive Work-Integrated Learning

Formal models are used for realizing adaptivity in adaptive learning systems. These formal models together fulfill the functions of a *domain model*, a *user model*, and a *teaching model* [1].

The *domain model* contains the structured expert knowledge in the learning domain, i.e. those *domain concepts* which are relevant for learning. In many cases, the domain model also specifies relations among domain concepts. For example, *statics*, *scale*, or *construction material* might be relevant domain concepts in the domain of *Architecture*. Properties of the user (knowledge, or skills, but also preferences, misconceptions etc.) are represented in the *user model*. In other words, the user model contains any information that the system knows about the learner.

The user model constitutes the rationale for individualized learning opportunities, and it is used throughout the interaction of the learner with the learning system, in order to adapt to the needs of that learner [2]. Following the example from above, an experienced architect might have high values, and thus "a high degree of knowledge" for all three domain concepts (*statics, scale, construction material*). Within this conception, the user model keeps track of how much the user knows about each of the concepts in the application domain. The *teaching model* designates the learning opportunities that are offered to the user in a certain situation, based on the actual *learning need* of a user. The actual *learning need* is derived from a discrepancy between situational requirements (e.g. a task at hand), and knowledge, skills and abilities of the user that are stored in the user model. Conceptually, the teaching model applies didactical strategies (realized as algorithms) for providing a user with accurate learning content. For instance, if the architect from the example above would have to perform the task *Select material for the building based on its groundplan and height*, the task might require knowledge about *statics*, and *construction material*. If the architect does

W. Nejdl et al. (Eds.): AH 2008, LNCS 5149, pp. 416–420, 2008.

not have knowledge about these domain concepts, the two concepts constitute the learning need of the architect.

Validation of formal models for adaptive technology enhanced learning can address different aspects of the models. The concrete research questions to be answered with validation studies are strongly depending upon the theories that are underlying the respective modeling approach. Therefore, in the next section, I will sketch the theoretical foundation that was chosen for modeling the application domains of the learning system under consideration.[1]

2 Competence-Based Knowledge Space Theory

Competence-based Knowledge Space Theory was chosen as a theoretical framework for building formal models of the work-integrated learning system under consideration. With this, Korossy [3] has introduced an extension of Knowledge Space Theory [4] which has been developed in the 1980s and 90s as an attempt to model a person's competence as close as possible to observable behavior. It is predominantly concerned with the diagnosis of knowledge and has been applied in adaptive testing and tutoring scenarios and system (e.g. [5], [6]).

Competence-based Knowledge Space Theory assumes that a learning domain can be structured as a set of tasks. In the domain *Architecture*, for instance, a task could be *Draw rough plan of a building*, or *Select material for the building*. Each task requires a specific set of competencies (e.g., *scale, construction material*) that are represented as domain concepts in the domain model. The set of competencies that is required for performing a task is termed the *task demand* of a task.

Strongly simplified, the domain model is structured by a set of tasks, a set of competencies, and a mapping of tasks and competencies (task demand). The user model is regarded as the collection of the competence states of all users. The competence state of a user is represented as a vector of the length n, where n is the number of competencies in the domain model. Each position of the vector contains a value that refers to one of the competencies. After a task execution, the competence state of a user is updated by raising the value of the competencies that constitute the task demand of the task. The higher the value in the competence state, the more often the user has "proven" the competency in a task execution. The teaching model is also based on the task demand of a task: The task demand of a task at hand is compared with the competence state of the user, and the learning need is derived.

One decisive advantage of the Competence-based Knowledge Space Theory is that modelling can immediately become the object of validation studies. Strongly simplified, model predictions are tested against observable performance, which has been conducted in several domains, such as Mathematics, Chess, or Word Problems ([5], [7]). Different methods and measures have been suggested for testing the model fit, and thereby assessing the overall model validity of the domain model and the user model ([8], [9], [10]).

[1] APOSDLE is partially funded under the FP6 of the European Commission within the IST Workprogramme (project number 027023). The Know-Center is funded by the Austrian Competence Center program Kplus under the auspices of the Austrian Ministry of Transport, Innovation and Technology (www.ffg.at) and by the State of Styria.

However, in work domains, a direct empirical validation by comparing observed solution patterns with predicted performance states is difficult, or even impossible for several reasons. A sufficient number of workers is required, who are neither able to achieve every task nor fail at every task. And, probably even more problematic, in order to obtain accurate solution patterns, every person under consideration must have tried to perform every task of the domain. Both these conditions may be hard to meet in a knowledge intensive work domain. Alternative validation methods focusing on construct validity have been applied for Competence-based Knowledge Space Theory in knowledge management approaches (e.g. [26], [27]). The latter are regarded to be a promising starting point for developing alternative methods in empirical validation studies.

3   A Multi-method Approach for Model Validation

In the course of my thesis, based on existing research, innovative ways shall be found for validating the formal domain model, user model and teaching model. The validation framework shall be applied in four different realistic work settings[2], in order to test its general applicability.

Firstly, the methodology shall allow for identifying inaccuracies of the domain model, and for deriving concrete implications for model revision. As the mechanisms for updating user models are based on the task demand which is part of the domain model, a valid domain model is a pre-condition for a valid user model. Secondly, the methodology shall be useful for assessing the validity of an existing user model (i.e., the collection of competence states of all users). Thirdly, the adaptation mechanisms of the teaching model shall be evaluated, especially with respect to the detection of the learning need. Moreover, the existing modeling methodology shall be improved, based on the results of model validation and evaluation. Eventually, the usefulness of the validation framework itself shall be assessed.

More concretely, the following research questions should be addressed by the validation methodology:

- Are the tasks complete and correct? Are the task demands, i.e. the mappings from tasks to competencies complete and correct?
- Are the competence states accurate, i.e. do the competence states in the user models depict the users "true" competence states?
- Is the learning need that is detected by the learning system accurate, i.e. is the adaptation rule of the teaching model accurate?

A multi-method-approach shall be developed for validating the formal.

Validation studies will be performed "online", i.e. with the prototype of the learning environment in use, as well as "offline". The participants will be both, domain experts, and regular knowledge workers. Data gathering will make use of structured face to face interviews, questionnaires, and user logs. Lessons learned during validation studies will be used to further improve the framework.

---

[2] The four application domains are sub-domains of the *European Aeronautic Defence and Space Company* (EADS France), the *Innovation Service Network* (ISN Graz, Austria), the *Chamber of Commerce and Industry* (CCI Darmstadt, Germany), and of *Statistical Data Analysis* (company independent).

With regard to the domain model, the aim is to answer the questions, whether the tasks, competencies and task demands are valid. For addressing the question of whether the tasks are complete and correct, structured interviews will be conducted (offline), and log data will be reviewed (online). Currently, different types of interview questions are being tested in the course of extensive pre-studies. This is for finding out which type of question an expert is able to answer, who is not familiar with the rationale of modeling.

The validity of the task demands and the completeness of the competencies will also be tackled using both, offline and online techniques. A validation questionnaire has been developed, tested and refined in the course of pre-studies. In this questionnaire, for each task, the expert is asked to (re-) assign the competencies that constitute the task demand of a task, or to add missing competencies. The responses of the expert are then correlated with the domain model under consideration. A high correlation is regarded as an indicator for high validity. By reviewing the results task-wise, tasks with low agreement can be identified, and the task demand can be improved. Besides the offline technique of a validation questionnaire, log data will be used for validating, and improving the domain model. For instance, if a competency is included in the task demand of a task, but no one of the users selects learning content for this competency, if he or she arrives at the task, then the validity of the task demand would have to be reconsidered. Furthermore, an automated self-assessment questionnaire will be used for cross-validating model predictions. Regular knowledge workers with different degrees of expertise will be asked to fill the questionnaire. A cross-validation technique will then be applied to investigate overall model validity based on the self-assessment patterns of the users.

The user model will be validated by assessing the fit of automatically generated competence states, and the self-perception of the users, or the perception of supervisors or peers. Therefore the outcomes from various sources of assessment (self-assessment questionnaires, interviews, assessment of colleagues, or supervisors, etc.) will be correlated with a user's competence state according to the user model. Additionally, log data will be used for comparing the actual selection of the learning content with the current competence state of a user. If the user, for instance, always selects content that is not in line with his or her competence state, this might serve as an indicator for low validity of the user model. However, it might also point out the fact that the adaptation mechanisms of the teaching model are not valid.

For validating the teaching model, besides reviewing log data, structured expert interviews will be performed. Experts will be asked questions of the following type: *Given an existing competence state of a user, what knowledge would the user need for successfully performing the task at hand?* Then, the expert's answers would be compared to the adaptation performed by the teaching model of the learning system. For further refining the teaching model, different algorithms for predicting user behavior from the competence states of users will be designed, and applied for predicting user behavior.

It becomes obvious that the interpretation of results of single validation studies as described above is not always straightforward because (at least in the application under consideration) the domain model, user model and teaching model are strongly interwoven. Consequently, none of these techniques and methods alone is sufficient for validating and refining that kind of formal models for adaptive technology enhanced work-integrated learning.

In the course of this thesis, a variety of methods will be applied in different work settings. The single methods will be carefully tested, and enhanced. That way, the outcomes of model validation will serve as a basis for improving the formal models, the modeling methodology, and the validation framework itself.

References

[1] De Bra, P., Houben, G., Wu, H.: AHAM: A Dexter-based Reference Model for Adaptive Hypermedia. In: Proceedings of the tenth ACM Conference on Hypertext and Hypermedia, pp. 147–156 (1999)

[2] Brusilovsky, P.: Methods and techniques of adaptive hypermedia. User Modeling and User Adapted Interaction 6(2-3), 87–129 (1996)

[3] Korossy, K.: Extending the theory of knowledge spaces: A competence-performance approach. Zeitschrift für Psychologie 205, 53–82 (1997)

[4] Doignon, J., Falmagne, J.: Knowledge Spaces. Springer, Heidelberg (1999)

[5] ALEKS Corp.: ALEKS - A Better State of Knowledge, http://www.aleks.com

[6] Hockemeyer, C., Conlan, O., Wade, V., Albert, D.: Applying Competence Prerequisite Structures for eLearning and Skill Management. Journal of Universal Computer Science 9(12), 1428–1436 (2003)

[7] Albert, D., Lukas, J. (eds.): Knowledge Spaces: Theories, Empirical Research, and Applications. Lawrence Erlbaum Associates, Mahwah (1999)

[8] Falmagne, J., Doignon, J., Koppen, M., Villano, M., Johannesen, L.: Introduction to Knowledge Spaces: How to Build, Test, and Search Them. Psychological Review 97(2), 201–224 (1990)

[9] Baumunk, K., Dowling, C.: Validity of Spaces for Assessing Knowledge about Fractions. Journal of Mathematical Psychology 41, 99–105 (1997)

[10] Kambouri, M., Koppen, M., Villano, M., Falmagne, J.: Knowledge assessment: tapping human expertise by the QUERY routine. International Journal of Human-Computer Studies 40, 119–151 (1994)

[11] Ley, T.: Organizational Competency Management - A Competence Performance Approach. Shaker, Aachen (2006)

[12] Ley, T., Albert, D.: Identifying Employee Competencies in Dynamic Work Domains: Methodological Considerations and a Case Study. Journal of Universal Computer Science 9(12), 1500–1518 (2003)

A Scrutable User Modelling Infrastructure for Enabling Life-Long User Modelling

Demetris Kyriacou

Learning Societies Lab
School of Electronics and Computer Science, University of Southampton
Highfield, Southampton, SO17 1BJ, United Kingdom
dke06r@ecs.soton.ac.uk

Abstract. User Modelling is the core component for the majority of personal-isation systems. By keeping a model for every user, a system can successfully personalise its content and utilise available resources accordingly. While re-searching the literature, one can recognize the importance of achieving interop-erability across various platforms and systems while attempting to personalise a large diversity of web resources. Furthermore, scrutable solutions allow users to control any modelling process that uses their information. Finally, privacy of user data while exchanging user models from one source to another must be taken in mind. With this paper, a Scrutable User Modelling Infrastructure is presented which blends together these user modelling 'ingredients' and, by adopting Semantic Web technologies, attempts to model a range of life-long user interactions with a variety of web-based systems from the educational, business and social networking domains.

1 Introduction

Consider the following imaginary scenario: Maria is a computer engineering student and for her assignment is required to develop a system written in Prolog. Maria knows only the basics around the Prolog programming language since she has read a book, bought from Amazon, and has gone through a couple of tutorials found on the course's website. In order to cope with the requirements of the assignment, Maria needs to register with personalisation system XYZ and follow a short course on ad-vanced concepts of Prolog. Maria logs on this new service, which it is proposed in this paper, and exports her Amazon model to XYZ, having previously set her Amazon model's privacy status to public. Furthermore, Maria filters her browsing history and selects to send to XYZ only the part that shows that she has gone through the Prolog tutorials. Now, XYZ knows what Maria is familiar with according to her various models and adapts its content accordingly to teach Maria Prolog concepts and features that she is unfamiliar with but are essential for the completion of the assignment.

What if each one of us had a user model for life from the moment we were born and that model was updated constantly with our every day interactions with various online services from the educational, business and social networking domains? What if we had absolute control over it and we decided which system gets access to which part of our model? What if we could set the privacy status of our information? Then,

W. Nejdl et al. (Eds.): AH 2008, LNCS 5149, pp. 421–425, 2008.

we would be able to scrutinise it the way we wanted and benefit from any interactions we chose to make with any service out there, by providing our model before the inter-action, and receiving it back at the end, updated with the new resulting data based on how we interacted with that service.

2 User Modelling

While trying to move a step further and model a dynamic user in a variety of contexts, life-long User Modelling (UM), the ability to model a dynamic and changing user throughout lifetime interactions with a diversity of resource providers, appears to be an attractive solution [6]. Focusing on some key UM areas is essential for coping with existing and arising challenges:

2.1 Interoperability

Interoperability can be described as "a condition that exists when the distinctions between information systems are not a barrier to accomplishing a task that spans mul-tiple systems" [1].

With the recent evolvement of the World Wide Web to the Semantic Web [2], the issue of interoperability has become a burning issue in the area of UM. Exchanging user profiles across various sources in a distributed eLearning (and not only) envi-ronment can not be achieved if explicit and widely accepted protocols are not being developed and adopted that will allow description, discovery and exchange of user models, stored in various systems - written in different languages and for different platforms [4, 5].

2.2 Scrutability

The term scrutability means that the model of every user can be controlled by the user him/her self to determine what has been modelled about him/her and how the model-ling process was conducted [7].

By adopting srutability in UM, users gain control of their models and therefore they can set their preferences on how the modelling process is applied on them. In addition, users can select in which stereotypes they should be included and which ones they should not. Furthermore, the users can alter the value of any single infer-ence that is used for drawing conclusions about them [7].

2.3 User Privacy

Privacy-Enhanced Personalisation is an area that aims at merging together the tech-niques and goals of UM with privacy considerations and apply the best possible per-sonalisation inside the boundaries set by privacy rules [8].

As the research in this area shows, there is no ideal solution while attempting to combine these two important elements. Instead, numerous small enhancements must be implemented, depending on the user and application domains in each case, in order to achieve the best possible solution.

The most important considerations while attempting to model a large diversity of users appear to be the issues of:

- Informing the users about the process of gathering their information.
- Allowing users to know how their data is stored and processed in order to draw conclusions about them.
- Acquiring users' approval when their data is being exchanged from one system to another in order to achieve effective and efficient personalisation.

2.4 User Modelling Standards

It is obvious that in such environment, agreement on common structures and scope of user information modelled is needed. The need for standards was naturally raised and was addressed by two significant organisations, IEEE and IMS and resulted in two widely accepted UM standards PAPI (IEEE) and LIP (IMS) [3].

2.5 Semantic Web Technologies in User Modelling

New directions and guidelines for UM have arisen with the introduction of the Semantic Web [2]. New technologies, such as XML, XML Schema, RDF, RDF Schema, OWL and Web Services, have emerged that allow the content of user models to be expressed in a format that can be read and processed by software agents, thus permitting them to find, share and integrate information more easily and efficiently.

3 Research Questions

Listed below are the research questions that will attempt to answer by the completion of my PhD.

What are the requirements for adopting a scrutable user modeling architecture and a communication protocol, for users AND providers of user models, for enabling exchange of user models amongst them?

Immediately, further questions arise which will contribute to answering the main question set above:

- Interoperability
    - How can we map all these different data models while enabling communication amongst them?
    - How can we allow providers of user models to define their data models for importing and exporting user data in order to enable effective and efficient exchange of user models?
    - What is the optimal solution for storing user data while adopting such architecture, i.e. where is it best to keep all this user information that it is been used for user modelling? What are the advantages and disadvantages of each choice?

- How can we enable this scrutable user modeling architecture to reflect the educational, business and social networking domain of every user in a way that will impose no barriers on merging and exporting data from any of these three domains, in order to explore the potential for interoperability across these three domains?

- Can Semantic Web technologies assist on the development of such architecture? If yes, which technologies are fitter for such implementation?
- What are the requirements for providers of user models, especially commercial providers, to employ this scrutable architecture and take advantage of the proposed communication protocol, in order to enable exchanging of user models to take place?
  - o What format should be used when providing user information to personalisation systems for adaptation purposes?
- To what extent it is possible for such architecture to allow users to scrutinise their models and express their data privacy preferences?
  - o How should we define a user model part and how can we allow SUMI users to export parts of their models to subscribed services?

4 Proposed Solution

An initial architecture, a Scrutable User Modelling Infrastructure (SUMI), is proposed, which will be used for demonstration (prototype) and evaluation purposes while attempting to answer the research questions set above

A prototype has already been designed and implemented to meet the majority of the initial core requirements mentioned above. More specifically:

- Every model in SUMI is a representation of an integrated variety of user models every user holds, by interacting with various services on the World Wide Web. The SUMI models' architecture will be later divided into three categories: educational, business and social networking data.
- A SUMI ontology will be developed, while taking in mind the structure of representative services from the educational, business and social networking domains, in order to enable mapping of the various providers' data models for successful communication between them via SUMI.
- Every user has absolute control over his/her SUMI model. The user can decide which models to integrate in SUMI and also who gets to see which part of his/her SUMI model.
- Importing models from services will be achieved by adopting the SUMI import protocol, based on Semantic Web technologies.
- Every user can define the status of the data retrieved by his/her various models. The three categories of data are public, private and hidden.
- The most important feature of SUMI is the users' ability to export a part of their SUMI model to any registered service they prefer. This will be achieved by adopting the SUMI export protocol, again based on Semantic Web technologies.

5 Evaluation Plan

For the evaluation of SUMI, simulation testing will be conducted which will consist of various generated queries, in order to demonstrate and evaluate the architecture of SUMI, the communication protocol and any potential features. This include the designing and developing of sample services, based on real educational, business and social networking providers of user models, in order to test the SUMI architecture and communication protocol against the pre-defined requirements. The queries will represent hypothetical requests made from (and to) the sample services that will be implemented, for enquiring various user information located in several user models that these services will hold. The SUMI architecture will be used to bring these sample services together, while offering a level of scrutability to the owners of the user models, whereas the introduced communication protocol will enable the exchange of user models to take place in an effective and efficient way.

References

1. Aroyo, L., Dolog, P., Houben, G.J., Kravcik, M., Naeve, A., Nilsson, M., Wild, F.: Interoperability in Personalised Adaptve Learning. Educational Technology & Society 9(2), 4–18 (2006)
2. Berners-Lee, T., Hendler, J., Lassila, O.: The Semantic Web. Scientific American 284(5), 34–43 (2001)
3. Dolog, P., Nejdl, W.: Challenges and Benefits of the Semantic Web for User Modelling. In: Proceedings of AH 2003 workshop at 12th World Wide Web Conference, Budapest, Hungary (2003)
4. Dolog, P., Schaefer, M.: A Framework for Browsing, Manipulating and Maintaining Interoperable Learner Profiles. In: Ardissono, L., Brna, P., Mitrović, A. (eds.) UM 2005. LNCS (LNAI), vol. 3538, pp. 397–401. Springer, Heidelberg (2005)
5. Dolog, P., Schaefer, M.: Learner modelling on the semantic web. In: Proceedings of PerSWeb-2005 Workshop: Personalisation on the Semantic Web at User Modelling 2005: 10th International Conference, Edinburgh, UK (2005)
6. Kapoor, A., Horvitz, E.: Principles of Lifelong Learning for Predictive User Modeling. In: Proceedings of the 11th International Conference on User Modeling, Corfu, Greece (2007)
7. Kay, J.: Stereotypes, Student Models and Scrutability. In: Gauthier, G., Frasson, C., VanLehn, K. (eds.) ITS 2000. LNCS, vol. 1839, pp. 19–30. Springer, Heidelberg (2000)
8. Kobsa, A.: Privacy-Enhanced Personalization. Communications of the ACM 50(8), 24–33 (2007)

Merging Adaptive Hypermedia and Intelligent Tutoring Systems Using Knowledge Spaces

Amanda Nicholas and Brent Martin

Intelligent Computer Tutoring Group
Department of Computer Science and Software Engineering
University of Canterbury
Private Bag 4800, Christchurch, New Zealand
amanda.nicholas@pg.canterbury.ac.nz,
brent.martin@canterbury.ac.nz

Abstract. Adaptive Hypermedia and Intelligent Tutoring Systems are both used for computer-based instruction, but their strengths lie in different areas. Adaptive Hypermedia is better suited to the instruction of concepts, while Intelligent Tutoring Systems generally assist in the use of these concepts to solve problems. A general instruction system requires both of these methods of instruction to provide a full learning environment. This paper describes a proposed method of combining Adaptive Hypermedia and Intelligent Tutoring Systems using Knowledge Spaces, a method of mathematically modeling a domain.

Keywords: Intelligent Tutoring Systems, Adaptive Hypermedia, Knowledge Spaces, Constraint-Based Modeling.

1 Introduction

Intelligent Tutoring Systems (ITS) are designed to assist students in the acquisition of skills rather than the complete mastery of a domain. ITS are primarily used as instruction during the tutorial section of a lecture course, or in conjunction with an alternate method of instruction. Conversely, Adaptive Hypermedia (AH) systems are primarily designed to impart the concepts of a domain that a student must know to utilise these skills. While some Adaptive Hypermedia systems do provide instruction in skills, it is generally less advanced than comparable ITS instruction. For a system to provide a standalone solution comparable to a lecture course it must provide instruction in both concepts and skills. We propose to achieve this using Knowledge Space Theory.

This paper describes a framework for integrating ITS and AH components into one system using Knowledge Space Theory, a method of mathematically modeling a domain. Background information on these areas is described, before the motivation and methodology of this research is expanded upon. Finally, the conclusions are presented.

W. Nejdl et al. (Eds.): AH 2008, LNCS 5149, pp. 426–430, 2008.
© Springer-Verlag Berlin Heidelberg 2008

2   Background

2.1   Intelligent Tutoring Systems

Of all teaching methods, it has been shown that one-to-one human tutoring provides the best learning gains [1], raising the average performance of students by two standard deviations. However, due to economic considerations it is not possible to provide a human tutor for every student. The aim of ITS is to achieve the results of one-on-one human tutoring without the resource requirements. Currently the best ITS achieve an improvement of one standard deviation over classroom teaching. They achieve this by maintaining models of the domain and student, allowing instruction to be tailored to the specific needs of the user. The primary type of instruction provided by an ITS is in the development of skills. A number of methods exist for modeling a domain, two of which are Cognitive Tutors, based on Anderson's ACT-R theory [2], and Constraint-Based Modeling (CBM).

Constraint-Based Modeling [3] is based on Ohlsson's theory of learning from performance errors [4]: people learn from making mistakes during practice. The purpose of the tutor within this theory is to detect student errors and provide feedback on these errors and how to correct them [5]. Principles of the domain are modeled as constraints. When a student solution does not conform to the rules of the domain – detected by a constraint being violated – a feedback message is given so the student can correct their error. This feedback message refers the student to the rule of the domain that has been broken, thus imparting declarative knowledge about the domain. Although these feedback messages provide declarative knowledge, there is currently no facility in CBM tutors to instruct the student in the concepts of the domain at a more general level.

2.2   Adaptive Hypermedia

AH combines Hypermedia with User Modeling [6]. The content presented by the system is adapted to the user's knowledge, goals and preferences by maintaining a model of the user. In the context of educational hypermedia, the topics suggested to the student for subsequent study would be determined by the student's existing knowledge. AH systems may contain a problem solving component, but this is primarily a static component, with the questions a student is asked determined by progress through the AH system and not by answers to prior questions. In practice, this means that different students are always asked the same questions although the order of these questions in relation to the material presented by the system may vary.

2.3   Knowledge Spaces

Knowledge Space Theory (KST) is a mathematical model of knowledge first described by Falmagne and Doignon [7]. It was originally developed for use in assessing knowledge, but the field has evolved to also address the instruction of knowledge. In KST, a domain is modeled as a set of generic questions or problems, known as items. An item may have as many instances as desired, that is there may be as many questions of a particular type as can be constructed. Between items, dependencies, known as surmise relationships, exist such that if a student answers a question x correctly, we can infer that they would answer y correctly also. These relationships provide guidance for determining which topic the student should be introduced to next, as students should only progress to a topic if they have learnt all of the prerequisites. Instruction in a Knowledge Space (KS) system may be incorporated by attaching to each item a teaching element that provides information on how to solve the current problem type.

At least three systems exist that utilise KST: ALEKS, RATH and AdAsTra. ALEKS (Adaptive LEarning in Knowledge Spaces), the first system to utilise KST for assessment and instruction, is a commercial system for teaching mathematics to students from primary school to university level. Concepts are taught by asking the student to solve a problem, and, if they are unable to do so, walking them through how the solution is found. Minimal feedback is given on the particular mistake the student has made: the standard feedback is to display the solution. RATH (Relational Adaptive Tutoring Hypertext WWW-environment) combines KST with hypertext. Instruction is split into two different types: teaching content and problem solving. The teaching content consists of a lesson and several examples; at present it is not adaptive. The problem solving nodes are structured using KST while the concept instruction nodes are structured using a hypertext model. The two models are combined to provide the overall tutoring system [8,9]. AdAsTra (ADaptive ASsessment and TRAining) is a problem-based system. Students are given problems to solve in two modes: assessment mode and training mode. The system marks the answer in both modes, and in training mode provides some feedback on errors [10].

3   Motivation

Constraint-based ITS were developed to help the user to achieve skills. Although the concepts of the domain are an important part of the feedback provided, currently no system exists that provides instruction at a more general level. Adaptive Hypermedia systems, conversely, provide instruction in concepts, but generally skill instruction is either not included or not fully adapted to the student's knowledge. By developing a system that contains both an ITS and an Adaptive Hypermedia element, a more complete instructional system could be constructed.

In addition, CBM tutors model the domain at a very fine level in order to provide feedback on individual errors. This means that when selecting a new concept to introduce to the student, the tutoring system has no information to use to determine which skills are appropriate for introduction. As a Knowledge Space contains domain information at a higher level, including prerequisites between concepts, using a KS to drive these decisions will result in skills being introduced in an appropriate order and context.

We intend to create an educational system that contains both an ITS component and an AH component by using a Knowledge Space as the overall student model that controls these components. By using a Knowledge Space to combine an ITS and AH into one system, overall decisions, such as determining the direction of instruction, can be made at a higher level in the domain. Feedback on attempted solutions and other lower-level decisions can be managed by the ITS component and concept instruction can be managed by the AH component. Both will draw on the Knowledge Space to drive their decisions and will return information about the student to the KS. Systems that use KST are in existence, but at present none of them contain a fully fledged ITS.

Our hypothesis is that using KST to guide problem selection will increase student learning of new concepts, which will be demonstrated by fewer violated constraints. We also hypothesise that the addition of an Adaptive Hypermedia component will improve student learning and reduce student frustration.

4   Methodology

We will implement a combined AH and ITS system. To allow these components to interact and share information about the user, a Knowledge Space component will be implemented as the driver of the ITS and AH. The Knowledge Space will hold the model of the domain and the model of the student, and will be able to give this information to the AH and ITS when necessary, so they can take appropriate instructional action. Our intention is to design a combined system which is generic enough to allow the use of components, whether AH, ITS, or KS, that have been independently authored.

A standard ITS and a standard Knowledge Space both maintain a model of the student's knowledge. In the KS this is captured as the student's knowledge state – the set of items that they have mastered. In the ITS, the student model is recorded as a level of mastery for each constraint. In the combined system, the Knowledge Space will act as an overlay on the constraints: each KS item will have a set of related constraints associated with it. The Knowledge Space will give information to the ITS about which constraints are currently being learned by the student, corresponding to the current item being targeted. The ITS can use this information to choose appropriate problems that involve skills tested by these constraints, and give feedback the emphasises the feedback messages from the constraints currently being learned. In return, the ITS will inform the Knowledge Space about the student's mastery of each constraint, which will allow the Knowledge Space to determine when an item has been learned.

The Adaptive Hypermedia component will have instruction that relates to each node in the Knowledge Space, and, when requested, it will display the appropriate information to the student. It will then inform the Knowledge Space about the instruction the student has encountered.

The efficacy of the system will be investigated in a study to be performed in late 2008. This study will compare the learning gains of two groups of students, one using a standard ITS, the other using the altered ITS described in this paper.

As the students will have had previous instruction in the domain outside of this study, the study will investigate whether the addition of instruction increases learning when students have already been taught the domain concepts.

5   Conclusion and Future Work

Adaptive Hypermedia and Intelligent Tutoring Systems are both effective methods of computer-based education. At present, however, little work has been dedicated to combining these systems. We propose a combined system, using Knowledge Spaces to drive the connection. The Knowledge Space will serve as a combined student model for the two systems, allowing them to share information on the student's achievements. We hope that this level of coupling between concept instruction and skill practise will provide increased learning.

References

1. Beck, J., Stern, M., Haugsjaa, E.: Applications of AI in education. ACM Crossroads 3(1) (1996)
2. Anderson, J.R., Corbett, A.T., Koedinger, K.R., Pelletier, R.: Cognitive Tutors: Lessons Learned. The Journal of the Learning Sciences 4(2), 167–209 (1995)
3. Ohlsson, S.: Constraint-Based Student Modelling. In: Greer, J.E., McCalla, G.I. (eds.) Student Modelling: The Key to Individualized Knowledge-based Instruction. Computer Systems and Sciences, vol. 125, pp. 167–189. Springer, Berlin (1994)
4. Ohlsson, S.: Learning From Performance Errors. Psychological Review 103(2), 241–262 (1996)
5. Ohlsson, S.: Learning and Instruction: An Introduction. COSC420 Course Reading Material (July 2004)
6. Brusilovsky, P.: Adaptive hypermedia. User Model. User-Adapt. Interact. 11(1-2), 87–110 (2001)
7. Doignon, J.P., Falmagne, J.C.: Spaces for the assessment of knowledge. International Journal of Man-Machine Studies 23, 175–196 (1985)
8. Hockemeyer, C.: Rath — a relational adaptive tutoring hypertext www-environment (1997)
9. Hockemeyer, C., Albert, D.: The adaptive tutoring system RATH. In: Auer, M.E., Ressler, U. (eds.) ICL 1999 Workshop Interactive Computer aided Learning: Tools and Applications. Carinthia Tech Institute, Villach, Austria (1999)
10. Dowling, C.E., Hockemeyer, C., Ludwig, A.H.: Adaptive assessment and training using the neighbourhood of knowledge states. In: Lesgold, A., Frasson, C., Gauthier, G. (eds.) ITS 1996. LNCS, vol. 1086, pp. 578–587. Springer, Heidelberg (1996)

SemWeB: A Semantic Web Browser for Supporting the Browsing of Users Using Semantic and Adaptive Links

Melike Şah, Wendy Hall, and David C. De Roure

Intelligence, Agents and Multimedia Group, School of Electronics and Computer Science,
University of Southampton
{ms305r,wh,dder}@ecs.soton.ac.uk

Abstract. Web browsing is a complex activity and in general, users are not guided during browsing. The aim of this research is to support the browsing of users using semantic and adaptive hyperlinks using Semantic Web technologies and personalization methods. In this paper, we propose a novel Semantic Web browser (SemWeB), which uses a behavior-based and an ontology-driven user modeling architecture. In our approach, semantic links and adaptive hypermedia can be achieved on different websites. In addition, user profiles can be easily updated with semantic metadata coming from the Semantic Web browser.

Keywords: Semantic Web Browser, Semantic Web, User Modeling, Ontology, Personalization.

1 Introduction

Browsing is an important activity on the Web and in general users are not guided during browsing. Our hypothesis is that browsing can be supported better by using Semantic Web technologies and personalization methods. Semantic Web technologies supply powerful knowledge representation formalisms and inferencing mechanisms on the Web. Browsing can be enriched by using this power. Additionally, different users have different browsing needs and the page content and hyperlinks should be adapted accordingly. Adaptive hypermedia is a solution, where personalization mechanisms adapt information to the needs of the users.

On the other hand, browsing is a complex activity and it is important to understand its nature to better help users. Bawden [1] categorize browsing into three groups: purposive browsing (looking for a definite piece of information), capricious browsing (randomly examining material without a defined goal) and exploratory browsing (deliberately searching for inspiration). Cove and Walsh [2] also divide browsing into three categories: search browsing (searching for defined information), general purpose browsing (looking for items of interest) and serendipity browsing (random). Based on these definitions, we can say that browsing tends to be used in three broad senses: a purposeful activity (directed), searching for inspiration (semi-directed) and capricious behavior (undirected). In our opinion, to better support browsing, user profiles should contain information about the user's browsing behaviors.

W. Nejdl et al. (Eds.): AH 2008, LNCS 5149, pp. 431–436, 2008.

2   Research Aim and Contributions

The aim of this research is investigating Semantic Web technologies and user modeling approaches to better support the user's browsing using adaptive hypermedia and enriched semantic links. From this point of view, first we attempt to create a personalized semantic portal with adaptive and enriched semantic hyperlinks [3], [4]. Although we achieved personalization and semantic linking on a static database, our main research question was how to achieve personalization and semantic linking on the Web scale. Therefore, this research question let us to think about existing Semantic Web architectures and user modeling approaches.

COHSE [5] and Magpie [6] are two systems that aim to provide useful browsing links using Semantic Web technologies. However, they both use static databases for linking. In addition, they paid little attention to the user's role and they do not supply adaptive links or contents. Existing personalization mechanisms on the Web require users to log in to multiple websites and the user profiles change from site to site. There is a need for generic user profiles and personalization architectures, which can achieve adaptive hypermedia on diverse websites. Our hypothesis is that Semantic Web technologies can offer the solution to these problems. Ontology-based user profiles are interoperable, and they can be easily extended and combined with semantic metadata on the Web. Therefore, user modeling approaches take advantage of semantic metadata; IMS LIP [7] and IEEE PAPI [8] are well known user modeling standards. Although these standards can be applied to any domain, they do not contain data about the user's browsing interests, browsing goals and browsing strategies.

In this research, we attempt to provide a personalized Semantic Web browser, which can be used on different domains for supporting browsing of users using semantic and adaptive links. Our main contribution is the integration of a behavior-based and an ontology-driven user modeling architecture into the Semantic Web browser. We also attempt to provide semantic links using Web as source for linking.

3   Results Achieved

This research can be divided into different stages: (1) *analysis*, (2) *system design*, (3) *information extraction*, (4) *creating semantic hyperlinks*, (5) *user modeling*, (6) *creating adaptive hyperlinks*, (7) *SemWeB evaluation*. Part 1 has finished. Parts 2, 3, 4, 5, 6 are ongoing and part 7 of this research will begin in May 2008.

3.1   Analysis

This part of research investigates existing Semantic Web enabled systems, semantic annotation platforms and user modeling approaches. Existing Semantic Web enabled systems, such as COHSE and Magpie do not supply adaptive links and contents. In user modeling, the browsing behaviors are not taken into account.

3.2   System Design

For understanding interactions of users with Web and enable adaptive hypermedia on different Web sites, we implemented SemWeB as a browser extension of the Mozilla Firefox Web browser (Fig. 1). SemWeB extends the Web browser with a vertical sidebar. The sidebar has two tabs: the navigation tab and the personalization tab. The navigation tab is used for highlighting ontological concepts found on the page and adding semantic and adaptive hyperlinks (Fig. 2). The personalization tab is used for updating user profiles.

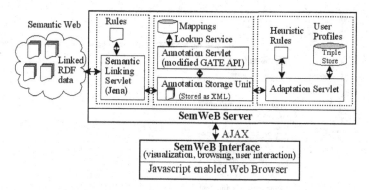

Fig. 1. The architecture of SemWeB

3.3 Information Extraction

For information extraction (IE), SemWeB uses ontologies and an ontology-driven lexicon based on a modified GATE [9] framework. GATE is a text engineering archi-tecture for extracting named entities from text. To improve IE, we added new gazet-teers and rules. In addition, we extend GATE with a lookup service and annotation storage unit. Lookup service returns the URIs of found concept instances and annota-tion storage unit stores created annotations as XML files at server-side. When the same page is requested again, the stored annotation is returned. In this way, we prevent undesired delays during semantic annotation. Because IE requires some pre-processing (creating mappings, etc.), SemWeB uses predefined ontologies, particu-larly ECS ontology [10] and instances. In ECS, every Web page has an RDF file associated to it. RDF files are crawled for the creation of gazetteers and mappings. SemWeB can also be adapted to different ontologies since interface, semantic and adaptive links are created independent of ontologies. GATE can also be adapted to different ontologies. In future, IE will be tested on large scale.

3.4 Creating Semantic Hyperlinks

Semantic links are added using the navigation tab. When user highlights a concept, SemWeB embeds an icon next to recognized instance on the page (Fig. 2). To prevent long delays, the semantic link injection is not automatic. The user is required to click the icon next to recognized instances. Once user clicks, URI of the recognized in-stance is sent to SemWeB server using AJAX. Service firstly dereferences URI over Web using HTTP content negotiation. Then parses RDF file using Jena and identifies more RDF link URIs. If necessary, more URIs are dereferenced. Possible link anchors and targets are identified and an XML response to client's browser is created. Links to open data sources (i.e. DBpedia, DBLP, etc.) are investigated. For this purpose, we are using Sindice Semantic Web search engine [11]. By using Sindice, we identify more related URIs on the Web. Related semantic hyperlinks are obtained by querying

SPARQL endpoints of data sources. For example, links to DBLP recent publications, and Wikipedia broader/narrower topic links are created. Finally, the semantic links are sent back to client as XML, and links are presented in a new Web page (Fig. 2).

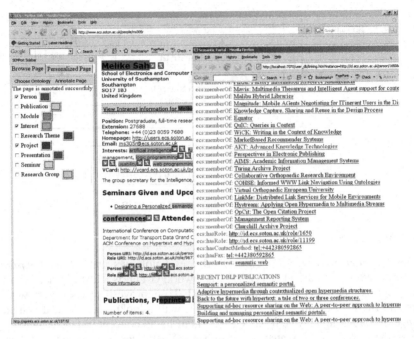

Fig. 2. SemWeB browser extension

3.5 User Modeling

For user modeling, we developed a new ontology-based user model, which uses the user's browsing behaviors for adaptation. The model can also be applied to different domains. In our model, currently we use seven categories: identification, preference, security, *browsing goal*, *interest*, *expertise* and *browsing behavior* (our main contributions are in italic). The browsing goal concept represents browsing aims of users and it is divided into two sub-concepts: short-term browsing goal and persistent browsing goal. The interest category represents browsing interests of users and it is divided into bookmark (interest to a page) and browsing interest (interest to a semantic instance). Users can also rate their interests (*low, medium, high*). The expertise category represents knowledge of users for a semantic instance (*novice, intermediate, expert*). Browsing Behavior category is used to understand the activities of users. The browsing behavior has browsing_level and browsing_type properties. Browsing_level is the number of clicks made by a user in a browsing session. Browsing_type indicates browsing aims of users as suggested by Cove and Walsh [1] and Bawden [2]. When the user has a short-term browsing goal, it is assumed that user is looking for a defined piece of information and browsing_type is set to "*directed*". When the user has a browsing interest or has bookmarked current Web page, then it is assumed that the user is looking for items of interest and browsing_type is set to "*semi-directed*". When the user does not have short-term browsing goals or browsing interests, browsing_type is set to "*undirected*".

Users can log in and register to personalization from the personalization tab. User profiles are kept at a server-side triple store. Users can explicitly update profiles from their browsers using SemWeB interface. In our ongoing work, profiles will be implicitly updated based on interactions with SemWeB (i.e browsing behavior).

3.6 Creating Adaptive Links

In our ongoing work, adaptation will be achieved on the recommended semantic links by calculating semantic distance between user model and semantic hyperlinks based on the following conditions. If it is directed browsing, show related links according to short-term browsing goals. If it is semi-directed browsing, use most recently added interests to supply related links. If it is un-directed browsing, make use of semantics. When a link is requested by a novice user, provide Wikipedia links. When the user is an expert, provide detailed semantic links. Also, link sorting and link annotation can be done based on interest ratings, goal priorities, expertise and browsing levels.

3.7 SemWeB Evaluation

We are planning to perform a system-based evaluation. Adaptability of SemWeB to different URIs and ontologies will be tested. Adaptability of user profiles to different ontologies will be checked. Interoperability of SemWeB to diverse RDF metadata will be analyzed. Finally, scalability of IE and user profiles will be evaluated.

4 Conclusions

This research investigates Semantic Web technologies and user modeling approaches and tries to find new architectures and user models to better support the user's browsing using adaptive hypermedia and semantic links. In this paper, we have presented our ongoing research for personalized Semantic Web browser (SemWeB).

References

1. Bawden, D.: Information Systems and the Stimulation of Creativity. J. of Information Science 12, 203–216 (1986)
2. Cove, J., Walsh, B.: Online Text Retrieval via Browsing. Information Processing and Management 24, 31–37 (1988)
3. Şah, M., Hall, W.: Building and Managing Personalized Semantic Portals. In: Proceedings of International World Wide Web Conference, pp. 1227–1228 (2007)
4. Şah, M., Hall, W., Gibbins, N.M., De Roure, D.C.: SEMPort – A Personalized Semantic Portal. In: 18th ACM Conference on Hypertext and Hypermedia, pp. 31–32 (2007)
5. Carr, L., Hall, W., Bechhofer, S., Goble, C.: Conceptual Linking: Ontology-based Open Hypermedia. In: International World Wide Web Conference, pp. 334–342 (2001)
6. Dzbor, M., Domingue, J., Motta, E.: Magpie – towards a semantic web browser. In: International Semantic Web Conference (2003)
7. IMS Learner Information Package Specification,
   http://www.imsglobal.org/profiles/lipinfo01.html

8. IEEE PAPI (Public And Private Information for Learners),
   http://edutool.com/papi/
9. Cunningham, H., Maynard, D., Bontcheva, K., Tablan, V.: GATE: A Framework and Graphical Development Environment for Robust NLP Tools and Applications. In: ACL (2002)
10. ECS Ontology, http://id.ecs.soton.ac.uk/docs/
11. A Semantic Web Search Engine, http://www.sindice.com/

Author Index

Lecture Notes in Computer Science

Sublibrary 3: Information Systems and Application, incl. Internet/Web and HCI